I0084393

BIOGRAPHICAL

AND

HISTORICAL SKETCHES

OF

EARLY INDIANA

William Wesley Woollen

> *He that writes*
> *Or makes a feast, more certainly invites*
> *His judges than his friends; there's not a guest*
> *But will find something wanting or ill-drest.*
> —Sir R. Howard

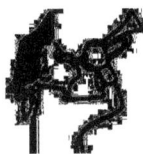

HERITAGE BOOKS
2015

HERITAGE BOOKS
AN IMPRINT OF HERITAGE BOOKS, INC.

Books, CDs, and more—Worldwide

For our listing of thousands of titles see our website
at
www.HeritageBooks.com

A Facsimile Reprint
Published 2015 by
HERITAGE BOOKS, INC.
Publishing Division
5810 Ruatan Street
Berwyn Heights, Md. 20740

Copyright © 1883 Emma W. Hubbard

Originally published
Indianapolis:
Published by Hammond & Co.
1883

— Publisher's Notice —
In reprints such as this, it is often not possible to remove blemishes from
the original. We feel the contents of this book warrant its reissue despite
these blemishes and hope you will agree and read it with pleasure.

International Standard Book Numbers
Paperbound: 978-0-7884-5643-5
Clothbound: 978-0-7884-6221-4

TO

EMMA W. HUBBARD

WHO GREATLY AIDED ME IN THE PREPARATION OF THESE

SKETCHES, THIS BOOK IS

Affectionately Inscribed

BY HER FATHER

THE AUTHOR

PREFACE.

MANY of the sketches contained in this book were originally published in the *Indianapolis Journal*. These, and such as have been given the public in other papers, have been carefully revised and rewritten. Some of the sketches, however, were prepared expressly for this work.

I have not written of living men, but only of those who have passed away. The dead Governors of Indiana—both Territorial and State—are sketched, and monographs of other distinguished men are given. The book contains other papers, of a historical character, the whole making a work which, I hope, will prove of permanent value.

The information contained in this book, which necessarily develops much of the early political history of the State, was obtained from various sources, and can not elsewhere be found without great research and labor. No inconsiderable part of it is derived from the author's own observation and recollection, and would pass away with him were it not committed to writing.

Should this book be favorably received by the public, it will, most probably, be followed by another of similar character, for the author is in possession of abundant material for such a work.

Such as the book is, I send it forth. Whatever may be the verdict of the public upon it, I shall have the satisfaction of knowing that it was conscientiously written. It contains nothing which I do not believe to be true, and in its preparation I accepted nothing as evidence which I did not regard as conclusive. I ask for the work the public's considerate judgment, and I shall be content to abide its verdict.

WILLIAM WESLEY WOOLLEN.

INDIANAPOLIS, MAY, 1883.

TABLE OF CONTENTS.

WILLIAM HENRY HARRISON.

INDIANA TERRITORY, when organized, embraced all the country lying between the present Ohio State line and the Mississippi river, the great northern lakes and the river Ohio, excepting a small part of Michigan and that portion of Southeastern Indiana ceded to the United States at the treaty of Greenville. It was created by an act of Congress passed May 7, 1800, and remained under territorial government until December 11, 1816, when the State of Indiana was admitted into the Federal Union.

The first Governor of Indiana Territory was William Henry Harrison. He was born in Berkeley, Charles City county, Virginia, February 9, 1773. He was the youngest son of Benjamin Harrison, one of the foremost men of the revolutionary era, and he lived to add new luster to his father's name. When nineteen years old he entered the army as an ensign, and fought under both St. Clair and Wayne. In 1795 he was appointed a captain, and assigned to the command of Fort Washington, a fortress standing on the present site of Cincinnati. Two years afterward he resigned his place in the army, and was appointed Secretary of the Northwestern Territory, of which his old commander, General St. Clair, was Governor. On the 3d of October, 1799, the Territorial Legislature elected him a delegate to Congress by a vote of eleven to ten, the latter number being cast for Arthur St. Clair, Jr., a son of the Governor. On the 13th of May, 1800, he was appointed Governor of Indiana Territory, and on the 10th of January following he arrived at Vincennes and took possession of his office. He remained in control of the executive department of the Territory until September, 1812, when he was appointed a brigadier-general of the army and assigned to the command of the northwestern fron-

tier. The next year he was promoted to the rank of major-
general, and continued in the military service of the country
until the close of the second war with Great Britain, when he
threw up his commission and retired to his farm near Cincinnati. But he did not remain long in private life. In 1816 he
was elected to Congress from the Cincinnati district, and continued a member of that body for three years. In 1849 he was
chosen a member of the Ohio Senate, and served two years as
a Senator. In 1824 Ohio sent him to the Senate of the United
States, where he sat until 1828, when President John Quincy
Adams appointed him minister plenipotentiary to Colombia.
But his residence abroad was short, as General Jackson recalled
him soon after becoming President. On his return to the United
States he went back to his old home at North Bend, and soon
afterward was elected clerk of the Court of Common Pleas of
Hamilton county, an office he held for twelve years. In 1836
he was a candidate for President of the United States and re-
ceived seventy-three electoral votes, being those of the States
of Vermont, New Jersey, Delaware, Maryland, Kentucky,
Ohio and Indiana. The electors who cast the vote of Indiana
for him were John C. Clendening, Achilles Williams, Hiram
Decker, Austin W. Morris, Milton Stapp, Albert S. White,
Enoch McCarty, Marston G. Clark and Abram P. Andrews.
In 1840 he was again the Whig candidate for the presidency,
and this time was triumphantly elected, receiving 234 electoral
votes to 60 cast for Martin Van Buren. The electors for Indiana this year were Jonathan McCarty, Joseph G. Marshall,
John W. Payne, Joseph L. White, Richard W. Thompson,
James H. Cravens, Caleb B. Smith, William Herod and Samuel C. Sample, several of them being among the most brilliant
men Indiana has ever produced. Thus, for the second time,
did Indiana vote for her first Territorial Governor for the highest office in the gift of the people. He was bound to her citizens by the strongest ties, for he had scattered the savage hordes
at Tippecanoe, and at the Thames, and saved the homes of the
pioneers from pillage. General Harrison was inaugurated President of the United States, March 4, 1841, and in one month
afterward—on the 4th of April, 1841—he died. His remains
were taken to his home at North Bend and there interred. The

soil of Ohio never hid from sight one more dearly beloved than he.

General Harrison was educated at Hampton Sidney College, and afterward studied medicine. But his entrance into the army, and his subsequent active service in the military and civil departments of the government, made its practice impossible. America has had no more illustrious family than that of the Harrisons. For four generations its members have sat in the national councils. General Harrison's father, Benjamin Harrison, was a delegate to the Continenal Congress, and signed the Declaration of American Independence. He was three times elected Governor of Virginia, and was a member of the convention called to ratify the Federal constitution. The General's son, John Scott Harrison, was a member of Congress from 1853 to 1857, and his grandson, General Benjamin Harrison, is now a Senator of the United States from Indiana. What a line of glorious ancestors has the Senator!

General Harrison's career as Territorial Governor of Indiana was an eventful one. For a time faction was rampant about him, fomented by able and ambitious men. These men sought to break him down, but he was too strongly entrenched in the affections of the people. Among the private papers of Thomas Randolph, a warm personal and political friend of General Harrison, is an unfinished and unsigned letter, believed to have been written by Benjamin Parke, the first delegate to Congress from Indiana Territory. It has never hitherto been published, and is exceedingly valuable, giving, as it does, a graphic account of the intrigues against Governor Harrison, and naming the men engaged in them. It is to be regretted that the narrative was not brought down to a later day. The following is a copy of the paper:

"VINCENNES, 5 September, 1808.

"SIR—The moral and political history of the people of this government exhibits numberless instances of the most barefaced inconsistency, duplicity, cunning and depravity. Remorse has lost its sting, shame its blush, and probity, justice, honor have all been supplanted by the most unblushing hypocrisy.

" To comply with your request, it will be needless to enumerate many cases. The leading features will enable you to form

a complete idea of the whole. In fact, a profile will give you
ample materials for a miniature.

" In 1801, about a year after the Territorial government commenced, I came to this place. At that time I found Colonel
Edgar and Robert Morrison eager for the establishment of the
second or representative grade of government. The partisans
of the measure were principally in the two western counties.

" R. M. went so far as to address circular letters to the people of the Territory, showing the ease with which it might be
attained and the advantages that would result from it. It was
notorious that he expected, from the standing of himself and
party, to be the first delegate to Congress. But the measure
was opposed upon the following grounds: By the census of
1800 the population of the Territory amounted to about 5,600
souls. Comparatively speaking, there was no emigration and
no prospect of there being any for some time. The county of
Dearborn was then within the limits of the Northwest Territory.
No purchase had then been made of the Indians, and they all
appeared to be averse to selling a single acre, and boundaries
between us and the Indians on the Mississippi and in this county
were not defined. The lines of Clark county, containing 150,-
000 acres, had been run. In fact there was scarcely an acre
of ground for settlement save in Clark county and the two do-
nations. Those who had removed to the county had principally
to settle on the public lands in the neighborhood of the old settlements, and, in fact, to which we had no title, as the Indian
lines had not been run. The expenses of the second grade were,
by some, estimated at about from $12,000 to $15,000. However, the smallness of the population; the barren prospects of
a speedy increase of it; our confined situation with regard to
the Indians; their aversion to selling any of their lands, and
the supposed expenses of the establishment, influenced a great
majority of the people against the measure. Some expressed
their sentiments on the subject to the Governor, by petition.
However, the project failed. There was little stir made in regard
to it for some time after.

" In 1803 the politics of the West took a new direction. Satisfied with no establishment from which they could not derive
either office or emolument, they seized with avidity every cir-

cumstance that might effect a change in our political situation. In the summer of that year we received information of the cession of Louisiana. Instantly the project was formed by the Edgar and Morrison party to connect the counties of St. Clair and Randolph to the country now called the Louisiana Territory, and make one government of the whole. Edgar was to be the Governor and R. Morrison the secretary, and all the posse were to be amply provided for in this new arrangement. A slight schism, however, took place in their party about this time. James Higgin, an attorney, notorious for his avarice, impudence and cowardice, proposed Judge Dowis as Governor of the new Territory, promising himself an office if the Judge succeeded. These projects failed also.

"It ought to have been observed that in 1802 a convention of delegates assembled at this place to take into consideration the situation of the Territory, and to petition Congress for redress on certain subjects. The petition was agreed to, and the majority of the delegates voted a clause for the introduction of slavery for ten years, or rather a suspension of the sixth act of the compact for ten years. It was then proposed to elect an agent to go forward with the petition. I, with others, was proposed. Morrison was violently opposed to my being appointed. I have been told, for I was in Kentucky at the time, that he wished the appointment himself. I was appointed, and this affair satisfied him and his party that their influence was trifling, and some change must be wrought to place them in the situation desired.

"After the golden prospects which the cession of Louisiana opened to this Territory had vanished, a project for dividing the territory and forming a distinct government of the counties of Randolph and St. Clair was brought forward. However, little more than conversation was had on it at that time. It was soon entirely suspended by the agitation produced by another project, that of going into the second grade of government.

" In the autumn of 1802 a treaty with the Indians was made at this place, by which the United States became possessed of the country from Point Coupie to the mouth of White river; and from twelve miles west of the Wabash to the distance of seventy-two miles east. This was the first purchase that was made. In August, 1803, the Kaskaskian Indians sold their

land to the United States. In March, 1804, Congress passed a
law for establishing land offices at Kaskaskia and Vincennes,
and authorizing the survey and sale of the lands purchased by
the above treaties. In August, 1804, the Delaware treaty was
made, by which the United States acquired the lands of the
Wabash, south of the first mentioned purchase and the road
leading from this place to Clarksville, thence down the Ohio to
the mouth of the river Wabash. (See the several treaties and
act of Congress in the laws of the United States.)

" In the year ——, the Northwestern Territory assumed a
State government, by which the counties of Wayne and Dearborn were annexed to the Indiana Territory.

" The purchases from the Indians had increased the emigration
to the Territory. It was also accelerated by the establishment
of land offices at Kaskaskia and Vincennes. In the summer of
1804 the subject of adopting the second grade of government
was agitated with considerable warmth.

" With agriculture improved, population increased, the counties of Dearborn and Wayne added to the territory; possessed
of all the lands from the falls of the Ohio to the Mississippi, with
the exception of the Pyan Kaskaw claim, of no great extent,
and which was shortly purchased; and offices established at
Kaskaskia and Vincennes for the sale of public lands, it was
thought that the measure might be safely gone into. To this advantageous change in our situation was added, that the expenses
of the establishment would not exceed $3,500 (I thought about
$3,000); that the people would be entitled to a partial repre-
sentative government; that they would have the absolute control over one branch of the Legislature; that it would give them
a Representative in Congress, and, although he would not be
entitled to vote, yet from his situation he would acquire respect
and attention, and would give a faithful representation of our
situation, and that some sacrifices ought to be made to obtain
even the partial exercise of the rights considered so dear and of
such universal importance to the several States.

" But strange as it may seem, to a case so plain, and principles resulting from it so obvious, forgetting former professions,
and lost to all sense of shame, Edgar, Morrison & Co. were opposed. In 1801 raising $10,000 or $15,000 would have been a

slight tax and no burden ; yet, in 1804, with an increased population, an immense purchase of lands, offices opened for their sale, and our situation in every respect changed infinitely for the better, between $3,000 and $4,000 would be ruin to the people ; although the office of Governor was obnoxious on account of the extent of its prerogatives, and the conduct of the Governor reprehensible for the tyranny of his conduct, yet it would endanger the rights and liberties of the people to diminish his prerogatives and contract the sphere of his duties ; and although in 1801 the Edgar and Morrison party were so violently in favor of the measures, in 1804 they were its most bitter opponents.

" In this county J. R. Jones, Vigo, Hurst, the Governor, the Johnsons and myself were in favor of the measure. Vanderburg and McIntosh were opposed to it. In Randolph, Fisher and Menard were in favor of it.

" By the act of Congress of May, 1800, (the Division act) the Governor of the Territory was authorized that whenever in his opinion a majority of the freeholders of the same were in favor of the second grade of government, to declare the Territory to be in the second grade, and issue his writ for an election of Representative. An absolute and undefined discretion was devolved on him as to the mode of collecting the evidence, its kind and qualities, upon which this fact depended in his own mind. Petitions had been presented to him both for and against the measure. From them he could form no definite opinion. He had neither evidence of the signing nor of the signers being freeholders. Thus situated, and conscious it was necessary, from the clamor, that the question should be put to rest, he wisely determined to authorize, by proclamation, an election in the several counties, on a certain day, at which, under the regulations of the election law, the freeholders could express their voice.

" This was public, open, fair and just. The notice was public and general, and an opportunity afforded to all of a candid expression of their will. This was particularly the case as to Randolph, St. Clair, Knox, Clark and Dearborn. It was not the case as to Wayne, as I will hereafter explain.

" In the month of ——, 1804, the election accordingly took place. The vote stood as follows :

	For.	Against.
" St. Clair	22	59
Randolph	40	21
Knox	163	12
Clark	35	13
Dearborn	.	26
Totals	269	131
	131	
Majority	138	

" Giving a majority of 138 in favor of the second grade of government.

"As to the county of Wayne, a proclamation was sent to Detroit by mail, and another by express by way of Fort Wayne. This to increase the chances of their receiving the information in time. However, no election was holden in that county. My memory does not enable me to state correctly the cause that prevented it; but it has been said that it was received before that day elapsed, but not in time to give it the necessary publicity, as it ought to have been published a certain number of days before the election; but as the proclamation was issued on the —— day of ——, in 1804, and the election authorized to be holden on the —— day of the next ——, and as it was immediately forwarded, and in time to attain the object in view, according to the source or mode of conveying intelligence to that county, the failure of the election in that county ought not to have affected the result of the election in the other counties. This from an obvious principle and notorious examples. In a general election the result is not to be affected by want of its possibility in every district; or, if known, by the electors failing to give their votes, or from the officers conducting it illegally. —— so —— is this principle in elections, that had the county of Knox, which was in the majority, or the county of St. Clair, which was in the minority, alone expressed its voice, it would unquestionably have settled the question. The principle is limited to this alone: If the proper officer performs his duty; if there is a fixed time in which proclamations shall be issued; that it be done in the time prescribed by law; or, if not fixed by law, if it be issued so as to afford reasonable time for its distribution ; with a view to its being done by mail or by private express ; distance of place, roads, season of the year, etc., the law and reason and common sense are complied with. As to examples, the case of Mr. Adams in —96 ; Governor Strong, of Massachusetts, in —— ; C. Mead, elected to Congress from Georgia in 1805, are conclusive.

" Upon the receipt of the returns, and learning that no election had been held at Detroit, the Governor declared the Territory to be in the second grade of government, and issued writs for an election of members of the House of Representatives. Yet it has been stated ten thousand times, and is now repeated with much confidence by Rice Jones, that the Governor thrust the people of the Territory into the second grade against their will. This view brings us down to the fall of the year 1804. I will proceed to recount a few things that grew out of this change in the political character of our government."

Here the paper ends.

I shall not attempt to do that which the author of this letter proposed to do, for I am not writing the history of the Territorial government, but attempting to sketch the life of its head, of the most influential and important man within its jurisdiction.

General Harrison was emphatically a man of the people. The pioneers of Indiana loved and honored him as they did no other man. They testified to this on every occasion that offered. Both times he ran for the presidency Indiana voted for him, although a majority of her citizens were averse to the party whose candidate he was. He was an honest man. No taint of dishonor attaches to his name. William McIntosh, his territorial treasurer, once accused him of official dishonesty, but was mulcted in heavy damages by a jury of his peers for the libel.

General Harrison was Southern-born, and grew up under the influence of human slavery. It is no wonder, then, that he favored the abrogation of the article in the ordinance of 1787 prohibiting slavery in the Northwestern Territory, but fortunately for Indiana, as well as for the General's fame, Congress refused its consent to the change.

When General Harrison was a candidate for the presidency his political opponents belittled his talents, and tried to make the people believe he was an ignorant and ordinary man. They said he was a backwoodsman, living in a log cabin ; a man who treated his guests to hard cider. His supporters accepted these charges as true, and utilized them in his'behalf. Log cabins, with corn-cobs tied to the latch-strings of their doors, were carried in the processions of his partisans and made to do duty in his cause. The result proved that it never renders a man unpopular with the people to have them believe he is one of themselves.

The house in which General Harrison lived while Governor of Indiana Territory still stands. The intelligent stranger seldom visits Vincennes without asking to see it. In the yard near it stand the trees under which the Governor held his celebrated conference with Tecumseh. The house and its surroundings are held in veneration by the inhabitants of the " Old Post," and the time will come when the people of the country will visit the spot and the grave at North Bend as they now do Mount Vernon, Monticello and the Hermitage. It was in this house that the civil government of Indiana Territory was planned, and its master was the one, of all others, who did most to rear the structure. He was a master builder, and builded well.

JOHN GIBSON.

John Gibson, Secretary of Indiana Territory from its organization until it became a State, and for a while Acting Governor of the Territory, was born at Lancaster, Pa., May 23, 1740. He received a good education, and when eighteen years old joined General Forbes's expedition against Fort Du Quesne, which stood on the present site of Pittsburg. The expedition was successful, resulting in the capture of the fort, and when peace was declared young Gibson settled at Fort Pitt, formerly Du Quesne, as an Indian trader. Soon afterward he was taken captive by Indians, and, with other white men, condemned to be burned at the stake. An aged squaw, however, who had lost a son in battle, adopted the young trader, and thereby saved his life. He remained with the Indians several years, and learned their language, manners and customs. During his residence with them he maintained conjugal relations with a sister of Logan, the chieftain made immortal by his speech on the murder of his family. The life he was compelled to lead among the Indians did not suit Gibson, and he determined to abandon it. A suitable opportunity offering, he left his savage associates, returned to Fort Pitt, and resumed his business as a trader.

In 1774 Mr. Gibson accompanied Lord Dunmore in his march against the Shawanee towns. Previous to this expedition the family of Logan, including his sister, known as "Gibson's squaw," were killed at Yellow creek by a family named Greathouse. The Indians, at the time of their murder, were on a friendly visit to the Greathouses, and their "untimely taking off" was an act of treachery of the basest kind. Logan laid the blame of the foul murders at the door of Colonel Cresap, a celebrated Indian fighter of that day, but history exonerates

Cresap from the charge. In a deposition made at Pittsburg, on the 4th of April, 1800, General Gibson gives this account of Dunmore's expedition, and of Logan's celebrated speech:

"This deponent further saith that in the year 1774 he accompanied Lord Dunmore on the expedition against the Shawanees and other Indians on the Scioto; that on their arrival within fifteen miles of the town they were met by a flag and a white man by the name of Elliott, who informed Lord Dunmore that the chiefs of the Shawanees had sent to request his lordship to halt his army and send in some person who understood their language; that this deponent, at the request of Lord Dunmore and the whole of the officers with him, went in; that on his arrival at the town, Logan, the Indian, came to where this deponent was sitting with Cornstalk and other chiefs of the Shawanees and asked him to walk out with him; that they went into a copse of wood, where they sat down, when Logan, after shedding abundance of tears, delivered to him the speech nearly as related by Mr. Jefferson in his ' Notes on the State of Virginia;' that he, the deponent, told him that it was not Colonel Cresap who had murdered his relatives, and although his son, Captain Michael Cresap, was with a party who had killed a Shawanee chief and other Indians, yet he was not present when his (Logan's) relatives were killed at Baker's, near the mouth of Yellow creek, on the Ohio; that this deponent, on his return to camp, delivered the speech to Lord Dunmore, and that the murders perpetrated as above were considered as ultimately the cause of the war of 1774, commonly called Cresap's war."

The speech referred to was as follows:

"I appeal to any white man to say, if he ever entered Logan's cabin hungry, and he gave him not meat; if he ever came cold and naked, and he clothed him not. During the course of the last long and bloody war Logan remained idle in his cabin, an advocate of peace. Such was my love for the whites, that my countrymen pointed as they passed and said: 'Logan is the friend of white men.' I had even thought to have lived with you, but for the injuries of one man, Colonel Cresap, who, last spring, in cold blood and unprovoked, murdered all the rela-

tives of Logan, not even sparing my women and children.
There runs not a drop of my blood in the veins of any living
creature. This called on me for revenge. I have sought it; I
have killed many; I have fully glutted my vengeance; for my
country, I rejoice at the beams of peace. But do not harbor a
thought that mine is the joy of fear. Logan never felt fear. He
will not turn on his heel to save his life. Who is there to mourn
for Logan? Not one!"

On the breaking out of the revolutionary war, Colonel Gibson raised a regiment and marched at its head to the scene of
hostilities. He and his regiment were with the army at New
York, and remained with it during its retreat through the Jerseys. Soon after this he was assigned to the command of the
Western frontier, a position he was admirably qualified to fill.
When the war had ended, and the independence of the colonies
was assured, he returned to Pittsburg and resumed his former
avocation of a trader.

In 1788 General Gibson was elected a member of the convention that made the first constitution of Pennsylvania. Subsequently he was, for several years, a judge of the Court of Common Pleas of Alleghany county, and at the same time he served
as general of the State militia.

In April, 1793, President Washington appointed Benjamin
Lincoln, of Massachusetts, Beverly Randolph, of Virginia,
and Timothy Pickering, of Pennsylvania, commissioners to
treat with the Indians northwest of the river Ohio. These gentlemen requested General Gibson, under date of May 26, 1793,
"to point out the most suitable persons for interpreters, and we
request your aid in engaging them," etc. They also asked him
to procure for them 80,000 white wampum, to use in their negotiations with the Indians. At that time General Gibson was
a general of the Pennsylvania militia, and under date of July
11, 1794, he wrote Governor Mifflin as follows:

"I have written to the different inspectors of my division,
pressing them to have the men ready, agreeably to the requisition of the adjutant-general, and you may rely on my using
every means in my power for the protection of the western
frontiers."

The historian of St. Clair's defeat gives this account of the Gibson family:

" Colonel George Gibson, who was mortally wounded at St. Clair's defeat, was the father of General George Gibson, of the War Department, and of the late Chief Justice of Pennsylvania. He was the brother of General John Gibson, commonly called by the *nom de guerre* ' Horsehead,' the well known Indian interpreter in Dunmore's war. Colonel George Gibson, besides being a gallant soldier, was an accomplished gentleman, a man of wit and of fine imagination. Had he, instead of his brother, been at the treaty of Camp Charlotte, and present at the delivery of Logan's speech, that posthumous leaf from the plants of Sir William Johnson might have been imputed to him."

On the 7th of May, 1800, Congress passed an act dividing the Northwestern Territory, and creating that of Indiana. Soon afterward, President Jefferson appointed General Gibson Secretary of the new Territory, and he at once started for its capital. He reached Vincennes in July, 1800, and the Governor, William Henry Harrison, not having arrived, he commenced to organize the Territorial government. He made several appointments of Territorial officers, and did other things in the direction of creating a civil government. He continued in charge of the executive department of the Territory until the arrival of Governor Harrison, the next January, when his executive functions ceased. He confined himself to the Secretary's office until the summer of 1812, when he again became Acting Governor, administering the affairs of the Territory at the most critical period of its existence. On the 18th of June, 1812, Congress declared war against Great Britain, and on the 4th of the next September, Fort Harrison, then commanded by Captain Zachary Taylor, afterward President of the United States, was attacked by a large body of Indians. The day after the attack, and even before the news of it had reached Vincennes, Governor Gibson took active measures for the gathering of military forces at Vincennes, in anticipation of trouble with the Indians. He wrote to Governor Harrison, at Frankfort, Ky., for one company of regular troops and two companies of Kentucky militia, with stores, wagons, etc., asking that they be sent as expeditiously as possible. There being some delay from lack of arms and equipments for some six hundred men, who were at Louisville, and Governor Gibson meantime being advised of the investment of Fort Harrison, on September 9, 1812, wrote a second letter urging the immediate march of the troops without their baggage, as the danger seemed imminent. Responding to this appeal, by the 20th of September General Winlock reported at White river, sixteen miles from Vincennes, with six hundred and forty infantry and six hundred mounted men, but one day behind. Nor was the commandant at Louisville the only officer to whom Governor Gibson applied for help. He also informed General Samuel Hopkins, of Henderson county, Kentucky, of Indiana's emergency, and asked for volunteers from Kentucky at once, saying, "The exigency is such as to preclude the possibility of applying for aid from your quarter through the proper channel." In response to this, Colonel Philip Barbour, at Henderson, on the 11th of September, dispatched Major William R. McGary, with two hundred and forty-one men, for Vincennes, with promise of the rest of the regiment just as soon as arms could be procured for them. Barbour wrote of Major McGary to Governor Gibson:

"The Major is brave, firm and determined, and, I doubt not, will give you a good account of any command you may be pleased to order him on."

In the latter part of September General Hopkins reached Vincennes with two thousand mounted volunteers from Kentucky. Colonel William Russell, of the United States Army, was also there with a considerable number of men. These, with the soldiers of General Winlock and Major McGary, made a large army, and one which had been mainly gotten together within a single month.

Meantime, Captain Taylor, in command at Fort Harrison, informed Governor Gibson by messenger that he had been able to maintain his garrison against a severe assault by the Indians, lasting seven hours. On September 12, Governor Gibson instructed Colonel Robert Robertson to use such militia as could be so employed to guard the boundaries of Clark and Harrison counties, "taking care to have an eye to Linley's settlement, the Drift Wood and Pigeon Roost settlements." He added, "You will give particular orders to the officers commanding to employ their men continually in reconnoitering and scouring through the country on the frontier, and should anything extraordinary or alarming occur, you will give me the earliest information thereof by express." Colonel Paddock, at the same time, received instructions identical with the above.

September 9, 1812, Governor Gibson wrote Colonel Robertson, who, at the head of a body of men, was on the way to the Delaware towns, as follows :

"VINCENNES, September the 9th, 1812.

"SIR—I have just been informed that a body of men have undertaken an expedition against the Delaware towns, under an impression that the Delawares had done or countenanced the murders which have been committed on the frontiers of Clark county. I have official information that the great body of the Delaware tribe are now in council at Piquea, with commissioners appointed by the President, to hold a treaty with the Indians, or such of them as wish to remain the friends of the United States. They being under the immediate protection of the United States, I do hereby forbid all citizens of this Territory from proceeding against the Delawares without permission from government, assuring you, at the same time, that no person will be more willing to punish them than myself if they are found to be guilty.   Very truly,

"JOHN GIBSON,

"*Acting Governor.*"

The above letter shows Governor Gibson to have been a just man. In the excited state of the people at that time there are few who would have troubled themselves about seeing that justice was done an Indian. Retribution, not justice, was what the people were clamoring for.

Colonel Russell reached Fort Harrison in due time, and soon after General Hopkins followed him with his army. In a letter written to Governor Gibson by General Hopkins, dated Fort Harrison, November 8, 1812, he says:

"Letters, etc., sent to Fort Harrison by safe hands might probably find their way to us ; we are kept wholly uninformed of everything passing. We feel the want of whisky badly ; any other thing could be better done without. General Butler informs me the contractor had a supply, which, by this time, might have arrived here had it been sent on. Our supply of bread-stuffs and meat will, I hope, suffice."

It seems the pioneer soldiers of Indiana loved their grog. General Hopkins puts it before powder and ball in importance, and, in fact, it might have done about as good execution if it had possessed the qualities of the modern article.

The temptation to outline the history of the Wabash and Illinois campaigns of 1812 is a strong one, as I have original materials at hand which could be used for the purpose, but my object is not to write history, except incidentally, but to sketch men. I have made these slight digressions to show the reader that Governor Gibson was equal to the occasion, that he took good care of the people under his jurisdiction, and that, too, when great watchfulness and discretion were demanded.

Governor Gibson was in charge of the Governor's office for about one year, and then gave place to Governor Posey. All this time—that is to say, from the day of his arrival at Vincennes until the commencement of Governor Posey's administration, and thence on until Indiana became a State—General Gibson was in charge of the Secretary's office. No complaint was ever made of the way he discharged its duties ; nor was there of his actions as Governor. In his double capacity of Secretary and Governor he so conducted the affairs of the Territory as to escape criticism from the ambitious and plotting men around him, something his chief, General Harrison, a good and patriotic man, was unable to do. He kept aloof from the cabals and intrigues of Territorial days, confining himself to the discharge of his public duties. He did not become involved in the quarrels about him, and as a consequence enjoyed the good-will and friendship of those who were hostile among themselves.

While Secretary of Indiana Territory General Gibson was not conspicuous in public affairs outside of his official duties. He seemed content with attending to his business, leaving to

2

others the task of righting neighborhood wrongs and settling private grievances. It was only on extraordinary occasions that his name appears in the proceedings of the public gatherings of these days. In July, 1812, a public meeting was held at Vincennes to consider the subject of the war with England. General Gibson was chosen its president, and strong resolutions were passed approving the declaration of war, and indorsing the course of the Madison administration. The *Western Sun*, a paper published at Vincennes by Elihu Stout, the grandfather of Hon. Henry S. Cauthorn, makes frequent mention, during the summer of 1812, of the valuable information furnished by General Gibson, then the Acting Governor of the Territory, in relation to public matters generally, and particularly in regard to Indian affairs. In the *Sun* of September 1, 1812, is a proclamation of General Gibson, as Acting Governor, requiring all aliens in the Territory to report, conformably to the law of Congress passed July 6, 1798, to him in person, in the county of Knox, and to certain persons named by him in the other counties of the Territory.

On the 26th of December, 1812, the *Sun* contains General Gibson's proclamation, as Acting Governor of the Territory, convening the Legislature, and naming February 1, 1813, as the time for its meeting.

On the 16th of January, 1813, the *Sun* contains the general orders of General Gibson as commander-in-chief of the Territorial militia, promoting Daniel Sullivan to the rank of colonel, and ordering that " on account of the present aspect of affairs the whole of the militia of the Territory hold themselves in readiness to march at a moment's warning, and when warned, will rendezvous according to law."

In the *Sun*, of February 6, 1813, is the address of General Gibson, as Acting Governor, delivered before the Legislature on the previous Tuesday. It is plain, pointed and brief. He says he is no speaker. The topics alluded to by him are " the devolving of the gubernatorial duties upon him ; " " his promise to discharge them fairly and justly," etc. He alludes " to the just war with England," and approves of the course of President Madison. Attention is called in the address " to the frequent and numerous Indian massacres, and the uncertainty of life and property in the Territory." He calls attention to the necessity of reform in "the militia organization of the Territory, the revenue laws and the salaries of public officers."

On the 6th of March the *Sun* contained the reply of James Scott, the Speaker of the Territorial Legislature, to General Gibson's speech before that body, in which the Speaker said:

"Your patriotism has long drawn down the attention of the only nation upon earth enjoying the liberal exercise of national liberty. We are happy, sir, in congratulating you that, notwithstanding the many years that the critical eye of envy has had an opportunity of observing you in the discharge of your duties of a national concern, and important trusts confided in you by your nation, that yet, for the most cogent reasons, national patronage is extended to you in the evening of your life."

This florid and prolix speech does not indicate an embryo jurist; nevertheless, the Speaker afterwards became a very eminent judge of our Supreme Court. On the 12th of March, 1813, Governor Gibson prorogued the Legislature, after a session of forty days, and directed it to reassemble at Corydon on the first Monday of the next December. In the meantime the records and offices of the Territorial government were removed to Corydon, Governor Gibson accompanying them. In May, 1813, he was superseded in the Governor's office by General Thomas Posey, and from that time until the admission of Indiana into the Union he acted as Territorial Secretary.

General Gibson's knowledge of the Indian language most probably once saved General Harrison's life. At a conference between the latter and Tecumseh, at Vincennes, the Indian, becoming angry, arose to his feet, flourished his tomahawk, and directed his followers to be ready to obey his command. General Gibson, who was present, understanding the Shawanee tongue, called the guard, which he had stationed near by, and on their appearance the cowed savage resumed his seat. When his threatening language was translated for the Governor, he broke up the conference and ordered Tecumseh away.

After much research I have been unable to find the origin of General Gibson's pseudonym of "Horsehead." I assume that it was his Indian name; at least that it was given him by the

Indians.   He was known by it long before he came to Indiana
Territory, and it clung to him while he lived.   It may be that
it was given to him because of his strong common sense, common sense sometimes being denominated "horse sense."

When the State government of Indiana was formed, General
Gibson went back to Vincennes, his old home, to live.   Soon
afterward he left Indiana, and during the remainder of his life
resided with his son-in-law, George Wallace, at Braddock's
Field, near Pittsburg, Pennsylvania, at whose house he died
April 10, 1822.

The *Western Clarion*, a paper published at Madison, Indiana,
in its issue of June 10, 1822, contains a letter supposed to have
been written by Mr. Wallace, dated Pittsburg, April 19, 1822,
which says that "General Gibson died recently at Braddock's
Field, near Pittsburg."   It also says that "he had been carefully educated, with uncommon pains, as he was a good scholar,
and his classical attainments were considerable."   It gives a
summary of the leading incidents of his life, to the time Indiana became a State, and concludes as follows:

"At this period, having become somewhat infirm, and being
afflicted with an incurable cataract, he, with his amiable wife,
removed from Vincennes to the residence of his son-in-law,
Mr. George Wallace, in the neighborhood of this place, where
he was attended till the moment of his death with the most ex-
emplary filial piety."

Having safely passed the dangers of field and flood, of both
civilized and savage warfare, he was mercifully permitted to
live far beyond the allotted years of man, and to die with his family about him.   God was with the old pioneer to the end.   Gibson county, in this State, was named in his honor, and it is,
therefore, his most enduring monument.

THOMAS POSEY.

Thomas Posey, the last Governor of Indiana Territory, was born in Virginia, on the banks of the Potomac, July 9, 1750. He was the son of a farmer, and grew up a farmer's boy. His education was scanty, being confined to those branches ordinarily taught in the country schools of that day. The family was respectable, but not wealthy, and the high distinction afterward reached by General Posey can not be attributed to family influence, nor the efforts of powerful friends. It was the work of himself.

When nineteen years old young Posey left his paternal home and went into the western part of the State, then the frontier of civilization. He was, no doubt, prompted to this change by a spirit of adventure and a desire to find full scope for his daring nature. Soon after locating in his new home the occasion offered for him to go soldiering, and he eagerly embraced it. It was in the year 1774, the year of Dunmore's expedition against the Indians, that he first put on the knapsack and shouldered his musket. Dunmore's army was in two divisions, one of which was commanded by himself and the other by General Lewis. The plan of the campaign was for Dunmore to march to Pittsburg and thence down the Ohio river to the mouth of the Kanawha, where the united army was to rendezvous. Lewis was to cross the mountain, march down the Kanawha valley and join Dunmore. Posey was with Lewis, and when that General reached the appointed rendezvous he encamped, to await the arrival of his superior. But when Dunmore reached Pittsburg he changed his mind, and, instead of going forward to join Lewis, he marched his army against the

Shawanee towns on the Scioto. On the 10th of October, 1774, Lewis was attacked by a large body of Indians under Cornstalk, and one of the bloodiest battles ever fought by Indians and white men took place. Seventy-five Virginians were killed outright and one hundred and forty wounded, while the loss of the Indians was still greater. The latter were defeated and driven away, and soon afterward peace was established, at Camp Charlotte, by the treaty between Lord Dunmore and the Indians. The battle between General Lewis and Cornstalk is known in history as the battle of Point Pleasant. Posey behaved with great gallantry, giving evidence of the coolness and bravery which afterward made him one of the most conspicuous figures in the military service of his country.

The war having ended, Posey went back to his home in Western Virginia, but did not long pursue his peaceful avocations. The next year (1775) war broke out between the colonies and Great Britain. Posey was elected a member of the committee of correspondence of his county, similar committees being chosen in the other counties of the colony, the purpose being to keep the people advised of what was going on and to draw them together in closer union. Shortly after hostilities had commenced Posey raised a company of infantry and took it to the field. His commander was the General Lewis under whom he had already fought, and the enemy against whom he marched was led by Lord Dunmore, who had been Lewis's superior officer the year before. The two armies met at Gwyn's Island, and in the battle which followed Dunmore was beaten and driven off the field.

After the Virginia campaign had ended, the regiment to which Captain Posey was attached joined the army of Washington in the Jerseys. The company then became a part of a regiment of picked men, armed with the rifle and commanded by Colonel Morgan, which did gallant service on many a field. At Piscataway it was surrounded by the enemy and cut its way out in a hand to hand fight, which left many a brave man on the ground. Afterwards it was with Gates at Saratoga, and helped compass the surrender of Burgoyne there. Subsequently Captain Posey was given command of this noted regiment, and headed it at the drawn battle of Monmouth. In 1778 the regiment was sent to the relief of the people of Wyoming, whose calamities have been made the subject of one of our finest poems.

In the spring of 1779 Colonel Posey joined the main army under Washington, and was assigned to the command of the Eleventh Infantry. Subsequently his regiment was transferred to the army of Wayne, and was with it at the taking of Stony Point. Marshall gives this account of Posey's actions in this battle:

"Colonel Fleury was the first to enter the fort and strike the British standard. Major Posey mounted the works almost at the same instant, and was the first to give the watchword, 'The fort's our own.'"

After the taking of Stony Point Colonel Posey went to South Carolina, and subsequently to Yorktown, at which place he witnessed Cornwallis's surrender. In the winter of 1781-2 he served with Wayne in Georgia, and on the 24th of June, 1781, was in the battle, near Savannah, fought with Guristersigo and his Indian followers. In this battle Posey killed several Indians with his own hands, displaying the greatest gallantry throughout the entire engagement. After this he served with Greene in South Carolina, being with him when peace was declared.

During the Revolutionary war Colonel Posey lost the wife of his youth. After the peace he married again, and settled in Spottsylvania county, Virginia.

In 1785 Colonel Posey was appointed colonel of the militia of his county, and the next year was made county-lieutenant, an office of much honor and dignity. He continued to act as county-lieutenant and magistrate until 1793, when he was again called into the military service of his country.

The Indians in the Northwest continued hostile. Many had been the expeditions sent against them, and many the chastisements they had received, but they had not been conquered. Washington determined to break their spirit and subdue them, and with these ends in view he appointed Mad Anthony Wayne to conduct an expedition against them. He also selected Generals Wilkinson and Posey as his lieutenants. These men were all revolutionary soldiers and had large experience in fighting the foe they were chosen to conquer. General Posey was with Wayne for some time and aided greatly in rendering successful the campaign of that able and patriotic man.

Early in the winter of 1793 General Posey applied for leave of absence in order to visit his home. The following is Wayne's letter granting it:

> " HEADQUARTERS, GREENVILLE,
>   " December 5, 1793.

" DEAR SIR—I must acknowledge that it was with difficulty I at length prevailed upon myself to grant you leave of absence at a crisis when I was conscious that your aid and advice were extremely necessary to me, perhaps to the nation. Friendship may have prevailed over duty on this occasion, but I have the consolation that it may eventually be in your power to render as essential services to your country during your absence in the Atlantic States as you could have done in the wilderness of the West. I have only to regret the temporary absence of a friend and brother officer with whom I have participated in almost every vicissitude of fortune from the frozen lakes of Canada to the burning sands of Florida. I have, therefore, to request that you will endeavor to return to your command on or before the last of March ensuing, and, in the interim, I pray you to make a point of impressing every member of Congress with whom you may converse with the absolute necessity of the immediate completion of the Legion, and that you also pay a visit to the seat of government, and wait personally upon the President and Secretary of War, and give them every information, *viva voce*, that they may wish to receive relative to the situation of the Legion, together with the motives and circumstances which influenced an advance and halt at this place. You will also suggest the expediency and policy of permitting settlers to take possession of it the moment the Legion takes up its line of march in the spring.

" Wishing you a safe and quick passage through the wilderness and a happy meeting with your family and friends, I am, with the truest and most lasting friendship and esteem, etc.,

                                  "ANTHONY WAYNE."

When the war was over, General Posey resigned his commission in the army, and soon afterwards removed to Kentucky. In a short time after settling there he was elected a member of the State Senate, and was chosen Speaker of that body. He thereby became ex-officio Lieutenant Governor of the State, and held the place during his entire service in the Senate.

In 1809, on account of the unsatisfactory conditions of our relations with France and England, Congress ordered the raising of an army of 100,000 men, and the President fixed the quota of Kentucky at 5,000. General Posey was commissioned a major general and assigned to the command of the Kentucky troops. He at once proceeded to organize and equip his forces, but the call for troops was premature. War was not declared, and the forces were disbanded. Soon after this General Posey removed to Louisiana. He never seemed contented except when on the frontier, and whenever his home ceased to be near the dividing line between civilization and the woods he moved away.

In 1812, when war was about to be inaugurated with Great Britain, General Posey, then a citizen of Louisiana, raised a company of infantry at Baton Rouge, and for some time was its captain. Seldom in the history of military men do we find one who, having held a major-general's commission, consents to command a company. But with General Posey patriotism was stronger than pride. Had he believed it best for his country, he would have shouldered a musket and marched in the ranks.

John N. Destrihan was one of the first Senators sent by Louisiana to the Senate of the United States. Soon after his election he resigned, and Governor Claiborne appointed General Posey to fill the vacancy. He sat in the Senate until March 3, 1813, when President Madison appointed him Governor of Indiana Territory. He reached Vincennes the next May and entered upon the discharge of his official duties. Soon after this the Territorial capital was removed to Corydon, necessitating a change of the Governor's residence to that town. On the 6th of the next December he delivered his first message to the Legislature. He was in delicate health at the time, and on the 27th of the same month he addressed a letter to the president of the legislative council, in which he said :

" I wish you to communicate to your honorable body that the delicate state of my health will not admit of my longer continuance at this place [Corydon]. I find myself badly situated on account of the want of medical aid. My physician is at Louisville, and I have taken all the medicine brought with me. The weather is moderate now, which will be favorable to my going to Jeffersonville, where any communication that the two houses of the Legislature may have to make will find me. Mr. Prather will, in the most expeditious manner, bring them on ; and it will take but a short time for me to act upon them and for his return, which would not detain the Legislature in session more than a day longer. Be assured, sir, that nothing but imperious necessity compels me to this step."

On the 6th of January, 1814, the legislative council passed the following preamble and resolution :

" WHEREAS, Both houses of the Legislature did, on the 4th inst., inform the Governor that they had gone through their legislative business, and were ready to be prorogued ; and,

" WHEREAS, The expense of near fifty dollars per day doth arise to the people of the Territory by reason of the Legislature being kept in session—all of which evils and inconvenience doth arise from the Governor leaving the seat of government during the session of the Legislature and going to Jeffersonville, and the Legislature having to send their committee of enrolled bills to that place to lay them before him for his approval and signature ; be it, therefore,

" *Resolved*, That in order to prevent any further expense accruing to the Territory at the present session, that the President of the Legislative Council and the Speaker of the House of Representatives be, and are hereby authorized to receive the report of the Governor of the laws by him signed or rejected, and his order of prorogation, and communicate the same to the clerks of their respective houses, who shall insert the same in their journals in the same manner as if the two houses were in session."

The House of Representatives concurred in this resolution, whereupon the two houses adjourned without day.

On the first Monday in December, 1815, the Legislature of the Territory met in session at Corydon. Governor Posey, who resided at Jeffersonville, was too unwell to be present, and sent his message to the two houses by his private secretary, Colonel Thom. The message was a brief one, treating principally upon questions affecting the internal affairs of the Territory. This was his last formal communication to the Legislature, and to it that body responded in the following complimentary language:

" They (the Legislature) can not refrain from declaring their perfect approbation of your official conduct as Governor of this Territory. During your administration many evils have been remedied, and we particularly admire the calm, dispassionate, impartial conduct, which has produced the salutary effects of quieting the violence of party spirit, harmonizing the interests as well as the feelings of the different parties of the Territory. Under your auspices we have become one people."

In May, 1816, delegates were elected to make a State constitution, and in the following June they met at Corydon and performed the work. The next August officers were elected for the new State. At this election General Posey was a candidate for Governor, but was beaten by Jonathan Jennings, by a very decisive vote.

When Governor Posey's official term had expired, by reason of the admission of Indiana into the Union, he was appointed Indian agent for Illinois Territory, with headquarters at Shawneetown. Early in the spring of 1818, while descending the Wabash river from Vincennes, he caught a deep cold, which threw him into a fever. When he reached Shawneetown he was compelled to take to his bed. He continued to grow worse until the 19th of March, when he died.

Governor Posey was a most amiable man in private life. He was a member of the Presbyterian church, and very active in church work. He was president of a Bible society, and did much to distribute the Scriptures among the poor and needy of the Territory.

In person, Governor Posey was exceedingly attractive and commanding. He was tall, athletic, and had a handsome face.

His manner was graceful and easy, denoting the gentleman he was. Some ten years ago a correspondent of the *Cincinnati Commercial* started the story that Governor Posey was a natural son of George Washington, but the romance did not take root. Had he been Washington's son, begotten in wedlock, he would have honored his father's name.

Dillon, in his history of Indiana, says that when General Posey was appointed Governor of Indiana Territory, "he was at the time a Senator in Congress from the State of Tennessee." This is a mistake. He never lived in Tennessee, and never served her in any official capacity whatever. Five States might properly claim that he once lived within their borders, but Tennessee is not one of the five. She must be content with Jackson and Polk, and other eminent men who have served her ably and well, and leave to Virginia, to Kentucky, Louisiana, Indiana and Illinois the honor of having once been the home of Thomas Posey, a revolutionary patriot, and the last Territorial Governor of Indiana.

JONATHAN JENNINGS.

JONATHAN JENNINGS, the first Governor of Indiana, was born in Hunterdon county, N. J., in 1784. His father was a Presbyterian minister, and, soon after Jonathan's birth, removed to Fayette county, Pa. It was here that the future Governor grew to manhood. After obtaining a common school education he went to a grammar school at Cannonsburg, Pa. Here he studied Latin and Greek, as well as the higher branches of mathematics. Thus liberally educated, he commenced the study of the law, but before being admitted to the bar he left Pennsylvania and started for Indiana Territory. Arriving at Pittsburg, he took passage on a flatboat and floated down the Ohio river to Jeffersonville, where he landed, having determined to make that town his home. He was then very young, and in appearance younger than he really was. He resumed his legal studies, and in a short time was admitted to the bar. But clients were few, and the young attorney sought other means for a living besides the practice of his profession. He wrote an unusually good hand, and was soon made clerk of the Territorial Legislature. While filling this place he became acquainted with most of the leading men of the Territory, and in 1809, when the Territory entered into the second grade and the people became possessed of a right to elect a delegate to Congress, he became a candidate for the place. His opponent was Thomas Randolph, then Attorney-general of the Territory, and a man of much learning and ability. The contest between Jennings and Randolph was exceedingly exciting and bitter. Randolph was Virginia born, and believed in the divinity of slavery, while Jennings, a native of a free State, considered slavery a blight and a curse. The Terri-

tory was but sparsely inhabited, the settlements being on its
eastern and southern borders, with one at Vincennes, on the
Wabash.   The question at issue was that of slavery.   The
Governor of the Territory, William Henry Harrison, and the
Virginians about him, were striving to have the provision of the
ordinance of 1787 prohibiting slavery in the Northwestern Territory suspended or repealed, and Jennings and other free-state
men were trying to prevent this.   The territorial delegate would
have much to do in determining the matter, hence the two parties battled fiercely for the election of their respective favorite.
The intelligent reader need hardly be told that the Territory was
then virtually a slave Territory.   Negroes were bought and
sold in the market at so much a head.   The author has been
permitted to examine the private papers of Mr. Randolph, and
among them are two bills of sale for negroes, executed at Vincennes in 1809.   There is, also, among Mr. Randolph's papers,
a letter from General James Dill, Randolph's father-in-law,
written from Vincennes to his wife at Lawrenceburg, saying he
had not bought her a negro servant because they rated too high,
but he hoped soon to find one at a price he could stand.   Public
sentiment at Vincennes was then as pro-slavery as it was at
Richmond.   Randolph was its representative and exponent,
and it rallied to his support with all the dogmatism that used to
characterize its adherents.   Jennings was then a young man—
a mere youth—but he met the assault of the pro-slavery men
with the courage of a hero.   He made a thorough canvass of
the Territory, riding on horseback to all the settlements.   As is
known, the eastern part of Indiana was mainly settled by Quakers from the Carolinas.   These people hated slavery, and they
supported Jennings almost to a man, Randolph hardly getting
enough votes in the Whitewater country to pay for the counting.
General Dill, who followed Jennings in the canvass, hoping to
counteract his work, in a letter to Randolph says that " wherever Jennings goes he draws all men to him."   In a letter from
Brookville, he says the only man he finds for Randolph is
Enoch McCarty, and that he publicly declares that Jennings
will be elected.

The election for delegate came off in May, and Jennings was
victorious.   His total vote in the Territory was 428, and that of

Randolph 402. John Johnson received 81 votes at the same election ; so it will be seen that Jennings was elected by a plurality and not by a majority. To us of the present day the vote which elected Jennings seems too insignificant to make a congressman. Wards in some of our cities now contain more voters than did the Territory of Indiana at that time. But the vote, meager as it was, virtually fixed the status of Indiana upon the subject of slavery for years to come. Had Randolph been elected, the clause in the ordinance of 1787 prohibiting slavery in the Territory would have been abrogated and the "peculiar institution" established by law. This done, it would have remained to curse our people until the day that American slavery went down in blood.

Governor Harrison gave Mr. Jennings his certificate of election, and the delegate went to Washington and took his seat in the National Congress. But he was not permitted to hold it unchallenged. Mr. Randolph contested his election on the ground that at one of the voting places in Dearborn county, the election was not legally held. At this precinct Jennings received a greater majority than that given him in the Territory ; consequently, if the vote of this precinct could be thrown out he would be defeated. There was a grave question as to the legality of the entire election, but as Mr. Randolph had advised the Governor that an election could be held under the law, he refused to raise the point. Both Jennings and Randolph appeared before the committee on elections and stated their cases. The committee reported to the House " that the election held for a delegate to Congress for the Indiana Territory, on the 22d of May, 1809, being without authority of law is void, and consequently the seat of Jonathan Jennings as delegate for that Territory is hereby declared to be vacant." The report of the committee was considered in committee of the whole, and adopted, but on being reported to the House, that body refused its concurrence, and confirmed Jennings in his seat.

Much bad feeling grew up between Jennings and Randolph on account of this election and contest. Each resorted to handbills and scattered them far and wide. Randolph was the more sarcastic and bitter ; Jennings, the more persuasive and convincing. In a circular dated "Jeffersonville, Indiana Territory, Oct. 10, 1810," addressed to the people of the Territory, he says :

" If Mr. Randolph succeeds in his wishes by fair means, without injuring me, rely upon it, that I shall never envy his success,
nor take the advantage of his absence to traduce him. But, if
he expects to ascend the political ladder by slander and detraction, he ought not to be surprised if his borrowed popularity
should forsake him and leave him, like other thorough-going
politicians, without so much as the consolation of an approving
heart."

The friends of Mr. Randolph partook of that gentleman's
hatred of Mr. Jennings. Waller Taylor, then a territorial
judge, in a letter to Mr. Randolph dated June 3, 1809, says he
had publicly insulted Mr. Jennings without the latter's resenting
it, and that Jennings was a " pitiful coward." He also says:
" Jennings revenges himself on me by saying he never did anything to injure me, and professes esteem." Surely, if it be true,
that " He that ruleth his spirit is greater than he that taketh a
city," Jonathan Jennings was a great man. It is evident that
Taylor's purpose was to provoke him to a duel, but he kept his
temper and gave the hot-blooded Virginian no excuse for challenging him.
In 1811 Mr. Jennings was re-elected to Congress, his opponent being Waller Taylor, the same man, who, two years before had tried to provoke him to mortal combat. In 1813 he
was again re-elected, his competitor this time being Judge
Sparks, a very worthy and popular man.
The Territory of Indiana was now ready to pass from its
chrysalis condition and become a State. Early in 1816 Mr.
Jennings reported a bill to Congress enabling the people of the
Territory to take the necessary steps to convert it into a State.
Delegates to a convention to form a State constitution were
elected in May, 1816, Mr. Jennings being chosen one from the
county of Clark. The delegates met at Corydon, June 10, and
organized the convention by electing Mr. Jennings president
and William Hendricks secretary. The convention continued
in session nineteen days, and then adjourned, having made the
constitution under which the people of Indiana lived and prospered for thirty-four years. The constitution required that an
election should be held on the first Monday in August, 1816,

for the election of a Governor, Lieutenant-governor and other officers, the Territorial officials in the meantime continuing in office. The candidates for Governor were Jonathan Jennings and Thomas Posey, the then Territorial Governor. Governor Posey was a Virginian by birth. He was a gallant soldier in the revolutionary war, and for a time served in the Senate of the United States from the State of Louisiana. He was considered the pro-slavery candidate, and, although the question of slavery had been settled in Indiana by the adoption of the State constitution, the pro-slavery men of the Territory still kept up their organization. Jennings had been a leader of the free-state party since his entrance into public life, and now that he was a candidate for governor, that party rallied to his support. He received 5,211 votes, and Governor Posey 3,934, his majority being 1,277.

The making and putting into motion of the machinery of a new State requires ability of a high order. Revenue is to be created, laws for the protection of life and property to be drawn and passed, and divers other things to be done that the foundations of the government may be properly laid. The Governor proved himself equal to the task. The State machinery started off without impediment and ran without friction. It did its work well, for it was guided by a master hand.

In his first message to the Legislature, delivered Nov. 7, 1816, Governor Jennings says:

"I recommend to your consideration the propriety of providing by law to prevent more effectually any unlawful attempts to seize and carry into bondage persons of color legally entitled to their freedom ; and at the same time, as far as practicable, to prevent those who rightfully owe service to the citizens of any other State or Territory, from seeking, within the limits of this State, a refuge from the possession of their lawful owners. Such a measure will tend to secure those who are free from any unlawful attempts to enslave them, and secure the rights of the citizens of the other States and Territories so far as ought reasonably to be expected."

3

In his message to the Legislature of 1817, he thus refers to the subject of fugitive slaves coming into the State :

" Permit me again to introduce to your attention the subject of slaves escaping into this State, and to suggest the propriety of making further provisions by law calculated to restrain them from fleeing to this State to avoid their lawful owners, and to enable the judges of our Circuit Courts, or any judge of the Supreme Court, in vacation, to decide, with the aid of a jury, upon all claims of this character without delay. This subject, in the adjoining State of Kentucky, has produced some excitement in the citizens and an interference on the part of their Legislature. To preserve harmony between our State and every other, so far as may depend on our exertions, is a duty the discharge of which is intimately connected with our best interests as a State, and solemnly required of Indiana as a member of the Union."

On the 10th of December, 1817, Governor Jennings sent to the House of Representatives a letter from Governor Slaughter, of Kentucky, and his answer thereto. The letter was referred to a special committee, of which General Samuel Milroy was chairman. In his letter Governor Slaughter complains of the difficulty the citizens of Kentucky encounter in reclaiming their slaves who escape into Indiana, and says : " You must be sensible, sir, that occurrences of this sort can not fail to produce discontent here and a spirit of animosity toward your State, which is equally the interest of all to avoid." In his reply Governor Jennings says :

" With regard to the subject matter of your letter—the difficulty said to be experienced by your citizens in reclaiming their slaves who escape into this State—allow me to state in relation to my views on this subject, that I have been and still am desirous that every municipal regulation, not inconsistent with the constitution of the United States or of this State, may be adopted by the legislative authority of the latter, calculated to secure to the citizens of every State or Territory of the Union the means of reclaiming any slave escaping to this State that may rightfully belong to them or either of them with as little delay as the operation of the law will admit."

The committee to which this matter was referred made a lengthy report, in which they said:

" On the subject of the difficulties said to be experienced by the citizens of Kentucky in regaining their fugitive slaves, your committee are of opinion that the feelings of His Excellency, as well as of the Legislature of Kentucky, have been governed in a great degree by the improper representations of individuals who have been disappointed in their attempts to carry away those whom they claim as slaves from this State, without complying with the preliminary steps required by law, together with the groundless assertions of unprincipled individuals who have attempted, in many instances, to seize and carry away people of color, as slaves, who were free, and as much entitled to the protection of the laws as any citizen of Indiana. * * * It is a well-known fact that, whatever may be the opinion of our citizens on the abstract principles of slavery, and however repugnant it may appear, in their estimation, to the principles of moral justice, there is but one sentiment prevalent on this subject of people of color migrating, in any circumstances, to this State. It is believed, if not restricted, it would, in time, become an evil of not much less magnitude than slavery itself. * * * Your committee, in the further prosecution of the duties assigned them, will take into consideration the laws on the subject of slaves escaping into this State, as well as the laws for the punishment of the crime of man-stealing, and, if it shall be found that any new provisions are necessary on either of these subjects, they will form the subjects of future reports."

In the last paragraph the committee showed its teeth, and told kidnappers to beware, or they would get bitten.

I have spoken thus fully of Governor Jennings's recommendations upon the subject of the rendition of fugitive slaves, because it was a question that confronted the young Commonwealth at its birth, and the people of the present day should know how it was met. That it was considered in a statesmanlike way and disposed of to the best interest of the people must be admitted by those who study it in the light of this time. Public sentiment upon the question of slavery was then widely different from what it is now, and in coming to a correct conclusion as to its treatment this fact should not be forgotten. Governor Jennings was far in advance of the public men of his day in Indiana upon this subject, and while his utterances seem to us exceedingly conservative, they are those of one of the most pronounced anti-slavery men of his time.

In 1818, President Monroe appointed Governor Jennings a commissioner to negotiate a treaty with the Indians, his associates being General Cass and Judge Benjamin Parke. The commissioners reached St. Mary's in September of that year, and proceeded with their work. On the 3d of October Governor Jennings wrote from St. Mary's to Christopher Harrison, the Lieutenant-governor, that " Understanding some official business is necessary to be transacted, permit me to inform you that my absence is still necessary, and that it may be necessary for you to attend the seat of government to discharge such duties as devolve on the executive of Indiana." Lieutenant-governor Harrison thereupon went to Corydon, took possession of the executive office, and performed the duties of Governor until Jennings's return from Saint Mary's. The constitution of the State prohibited the Governor from holding " any office under the United States," and Governor Jennings, having accepted and performed the duties of Indian Commissioner, contrary to this provision, the Lieutenant-governor claimed that the Governor had thereby forfeited his office, and that he, the Lieutenant-governor, had become Acting Governor of the State. Governor Jennings refused to accept this interpretation of the law, and demanded possession of the executive office. The Lieutenant-governor left the room he had been occupying, and taking with him the State seal, opened an office elsewhere. The State officers were in a quandary what to do. Two men were claiming to be Governor, and they did not know which to recognize. Such was the condition of affairs when the Legislature of 1818 convened. On the 10th of December of that year Ratliff Boon, then a senator from the county of Warrick, appeared upon the floor of the House and said :

" Mr. Speaker, I am directed by the Senate to inform this House that the Senate has appointed a committee on their part to act with a similar committee which may be appointed on the part of the House of Representatives to wait on the Lieutenant-governor, and late acting Governor, and inform him that the two houses of the General Assembly have met, formed a quorum, and are now ready to receive any communications which he may please to make relative to the executive department of government, and request a similar committee be appointed on the part of the House of Representatives, and that on the part of the Senate Messrs. Boon and DePauw were appointed that committee.

" Whereupon, on motion of Mr. Milroy, the House ordered ' that a similar committee be appointed on the part of this House to act with the committee on the part of the Senate, and to learn from the Lieutenant-governor, if he should please to make any communications, at what time and in what manner the two houses may expect them.' "

Thus it will be seen that the Lieutenant-governor was acknowledged to be the chief executive by both branches of the Legislature. The next day Mr. Sullivan, chairman of the House committee under the resolution above quoted, reported to the House that the committee had waited on " His Excellency Lieutenant-governor Harrison, and had informed him that a quorum of both houses of the General Assembly had convened and were ready to receive any communication he might be pleased to make to them," and that the Lieutenant-governor, had replied, " That, as Lieutenant-governor he had no communication to make to the Senate or House of Representatives, but as Lieutenant and Acting Governor, if recognized as such, he had."

The same day a committee was appointed by the House to investigate the troubles in the Executive Department, and next day reported through their chairman, General Milroy, that they " are of the opinion, from the testimony herewith transmitted, that His Excellency, Governor Jonathan Jennings, did, in the months of September and October last, accept an appointment under the government of the United States, by virtue of which he, together with others, did repair to St. Mary's, and then and there did negotiate and conclude a treaty with various tribes of Indians on behalf of the United States ; and that he did sign said treaty as the agent or officer of the United States, and he did thereto subscribe his name with others."

The committee addressed Governor Jennings a note, informing him that they had been appointed to investigate his actions in relation to the treaty of St. Mary's, with a view of determining if he had forfeited his office of Governor, and asking him to appear before them and make his defense. He replied in a courteous note, in which he said :

"If the difficulty, real or supposed, has grown out of the circumstances of my having been connected with the negotiation at St. Mary's, I feel it my duty to state to the committee that I acted from an entire conviction of its propriety and an anxious desire, on my part, to promote the welfare and accomplish the wishes of the whole people of the State in assisting to add a large and fertile tract of country to that which we already possess."

Governor Jennings declined to appear in person before the committee, but wrote General Milroy to " receive and introduce Mr. C. Dewey as my counsel to the committee of which you are chairman."

The committee took the testimony of several persons, from which it conclusively appeared that Governor Jennings had acted as a commissioner of the United States at St. Mary's. The testimony was reported to the House, and that body, on the 16th of December, passed a resolution " that it was inexpedient to further prosecute the inquiry into the existing difficulties in the executive department of the government of the State," and thereupon recognized Governor Jennings as the rightful Governor by receiving his message. The vote by which this resolution was passed was 15 yeas and 13 nays ; so it will be seen that a change of two votes would have put Governor Jennings out of office. Indeed, had a vote been taken directly upon the question, a majority of the House would probably have declared that he had forfeited the governorship, for this he most unquestionably had done. But the Legislature, appreciating the motive of his action, avoided the issue, and he remained in office.

So soon as the Legislature recognized Jennings as Governor, the Lieutenant-governor resigned, saying in a note to the House that " As the officers of the executive department of the Government and the General Assembly have refused to recognize that authority which, according to my understanding, is constitutionally attached to the office, the name itself is not worth retaining." The next year he ran against Mr. Jennings for Governor, and was badly beaten, receiving but 2,008 votes in a total of 11,256.

In May, 1820, Governor Jennings left Corydon with General Tipton, to meet the commissioners appointed by the Legislature to locate and lay out a permanent capital of the State. As is known, the ground upon which Indianapolis stands was selected, and although Governor Jennings was not officially a party to the selection, he was present when it was made, and no doubt advised it.

In August, 1822, Governor Jennings was elected a representative to Congress from the Second congressional district, and on the 12th day of next month—September—resigned the governorship. The remainder of his term—until Dec. 5, 1822—was filled by Ratliff Boon, the Lieutenant-governor. Governor Jennings was re-elected to Congress in 1824, in 1826, and in 1828, serving his district continuously for eight years. In 1830 he was again a candidate, but was beaten by General John Carr, a gallant soldier of the war of 1812. The defeat of Governor Jennings at this election was not because the people had lost confidence in his judgment or ability to serve them, but because they believed such a result would conduce to his good. He was of convivial habits, and at Washington had become a regular drinker. His friends saw the habit was growing on him, and were fearful that if they continued him in public life he would become a drunkard. Therefore many of them voted against him, believing such a course was best for him. The habit, however, had become so fastened upon him that his retirement to private life did not cause him to leave it off. He continued to drink while he lived, and in his later years was often incapacitated for business by the too free use of the liquor he

made on his farm. This habit—the single vice of his life—followed him to the grave.

On leaving Congress, Governor Jennings retired to his farm
near Charlestown, where he remained until his death. In 1832,
President Jackson appointed him a commissioner to negotiate
a treaty with the Indians for the Indian lands in northern Indiana
and southern Michigan. His associates in the commission were
Dr. John W. Davis and Mark Crume, the treaty being held at
the forks of the Wabash river, near where the city of Huntington now stands. Mr. John H. B. Nowland, of Indianapolis, was
at the treaty, and tells this story of what happened there :

" During the preliminary council, Dr. Davis, who was a pompous, big-feeling man, said something that gave offense to Oba-
noby, one of the head chiefs of the Pottawatomies. The chief
addressed Governor Jennings saying : ' Does our Great Father
intend to insult us by sending such men to treat with us?
Why did he not send Generals Cass and Tipton? You (pointing to the Governor) good man, and know how to treat us.
(Pointing to Crume). He chipped beef for the squaws at Wabash. (Meaning that Crume was the beef contractor at the
treaty of 1826.) Then pointing to Dr. Davis, he said : ' Big man
and damn fool." The chief then spoke a few words to the Pottawatomies present, who gave one of their peculiar yells and
left the council house, and could only be induced to return after
several days, and then only through the great influence of Governor Jennings."

The signing of the treaty at the forks of the Wabash was Governor Jennings's last official act. He remained on his farm, cul-
tivating the soil and spending his leisure in his library, until
July 26, 1834, when the end came. He died at home, surrounded by his family and friends, beloved by them all. The
next day his body was placed in a common farm wagon and
taken to Charlestown and buried. The day was intensely hot,
and but few were at his burial, these few being members of his
family and particular friends. He was laid at rest on a hill
overlooking the town, and his grave was unmarked by head or
foot stone. Thus it has remained until the present time, and

were it not that a few men and women still live who were present at his burial, no one would certainly know where the remains of the First Governor of Indiana are interred.

Men who plant civilization in the wilderness, who organize
backwoodsmen into communities, and throw around them the
protection of the law, should not be forgotten. They render
mankind a priceless service, and those who come after them and
enjoy the fruits of their labor and their sacrifices should never
tire in honoring their memory. Jonathan Jennings was such a
man, and Indiana owes him more than she can compute. He
fought slavery to the death when it sought to fasten itself upon
her territory; he helped secure for her sons and daughters the
best portion of her rich and fertile lands, and yet he sleeps the
long sleep without a stone to mark his resting place. Shame
on Indiana!

The first Governor of Indiana, like the first President of the
United States, died without issue. He was twice married, but
no child was born in his household to call him father.

Governor Jennings was a man of polished manners. A lady
who knew him well, and was often a guest at his house, told the
author that she never met a more fascinating man. He was always gentle and kind to those about him. He was not an orator,
but he could tell what he knew in a pleasing way. He wrote
well, as well perhaps, as any of his successors in the Governor's
office. He was an ambitious man, but his ambition was in the
right direction—to serve the people the best he could. He had
blue eyes, fair complexion and sandy hair. He was about five
feet eight and one half inches high, and in his latter days inclined to corpulency. He was broad-shouldered and heavy-set,
and weighed about 180 pounds. He died comparatively young,
but he did as much for the well-being of Indiana as any man
that ever lived. Will not she do something to mark the spot
where he lies?

RATLIFF BOON.

THERE is some uncertainty as to the birthplace of Ratliff Boon. Lanman, in his "Biographical Annals of the Civil Government," says he was born in Franklin county, North Carolina, in 1781. Boon's grandson, David N. Boon, in a letter to the author, says he was born January 18, 1781, in the State of Georgia. Lanman is usually correct, and his account should not be lightly considered, but I assume that the statement of the grandson is true, and that the Empire State of the South has the honor of being the birthplace of one of Indiana's most influential pioneers.

When Ratliff Boon was a boy his father emigrated to Kentucky, and settled in Warren county. Ratliff learned the gunsmith's trade in Danville, and in 1809 came to Indiana Territory, and located in what is now Boon township, Warrick county. In 1813, on the organization of Warrick county, Boon was appointed its first treasurer, which office he held for several years. He was a member of the House of Representatives in the session of 1816–17, and in 1818 was elected from Warrick county to the State Senate, and took his seat in December of that year. He possessed, in an unusual degree, the qualities which make a leader, and at once drew to himself a large following. Three years afterward (in 1819) he was elected Lieutenant-Governor of the State on the ticket with Jonathan Jennings, and on the resignation of that gentleman, September 12, 1822, to accept a seat in Congress, Lieutenant-Governor Boon filled out the unexpired term of the Governor.

In August, 1822, Governor Boon was re-elected Lieutenant-Governor of Indiana on the ticket with William Hendricks.

He served as Lieutenant-Governor until the close of the legislative session of 1824, and then resigned to become a candidate for Congress in the First District. His letter notifying the Senate of his resignation, dated January 30, 1824, was as follows:

"GENTLEMEN OF THE SENATE—This day closes with me, perhaps forever, the honor of presiding over your honorable body. Circumstances combined have made it necessary for me to resign into the hands of the people from which it emanated the office of Lieutenant-Governor; the object of which, when explained, I flatter myself will be received as a sufficient apology for making it.

" I shall carry with me, from this into whatever situation I may be placed, a grateful recollection of the civilities which I have received from many of you, and of the almost unlimited confidence which has been reposed in me by a generous public. No one can estimate more highly the value of your favor, nor could any one with more unfeigned gratitude than I do the honors which have been conferred on me. And, in conclusion of this address, permit me to solicit you to accept assurances of my best wishes for your present felicity, and a hope for your future prosperity.

" I have the honor to be, with sentiments of regard and esteem, yours and the public's obedient humble servant.

" CORYDON, January 30, 1824. R. BOON."

On the same day the Senate was notified by a communication from Robert A. New, the Secretary of State, that the resignation of Governor Boon had, that day, been filed in his office.

Governor Boon was elected to Congress in August following, and two years afterward was a candidate for re-election, but was defeated by Colonel Thomas H. Blake. In 1829 he was again a candidate for Congress, and this time was successful. He was re-elected in 1831, in 1833, in 1835, and in 1837, most of the time serving as chairman of the Committee of Public Lands. In 1836 he was a candidate for United States Senator, but was defeated by Oliver H. Smith. His congressional career ended in March, 1839, and a few months afterward he removed from Indiana and settled in Pike county, Missouri.

In Missouri Governor Boon at once became active in public affairs, and soon was one of the leading men of the State. At that time Missouri elected her congressmen on general ticket, and not by districts, as is now the case. Colonel Thomas H. Benton was then the political dictator of Missouri, and controlled its politics as absolutely as a feudal lord controlled the action of his dependents. A rebellion against the autocratic rule of Benton was inaugurated, and Boon became its principal leader. He placed himself in antagonism to Benton, and thereby incurred the latter's deadly hostility. Early in 1844 Boon became a candidate for Congress, and at once went to work to secure his election. He espoused the measures of reform then in agitation, and although he did not live to see them consummated, justice to his memory requires me to say that he gave them the momentum that insured them success. Before he had formally announced himself as a candidate he received the following letter from a committee of St. Louis Democrats:

"St. Louis, January 31, 1844.

"*Hon. Ratliff Boon:*

"Sir: At a meeting of the Democratic party of the city and county of St. Louis, convened on the 8th inst., at the court house in said city, a committee was appointed to interrogate the aspirants to important offices in this State. In the absence of S. Penn, Jr., Esq., chairman of said committee, the undersigned beg leave to submit the following questions, to wit:

"1. Are you in favor of a convention to amend the constitution so as to equalize representation according to population, and to limit the judicial tenure according to established Democratic principles?

"2. Are you in favor of the passage of a law by the next General Assembly to lay off the State into districts, and to provide that each district shall elect one member?

"3. Are you in favor of the bills, as originally introduced last session, commonly denominated 'the currency bills?'

"4. Are you still in favor of the principles and will you sustain the doctrines embodied in the address adopted and published by the Democratic National Convention held at Baltimore in May, 1840?

"You are most respectfully requested to furnish, at your earliest convenience, direct and categorical answers to the foregoing interrogatories.   Very respectfully,

> "THOMAS B. HUDSON.
> "L. T. LABEAUME.
> "N. RANNEY.
> "D. H. ARMSTRONG."

To this letter Governor Boon replied as follows:

> "LOUISIANA, Mo., February 14, 1844.

"GENTLEMEN—I have the honor to acknowledge the receipt of your communication of the 31st ult., in which you say that at a meeting of the Democratic party of St. Louis you were appointed a committee to interrogate the aspirants to important offices in this State.

"Whilst I am insensible of having authorized the use of my name as an aspirant to any office at the next August election, I am, nevertheless, proud of the opportunity thus afforded me to express my sentiments touching some of the leading questions of political economy, about which there exists so great a diversity of opinions among the Democrats of Missouri. And in my answer to your several interrogatories, I will respond to each one of them in the order in which they stand arranged.

"To your first interrogatory I answer—I am.

"To your second, I answer—I now am and ever have been in favor of electing members of Congress by single districts.

"To your third interrogatory I answer—I now am and ever have been opposed to those bills, from their first introduction into the Missouri Legislature.

"To your fourth interrogatory I answer—That I have not before me the address of the Democratic convention held in Baltimore in 1840, but from my present recollection of the principles therein set forth, they will continue to receive from me a cordial support.   Very respectfully,   R. BOON.

"Thomas B. Hudson and others, Committee."

The contest became exceedingly bitter between the reformers and the adherents of Benton. In looking over some newspaper clippings sent me by a grandson of Ratliff Boon, I am reminded of the contest in Indiana in 1860, between the administration men and the friends of Judge Douglas. On the 1st of March, 1844, a committee of St. Louis Democrats wrote Governor Boon, asking him questions upon various subjects, and ending as follows: "We also desire to learn from you whether you are willing to submit your pretensions to the convention above named (the State convention), abide its decision and support its nominees." To this letter Governor Boon replied as follows:

"LOUISIANA, Mo., March 7, 1844.

"GENTLEMEN—Your letter of the 1st inst. came to hand last evening. And as I have determined to submit my pretensions to a seat in the next Congress of the United States, subject to the untrammeled decision of the freemen of Missouri, in the exercise of the elective franchise, it will, for the present, supersede the necessity of my going into detail touching my views of national policy. Suffice it to say that I am a Democrat of the true Jeffersonian stamp, and will, in due season, write out for publication a full expose of my political creed.

"Very respectfully,   R. BOON."

From this time on the battle between the two wings of the party waxed hotter and hotter. As a sample of the political literature of that day, I copy the following communication published in an organ of the Reformers:

"OLD PIKE.

"Doubtless it will be gratifying to the friends of the Democracy everywhere, and to the warm admirers of Hon. R. Boon in particular, to learn that this war-worn veteran, who for the last thirty years has bravely battled side by side with the noble spirit of the nation against every species of fraud upon the rights of the people, 'is himself again;' that by the superior skill of his accomplished physician, Dr. W. B. Gorin, a disease which had fastened itself upon him, and for several months seemed to leave little hope of his recovery, has been, in a measure, removed, and that he is once more actively associated, as was his wont, with the unterrified Democracy—confirming the doubting, giving strength and efficacy to their action—aiding and assisting the pure and disinterested in combatting alike the open and disguised enemies of republicanism, and lending dignity to their councils. I have been drawn into these reflections by unexpectedly seeing this time-honored father of Democracy called, a few days since, to preside, at Louisiana, over one of the largest and most respectable political meetings ever assembled at that place. SPECTATOR."

The editor of the paper which published this communication says, " Colonel Boon was one of the most sterling Democrats in Indiana, and is one of the best in Missouri ; yet his Democracy, past services and unflinching integrity have not saved him from the machinations of those whose instrument the editor of the *Missourian* is."

" Spectator " was at fault in relation to the success of Dr. Gorin's skill, for Governor Boon soon had a relapse and was compelled to take to his bed. His health was such that he determined to withdraw from the canvass. This he did, very much to the regret of his friends. He recovered his health sufficiently to get about the town, but not to travel. He was very anxious for the election of Mr. Polk, and as the election hinged on the result in New York, he was at the wharf boat all day November 20, 1844, in hope of learning how New York had voted. He said during the day that if the boat brought the news of Polk's election he would be willing to go home and die. When the boat came with the information that New York had voted for Polk and he was elected, Ratliff Boon went home, and in a few hours afterward died. He was buried in the cemetery at Louisiana, and his son, Baily Hart Boon, caused a monument to be erected at his grave bearing this inscription :

" RATLIFF BOON,
" Born January 18, 1781 ; died November 20, 1844."

And the earthly career of Indiana's second Lieutenant-Governor was ended.

E. C. Murray, Esq., of Louisiana, Mo., who married a granddaughter of Ratliff Boon, has furnished the author the following account of Governor Boon's career in Missouri, written by Colonel N. P. Minor :

"In 1839 Hon. R. Boon came to Missouri from Indiana, and settled at Louisiana permanently with his family, Mrs. Luce, Baily H. Boon and Matilda, afterward intermarried with John Folks, Jr. He was then apparently a long ways on the shady side of life, and yet full of pluck and vigor, and there was never more vitality concentrated in one small body than in his. He was the very embodiment of courage and daring, and as we listened to his fierce philippics on his enemies, and looked into his small but deep-set eyes, we could not but realize the truth of General Jackson's encomium on Boon, when he called him 'faithful among the faithless.'' The *Missouri Republican*, the Whig organ, called him 'Collar Boon,' because they said he wore the collar of General Jackson, for whom he had intense admiration. But it was all words; he was a born partisan, loved his friends and hated his enemies, but at heart he was too honest and independent to fawn on any man, and if General Jackson, as much as he loved him, had been recreant to his trust, Boon would have branded him as he afterward did Colonel Benton. His interest in politics never abated by his change of location; in fact he always wore his harness, and he was always ready to strike heavy blows for what he thought was right. About this time Benton began to show treachery to the Democratic party, although he did not go off then boldly with Van Buren, Dix and others. He had his currency bills pass the Legislature, the object being to suppress the circulation of small bank bills, the passing or receiving them being made a felony. Of course, no one regarded the law, and it fell still-born. In 1843, I think, a Whig Congress had passed their mandamus act ordering the State to district before electing their members of Congress. As 1844 approached it was evident that Benton's heart was with Van Buren and Blair, then avowed Freesoilers, although I believe he voted for Polk. The Democracy divided, and a fierce war followed. Colonel Boon became the candidate of what was called the soft wing of the Democracy on account of their opposition to the folly of Benton's currency bills, and he made a splendid canvass of the State. Much might be written of Colonel Boon's career in Missouri, to demonstrate how profound and fixed he was in his views, and how unyielding he was in all things. The labor of the canvass and advancing years had worn out the old man, and he was admonished to set his house in order. He was willing to go, but he wanted to know that James K. Polk was elected before his eyes closed in death. The November election came at last, but the result was so close that none knew who the lucky man was. The State of Louisiana, long in doubt, after weary weeks, declared for Polk, and then the Empire State, New York, trembled in the balance. Then a single county in that State, then a single township in that county of that State, hung fire, until some time in November, when the news reached us that New York had voted for Polk, which made him President. Then the venerable old man, with the spray from the Jordan of death beating in his face, exclaimed, ' Polk has beaten Henry Clay ; I am willing to go ;' and with the evening tide he entered that undiscovered land we call death.   N. P. Minor."

Knowing that the Hon. Charles H. Test was familiar with the prominent men of early Indiana, I wrote him, requesting his recollections of Ratliff Boon, and in reply received the following :

" Dear Sir—I had but a slight acquaintance with Ratliff Boon. He lived on the west side of the State and I on the east. The first time I ever saw him was in 1817, at Corydon. He was a member of the first Legislature after the admission of Indiana as a State, and appeared to be an active member of the body. I recollect a circumstance occurring at that session of the General Assembly, strongly illustrative of the spirit of the times in regard to the negro race. A gentleman of Kentucky, by the name of Sumner, had determined to manumit his slaves, some forty in number, and with that view petitioned the Legislature to be allowed to settle them in Indiana, promising to provide for them until such time as they were able to take care of themselves. The petition was referred to a select committee of which Boon was a member. The committee reported to the House a letter addressed to Mr. Sumner, in which they complimented Mr. Sumner as a philanthropist, but could not consent to his proposition to settle his freedmen in Indiana, as it set a dangerous precedent. They declared it would not do to allow

4

free negroes to settle in Indiana, as in process of time they might inaugurate all the horrors of the massacre of St. Domingo. The reasons given for rejecting the petition of Mr. Sumner are at this day somewhat laughable, but the manner in which it was done was quite as much so. The idea of a sage Legislature addressing a letter to a private individual is quite as ludicrous as the fears that at some future day we might all be murdered by the freedmen if allowed to live within our boundaries. Amos Lane, of Dearborn, was the only member who opposed the report of the committee.

"In those early days the whole State was infested by wolves. Farmers could raise no sheep. The Legislature undertook to give some protection in this particular, and passed a law allowing a premium on wolf scalps, to be paid out of the State treasury. The whole revenue of the State did not amount to much more than the expenses of an incorporated small city do now. The law failed to designate the kind of wolf for the killing of which the premium should be paid. It was intended, without doubt, to embrace the large gray species, for they were the most to be feared among the farmers' sheep. Boon, however, went to hunting prairie wolves, found in great numbers in the Wabash country, and at one haul drew from the treasury about $700. The next year the Legislature repealed the wolf law to save the treasury from bankruptcy.

"Boon was a lithe, active man when I last saw him. In height he was about five feet ten inches, spare in person, and as straight as an Indian. His forehead was low and receded rapidly from his eyebrows. His face in this particular was peculiar. Without doubt he was closely connected with the Boones of Kentucky.   Yours truly,

"CHARLES H. TEST."

There are few men now living who knew Ratliff Boon, and these few are widely scattered. He belonged to a type of men suited to frontier life, and his career, both in Indiana and Missouri, was that of a courageous and self-reliant man. He was a pioneer of two States, and he left his impress upon them both.

WILLIAM HENDRICKS.

WILLIAM HENDRICKS, Governor of Indiana from 1822 to 1825, was born at Ligonier, Westmoreland county, Pennsylvania, in 1783. He was educated at Cannonsburg, having for a classmate Dr. Wylie, afterward a distinguished president of the State University at Bloomington. They both became eminent, one as a statesman, the other as an educator, but their diverse pathways did not sever their early friendship, which terminated only with their lives.

After reaching manhood Mr. Hendricks left Pennsylvania and located at Cincinnati, Ohio. He remained there but a year or so, and during that time studied law and was admitted to the bar. In 1814 he left Cincinnati and took up his abode at Madison, this State, and resided there until he died.

Indiana was then a Territory, and the same year, 1814, he was elected a member of the House of Representatives of the Territorial Legislature from Jefferson county, and was chosen Speaker of that body. The question of a State government was then agitating the people, and in 1816 a convention was held at Corydon to form a State constitution. · This was but two years after Mr. Hendricks settled at Madison, but during this time he became so well known that on the organization of the convention he was made its secretary. He so discharged the duties of this office as to win the good opinion of the delegates, and when the convention adjourned he had established for himself a reputation for business aptitude and political sagacity equal to that of any man within the boundaries of the State. At the next August election—the first held under the State government—he was elected the sole representative of the people of the new

State to the National Congress.   He was re-elected in 1818 and in 1820, thus serving the people of Indiana in Congress for six consecutive years.   He discharged the duties of his high position with so much acceptability that at the end of his third term, in 1822, he was elected Governor of the State without opposition, receiving 18,340 votes, all that were cast.   Thus he and Jonathan Jennings, the first Governor, exchanged places.

Before Governor Hendricks's term as Governor had expired the Legislature elected him a Senator of the United States, and on Saturday, February 12, 1825, he filed his resignation as Governor in the office of the Secretary of State, and notified the Senate thereof in the following communication, dated at Indianapolis the day aforesaid :

" GENTLEMEN OF THE SENATE—Permit me to inform you that I have filed in the office of the Secretary of State my resignation as Governor, and to assure you of the great degree of gratitude, which, under all circumstances, I must ever feel for the many signal instances of confidence reposed and honor conferred by the people and Legislature of the State.   I have the honor to be, with the greatest respect, your obedient servant,

" WILLIAM HENDRICKS."

In 1831 he was re-elected, and at the expiration of this term— in 1837—he retired to private life, and never afterward took upon himself the cares of public office.   Thus it will be seen that for twenty-one years—from 1816 till 1837—he served without intermission the people of Indiana in the three highest offices within their gift.

Men who found empires should not be forgotten.   They plant the tree of civil liberty, and water its roots, while those who come after them but trim its branches to preserve its symmetry. If they plant carelessly and in poor soil the tree will have but a sickly growth.   That the men who planted Indiana in the wilderness sixty-seven years ago planted wisely and well, is evidenced by its wonderful growth.   It was then inhabited only by a few thousand hardy pioneers, who had settled on its southern and eastern borders ; now it contains two millions of prosperous people, its whole area being covered with happy homes.

William Hendricks had as much to do with laying the foundations of this great State and commencing its superstructure as any other man, excepting Jonathan Jennings only, and yet how few there are who know he ever lived. How transitory is the fame of human greatness.

> "This is the state of man; to-day he puts forth
> The tender leaves of hope, to-morrow blossoms,
> And bears his blushing honors thick upon him;
> The third day comes a frost, a killing frost,"

and he dies and is forgotten.

Worldly honors are not easily won, although the bard tells us that some men have greatness thrust upon them. In the contest for fame there is sharp competition, and those only win who have endurance and mettle. A number of educated and talented young men had come to Indiana in quest of fortune, and had William Hendricks been a dolt or a laggard he would have been distanced in the race. But he was neither. He was talented and energetic, and he won. He also knew how to utilize the means at his command and to make the most of the situation. When he came to Indiana he brought with him a printing press, and soon afterward commenced the publication of a weekly paper. It was called the *Eagle*, and, I believe, was the second newspaper published in the State, the *Vincennes Sun* being the first. Through his paper he became known and paved the way for his political fortune. He made the first revision of the laws of the State and had it printed on his own press. The Legislature offered to pay him for this work, but he declined all pecuniary compensation. It then passed a resolution of thanks, the only return for his labor he would take.

Governor Hendricks was a friend to education. Hanover College and the State University at Bloomington both received his fostering care. He took an active interest in public enterprises, and frequently aided them with his purse. He was very politic in his actions, never antagonizing a man when he could honorably avoid it. He had a large estate, and after leaving the Senate he spent his time in managing it and practicing law. He held on to his real estate with great tenacity, leasing it for a term of years when practicable, instead of selling it. Many houses were erected at Madison on property leased of him, and, like most houses built under such circumstances, they were poorly and cheaply constructed. His disposition to lease rather than sell his property caused much dissatisfaction among the people, and very greatly lessened his influence.

On the 16th of May, 1850, Governor Hendricks rode out to his farm, just north of Madison, to oversee the building of a family vault. While assisting in the preparation of a receptacle for his body "after life's fitful fever" was over, he was taken ill and soon afterward died. The author is not certain whether he died at the farm-house or was taken back to his home in the city, but is inclined to the opinion that he breathed his last near the spot where he is buried and where his remains have crumbled to dust.

The *Indiana Gazetteer* of 1850 thus speaks of him:

"Governor Hendricks was for many years by far the most popular man in the State. He had been its sole representative in Congress for six years, elected on each occasion by large majorities, and no member of that body, probably, was more attentive to the interests of the State he represented, or more industrious in arranging all the private or local business entrusted to him. He left no letter unanswered, no public office or document did he fail to visit or examine on request; with personal manners very engaging, he long retained his popularity."

Governor Hendricks was of a family that occupies a front place in the history of Indiana. There is probably no other one in the State that has exerted so wide an influence upon its politics and legislation as his. His eldest son, John Abram, was a captain in the Mexican war, and a lieutenant-colonel in the war of the rebellion. He was killed in the battle of Pea Ridge while in command of his regiment. Another son, Thomas, was killed in the Teche country during General Banks's campaign up Red river. A brother and a nephew sat in the State Senate, and another nephew, Hon. Thomas A. Hendricks, has received the highest honors his State could confer upon him.

Governor Hendricks was about six feet high and had a well-proportioned body. He had auburn hair, blue eyes and a florid complexion. His manners were easy and dignified, and his address that of a well-bred gentleman. He was not a great lawyer, nor an eloquent advocate, but he prepared his cases with care and was reasonably successful at the bar. In early life he was a Presbyterian, but in his later years he joined the Methodist church and died in her communion. He never had a picture taken of himself, so there is no portrait of him in the State library, while portraits of the other Governors are there. This is to be regretted, for the people whose ancestors honored him so highly would like to know something of his form and features. The only picture they can have of him must be drawn with the pen, and the author submits this sketch as an effort in that direction. Would that the work were better done.

JAMES BROWN RAY.

ONE of the most noted and influential men of early Indiana was James Brown Ray. He was born in Jefferson county, Kentucky, February 19, 1794, and when quite a youth went to Cincinnati, Ohio, and read law with General Gano, of that city. On the 10th of December, 1818, he married Mary Riddle, and soon afterward removed to Brookville, Indiana, and commenced the practice of the law. Brookville was then the home of many ambitious and able men, but the young Kentuckian soon took rank among the ablest and most influential of them. In August, 1822, he was elected to the State Senate from Franklin county, and took his seat on the 2d of December following. On the 30th of January, 1824, Ratliff Boon, then Lieutenant-Governor of the State, resigned his office, and on the same day Mr. Ray was elected President *pro tempore* of the Senate. The Senate journal shows that, on motion of Mr. Stapp, it was "resolved that a committee be appointed to wait on His Excellency, the Governor, and inform him that the Hon. Ratliff Boon having resigned the office of Lieutenant-Governor, the Senate has elected James B. Ray as President *pro tempore*." Mr. Ray presided over the Senate for the balance of the session, and when that body met, in January, 1825, on motion of Dennis Pennington, the Senator from Harrison county, Mr. Ray again took the chair as President. A very interesting debate took place as to whether the election of Mr. Ray at the previous session continued him as President *pro tempore* of the Senate, and, a vote being taken, it was decided that it did not; whereupon he called General Stapp to the chair and took his place upon the floor. An election then took place for President *pro tem-*

porc, which resulted in the re-election of Mr. Ray, who thereupon resumed his seat as the Senate's presiding officer.

Governor William Hendricks having been elected to the United States Senate, resigned the Governorship on the 12th day of February, 1825. When the Senate received notice of his resignation Mr. Ray left the presiding officer's seat and at once entered upon the discharge of his duties as Acting-Governor. The Senate unanimously passed a resolution thanking him for the ability and fairness with which he had discharged his duties as presiding officer, an honor fairly won, for he had been impartial in his rulings and courteous in announcing them. He was then a young man, but he was one of the most popular and influential politicians in the State. He became a candidate for Governor, and the next August was elected to that office over Isaac Blackford by a majority of 2,622. Three years afterward—in August, 1828—he was a candidate for reelection, his competitors being Dr. Israel T. Canby and Harbin H. Moore. Governor Ray received 15,141 votes; Dr. Canby, 12,315, and Mr. Moore, 10,904. Governor Ray having received a plurality of the votes was re-elected, and held the office of Governor until the inauguration of Noah Noble, in 1831.

During Mr. Ray's service as Governor no exciting questions agitated the people of the State. In 1830 the terms of the Supreme Judges expired, and he determined to reorganize the court. He reappointed Judge Blackford, but refused to nominate to the Senate Judges Scott and Holman. It was charged at the time, and very generally believed, that his refusal to reappoint Judges Scott and Holman was because they had declined to aid him in his senatorial aspirations. Be this as it may, he would not send their names to the Senate, but, in their stead, nominated Stephen C. Stevens and John T. McKinney. This action of Governor Ray cost him many friends. Up to that time no man in the State was so popular, but after this his popularity waned, and finally almost disappeared. The people believed this action of Governor Ray was prompted by personal reasons and not for the public good, hence they withdrew their support and confidence from him. A sad example was this of what one false step will do.

In 1826, while filling the executive chair of Indiana, Gov-

ernor Ray was appointed a commissioner, on the part of the
United States, to negotiate a treaty with the Miami and Pottawatamie Indians.   His associates in the commission were Generals Cass and Tipton, and the result of the treaty was the
ceding of a tract of land ten miles wide, on the north line of
the State, and the cession of a small body lying between the
Wabash and Eel rivers.   Through the exertions of Governor
Ray the Indians donated to the State one section of land for
each mile, to aid in building the road from Lake Michigan to
the Ohio river, known as the Michigan road.   This was an important cession, and Governor Ray deserves the gratitude of the
people of Indiana for obtaining it.

The constitution of the State prevented the Governor from
holding any office of honor or profit under the government of
the United States, and when Governor Ray asked to be appointed a member of the commission to negotiate the treaty
which I have named, he requested that no commission, but
merely a letter of authority should be sent him.   He remembered the difficulty Jonathan Jennings had encountered by acting as commissioner to negotiate an Indian treaty while holding
the office of Governor, and sought to avoid a similar difficulty
by acting without the authority of a regular commission.   But
his precaution did not save him from trouble.   The Legislature
took cognizance of his action, as it had done with Governor
Jennings, and, as in that case, settled the matter by evading it.

The record of this controversy is as follows.   It is of interest
in showing the somewhat stilted dignity of those early statesmen in the exercise of their official functions :

In the Legislature of 1826 Mr. Craig, a representative from
Ripley county, offered the following resolution:

"*Resolved*, That it is the opinion of this House that James B.
Ray, Esq., who now is acting in and filling the office of Governor of this State, has forfeited his right to act in and fill said
office of Governor by accepting of and exercising at Mississin-
awa, during a part of the year 1826, the office of commissioner
under the United States, together with Lewis Cass, Esq., Governor of the Territory of Michigan, and John Tipton, of Fort
Wayne, Indian agent, to treat with the Pottawatamie and Miami

tribes of Indians, for the purchase of lands lying within the State of Indiana; and that the Senate be informed of this opinion, and their opinion requested."

The resolution was offered on the 5th of December, 1826. The next day the House passed a resolution " That a committee be appointed to wait on James B. Ray, Esq., and inform him that there is now a resolution before this House tending to declare his office as Governor of the State vacated, in consequence of his having accepted and exercised the authority, under the President of the United States, of treating with certain Indian tribes within this State during the present year; and that he, the said James B. Ray, has leave, should he judge proper, to avail himself of the privilege to appear before this House and defend himself, either in person or by counsel." The Speaker appointed Messrs. Johnston and Bassett the committee, who served Governor Ray with a copy of the resolution, and the following day the Governor sent the House a letter, of which the following is a copy :

" GENTLEMEN OF THE HOUSE OF REPRESENTATIVES—As the Executive of the State, it will at all times give me pleasure to answer any suitable requisition made of me by either branch of the General Assembly, and I acknowledge the resolution which I have had the honor of receiving from the House of Representatives, through the gentlemen composing their committee, to be full evidence that I had reason to have the confidence in the members composing your body, that you would not arraign my conduct whilst holding the important and responsible situation to which the voice of the people of the State has called me, without in the first place allowing me the sacred constitutional privilege to which the humblest citizen is entitled, of being heard in my defense. At the same time, feeling conscious of having committed no act since I have been honored with the office of Governor, incompatible with its high obligations and duties, and which was not intended, to the best of my ability, for the prosperity of the State of our choice, I must express my conviction that the harmony of the co-ordinate branches of this government, the laws of delicacy, and the true interests of our common country at this late period, with which I have been favored through your committee ; asking to be permitted to add, that in no transaction of mine, official or other, have I anything proper to be communicated, which shall not be at all times subject to the inspection of my fellow citizens of the State, or their representatives.   If I have erred in the manner intimated in a resolution sent me, I have erred with the fathers of the republic, the first patriots of the age, and in attempting to do good and advance the highest interests of our beloved country.   As custom, precedent and example passed in review before me, I could not be insensible of their force, and have been made to feel as if I had done my duty to my conscience and the State.

" I have the honor to be, very respectfully, your most obedient servant,   J. BROWN RAY."

This exceedingly diffuse and muddy communication was received and the question debated by the House until just before the close of its sitting that day, when a vote was taken on Mr. Craig's resolution, which resulted in 28 yeas and 30 nays.   The House then, by a vote of 31 yeas to 27 nays, passed a resolution to receive the message of Governor Ray, whereupon the message was delivered, and the effort to declare the Governorship vacant ended.

In Governor Ray's messages to the Legislature he argued forcibly and eloquently the great advantage that must accrue to Indiana by the construction and operation of railroads, and predicted much which, although at the time seemed chimerical, has really come to pass.   Many considered him insane and his utterances those of a madman, but time has demonstrated that in the main he was correct.   He saw more plainly than any other man of his day the future of the State in which he lived. After he left office he continued to dilate upon his favorite subject, and to predict a great future for Indianapolis.   A writer, who seems to think the Governor was somewhat off his mental balance, thus speaks of him in a late article in an Indianapolis paper :

" During a long period of mental disturbance in his old age, Governor Ray was fond of discussing his ' grand scheme ' of railroad concentration at Indianapolis.   Here was to be the head of a score of radiating lines. At intervals of five miles were to be villages, of ten miles towns, and of twenty miles respectable cities. This crazy whim, as everybody regarded it, has been made a fact as solid as the everlasting hills. The only point of failure is the feature that possessed special interest to the Governor. The Union Depot and point of concentration of the radiating lines are not on his property, opposite the Court-house, where, by all the requirements of symmetry and consistency, they should have been. Oddly enough, one expedient in construction, which certainly looked silly, has been actually put in use successfully in some one or another of our far Western lines. Where deep gorges were to be crossed, he thought that trestle-work might be replaced by cutting off the tops of growing trees level with the track and laying sills on these for the rails. It is not many months since the papers published a description of exactly that sort of expedients in crossing a deep and heavily timbered hollow on a Western railway— the Denver and Rio Grande probably. So thoroughly has the great ' hub ' scheme and its connections and incidents been identified with Governor Ray and his hallucinations, that there are few who know anything of the matter at all who will not be surprised to learn that the origination of it is at least as likely to be the work of Governor Noble's deliberate reasoning as of Governor Ray's fantasies. In his annual message of 1833-4, he discusses the importance of the internal improvement system, then projected and widely debated, but not adopted by the State, and only partially pursued by the help of canal land grants by Congress, and he argues for the concentration of artificial facilities for transportation here. In other words, without saying it, he wants Indianapolis to be exactly the ' hub ' that Governor Ray predicted it would be. Whether the rational Governor in office got his notions from the fancies of the deranged ex-Governor, or the latter only expanded in his fantastic projects the official suggestion of the other, we shall never know. But the probability is that the sane Governor profited by the hints he saw in the wild talk of the insane Governor. For Governor Noble was not a strikingly original genius, and Governor Ray, as eccentric and egotistical as he was, had more than an average allowance of brains."

After Governor Ray ceased to be Governor he resumed the practice of law, but he did not succeed in getting much legal business. He seemed to have "run down at the heel," and, although he was in the prime of life, the public appeared to think him superannuated, as having passed his day of usefulness. In 1835 he became a candidate for clerk of Marion county against Robert B. Duncan, Esq., and, for a time, seemed bent on making a lively canvass. But, before the election came off, he had virtually abandoned the contest. Although he did not formally withdraw, he had no tickets printed, and when the ballots were counted, it was found that few of them had been cast for him. In 1837 he ran for Congress, in the Indianapolis district, against William Herrod, and was defeated, receiving but 5,888 votes to his competitor's 9,635. This want of appreciation by the public soured him, and made him more eccentric than ever.

In the summer of 1848 Governor Ray made a trip to Wisconsin and returned home by way of the Ohio river. While on the river he became unwell and, on reaching Cincinnati, was taken to the house of a relative. The disease proved to be cholera, and terminated in his death August 4, 1848. He was buried in the Spring Grove Cemetery, near Cincinnati, outside the State he had helped to found.

Governor Ray's first wife died while he was in the Senate, and in September, 1825, he married his second wife, Mrs. Esther Booker, of Centreville, Indiana.

Governor Ray was egotistical, very dressy and fond of display. He liked sensations, and more than once, while Governor, exercised his executive functions in a manner that was highly tragical. In the summer of 1825 three executions of white men were to take place at Pendleton for the killing of some Indians. The day arrived and two of the murderers were hung, the sheriff delaying the execution of young Bridges, a mere boy, in hope the Governor would interfere. Mr. John H. B. Nowland, in his "Prominent Citizens of Indianapolis," thus speaks of this event:

"After they (Bridges, senior, and Sawyer) had hung about thirty minutes they were taken down and placed in coffins at the foot of the gallows. The young man, who had witnessed the scene, was then placed in the wagon (which had been readjusted on the hillside) with the intention of waiting until the last moment for Governor Ray or a pardon. He had not been in this situation long before the Governor made his appearance (which created a shout from all present) on a large, fancy gray horse. He rode directly up to the gallows, where the young man was seated on a rough coffin in the wagon. The Governor handed the reins of the bridle to a bystander, commanding the prisoner to stand up. 'Sir,' said the Governor, 'do you know in whose presence you stand?' Being answered in the negative, the Governor continued: 'There are but two powers known to the law that can save you from hanging by the neck until you are dead; one is the Great God of the Universe, the other is J. Brown Ray, Governor of the State of Indiana. The latter stands before you (handing the young man the written pardon); you are pardoned.'"

Had Governor Ray turned his attention to dramatic literature, the Buffalo Bills of Indiana would have had no occasion to go outside the State for their blood-and-thunder plays.

In traveling it was the custom of Governor Ray to register his name on steamboats and at hotels as "J. Brown Ray, Governor of Indiana." But, then, he was not the only great man who has been vain. Either Sir Walter Raleigh or Murat would have registered with all his titles.

Governor Ray was a brave man, and sometimes a belligerent one. When a young lawyer at Brookville, James Jones, a farmer, attacked him, and in a hand to hand fight was worsted. When he and Calvin Fletcher were in the active practice of the law they had a personal difficulty at Danville, which caused a good deal of talk at the time. The court was in session, and one morning while the lawyers in attendance were warming their backs at the hotel fire, Governor Ray and Mr. Fletcher got into a controversy about something the former had said in one of his messages to the Legislature. The dispute begat bad blood, and eventually Governor Ray told Mr. Fletcher that if he repeated the offensive remark he would thrash him. Those who knew Mr. Fletcher are aware that threats had but little terror to him, so he reiterated the accusation, whereupon Governor Ray caught him by the nose. At this Mr. Fletcher struck the Governor in the face, but before he could repeat the blow his arm was caught by the bystanders and the belligerents separated. Both these men had the courage of their convictions, and were ever ready to maintain them in the old Western style.

In his latter days Governor Ray was so eccentric that most people thought his mind diseased. He always walked with a cane, and sometimes he would stop on the street and, with his cane, write words in the air. It is no wonder that those who saw him do this believed him insane. A short time before he died he advertised, in an Indianapolis paper, a farm and a tavern-stand for sale, and for a proposition to build a railroad from Charleston, South Carolina, through Indianapolis to the northern lakes, all in one advertisement.

In person, Governor Ray, in his younger days, was very prepossessing. He was tall and straight, with a body well-proportioned. He wore his hair long and tied in a queue. His forehead was broad and high, and his features denoted intelligence of a high order. For many years he was a leading man of Indiana, and no full history of the State can be written without frequent mention of his name.

NOAH NOBLE.

Noah Noble, fourth Governor of Indiana, was born in Clark county, Virginia, January 15, 1794. When he was a little boy his father emigrated to Kentucky with his family, and there Noah grew to manhood. About the time Indiana was admitted into the Union Mr. Noble came to the State and located in Brookville. His brother James had preceded him to Brookville, and had become quite prominent in public affairs. In 1820, a few years after Mr. Noble settled at Brookville, he was elected sheriff of Franklin county, and was re-elected in 1822. In August, 1824, he was chosen a representative to the State Legislature from Franklin county, virtually without opposition, there having been but twenty votes cast against him. At that time he was probably the most popular man in Franklin county. Enoch McCarty was then clerk of the county, and, being a candidate for re-election, was considerably disturbed when he heard that the friends of Mr. Noble were talking of him for the office. In a conversation between the partisans of McCarty and those of Noble about the clerkship, one of them said: "Let's elect Enoch McCarty clerk, and Noah Noble Governor." In this way was the movement started that landed Governor Noble in the executive chair. Lazarus Noble, a younger brother of Noah, was receiver of public moneys for the Brookville land district. In 1826 the office was changed to Indianapolis, and while on his way to that place with his books and papers, Lazarus Noble died. President Adams appointed his brother Noah to the vacancy, and the new receiver at once came to Indianapolis and opened his office. He filled the place with great acceptability until 1829, when he was removed by President Jack-

5

son for political considerations, and the office given to James
P. Drake. While receiver of public moneys Mr. Noble was
brought into contact with many people, and he made friends of
them all. He often assisted the immigrant with money to enter
his land, and in other ways accommodated and befriended him.
In 1830 he was appointed one of the commissioners to locate
and lay out the Michigan road. In 1831 he was a candidate
for Governor of the State, and although he was a Whig and
the Democracy had a large majority in the State, he was elected
over James G. Reed (Democrat) by 2,791 majority. This was
a remarkable result, for Milton Stapp, also a Whig, was a candidate, and polled 4,422 votes.

In 1834 Governor Noble was a candidate for re-election. He
received 27,676 votes, and his opponent, James G. Reed, 19,994.
In 1839, after his gubernatorial term had expired, the Legislature elected him a member of the Board of Internal Improvements. In 1841 he was chosen a Fund Commissioner, a very
important and responsible position. Early in 1841 he was offered by the President of the United States the office of General
Land Commissioner, but he declined the place because he
thought he was needed in Indiana to help the State out of her
financial embarrassments.

Governor Noble died at his home near Indianapolis (now
within the city limits), February 8, 1844, and was buried in
Greenlawn Cemetery. About five years ago his remains were
taken up and reburied at Crown Hill by the side of his wife.

That Governor Noble was beloved by his neighbors is evinced
by the way they received news of his death. So soon as it was
known in the city that he was dead a meeting was held at
Browning's hotel, at which Nicholas McCarty presided. A
committee of arrangements, consisting of forty-three persons,
was appointed, and as evidence of the mutability of earthly
things, it may be noted that Alfred Harrison is the only one of
of the forty-three now (1883) living. The next day a meeting
was held at the Court-house, to which the committee of forty-
three made report. Samuel Merrill, chairman of the committee, reported the following resolutions :

" WHEREAS, It has pleased Almighty God to remove from us
by death our respected fellow-citizen, Noah Noble, who, as

Governor of the State for six years, and in the performance of various other official duties, acquired for himself the approbation and respect of a large portion of the community ; and,

" WHEREAS, The ability, integrity and patriotism of Governor Noble as a public officer, and his uniform kindness, liberality and anxiety for the welfare of others as a private citizen, secured to him to an extent unexampled amongst us the friendship and good wishes of his neighbors and numerous acquaintances ; therefore,

" *Resolved, unanimously*, That this assembly deeply sympathizes with the bereaved family of Governor Noble in the loss they have sustained.

" *Resolved, unanimously*, That the public services and private character of the deceased have been such that his death inspires general gloom and deep regret in the community and State of which he was so distinguished an ornament.

" *Resolved, unanimously*, That, as a mark of respect for the memory of Governor Noble, this assembly will attend the funeral at two o'clock to-morrow, and will wear the usual badge of mourning for thirty days.

" *Resolved*, That copies of the foregoing preamble and resolutions be sent to the widow and children of the deceased, and also to the *Journal* and *Sentinel* for publication."

Messrs. Douglas Maguire, Samuel Merrill, Judge James Morrison, Dr. Richmond and others, made speeches in favor of the resolutions, and, on the vote being put, they were unanimously adopted. The next day the remains of Governor Noble were taken from his home to the Methodist church in Indianapolis, where appropriate religious services were held. Rev. Dr. Gurley led in prayer, after which Rev. L. W. Berry preached the funeral sermon. The exercises closed with a prayer by Rev. Henry Ward Beecher, after which the corpse was taken to Greenlawn and buried.

Governor Noble's father was a slaveholder, and some of the negroes once owned by him, and with whom the Governor had played when a boy, were sold out of the family. After Governor Noble had removed to Indianapolis he sought out these negroes, bought them, and brought them to his home. He looked after them while he lived, saw they wanted for nothing necessary for their comfort, and in his will provided for their maintenance and support. This incident illustrates his goodness and kindness of heart, and his interest in the race which for centuries had worn the bondsman's yoke.

Governor Noble once gave public notice that if any one hunted on his farm " with dog or gun," he would be prosecuted to the full extent of the law. One day the late George McOuat, then a lad, and his younger brother, Andy, while hunting on the Governor's farm flushed a flock of quails, which sought refuge in some beech trees near the Governor's house. The young hunters were under the trees trying to get a favorable position to shoot when they saw the Governor running toward them with a gun in his hand and shouting, "Get out of my inclosure; don't you dare to shoot in my woods." Andy was scared, and started to run, but his brother George commanded him to stop, and he obeyed. George paid no attention to the Governor, and getting a favorable position, pulled the trigger and brought down five birds. The Governor looked on with a certain degree of admiration, for he loved a good shot, and was proud of his own ability to make one, and when the birds fell, in a pleasant tone he said: "Well, I believe there is no scaring a Scotch boy." "You are right, Governor," said the elder of the brothers, "and particularly when that boy is a Macgregor." The McOuats are descendants of the Macgregors.

Governor Noble had a laudable ambition to go to the United States Senate, but it was never gratified. In 1836 he was a candidate to succeed William Hendricks, but was defeated by Oliver H. Smith. He led on the first ballot, and continued in the lead until the eighth, when Mr. Smith ran ahead of him, and on the next ballot was elected. In 1839 he was again a candidate for the Senate, to succeed General John Tipton, but was defeated by Albert S. White, on the thirty-sixth ballot. Governor Noble occupied about the same position in Indiana that Henry Clay did in the United States. He was the strongest man in his party, but his antagonisms were such that he could not draw from the opposition. The consequence was, that while leading off with a large plurality, he never could get a majority. His political opponents preferred any other candidate to him, and when they found they could not elect their own man they always went to the one who could beat Governor Noble. This fact shows he was a positive man. A negative man is the one to draw from an opposing party; the positive one, however, keeps his friends.

Governor Noble was one of the most efficient promoters of the internal improvement system, and when the system broke down his popularity waned. He never lost his hold upon his friends, but he never had enough of them to reach the goal of his ambition—the Senate of the United States.

Governor Noble was a remarkable man. "Self taught, almost, he readily acquired a capacity for managing all kinds of important business; with a very feeble constitution, he could endure almost any fatigue; and so much of an invalid as seldom to be free from pain, and always living on the diet of a hermit, he was never otherwise than cheerful, and few persons ever did so much to promote good feeling in the society in which he lived. His benevolence was not manifested merely by professions, but his kind looks and kinder words were always attended by the most substantial aid whenever distress or difficulty appealed to his sympathy."

Oliver H. Smith says that Governor Noble "was one of the most popular men with the masses in the State. His person was tall and slim, his constitution delicate, his smile winning, his voice feeble, the squeeze of his hand irresistible. He spoke plainly and well, but made no pretense to eloquence. As Governor he was very popular; his social entertainments will long be remembered." John H. B. Nowland says of him: "In his friendships he was warm and devoted, and confiding to a fault. He had a mild and benevolent countenance, and a smile for all with whom either business or circumstances brought him in contact."

DAVID WALLACE.

DAVID WALLACE, Governor of Indiana from 1837 to 1840, was born in Mifflin county, Pennsylvania, April 24, 1799. When he was a little boy his father emigrated to Ohio, and settled near Cincinnati. General William H. Harrison lived in the neighborhood, and between him and the Wallace family a friendship was formed that lasted while they lived. General Harrison was then in Congress, and through his influence young David secured the appointment of a cadet to West Point. This act bound the young emigrant to the old pioneer with hooks of steel, and he lived to repay the debt thus contracted with interest compounded.

Mr. Wallace graduated at West Point in 1821, and afterwards, for a short time, was a tutor in that institution. He then entered the army as a lieutenant of artillery, and in about one year resigned his commission. His father having emigrated to Indiana in 1817, and settled at Brookville, the son came to his paternal home and commenced the study of the law in the office of Miles C. Eggleston, a distinguished jurist of that day. In 1823 he was admitted to the bar, and soon obtained a large practice. He entered politics, and was elected to the Legislature in 1828, 1829 and 1830. In 1831 he was elected Lieutenant-Governor of the State, and in 1834 was re-elected. Indiana never had a Lieutenant-Governor who excelled him as a presiding officer, and but few who equaled him. His voice was good, his manner dignified, and his decisions just and impartial. In 1837 he was elected Governor, defeating for the office John Dumont, an able and distinguished lawyer who lived at Vevay, on the southern border of the State. He had been closely identified with the internal improvement system, and was elected Governor upon that issue, but during his term of office the system broke down and took him with it. It is the nature of the American people to go from one extreme to the other, and the measure that gave him office in 1837 defeated him in 1840. When the Whig State convention met that year it passed him by and nominated for Governor Samuel Bigger, a man who had not been identified with the internal improvement system. He stepped aside without a murmur, and at once resumed the practice of the law. The next year, 1841, he was elected to Congress from the Indianapolis district, defeating Colonel Nathan B. Palmer. Two years afterward, 1843, he was a candidate for re-election, but was defeated by William J. Brown 1,085 votes. In 1846 he was chairman of the Whig State central committee. He again went back to the law, and practiced it uninterruptedly until 1850, when he was elected a delegate to the constitutional convention from the county of Marion. In this body he was chairman of the Committee on Public Institutions, and was a member of the Committee on the Practice of Law and Law Reform. He took but little part in the deliberations of the convention, his name only appearing nine times in its records, except on the call of the roll. It seems strange that a man of his talents and experience in public life should have taken so insignificant a part in the proceedings of the convention; but strange as it is, it is true. He made one speech in opposition to the proposition of Judge Pettit to abolish grand juries, which was a strong presentation of the reasons why it should not be done.

In another speech delivered on a series of resolutions introduced by Mr. Rariden, approving of Mr. Clay's compromise measures, Governor Wallace made the following rather noteworthy statement. He said:

"Mr. President—I hope that the charge of being an abolitionist will not be made against me because I vote against the postponement of these resolutions. I ought to be above suspicion, for when I had the honor of a seat in Congress I voted to expel the high priest of abolitionism from that body—Joshua R. Giddings. I voted for that expulsion, and I speak of it now as an act that, under the same circumstances, and influenced by the same impressions which then operated on me, I would cheerfully do again. I voted on that occasion regardless of consequences, honestly believing that the welfare of the country demanded such an example."

In 1856 Governor Wallace was elected Judge of the Court of Common Pleas, and held the office until he died. As a judge he was impartial and able, and made the best record of his life.

He died suddenly on the 4th of September, 1859, and the next day the Indianapolis bar convened to take action upon his death. Judge David McDonald presided at the meeting, and John Coburn acted as secretary. Several gentlemen delivered addresses, and a committee on resolutions was appointed. The resolutions were reported by Mr. Coburn, one of them declaring that the dead jurist "was a just judge—firm, upright, clear, patient, laborious, impartial and conscientious." Mr. Coburn was appointed to present the resolutions to the Circuit Court, and twenty-one days afterward he performed the duty, accompanying the presentation with an eloquent eulogy upon the life and character of the deceased. The address was a chaste and elegant production, and worthy of its distinguished subject. Speaking of Governor Wallace's ability as a speaker, Mr. Coburn said :

"As an orator Governor Wallace had few equals in the nation. With a voice modulated to the finest and nicest precision, an eye sparkling and expressive, a countenance and person remarkable for beauty and symmetry, he stepped upon the speaker's stand, in these respects, far in advance of his compeers. His style of delivery was impressive, graceful, and at times impassioned, never rising to a scream or breaking into wild gesticulations, and never descending into indistinctness or lassitude. His style of composition was chaste, finished, flowing, and beautiful, often swelling up into rarest eloquence or melting down into the tenderest pathos.   *   *   *   His prepared orations were completed with the severest care. As the sculptor chisels down and finishes his statue, chipping and chipping away the stone to find within his beautiful ideal, so did he elaborate his thoughts till they assumed the shape he would give them, and so will retain them forever."

Previous to ordering the resolutions placed upon the records Judge Wick said:

"The political and official history of the deceased would lead one, in the absence of knowledge of his personal character, to expect that he had become more or less imbued with the spirit of the times. But those who have known him longest, and the most intimately, can unite their voices in calling for proof or allegation that he ever knowingly wronged a fellow-creature, or pocketed a single cent in dishonesty or corruption.

"Few persons born at the close of the last century, and flourishing during more than half the present one, prominent in both private and political station, can present such a record as this.

"Verily, the absence of evil is the best evidence of the presence of good—far better than all the monuments ever erected by either real or Pharisaic piety."

On the 7th of November, 1835, a convention was held on the Tippecanoe battle-ground, at which General Harrison was formally put forward for the presidency. William Ross Wallace read a poem, and Governor Wallace, in replying to a toast, said:

"We have been told by the magic genius of our youthful poet that we are standing on one of the proudest battle fields of our country, the very soil of which has been rendered holy by the blood of heroes; that some of the noblest of Kentucky chivalry are sleeping beneath our feet, inclosed in the same grave, mingling their dust with the bravest of the sons of Indiana; that, although no monument as yet arises to commemorate their deeds, no inscription to claim the homage of gratitude from the traveler, scarce a vestige to indicate the exact place of their repose, still—still they are not forgotten. Their memories and their sacrifices have found an abiding place and a sanctuary in the hearts of the living who are here, and of every son and daughter of Indiana who is absent, and there they remain, to be forever fondly and devotedly cherished while man has a soul to worship at the altar of patriotism, or woman a tear to shed at the tomb of the fallen brave."

He then pronounced a glowing eulogy upon General Harrison, during which he said:

"It is the first time in my life that the opportunity has presented itself enabling me to pay a long-existing debt of gratitude to one whose name and whose services are identified with the history and the glory of this field. Twenty-four years ago, and you all recollect how consternation and dismay pervaded the whole line of our Western frontier; how conflagration and murder and massacre were the ordinary scenes of the day; and how the fiend-like yell of the savage was often the last sound that rang upon the ear of the dying pioneer as he sank beneath the assassin blow of the Indian knife or tomahawk. And there, too, you recollect, there was in the field that mighty genius— that man—I scarce know where to place or what to name him— the sworn, the inveterate enemy of our race, who grasped so astoundingly the scepter of power, and with a giant's strength and a god's ability, seemed to wave it over the wilderness, and to make the tribes and nations there bow to its supremacy; to forget the national feud and private animosities, and to catch from it the same fierce, terrible and unrelenting hate toward us which fired and burned and blazed in his own bosom. But why this allusion to the past?   *   *   *   Why, that you may recollect more vividly the thrill of joy and shout of exultation with which you received the tidings of the battles fought and victory won on this field; that you may recollect with what sincerity of heart you hailed the victor's return, and blessed the memory of those who gallantly perished in the fight; that you may recollect in all its freshness the unbribed, unasked burst of approbation and applause which everywhere rose to greet and welcome the honored chieftain of the battle; how, with one voice, you proclaimed him your preserver; the restorer of peace to your firesides; the matchless warrior, who, on Tippecanoe, had broken and dispersed the fierce legions of the border foe; who rolled back with one sweep of his arm the destructive war-cloud which the charmed genius of the savage had so wonderfully gathered and concentrated and suspended over your boundless forests, shading them with terror and bristling them with death."

While Governor of the State, Governor Wallace issued a proclamation appointing a day for thanksgiving and prayer. It was the first paper of the kind issued by a Governor of Indiana, and it established a precedent which has been followed to the present time. Governor Wallace, in this matter, but followed the custom of the Governors of the New England States, who for a long time previous had been in the habit of annually calling upon the people to meet together and give thanks for the blessings they enjoyed.

When in Congress Governor Wallace was a member of the Committee of Ways and Means, and in committee gave the casting vote in favor of assisting with a donation, Professor Morse to develop the magnetic telegraph. This act was ridiculed by his political opponents, and cost him many votes the last time he ran for Congress. But he lived to see the telegraph established in nearly all the countries of the world and the wisdom of his action acknowledged by all.

Governor Wallace was not a money-making and money-getting man. He took more pleasure in filling his mind with knowledge than in filling his pockets with money. He entered into a business venture at Fort Wayne which, proving unfortunate, cost him his entire estate. One day, while sitting in his yard talking with his oldest son, the sheriff came with an execution which he sought to levy upon the Governor's property. After some parleying the sheriff left, and the Governor, addressing his son, said: "William, I want you to remember that it will be a good deal better to have a few thousand dollars laid away for old age than to have been Governor of the State or a member of Congress."

Governor Wallace was a man of great equanimity of temper. He was never known to exhibit anger in his family, but in his home and in his business affairs he was uniformly courteous and kind. He was a lover of books, and was one of the most delightful of readers. In this respect he was superior to most men who make reading and elocution a profession. It was his custom of evenings, at his home, with his family and friends around him, to read aloud choice selections from the writings and speeches of poets and statesmen. Those who were so fortunate as to be admitted to his family circle, and had the privilege of being present on such occasions, will ever remember the pleasure the exhibitions afforded.

Governor Wallace was twice married. His first wife was a daughter of John Test, and his second a daughter of Dr. John H. Sanders. The latter still lives, and is prominent in reformatory work. She is one of the leaders of the woman's suffrage movement, and is quite active in the temperance cause. She is a good public speaker, and is a woman of great force of character and large influence.

When a young man, Governor Wallace had a well-proportioned body, but in his latter years its symmetry was marred by an undue amount of flesh. He had black hair, dark eyes, and a ruddy complexion. He was cultured and well-bred. His address was good, and his manners unexceptionable. He was prominent at a time when Marshall and Dunn, the two Smiths, Whitcomb, Bright and Howard lived, and had he not been a man of talent he would inevitably have been obscured by their greatness. That he was not is the best evidence that can be adduced of his ability and acquirements.

SAMUEL BIGGER.

The life-journey of a man like Samuel Bigger is difficult to sketch in a way that will interest the reader. From the time he grew to manhood he occupied the table-lands of life. There were no mountains in his pathway nor gorges for him to cross. If his road was not smooth it was level, and if not macadamized it was solid enough to bear his weight. He ever occupied a respectable plane; he never fell below it, and his altitude was never much above it.

Samuel Bigger, Governor of Indiana from 1840 to 1843, was born in Warren county, Ohio, March 20, 1802. He was the eldest son of John Bigger, a Western pioneer, and for many years a member of the Ohio Legislature. The son loved his books, was fonder of them than of farm work, a disposition which remained with him while he lived. When eighteen years old he contracted a deep cold which settled on his lungs and came near costing him his life. His feeble health unfitted him for manual labor and determined his father to qualify him for a profession. He was prepared for college in the neighborhood, and then entered the one at Athens, from which he graduated with honor. Subsequently he studied law, and in 1829 removed to Liberty, Indiana, and commenced the practice of his profession. He remained at Liberty but a short time, when he removed to Rushville, where his public life began. He was elected to the Legislature in 1834, and re-elected in 1835. In the Legislature of 1834 Mr. Bigger was a candidate for Speaker of the House, his opponent being Colonel James Gregory. On the first ballot he received 37 votes, Colonel Gregory 38, and one vote was cast scattering. On the second ballot each of the candidates received 38 votes. The vote continued about even until the sixth ballot, when Colonel Gregory was elected, receiving 39 votes, one more than a majority. The next year Mr. Bigger was chosen judge of his judicial circuit, and served acceptably until called to a higher office. In 1840 he was nominated for Governor by the Whig State convention, and, after an exciting race, was elected, beating General Tilghman A. Howard. He was a candidate for re-election in 1843, and was defeated by James Whitcomb, one of the ablest of Indiana's Governors. Soon after leaving the gubernatorial office he removed to Fort Wayne and resumed the practice of law. His professional career at Fort Wayne was honorable, but was too brief for him to obtain a lucrative practice. He died at Fort Wayne in 1845, and was buried in the cemetery there.

While Governor Bigger was Chief Executive of Indiana the State was overwhelmed with debt. The internal improvement system broke down the year before his election, leaving the people in the slough of despond. Little was done during his administration to relieve the State from its financial embarrassments, that being reserved for his successor, Governor Whitcomb.

In February, 1841, the Legislature appointed Governor Bigger " to prepare a compilation and revision of the general statute laws of this State, and to suggest such amendments and alterations in any of said statutes, and to prepare such additions as he might deem proper, with a view to the adoption and enactment by the Legislature of a full and complete code of general laws." This was a work Governor Bigger was well qualified to do. He entered upon it at once, but becoming convinced that he could not, of himself, prepare the revision in the time fixed by the law, he asked the next Legislature to allow him an assistant. His request was granted, and George H. Dunn became associated with him in the work. The revision was reported to the Legislature in 1842, and passed that body almost as it came from the hands of the revisers. It was intelligently and carefully done, and is a memento of the painstaking care and legal ability of its author.

The Hon. Finley Bigger, in a note to the author, gives this graphic account of his brother's early life:

"When a boy, his (Governor Bigger's) temper was very equable, and it was seldom any one ever saw him angry, or even vexed. He was nevertheless high-strung and sensitive, and to have been decoyed or hurried into a wrong act would have mortified him greatly. A cowardly or unmanly act in another would sometimes throw him off his guard and prompt him to action. I recollect, when at school, an instance which I will name. A boy, much larger than his victim, struck and knocked a small boy down and then kicked him. Samuel broke a gad from a bush, took the large boy by the arm, and gave him a severe flogging. This was the only time in his whole life that I ever saw him evince what one might call hot temper.

"When quite a boy he was noted for expertness in wearing out the seat and knees of his breeches; a good pair would last him about a week. I have heard my mother say that, as a matter of economy, she once made him a buckskin suit, and that even the pants of this didn't stand his gyrations long.

"He was always, in his young days, fond of his books, but the state of his health compelled him to moderate this desire. His early life was passed in the midst of great men—the Western pioneers, who felled dense forests and cultivated farms, and at the same time built log houses, barns, school-houses and churches, employed and paid teachers and preachers, lived at first on venison, wild turkeys and bear meat killed with their rifles. Sometimes they dropped the ax and hoe, shouldered their rifles, and hastened to some point to defend their homes from an invasion of savages. A common necessity and a common danger made all these men brothers. Among such men Samuel began his life and grew to manhood. No one knew him better than I, and it may look unseemly in a brother, but I only do just reverence to his name and memory when pronouncing him a great man in goodness, great in heart, and great in soul."

Governor Bigger's talents were not of the showy kind. As a speaker he was plain and simple. He made no attempt at florid oratory, and would have failed if he had. His mind was of the judicial order. He carefully weighed a question before deciding it, and reached his conclusions by feeling his way.

Governor Bigger was beaten for Governor in 1843 mainly by the influence of the Methodist church. His opponent, James Whitcomb, was a member of that denomination, and during the canvass it was charged that in opposing some legislation which resulted in the establishment of Asbury University, Governor Bigger had said that the Methodist church did not need an educated clergy; that an ignorant one was better suited to the capacity of its membership. The vote of the church was cast almost solid against him and caused his defeat. The author well remembers hearing the late Bishop Ames say, in 1846: " It was the amen corner of the Methodist church that defeated Governor Bigger, and I had a hand in the work."

Governor Bigger was a Presbyterian, and for many years was a ruling elder in the church. He was a capable musician, being a good bass singer, and a skillful performer upon the violin. For many years he led the church choir, and took much delight in the work. He was a man of fine form and presence. He was six feet two inches high, and weighed two hundred and forty pounds. His hair was black, his eyes a blue hazel, and his complexion dark. The expression of his face was kind and benignant, and denoted the goodness of his heart. His talent was not of the highest order, but he accomplished more in life than others more brilliant than he. He was a patriotic citizen, an incorruptible judge, and an executive officer of very respectable ability.

JAMES WHITCOMB.

THE student of Indiana history will look in vain for a more eminent name than that of James Whitcomb. It is a name which should excite love and veneration in the bosom of every Indianian, for his State gave Whitcomb her highest honors, and he bore them honestly and well.

James Whitcomb was born near Windsor, Vermont, December 1, 1795. When James was a little boy his father left the barren fields of the Green Mountain State and came to the Great West. then the El Dorado of the enterprising and ambitious. The family settled near Cincinnati, Ohio, and at once began the work of opening up and improving a farm. Hard work and coarse fare were their lot, their new home being in a barren pasture for the cultivation of the mind, but a rich one for the growth of a steady independence and a true manhood. The future Governor and Senator was known in the neighborhood as a studious boy, one who read all the books he could lay his hands upon. His father often complained of his son's love of books rather than of manual labor, and more than once told him he would never amount to anything in life; for, be it known, that old John Whitcomb, like many another pioneer, thought it more important that his son should be able to lay off a straight corn row and to deftly handle the sickle and the scythe than to read Homer and Virgil in the original. But the son did not agree with the father, and continued to borrow books and to read them when his daily work was done. In this way he acquired a great fund of information, and was noted throughout the settlement as the most studious and intelligent boy in it. Indeed, so well established was his reputa-

6

tion for diligence and knowledge, that a Mr. Johnson—a neighbor—once said to him, " Jimmy, some day you will be a United States Senator; you study while others play." This incident Governor Whitcomb related to a friend a few moments after he was elected to the United States Senate in 1849.

When the lad had fitted himself for college he entered Transylvania University, and by teaching during vacation managed to maintain himself at college until he graduated. On leaving college he entered a law office and bent his best energies to acquiring a knowledge of the profession in which he afterward became eminent. In March, 1822, he was admitted to the Fayette County, Kentucky, bar, and two years after this he came to Indiana and settled at Bloomington, then one of the most promising towns in the State. He soon became known as an able advocate and practitioner, and in 1826 was appointed Prosecuting Attorney of his circuit by James Brown Ray, then Governor of the State. In discharging the duties of this office he traveled over a large scope of country and became acquainted with many leading men. In 1830 he was elected to the State Senate, and was re-elected in 1833. In the Senate he had for associates Calvin Fletcher, John Dumont, and other men of distinction, but it is saying only what is known to those who are familiar with the history of that day, that in ability and influence he outranked them all. The internal improvement fever was then at its highest point, and Whitcomb did more to stay its progress than any other man in the State. On the roll-call, there were but nine votes against it, Whitcomb being one of the nine.

While in the Senate Mr. Whitcomb participated largely in the debates of that body, and during most of the time was chairman of the Judiciary Committee. He was felt in the Committee-room as well as in the Senate chamber.

In October, 1836, General Jackson appointed Mr. Whitcomb Commissioner of the General Land Office, and the next June he was reappointed by President Van Buren, and served as commissioner until the end of Mr. Van Buren's term. On taking charge of the land office Mr. Whitcomb found himself embarrassed by reason of his inability to read French and Spanish, many of the land grants being printed in these tongues; he therefore commenced at once to study these languages, and soon qualified himself to read them with facility and ease.

Early in 1841 Mr. Whitcomb left Washington and returned to Indiana. He located at Terre Haute, opened an office and commenced the practice of law. Business came to him quickly, and he soon commanded a large and lucrative practice. He was then one of the best known and most popular members of his party, and at the Democratic State convention of 1843 he was nominated for Governor of the State. His opponent was Samuel Bigger, who, three years before, had beaten Tilghman A. Howard, one of the ablest and purest men in the State, 8,637 votes. Mr. Whitcomb entered the canvass with confidence and zeal, and was elected Governor by 2,013 majority. Three years afterward, in 1846, he was re-elected, beating Joseph G. Marshall, the Whig candidate, 3,958 votes.

Governor Whitcomb occupied the executive chair during an eventful period of the State's history. He entered the office with the State loaded down with debt, upon which no interest had been paid for years; he left it with the debt adjusted and the State's credit restored. "He smote the rock of national resources, and abundant streams of revenue burst forth; he touched the dead corpse of public credit, and it sprang upon its feet." It was at his suggestion and on his recommendation that the Butler bill was passed, whereby one-half the State's debt was paid by a transfer of the Wabash and Erie canal, and the other half arranged for by the issuance of bonds drawing a low rate of interest. The settlement was alike satisfactory to the bondholders and the people, and in Governor Whitcomb's own words, restored "the tarnished escutcheon of Indiana to its original brightness." Had he done nothing else, he would deserve the gratitude of all, but this was only one of the many things he did for the good of the people and the honor of the State. It was by his efforts that a public sentiment was created which demanded the establishment of our benevolent and reformatory institutions, and he it was who awakened the people of Indiana to the importance of establishing common schools and providing a fund for their maintenance. It was while he was Governor that the Mexican war broke out, and Indiana was called upon for soldiers to assist in "conquering a peace."

Five regiments of infantry were organized and mustered into the service under his direction, and the ease and rapidity with which it was done proved him as able in organization as in finance.

The Legislature of 1849 elected Governor Whitcomb to the Senate of the United States for the term commencing in March of that year. He was qualified by talent, by education, and by experience for the place, and he would have added luster to a name already great by his service there, had his health been good and he permitted to serve out his term. But disease had fastened itself upon him, and therefore he was unable to discharge his senatorial duties as he otherwise would have done. He often left the capital in quest of health, but he found it not. His disease (gravel) was painful in the extreme, but he bore it with Christian fortitude. He died at New York, October 4, 1852, away from the State whose representative he was. His remains were brought to Indianapolis and buried in Greenlawn Cemetery, where they have mouldered to dust. The State erected a monument to his memory, and it still stands to point out the spot where lies all that is mortal of one whose influence upon public sentiment is felt even at the present day.

Governor Whitcomb's poverty in early life forced upon him habits of economy which never left him. By many his economy was considered parsimony, and indeed, if it were not such, it it was near akin to it. It cost him a seat in the Senate of the United States at a time when he very much desired the honor. In 1843 he wrote a remarkable pamphlet, entitled " Facts for the People," the most effective treatise against a protective tariff ever written. In those days corruption funds to carry elections were unknown, and after the Democratic State convention of 1843 had nominated him for Governor, and Jesse D. Bright for Lieutenant-Governor, a proposition was made in the convention to raise a fund to publish Whitcomb's pamphlet for gratuitous circulation. Whitcomb headed the paper with a donation of twenty dollars, and after him came Bright with a two hundred dollar subscription. In 1845, when a United States Senator was to be chosen, Mr. Bright was selected instead of the Governor; his two hundred dollars contribution brought its reward. The remarkable pamphlet to which reference has been made is out of print, and can only be found in the libraries of those antiquarians who delight in preserving the treasures of the past. It was with great difficulty that the author was able to procure a copy, and he has transcribed a page or so for the edification of the reader. This was done to show Governor Whitcomb's style and the simple manner in which he gave his thoughts to the public. It is extracted from a chapter entitled "A Familiar Example : "

" Suppose one of our incorporated towns in Indiana should pass a law, or ordinance, that all articles brought within the town limits to market from the country should pay a tax. Among others, suppose the tax of fifty cents on every bushel of potatoes. Suppose a bushel of potatoes could be raised for fifty cents. The farmer taking them to market, ' to make himself whole,' would be obliged, then, to charge one dollar a bushel ; that is, fifty cents for the trouble of ' raising and hauling ' them to town and fifty cents for the tax which he would be obliged to pay for the privilege of selling them.

" Now, one raising potatoes in town, in his garden, or on his outlot, with the same trouble or expense of fifty cents a bushel, could get his dollar a bushel in market also, although he would have to pay no tax, because he would ask and could get the highest price in market, for the tax on the farmer's potatoes would keep them up to a dollar, and the town people must pay that or do without ; and it is manifest that the tax, although paid by the farmer in the first instance, would, after all, be paid by the people in town, who were the buyers, the farmer being obliged to charge just so much more. So a high tax, to be sure, would cause fewer potatoes to be eaten, and, of course, fewer would be sold by the farmer. The farmer, also, could not buy as many articles in town as he would have done had he sold more potatoes. He couldn't be as good a customer to the mechanics in town, nor get as much sugar, tea, coffee, salt, iron, etc., as he would have done if he had sold or exchanged more of his potatoes. He can't, for instance, get leather from the tan-yard in town, because the people in town can't afford to give the money for his produce. He is not well prepared for tanning leather on his farm, and besides he has too many other matters to attend to ; but leather he must have, and the time it takes to tan an inferior article would have enabled him to raise potatoes enough to buy twice as much from the tanner, if the tax was not in the way.

" So far, such a tax would diminish trade and be injurious to both parties.

" Now, the operation of such a law between town and country is precisely that of a tariff between this and a foreign country.

" The most difficult national question can be understood by any man who is able to attend to his own business without the aid of a guardian, if exhibited to him by a familiar example, and if he will think for himself. There are too many who are interested in veiling such questions beneath the mist of deceptive words and pompous declamation.

" But to return. Another and more important effect would be produced by this town tariff. The advanced price on potatoes, occasioned by the tax, would not all be paid into the town treasury. That part paid on the potatoes sold by the farmer would go into the treasury, but the extra fifty cents a bushel paid for those raised in town would go into the gardener's pocket. The gardener would be benefited by that part of the operation, and not the town government, for carrying on which the tax was imposed.

"Again, if the tax on potatoes should be so high that the farmers would take theirs to other towns where the taxes were not so high, then none would be brought from the country to the first town, and no tax would be derived from that source. That would be a prohibitory tariff; and the first town would be compelled to resort to direct taxation to pay the town expenses. The farmers, too, being compelled to trade with other towns, the mechanics, merchants, etc., in the first town would lose the benefit of their custom.

" But the potatoes that might yet be raised in our own town would still bring a dollar a bushel, although it would cost the gardener but fifty cents a bushel to raise them. The remaining fifty cents would then be a tax on the rest of the community for the exclusive benefit of the gardener, not a cent of it going into the treasury, for the common benefit of the citizens.

"All this would be bad enough. But the argument of the town council would be, that they wanted to protect the gardeners until they could raise and sell potatoes as cheap as the farmers, and make the town independent of the country. Well, suppose the ten or a dozen gardeners should have bought up nearly all the outlots for that purpose, and having no other cultivation to attend to, should, by the aid of machinery, wealth, etc., actually raise potatoes so cheap that after the people of the town had bought all the potatoes they wanted of them, at a high price, there would still be an overplus, which the gardeners could afford to be at the expense of sending to the other towns and undersell the farmers. Would the gardeners need a tax on their neighbors for their own protection any longer?

" But perhaps it might still be urged that if the profits of the gardeners were so high, it would encourage others to turn gardeners also, and so cheapen the article. But, to make the comparison just as to our large manufactories, suppose it required great wealth to procure machinery, etc., to engage in the business; that it could generally be done only by rich companies; they could then undersell any new beginner, and break him up, and then indemnify themselves by again raising their prices. Besides, it is seen that they already raised more potatoes than were used in the town. And would the gardeners ask for an increased tax if they believed it would cheapen the article and diminish their profits?

"Another argument is that, by encouraging others in town to turn gardeners, there would be fewer mechanics, etc., left to attend to their old business and more gardeners to buy their work. But there are but few gardeners needed, as their work is carried on by machinery, etc., and it is not machinery, but human beings, that need shoes, leather, salt, sugar, coffee, etc. A gardener can use only a small part of these articles which are for sale in town, and, by their high tax, they have driven off the farmers who would have used them in exchange for their productions. Is it strange that under such circumstances the gardeners should become rich, and the rest of the town complain of ' hard times?'

" Not satisfied with all this, however, suppose the gardeners, made wealthy by this very tax, should beg the town council to lay a still higher tax on potatoes. Would there be any reason or justice in it? It might be natural enough for the gardeners to ask, but would you suppose that a town council, fairly elected by all the citizens, would pass such a law? Would you suppose that, to gratify one-tenth part of the people in the town, they would be willing to increase the already heavy burdens of taxation on the other nine-tenths?"

After this sketch was prepared and published, in February, 1882, by request, the *Indianapolis Sentinel* reproduced the pamphlet named, and it was widely distributed during the political campaign of 1882. In respect to the document and its author, the *Sentinel*, of August 26, spoke editorially as follows:

"The *Sentinel* has no hesitancy in recommending the widest possible circulation of this remarkable production by one of the most remarkable men that was ever connected with public affairs in Indiana. Governor Whitcomb was an intellectual giant. He was a man of lofty integrity. He was *sans peur et sans reproche*. He was a man of the people. His colossal mind grasped every problem of statecraft and mastered it. No question was too occult for his analytical powers. In the crucible of his reasoning faculties the pure gold of fact was brought forth from the dross of fiction. Sophisms were exposed, duplicity was throttled, subterfuges were swept away and plain people were permitted to comprehend the most intricate questions relating to their welfare, and the pamphlet in question is a monument to his clear-sightedness."

Besides being an inveterate user of snuff, Governor Whitcomb was addicted to smoking. But his habits of economy were such that when his cigar was so far consumed that he could no longer manipulate it with his fingers, he would insert a pin in the stump to hold by, and thus get all the good (or bad) there was in it. One day he was in the office of Horatio J. Harris, then Auditor of State, when Mr. Harris used a match to light a cigar. A fire was in the grate at the time, and the Governor thus reproved the Auditor for his reckless extravagance: "Why didn't you light your cigar by the fire?" said the Governor. "A man has no right to wantonly destroy a thing of value. A match has its value, and the one you used could have been saved."

Governor Whitcomb was as economical of time as of money. He wasted neither. It was his custom to read as he walked, and those who used to see him going from his boarding house to his office will remember that he was nearly always reading a book.

While he had a remarkable memory in most things it was very defective in relation to names. He was often unable to recall the names of his friends, an imperfection which caused him much annoyance and inconvenience.

Governor Whitcomb was a very able lawyer. Governor Porter rates him as the first in the State of his day, but the estimate I think is too high. But if he did not stand at the head of his profession, his place was very near him who did. In arguing his case before a jury it was his custom to first present the side of his opponent, and then demolish it. Like the player in the bowling alley, who puts up the pins to knock them down, he set up his adversary's arguments that he might scatter them with his own.

During the Legislature of 1845 Governor Whitcomb became involved in a quarrel with the Senate over the appointment of Supreme Judges. The terms of Judges Dewey and Sullivan having expired, he refused to reappoint them. He sent the names of Charles H. Test and Andrew Davidson to the Senate as successors to Dewey and Sullivan, but the Senate refused to confirm them. He then nominated E. M. Chamberlain and Samuel E. Perkins, but they were also rejected. He then designated William W. Wick and James Morrison for the places, but the Senate refused its consent. After the Senate adjourned he appointed Samuel E. Perkins and Thomas L. Smith, who served until their successors were chosen. The opposition to Governor Whitcomb in these appointments was led by Joseph W. Chapman, then a Democratic Senator from Laporte, and afterward a distinguished judge of the Madison circuit. The reason the Governor gave for his refusal to reappoint the old judges was the fact that the court docket was behind, and he believed it needed younger men to bring it up.

Governor Whitcomb was a member of the Methodist church,

and an active worker in its cause.   He frequently led in public
prayer, and for some time was a class-leader in the church.
In his public utterances he often referred to the Deity, and always in a reverential manner.   In December, 1844, Mr. W. P.
Dole, a Senator from Vermilion county, offered a resolution in
the Senate "to refer so much of the Governor's message as
referred to the goodness of God to the priesthood."   This irrev-
erent proposition met with no favor, even from the Governor's
political opponents.

When he died, Governor Whitcomb was Vice-President of
the American Bible Society, an organization he loved, and to
which he contributed with his means.   He willed his library to
Asbury University, an institution he favored in many ways.
The library was large, containing many rare books, but the
collection was ill-assorted and disjointed.   It showed that he
gathered his books without a system, picking them up here and
there as he came across them.

Governor Whitcomb was one of the best amateur musicians
in the country.   He composed many pieces of music for the
violin, an instrument upon which he played with rare skill and
ability.   Many stories are told of him and his "fiddle," but
one must suffice for this biography.

Oliver H. Smith, in his book entitled "Early Indiana Trials
and Sketches," tells of a trip he took with Governor Whitcomb
from Indianapolis to Eastern Indiana.   They stopped for the
night at a house standing on the present site of Knightstown.
Mr. Smith says:

"Entering the cabin, there sat before the fire a lame young
man by the name of Amos Dille, with an old violin in his hand,
scraping away, making anything but music.   He laid the violin
on the bed and started with our horses to the stable.   As he
closed the door, Mr. Whitcomb took it up, soon put it in tune,
and when Amos returned was playing light and beautiful airs.
Amos took his seat by me seemingly entranced, and as Mr.
Whitcomb struck up 'Hail, Columbia' he sprang to his feet.
'If I had fifty dollars I would give it all for that fiddle; I never
heard such music before in my life.'   After playing several
tunes Mr. Whitcomb laid the instrument on the bed.   Amos

seized it, carried it to the fire where he could see it, turned it over and over, examined every part, and sang out, 'Mister, I never saw two fiddles so much alike as yours and mine.'"

Governor Whitcomb was always well dressed, was always clean. It was his custom when traveling over the circuit to take a night-shirt, which he would put on before retiring. This custom was so different from that of the ordinary itinerant lawyer that his brother attorneys resolved to play a prank upon him. While at a tavern in the eastern part of the State, kept by one Captain Berry, the resolve was carried out. I again quote from Mr. Smith:

"Taking the Captain to one side, Fletcher said: 'Do you know, Captain Berry, what Mr. Whitcomb is saying about your beds?' 'I do not; what did he say?' 'If you will not mention my name, as you are my particular friend, I will tell you.' 'Upon my honor, I will never mention your name; what did he say?' 'He said your sheets were so dirty that he had to pull off his shirt every night and put on a dirty shirt to sleep in.' 'I'll watch him to-night.' Bed-time came, and Captain Berry was looking through the opening of the door when Mr. Whitcomb took his night-shirt out of his portmanteau and began to take off his day-shirt. Captain Berry pushed open the door, sprang upon Whitcomb and threw him upon the bed. The noise brought in Mr. Fletcher and the other lawyers, and after explanations and apologies on all sides the matter was settled."

In his remarkable address entitled "The Advocate," delivered before the Central Law School, in April, 1882, Governor Thomas A. Hendricks pays the following eloquent tribute to the subject of this sketch:

"Governor Whitcomb was a great scholar. He was capable not only of acquiring but of using the accumulations of learning. With him learning became an influence, an instrumentality, a power. His tastes were cultivated. He commanded beautiful and strong language, and in it he clothed his thoughts, that were always appropriate to the subject and the occasion. I heard him address the people in his first candidacy for Governor. It was the greatest political speech I have ever heard. There was not in it a vulgarism or an appeal to low sentiment. He addressed reason, emotion, sympathy. The multitude stood enraptured. As men went from the place of the meeting they fell into grave and serious conversation about what they had heard, and the impression remained. From that day he was a leader, but not as men commonly speak of leadership; he maneuvered for no combinations; he was a leader in a higher sense. He declared what he believed to be the truth, and trusted to its influence upon men's minds to bring them into common action. He led legislators because it was safest for them to follow. His manner was grave and serious, his voice was full and musical, and his delivery almost without gesture. I never heard him in court, but am sure he was a formidable antagonist before either court or jury."

Governor Whitcomb was an active Freemason. He was the first man knighted in Indiana, the honor being conferred upon him May 20, 1848. Raper Commandery was organized in his house, and for some time held its meetings there. He was proud of his connection with Masonry; in his affections Masonry stood only second to his church.

Governor Whitcomb was married March 24, 1846, to Mrs. Martha Ann Hurst. His wife died July 17, 1847, shortly after giving birth to a daugher, now the wife of Claude Matthews, Esq. He recorded her death in the family Bible, and followed the record with these words: "How brief our happy sojourn together."

If not universally loved, Governor Whitcomb was universally respected. He was kind to the young and aspiring. Professor Collett, the distinguished geologist, says he feels he is indebted to Governor Whitcomb's advice for whatever success in life he has attained. On being asked what the advice was he replied: "Follow one line of thought and research with your whole mind and soul; take no active part in politics until maturity has brought you settled thought. The life of a politician is not always reputable; it has so many elements of deceit and dishonesty that it is hard to follow it and keep clean one's hands and soul."

Governor Whitcomb was compactly and strongly built; he was somewhat above the average size of man; he had a dark complexion and black hair, which usually fell in ringlets to his shoulders. His features were good and expressive, and his manners the most elegant. His appearance was that of a courtier, and in any circle of society he would have been considered a pattern of propriety. He was not a fop, but, like many other eminent men, he had a weakness in that direction. Foibles he had, but they were insignificant in comparison with his many virtues. He was a talented and an honest man, and when the roll of Indiana's great is made up, among the first in the list will be the name of Whitcomb.

JOSEPH A. WRIGHT.

THERE are many examples of self-made men, but there are few more striking and worthy of study than that of Joseph A. Wright. Some men have reached a higher eminence than he, but they are few. Where one attained his altitude, thousands fell by the way. His career shows the possibilities of life, and ought to stimulate young men to new exertions when they are faint and ready to fall.

Joseph A. Wright, for seven years Governor of Indiana, was born at Washington, Pa., April 17, 1810. When a boy he emigrated to Indiana with his parents and settled at Bloomington. They were poor and unable to give their son the education he desired, but this did not prevent him from securing it. "Where there is a will there is a way," says the proverb, and so said the boy. He entered the State University as a student, and paid his way by ringing the college bell and doing the janitor's work. To get money to buy his books and clothing he bore off brick from the brick-yard, and gathered nuts from the woods.

Being also trained in the use of the trowel, and doubtless glad of a chance to use it, he proved to be a convenience in doing small jobs around the premises. Proof of this appears on the records of the Indiana college to-day, as the following passages which the author has taken pains to copy show:

EXTRACTS FROM THE RECORDS.

"FRIDAY, May 6, 1828.

"*Ordered*, That Joseph A. Wright be allowed for ringing the college bell, making fires, etc., in the college building during the last session of the College Seminary, the sum of $16.25 ; also,

FIRST PRESIDENT OF THE INDIANA STATE BOARD OF AGRICULTURE.

for a lock, bell-rope and brooms, the sum of $1.37½, and that the treasurer of the State Seminary pay the same."

" BLOOMINGTON, Friday, October 31, 1828.

"*Ordered by the Board of Trustees*, That Joseph A. Wright be and he is hereby allowed the sum of one dollar for repairing the top of one of the college chimneys, and that the treasurer pay the same."

" NOVEMBER 18, 1828.

" Joseph A. Wright is allowed for repairing arches in the small seminary building and kitchen the sum of $1.25."

By such expedients and humble yet persistent exertions he defrayed his expenses for a couple of years, and then he left college and entered the law office of Judge Hester as a student. In 1829, when less than twenty years old, he stood his examination, and obtained his license to practice law. Soon after this he removed to Rockville, and hung out his shingle as a lawyer. In 1833 he was elected a member of the State Legislature.

A rather amusing incident, given by Robert Dale Owen in *Scribner's Monthly*, should not be omitted. It happened while he and Mr. Wright were members of the House of Representatives. Mr. Owen writes:

" The most flowery speech on our side was made by a promising young man, then fresh from college and classical recollections, Joseph Wright. A poor boy, he had entered the State University as janitor, and afterwards became, first, Governor of the State, and then foreign minister. I remember that he was descanting, in a somewhat sophomoric strain, on the duty of Indiana toward the children of the State—her best treasures— when his eye was arrested by a chubby little fellow of seven or eight, son of one of our members, who had been sitting on his father's knee and had strayed off, coming down the center aisle toward the orator.

" ' Ah, there !' said Wright, extending his arms to the boy, who stopped, abashed at the sudden address. ' Look there ! I am reminded, when I gaze upon that little one, of a pleasant story from the annals of Rome, in her old republican days. It is related of the mother of the Gracchi, when several of her lady friends were exhibiting to her, somewhat vauntingly, no doubt, their costly ornaments, while she, simple in her tastes, had little to show them in return, that she turned to her children, playing in the room, and exclaimed, ' These are my jewels!' Let us learn wisdom, gentlemen, from the mother of the Gracchi.'

" ' The mother of the what?' exclaimed, in an under-tone, a rough young country member, named Storm, and whom, because he seldom opened his lips except to move the previous question, we had nicknamed ' Previous Question Storm.' His exclamation was addressed to the member next to whom he was sitting, Thomas Dowling, of Terre Haute. Now, of all things, Dowling loved, from his heart, a good joke; and this was too good a one to be lost. So, composing his features, he replied gravely to Storm: ' Why, don't you know her? It is a noted old woman in Parke county, where Wright comes from. Everybody knows her there. You get up and ask Wright, and no doubt he'll tell you all about her.' "

In 1840, the year of the Harrison political tornado, Mr. Wright was elected to the State Senate. In 1843 he was elected to Congress, and two years afterward was beaten for that office by Edward W. McGaughey 171 votes. In 1849 he was nominated for Governor, and defeated John A. Matson 9,778 votes. In 1852 he again ran for Governor, and defeated Nicholas McCarty 20,031 votes. In 1857 he was appointed United States Minister to Prussia, and served four years as such. In 1862 he was appointed by Governor Morton United States Senator, and sat in the Senate until the next January. In 1863 President Lincoln appointed him a commissioner to the Hamburg Exposition. In 1865 he again went to Prussia as United States Minister, and remained there until he died. His death occurred at Berlin, March 11, 1867, and his remains were brought to New York, and there buried. This is an epitome of the life and death of Joseph A. Wright.

Governor Wright will be best remembered as Governor of Indiana. His service in Congress, one term in the House and one year in the Senate, was too brief for him to make much impression there. As Governor, he was an important factor in shaping legislation and moulding public opinion in his State. It was while he was Governor that the constitution under which we live was made. It was while he was Governor that the State Agricultural Society was formed, and it was while he was Governor that the Free banking law was passed, and the charter for the Bank of the State of Indiana granted. In 1852, on the organization of the State Board of Agriculture, he was chosen its President. He was re-elected in 1853 and in 1854. He took great pride in the work of this society. He used to quote the saying of Horace Greeley, that "the man who makes two blades of grass grow where but one had grown before, is a public benefactor." Agriculture was a "hobby" with him. From the fact that he had never been a farmer his political opponents made sport of his farming pretensions. They used to tell a story on him, which is too good to be omitted here. It was said that in one of his speeches before an agricultural society, he advised farmers to buy hydraulic rams to improve their sheep! The story, although apochryphal, had great credence at the time. Another, which was true, will bear repeating: Some one brought him a bunch of hog bristles, taken from the paunch of a cow. He exhibited this as a great curiosity, and was wont to descant upon it for the edification of his farmer friends. At last it was discovered that the cow from which the bristles were taken was in the habit of browsing near a pork-house where hog's hair was spread to dry. While eating grass she had swallowed the bristles, and, as they were indigestible, they remained in her stomach until she died. This discovery spoiled the Governor's lecture on the cow.

Governor Wright was an anti-bank man, and opposed with the whole weight of his influence the free bank law and the bill chartering the Bank of the State of Indiana. He vetoed both these measures, but the Legislature passed them, notwithstanding his opposition. The bill to charter the Bank of the State passed the Senate at the session of 1855, in its closing hours, and when the Senate had adjourned the Governor ascended the President's chair and made a bitter speech against the bill, asserting that it was passed by corruption and fraud. This

7

speech caused much bad feeling between the Governor and the members of the Legislature, and also the Lieutenant-Governor, who had been an advocate of the bill. The Legislature having passed the bank bills over the Governor's veto, he sought to bring the laws into disrepute, and thereby impede the organization of banks under them. He commenced a suit in the Marion Circuit Court against John D. Defrees and others for the purpose of having the charter of the Bank of the State declared null and void. The case was decided against him, but he appealed to the Supreme Court, and that tribunal affirmed the judgment of the court below. Having exhausted all legal measures, he was compelled to retire from the contest, which he very reluctantly did. But he renewed the fight in the Legislature of 1857. In his message to this Legislature he said:

"The means and appliances brought to bear to secure the passage of this charter would, if exposed to the public gaze, exhibit the nakedest page of fraud and corruption that ever disgraced the Legislature of any State. While men of pure and honorable sentiment were led into its support in the belief that the approaching close of the existing bank required them thus early to provide a successor, others supported it upon promise of stock, equivalents in money, or pledges as to the location of certain branches. To make up the constitutional vote in its favor the names of members were recorded on its passage who were at the moment absent, and many miles distant from the capital."

Upon the delivery of this message the Senate raised an investigating committee of five, at the head of which was Horace Heffren, the Senator from Washington. The examination of the committee was thorough and exhaustive, and, although some suspicious transactions were discovered, nothing was developed to justify the sweeping charges of the Governor. A majority of the committee reported that many dishonorable things had been done by the speculators who engineered the bill through the Legislature, and recommended that the charter be revoked. Mr. Heffren, the chairman, dissented from the opinion of a majority of the committee, taking the ground that one Legislature had no right to review and pass judgment upon the acts of another. The investigation and reports of the committee practically amounted to nothing, for the bank was organized, and made for itself one of the most honorable records known in the history of banking.

Governor Wright was more fortunate in his contest with the free banks than with the Bank of the State. He sent a messenger to a small town near the Illinois line with some $2,000 of the bills of a bank located there for the purpose of testing its bottom. The messenger demanded payment of the bills, and the bank being unable to redeem them, suffered the dishonor of protest. The result justified the Governor's often expressed opinion, *i. e.*, that some of the free banks were merely banks of circulation. His action in testing the solvency of a single bank brought on a crisis with the system. Those which could not stand the test of solvency—the redemption of their bills—were forced to suspend and wind up their affairs. For some time the value of Indiana free bank bills was an uncertain quantity. The banks of Indianapolis fixed a price upon these bills, and this price was as fluctuating as the mercury in March. It often varied as much as ten per cent. a day; sometimes down, and then up. This state of affairs continued until all the illegitimate banks were closed, leaving only those standing which had been organized with capital, and were under the control of reputable men.

Until the summer of 1861 Governor Wright acted and voted with the Democratic party. He favored the compromise measures of 1850, being their zealous advocate. During their pendency in Congress he invited John J. Crittenden, then Governor of Kentucky, to visit Indiana. This eminent Kentuckian was warmly received wherever he appeared, and when he returned to his home he took with him the best wishes of the people of Indiana. It was believed at the time that this visit did much to allay sectional animosity and assuage the bad feeling existing between the North and the South. About one year and a half after Governor Crittenden's trip to Indiana Governor Wright was invited to visit Kentucky. He accepted the invitation, and at Frankfort was received with great honors. The welcoming address was made by Lazarus W. Powell, then Governor of the

State, one of the most eloquent men of that time. In his reply, Governor Wright said :

"Governor Powell, you refer to the invitation extended to Governor Crittenden to visit our State in 1850, and have alluded to me in connection therewith. That invitation, sir, came from the people of Indiana, and it was due to the exalted worth, talents and services of your then distinguished Executive. It was peculiarly appropriate, in the dark hour of our country's history, when the tempest of disunion frowned in the political horizon, that the people of two States like Kentucky and Indiana, differing in their institutions, should meet together, smoke the pipe of peace, and pledge themselves to the support of the constitution. It was eminently proper, in this dark and trying hour, that the heart of this nation should speak, and when Kentucky and Indiana spake, the heart did speak.

"On crossing the beautiful Ohio, yesterday, I was reminded of the custom of some of the aboriginal inhabitants of this country, in performing the marriage ceremony of the tribe. The bride stood upon one side of the stream and the groom upon the other, their hands plaited together, and the clear, living waters of the rivulet, emblematical of their virtue and purity, and tending to a common union, the great ocean of love. Kentucky and Indiana have clasped hands upon the Thames and the Tippecanoe, and at Buena Vista, and for forty years, in peace and in war, they have been shaking hands; and to-day (shaking the hand of Governor Powell) they renew the covenant afresh, that Kentucky and Indiana will live by the bond of their union, the ark, the covenant, the pillar, the cloud, the constitution! They theoretically and practically carry out the doctrine of non-intervention, each State attending to its own municipal affairs."

During Governor Wright's official term the Washington Monumental Association requested the several States to contribute blocks for the Washington monument. At that time there were but few stone quarries open in Indiana, the principal ones being those at Vernon, in Jennings county, and at Saluda Landing, in Jefferson county. Governor Wright had a block from the Saluda quarry properly dressed and prepared at Madison, and sent to Washington. It bore this inscription, dictated by the Governor: "Indiana knows no East, no West, no North, no South; nothing but the Union." The stone was placed in the Washington monument, a work which was commenced over thirty years ago, and is still unfinished.

In the report of Postmaster General Barry, made in 1830, under the caption of "Contracts made for carrying the mails," the following may be found: "The Postmaster General reports route No. 10, from Brownstown to Terre Haute, Ind., once a week, 134 miles, awarded to Alfred J. Athon, at $398. Joseph A. Wright bid $334 per annum. Wright was not sufficiently known nor recommended; therefore his bid was rejected." Mr. Wright was then a young lawyer of Bloomington, and being badly in need of money sought to make a few dollars by getting a mail contract. As will be seen, he was not sufficiently known for his bid to be regarded. What a commentary on the possibilities of life is this! The man who was then too insignificant to be considered, afterward sat in both branches of the Legislature of his State, and for nine years was its Governor. Not only this, but he served in both houses of Congress, and twice represented his country at a foreign court. I have told the reader who the unsuccessful bidder was; can he tell me who was the successful one, and what became of him? I imagine not.

Governor Wright was a Democrat of the straightest sect. He stood high in the councils of his party, and contested with Jesse D. Bright for the leadership, but without success. He was strong with the people, but weak with the leaders. Mr. Bright always kept the upper hand of him, and when he aspired to the United States Senate, in common parlance, Mr. Bright sat down upon him. The rivalries of these party leaders begat bad blood, and Mr. Bright was outspoken in his denunciations of the Governor. In a letter, now in possession of the author, he thus speaks of him:

"While the Governor is active in getting up his certificates to prove a lie the truth, I am wagging on in the even tenor of my way, a firm believer in the correctness of that old, time-honored maxim, 'Truth is mighty and will prevail.' He has begged a truce out of Governor Whitcomb, I understand. The latter shows he is a man of peace; though very timid, he will make good all he has uttered or written as to that prince of liars and hypocrites."

Governor Wright was in Europe when the rebellion began, but he warmly espoused the cause of the government, and did much to create a correct sentiment at the court to which he was accredited. He returned home in the fall of 1861, reaching Indianapolis on the 7th of September of that year. He was warmly received by his old neighbors and friends, General Dumont making the welcoming speech. The next February Mr. Bright, his old rival and enemy, was expelled from the United States Senate, and Governor Wright was appointed to the place. Will Cumback wanted the appointment, but Governor Morton said there was poetic justice in Governor Wright's taking the place of Mr. Bright, and he gave it to him. The appointment only lasted until the meeting of the next Legislature, and the Democracy, having a majority in that Legislature, elected Hon. David Turpie to fill out Mr. Bright's unexpired term. Thus it will be seen that as a Democrat, Governor Wright never reached the Senate. It was only after he had cut loose from his party and affiliated with those he had ever fought that he reached the coveted honor.

In 1863 Governor Wright was appointed by President Lincoln Commissioner to the Hamburg Exposition, and remained some time abroad. Two years after this President Johnson appointed him Minister to Prussia. This was the second time he represented his government at Berlin. He made many friends at the Prussian capital, among them Baron von Humboldt, with whom he maintained a very close intimacy. As previously stated in this sketch, he died in Berlin while United States Minister there.

Governor Wright was an able canvasser. He had the faculty of getting at the people and getting hold of them. In his speeches he used to say the people were more interested in selecting good County Commissioners than good Congressmen. He was a member of the Methodist church, and many believed he used his church connection to advance his political fortunes. In the canvass of 1852 he went to Madison and remained there over Sabbath. On Sunday morning he attended Third Street

Methodist Church, and afterward dined with William Griffin, a leading Roman Catholic. In the afternoon he attended the Wesley Chapel Sunday-school, and delivered a lecture to the scholars; and in the evening he attended the services of Wesley Chapel. Thus it will be seen that he put in his whole time on Sunday, and when the votes were counted that fall it was found that he had carried Jefferson county, Whig though it was. His most effective electioneering was done in the circles of his church.

Governor Wright was tall and raw-boned. He had a large head, and an unusually high forehead. His hair was light and thin upon his head, his eyes blue, and his nose and mouth large and prominent. He was an effective speaker, mainly on account of his earnestness and simplicity. He was not an eloquent man, and did not compare with Willard as a stumper, but the people liked to hear him talk, and listened attentively to what he said. While not the greatest man in the State, he was one of the most influential; and, to his honor be it said, his influence was exercised for the public good. Economy and honesty in public life, and morality and religion in private station, had in him an advocate and an exemplar.

ASHBEL PARSONS WILLARD.

Robert Pollock, author of "The Course of Time," died before he was 28 ; Lord Byron, of whom it had been said,

> "He laid his hand upon the ocean's mane,
> And played familiar with his hoary locks,"

died at 36 ; William Pitt was Prime Minister of England at 25, and Ashbel P. Willard was Governor of Indiana at 36. What a lesson for young men !

Ashbel Parsons Willard was born October 31, 1820, in Oneida county, New York. He was educated at Hamilton College, and studied law with Judge Baker in his native county. He emigrated to Marshall, Michigan, in 1842, and lived there for a year or so. He then made a trip to Texas on horseback, and on his return stopped at Carrolton, Kentucky, and there taught school for a while. After this he went to Jefferson county, Kentucky, and took a school near Louisville. His spare hours were employed in reading, and the knowledge he gained at this time was of great benefit to him in after life.

The contest for the presidency in 1844 between Clay and Polk was an exciting one, and in no part of the country did party spirit run higher than in Kentucky, the home of Clay. Young Willard was a Democrat by birth and by education, and was firmly grounded in the faith. He had a natural love for politics, and he soon left the school-room for a more exciting theater. He commenced stumping for Polk, and during the campaign spoke at New Albany, just across the river from Louisville. He made such a favorable impression that many of the first men of the town solicited him to come and settle among them. What they said impressed him, and next spring he left Kentucky and took up his abode at New Albany. He lived there until he died, except when at the State capital attending to his official duties.

He opened a law office at New Albany, but clients were tardy in coming, and to get money to pay his necessary expenses he supplemented his professional income by a small salary received for writing in the office of the county clerk. The first office Mr. Willard held was that of common councilman. He took pride in the place, and won the good opinion of the people without respect to party. The next year, 1850, he was elected to the State Legislature, and from that time until he died he occupied a conspicuous place in the public eye. On the organization of the House he was chosen chairman of the Committee on Ways and Means, and thus became leader of the House. We now find him, at thirty years of age, the acknowledged chief of his party in the popular branch of the Legislature, and never was chieftain more lovingly followed. Alert and watchful, he was always ready for the contest. He could parry a blow or give one with as much dexterity as an old knight of the lance. His address and manner were so captivating that before the session closed he had made prisoners the hearts of his fellow members. Those who did not like his politics liked the man, and when the members separated and went to their homes they took with them the fondest recollections of the gallant young leader of the House.

When the Democratic State Convention of 1852 convened, the delegates were met by an overwhelming public sentiment demanding the nomination of Willard for Lieutenant-Governor. The demand was recognized and the nomination made. Joseph A. Wright, the nominee for Governor, was an able and popular man, but he was not the equal of Willard on the hustings. Indeed, I only state a fact well known to those familiar with the public men of that day, when I say that, as a political stumper, Mr. Willard had no equal in the State, with the exception of Henry S. Lane. There were men who surpassed him as debaters and logicians, but none who matched him in impassioned oratory, with the exception named. He was elected and, at the next session of the Legislature, took his seat as President of the

Senate. As a presiding officer he was courteous, prompt and decisive. He was a warm partisan, and his decisions were sometimes influenced by party zeal; but, on the whole, he averaged well. In politics he met fire with fire, and believed in doing evil that good might come. Witness his casting vote in the Senate in 1855 on the resolution to go into an election for United States Senator. The People's party, having a majority on joint ballot, nominated Joseph G. Marshall, of Jefferson, for United States Senator. The Senate was a tie, and, by the casting vote of Lieutenant-Governor Willard, refused to go into an election. There can be no justification for this act. The most that can be said in its defense is that the Lieutenant-Governor followed a line of bad precedents. Several times in the history of Indiana politics has a legislative minority failed to discharge its constitutional duty by refusing to go into an election for Senator. Happily the law has been so changed as to break up this reprehensible practice.

In 1856 Willard was nominated for Governor. Two years before the Know-nothing party had swept the State. Willard had antagonized it from the first, having fought it bitterly and unrelentingly. It had gone to pieces, but those of its members who entered the Republican party took with them an intense hostility to the Democratic candidate. Oliver P. Morton, then a young lawyer of Wayne county, and afterwards the great war Governor of Indiana, was Willard's opponent for Governor. The contest between them was memorable. It was a battle of giants. Morton fought with the battle-ax of Richard Cœur de Lion, and Willard with the sword of Saladin. The sword conquered, and the young man who, eleven years before, had come to Indiana poor and friendless, was now the Governor-elect of a great State. I shall not speak of Governor Willard's administration of the State government further than to say that it commanded the approbation of his political friends and met the condemnation of his political enemies. The time is too recent to examine it without political bias, so I will pass it by.

In the summer of 1860 Governor Willard's health gave way. It had been bad for years, but his strong will enabled him to keep up and attend to his official duties. The last speech he attempted to make was at Columbus, this State. At that time the Democratic party was suffering from internal disorders. The Nebraska bill had disrupted it, and the wonder is that a man of Governor Willard's discernment and sagacity did not see it was doomed to defeat. But he continued hopeful of its future, and did all he could to insure its success. He attended many of its conventions and labored hard to heal its wounds. He went to Columbus as a peacemaker, but he had his labor for his pains. The convention, after much wrangling, nominated Dr. William M. Daly, a Methodist preacher, for Congress. The delegation from Jefferson was intensely hostile to him, although that county was his home, and, when the nomination was made, one of the delegates arose and proposed three cheers for McKee Dunn, the Republican candidate. To hear a member of a Democratic convention propose cheers for a Republican was, indeed, shocking to Willard, and he at once mounted the rostrum and commenced to speak. His voice was as musical, and he controlled it as artistically as ever, but in the midst of an impassioned appeal for harmony he suddenly stopped. He was taken ill, having a hemorrhage of the lungs, but the bleeding soon stopped, and he left the room.

Soon after the convention at Columbus Governor Willard went to Minnesota in quest of health. But the trip had been too long delayed to do him permanent good. Disease was eating at his vitals, and refused to release its hold at the bidding of the bracing air of the Northwest. On the 4th of October, 1860, he became suddenly worse, and on the evening of that day breathed his last, and there went from the face of the earth one of the brightest intellects of the day.

Governor Willard was the first Governor of Indiana to die in office. The people, without respect to party, paid homage to his remains as they passed through the towns and cities of the State. They were brought to Indianapolis, and for three days lay in state, being viewed by thousands who loved the young man eloquent. On the day after the October election, 1860, they were taken to New Albany, his old home, and there interred.

Some incidents illustrating Willard's character, and his power as an orator, may appropriately conclude this sketch of his life and death.

On the Saturday before the presidential election in 1856, Governor Willard went to Madison to deliver a political address. It had been announced that he would speak in the Court-house, but the deputy sheriff had let the Fillmore men have it that evening for the purpose of holding a political meeting. There was but a handful of these men, and it was believed that this was but a ruse to prevent Governor Willard from speaking. A party of Democrats, headed by Joseph W. Chapman, went to the deputy sheriff and charged him with being a party to the trick. They told him that Willard should have the Court-house, and if he—the deputy sheriff—did not open its doors, they would break them down. Judge Chapman and his friends went to Governor Willard and told him the situation, and what they intended to do. He said there should be no trouble, and that he would speak in the market-house. His friends objected to this, but he remained firm, saying that as the Democracy was "on top" it could afford to be generous. That evening he addressed an immense crowd in the market-house in his happiest vein. He was never more eloquent and effective. During the delivery of his speech he was interrupted by huzzas for Fremont. Some of his friends started for the offender with a view of putting him out of the house, but Willard stopped them, saying: "Let him alone. Enjoy the music while you can. After Tuesday 'hurrah for Fremont' will be the dearest music you can buy."

Soon after the election in 1856, Governor Willard was invited by the Legislature of Mississippi to visit Jackson as a guest of the State. Being acquainted with a gentleman who is familiar with public events in Mississippi, the author requested him to give an account of this event. The following is his response:

"MR. WOOLLEN—Of course my recollection of details must be somewhat imperfect, as I was then a lad of fifteen years. I will give them as I remember them. It was in December, 1856, after the Democratic victory, the Legislature being in regular session. Governor Willard and other prominent Democrats were invited to visit the capital of the State, Jackson. I remember his speech was full of vigor and patriotic sentiments, and overflowing with kindness towards his entertainers and the

whole Southern people. I can not now recall any expression
of his, but I know his address was received with the greatest
enthusiasm. After the speech-making, reception and general
hand-shaking, a banquet at the Spengler House was given, and
three hundred people were present. Wit flowed as freely and
sparkled as brightly as the generous wines which graced the
board. General good feeling prevailed. David C. Glenn was
the newly appointed Attorney-General of the State, just barely
of the constitutional age. He was considered one of the brightest lawyers of the commonwealth, and was a brilliant and eloquent writer. He came from the sea-coast country, or the
" Piney Woods " district, as it was then called. His brilliancy
and eloquence were famous throughout the State. His capacity
for a drinking bout was also well established. In fact, he was
considered the best, heaviest and solidest drinker in the Southwest. The reputation of Governor Willard in this particular
had preceded him, and it was determined to pit Glenn against
him. The result was that Glenn was put *hors du combat* at an
early stage of the proceedings, and Willard held his own as
cool and clear-headed and as steady on his pins at the close of
the banquet as he was at the commencement."

Colonel John S. Williams thus speaks of Governor Willard
in the *Lafayette Times:*

"As a political organizer and mere party man the late Governor Willard never had an equal in the State of Indiana. I
will not except his great rival, Governor Morton. I remember
the Saturday before the State election, in 1856, his arrival in
Lafayette to make the closing speech of the campaign. Coming into my apartments, he found me, in company with the late
Senator Hannegan, talking over the political situation. We at
once asked him what he thought of the political situation and his
chances of election. 'I've got 'em sure.' 'Can you give the
figures!' I inquired. 'Yes,' he responded; 'get your paper
and I will give you the vote of every county.' Commencing
with Posey county, in the southwest corner of the State, and
without any list before him, he named every county, giving his
estimate of majorities in each one. Strange to say, he had not
missed a single county. I have his figures now before me. In

several counties they correspond with the official vote, and, in the aggregate, do not vary three hundred votes as declared by the board of State canvassers. His majority over Governor Morton was about six thousand."

In 1857 news came to Indianapolis of the John Brown raid. Among those connected with Brown was John E. Cook, a brother-in-law of Governor Willard. Governor Willard's family had not heard of Cook for years, and, when it was published that one John E. Cook was arrested for participating in the Harper's Ferry tragedy, they could hardly believe it was Mrs. Willard's brother. But it was he, and when Governor Willard knew this fact he determined his course at once.

The raid of John Brown on Harper's Ferry was reprobated by all save a few abolitionists, and they were hushed to silence. Willard was young, was ambitious, and had great expectations of the future. He had a national reputation as an orator, and visions of the first office in the people's gift no doubt flitted before him. To identify himself as a friend of one connected with the detested raid would surely damage him at the South, and might do so at home. But he hesitated not. He determined to go to the rescue of his kinsman. He sent a special messenger to his friend, Daniel W. Voorhees, requesting his immediate presence. The messenger found Mr. Voorhees at Vincennes engaged in an important trial, but the eloquent advocate turned the case over to another and went to his friend as fast as the cars could take him. He found him in sore distress. He comforted him as best he could, and without delay the two started for Charleston, Virginia, where young Cook was imprisoned. The meeting between Willard and his brother-in-law was deeply affecting. One was Governor of a great State, the other a prisoner, charged with crime, but the difference between them did not stop the flow of affection from one heart to the other. And, here, let it be recorded, that Cook's love for Willard probably cost him his life. It was stated at the time, and not contradicted, that after Governor Willard left the prison the keeper opened a way for Cook's escape. But he would not embrace it. He said if he escaped the blame would be laid on Willard, and would ruin his prospects for future preferment; hence he staid in prison and met his fate. Brave and considerate man! Prisoner though you were, convict though you were to be, this act of self-abnegation proves you to be a hero.

On the 8th of November, 1859, Cook was put upon his trial. He was defended by Mr. Voorhees in a speech of transcendent eloquence, but it availed him naught. The fiat of a frenzied public had gone forth that he should die, and there was no putting it aside. After he was convicted Governor Willard appealed to Governor Wise for his pardon, but the appeal was in vain, and the young man suffered the extreme penalty of the law.

Governor Willard's efforts to save Cook's life, instead of lessening his popularity at home, increased it. People admired his courage and commended him for what he had done. Particularly was this true of his political opponents, and from that time until he died they respected and esteemed him as they had never done before.

In the Legislature of 1857 the Democrats had a majority on joint ballot, but the Republicans had the Senate. The two houses met in joint convention to count the vote for Governor, and when this was done, adjourned to a subsequent day. The purpose of thus adjourning was to elect United States Senators. The Republicans refused to go into another joint convention, so the Democrats were in a great strait to know what to do. It was contended that there having been a joint convention, a majority of the members of the Legislature could meet on the day appointed and legally elect the Senators. The Republicans controverted this position, and contended that it took a majority of each branch of the Legislature to constitute a legal convention. Senator Bright was disposed to consider this as the correct view of the question, and refused to accept an election which he believed to be tainted with illegality. The subject was referred to Samuel E. Perkins, Joseph W. Chapman and James Hughes, three lawyers of the highest standing. After examining it, these gentlemen came to the conclusion that an election held, as proposed by the Democrats, would be legal. A caucus of the Democratic members of the Legislature was held in the hall of the House to receive the report of the committee. The report was read by Judge Chapman, and when he had concluded Governor Willard arose and said that if a majority of all the members of the Legislature met in joint session and elected Messrs. Bright and Fitch to the Senate, he would commission them, and he had no doubt they would get their seats; that the Senate of the United States would not refuse to receive men whose commission bore the great seal of the State of Indiana. The author was present at the caucus, and well remembers the effect of Governor Willard's speech. Although one of the youngest men in the hall, he was looked to for advice and guidance. His emphatic declaration that he would commission Messrs. Bright and Fitch if they were elected in the manner proposed, and that he had no doubt of their admission in the Senate, caused the doubting Thomases to give way and cease their opposition.

In person Governor Willard was very prepossessing. His head and face were cast in the finest moulds, his eyes were blue, his hair auburn and his complexion florid. By nature he was open and frank. He was generous to a fault, carrying his heart on his sleeve. A more magnetic and attractive man could nowhere be found, and had he lived to the allotted age of mankind, he must have reached still higher honors.

The *Western Democratic Review*, in its October number, 1854, thus sums up Governor Willard's characteristics as an orator:

"Willard, though a young man, is the best popular orator in the United States. His language is chaste and elegant, utterly void of commonplace and provincialisms, his manner that of a practical speaker, his voice one of the best we have ever heard for an orator. He speaks with rapidity, precision and uncommon emphasis, and can be heard distinctly by an immense number of persons at once. His commanding talents will, one day, lift him far above the reach of the most bitter stings of prejudice and the boldest shafts of enmity."

a A Hammond

ABRAM ADAMS HAMMOND.

Abram Adams Hammond, once Governor of Indiana, was born at Brattleboro, Vt., March 21, 1814. He came to Indiana when six years old, and was raised at Brookville, where he studied law with John Ryman, a lawyer of note of that place. In 1835, having previously been admitted to the bar, he removed to Greenfield, in Hancock county, and commenced the practice of his profession. In 1840 he removed to Columbus, Bartholomew county, and soon afterward formed a partnership with John H. Bradley in the practice of the law. While a resident of Columbus he was chosen Prosecuting Attorney of his circuit, and acquitted himself with decided ability in the office. In 1846 Mr. Hammond and Mr. Bradley removed to Indianapolis, and the next year to Cincinnati. But not being satisfied with their location, they returned to the former city in 1849, and Mr. Hammond formed a partnership with Hugh O'Neal, a celebrated criminal lawyer of his day. In 1850 the Legislature of Indiana passed a law creating a Court of Common Pleas for Marion county. Mr. Hammond was chosen the first judge of this court. He, however, held the office but a short time, resigning it to leave for the West. In 1852 Judge Hammond went to San Francisco, Cal., and became a partner in the practice of the law with the eminent Rufus A. Lockwood. The next year he returned to Indiana, and in 1855 removed to Terre Haute and formed a partnership with Hon. Thomas H. Nelson in the practice of the law. He lived in Terre Haute until elected Lieutenant-Governor of the State.

In 1856 the Democratic State Convention of Indiana nominated the late John C. Walker for Lieutenant-Governor. Soon

8

after the nomination had been made it was discovered that Mr. Walker was not eligible for the office by reason of his not having reached the constitutional age. He therefore withdrew from the ticket, leaving the vacancy to be filled by the State Central Committee.

On the dissolution of the Whig party, after the disastrous campaign of 1852, many of its members entered the ranks of the Democracy. There was but little difference in the national platforms of the two great parties in that year, so these recruits had not far to go. Judge Hammond was one of the most prominent men in Indiana who took the new departure, and as there was a disposition to recognize this element of the Democratic party, the State Central Committee put him on the ticket in the place of Mr. Walker. He had not been a prominent politician, but he was well known over the State as an able lawyer. He made an active canvass, speaking in the principal cities, and when the election came off was chosen Lieutenant-Governor. He made a most excellent presiding officer of the Senate, his rulings being so fair and his decisions so just that even his political opponents bestowed encomiums upon him.

During the time that Mr. Hammond was Lieutenant-Governor and Governor, the Democratic party was greatly distracted by the slavery question. The President, Mr. Buchanan, and his cabinet held the doctrine that the constitution of the United States protected slavery in the Territories, and that slaveholders had the legal right to take their slaves into the Territories of Kansas and Nebraska. Mr. Douglas, the great apostle of popular sovereignty, controverted this position, and contended that the people of the Territories had the right of determining the question for themselves so soon as they had organized a civil government. In an elaborate paper, published in Harper's Magazine, he argued to this effect with great force and plausibility, if not with irresistible logic. There was an "irrepressible conflict" between the two wings of the Democracy, which culminated at the Charleston convention in 1860, and severed the party in twain. That convention adjourned without making a nomination, and subsequently reassembled at Baltimore, where one wing of the party nominated Mr. Douglas for the presidency, and the other John C. Breckenridge. The fight between the factions was bitter and relentless—more bitter than against the Republicans. The mass of the party in Indiana followed the lead of Douglas, but many of the politicians tried hard to compass his overthrow. Previous to the meeting of the Democratic State Convention of 1860 Governor Hammond went to several county conventions for the purpose of using his influence to have administration delegates sent to the State convention. The author saw him at the convention in Jefferson county, and well remembers his efforts to have delegates chosen who would sustain Mr. Buchanan. He was fully in accord with Senator Bright, Governor Willard, United States Marshal Robinson, and others in their opposition to popular sovereignty as expounded by Douglas, and, with them, he favored the admission of Kansas under the Lecompton constitution. But he did not follow Senator Bright into the Breckenridge movement. The organization of the party in Indiana was for Mr. Douglas, and Governor Hammond stood by the organization. He, however, gave Mr. Douglas but a passive support, his heart not being in the fight. A Breckenridge electoral ticket was formed, which received 12,295 votes in the State, but, had these votes been added to those cast for Mr. Douglas, Mr. Lincoln would still have carried Indiana. His vote was 139,033, that of Mr. Douglas 115,509, that of Breckenridge 12,295, and that of Bell (Union) 5,306. It will thus be seen that Mr. Lincoln's majority in the State over all opposition was 5,923.

Governor Willard died at St. Paul, Minnesota, October 5, 1860, and Mr. Hammond became Governor. On Friday, January 11, 1861, he delivered his first and only message to the Legislature. In it he refers to the death of Governor Willard; to the borrowing of $125,000 of Winslow, Lanier & Co., of New York, to pay the semi-annual interest on the State debt, the necessity for which he declares was occasioned by "the failure of the Senate of Indiana to pass a revenue bill for the years of 1857-8." He recommends legislation to protect the ballot-box, a law requiring "the collection of the debts due the State in gold and silver," and the establishment of a sub-treasury in which to keep the funds of the State. He says "the establishment of a house of refuge upon the grounds selected and purchased for that purpose [one hundred acres lying four miles

west of Indianapolis, bought of Colonel Drake], is imperatively
demanded—demanded alike by good morals and sound policy—
and I recommend that prompt and adequate action be taken by
the Legislature in the matter, and that an appropriation for that
purpose be made." He closes his message as follows :

"It gives me great pleasure to say that Indiana, as a State,
has hitherto faithfully kept the bond of union with all her sister
States. Her record is unstained by any act of bad faith. She
has never attempted, directly or indirectly, to evade or avoid
any of the requirements of the Federal constitution, and no man
can doubt that if the same could be said of every other State,
instead of discord, peace and harmony would reign throughout
our borders. Let us then take pride in maintaining the high
position we have thus far occupied as a conservative, union-
loving State, and while we throw our weight into the scale in
favor of any practical mode of settling the present trouble, let
us endeavor to aid in that more permanent and lasting settlement that must flow from a restoration of amity and cordiality
among all our people, North and South. Then, as you have
met in a legislative capacity, you should place Indiana, in this
controversy, where she rightly belongs, as a conservative, law-
abiding and Union State. Show to the people of the Confederacy that Indiana will maintain the constitutional rights of
every State in this Union; that she will extend to the South all
rights in the Territories belonging to this government that she
would claim for herself; that she will look to the constitution
and the laws to determine rights of property, and not permit
any moral question to interfere to affect that determination, and
that all property recognized by the constitution and laws shall
be alike protected. This position, although it may not affect
the action of the extreme Southern States, yet it may do much
to bring about a convention of the border free and slave States.
And regarding, as I do, these States to be conservative, and in
favor of maintaining the Union as it is, it would be well for the
peace of this country if they could meet in convention and consult together in regard to the present unhappy differences existing between the North and South. They might, by their conservative action, induce the extremists of the North and South

to pause and reflect upon the consequences which must necessarily result from their fanatical course, and if, by their action,
this much could be gained, there would then be hope that by
a union of the conservative elements of the country these unhappy differences might be satisfactorily settled, and the best
government under heaven saved from the horrors of disunion
and civil war."

These recommendations of Governor Hammond were favorably received and acted on by the Legislature. Subsequently
a sub-treasury law was passed, and is still upon the statute
books. Although the Legislature he addressed failed to provide
for the creation of a house of refuge for juvenile offenders, a
subsequent one passed such a law. It was during the administration of Governor Baker that the institution at Plainfield was
established, but a part of the honor for its creation justly belongs
to Governor Hammond.

Governor Hammond's recommendation that Indiana should
be represented in a convention of the border States, then about
to be held, was adopted. Five days after the delivery of his
message, Lieutenant-Governor Morton became Governor by
reason of the resignation of Governor Lane, who had been
elected to the United States Senate. Governor Morton was
opposed to Indiana's sending delegates to the Peace Congress,
but the Legislature passed a joint resolution for their appointment, whereupon the Governor named Caleb B. Smith, Pleasant A. Hackelman, Godlove S. Orth, Thomas C. Slaughter and
Erastus W. H. Ellis as the delegates.

The Peace Congress met at Washington City, February 4,
1861, and organized by the election of John Tyler, once President of the United States, as its president. Much was hoped
from it, but nothing obtained. There were several propositions
before it, notably the one named for Mr. Crittenden, looking to
a compromise of the differences between the sections; but they
were all rejected. The delegates from Indiana opposed all
compromise or concessions to the South, and after several days
of fruitless efforts to reach an accommodation the convention
adjourned. Governor Hammond was in favor of the Crittenden
compromise, and if he had had the selection of the Indiana del-

egates he would have chosen men who would have supported
that measure.

About the time Governor Hammond went out of office his
health gave way. Rheumatism fastened itself upon him and
never let go its hold. After this time he suffered almost continuously and was compelled to walk with crutches. He tried
all manner of remedies to get relief, but to little purpose. After
awhile asthma attacked him, and in the summer of 1874 he went
to Colorado, hoping to be benefited by its climate. But the
dry air of the mountains failed to work a cure.   e died at Denver, August 27, 1874, and four days afterward his remains
reached Indianapolis and were taken to the house of John M.
Talbott, an old friend of the Governor. On the day of their
arrival Governor Hendricks issued an order for the closing of
the State offices during the obsequies. On the afternoon of
September 1, the funeral took place at Mr. Talbott's residence,
Rev. F. M. Bird officiating. The pall-bearers were Governor
Hendricks, Major Gordon, Judge Roache, Aquilla Jones, Captain Dodd, Hon. Joseph E. McDonald, William Mansur and
Simon Yandes, who escorted his remains to Crown Hill Ceme-
tery, where they were buried.

Governor Hammond was the first Lieutenant-Governor of
Indiana to become Governor on account of death. In 1822
Lieutenant-Governor Boon became Governor, succeeding Jonathan Jennings, and in 1825 James Brown Ray, President of the
Senate, became Governor, as the successor of William Hendricks, but in both cases the vacancies were caused by resignation, and not by death.

Governor Willard died October 5, 1860, and Governor Hammond served until the inauguration of Governor Lane, January
14, 1861. Two days afterward Governor Lane resigned and
Lieutenant-Governor Morton became Governor. Thus it will
be seen that in a period of one hundred and three days Indiana
had four different Governors, a fact without a parallel in the
history of the country, so far as my knowledge goes.

Governor Hammond was not a showy man, but he was an
able one, much abler than the public gave him credit for. He
had an analytic and logical mind, and was remarkably clear in
stating his positions and drawing his conclusions. He had not

great learning, but he was a close observer of events, and during life gathered a mass of information not found in books. He was not particularly well read in the law, but he was a good lawyer, for he comprehended principles and was able to apply them in his practice.

While Governor Hammond's residence was at Indianapolis from 1849 until he died, except the year he was at Terre Haute, yet he made several changes in the location of his business. He would have succeeded anywhere, for in ability he was far above most of his competitors at the bar, but he would hardly be well settled at one place before he would close his office and open one elsewhere. He was not content to " watch and wait," but wanted the business to come at once.

Until he became afflicted with rheumatism Governor Hammond was an unusually fine specimen of physical manhood. He walked with a spring and moved with the agility of an athlete. He was of medium height, compactly built, and of dark complexion. His head was large and well-shaped. While the expression of his countenance was kind and gentle, it never betrayed passion or emotion. He was cool, deliberate and self-possessed, keeping his feelings and temper under perfect control. He was frank in his manners, honorable in his dealings and dignified in his deportment. Although not one of the most learned Governors of Indiana, he was, by nature, one of the ablest.

HENRY SMITH LANE.

HENRY SMITH LANE, for two days Governor of Indiana, was born in Montgomery county, Kentucky, February 11, 1811. He was well educated, and when eighteen years old commenced the study of the law. Soon after reaching his majority he was admitted to the bar, and in 1835 came to Indiana and settled at Crawfordsville. He had a winning address, abounded in anecdote, and was fluent in speech. He soon obtained a good legal practice, particularly in criminal cases. He became very popular, and in 1837 was elected to the State Legislature from his county.

In 1840 the Democracy of Indiana nominated General Tilghman A. Howard, then a member of Congress from the Seventh District, for Governor of the State. General Howard resigned his seat in Congress to make the race, and Edward A. Hannegan and Henry S. Lane became candidates to fill the vacancy. In many respects they were alike. They were both wonderfully eloquent, but neither very logical. Mr. Lane was elected, defeating his competitor some 1,500 votes. The next year he was again a candidate for Congress, and defeated John Bryce by an immense majority. He never was elected to Congress after this.

In 1844 Mr. Lane stumped Indiana for Henry Clay, and none mourned the defeat of the Kentucky statesman more than he. On the breaking out of the Mexican war he engaged earnestly in the work of raising troops and stimulating the war spirit among the people. In May, 1846, he attended a war meeting at Indianapolis and participated actively in its proceedings. He was a member of the committee on resolutions, and assisted in drawing those adopted by the meeting. The resolutions were preceded by the following preamble:

" WHEREAS, The cherished malice of the Mexican government toward the United States has at length resulted in the audacious invasion of our territory by her troops, and the shedding of American blood on American soil."

This preamble was followed by a series of resolutions, one of which pledged the government the support of the West " without regard to political distinctions." The account of this meeting. published at the time, says that " Henry S. Lane being called for by the meeting, addressed it in that peculiar strain of inspiring eloquence for which he is so distinguished, and which is possessed by few other men of our country." No man in the State was warmer in his support of the war than Mr. Lane, and few did so much to enthuse the people and unite them in its support. But he did other things besides talking to aid the country in its war with Mexico. He raised a company of volunteers, and when the first regiment was organized, he was chosen its major. While in the field he was promoted to the lieutenant-colonelcy, and served as such until the regiment disbanded. His regiment was engaged most of the time it was in Mexico in guarding supply trains and protecting posts, but nevertheless its services were valuable to the government.

After the expiration of the term for which Colonel Lane had enlisted he returned to Indiana, landing at Madison. The night of his arrival he made a speech in the Madison Courthouse in support of the war. He was a leading Whig, and in this speech he severely attacked those men of his party who opposed the war with Mexico. He declared that if Governor Corwin and others of his school were to shape the policy and lay down the principles for the Whig party, it would become the duty of all patriotic men to abandon it. The fiery eloquence of the speaker kindled anew the war spirit at Madison, and a company was soon organized, which went into the field as part of the Fifth Indiana Regiment, commanded by Colonel James H. Lane.

In 1849 Colonel Lane was again a candidate for Congress in his district. His opponent was Hon. Joseph E. McDonald, afterward a Senator of the United States. The contest between these distinguished men was conducted with entire good feeling, and resulted in the election of Mr. McDonald.

On the organization of the People's party in 1854, Colonel Lane entered it. That party having a majority of the Legislature that year, Colonel Lane came to Indianapolis and labored for the election of Joseph G. Marshall to the United States Senate. But the Democrats, having control of the Senate, refused to go into an election for Senator, and none took place.

When the Republican party was formed, Colonel Lane took a position at its head in Indiana, and such was his reputation throughout the country that when the national convention of the Republican party met in 1856 he was chosen its president. His speech on taking the chair was wonderfully eloquent and spirit-stirring. The delegates became so enthused during its delivery that they cheered the speaker to the echo. The convention nominated Fremont and Dayton for President and Vice-President, and Colonel Lane at once took the stump in Indiana in their support. They were defeated at the election which followed, but the principles they represented soon became dominant in the country.

In 1859 Colonel Lane and Colonel William M. McCarty received the votes of a majority of the members of the Indiana Legislature for United States Senators. They went to Washington and contested the seats held by Senators Bright and Fitch, but the Senate decided against them.

The Republican State convention of 1860 nominated Colonel Lane for Governor and Oliver P. Morton for Lieutenant-Governor. Their Democratic competitors were Thomas A. Hendricks and David Turpie. It is questionable if four men of equal ability were ever pitted against each other as candidates for Governor and Lieutenant-Governor in Indiana. They started out to make joint canvasses, and for some time continued their debates. The candidates for Governor began their canvass at Jeffersonville. They then went to Charlestown, thence to New Albany, and then down the river, stopping at the leading towns, until they reached Evansville. Soon after they spoke at Evansville Colonel Lane left Mr. Hendricks and went to Chicago to attend the convention which nominated Abraham Lincoln for

President. When the convention was over he returned to Indiana and resumed his debates with Mr. Hendricks, speaking
first at Fort Wayne, and afterward at several other towns in the
northern part of the State. After filling these appointments
Colonel Lane refused to further extend the joint discussion, and
during the remainder of the campaign canvassed by himself.
In this he acted wisely, for while he was Mr. Hendricks's superior as a popular orator, he was not his equal as a debater.
The election resulted in the choice of Colonel Lane by a large
majority, and on the 14th of January, 1861, he took the oath of
office and entered upon his official duties. In his message to
the Legislature he said:

"The novel, alarming and treasonable assumption that any
State in the Union has a right, under the Federal constitution,
to secede at pleasure is a doctrine unknown to the constitution,
at war with the principles on which our government was established, and destructive of those high and sacred objects
sought to be accomplished by the confederation. * * The
doctrine of secession, peaceable or forcible, now or at any other
time, is a dangerous heresy, fraught with all the terrible consequences of civil war and bloodshed, and leading directly to
the utter ruin of all our institutions. This heresy has not yet
poisoned the public sentiment of Indiana, and may God, in
his kind providence, put afar off the evil day which shall witness its prevalence amongst us. I most sincerely believe, and
am proud to declare, that the people of Indiana, of all parties,
are true to the constitution and loyal to the Union; and that
they will always be in the future, as they have shown themselves to have been in the past, will'ng to yield a ready and
cheerful obedience to all the requirements of the constitution
of the United States, and to maintain and uphold at all times,
under all circumstances, and at every hazard, the glorious form
of free government under which we live."

Two days after the delivery of this message Governor Lane
was elected to the Senate of the United States. He at once
resigned the governorship, having held the office but two days—
the shortest term in that office on record in Indiana.

In the Senate Colonel Lane did not attain any great distinction. It was not the place for the exercise of his peculiar talents. These were better suited to the hustings than to a legislative body. He was placed upon the Committee of Military Affairs, and upon that of Pensions, and reached the chairmanship of the latter committee before his senatorial term expired. He zealously sustained the government in its war for the Union, voting it all needful supplies, and upholding its hands in every way he could. But he was not an ultra man, and did not advocate ultra measures. In the beginning of the trouble he had favored concessions to the South not inconsistent with national honor and national union, but when the flag was fired on at Fort Sumter the compromising spirit left him. Absolute and unconditional obedience to the law was the only condition he had to offer the South after that.

When Colonel Lane's senatorial term expired he returned to his home at Crawfordsville, and never afterward held public office, unless the appointment of Indian Commissioner, tendered him by General Grant, may be said to have been a public one. He lived at his pleasant home, at peace with the world and enjoying the affection of his neighbors and friends until the end came. And when it did come grief abounded throughout the State.

On the afternoon of Friday, June 18, 1881, Colonel Lane was upon the streets of Crawfordsville enjoying his usual health. In the evening he entertained some of his friends at his residence, and after they had gone, retired to bed as usual. He was taken sick in the night, suffering from smothering spells and pains in the region of the heart. The next morning, however, he arose, dressed himself, and for some time sat on his porch, smoking. About 11 o'clock that morning he complained of being unwell. He undressed himself and went to bed, and continued to grow worse until half-past one o'clock that afternoon, when he died.

The news of Colonel Lane's death was telegraphed over the country, and created a profound sensation. He was universally popular in Indiana, and his death was mourned as sincerely by his political opponents as by his political friends. The people of his town held a meeting the day he died, and passed resolutions testifying of their love for the dead statesman. When the news reached Indianapolis Governor Porter issued an order that " the State offices be draped in mourning for a term of thirty days, and that on the day of the funeral they be closed." On Monday, June 20, the State officers met and resolved to attend the funeral in a body. The same evening a public meeting was held at Indianapolis, over which ex-Governor Hendricks presided, to testify of the high respect in which the deceased was held by the people of the State capital. In his speech stating the object of the meeting, Governor Hendricks said:

" It is now twenty-one years since we were the candidates of our respective parties for Governor, and I came out of that campaign respecting him most thoroughly, and have so continued to do ever since."

In his speech at this meeting Senator McDonald said:

" In 1849 we were competitors for Congress. He was always the soul of honor, and generous to his opponents alike in the practice of the law and on the stump."

General Coburn said:

" Caleb B. Smith was a more fluent and graceful speaker, perhaps, General Howard more stately and polished, Samuel Parker excelled him in the keenness of satire and ridicule, but in the intensity of force, point, and a wonderful drollery, Lane was simply unapproachable."

General Harrison said of him:

" There was no personal malice in his speeches; if they contained hostility or bitterness it was directed towards the political principles of his opponents. He was, to an eminent degree, a man of the most genial and kindly feeling, of an open-hearted, sympathetic disposition."

Judge Gresham said:

" The conditions under which Colonel Lane came forward and gained his power do not now exist, and perhaps never will again. That power consisted largely in his ability to speak to the feelings of men. He depended greatly upon the inspiration of the moment. Thoughts came as he spoke, and he made a better speech *ex tempore* than by writing it out."

The Committee on Resolutions, consisting of Major Jonathan W. Gordon, John M. Butler, Thomas A. Hendricks, Albert G. Porter and Joseph E. McDonald, reported to the meeting a memorial, in which they said:

" In private and social life he was a model man and citizen. * * * His peculiar gifts as an orator fitted him for the field of politics, and he entered it with all the enthusiasm of his nature. * * * He was a wise man, just and generous withal; and many a charitable act that was known only to his giving hand will be revealed by Him who seeth in secret and rewardeth openly. He was capable of intense enthusiasm and passion, but able to restrain and direct them to ends of beneficence and order. His last year was like the hour of a glorious and cloudless sunset; and even now, that he has left us, his light still streams far up our skies to enlighten and cheer us amid the gloom of the present."

Tuesday, June 21, was designated as the day the remains of Colonel Lane would be laid at rest. The hour of the funeral was 1 o'clock, but long before the time arrived, business in Crawfordsville was suspended, and the people began to meet in the grounds about the home of the distinguished dead. The bells were tolled, and gloom hung over the city like a pall. Among the distinguished persons from a distance were ex-Senators Hendricks and McDonald, Governor Porter, Senators Harrison and Voorhees, Judge Gresham, and many other noted men. The religious services were conducted by Rev. John L. Smith, after which the remains, followed by an immense concourse of people, were taken to Oak Hill Cemetery, deposited in a vault, and subsequently buried. The pall bearers were Samuel Binford, Governor Porter, James Heaton, R. B. F. Peirce, Peter S. Kennedy, Senators Voorhees and Harrison, B. F. Ristine, Prof. Campbell and Governor Hendricks. Some of these gentlemen had often met him on the hustings and been the objects of his keenest satire and inimitable drollery, but these contests had left no stings, and they mourned him as a friend.

The monument erected to the memory of Colonel Lane is thus described:

"It is an obelisk of Scotch granite, from the quarries of Aberdeen, Scotland, resting upon a double base of American granite, which is eight feet and two inches square. Upon the first Scotch granite base is the name 'Lane' in raised, large block letters. Within the die is a polished panel, upon which inscriptions are to be carved. On the die, which is bordered by polished columns, are the letters, 'H. S. L.,' forming a beautiful monogram. The shaft is thirteen feet high, and is surrounded by a finial, the terminal of which is a polished ball. The height of the entire structure is thirty-two feet. The monument weighs forty-five tons. It is a magnificent piece of workmanship, and is a worthy memorial of the distinguished man whose resting place it marks."

In October, 1831, when but twenty years old, Mr. Lane delivered an address before the Colonization Society in Bath county, Kentucky, which proves him to have been opposed to slavery in his youth. In his speech he said: "This society presents the only plausible way of removing the evil of slavery from this country." He was not an abolitionist, but a colonizationist. In this respect he was like Henry Clay, at whose political shrine he was a worshiper. He also declared that "The history of all times admonishes us that no nation or community of men can be kept in slavery forever; that no power earthly can bind the immortal energies of the human soul; and however unpleasant the reflection may be, it is nevertheless true that we must free our slaves, or they will one day free themselves. Perhaps they may soon rise in their might and majesty of freemen and cast their broken chains at their feet with a mighty effort, which will shake this republic to its center. The light of history shows us that men determined to be free can not be conquered." The speaker lived to see the negro free and enfranchised, but the work was not accomplished by the

Colonization Society. The great evil of human slavery could only be destroyed by the sword.

While Colonel Lane was an anti-slavery man, he did not, until after the repeal of the Missouri Compromise, favor anti-slavery agitation. In 1842, when in Congress, he voted to censure Joshua R. Giddings for introducing his celebrated resolutions in the Creole case. The passage of the vote of censure on Mr. Giddings caused the sturdy old abolitionist to resign his seat and appeal to his constituents for vindication.

Colonel Lane became popular at a time when the world was in love with his peculiar oratory. He abounded in anecdote, was very felicitous in illustrations, and extremely happy in his applications of them. He spoke easily and fluently, and there was a peculiar charm in his delivery. He could enthuse a crowd as but few other men could do ; but he was not a logical speaker, and as a debater he was excelled by many of far less reputation as an orator than he. While in the United States Senate he seldom said a word. The debates of that body were not suited to one of his type, and, as a consequence, he seldom or never participated in them. On the hustings he was the equal of any man who sat in the Senate with him, but he felt his deficiencies as a Senator, and when his term expired refused to be a candidate for re-election. But in a canvass before the people he was superb. We never had a man in Indiana who excelled him in this respect, and but few who equaled him. While mingling among the people, addressing them from the stump, he felt his power, and was at home. He could then say, without the semblance of egotism, "My foot is on my native heath, and my name is Macgregor." It may truly be said of Colonel Lane that "He was not analytical or philosophical. He rarely attempted to make a speech instructive to the uninformed or convincing to the undetermined. His mission, fixed by the character of his intellect and the intensity of his feelings, was rather to stir men up to act, to give them impulse and motive, than to arm them for controversy or determine the direction of their action."

Colonel Lane was a speaker, not a writer. He wrote nothing, unless it were a letter, or a paper designed for use at the time. He never wrote his speeches, and did not care whether they were published or not.   He made them to influence those who heard them, and not those who were to come after him.

Colonel Lane was a member of the Methodist church, and was a God-fearing man.   He was a gentleman, a patriot and a Christian, and was esteemed as such by those who knew him.

In person Colonel Lane was tall and slender and somewhat stoop-shouldered.   His face was thin and wore a kindly expression.   In his latter days the long beard he wore was as white as snow.   He moved quickly, and his bearing was that of a cultured man.

> "None knew him but to love him,
> None named him but to praise."

OLIVER P. MORTON.

FULLY realizing the difficulty before me I commence this sketch of Oliver P. Morton. Sufficient time has not elapsed since he was a leading factor in the politics of the country for him to be correctly weighed and judged. He held high official positions and great power during a great civil war, a war that fanned the passions of the people to the fiercest heat. By many he was considered little less than a god, by some as little better than a devil. History will accord him the place of a man who accomplished great results; of a man of strong will and passions; of intense love of country and of great intellect. He had the weaknesses inherent in mankind, but his great deeds obscured them, and he will go down to future ages as the foremost man Indiana has yet produced.

Oliver Perry Morton, the War Governor of Indiana, was born in Saulsbury, Wayne county, Indiana, August 4, 1823. The original name of his family, which was of English origin, was Throckmorton, but the last member to so write it was his grandfather. The father of the late Governor left off "Throck" from the family name, writing it "Morton," which example was followed by his children. He called the boy Oliver Hazard Perry, but when the future statesman reached an age when he could determine for himself he eliminated Hazard from his name.

When Oliver was a boy he attended the academy of Prof. Hoshour at Centerville, but the family being poor he was placed, at the age of fifteen, with an older brother to learn the hatter's trade. He worked some four years at this business, and I doubt not became proficient in his calling, for he always

Oliver P. Morton

ENGRAVED AND PRINTED
AT THE
BUREAU OF ENGRAVING & PRINTING,
U. S.
TREASURY DEPARTMENT.

mastered anything he undertook. Concluding that the hatter's business did not suit him he resolved to abandon it and qualify himself for the profession of the law. With this object in view he entered Miami University in 1843, and remained there a couple of years. He then returned to Centerville and commenced the study of the law with the late Judge Newman. He soon secured a good practice and rose to prominence at the bar. In 1852 he was elected Circuit Judge. He served on the bench about a year, when, preferring the practice to judicial service, he resigned. He then attended a law school at Cincinnati for one term, and resumed his legal practice.

Up to this time Judge Morton had been a Democrat. The county in which he lived was largely Whig, thus virtually precluding him from holding elective offices. Had he been in political accord with the majority in his county he would, no doubt, have become prominent in the politics of the State at an earlier day than he did. But in 1854 politics underwent a change that brought him to the front. The repeal of the Missouri Compromise created a rebellion in the Democratic party, and Judge Morton became a political rebel. He entered the " People's " movement in 1854, and in 1856 became one of the creators of the Republican party. He was a delegate to the Pittsburgh convention of that year, a convention that gave the Republican party form and shape, and breathed into its nostrils the breath of life. His prominence was such that in May, 1856, he was unanimously nominated for Governor of the State. His opponent was Ashbel P. Willard, a brilliant man, and the superior of Morton as a stumper, but greatly his inferior as a logician and a debater. Both the candidates were young and able. They canvassed the State together and drew immense crowds of people to hear them. The speeches of Willard were florid and spirit-stirring, those of Morton plain and convincing. He made no effort to be eloquent or witty, but addressed himself to the reason and conscience of his hearers. Although he was beaten at the polls, he came out of the contest with his popularity increased and with the reputation of being intellectually one of the strongest men in the State.

The defeat of Judge Morton for Governor in 1856 had a depressing effect upon him, as, indeed, did all his defeats. Mr.

Murat Halstead, of Cincinnati, gives this account of a meeting between him and Judge Morton:

" The night after the day when he was beaten by Willard for Governor of Indiana, Morton called at my office, and was weary and depressed. His first State campaign had ended in disaster, and he seemed to have no political future. He was himself of the opinion at the time that that was the end of his career as a politician. Could he have looked ten years ahead he would have beheld himself a leading man of the country."

In 1860 Judge Morton was nominated for Lieutenant-Governor of Indiana on the ticket with Henry S. Lane. Colonel Lane was a more popular orator than Judge Morton, but far behind him in executive ability. Both were able, and they had able men to contend with. Judge Morton's opponent was David Turpie, afterward a United States Senator, and one of the strongest writers and debaters in the State. They made a joint canvass, and ably discussed the issues then before the country.

The election resulted in the choice of Lane and Morton, and when the Legislature convened in January, 1861, the latter was duly inaugurated Lieutenant-Governor of the State. Two days afterward Governor Lane was elected to the United States Senate, and resigned the governorship, whereupon Lieutenant-Governor Morton became Governor. It was while filling this term as Governor that Morton did his best public work, and created for himself a fame as lasting as the State itself. A civil war was about breaking out when he became Governor, and few so well comprehended what would be its magnitude as he. While many believed the trouble would pass away without an armed conflict, and that if one did commence it would be of short duration, Governor Morton plainly saw its coming, and knew it would be one of the hardest fought and bloodiest contests the world ever saw. Many of Governor Morton's party friends, and among them Governor Lane, had favored concessions to the South before hostilities began; but not so Governor Morton. The only compromise he had to offer the South was absolute obedience to the laws of the land. He opposed the scheme of a peace congress, and when the Legislature passed a joint resolution providing for the appointment of peace commissioners, he selected men who were publicly known to be opposed to any compromise or concessions. He commenced preparing for the conflict that he knew was coming, and when Beauregard fired on Sumter, April 12, 1861, the Governor of Indiana was neither surprised nor appalled. On the 15th of April, three days after the attack on Sumter, President Lincoln called for seventy-five thousand men to put down the rebellion. The same day Governor Morton telegraphed him as follows:

"INDIANAPOLIS, April 15, 1861.

"To Abraham Lincoln, President of the United States:

"On behalf of the State of Indiana, I tender to you for the defense of the nation, and to uphold the authority of the government, ten thousand men.   OLIVER P. MORTON,
"Governor of Indiana."

In seven days from the date of this offer, over three times the number of men required to fill Indiana's quota of the President's call offered their services to the government. The struggle was to get into the army, not to keep out of it. Never, in the world's history, did the people of a State respond more cheerfully and more enthusiastically to the call of duty than did the freemen of Indiana in the spring of 1861.

On the 24th of April Governor Morton reconvened the Legislature, which had adjourned a short time before. In his message to that body he particularly described the condition of public affairs and asked that one million of dollars be appropriated to meet the emergencies of the occasion. At this special session there was little or no division among the members upon the subject of the war. They voted a loan of two millions, provided for all needful supplies, and sustained the Governor in his efforts to put Indiana in the fore-front in the war for the Union. It was only when the war pointed to the abolition of negro slavery that division among the people of Indiana began.

There is not room in a sketch like this to go into the details of Governor Morton's public acts. He displayed extraordinary industry and ability in putting troops into the field, and in providing for their needs while there. He never tired in working for their comfort, and his efforts in their behalf justly earned him the title of " The Soldiers' Friend."

The Legislature of 1862 was not in accord with the political opinions of Governor Morton. It refused to receive his message, and in other ways treated him with want of consideration and respect. While a bill was pending in the House to take from the Governor the command of the militia and give it to a board composed of State officers, his friends in that body left the capital and went to Madison. The Legislature was thus broken up before the appropriation bills had passed, and the Executive was left without money to run the government. In this emergency he applied to certain county boards and banks for funds to defray the expenses of the State government. Large amounts were furnished him, but not enough to answer his purpose ; so he went to Washington and obtained from the national government a quarter million of dollars. He established a Bureau of Finance and appointed General W. H. H. Terrell his financial secretary. This bureau was created in April, 1863, and continued in existence until January, 1865. During the intervening time all the disbursements on account of the expenses of the State, except salaries, were made by this bureau. It received a total of $1,026,321.31, every cent of which was properly accounted for. Its creation was without authority of law, but it served a necessary purpose, and was in consonance with many things done during these troublous and exciting times. I know of no parallel to this action of Governor Morton in the history of the country. He ran, for many months, the State government outside of legal channels, but he ran it so honestly and well that the people not only excused the act, but applauded it. By assuming great responsibilities he kept the machinery of the State government smoothly in motion in all of its departments, and preserved the financial credit of the commonwealth by securing an advance of about $600,000 through a New York banking house to pay the interest on the public debt.

In 1864 Governor Morton was again nominated for Governor of Indiana, and this time was elected, defeating his opponent, Hon. Joseph E. McDonald, by a majority of 20,883 votes. He and Mr. McDonald made a joint canvass of the State, and

passed through it with the utmost good feeling. Although
standard-bearers of their respective parties, during one of the
most exciting canvasses ever made, nothing occurred to mar
the personal friendship long existing between them. This
friendship continued while Governor Morton lived. After he
had been prostrated by disease, and, indeed, was on his death-
bed, Mr. McDonald, then his colleague in the Senate, visited
him and assured him that should he be unable to attend the next
session of the Senate, without injury to his health, he, Mr.
McDonald, would pair with him upon all political questions.
For this generous offer Senator McDonald was severely criticised by the Democratic press at the time, but, nevertheless, it
detracted nothing from his popularity, but rather added to it.

In the summer of 1865 Governor Morton received a partial
paralytic stroke, from which he never recovered. The disease
struck the lower part of his body, affecting his limbs to that
extent that he never walked afterward without the assistance of
canes. At this time he was in the prime of life, with great
physical and mental vigor. His mind was in no wise affected
by the shock, but continued to grow stronger while he lived.
In December following this attack of paralysis Governor Morton
turned over the executive department of the State to Lieutenant-Governor Baker and went to Europe. While there he received medical attention from the most eminent specialist in the
treatment of nervous diseases on the continent, but although
the treatment benefited him, it did not restore him to health.
He remained in Europe until the next March, and then returned
home and resumed his official duties.

In January, 1867, Governor Morton was elected to the United
States Senate. He resigned the governorship and was succeeded by the Lieutenant-Governor, Conrad Baker, who served
the remainder of the gubernatorial term. In 1873 Mr. Morton
was re-elected to the Senate and continued a member of that
body while he lived.

In the Senate Mr. Morton ranked among its ablest members. As a party leader he stood like Saul, the son of Kish,
among his fellows. He was chairman of the Committee of
Privileges and Elections, and did more to determine the policy

of the Senate, and of the Republican party of the country, upon
political questions, than any other member of that body.

Mr. Morton served in the Senate during a most exciting and
troublous time. It was while he was there that the question of
reconstruction of the rebellious States was before the country.
He supported the most repressive and radical measures affecting these States and their inhabitants, treating them as conquered provinces subject to rehabilitation by Congress. He
favored the impeachment of President Johnson on account of
his differences with Congress upon the reconstruction question,
and when the impeachment failed none regretted it more than he.

In 1874 Senator Morton voted for the inflation bill vetoed by
President Grant, and the next year he supported the redemption
act. He opposed the electoral commission bill of 1877, holding
that the President of the Senate had the right to open and count
the votes. But when Congress passed the act he accepted a
place upon the commission and voted against going behind the
returns as certified to the Senate. In a speech delivered at
Richmond, Indiana, in the summer of 1865, he argued against
conferring upon negroes the right to vote, and soon afterward
became a champion of negro suffrage. Once, after making a
speech in the Senate in its favor, he was twitted by Senator
Doolittle with inconsistency, and replied as follows:

" I confess, and I do it without shame, that I have been
educated by the great events of the war. The American people have been educated rapidly ; and the man who says he has
learned nothing, that he stands now where he did six years ago,
is like an ancient mile-post by the side of a deserted highway."

In the spring of 1877 Senator Morton went to Oregon as
chairman of a Senate committee, to investigate matters connected with the election of Senator Grover of that State. His
associates on the committee were Senators Saulsbury, of Delaware, and McMillen, of Minnesota. The committee sat eighteen
days and took a large amount of testimony, which was subsequently submitted to Congress. While in Oregon, Senator
Morton delivered a political speech at Salem, the last speech
he ever made. It was characteristic of the man, being strong,
logical, and exceedingly hostile to the South. On his way

home from Oregon he stopped awhile at San Francisco for rest. On the evening of the sixth of August, being still in that city, he ate a hearty supper and retired to rest. He awoke in the night and found his left side paralyzed. The next day he started home in a special car, and was met by his brother-in-law, Colonel Holloway, at Cheyenne, and by his family physician, Dr. Thompson, at Peoria. These gentlemen accompanied him to Richmond, Indiana, when he was taken to the residence of Mrs. Burbank, his mother-in-law. He remained there until October 15, when he was removed to his home in Indianapolis. There, surrounded by his wife and children and intimate friends, he remained until Thursday, November 1, 1877, when the end came.

After his paralytic stroke in 1865, Senator Morton always sat while making a speech. As he was never profuse in gestures, the unusual posture did not militate against the effectiveness of his addresses. In the Senate he had a "rest" to support him while standing, but he was never long upon his feet, always conducting his debates and making his set speeches sitting in his chair.

In 1870 President Grant offered Senator Morton the English mission. It was declined for the reason that should he resign his seat in the Senate, a Democrat would be elected in his place. He was too good a party man to accept office at the expense of his party, and besides, I doubt not, his work in the Senate was more congenial to his tastes than the negotiation of treaties. His nature was to reach his ends in a straightforward way, and not by the tortuous road of diplomacy.

During the time Senator Morton lay sick nigh unto death the interest of the people in his condition was intense. The great newspapers sent special correspondents to Indianapolis to keep them advised of his pulse-beats. Bulletins were issued every hour, which were telegraphed over the country and posted at the newspaper offices. Previous to that time the health of no public man had created so much concern among the people.

The death of no man, with the exception of that of President Lincoln, ever created so much grief in Indiana as did that of Senator Morton. At Indianapolis, gloom hung over the city like a pall. Bells were tolled, and public and private buildings

were draped in mourning. Men walked the streets with sad-
dened faces and measured footsteps. The city legislature met,
passed suitable resolutions and appropriated money to defray
the expenses of the city government in attending the funeral.
Nor were the manifestations of grief confined to Indiana. The
President of the United States issued an order directing the
flags on all the public buildings to be placed at half-mast. He
also ordered that the government departments should close on
the day of the funeral. The city council of Cincinnati, which
had previously placed a portrait of Senator Morton in its hall,
met and appointed a committee to go to Indianapolis to attend
his funeral.

The remains of the great Senator were taken from the family residence to the Court-house, where they lay in state during
the Sunday and part of Monday succeeding his death. They
were then conveyed to Roberts Park Church, where the funeral
exercises were conducted, and thence to Crown Hill Cemetery,
where they were placed in a vault, and afterwards buried on
the spot where he stood on Soldiers' Decoration or Memorial
Day, in May, 1876, when delivering his great speech to the people there assembled. The procession, which followed the remains to Crown Hill was an immense one, and was under the
command of General Lew Wallace, as chief marshal, who
ably directed its movements.

Never before did so many distinguished men attend the funeral of a citizen of Indiana. A son of the President of the
United States, two cabinet ministers, six United States Senators, seven members of the national House of Representatives,
besides other men eminent in the politics and legislation of the
country, were present, as well as thousands of people from all
parts of Indiana and from other States of the Union.

The day after Senator Morton died his colleague, Senator
McDonald, announced the fact in the Senate, whereupon the
Vice President appointed Senators McDonald, Davis of Illinois,
Burnside, Bayard, Cameron of Pennsylvania, and Booth, a
committee to attend the funeral on behalf of the Senate.

On the 17th of the next January Mr. McDonald offered in
the Senate a series of resolutions in relation to Senator Morton's

death, which was unanimously adopted. In speaking to these resolutions, Senator McDonald said:

"Naturally combative and aggressive, intensely in earnest in his undertakings, and intolerant in regard to those who differed with him, it is not strange that while he held together his friends and followers with hooks of steel, he caused many whose patriotism and love of country were as sincere and unquestioned as his own to place themselves in political hostility to him. That Oliver P. Morton was a great man is conceded by all. In regard to his qualities as a statesman, men do differ now and always will. But that he was a great partisan leader—the greatest of his day and generation—will hardly be questioned, and his place in that particular field will not, perhaps, be soon supplied."

Senator Edmunds said:

"He was a man of strong passions and great talents, and was, as a consequence, a devoted partisan. In the fields in which his patriotism was exerted, it may be said of him, as it was of the Knights of Saint John in the holy wars : 'In the fore-front of every battle was seen his burnished mail, and in the gloomy rear of every retreat was heard his voice of constancy and courage.'"

Senator Thurman said of him:

"He evaded no duty however onerous ; he asserted his claim to leadership at all times and under all circumstances, however great might be the sacrifice of comfort, repose or health."

Senator Conkling paid this eloquent tribute to his memory:

"As a party leader he was too great for any party or any State readily to supply his place. As an efficient, vigilant, and able representative he had no superior in either House of Congress. Oppressed and crippled by bodily infirmity, his mind never faltered or flagged. Despite pain and sickness, so long as he could be carried to his seat he was never absent from the Senate or the committee. No labor discouraged him, no contingency appalled him, no disadvantage dismayed him, no defeat disheartened him.   He will go down to a far hereafter, not as one who embellished and perpetuated his name by a studied and scholastic use of words, nor as the herald of resounding theories, but rather as one who day by day on the journey of life met actual affairs and realities and grappled them with a grasp too resolute and quick to loiter for the ornament or the advantage of protracted and tranquil meditation."

Senator Burnside said :

" Morton was a great man.   His judgment was good ; his power of research was great, his integrity was high, his patriotism was lofty, his love of family and friends unlimited, his courage indomitable."

The closing speech in the Senate upon the adoption of the resolutions was made by Mr. Voorhees, Mr. Morton's successor. In it Mr. Voorhees said :

" Senator Morton was, without a doubt, a very remarkable man.   His force of character can not be overestimated. His will power was simply tremendous.   He threw himself into all his undertakings with that fixedness of purpose and disregard of obstacles which are always the best guarantees of success. This was true of him whether engaged in a lawsuit, organizing troops during the war, conducting a political campaign or a debate in the Senate.   The same daring, aggressive policy characterized his conduct everywhere."

At the close of his speech Senator Voorhees moved the adoption of the resolutions, and they were unanimously agreed to by the Senate.   Similar resolutions passed the House of Representatives, and eulogies were delivered upon the dead Senator by several of the people's representatives.   One of the best and most just estimates of Senator Morton is the following, taken from an address delivered by ex-Governor Hendricks before the Central Law School of Indiana.   Governor Hendricks said :

" Governor Morton was not what is called a ready speaker, in the sense of speaking upon the spur of the moment.   He was one who became ready by careful forethought and preparation. The order of arrangement received great care. The positions followed one after another in adroit sequence, with studied effort, to the close. The matter was carefully chosen and considered. The manner or style did not share the same attention. His sentences were not always smooth, sometimes, indeed, rough, but always strong and forcible. Sometimes a passage occurred, as if not noticed by himself, of almost classic force and beauty. His voice was clear and strong, his gesture heavy and not frequent, and his utterance deliberate and distinct. As he spoke the impression was felt that he had other and further forces which he might summon to his aid if needed either to establish his own position or attack that of his adversary. Force was the marked quality of his style. He chose the shortest, boldest and most direct method both of attack and defense. When stated, his proposition was understood, and he would not delay to repeat it. He lacked the power of persuasion. It was probably a weakness in the court-house, as it was at the head of a political party. In debate he was a combatant. He could not conciliate. The development of that quality was probably the result of the turbulent times in which he was an actor."

After having quoted so largely from others, it may seem a work of supererogation for me to attempt an analysis of Senator Morton's character. But as some of his leading traits have not been touched upon in the extracts I have given, I will essay the task.

A prominent characteristic of Senator Morton was tenacity of purpose. When he attempted a thing he did it. If he could not succeed in one way, he would in another. He never tired and he never let up. He would abandon a position at once, if by so doing he could better succeed in his ultimate purposes. But he was never conciliatory. If an obstruction appeared in his pathway and he wanted to continue his journey, he would take a club and knock it aside. If, however, he believed it best to retrace his steps and take another path he did not hesitate to do so. In 1868 he delivered a speech in the wigwam on the Court-house square, Indianapolis, and replied to the charge of inconsistency made against him by Governor Hendricks two nights before, by confessing that his course was inconsistent with the sentiments of his Richmond speech, but declared it to be " consistent with the logic of events." Most men would have hunted evidence to defend their consistency, but he admitted the contrariety of his public life upon the negro question, and justified it.

Another marked trait in Senator Morton's character was fore-sight or looking ahead for what was coming. The author had opportunities for observing this characteristic of the Senator during a trip they took together in 1865. At that time travel was so great that seats in railroad cars were hard to get, and sleeping-car accommodations only secured by industry and fore-sight. In these matters he succeeded because he was always in advance of others. At Harrisburg, where we had missed connection with the train from Philadelphia, and were compelled to lie over until the next one arrived, the Senator had an oppor-tunity of exemplifying the trait I have named. On the arrival of the Philadelphia train it was observed that it was full to over-flowing. There was not a vacant seat in it, and the effort to secure one was hopeless. While taking in the situation, the Senator observed a passenger car attached to an engine on a side track some distance from the depot, and saying, " That car will be added to the train," broke and ran for it. He boarded it and secured the most comfortable seat in it for himself and the author. When the car was attached to the train and the crowd entered it, it found him seated and at his ease. When we reached Pittsburg he gave another evidence of his care and forethought. No one was permitted to pass the gate that leads to the western bound train without exhibiting a ticket. Before we reached the Pittsburg depot Senator Morton had selected a Pan-Handle pass from among many others, and, holding it in his hand he took a position on the steps of the car, and at the earliest possible moment sprang from it and rushed to the gate. He was the first to pass its portals, and when the author, who was among the first to follow him, entered the sleeping car, he found that the Senator had secured berths for both.

Senator Morton was well versed in the sciences. He knew as much of geology as some who make it a study, and he knew more of theology than many whose province is to teach it. He was familiar with all creeds, and knew the arguments that best sustained them. He was particularly conversant with those which infidels use against Christianity, and could designate the strongest points as readily as he could the weakest of an opponent in a political debate.

But it was as a politician and statesman that he made his great reputation, and no estimate of his character would be at all complete without weighing and considering his political actions.

As Governor of Indiana Senator Morton displayed wonderful energy, tact and forethought. He distanced all contemporary Governors in putting troops into the field, and excelled all in providing for their wants while there. His best claims to fame rest upon his administration of the office of Governor. In that office he showed remarkable powers of organization and ability to use that organization to accomplish his purposes. In these respects he had no peer in the Union.

While having charity for the masses of the South who went into the rebellion, Senator Morton hated their leaders with intense hate. The last public letter he wrote and the last public speech he made showed that his animosities toward them were neither allayed nor placated. They were rather intensified by the fact that the policy he had advocated was being abandoned and the people of the South were being restored to self-government. He seemed to forget that the war was ended and the country at peace. He wanted a policy continued which might be justified by the exigencies of war, but which was without defense in time of peace. In these extreme views he was not sustained by the country, nor even by his party. This was evinced by the vote he received at Cincinnati in 1876. Although the ablest man in his party, and confessedly the best organizer and leader it contained, he received but a single Northern vote for the nomination for President except those cast by the delegates from his own State. His main support came from the extreme South, and was rendered by men who did not represent the people of that section. They were mostly negroes lately freed from slavery, Northern men who had gone South for pelf and personal aggrandizement, and Southern men who had separated themselves from the masses of their section.

It is greatly to the honor of Senator Morton that, living and holding office during an era of venality and corruption, he kept his hands clean. With opportunities to enrich himself possessed by few, he contented himself with a moderate competency, and illustrated by the simplicity of his habits the principles of the democracy he professed. If he had vices cupidity was not one of them.

Senator Morton was not what is called a society man. After he entered politics he became so much absorbed that he had but little time for social gayeties and pleasures. But he was a family man, of domestic habits and tastes, passionately loving his wife and children and spending his happiest hours in their society.

The State pride of Senator Morton was intense. Indiana had been a butt for the ridicule of men for years who knew but little about her, and he determined to raise her to a plane where she could be ridiculed no longer. And he did it. In the great civil war, which tried the mettle and patriotism of the people, Indiana came, under his guidance, to the front, yea, to the forefront of the line. Senator Morton was an untiring worker, but he had no taste for the drudgery of details. He left this to others, and was very careful who they were. His brother-in-law, Colonel W. R. Holloway, and General W. H. H. Terrell were his most trusted lieutenants, and rendered him services of incalculable value. Senator Morton was not a member of any church, but he was a believer in the Christian religion. In a letter to a friend, written from New York on the eve of his departure for Europe, in 1865, he said:

"You are right when you say you believe that I deeply appreciate the prayers which have been offered up by the praying friends whom I have left behind me. I am no infidel. I was educated by pious grandparents to a professed belief in Christianity, and taught to reverence holy things; and though I may not, in many things, have led a Christian life, yet I have never fallen into disbelief, nor have I been the immoral man some would have the world to believe. The Christian gentleman is

the noblest and loveliest character on earth, for which I entertain the highest respect and love. I recognize the hand of
Providence in all the affairs of man, and believe there is a divine economy which regulates the lives and conduct of nations."

These are not the sentiments of a scoffer, nor of an unbeliever.

The mind of Senator Morton was massive and logical. He
possessed the faculty of getting at the "bottom facts," and of
weighing them with deliberation and judgment. He was never
superficial in the examination or treatment of a subject. His
comprehension was broad and far-reaching, his perception acute
and penetrating, enabling him, with singular clearness, to present his opinions and arguments in a convincing and masterly
manner.

As a legislator it can be said of Senator Morton that he orig-
inated and accomplished much. He introduced many important measures and followed them up with persistent advocacy
until they were disposed of. Many of them passed and became
laws. He showed large capacity and fertile expediency as a
law-maker, and as a party man never lost sight of the important
bearing congressional action would have on the success of his
party. And thus it was that he always took a leading part in
such legislation as affected the political destiny of the organization to which he belonged. He was quick to observe the strong
points of political advantage and the weak points in the record
and programme of his opponents. These he pressed with a
vigorous industry, scarcely equaled in Senatorial annals. He
was far-seeing in the political future, full of well-defined expedients, comprehending, as if by intuition, the political situation, and was undoubtedly the most aggressive, bold and clear-
headed Republican politician of his time.

A statue of Senator Morton has been made and will soon be
placed in one of the public parks at Indianapolis. It is of
bronze, is of life size, and represents the distinguished statesman in a standing posture. It was executed by Francis Sim-
mons, an American artist residing in Rome. He made the
statue of William King, contributed by Maine to the collection
in the national capitol. He also designed the army and navy

10

monument at Washington, and is known throughout the civilized world as a man eminent in his profession. Although the
remains of Governor Morton were buried at Crown Hill, near
Indianapolis, the statue of him will be placed in the heart of the
city. It will stand where visitors to the State's capital can see
the form and lineaments of the great War Governor, and be reminded of his public work and patriotism. The money which
is to pay for this monument was contributed by a generous public; therefore the monument will be an acknowledgment of the
people's love and veneration for the man whose memory it was
erected to perpetuate, and who was Indiana's most distinguished son.

JAMES D. WILLIAMS.

In a book entitled " Eminent and Self-Made Men of Indiana," published at Cincinnati, by the Western Biographical Publishing Company, is the following monograph of the late Governor Williams, written by the author of these sketches:

James Douglas Williams, Governor of Indiana, is a type of the Western pioneer now seldom seen east of the Mississippi river. Born in Pickaway county, Ohio, January 16, 1808, he moved with his father's family to Indiana in 1818, and settled in Knox county, near the historic city of Vincennes. He grew to manhood there, and there remained until January, 1877, when he came to the capital of Indiana to take the reins of the State government, at the command of over 200,000 American freemen.

When Governor Williams arrived in Indiana, and for many years afterward, the State was sparsely populated. In many parts of it there were no white men or women, and where there were white settlements dwelling houses were far apart, and communication with the outside world difficult and unfrequent. Therefore, it was hard to establish and maintain schools and churches, and the newspaper was an unusual visitor at the fireside of the pioneer. It was under such circumstances as these that Governor Williams grew to manhood and entered upon the duties of life. The little schooling he received was obtained in the log school-house, at times when his services could be spared from the farm. But, if the advantages of the school-room were measurably denied him, he was somewhat compensated for their loss by mingling with the best people in his settlement, and learning from them something of the outside world. Therefore, when he reached his majority he was unusually well versed, for one in his circumstances, in the news of that day and the history of the past. Added to this, he had a well-knit, hardy frame, was supple and agile in his movements, and, taken all in all, was the most promising young man in the settlement. He could make a full hand at the plow, in the harvest-field, or at the log-rolling, and was known throughout the neighborhood as a young man of industrious habits and of more than ordinary culture.

When Governor Williams was twenty years of age his father died. Being the oldest of six children, the care of the family devolved on him. He accepted this responsibility and acquitted himself well, as he has always done when charged with important duties. Three years afterward, at the age of twenty-three, he married Nancy Huffman, who lived until this year to bless and comfort him in his declining years. By her he has had seven children, two of whom only are living. His wife, like the mistress of the Hermitage, was wedded to her country home, and throughout his long life, most of which has been spent in the public service, has remained on his farm and participated in its management. Her death occurred June 27, 1880.

Governor Williams entered public life in 1839, as a justice of the peace. For four years he held this office and decided the controversies and adjusted the difficulties of his neighbors with great judicial fairness. His decisions were sometimes dissented from, but in no case were corrupt motives imputed to him. His neighbors knew his integrity, and while they sometimes criticised his conclusions they never impugned the motives by which he reached them. In 1843 he resigned his office of justice of the peace, and the same year was elected to the lower branch of the State Legislature. From that time until 1874, when he was elected to the national Congress, he was almost continuously in the legislative service of the State, sometimes in the House of Representatives, and then in the Senate. A history of his legislative work would be a history of the legislation of Indiana from 1843 to 1874. No man in the State has been so long in public life as he, and no one has more faithfully served the people. He is identified with most of the important measures of legislation during this time, and is the author of many of them. It is to him that the widows of Indiana are indebted for the law which allows them to hold, without administration, the estates of their deceased husbands, when they do not exceed three hundred dollars in value. He is the author of the law which distributed the sinking fund among the counties of the State; and to him more than to any other man, with probably the exception of the late Governor Wright, are the people indebted for the establishment of the State Board of Agriculture, an institution that has done so much to foster and develop the agricultural interests of Indiana. He was for sixteen years a member of this Board, and for four of them was its President. During his management of its affairs it was a self-supporting institution, and, besides, it accumulated an extensive and valuable property during the time he was at its head. It has happened, since he ceased to control its direction, that its finances have become so disordered that to preserve its existence the Legislature of the State has been compelled to take from the public treasury large sums of money and bestow them upon the society. It is safe to say that had he continued at its head no such necessity would have arisen.

In 1872 Governor Williams was the nominee of the Democratic members of the Legislature for United States Senator, but his party being in the minority he was defeated for the office by the late Senator Morton. In 1874 Governor Williams was elected to Congress from the Vincennes district, and took his seat the ensuing fall. He was made chairman of the Committee on Accounts of the House. Abuses had crept into this branch of the public service. Officers and employes acted upon the theory that "Uncle Sam" was a rich goose, from which every one had the right to pluck a quill. He soon taught them that public property was as sacred as private property, and that no one had a right to its use without rendering an equivalent. This brought upon him the maledictions of those who hover about the capital to fatten upon the rich pickings there to be found; but it endeared him to those whose money supplies them. It was while at his post at Washington, attending to his public duties, that a telegram was handed him announcing his nomination for Governor of Indiana by the Democratic convention of that State. He had not been a candidate for the place, and was as much surprised as any one when informed that the nomination had been made.

The campaign of 1876 in Indiana was a memorable one. It never had its counterpart in this country, except in 1858, when Douglas and Lincoln, in Illinois, contested for the Presidential stakes in 1860. Senator Morton announced early in the canvass, in a speech he delivered in the Academy of Music in Indianapolis, that the election of Williams as Governor meant the election of Tilden as President. Events proved the truth of the Senator's declaration; for neither the decision of the electoral commission nor the legerdemain practiced by the returning boards can obscure the fact that the United States voted in November as Indiana did in October. Hendricks and McDonald, Landers and Gooding, Voorhees and Williams, and many other able men, entered the fight as champions of the Democracy; while Morton and Harrison, Cumback and Butler, Gordon and Nelson, and other men of prominence and ability, marshaled the forces of the Republicans. The conflict was so fierce that it shook the whole country. The Republican speakers and journals ridiculed the Democratic candidate for Governor, and made sport of his homespun clothes and plain appearance; but the Democracy seized upon his peculiarities and made them watchwords of victory. Blue Jeans clubs were formed throughout the State, and the name the Republicans had given the Democratic candidate in derision was accepted by his friends and made to do service in his behalf. When the campaign was ended and the ballots were cast and counted, it was ascertained that the plain and honest old farmer of Knox had beaten his opponent—General Benjamin Harrison—over 5,000 votes. The result was as gratifying to his friends as it could have been to him, for they knew he had never been found wanting in any place he had been called upon to fill; and they felt entire confidence that his legislative and congressional laurels would not turn to gubernatorial willows. The predecessors of Governor Williams for more than two decades have been eminent men. The three immediate ones were Morton, Baker, and Hendricks, the first and the last of whom have national reputations. While he has not the organizing ability and aggressiveness of Morton, the reading and legal erudition of Baker, nor the elegance and symmetrical development of Hendricks, he has other qualities as an executive officer as valuable as those possessed by any of them. He is careful and painstaking, and enters into the minutest details of his office ; and he performs no official act without thoroughly understanding its import and effect. He is self-willed and self-reliant, and probably consults fewer persons about his official duties than did any of his predecessors for a generation.

During his canvass for Governor it was charged by his political opponents that his selection would place in the executive chair one who would be influenced and controlled by others, but experience has proved the falsity of the charge. If any just criticism can be made upon him in this regard, it is that he has not sufficiently given his confidence to his friends. Instead of being swayed to and fro by others, he goes, perhaps, to the other extreme, and refuses to be influenced by any. Better, however, be stubborn than fickle, for the first insures stability and fixedness of purpose, while the latter always results in uncertainty and doubt.

Governor Williams is economical and simple in his tastes and habits. By industry and care he has accumulated a handsome competency, which, no doubt, will increase each succeeding year of his life. The necessities of his youth caused him to be careful and saving of his earnings, and he has clung to the habits then formed to the present day. He is fond of amusements and is an adept in social games and pastimes. He frequently visits the theater, and it is as pleasant as it is common to see him enter a place of public amusement accompanied by his grandchildren or some of his country neighbors. He is courteous in his intercourse with others, is a good conversationalist, and is never at a loss for words to express his thoughts. He stands six feet four inches in his boots ; is remarkably straight and erect for one of his years ; has large hands and feet ; has high cheek bones ; a long, sharp nose ; twinkling gray eyes ; a clean shaven face, skirted with whiskers upon his throat, and a head covered profusely with black hair, in which scarcely a gray filament is to be seen. His physiognomy denotes industry and shrewdness, and does not belie the man. He dresses plainly but with scrupulous neatness. He is a good judge of human nature, and he

who attempts to deceive or overreach him will have his labor
for his pains. Such is James D. Williams, the Centennial Governor of Indiana.

Governor Williams will retire from his office in January, 1881.
His age is such that it is probable that his public life—forty-two
years in the service of the people—will then be ended. That
he has acquitted himself well in all the positions he filled; that
he has made the world better by having lived in it, and that he
is entitled to honorable mention in the history of his adopted
State, will be the verdict of the people, when, like Cincinnatus
of old, he lays aside the robes of office and retires to his farm,
there to spend the evening of his life in quietude and rest.

On Saturday evening, October 30, 1880, Governor Williams
attended the dedication of the dining hall of the House of Refuge, at Plainfield. During the dedicatory exercises he was
called out by a toast to "Our present Governor," and responded
in a neat speech of some ten minutes, the last speech he ever
made. He told the boys when they left the House of Refuge
to go into the country, to keep away from towns and cities,
which, he said, were filled with pit-holes and sinks of iniquity.
He declared that he had fully realized this to be true during the
four years he had lived in a city, and that as soon as his term
as Governor expired he was going back to his farm to stay
while he lived. (Alas! he was taken there before another put
on his official robes.) That night Governor Williams and the
author slept in the same bed. He was up many times, a dozen
or more, on account of discharges from the bladder, and next
morning I said to him that I thought he ought to consult a physician, as he evidently had disease of the kidneys or bladder.
He replied, he thought not, that the trouble was "a breaking
down of the fence all along the line." It struck me at the
time that the words were very expressive, and they sank deep
into my memory. The illustration was drawn from the farm,
a place he never forgot, no matter where he was, nor in what
business he was engaged. The next day Governor Williams,
Governor Baker, Senator Briscoe and myself drove from Plainfield to Indianapolis in a two-horse carriage, Governor Baker
holding the reins. During most of the trip the conversation ran

upon farm-life and its effect upon boys. Both the Governors expressed great concern about the future of the boys at Plainfield, and agreed that the farm was the place for them to go when they left the Reformatory.

On the Tuesday after the dedication at Plainfield, Governor Williams walked to the polls and cast his ballot for electors for President and Vice-President of the United States. He was unwell at the time, and after exercising this right of citizenship he returned to his rooms at the Washington Club House, never to leave them again. For several days he retained his cheerfulness and saw those of his friends who called upon him. He also dispatched such public business as demanded immediate attention, his last official act being to respite a man sentenced to be hanged. During his illness he had the best of medical attention, careful nursing and the presence of several personal friends, among them Hon. John T. Scott, who remained with him almost constantly. He continued to grow worse until Saturday noon, November 20, when he died.

The news of Governor Williams's death spread over Indianapolis with great rapidity. In an hour or two flags were placed at half-mast on all the public buildings, and upon many private ones. That afternoon a meeting of citizens was held in the parlors of the Washington Club House to take action in relation to the Governor's death. A committee was appointed to prepare a memorial, and it was determined that the remains should lie in state at the Court-house at Indianapolis on Monday, on Tuesday morning be taken to Vincennes, and lie in state at the Court-house there until that evening, and then be conveyed to the homestead near Wheatland, and the next day be buried.

On Sunday the remains lay in state in the parlors of the Washington Club House. On Monday morning they were taken to the Marion county Court-house and placed on a bier in the main hall. Thousands of people—white and black—citizens of Indianapolis, and citizens from other parts of the State, passed by the casket and viewed, for the last time, the face of the farmer Governor. The same day a meeting of the citizens was held in the Court-house, at which Hon. Joseph E. McDonald presided and the author of this sketch acted as secretary. Hon. Walter Q. Gresham, Solomon Claypool, Thomas

F. Davidson, Augustus N. Martin and William P. Fishback, the committee appointed the Saturday previous, reported a memorial, from which I make the following extracts :

" He never lost his fondness for the soil, nor for the men who till it ; and in the midst of his most pressing official engagements it was his wont to seek a respite from public care in the active management of his farm at Wheatland. * * * It is worthy of note and emphasis that Governor Williams was a man of singular purity of character. His private and domestic virtues are attested by all who enjoyed the intimacy of his personal friendship, and his official integrity was never blurred by even an imputation of dishonesty. His conception of official station was that it was a public trust, to be administered with the same care, prudence and frugality which a wise man would bestow upon his private affairs. It is to his honor that at a time when the tendencies in official station were in the direction of a lavish and careless expenditure of the public moneys, he used his influence in Congress to check those tendencies and expose existing abuses. As Governor he evinced the same watchful care of the public interests, and, though a warm partisan, no alleged party necessity, no consideration of personal friendship, could swerve him from what he believed to be the path of duty.

*   *   *   *   *   *   *   *

" Measured by the best standards Governor Williams was a worthy citizen, a faithful public servant, a good man. His virtues were many and conspicuous,

"' And e'en his failings leaned to virtue's side.' "

Hon. William H. English arose and seconded the adoption of the memorial, and in a very appreciative speech said, among other things :

" When I say he represented the people, I mean it in the broadest and best sense, for he was literally of the people, and always especially devoted to their interests—himself a hard-working tiller of the soil, a true type of that class of sturdy pioneers whose stout hearts and strong arms have made Indiana the great and prosperous State it is to-day. The masses of the people did honor to themselves in honoring him, for he was their true representative. He was not a man learned in the lore of books—not in one sense a man of culture—but he was a man of most excellent judgment, and his mind was well stored with useful and practical information ; and what is more than all, and better than all, he was what is said to be God's noblest work, an honest man."

Ex-Governor Hendricks said :

" I believe that no man living has served the people of the State in so many important respects for so long a period, commencing, as I perceive by the memorial, in 1839, almost continuously. He was a public servant until the day of his death, more than forty years—not all the time in public service, but for the greater portion of that period, and what gives emphasis to this circumstance, is the fact that for the most of the time he was selected by his immediate neighbors, among whom he was raised, and with whom he had all the relations of life. Such a man, so indorsed, is worthy of the respect which we pay him to-day. It is a great loss when such a man dies, and I feel that the public service suffers in his death. I wish simply, in rising, to express my profound regard for his character and for the excellence of his public service."

Hon. Jonathan W. Gordon closed a very eloquent speech, as follows :

" When a generation of men shall come—as it will come in the State of Indiana—that will believe that economy will be subserved by lavish expenditure of money in building a temple to preserve the memory of the great who have served the people, Governor Williams's name and memory and face and monument will be entitled to a conspicuous place in that temple."

General Benjamin Harrison, who was Governor Williams's opponent in the gubernatorial contest of 1876, paid this generous tribute to the memory of the departed Governor :

" If there were nothing to be said of Governor Williams's relation to the public affairs of Indiana at all, his life would be an honorable and successful one. I have always felt that the successful pioneer, one of those who pressed toward the edge of civilization in the early days, and made a successful fight with the wilderness, and cleared the primitive forest and made of it a meadow, and of the marsh a dry field, and who built up around him and for himself and for the family that God gave him, a competence, elevated them, that that life was an honorable life and worthy of mention in any assembly. This work Governor Williams has done conspicuously."

Ex-Governor Baker said :

" He was not a learned man, but not an uneducated man. I mean by that, he was a man who knew how to think. He had learned the art of thinking, but had he been an educated man he would have been a good lawyer. He had a discriminating mind. He was one of the best parliamentarians I ever knew, hardly ever making a mistake. He was a man of a strong, generous, emotional nature. I have seen him on several occasions when he could not control his emotions. I was with him a few weeks ago, at the house of a friend, when some songs of the little folks touched him so that he filled up and could not speak."

Rev. Dr. Bartlett spoke thus eloquently of Governor Williams :

" Cincinnatus was found at the plow when his promotion came. Our Governor, we may say, has never left the plow. It is a credit to the institutions of the country that you can take the plain workingmen, that you can take the early suffering pioneers, men who can only make headway by virtues that are rugged and severe and stern, virtue that labors with unremitting toil, the ingenuity that comes from making much out of little, building your house with a hammer and a saw rather than with the refined implements of a later day."

On Tuesday, November 23, the remains of Governor Williams, accompanied by the State officers and hundreds of leading citizens, were taken to Vincennes on a special train. They were met at the Vincennes depot by a committee and taken to the Court-house, where they lay in state during the day. The weather was intensely cold, but, notwithstanding this, thousands of Knox county farmers were in Vincennes to take a last look upon the remains of the man they loved so well. That evening the corpse was taken to the old homestead, and the next day buried in the cemetery near by.

During the present year, 1883, the family of Governor Williams procured a granite monument and placed it at the head of his grave. On the 4th of July it was unveiled with imposing ceremonies in the presence of thousands of his former neighbors and friends. Hon. D. W. Voorhees made a very eloquent address on the occasion, in which he said:

"He lived and died a practical farmer. He knew the laboring people better than any other public man Indiana ever produced. He was born in their ranks and remained there to the end. He was at home in the broad and wholesome field, and he was familiar with the wants and ways, the hardships and the hopes of those who eat their bread by the sweat of their faces. From the days of Cincinnatus to the present time, men seeking popular favor have been paraded and eulogized as farmers who could not tell a field of wheat from a field of oats, but the farmer in whose memory we are here to-day drove his team and held the plow; planted the corn, attended its growth, and gathered it in; sowed his small grain, and reaped his harvests; raised horses, cattle, sheep and hogs, and fed them with his own hands. He made more than two blades of grass grow where none grew before, and thus advanced the general welfare."

Speeches were also made on this occasion by Ex-Governor Baker, Ex-Senator McDonald, Senator Harrison and Hon. Jason B. Brown, all of them being eloquent and appreciative.

The monument which stands at Governor Williams's grave bears this inscription:

JAMES D. WILLIAMS,

Born January 6, 1808;

Died November 20, 1880.

A representative of the people for many years;

Was one term in Congress;

Governor of Indiana from 1877 until his death.

A faithful officer

and

An honest man.

Indiana honored him in life and cherishes his memory in death.

In the spring of 1880 the author of these sketches accompanied Governor Williams in a trip to the Gulf of Mexico. After leaving Nashville, at every point of importance upon the road he was received by large delegations of people. When he reached Mobile, he was met by the recorder, who is the chief executive officer of the city, the president of the Cotton Exchange and the president of the Board of Trade, who escorted him to his quarters at the Battle House. After dinner he held quite a levee in the parlors of the hotel, where many of the leading people of the city called upon him. While thus engaged, a young girl, some twelve or fourteen years old, called at the office of the hotel, with a large bouquet, and asked for him. The clerk, thinking she was a flower girl, seeking to dispose of her wares, tried to have her leave the hotel without seeing the Governor, but this she would not do. She came into the parlor where he was seated surrounded by a number of gentlemen and ladies, and approaching him, said: "This is Governor Williams, I believe?" "Yes, my daughter," he replied. She then presented him the bouquet, which he accepted with the grace of a courtier. She asked if he did not remember receiving a bouquet at Laporte, during the canvass of 1876, from a little girl who was sick. He replied that he remembered it well. She then said: "I am the girl who sent it to you, and your kind acknowledgment makes mamma very anxious to see you." "Where is your mamma?" asked the Governor. "At home," replied the girl, giving the street and number. "She shall see me," said the Governor, who then arose, excused himself to the ladies and gentlemen present and left the room. On reaching the street he called a hack and was driven to the mother's home.

This incident illustrates one prominent trait in his character— his love for children.

On our return home from the South we stopped one day in Nashville. While there I procured a hack and asked Governor Williams to accompany me to the Hermitage, as I wished to see the home and grave of Jackson. He did so, and on our return said to me: "This morning I went with you, now I want you to go with me." I asked him, "Where?" He replied, "To see the finest farm in America, if not in the world." He ordered a carriage and we drove to the farm of General Harding, some seven miles from Nashville. I shall not attempt to describe the farm. After seeing it I had no disposition to question the Governor's judgment. We went over the farm, chaperoned by General Jackson, General Harding's son-in-law, and saw some of the fine stock for which the farm is noted. A horse, for which $30,000 had been paid in Europe, particularly attracted the Governor's attention. He examined him critically, and pointed out his excellencies and his defects. I wondered at the time what Governor Williams thought of General Harding's investment, for I knew he would never have put $30,000 in a horse. He believed in utility, but not in show. As we walked over the farm Governor Williams, several times, plucked blades from the blue-grass sod and examined them with a critic's eye, some times tasting them. He spoke of the blue-grass of the Wabash country, which, he said, was as fine as any he had ever seen. Often, after our return home, did Governor Williams speak to me about our visit to General Harding's farm, but never once about that to the Hermitage. While he loved the memory of Jackson he loved still more fine stock and rich blue-grass pastures.

Governor Williams was the only farmer ever elected Governor of Indiana. He belonged to the class who till the soil and husband its increase. He loved his calling and was successful in it. The farmers of the State considered him their representative and were proud of his fame. Posterity will revere his memory and he will go down in history as the Farmer Governor of Indiana.

CHRISTOPHER HARRISON.

On the south bank of the Choptank river, fourteen miles from its confluence with Chesapeake bay, stands the beautiful town of Cambridge. It is one of the oldest towns on the Eastern Shore of Maryland, having been settled early in 1600 by immigrants from England, many of whom were of gentle blood. In the Episcopal burying-ground at Cambridge may now be seen tombstones covered with ivy, upon which are engraved the names and coats of arms of the early settlers of that country. The town is in Dorchester county, and is the most beautiful as well as one of the most populous on the peninsula lying between the Chesapeake and Delaware bays. In this town, sometime during the year 1775, Christopher Harrison, first Lieutenant-Governor of Indiana, was born.

Christopher Harrison's family were English. His parents emigrated to Maryland about the middle of the eighteenth century, and settled at Cambridge. The family was of good social standing in England, one of its members having held an important office in the city government of London. The Harrisons were received into the aristocratic circles of Maryland, for be it known that nowhere in the country were the lines dividing the people into classes more distinctly drawn than in the land first settled by Calvert. The abolition of slavery destroyed this, and now a man in that country is not measured by the negroes he owns, nor by the number of years his ancestors lived off the labor of others. During the war of the rebellion the author of this sketch, who is a native of Dorchester county, asked an old school-fellow about one of their early friends, and was told that he was sheriff of an adjoining county. Knowing that in the days of his boyhood the sons of slaveholders only were elected to office, the author remarked: "Well, Frank has risen in the world." "Yes," said his friend, "in this country the bottom rail has become the rider."

Christopher Harrison was liberally educated. He graduated at St. John's College, Annapolis, and soon after entered the counting-room of William Patterson, one of the merchant princes of Baltimore, as his confidential clerk. He was received into Mr. Patterson's family as an equal, a privilege to which he was entitled both by his birth and his education. Mr. Patterson was the father of Madame Bonaparte, then Elizabeth Patterson, one of the most beautiful and brilliant women America has ever produced. The young clerk became her friend, and for a while acted as her tutor. There is a tradition that an attachment grew up between the young people, resulting in an engagement of marriage. It is also said that the match was opposed by the lady's father, and that Harrison, finding his suit hopeless, left Baltimore and sought surcease of sorrow in the wilderness of the West. There is a good deal of evidence to support this tradition, but not enough, I think, to make the matter conclusive. It is, however, certain that Christopher Harrison had a love affair at this period of his life, and that it caused him to leave his native State and come to the new Territory of Indiana. Thomas P. Williams, of Baltimore, who married his niece, in a letter to Judge Banta, of Franklin (to whom I am indebted for much of the material for this sketch), thus speaks of this epoch in Mr. Harrison's life:

"In early life he was a confidential clerk of the late William Patterson, of this city, one of our princely merchants, and who was the father of Madame Bonaparte, who recently died in this city. He instructed, or rather aided her in her studies as a young girl, and has often spoken of her as the brightest and most ambitious person he ever knew. I have been informed that in a sketch of Madame Bonaparte it is incidentally mentioned that Mr. Harrison made love to this then beautiful woman, but this, I think, is a mistake. He had, however, a love affair, which was the cause of his leaving home, and of not being heard from for years. Both his family and the family of the lady objected to the marriage, and, while the young people were devotedly attached to each other, they did not marry, for Mr. Harrison said he would not enter a family where there was opposition; and seeing no end to this opposition, he preferred to go West."

The belief was quite general among Mr. Harrison's friends in Indiana that he and Madame Bonaparte had been lovers, and if there had been nothing of it, it is somewhat strange that the husband of his niece, at whose house he lived for many years after his return to Maryland, should have said anything about it.

In 1809, when Williamson Dunn settled in Jefferson county, where Hanover now stands, Christopher Harrison was living in a log cabin on the bluffs of the Ohio river, near by. When he came there I know not, but on a beech tree standing near his cabin door, were engraven these words:

"CHRISTOPHER HARRISON, JULY 8, 1808."

Perhaps he made the inscription as a memento of the day he located upon this beautiful and romantic spot. His cabin stood upon a point known as "Fair Prospect," a site which commands a view of the Ohio river for miles up and down. It had but a single room, and was roughly made, but inside were many things which testified of the culture of its occupant. Books were there, some of them classical, and paints and brushes and easels were to be seen, and pictures hanging on the wall. He also had about him man's most faithful friend—the dog. Back of his cabin, jutting against its chimney of clay, was a kennel, in which the companions of his solitude were wont to shelter themselves from the wind and the rain.

This hermit of the wilderness was quite a hunter. He supported himself mainly by his dog and gun, for the woods abounded in game, and his necessities were few. Thus lived Christopher Harrison until 1815, when George Logan came along and bought his land. It is supposed that by this time the keenness of disappointed love had worn off, for he threw solitude behind him and went out into the world. At that time Salem was one of the most important towns in the State, and thither the hermit of the Ohio bluffs determined to go. He and

Jonathan Lyons, one of the original proprietors of Madison, bought a miscellaneous stock of merchandise and took it to Salem, where they opened out a store. For many years they sold goods together, doing the largest business in their line in the place.

While at Salem Christopher Harrison lived alone. His dwelling was a little brick house of two rooms, one of them barely large enough for a bed. An old colored woman came each morning to tidy up the house and put things in order, and, with this exception, no one scarcely ever entered his door. But the lot upon which it stood was often visited. It was fifty feet one way by a hundred the other, and nearly every foot of it not covered by the house was planted in flowers. Here the boys and girls of the town would come for flowers, and seldom did they go away empty-handed. The master of the house made bouquets and gave them, drew pictures for them, and in many other ways sought to please and make them happy. One who remembers his Salem home says he painted a picture of a grape-vine clinging to his porch so perfectly that she once, on seeing it, reached out her hand, thinking she was about to pluck a bunch of grapes. About 1830 Governor Harrison left Salem and moved upon a farm a few miles away, where he lived until 1834, when he left Indiana and returned to his native State. While he lived on his farm it was his custom, in melon time, to fill his wagon with this delicious fruit for his little friends in town. He would cut the name of each favorite on the rind, and then deliver the melons to the delighted young folks. He evidently loved children. But I can not longer dwell upon his tastes and habits, and must hurry along and say something about his public life, else the reader will wonder why this sketch was written.

In 1816 Christopher Harrison was elected Lieutenant-Governor of Indiana, at the first election held under the State government. At the same election Jonathan Jennings was elected Governor over Thomas Posey, while Harrison's competitor was John Vawter. He served as Lieutenant-Governor for a couple of years, and then resigned in a pet, and went home. The cause of this unnatural act in an office-holder was this: In 1818, Governor Jennings, General Cass and Judge Parke were appointed by the President of the United States, commissioners to negotiate for the purchase from the Indians of the lands in the central part of the State. The constitution of the State forbade the Governor from holding " any office under the United States," but Governor Jennings accepted the office and discharged its duties. Lieutenant-Governor Harrison claimed that Jennings had vacated his office, and that he (Harrison) had become Acting Governor. He took possession of the executive office and attempted to assume its duties, but Jennings appealed to the Legislature, and that body recognized him as the legal Governor. This so incensed the Lieutenant-Governor that he resigned his office. The day he resigned his office of Lieutenant-Governor, he sent to the House of Representatives a letter dated Corydon, December 18, 1818, addressed to the Speaker, in which he said :

" I have this day delivered to the Secretary of State, to be filed in his office, my resignation of the office of Lieutenant-Governor of this State. As the officers of the executive department of government and the General Assembly have refused to recognize and acknowledge that authority which, according to my understanding, is constitutionally attached to the office, the name itself, in my estimation, is not worth retaining."

Upon the reading of this letter the House passed the following resolution :

"*Resolved*, That the House of Representatives view the conduct and deportment of Lieutenant-Governor Christopher Harrison as both dignified and correct during the late investigation of the differences existing in the executive department of this State."

The next year, 1819, he was a candidate for Governor against Governor Jennings, but was badly beaten, receiving but 2,088 votes in a total of 11,256.

But his defeat for Governor in 1819 did not end Christopher Harrison's public life in Indiana. In 1820 the Legislature elected him and James W. Jones, of Gibson county, and Samuel P. Booker, of Wayne county, commissioners to survey and lay off

Indianapolis, the new capital of the State. At the time fixed by law for the commissioners to meet none of them except Mr. Harrison appeared. He determined to act by himself, and at once proceeded to business. He appointed Elias P. Fordham and Alexander Ralston surveyors, and Benjamin I. Blythe clerk. This was in April, 1821, and the next October the lots were sold under the direction of General John Carr, the State agent. At this sale Christopher Harrison bought several lots, some of which he held until after he left the State.

On December 1, 1823, he made his report of the condition of the 3 per cent. fund, of which he was agent, and in 1824 the Legislature appointed him and Governor Hendricks commissioners to open a canal around the falls of the Ohio. This report dates January 18, 1825.

After Governor Harrison returned to Maryland he lived around among his relatives and friends. For many years he resided with his sister, Mrs. Lockerman, and spent his time, when not reading, in hunting and fishing in Chesapeake bay and its estuaries. Judge Banta has several of his letters written at this time, in which he very minutely describes his manner of life. He says he is "uncle" to all the young folks in the neighborhood. He tells of his success in hunting and fishing, of the number of canvas-back ducks and sheep's-head fish he brings home to "the pot."

Mr. Williams, in the letter heretofore referred to, says:

"He was a student all his life, and his acquirements were various and extensive. He was not satisfied with a superficial knowledge of anything; he went into matters thoroughly. He was reticent, and it was difficult to get at what he knew or thought on any subject. He was the soul of honor, and no man I ever knew had a more thorough contempt for a mean act. He was generous to excess. He had no love for money or its accumulation. He had opportunities for making a fortune, but he gave away as he made. From the simplicity and purity of the man and his great goodness I became greatly attached to him. He was the best informed man I ever met. At one time he lived in my family for ten years, and I know him thoroughly. He was an honest man and died poor.   He was a remarkable man, and deserves a place in history."

Governor Harrison died at the home of Mr. H. C. Tilghman, in Talbot county, Md., in 1863, at the ripe age of eighty-eight years.   And another Indiana pioneer was laid at rest.

When Christopher Harrison arrived at man's estate he was the owner, by inheritance, of a number of slaves.   To these he gave their freedom, and never afterward was he the proprietor of human flesh and blood.   In those days it was a rare thing for a young slaveholder to free his chattels, but Christopher Harrison stood not upon precedent; he acted for himself.

Governor Harrison was a well-built man, of medium height. While he lived in the cabin near where Hanover now is he was erect in carriage, but later in life he became bent or stoop-shouldered.   He had an oval face, light complexion and blue eyes, says one authority.   Another describes him the same, except that his eyes were gray.   He was always careful of his dress.   Usually he was cleanly shaved, and in his person was always scrupulously clean.   He was a free-thinker, but he had great respect for the Quaker church.   After he returned to Maryland he frequently extolled the virtues of the Quakers he knew in Indiana.   He was a great student, being a voracious reader of books.   Judge Banta has a couple of books, one of them printed in Latin, which once belonged to the old pioneer. They contain notes and emendations in his handwriting, and interspersed through them are beautiful pictures, in water colors, drawn by the deft hand of their owner.

Dr. Alexander H. Bayly, who lives at Cambridge, Maryland, the town in which Christopher Harrison was born, in a recent letter to the author of these sketches, says:

" Well, indeed, do I remember the sturdy old gentleman as he visited, for the last time, the home of his childhood.   I can see him now, dressed in the old style, slowly wandering around our town, lost, as it were, in the memories of ' the long, long ago.'   Sad, indeed, must have been his thoughts.   Being bald, he wore a black silk skull-cap, which gave rise to the report that he had been scalped by the Indians.   His father, Robert Harrison, was a proud, aristocratic Englishman, and all stood in awe of him.   He owned, lived and died on his farm, 'Appleby,' in the suburbs of Cambridge, on the Blackwater road, where old Dr. Joseph E. Muse once lived, and where he died. After his death it was bought by the late Governor Thomas H. Hicks, who resided on it at the time of his death.   You, no doubt, recollect the farm.   [The author remembers it well.]

"Christopher Harrison, or as he was most commonly called here, 'Old Kit Harrison," was a descendant of the John Caile, now resting in our old graveyard, and was related to William G. Harrison and others of Baltimore.   The family was highly respected and influential."

Christopher Harrison never married.   He lived his fourscore and eight years without a helpmeet, but he was blessed with loving friends.   These cared for him in his old age, and when the messenger came and called him to his fathers, they laid him away in his silent tomb and covered him with his native earth. There I will leave him at rest.

MILTON STAPP.

INDIANA owes much to Kentucky. She owes her for thousands of pioneers who helped cut down her forests and bring her lands into cultivation ; she owes her for statesmen of transcendent ability, and particularly does she owe her for the gallant rangers she sent to beat back the savage foe.

Among the men from Kentucky who came to the help of Indiana in her trials was Milton Stapp, the subject of this sketch. He was born in Scott county, Kentucky, in the year 1793. His boyhood was spent in the ordinary way, there being nothing unusual in his history until after he was nineteen years old. The tidings of Indian cruelty that came to him from across the Ohio river fired his blood and stimulated his patriotism to such a degree that he resolved to go to the rescue of his imperiled countrymen. He enlisted as a private soldier in the regiment commanded by Colonel Richard M. Johnson. He participated in all the skirmishes and battles of his regiment, and at the battle of the Thames, fought October 5, 1813, he was wounded in the neck by a musket ball. He carried the scar of this wound while he lived—a badge " more honorable than the star or garter," for it testified of blood spilled in saving women and children from outrage and butchery and their homes from pillage. When peace was declared, and the inhabitants north of the Ohio river no longer needed his musket, he returued to his Kentucky home. In his march through the Territory of Indiana to meet the Indians and their British allies, he saw a country rich in soil and natural advantages, and believing that such a land presented more inducements to the young and ambitious than the country where he lived, he determined to make it his

home. Therefore, in 1816, the year Indiana was admitted into
the Union, he left Kentucky and came to this State, making
his home at Madison, a town on the southern border. At that
time Madison was a leading town and the home of men who
subsequently became famous.

The young settler was ambitious, and knowing that the road
to political preferment usually ran through legal fields, he determined to study law. He entered the office of the late James
F. D. Lanier, as a student, and, after acquiring sufficient knowledge, was admitted to the bar. He began the practice as a
partner of his preceptor, but having chosen his profession more
as a means than as an end, he did not give it his sole attention.
His mind ran on other things, mainly on public employment,
and he was exceedingly active in trying to secure it. He was
fond of display, and the militia law of that time gave him scope
for the gratification of this propensity. It was then the custom
to have an annual muster at Madison, which all the able-bodied
soldiers of the town and its vicinage were required to attend.
The glories of these musters have departed, but the remembrance of them still gladdens the lovers of devastation and
carnage. Governor Corwin once described " parade day " so
graphically that the reader will pardon its insertion here :

" We all in fancy now see the gentleman from Michigan in
that most dangerous and glorious event of the life of a militia
general on the peace establishment—a parade day ! That day
for which all other days of his life seem to have been made.
We can see the troops in motion ; umbrellas, hoe and ax handles, and other deadly implements of war overshadowing all
the fields, when lo ! the leader of the host appears.

"Far off his coming shines;

his plume, white, after the fashion of the great Bourbon, is of
ample length, and reads its doleful history in the bereaved necks
and bosoms of forty neighboring hen-roosts. Like the great
Suwaroff, he seems somewhat careless in forms and points of
dress ; hence his epaulets may be on his shoulders, back or
sides, but still gleaming, gloriously gleaming in the sun."

This picture, though drawn of a Michigan general, portrays the aspects of the Indiana brigadier equally well. Napoleon was no fonder of drilling the Old Guard than was General Stapp of drilling the Madison militia. He and Major Cochrane would array themselves in the attire of warriors and march at the head of their columns. They were the boiler and engine that ran the military machine. To see them on their prancing steeds, their white plumes waving in the air, their swords flashing in the sunlight, was enough to drive Jupiter to cover and Mars to his temple. The General's renown as a militiaman spread throughout the land, and did much to bring him into public notice. But he did not devote all his time to the intoxicating militia drilling. He became a candidate for the State Legislature in 1822, and was elected from Jefferson county, and in 1823 he was chosen State Senator from Jefferson and Jennings counties, of which body he was made President *pro tem.*, in December, 1825, and in 1828 he was elected Lieutenant-Governor of the State, on the ticket with James B. Ray. His term expired in 1831, but he still continued in politics. In that year he ran for Governor, receiving only 4,422 votes, while Governor Noble received 17,959, and James G. Reed 15,168. Noble was elected, but he went to the Legislature again, and was an active and successful advocate of the internal improvement system of that time. In 1836 the system culminated, and in 1839 broke down. A debt of $15,000,000 had been contracted, upon which no interest was paid for years. Bankruptcy overtook the people, and ruin ran riot. The unfinished public works were abandoned, and afterward sold. A commission of three was appointed to settle this debt, General Stapp being one of the commission. After this he was elected Agent of State and charged with the care of the bonded debt. But neither his career as Fund Commissioner nor as Agent of State proved him a Morrison or a Gallatin. As Agent of State he placed a large amount of bonds with the Morris Canal and Banking Company for negotiation. The institution broke, with the money received for the bonds in its coffers, and all the State ever got from it were a few Brooklyn water lots, upon which was an old soap factory.

It will thus be seen that as a public financier General Stapp was not a success. But, in justice to his memory, be it said that no charge of dishonesty was laid at his door. Many thought him weak, but none believed him dishonest.

In 1834, when the Madison branch of the State Bank of Indiana was organized, General Stapp was appointed its cashier. In a short time he resigned this position, to take the presidency of the Madison Savings Institution, a bank of discount and deposit. He remained at the head of this institution so long as it transacted business.

In 1850 General Stapp was elected mayor of Madison, the last office he held in Indiana. He made a most excellent mayor, certainly as good a one as the city ever had. He administered the law fearlessly and without favor. He had the intelligence to know his duty and the courage to perform it. He never filled an office with so much honor to himself, and with so much acceptability to the people.

In the spring of 1853 General Stapp bought a half interest in the *Madison Daily Banner*, and took editorial charge of the paper. He continued to direct its columns until it died.

In 1860, when sixty-seven years old, General Stapp left Madison and removed to Texas. He was active and reasonably vigorous at the time, and bid fair to live many years in his new home, but the war soon coming on, he determined to leave. He had fought under the old flag when he was young, and he would not desert it now. Communication by public conveyance between the sections having ceased, he procured a spring wagon and a mule, and, taking his family with him, traveled overland from Goliad, Texas, to Sedalia, Mo. From there he came by railroad and steamer to Madison. He remained at his old home until the war had ended, and in 1865 returned to Texas as Collector of Internal Revenue for the Galveston district. Galveston was his home, but he traveled extensively over the State in attending to his official duties. On one of his trips, while crossing a stream between Goliad and Galveston, he suddenly became surrounded by a flood of water, and was compelled to climb a tree to save his life. The water continued to rise, and all communication with land was cut off. By hallooing he made himself heard, but there was no boat in which to go to his relief. This was in the afternoon, and he had to

stay in the tree top until the next morning. By that time a
boat had been constructed, and the General was relieved from
his perilous situation. It rained hard during the whole of his
water captivity, and when succor came he was found to be suffering from a burning fever. He was taken to his home at
Galveston, and soon after reaching there he died. The news
of his death reached Madison on the 4th of August, 1869, but
his remains were not removed from Galveston until the first day
of the next November, when they were shipped to Madison.

His funeral took place on the 9th of November, at the residence
of his nephew, William Stapp, in the house which was formerly
his home. After the services the body was taken to the Madison cemetery and there interred.

In politics General Stapp was a Whig, while the party existed, and on its dissolution he did not attach himself to either of
the great political parties. Hence, during the latter part of his
life, his was a free lance in politics. But, when the war came,
he took his position on the side of the Union, a place where all
who knew him expected him to stand.

General Stapp was a man of great energy and courage. He
had many ups and downs in life, but he bore his misfortunes
well, and, at a time when most men would have given up work
and sought ease in the chimney corner, he went to a new country to build up his fortunes anew. He was an active member
of the Baptist church and prominent in the religious work of
that denomination. In his credulity he was as simple as a child.
His heart was tender, and he was never happier than when
binding up the wounds of others. In person he was rather under the usual size. He had light hair with a somewhat golden
tinge, a fair complexion and light-blue eyes. His self-esteem
was great, but it hurt no one but himself. Sharp and designing
men worked upon it to his disadvantage; but, take him altogether, he averaged well. He was a kind and good neighbor,
a brave and patriotic citizen, and an active Christian worker—
qualities which more than compensate for the defects of his
character.

DAVID HILLIS.

DAVID HILLIS, Lieutenant-Governor of Indiana from 1836 to 1840, was born in 1785, and emigrated to Indiana in 1808, settling in Jefferson county, near Madison. He was, at the time, vigorous and healthy, with a body capable of enduring the privations incident to the life of a pioneer. He entered a large tract of land near Madison, much of it hilly and broken, but enough of it was level to make him a very desirable farm. He built him a cabin on the edge of a ridge that now bears his name, and commenced to open up a farm.

It was on such a spot as I have named that the young pioneer commenced the battle of life. There were no settlers near him; he was alone in the woods. His brother Ebenezer, and the Rykers—Colonel John, Samuel J. and Gerrardus—had come to the Territory about the same time as himself and settled some three miles away, but they lived too far from him to be considered neighbors. With the exception of them, no white man lived nearer than Madison. Christopher Harrison had settled some time before on the bluff of the Ohio river, near where Hanover now is, and the year after Mr. Hillis came to the Territory Williamson Dunn left his Kentucky home and located near the cabin of Harrison. With these and a few other exceptions all the territory now comprised in Jefferson county, outside of the settlement at Madison, was wild and uninhabited.

A short time after Mr. Hillis had built his cabin and commenced clearing up his land, the Indians became hostile. The settlers lived in constant fear of the tomahawk and scalping-knife, and well they might, for they were used with merciless severity. To protect the settlements from Indian incursions, a company of rangers, or mounted men, was organized at Madison and mustered into the service of the government. Williamson Dunn was captain of the company and David Hillis its first lieutenant. This was in the spring of 1813. For some time the rangers were engaged in the building of block-houses and in scouring the woods for Indians, but in June, 1813, they marched to the Indian towns on White river, and in the fall of that year made a campaign to the Wabash country. They went to Fort Harrison, near Terre Haute, where Captain Taylor, afterward President of the United States, was surrounded by the Indians. The presence of the rangers was most opportune, for had they not come when they did the garrison must soon have surrendered to the enemy. In the spring of 1814 Captain Dunn left the service, and from that time until the company disbanded it was commanded by Lieutenant Hillis. This company of rangers rendered great service to the settlers, and its commanders were not forgotten. Both Captain Dunn and Lieutenant Hillis were held in high esteem by the people. Both of them were time and time again given public office, and both of them honored the places given them.

When the company of rangers was mustered out of service, Lieutenant Hillis went back to his farm. He employed a large number of men in clearing his land and putting it in order for the plow and the harrow. No other farmer in the country gave work to so many men.

Lieutenant Hillis was a civil engineer, and one skilled in his profession. He was appointed government surveyor, and for several years was engaged in surveying the public lands of Northern Indiana, Michigan and Illinois.

Soon after the organization of the State government Lieutenant Hillis was elected an Associate Judge of the Jefferson Circuit Court. He displayed a legal acumen unusual in one not bred to the law, and when he left the bench he took with him the good will of the bar and his brother judges.

In 1823 Judge Hillis commenced his legislative career, and it was continued almost uninterruptedly while he lived. In that year he was elected to the State Legislature, and he was re-elected each succeeding year, with one exception, until 1830. Two years afterward, in 1832, he was sent to the State Senate, and in 1835 he was re-elected. At that time there were many able men in the Senate, but Judge Hillis ranked them all, being chairman of the Committee on Ways and Means, and, therefore, the Senate's leader.

Such was Judge Hillis's prominence and popularity that, in 1837, he was nominated for Lieutenant-Governor on the ticket with David Wallace. His competitor was James Gregory, an able and popular man, but Judge Hillis defeated him at the polls. The issue in this campaign was the internal improvement system, and upon that question Judge Hillis occupied the popular side.

In 1842 Governor Hillis was again elected to the Legislature. When the Legislature met he was nominated for Speaker of the House, but his party being in the minority, he was defeated.

In 1844 Governor Hillis was, for the tenth time, elected to the Legislature. Soon after the election he was taken sick and never recovered. When the Legislature met he was unable to leave his home, but hoping to regain his health, he did not resign his seat. The session ended without his being able to attend a single sitting, or, indeed, to come to the capital. He lingered through the spring and until midsummer, when he died. His death took place at his homestead, on the 8th day of July, 1845. Being known and beloved by almost every man and woman in his county, his death caused great public sorrow. The people from far and near came to his funeral, and many not of his blood wept at his grave. He was buried a few hundred yards north of his dwelling, and all that was mortal of the old pioneer has gone to dust.

Governor Hillis was kind and obliging to all who had dealings with him. He gave largely to the poor and to benevolent and religious purposes. He had the qualities which drew men to him and kept them there. His large estate had many tenants, and these tenants were always the landlord's friends.

In religion Governor Hillis was a Seceder of the straightest sect. Indeed he was the head and front of the Seceders' church at Madison. He would come to town on Sunday morning, bringing his family and dinner with him, and devote the day to religious services. He would listen to a two hours' sermon in the morning and return to church to listen to another equally as long. A sermon was never too long for him, if it abounded in gospel unction. The house of God was to him the best of all places. He never tired of being there. Were he now living he would consider the half-hour discourses of our preachers as mere exordiums of what gospel talks should be.

No guest left Governor Hillis's house on the Sabbath. Those who came to it on Saturday remained until Monday. He believed in the Bible injunction and kept holy the Sabbath day, and he saw that all his household obeyed the command. He would not permit his sons to pluck apples from the trees on Sunday. One of them once said to me that when a boy the sound of a falling apple or walnut, on the Sabbath, shocked him, so still was everything about his father's house.

Governor Hillis abhorred secret societies. He held them sinful, and thought no Christian should belong to one. He believed the singing of hymns in worship to be wrong, but took great delight in the singing of psalms of approved rendition. This pleasure was in nowise marred by faulty time or measure, when the words were according to Rouse.

Governor Hillis's old homestead still stands. It was one of the first brick farm-houses built in Jefferson county, and, when new, was the wonder of the people. It is located near a spring of ever-flowing water, and all around and about it great locust trees are growing. These trees were planted by the old pioneer, and he lived to see them grow large enough to protect him from the sun as he walked about his yard or sat under the branches of his trees. But the house has passed into the hands of strangers. Those who tread its halls and rest in its chambers have none of the builder's blood in their veins. They are not to the manor born.

When Governor Hillis died he left surviving him a widow, two sons and several daughters. His oldest son, William C. Hillis, represented Jefferson county in the Legislature of 1849–50, and subsequently served a term as treasurer of his county. He afterwards emigrated to Missouri, and subsequently to Iowa. He is now police judge of Des Moines, and Master Commissioner of the United States Court for the district of Iowa. The youngest son, David Burke Hillis, is a practicing physician of

Keokuk, Iowa, and occupies a high place in his profession. The sons detract nothing from their father's well-earned fame.

There are but few men living who knew David Hillis, but there are many who revere his name.

In person, Governor Hillis was about the average size of man. He had black hair and eyes, and a good face. He was well educated for the time in which he lived, but he was not a classical scholar. He was one of the most noted men in his section of the State—a section which has given Indiana several of her most distinguished sons.

JAMES NOBLE.

AT the time of the formation of the State government of Indiana, and for many years afterward, the politics and offices of
the State were controlled by a few families, chief among them
being the Nobles. It is James Noble, the head of this family,
that I now propose to sketch.

The Nobles were of Virginia stock, the family home being
near Fredericksburg, a city rendered famous by the great battle fought there during our civil war.

Near the close of the eighteenth century Thomas T. Noble,
the father of James, left Virginia with his family and emigrated
to Kentucky. His life was like that of other pioneers who settled in the wilderness of the West. His son James was a hardy
boy, inured to labor. He grew up strong and self-reliant.
When but seventeen years old he married Mary Lindsay, of
Newport, and soon afterwards entered the law office of a Mr.
Southgate as a student. After finishing his legal studies and
being admitted to the bar, he removed to Brookville, Ind., and
commenced the practice of his profession. He soon became
known as an eloquent advocate, his practice extending throughout the Whitewater country. In those days the bar of eastern
Indiana was very able. James Brown Ray, John T. McKinney, David Wallace, Oliver H. Smith, Amos Lane, George H.
Dunn, John Test and other noted men were contemporaneous
with James Noble, and were his competitors at the bar. But
as a speaker upon the hustings and as a jury lawyer he excelled
them all. Some of them were better judges of the law, and
stronger before the court, but none equaled him in swaying the
masses upon the stump and in influencing juries in the box.

When Indiana resolved to emerge from her territorial condition and become a State, the people of Franklin county sent General Noble to Corydon to help make a constitution. In the constitutional convention he was chairman of the Committee on the Legislative Department, and he was also a member of the Judiciary Committee. When the work of the convention was done he returned to Brookville and continued the practice of the law. The next August he was elected a member of the first Legislature under the State government. It met at Corydon, November 4, 1816, and adjourned January 3, 1817. Among the members of this Legislature who are remembered now, were James Noble, Amos Lane, John Dumont, Williamson Dunn, Davis Floyd, Samuel Milroy, Isaac Blackford and Ratliff Boon. Isaac Blackford was elected Speaker of the House, and John Paul President of the Senate. Three days after their organization the two houses met in joint convention and declared Jonathan Jennings to have been elected Governor, and Christopher Harrison Lieutenant-Governor, whereupon these gentlemen took the oath of office and entered upon their respective duties. The next day, November 8, 1816, the General Assembly, by a joint vote, elected James Noble and Waller Taylor to represent Indiana in the Senate of the United States. Thus it will be seen that in four days from the time General Noble took his seat in the Legislature he was elected a member of the highest legislative body in the world. This was not an accident; it was because his fellow-members knew his eminent qualifications for the place.

In the Senate General Noble had for associates the ablest men the country has yet produced. He was not dwarfed by their stature, but maintained a respectable standing among them. He continued in the Senate until February 26, 1831, when he died at his boarding-house in Washington. On Monday, February 28, 1831, William Hendricks, his colleague, arose in the Senate and said:

"Mr. President—It becomes my painful duty to announce to the Senate the death of my respected colleague. He departed this life on Saturday evening last, at 10 o'clock. His services in this body have been faithful and uninterrupted for

the last fifteen years. They have been honorable to himself and
useful to his country ; but man goeth to his long home, and with
him these services have terminated in the meridian of life.   He
had indeed lived to see his early associates in the business of
this house retire to other spheres of life, or, like himself, pass
silently to the grave ; yet his friends might reasonably have
hoped and expected for him a longer period of usefulness and
distinction.   On an occurrence like the present, and especially
standing as I do in the midst of a circle so intimately acquainted
with the deceased, it will not be expected of me to pronounce
his eulogy ; but I can speak, and I may be permitted to speak,
in the language of early and well-tried personal friendship of
one highly prized, not only by myself, but by the State he has
so long had the honor to represent ; of an individual idolized by
almost every circle in which he ever moved.   He was a bold
and fearless politician, warm and generous in his feelings.   He
had a heart that responded to every appeal of sympathy and
benevolence ; a heart formed for the most ardent attachment.
Open and undisguised, the prominent traits of his character
were always before the world ; but a long period of familiar acquaintance could only develop the ardor, the devotion and the
value of his friendship.   For such an associate it may well be
permitted us to mourn, and well assured am I that in paying
these last honors to his memory we are but giving expression to
the feelings of every member of the Senate.   His society I have
enjoyed when he was in health ; in sickness I have frequently
been near him and endeavored to soothe his hours of anguish
and distress, and I had an opportunity of watching, with intense
anxiety and great solicitude, the last moments of his life."

Mr. Burnet then submitted the following resolution, which
was agreed to :

"*Resolved, unanimously*, That a committee be appointed to
take order for superintending the funeral of the Hon. James
Noble, deceased, which will take place at half-past 11 o'clock
this day, and that the Senate will attend the same, and that notice of this event be given to the House of Representatives."

The chair stated that under the circumstances of the case,

upon being informed yesterday of the death of the late Senator from Indiana, he had appointed a committee of arrangements and pall-bearers, and hoped the course he had pursued would not be disapproved of.

Mr. Burnet then submitted the following resolutions, which were adopted :

"*Resolved, unanimously*, That the members of the Senate, from a sincere desire of showing every mark of respect due to the memory of the Hon. James Noble, deceased, their late associate, will go into mourning for him for one month, by the usual mode of wearing crape round the left arm.

Resolved, unanimously, That, as an additional mark of respect for the memory of the Hon. James Noble, the Senate do now adjourn."

On the same day a message was received in the House of Representatives from the Senate, notifying the House of Senator Noble's death, and informing it that his funeral would take place that day at 11:30 o'clock A. M., whereupon Mr. Test, the member representing the district in which Senator Noble had formerly lived, offered the following resolution and moved its adoption :

"*Resolved*, That the members of this House will attend the funeral of the Hon. James Noble, late a member of the Senate from the State of Indiana, this day at the hour appointed, and, as a testimony of respect for the memory of the deceased, they will go into mourning and wear crape around the left arm for thirty days."

The resolution was agreed to unanimously.
On motion of Mr. Vance it was then ordered :

" That for the purpose of attending the funeral of the late Senator Noble, the House take a recess until 3 o'clock P. M."

The committee of arrangements issued the following order in relation to the funeral of General Noble :

ORDER OF PROCESSION

FOR THE FUNERAL OF THE

HONORABLE JAMES NOBLE,

Senator of the United States from the State of Indiana.

The committee of arrangements, pall-bearers and mourners will attend at Mrs. Galvin's, the late residence of the deceased, at 11 o'clock A. M., to-morrow, at which time the corpse will be removed, in charge of the committee of arrangments, attended by the Sergeant-at-Arms, to the Senate Chamber, where divine service will be performed.

At 11:30 o'clock the funeral will move from the Senate Chamber to the place of interment in the following order :

Pall-Bearers:

Mr. Holmes.	CORPSE.	Mr. Burnett.
Mr. Clayton.		Mr. Woodbury.
Mr. Robinson.		Mr. Frelinghuysen.

February 27, 1831.

The funeral will take place this day at 11 o'clock.
February 28, 1831.

The body of the deceased was brought into the chamber of the Senate and placed in front of the secretary's desk, soon after which the House of Representatives, preceded by their Speaker and clerk, together with their sergeant-at-arms, entered the chamber, and were immediately followed by the President of the United States, the heads of departments, and the judges of the Supreme Court, who respectively took the seats prepared for them. The chaplain of the Senate (the Rev. Mr. Johns) then arose and delivered an eloquent and very impressive address, which was followed by a fervent prayer by the Rev. Mr. Gurley, the chaplain of the House. A procession was then formed and proceeded to the Eastern Branch burial ground, where the remains of the deceased were solemnly interred. There they have mouldered to dust.

Oliver H. Smith, in his " Early Indiana Trials and Sketches," makes frequent mention of General Noble. He thus speaks of a passage at arms between him and Mr. Calhoun, then Vice-President of the United States. Addressing the chair, General Noble said :

" I tell you, Mr. President, the Little Magician will spoil your dish with the old hero ; he is as cunning as a serpent and as harmless as a dove."

" The Senator will confine himself to the subject."

" Which subject?"

" The one before the Senate."

" I am trying to do so. I see but one subject before the Senate—the other is at the White House."

" The Senator will take his seat."

"As I was saying, the Little Magician—"

" The Senator was directed to take his seat."

" So I did, but the chair did not expect me to sit there the balance of the session."

Mr. Smith declares General Noble to have been one of the strongest and most effective speakers before a jury or a promiscuous assembly he ever heard. He gives his opinion of him as a party leader in these words :

" General Noble was, as the saying is, born for a leader. His person, his every act, look and motion suited the populace. He was emphatically a self-made man—quick, ready and always prepared. His taste was quite military, and the old settlers of Whitewater will not soon forget the General in full uniform, mounted on ' Wrangler,' at the head of his division."

There are but few men now living who were personally acquainted with General Noble. The Hon. Jacob B. Julian, of Indianapolis, has given the author the following account of a trial at which General Noble was a conspicuous figure :

" In the spring of 1821 Hampshire Pitt was placed on trial in the Wayne Circuit Court at Centerville, for the murder of William Mail, both men of color. Noble was the leading counsel for the defense, and made one of his ablest speeches. I was then a little boy, and was taken into the court-room while he was addressing the jury, by an older brother, and such was the violence of his actions, and so loud and terrific were his denunciations of the prosecution and all connected with it, that I became alarmed and demanded that I should be taken away.

I need not say that I have lived to learn that such performances are harmless. Of all the men connected with this trial, Samuel King, one of the jurors, only survives. He resides in the State of Iowa, and is ninety-four years of age."

General Noble was a large, well-proportioned man of fine address and bearing. His hair was black, his eyes dark and his complexion florid. He was, in fact, one of the finest looking men of his day in the Whitewater valley. With his easy and graceful manners, his fine conversational powers, added to his warm heart and generous nature, he was the idol of the people of his section of the country, and was perfectly invincible before them. He was a good lawyer, though he specially excelled as an advocate, in which department of the practice he had no equal in his part of the State. His style was what would be called Western, now. He had a voice of great compass to which he gave the fullest scope, and it was generally known for several squares around the Court-house when he was addressing a jury. There was no occasion for a juror to hold his hand behind his ear to catch the sound, or to use an ear-trumpet, when General Noble was pleading a case before him. He spoke loud enough to be heard.

Mrs. Austin H. Brown, a granddaughter of General Noble, has in her possession a miniature portrait of her distinguished ancestor. It is that of a man in the prime of life, with a full, round, ruddy face, large nose, small and unusually shapely mouth, dark eyes, and black hair gathered into a queue and hanging down his back. Such is the picture of James Noble, a Senator of the United States from Indiana from 1816 to 1831.

JOHN TIPTON.

Among the pioneers of Indiana few did a grander work than John Tipton. He was a great man in the council and in the field, and no history of the State can be written without honorable mention of his name. Many of his leading characteristics were inherited from his father, Joshua Tipton, who, born in Maryland, emigrated to East Tennessee, where he became a man of note and influence. He was well acquainted with Indian character, and led many a foray against the hostile Cherokees. He thus became an object of hatred to the wily savages, and on the 18th of April, 1793, was waylaid and murdered by them. It was from the loins of such a man that John Tipton sprang.

John Tipton, the subject of this sketch, was born in Sevier county, Tennessee, August 14, 1786. From a child he was used to the ways of the Indian. He knew his habits, his treachery, and his savageness. He could trail him like Chingachgook or circumvent him like Pathfinder. The Indian murdered Joshua Tipton, and John Tipton felt it his duty to avenge his father's death. And inexorably he did it. Many an Indian bit the dust at the command of John Tipton's rifle, and many a pioneer's home was saved from savage incursion by a healthy dread of the same terrible weapon.

When John Tipton had reached his majority he was known in the section where he lived as a man of untiring industry and of unquestioned courage. He became dissatisfied with his condition and opportunities, and determined to leave Tennessee and find a home in the territory northwest of the river Ohio. With him to determine was to act, so in the fall of 1807 he left Tennessee with his mother and her family, and came to Indiana. He settled in Harrison county, near Brinley's Ferry, on the Ohio river, and for many years made that place his home. Buying fifty acres of land, which he mainly paid for with money earned by splitting rails and clearing ground for his neighbors, he commenced the battle of life anew. In a short time he was the acknowledged leader of his neighborhood when leadership was required, and when it became necessary to organize the good people to drive out the horse-thieves and counterfeiters with which it was infested he was put in the van. They left the neighborhood without a fight, for when he told them they must go or take the consequences, they well knew what it meant.

In the summer of 1809 a military company called the " Yellow Jackets " was formed near young Tipton's home, of which he became a member. It was commanded by Captain Spier Spencer, and was designed for active service should the necessity occur. On the 10th of September, 1811, the company entered upon the campaign that culminated in the battle of Tippecanoe and the rout of the army under the Shawanee prophet. The young soldier kept a journal of this campaign, and it, with a journal of his trip to Indianapolis to locate the State capital, is in the possession of Mr. John H. Holliday, of Indianapolis. These journals are written upon common writing paper, folded and stitched, and are yellow with age. On the front page of that giving an account of the Tippecanoe campaign are these words :

" John Tipton,

September 11, 1811.

" Steal Not this Book for fear of Shame, for here you see the Oner's Name."

At the end of the journal is this certificate of its authenticity, written in General Tipton's own hand :

" This Day Book kept During the Campane in the year 1811 wherein His Excellency Governor Harrison was Commander in Chief and Col. J. B. Boyd of the 4th united States Riegement was Second in Command Everything therein Stated the Subscriber holds himself Ready to make appear to Bee fact from the Best information could be Had as it was duly kept by himself. JOHN TIPTON."

On a page at the back of the journal are these lines:

" Young major Dark received a wound,
    Just by his father's side,
  Those feeble hands shall be Revenged
    For my son's death he cry'd
  And like a man distracted
    Out of the lines he flew
  And like a bold Virgin-i-an
    A savage there he Slew."

The journal begins as follows:

"An acompt of the march and encampment of the riflemen of harrison County I. T. Commanded by Capt Spencer, consisting of 47 men, besides officers in Company with Capt. R. M. heath, with 22 men."

It commences Thursday, September 12, 1811, and ends Sunday, November 24, 1811, a period of seventy-three days. It gives a minute and particular account of everything that occurred under his notice during the time it covers, and is, perhaps, the fullest narrative in existence of the campaign it describes.

The battle of Tippecanoe was fought November 7, 1811, and I copy the entries in General Tipton's journal narrating the events of the day preceding the battle, the day of the battle and the day after. They are as follows:

" wednesday the 6 a verry Cold day we moved earley a scout sent out they Came back had seed indian sines. We marched as usel till 12. Our Spies caught four horses and seed some indians. Stopt in a prairie the foot throwd all their napsacks in the waggons. we formed in order for Battle—marched 2 miles then formed the line of Battle we marched in 5 lines on the extreme Right. went into a Cornfield then up to the above town and surrounded it they met us Pled for Peace they said they would give us satisfaction in the morning. All the time we ware there they kept hollowing. This town is on the west side of wabash—miles above Vincinnis on the Second Bank neat built about 2 hundred yards from the river. This is the main town, but it is scattering a mile long all the way a fine Cornfield, after the above moovement we mooved one mile farther up. Campd in timber between a Creek and Prairie after crossing a fine Creek and marching 11 miles.

"Thursday the 7 agreéble to their promised. Last night we ware answered by the firing of guns and the Shawnies Breaking into our tents a blood Combat Took Place at Precisely 15 minutes before five in the morning which lasted two hours and 20 minutes of a continewel firing while many times mixed among the Indians so that we Could not tell the indians and our men apart. they kept up a firing on three sides of us took our tent from the gueard fire. Our men fought Brave and By the timely help of Capt Cook with a company of infantry we maid a charge and drove them out of the timber across the prairie. Our Loost in killed and wounded was 179 and theirs graiter than ours. among the Dead was our Capt Spier Spencer and first Lieutenant mcmahan and Captain Berry that had been attached to our company and 5 more killed Dead and 15 wounded. after the indians gave ground we Burried our Dead. Among the Kentuckians was killed mayj Owen and mayj Davis badly wounded and a number of others in all killed and wounded was 179 but no company suffered like ours. we then held an Election for officers. I was Elected Capt, Saml. Flanagan first Lieut and Jacob Zenor second Lieut and Philip Bell Ensign. we then built Breastworks our men in much confusion, our flower been too small and all our beeve lost. Last night onley half Rations of whisky and no corn for our horses. my horse killed I got mcmahans to Ride. 37 of them had been killed wounded and lost last night. I had one quart of whisky.

"Friday the 8th a cloudy Day and last night was also wet and cold. we Lay all night at our Breastwork fire in the morning Spies sent out found the indians had Left their town, the horsemen was all sent to burn the town. We went and found grait Deal of Corn and Some Dead indians in the houses. loaded 6 waggons with Corn and Burnt what was Estimated at 2 thousand Bushels and 9 of our men Died last night."

The journal closes on the 24th of November, the day General Tipton reached his home. He describes that event in these words:

" Sunday the 24th a Cloudy and Rainy morning we moved Early Came to Corrydon at half past ten. I staid two hours and half took Breakfast mooved up to Coonrod's found my Lt and sick man. Staid 2 hours had my horses fed got some whisky, met one of my neighbors, mooved again and at 2 o'clock got safe Home after a campaign of 74 days. John Tipton."

It was reported by a member of General Harrison's staff that while the battle of Tippecanoe was raging, and after the death of Captain Spencer and his lieutenants, General Harrison rode up, and, addressing Ensign Tipton, asked where was his captain. " Dead, sir," replied the ensign. " Your first lieutenant?" " Dead, sir." " Your second lieutenant?" " Dead, sir." " Your ensign!" " He stands before you." " Hold your position, my brave lad, a little longer, and I will send you assistance." General Tipton says nothing about this incident in his journal, but nevertheless it may be true, as his modesty might have prevented him from recording it; but I think the probabilities are that it rests on no better foundation than the current gossip of the camp.

After the Tippecanoe campaign had ended General Tipton arose, by regular gradation, until he became a brigadier-general in the military service of the State. It may be mentioned that in 1813 he piloted Captain Dunn's company of rangers through the wilderness and in the same year acted as officer of the spies during the campaign to the Indian town on the West Fork of White river.

At the first election under the State constitution General Tipton was elected Sheriff of Harrison county. He was afterward re-elected, and continued to discharge the duties of the office until August, 1819, when he was elected a representative to the State Legislature.

On the 11th of January, 1820, the Legislature appointed George Hunt, John Conner, John Gilliland, Stephen Ludlow, Joseph Bartholomew, John Tipton, Jesse B. Durham, Frederick

Rapp, William Prince and Thomas Emerson, commissioners to select and locate a new capital for the State. In General Tipton's journal, giving an account of his trip for this purpose, he says :

" On Wednesday, the 17th of May, 1820, I set out from Corydon, in company with Governor Jennings. I had been appointed by the last Legislature one of the commissioners to select and locate a site for the permanent seat of government of the State of Indiana. We took with us Bill, a black boy," etc.

He gives a very particular account of the journey to the house of William Conner, where the commissioners were to meet and qualify. The commissioners were divided in judgment between Conner's farm, the mouth of Fall creek (Indianapolis), and the Bluffs near Waverly. The Fall creek site was chosen, upon General Tipton's motion, as will be seen from the following extract from his journal :

" Wednesday, 7th (June). A fine, clear morning. We met at McCormick's, and on my motion, the commissioners came to a resolution to select and locate sections numbered 1 and 12, and east and west fractional sections numbered 2, and east fractional section 11, and so much off the east side of the west fractional section number 3 to be divided by a north and south line running perelled to the west boundary of said section, as will equal in amount 4 entire sections in t. 15, n. of R. 3, E. We left our clerk making out his minuets and our report and went to camp to dine. Returned after dinner. Our paper not being ready B. (General Bartholemew), D. (Colonel Durham) and myself returned to camp at 4 ; they went to sleep, and me to writing. At 5 we decamped and went over to McCormick's. Our clerk having his writing ready, the commissioners met and signed their report, and certified the service of the clerk. At 6 :45 the first boat landed that ever was seen at the seat of government. It was a small ferry flat with a canoe tied alongside both loaded with the household goods of two families moving to the mouth of Fall creek. They came in a keel boat as far as they could get it up the river, then reloaded the boat and brought up their goods in the flat and canoe. I paid for some corn and w (whisky?) 62½."

During the nine years between the Tippecanoe campaign and the location of the State capital General Tipton had very much improved in composition, as is attested by his journals. The one recording his trip to Indianapolis and return is much more correctly written than the one giving an account of the Wabash campaign. He was a growing man, and he grew in ability to write, as well as in other things.

In August, 1821, General Tipton was re-elected to the Legislature from his county. At the session following he was chosen a commissioner on the part of Indiana to meet a similar commissioner from Illinois to fix and locate the boundary between these States. The work was done the ensuing summer, and the action of the commissioners ratified by the Legislature during the session of 1822–3.

In March, 1823, General Tipton was appointed by President Monroe general agent for the Pottawattomie and Miami Indians in Northern Indiana. He at once removed to Fort Wayne, where the agency was located. In the spring of 1828, at his suggestion, the agency was removed from Fort Wayne to Logansport. In 1826, two years before his removal to Logansport, he was mainly instrumental in securing from the Indians valuable lands for public settlement.

On the death of United States Senator James Noble, in February, 1831, Governor Ray appointed Robert Hanna to the vacancy. Soon after this appointment was made a movement was started to have the Legislature, when it met, elect General Tipton to the place. For some time he declined to allow his name to be used, but finally he gave way and became a candidate. The following letter, written to Dr. Stewart, of Delphi, will be read with interest:

"AT HOME, July 23, 1831.

"Dear Sir—Your note of yesterday has been received, and in reply I have to inform you that I would greatly prefer remaining in the situation I now hold, as Indian agent, to any other that could be given me. I have many letters on this same subject, and am of opinion we should weigh well this matter before we act. If, after the election, it is found best to use a name, and mine is best (strongest), I will go with my friends for the cause and for our country ; but believe me, that I am not seeking office, and will esteem it a sacrifice of peace and property to do this. My talent is not of the kind that I wish to see in the United States Senate.   JOHN TIPTON."

Such was General Tipton's hold upon the people of Indiana, and such their confidence in his integrity and wisdom, that, notwithstanding his opposition, he was elected in December, 1831, to fill out General Noble's term, and in 1833 he was elected for the full term of six years.   Politically, he was a friend of General Jackson ; but he opposed with all his power that great man in his warfare upon the Bank of the United States.   He believed the bank a necessity, and its issues the best currency the people had ever had.   When party stood in the way of conviction he put party aside.

General Tipton took great interest in the material and educational affairs of Logansport, the town where he lived.   On his removal there he took steps to organize the Eel River Seminary Society and to construct school-houses and raise money to pay teachers.   He built saw and grist mills, and, in fact, was "the motive power that gave form, and imparted energy to every movement calculated to improve society and induce progress toward the unfoldment and utilization of all the natural advantages with which Cass county has been and is so abundantly supplied."   He was the proprietor of additions to Logansport, and was interested with Mr. Carter in the original plat of the town.   In 1838 he was given discretionary powers to remove the disaffected Indians west of the Mississippi river.   He overcame many difficulties in this work and accomplished it with dispatch.

General Tipton was twice married ; the first time, about the year 1818, to Miss —— Shields, who died in less than two years after their marriage.   The second time was in April, 1825, to Matilda, daughter of Captain Spier Spencer, who was killed at the battle of Tippecanoe.   The second Mrs. Tipton died at their residence in Logansport on the 14th of February, 1839, a few days prior to the close of her husband's senatorial career.

The prestige of his name as a civilian and statesman, added to his fame as a military leader, did not completely fill his measure of honor. He was a member of the Masonic fraternity, and occupied a distinguished position in the order. He received the first degrees in Pisgah Lodge, No. 5, at Corydon, Indiana, in the year 1817. He was soon after elected Master, and as such represented that lodge at the first session of the Grand Lodge of Indiana, at which time he was elected Senior Grand Warden, holding that position until 1820, when he became Grand Master. Having served one term, he was again elected Grand Master in 1828. In 1822 he received the Chapter degrees at Louisville, Kentucky, at the hands of Companion Snow, of Ohio. Subsequently he filled many important positions in the Grand Lodge, and was chiefly instrumental in the institution of Wayne Lodge, No. 25, at Fort Wayne, and Tipton Lodge, No. 33, at Logansport, Indiana, in 1828, and also of Logan Royal Arch Chapter, No. 2, at the latter place, in 1837, in all of which he achieved the highest honors.

On the morning of April 5, 1839, having the day previous taken cold while superintending the proposed improvement of the extensive water privileges owned by him, after a few hours of apparently unconscious suffering, he died, in the meridian of life, honored and respected by all save the few who were unable to command his energies in behalf of what his judgment could not approve. He was buried with the honors of war and in accordance with the rites of his cherished order, on Sunday, April 7, 1839.

General Tipton was an excellent judge of land, and his opportunities were such that he was enabled to secure a large amount of the best in the State. He entered an extensive body in Bartholomew county, and donated sixty acres of it, where the city of Columbus now stands, to the county for the purpose of erecting public buildings. For awhile the county seat was called "Tiptonia," in honor of General Tipton, but after awhile the county officers, who were not political friends of the General, changed the name to Columbus. This action of the officials of Bartholomew county was very ungenerous, and deeply touched General Tipton. Afterward he took but little interest

13

in the affairs of that county, and seldom or never visited its capital. He was entitled to the name, by reason of his public services and private liberality, and to take it from him after it had been bestowed was an insult not to be forgotten.

There is an elevation on the bank of White river, at Columbus, probably one hundred feet high, which is known as "Tipton's Mound." In early times it was called "Tipton's Knoll," and the street leading to it was named Tipton street, but now "Knoll" has been changed to "Mound," and Tipton street to Third street. General Tipton's name may be stricken from the map of Columbus, but his donation to Bartholomew county will stand as a memento of his public spirit and private munificence. It was he, also, who donated to the State the beautiful Battle Ground of Tippecanoe. (See journal of constitutional convention.)

In a recent history of the Miami Indians, by Thad. Butler, Esq., it was stated that Samuel McClure, of Marion, was present at the Indian treaty of 1826. Desiring to know the facts in the case I addressed Mr. McClure a letter, and received the following reply:

"MARION, IND., April 10, 1882.

"WILLIAM W. WOOLLEN, ESQ.: Dear Sir—Yours of the 7th inst. at hand and contents noted, and in answer I will say that Mr. Butler got his statement a little wrong when he said that I was at the treaty of the Miami Indians in 1826. I was at the payment which occurred in November, 1826, and my recollection is that General Tipton and Martin M. Ray were there and made the payment at that time. I was but a boy, about nineteen years old, and they were strangers to me. My father, Samuel McClure, came to Wabash in January, 1827, and settled at the spring where the treaty was made, and lived in the cabins built for that purpose.

"I knew General Tipton, but was not intimate with him. Knew him to be a shrewd, smart and very decided man; positive in having his orders obeyed, and he made a good agent for the government and also for the Indians. I was at every payment he made the Indians.

"General Tipton lived in the fort at Fort Wayne when I came to the State, but in the fall of 1827, or in the spring of

1828, he moved from Fort Wayne to the mouth of Eel river, on the east side of the Wabash, and lived in a two-story hewed log house built by a man named Chamberlin, who moved from there to Rochester, or where Rochester now is. I think it was before Logansport was laid off. The General bought lands on the same side of the river and made quite a nice improvement, and lived there until his death. Yours very respectfully,

"SAMUEL McCLURE."

Oliver H. Smith, in his "Early Indiana Trials and Sketches," thus speaks of General Tipton:

"He was about the medium height, well set, short face, round head, low, wrinkled forehead, sunken gray eyes, stern countenance, good chest, stiff sandy hair standing erect from his forehead. He was not what is called an eloquent debater, still he was plain and strong as a speaker. He saw the question clearly, and marched directly at it without rhetorical flourishes. He was a strong, if not an eloquent debater, and was always formidable upon the subject he had in charge, and he seldom or never interfered with the business of others beyond a silent vote."

General Tipton was about five feet eight inches high, was slightly though compactly built, and weighed about 140 pounds. He was muscular and strong for one of his weight, and in manner he was quick and active. His stern features and sharp eyes denoted a man born to command and to see that his commands were obeyed. He had unconquerable will, and when determined upon a line of policy he moved forward with all the energy of his nature to execute it. He always took the lead, and others followed as a matter of course. A leading citizen of Fort Wayne said that Fort Wayne owed more to General Tipton in his day than to any other man. The same is true of Logansport, the city in which he died. Indiana, however, owes him more than any of her cities, for he did as much to free her from Indian depredations and to render her people secure in their homes as any other man of his time.

OLIVER HAMPTON SMITH.

OLIVER HAMPTON SMITH, Congressman and Senator, was born October 23, 1794, on Smith's Island, near Trenton, New Jersey. He came very near being drowned when a boy, having taken the cramp while swimming. In his "Early Indiana Trials and Sketches," he thus describes this incident:

"The breathing ceased, the pressure on my lungs was painful, my head rolled over on the gravelly bottom, my mind was clear as my eyes closed on a bright sun. I fell, as it were, into a sound sleep. Some thirty minutes afterward I felt very sick, the water was running from my mouth, and my eyes seemed to open involuntarily. There stood Isaac Fox bending over me. When I was drowning he ran down to the bank of the river, learned where I went down, floated over me, and saw me lying quietly on the bottom. I had been there near ten minutes. He dived down and brought me up, and took me, unconscious, to a tavern just by, and rolled and rubbed me into life. As I opened my eyes he cried aloud for joy."

Had it not been for the opportune presence and daring of young Isaac Fox this sketch would never have been written.

Young Smith commenced attending school when he was six years old, in a building near his home. He went to this school off and on until 1813, when, on account of the death of his father, he left home and went out into the world to seek his fortune. He visited New York, and then went to Pennsylvania, where for a time he worked in a woolen mill. On reaching his majority he received $1,500 from his father's estate, which he invested in an enterprise that proved to be unfortunate. On

closing it out the only thing he had to show for his patrimony
was a Canadian pony, upon which he rode to his brother Thomas's. He remained there a short time and then started West.
On his arrival at Pittsburg he engaged as captain of a coal boat
bound for Louisville, Kentucky. The boat had another lashed
to it, and during the trip down the river the captain discovered
that the consort of his boat was about to strike a snag. He
knew if she did she would sink and take down with her the one
upon which he stood. He met the exigency with promptitude.
Seizing an ax he cut the rope which bound the vessels together,
and in a moment afterward the fated boat struck the snag and
sank to the bottom. This incident illustrates Mr. Smith's judgment and promptitude.

In 1817 Mr. Smith came to Indiana. He first settled at Rising
Sun, but in a short time he removed to Lawrenceburg and commenced the study of law. In March, 1820, he was personally
examined by Miles C. Eggleston, then Judge of the Third Judicial Circuit, and licensed to practice law. Soon after this he
removed to Versailles, in Ripley county, and opened an office,
but, not liking the location, in a few months he removed to Connersville, where he lived until 1839, at which time he became a
citizen of Indianapolis. At Connersville Mr. Smith, notwithstanding the strong competition, soon obtained a large practice.
He came in contact with the lawyers of Brookville and Lawrenceburg, as well as those at his home, but his ability was such
that he was able to earn and maintain a position among them
equal to the best.

In August, 1822, Mr. Smith was elected to the Legislature
from Fayette county. On his way to Corydon, then the capital
of the State, he stopped over night at Madison and had his
horse taken to the stable by General Milton Stapp, and on the
organization of the House, when the county of Jefferson was
called, the "flaxen-headed hostler" stepped forward and took
the oath of office. General Joe Lane, afterwards famous as a
warrior and statesman, was also a member, as were Dennis Pennington, Isaac Howk, John Dumont, William A. Bullock, and
others whose names have come down to the present day. Mr.
Smith was made chairman of the Judiciary Committee, an important position, and one which is usually given to the ablest

lawyer in the body. It is, therefore, evident that his professional reputation was at that early day well established. In 1824 Governor Hendricks appointed Mr. Smith prosecutor of the Third Judicial Circuit. It was while he held this office that Hudson, Sawyer, Bridge, sr., and Bridge, jr., were indicted and tried for the killing of a party of friendly Indians near Pendleton, in Madison county. In an address delivered before the Marion County Agricultural Society, Mr. Smith thus speaks of this trial :

" I was circuit prosecuting attorney at the time of the trials at the falls of Fall creek, where Pendleton now stands. Four of the prisoners were convicted of murder, and three of them hung, for killing Indians. The court was held in a double log cabin, the grand jury sat upon a log in the woods, and the foreman signed the bills of indictment, which I had prepared, upon his knee ; there was not a petit juror that had shoes on—all wore moccasins, and were belted around the waist, and carried side knives used by the hunters."

In 1826 Mr. Smith became a candidate for Congress against Hon. John Test, who had represented the district for three full terms. The district comprised one-third of the State, and extended along its eastern border from the Ohio river to the Michigan line. Mr. Smith traversed the district from one end to the other, and spoke to the people whenever and wherever he could get an audience. He made a trip, under great difficulties, to Fort Wayne, and when the election came off he received just ten votes in Allen county. Allen county then, as now, voted pretty much one way. But the other counties of the district did better by Mr. Smith, for he was elected by over 1,500 majority. Mr. Smith served with distinction in Congress. His speech on the appropriation to build the Cumberland road was the ablest argument in its favor made in the House. He was attentive and industrious in his public duties. When his term expired he returned to the practice of the law and to the cultivation of his lands.

In December, 1836, he was a candidate for the United States Senate. His competitors were Noah Noble, William Hendricks and Ratliff Boon. On the first ballot he ran behind both Governor Noble and Governor Hendricks, but on the eighth he took the lead, and on the ninth was elected. The second night after the election he reached his home, and the next morning started to Cincinnati with a drove of hogs. But I will let him tell the story :

" Late in the evening I reached Henrie's Mansion House, in Cincinnati, covered with mud. There were many inquiries about the result of our senatorial election ; I was asked if there had been an election. 'Which is elected, Hendricks or Noble?' 'Neither.' 'Who, then, can it be?' 'I am elected.' 'You! What is your name?' 'Oliver H. Smith.' 'You elected a United States Senator! I never heard of you before.'"

In the Senate Mr. Smith was chairman of the Committee on Public Lands. He took great pride in the place, and filled it with distinguished ability.

In 1839, while holding the office of Senator, Mr. Smith removed to Indianapolis, and afterward resided there while he lived. He had a large law practice in the Federal courts as well as in the State courts, and when not in Washington attending to his public duties he was industriously engaged in his profession.

In 1842 Mr. Smith was a candidate for re-election to the Senate, but was defeated by Edward A. Hannegan. In March, 1843, his senatorial services terminated, and he came back to his home. Soon after this he turned his attention to railroads, and Indianapolis is mainly indebted to him for the building of the Indianapolis and Bellefontaine road, now known as the Bee Line. He was at different times president of two railroads, and he directed their affairs with the same energy and intelligence that he displayed in everything he undertook.

In 1857, having measurably abandoned the law, and his railroad enterprises being, in a manner, suspended, he commenced writing a series of sketches for the *Indianapolis Journal* on early times in Indiana. They attracted much attention, and the next year the publishing house of Moore, Wilstach, Keys & Co., of Cincinnati, brought them out in book form. The book is valuable as a record of early Indiana times, containing as it does many historical incidents which otherwise would have been forgotten. Had its extraneous matter been omitted, and the author confined himself to sketching Indiana men and their actions, the book, while not so bulky, would have been of more value than it is. There is a good deal of genuine humor in it, and its matter otherwise is interesting, but its style is not that of a practiced writer. It is, however, a most valuable contribution to the history of the times of which it treats, and will live while the State exists. As a sample of its style I copy the following from a sketch entitled, " Early Condition of Indiana : "

"At the time I came into the State, in March, 1817, there was not a railroad in the United States, nor a canal west of the Allegheny mountains. The telegraph had not been discovered, fire was struck by the flint and steel—the falling sparks were caught in ' punk ' taken from the knots of the hickory tree. There was not a foot of turnpike road in the State, and plank roads had never been heard of. The girdled standing trees covered the cultivated fields, the shovel plow the only cultivator ; no roads west of Whitewater ; not a bridge in the State ; the traveling all done on horseback, the husband mounted before on the saddle, with from one to three of the youngest children in his arms—the wife, with a spread-cover reaching to the tail of the horse, seated behind, with the balance of the children unable to walk, in her lap. We young gentlemen retained the luxury of a single horse ; not a carriage nor buggy in all the country. After some years Mr. Lovejoy brought a buggy without a top to Connersville, from New England. I borrowed it to ride to Wayne county, but I gave up the buggy and took my horse for fear the people would think me proud and it would injure my election to Congress."

Mr. Smith died on Saturday, March 19, 1859. On the Monday following, the Indianapolis bar met in the Court-house to take action upon his death. Governor David Wallace presided, and Simon Yandes, Esq., acted as secretary. Governor Hammond, Jonathan W. Gordon and Hugh O'Neal were appointed a committee on resolutions, and reported a series, in which the private worth and public service of the deceased were recounted and extolled. Speeches were made by Mr. Yandes, John L. Ketcham, Hugh O'Neal and Governor Wallace. The speech of the last gentleman was particularly able and discriminating. In it he said:

"He had no envy in his composition. He never tried to crush others. His egotism had been sometimes spoken of during his life, but it was the simplest egotism the world ever saw. He never assailed another, or tried to pull him down that he might raise himself. Detraction he was never guilty of. He was ambitious, but his ambition was to surpass you, not to ruin you. He would give you all the merit you deserved, and often more, and then claim that he excelled you. This was the extent of this feature of his character."

The meeting appointed Governor Willard, Lieutenant-Governor Hammond, R. L. Walpole, Albert G. Porter, John L. Ketcham, John Coburn, Robert B. Duncan and Governor Wallace Mr. Smith's pall-bearers, and Simon Yandes, Esq., to prepare a eulogy on his life and character. It adjourned to meet at the house of Governor Willard, from whence the members proceeded in a body to the residence of Mr. Smith to attend his funeral.

On the 29th of March Governor Wallace asked the Marion Circuit Court to have the resolutions adopted at the bar meeting spread upon its records. He accompanied the request with a few remarks, after which Simon Yandes, Esq., delivered a very appreciative and eloquent eulogy upon the life and character of the deceased. Mr. Yandes had long been his friend, and for many years was his law partner, and was, probably, better qualified to bring out the prominent and salient points in his character than any other man. In this address he said:

"It is said he was ambitious. It is true he was ambitious of excellence, and this was his greatest merit. He may have been but too ambitious of success, and it is perhaps but fair to admit that is a fault of our profession, especially among its leaders. It does not become me to pass upon a measure of intellect, or the comparative rank of a man so distinguished as he was. No man in the State more filled the public eye; and, indeed, it may be said that his senatorial and other services gave him a reputation that was national.   He and our lamented Marshall had this trait of greatness in common : they rose with the occasion, and always seemed to have a force in reserve.   He was of great and varied ability, prompt alike for the debates of the Senate or the bar ; in the argument of fact or law, and of all classes of cases, he intuitively fastened upon the leading and governing points."

Previous to making the order to have the proceedings of the bar meeting spread upon the records, Judge Majors said :

"As a lawyer Mr. Smith was ever true to the interest of his client.   In the prosecution of his cases in court he displayed much zeal and earnestness.   He was generally well prepared and ready for trial, and if unsuccessful, from inadvertence or oversight, it was a very rare occurrence.   He was an honorable opponent, and very liberal in his practice, yet very capable and sometimes ready to seize upon the weakness or oversight of an adversary.   Mr. Smith's career at the bar was a successful one. He well merits the tribute paid to his memory by his brethren of the bar.   The court takes great pleasure in directing that the resolutions be spread upon the record."

Mr. Smith was a jovial man, of a happy disposition, and he loved to make others happy, hence he would say things which, taken from their surroundings, would appear the height of egotism.   He was an irrepressible talker ; would talk to any one and every one he met.   A gentleman who knew him well, and who was also acquainted with Judge Story, says Mr. Smith, in this respect, more nearly resembled that distinguished jurist than any one he ever knew.   One day a boarder at a hotel kept by a Mr. Sloan (who was a good liver and had a rubicund face) complained, in Mr. Smith's presence, of the fare he had at his hotel, when Mr. Smith remarked, " What better could you expect?   Sloan eats all the good things himself ; there is nothing left for his boarders."   One day a friend said to him that he was too much given to self-praise, when, with a twinkle of the eye, he replied, " Why not praise one's self?   A man can praise himself more in a minute than his friends will in a year."   The reader should bear in mind Mr. Smith's wit and disposition to be facetious, else he will form a wrong idea of his character.

He had vanity, but, according to Governor Wallace, it was the simplest the world ever saw—it harmed no one.

Mr. Smith's disposition was such that he made the best of everything. He never grieved over things that could not be prevented, and when they came upon him he bore them with fortitude aad soon forgot them.

Indiana has produced few men who will be so long remembered as Mr. Smith. As a lawyer he ranked among the very first in the State, as a politician he had great influence, and as a statesman he maintained a very high standing while in the Senate of the United States. He was also an active promoter of railroads, and his book containing sketches of early Indiana will live when his other works are forgotten. He himself says :

"These sketches will live and be read by thousands when the author and his subjects shall sleep together in the silent tomb."

Mr. Smith is in his tomb. Most of the men he mentioned have gone the way of all the earth, but his book still lives, and is more highly prized as the years roll on. It is the only record we have of the men and times of which it treats, and will be read with more interest fifty years from now than it is to-day.

Mr. Smith was five feet ten inches high, and weighed about 180 pounds. He was broad-chested—was large from the waist up. The lower part of his body was correspondingly smaller than the upper, and, when he was subjected to great physical exercise it was too weak to bear him up. Often, when fatigued by travel and compelled to speak, he would address the people sitting. His eyes were dark, his hair was black and stood up upon his head. He had large, shaggy eyebrows, and the general outline of his features denoted energy, pluck and endurance. His place is in the front rank of the great men of Indiana.

ALBERT S. WHITE.

AMONG the most scholarly men who have attained eminence in the politics of Indiana was Albert S. White. His writings were copiously embellished with classical allusions, and his speeches were rich in references and quotations from the most noted thinkers and publicists of the world.

Albert S. White was born in Blooming Grove, New York, October 24, 1803. He graduated from Union College, New York, in 1822, having for a classmate the Hon. William H. Seward, one of the most eminent men of his time. Mr. White studied law at Newburg, New York, and in 1825 was licensed to practice his profession. Soon after this he emigrated to Indiana and located at Rushville. After practicing law a year or so in that town, he removed to Paoli, where he remained but a short time, and then took up his abode in Lafayette. This was in March, 1829, and from that time until his death, Lafayette, and its near neighbor, Stockwell, was his home.

During the session of 1828-29 Mr. White reported the proceedings of the Indiana Legislature for the *Indianapolis Journal*, the first work of the kind done in the State. He did it thoroughly and well, as the files of the paper will attest. In 1830 and 1831 he was the assistant clerk of the Indiana House of Representatives, and from 1832 to 1835 he was its clerk. During these years of service in the House he was brought in close contact with the leading men of the State, a circumstance which was of great benefit to him in his future political career. In 1833 he was a candidate for Congress against Edward A. Hannegan, and was defeated. He had neither the brilliancy nor eloquence of Hannegan, but he was the superior of that erratic man in education, culture, and in most of the qualities which go to make up the successful man. Four years after this he was elected to Congress from his district, defeating Nathan Jackson by a majority twice as large as the latter's vote. The year before he was on the Whig electoral ticket, and in the electoral college cast his vote for William Henry Harrison.

On the expiration of the senatorial term of General John Tipton, in 1839, Mr. White was chosen to succeed him. A protracted struggle took place over this election, the candidates being Governor Noble, Colonel Thomas H. Blake and Mr. White. It was not until the thirty-sixth ballot was reached that an election took place; on that ballot Mr. White received a majority of the votes. He was then a young man, but his training had been such as to acquaint him with public business, and when he took his seat in the Senate he was no novice in the duties of the place. He actively opposed the annexation of Texas, as he did every measure which was calculated to extend the area of slavery. He was of a conservative temperament, and usually voted with the moderate men of his party, but he was conscientiously an anti-slavery man, and always acted with those who strove to confine slavery to the territory it then polluted. He was active in securing grants of land to aid in the extension of the Wabash and Erie canal, and it was largely by his influence that such grants were obtained.

On the expiration of his senatorial term in 1845, Mr. White resumed the practice of the law, but in a short time he abandoned it and entered actively into the business of railroading. He was president of the Indianapolis and Lafayette railroad from its organization until 1856, and during three years of the time was also at the head of the Wabash and Western railway. He performed the duties of these places with ability, and to the satisfaction of the public and the roads.

In 1860, when the country had need of its strongest and most experienced men, Mr. White was again called into the public service. He was elected to Congress from his district, and having had experience both in the House and the Senate, he at once took high rank as a member. He was made chairman of a select committee raised to consider the question of compensated emancipation. Mr. White reported a bill appropriating

$180,000,000 to pay loyal men for their slaves, and $20,000,000 to aid in the colonization of the freedmen. This measure was recommended by Mr. Lincoln, and supported by him with all the influence of his position, but the madness of the Southern people prevented its adoption. Had the men of the South been wise they would have accepted this proffer as a solution of the slavery question. Had they done so there would have been no war, and the devastation that swept over the Southern States would have been avoided. In presenting the bill, Mr. White accompanied it with a report in which the social and political influences of slavery were elaborately argued. He contended that the white and black races should be separated, and the latter colonized in the equatorial regions of America. In his speech supporting the bill, he told the Southern members that if they did not accept the olive branch it would be withdrawn, and their slaves would be taken from them without compensation. The result is known. The offer was rejected and the slaves freed by a proclamation by the President.

Mr. White failed of a renomination to Congress mainly on account of his action in regard to the emancipation question. He was, however, appointed by Mr. Lincoln one of three commissioners to adjust the claims of citizens of Minnesota and Dakota against the government for Indian depredations. He discharged the duties of this position, as he did all his public trusts, honestly and well.

On the death of Hon. Caleb B. Smith, January 7, 1864, President Lincoln appointed Mr. White United States Judge for the District of Indiana. He had been out of law practice so long that many doubted the wisdom of the appointment, but it proved a good one. He soon adapted himself to his new position, and had he lived would have proven a worthy successor of the eminent man who preceded him. But his term was of short duration, for, on the 4th of the next September, eight months from the time of his appointment, he died at his home in Stockwell, a town of which he was one of the founders. His death caused a gloom throughout the State, but its darkest shadows rested over Lafayette, where he had lived so long. A special train left there for Stockwell the Wednesday morning after his death, and soon returned with his remains. They were met at the

Lafayette depot by an immense concourse of people, headed by the mayor, the city council, and the members of the bar. The procession moved to the Fifth-street Methodist church, where an appropriate discourse was delivered by Rev. John L. Smith, after which all that was mortal of Albert S. White was taken to the Greenbush Cemetery, and there interred. Subsequently, William F. Reynolds, a wealthy citizen of Lafayette, and a great admirer of Mr. White, erected over his grave a monument which still stands to mark the resting place of the scholar and jurist. It is of Bedford stone, and represents an oak tree, thunder-riven, blasted, dismantled, its branches shattered by the storm, but enough of the trunk standing to show how loftily and nobly it towered toward the heaven. A pair of doves nestle on a broken limb, and an ivy vine clings and clambers around the root. On a scroll fastened to the tree is inscribed the name, date of birth and death of Mr. White, and a simple tribute to his worth as a man, a legislator, judge, lawyer, citizen, friend. The inscription is as follows:

The grave of
ALBERT S. WHITE.
In all relations of life, admirable.
As a friend, sincere; as a citizen, public spirited; as a lawyer, honest;
as a legislator, wise; as a judge, without reproach.

It is a beautiful tribute of friendship to exalted worth.

In the *Fayette Observer*, of July 22, 1826, is the full text of an address delivered by Mr. White, at Rushville, on the Fourth of July of that year. It is a chaste and elegant production, abounding in classical allusions, couched in the choicest language. It could only have been prepared by a scholar of great erudition, one familiar with the classic authors. In apologizing for the space occupied by the speech, the editor says:

"We pretend not to be very lynx-eyed in historical politics, nor very sensitive to beauties or deformities in rhetoric and belles-lettres; nor, indeed, to profess the talents or to exercise the privileges of reviewing public performances; nevertheless, we can venture to express our belief that the speech of Mr. White, fraught, as it seems to us to be, with many historical incidents that can not fail to be pleasing to those who delight in the story of ' the times that tried men's souls,' will fully compensate its readers for time and labor."

Mr. White was then a young man, fresh from college, and his address was somewhat sophomoric, yet its diction is such as to stamp its author as one who had drunk deeply of the waters of classical lore.

Mr. White had but little in common with the typical Western pioneer, and it is, therefore, somewhat strange that he should have reached the eminence he did. He never sunk his manhood nor lowered his self-respect by trying to get down to the level of every man who approached him. He was in no sense a demagogue, and never sought to curry favor by pretending to be what he was not. He was always dignified, was always a gentleman. The last speech made by Mr. White was delivered on the 1st of June, 1864, at the dedication of Crown Hill Cemetery. It was an elegant production, entirely worthy of its distinguished author. The following extracts from this address will serve to show the author's style:

" You do well, friends, to leave for a day the busy pursuits of common life to plant these altars here. Your city is but little older than Jonah's gourd, but where are now the men who built it? Where are your Nobles, your Wallaces, your Merrills, your Coes, your Mitchells, your Coburns, your Stevenses, your Walpoles, your Footes, your Browns, your Morrises, your Saunderses, your McCartys, and your Blackfords?

" Of some the public history of our State, and of others the traditionary annals of your city, will have preserved the memory, but though their virtues may survive, their persons will have been forgotten. Let the honored remains of such be transferred to these guarded grounds, and here, side by side, let them sleep with other cotemporaries equally dear to memory. As time rolls round and the inmates of these grounds are counted by thousands; as strange guests are deposited here from the myriads of emigrants who will flock to our capital after its fortunes have been made, the story of the pioneer settlers will have a thrilling interest, and their graves a peculiar sanctity. In this respect your cemetery grounds will have a more classic interest than those of Mt. Auburn, Greenwood, Laurel

Hill or Spring Grove, or even the famous cemetery of Pere la Chaise, which is said to contain the dust of Heloise and Abelard."

While Mr. White was in Congress Mr. Lincoln promised him the Lafayette postoffice for a friend, but after he left Washington the President changed his mind, and appointed Mr. James P. Luse. Mr. Luse was not Mr. White's candidate, and when word came to Lafayette of the appointment, Mr. White at once went to Washington to remonstrate against it. As soon as Mr. Lincoln saw him he knew his business and sought to mollify him before he had time to speak. " I see how it is, White," said the President, " but before you proceed to business I want to tell you a story. In one of our large towns in Illinois a new hotel was opened to the public with a splendid entertainment to a large number of invited guests. Among these came a big, lean man, who was supposed to be a guest, and at the table he made tremendous havoc among the viands, eating with a voracity that struck everybody with astonishment. After dinner the man approached the landlord and said : ' I was not invited to your dinner, but I was very hungry, and came of my own accord. I have nothing with which to pay you for your bountiful dinner, and all that you can do in the case is to kick me out of doors, and I shall be greatly obliged if you do kick me out ! I shall feel in that case that I have paid the debt.' "Now, White, I promised you that Lafayette appointment; I admit it. Just before I left Springfield an old friend, with whom I had often fished and hunted and slept, came to see me, and I asked him if I could do anything for him, but he said there was no office he wanted. Well, the other day this good old friend of mine came on, and, of course, was my guest ; and before he left he asked me for the Lafayette postoffice for some friend of his, and I had to give it to him. You see, White, I admit I had promised it to you, but what could I do but give it to him? Now, if you will kick me out of doors, and go quits, I shall feel greatly obliged to you," whereupon the President turned his back to Mr. White, drew aside his coat tail, and asked for the kick. Mr. White used to tell this story, and add :

14

"Just think of it! The President of the United States asking
to be kicked!"

In person Mr. White was small and spare. He had a thin
visage, a large Roman nose and a narrow chest. Physically
he was weak ; intellectually he was strong. Had his career in
life depended alone upon his body he would have been a failure ;
but depending, as it did, upon his mind and heart as well, he was
a success. He was one of the first men of the Wabash country
and of the State, and his name will not be forgotten while learning and scholarship are cherished, and honor and patr otism
revered.

EDWARD A. HANNEGAN.

EDWARD A. HANNEGAN was born in Ohio, but early in life he moved to Lexington, Kentucky, and grew to manhood there. He acquired a good education, studied law, and, when twenty-three years old, was admitted to the Lexington bar. Not long after this he left Kentucky and started West in search of a location. When he reached Covington, a town on the Wabash, he stopped, and for many years afterward made it his home. He opened an office and commenced the practice of his profession. In a short time he obtained a lucrative business, his practice not being confined to the county in which he lived, but extending to many others in the western part of the State. But the law was too dry to satisfy his fiery nature, so he entered politics. He was elected to the State Legislature, and became a leading member of that body. He advocated the passage of a bill chartering the State Bank of Indiana, and was particularly active in trying to secure an appropriation for the improvement of the Wabash river at the rapids. This was in January, 1833, and the next August he was elected to Congress from his district, defeating Albert S. White, afterward his colleague in the United States Senate. He was re-elected in 1835, and during his two terms established a reputation for eloquence excelled by few in the House. In 1840 he was again a candidate for Congress, but, after a most laborious and exciting contest, he was defeated by Henry S. Lane, afterwards Governor of Indiana, and then a Senator of the United States.

The Legislature of 1842 was very evenly divided between the Whig and Democratic parties. Oliver H. Smith was the Whig candidate for United States Senator, and General Tilghman A.

Howard the Democratic. On the first ballot Mr. Smith received 72 votes; General Howard, 74 votes; Edward A. Hannegan, 3 votes; and Joseph G. Marshall, 1 vote. On the second ballot Mr. Smith received 75 votes; General Howard, 74 votes; and Mr. Hannegan, 1 vote. On the third ballot Mr. Smith received 73 votes; General Howard, 73 votes; and Mr. Hannegan, 3 votes. The fourth ballot was the same as the third, except that Governor William Hendricks received one of the votes which before was cast for Mr. Hannegan. On the fifth ballot Mr. Smith received 71 votes; General Howard, 73 votes; and Mr. Hannegan, 2 votes. On the sixth ballot Mr. Hannegan received 76 votes, and was elected, General Howard having withdrawn from the race.

This election caused much excitement at the time. David Hoover, of Wayne county, and Daniel Kelso, of Switzerland county, refused to vote for General Howard, and, as he could not be elected without their support, he withdrew from the contest. It was said that both Hoover and Kelso were pledged to the support of Mr. Smith. Hoover, who was a Democrat, elected from a Whig county, voted for Mr. Smith on the first and second ballots, and then went over to Mr. Hannegan. Kelso voted for Hannegan on every ballot; therefore it will be seen that Hoover and Kelso virtually selected the Senator.

Mr. Hannegan took his seat in the Senate on the 4th of December, 1843, and served until the 4th of March, 1849. During his service in that body he made several speeches which attracted the attention of the country, notably, one on the Oregon boundary. He occupied an extreme position on this question, being " for 54-40, or fight." In a letter to the committee inviting him to be present at a meeting of the friends of Mr. Dallas, held in Philadelphia, January 8, 1846, he sent the following toast:

" Oregon—Every foot or not an inch; 54 deg., 40 min. or *delenda est Britannia.*"

The committee replied: " The Hon. Edward A. Hannegan. The true-hearted American statesman, who truly represents the people on the Oregon question—the whole of it or none; Oregon or war!"

He attacked President Polk, who favored a compromise policy, in a most bitter manner. He said of him:

"So long as one human eye remains to linger on the page of history the story of his abasement will be read, sending him and his name together to an infamy so profound, a damnation so deep, that the hand of resurrection will never drag him forth. So far as the whole tone, spirit and meaning of the remarks of the Senator from North Carolina are concerned, if they speak the language of James K. Polk, then James K. Polk has spoken words of falsehood with the tongue of a serpent."

He closed the speech as follows:

"For the singleness and sincerity of my motives I appeal to heaven. By them I am willing to be judged now and hereafter, so help me God, when, prostrate at thy feet, I falter forth my last brief prayer for mercy on an erring life."

Mr. Hannegan's votes in the Senate were always in accord with those of his party friends. On the 1st of March, 1847, Mr. Upham, of Vermont, while the Mexican treaty was before the Senate, moved "that there shall be neither slavery nor involuntary servitude in any Territory which shall hereafter be acquired or annexed to the United States, otherwise than in punishment for crimes." Among the nays was Mr. Hannegan. In this, however, he but obeyed his party's will, for he had for company Senators Bright, Cass and Dickinson, from the free States, and all the Senators from the South.

The Thirtieth Congress expired March 4, 1849, and with it Mr. Hannegan's senatorial term. In its closing hours Mr. Polk nominated him for Minister to Prussia, and the Senate confirmed the appointment. He was commissioned on the 29th of March, 1849, and at once sailed for Berlin. Mr. Hannegan was unfitted for diplomacy both by nature and by habit. He was naturally open and frank, carrying "his heart upon his sleeve," and besides, his convivial habits were such as to make him an unsafe depository of secrets. It is therefore no wonder that his career at Berlin was such as added nothing to his character or that of his government. He was recalled on the 13th

of the next January, and with that recall the public life of Mr.
Hannegan ended. He returned to his home at Covington, and
the next year was a candidate for the State Legislature. At
that time the question of removing the county seat from Covington to a more central point agitated the people of his county,
and the canvass was made mainly upon that issue. Jacob Dice,
a Democrat, who favored the removal of the county seat to
Chambersburg, became a candidate against Mr. Hannegan, and
receiving the votes of those who favored a change, and also of
many Whigs at the county seat who were particularly hostile to
his opponent, was elected. Mr. Hannegan took his defeat
much to heart. Like many other generous and warm-hearted
men, he loved his cups, and his defeat caused him to drink the
harder. The habit grew upon him until, in a fit of madness, he
killed one whom he dearly loved. This tragic event took place
in his own house, and at the time created intense excitement
not only at Covington, but throughout the State. Mr. Hannegan and his brother-in-law, Captain Duncan, had been drinking
deeply, and angry words passed between them. Mrs. Hannegan, who was present, asked her husband to go up stairs, which
he did, and lay down upon his bed. Captain Duncan started
after him, when his sister requested him not to go, saying her
husband was drinking and trouble might ensue. But he refused
to heed her, and went up stairs and into Mr. Hannegan's room.
As he entered, the latter half arose and awaited the Captain's
coming. A Spanish dagger was within his reach, and as Captain Duncan approached he called Mr. Hannegan a coward and
slapped him in the face. Hannegan snatched the dagger, and
in an instant drove it to the hilt in the Captain's body. The latter, all wounded and bloody, walked into an adjoining room and
lay down to die. When his sister came, and friends gathered
about him, he told them no blame attached to Mr. Hannegan,
that the fault was all his own. Hearing this, Hannegan ran to
the wounded man, threw his arms around him, and madly kissed
him again and again upon the forehead, sobbing all the time as
though his heart would break. The wounded man died the
next day and was buried in the cemetery at Covington. Never
afterward did Hannegan enter that city of the dead. Not even

when his wife died and was there laid to rest would he cross its portals.

In the *Madison Banner*, of May 13, 1852, a paper conducted by the author of this sketch, is the following notice of Captain Duncan's death :

" Captain Duncan, whose unfortunate altercation with ex-Senator Hannegan we mentioned yesterday, died on Saturday, twenty-six hours after receiving the fatal blow. Captain D. was a brother of Mrs. Hannegan, and a member of her family. He was formerly a citizen of Newark, Ohio, and commanded a company of mounted riflemen during the Mexican war. His personal appearance was exceedingly prepossessing and commanding. He was about forty years of age, and had never been married.

"Nothing has transpired as to the cause of this lamentable affair, but it is generally attributed to the influence of liquor. No steps have yet been taken to arrest Mr. Hannegan. The anguish of his mind is said to be indescribable. His friends are apprehensive that the consequences of his rash act will drive him mad. What a lesson !

> "' Better be with the dead,
> Whom we, to gain our peace, have sent to peace,
> Than on the torture of the mind to lie
> In restless ecstasy. Duncan is in his grave ;
> After life's fitful fever, he sleeps well ;
> Passion has done its worst, nor steel, nor poison,
> Malice domestic, foreign levy, nothing
> Can touch him farther.' "

Mr. Hannegan was not indicted and tried for the killing of Captain Duncan, the universal sentiment of the people being in his favor. But had he been convicted it would have added nothing to his suffering. He sought surcease of sorrow by leaving the State and going to a distant place, but peace did not come. He removed to St. Louis in 1857, and on the 25th of January, 1859, he died in that city. His remains were brought to Terre Haute and deposited in the earth with imposing ceremonies, on the banks of his own beloved Wabash. Let us hope that the peace which came not to him on earth was found when he entered the dark portals of death.

Mr. Hannegan was warm in his friendships, and had a large personal following. He and Judge John R. Porter and Josephus Collett maintained the closest intimacy for many years. It was their custom to often meet at the home of Mr. Collett and spend days together. Hannegan was a brilliant conversationalist, Porter a fascinating talker, and Collett the best story teller in the country 'round about. When they met it was seldom they parted until

"Some wee short hour ayont the twal."

One evening they entered into a compact that the one who first died should return to his friends, if it were possible, and give them words or tokens of what was going on in the other world.

After this every time they met, before separating, they would clasp hands and renew the covenant. Judge Porter first "crossed the river," and soon afterward Mr. Hannegan wrote Mr. Collett a note stating that he would be with him the next Wednesday evening. He came at the time, and was received by Mr. Collett with all his wonted cordiality. But he was nervous and ill at ease. After supper the two friends conversed until bedtime without either of them naming Judge Porter. When the time for retiring arrived, Mr. Collett announced it, and proposed conducting Mr. Hannegan to his room, whereupon Hannegan sprang to his feet, and in an excited manner said : "Joe Collett, has John Porter been back to you?" "No, Mr. Hannegan," replied Mr. Collett; "has he appeared to you?" "No; and now I know there is no coming back after death. John Porter never broke his word." This instance illustrates Mr. Hannegan's faith in mankind, and his confidence in the veracity of his friend.

When Mr. Hannegan was on his way to Covington in search of a location, he was overtaken in the woods, one evening, by darkness. He saw a cabin, and, approaching it, asked for shelter for the night. It was given him, and next morning, when ready to resume his journey, he demanded his bill, and was answered there was none. This was a boon to the young man, for he had but a pittance in his pocket, and could ill have spared the small amount he expected to pay. He never forgot the kindness then shown him, and years afterward, when he had become famous, he repaid the debt with interest doubly compounded. A rich neighbor had killed the son of the woman who had given him shelter and bread in the woods, and Hannegan was employed to prosecute him. The attorney for the defense tried to make capital for his client by speaking of the efforts made to convict him, dwelling particularly on the employment of the most eloquent man in the country to prosecute him. Hannegan replied by telling the story of his stopping in the cabin in the woods, and saying that the woman who then gave him shelter and bread had come to him in her extremity, and requested his services in prosecuting the murderer of her son. "She said she had no money to give me," said Hannegan, "but she had a horse which I could send for when I pleased." With flashing eye and quivering lips, he continued: "When Edward A. Hannegan and his family are starving for bread, then, but not till then, will he send for the horse."

In some respects Mr. Hannegan was superstitious. He would not commence a journey or any important business on Friday. Neither would he pay out money on Monday, and so well was this fact known that his bills were never presented on that day.

For years a great rivalry existed between Covington and Attica. Hannegan headed it in Covington, and James D. McDonald in Attica. In 1848, when the water was being let into the Wabash and Erie Canal below Lafayette, the level at Attica was necessarily filled before the Covington level was reached. Some ten days before the latter level could be filled Mr. Hannegan and a party of his friends went to Attica for the purpose of having the water drawn into the Covington level. The boatmen prevented this from being done, and Mr. Hannegan left for home. A few days afterward he returned, with some two hundred followers, determined to turn on the water. The party took possession of the lock, placed guards around it, and turned on the water. Ezekiel M. McDonald, and some half dozen other citizens of Attica, were present, and mixed with the crowd in a friendly way. A Covington man knocked a Mr. Herr, of Attica, down, while he was in the water, and Mr. McDonald, on attempting to go to his assistance, was struck with a club and badly hurt. The Covington men, having accomplished their purpose, returned home and disbanded. Mr. McDonald determined to hold Mr. Hannegan personally responsible for the assault upon him, and punish him for it. Some six months afterward he and Hannegan met at the Brown Hotel, in Covington, and McDonald at once assaulted him. The parties were separated before either was hurt, and Hannegan left the hotel. He went home and armed himself and returned at the head of some forty of his friends, and demanded that McDonald be surrendered to him. The latter was secreted in the house, and knew what was going on. The landlord, however, told the mob that McDonald had gone, and it left in search of him. A horse was obtained, and McDonald left town by way of the Crawfordsville road, and by a circuitous route reached his home. Had he been caught he would have been killed, so excited and mad were Hannegan and his friends.

Two years after this, Mr. Hannegan made overtures to Mr. McDonald for a settlement of the feud between them. With the assistance of mutual friends a reconciliation was reached, and ever afterward they and their families were upon the best of terms.

Mr. Hannegan's manners were elegant. He was courteous to ladies and delighted in their society. While he was in the Senate, Mrs. Maury, an English woman, visited the United States and afterward published a book. She was fascinated with Hannegan, and in her book praises him to the skies. She says:

" This is a genuine son of the West; ardent, impulsive and undaunted; thinking, acting and daring with the most perfect freedom. His spirit is youthful and buoyant, and he is ever sanguine of success, though he feels acutely the bitterness of disappointment. Show me a gentler, more affectionate nature than Edward Hannegan, you can not; and believe me, the Western men in general resemble him. * * * When Mr. H. made his speech on the Oregon question, I was in the gallery immediately above, and in the excitement of the moment I threw down my glove to the speaker; it fell at his side. The chivalrous Hannegan instantly picked it up, pressed it to his lips, looked gratefully up to the gallery, bowed and placed it in his bosom. The fortunate glove was transmitted by the next day's post to the lady of the Senator, then in Indiana. I preserve the less happy fellow to it. * * *

" This Senator was not born in the State he represents, but in Kentucky (?), in the city of Lexington (??); consequently, in the very atmosphere of Henry Clay, and I can not well tell how he escaped being a Whig. He is a Presbyterian, but has committed his only son to the care of Dr. Hailandière, Catholic Bishop of Vincennes, in Indiana, to be educated at the college in that city. A devoted lover of the country and of its independence, he so pined at last in Washington that he was compelled to go home for a fortnight to refresh his spirits and recruit his health. I met him on the Ohio on his way. 'Come home with me,' said he to the Doctor and myself; ' come home with me, and I will show you the lovely valley of the Wabash. I can endure those hot and crowded halls no longer ; I must have free air and space to roam in ; I like to hunt when I please, and to shoot when I please, and to fish when I please, and to read when I please. Come home with me and see how I live in Indiana.' "

Mr. Hannegan, like most other men, did not enjoy a practical joke at his own expense. A jolly Irishman, still living at Covington, delighted in playing pranks upon his distinguished friend. On one occasion a Teutonic sausage-grinder was holding forth to a crowd upon the wonderful merits of his sausage, and declaring that " Meester Hannegan, he buys 'em," when the jolly Irishman, with a twinkle in his eye, said: " Pshaw ! Hannegan says you make your sausages out of dead hogs." " Did he say dot; did he say mine sausage was made from dead hogs?" asked the butcher, terribly excited. " Yes, he did," replied the Irishman, as he left and went on his way. The meat man wanted to hear no more. With coat off and shirt sleeves rolled up, he ran, butcher-knife in hand, to Hannegan's office door, which he pounded vigorously. Mr. Hannegan, who, at the time, was entertaining some friends, quickly turned the knob and met the irate butcher face to face. There stood the angry German, flourishing his butcher-knife, and pouring forth a torrent of broken words with such energy that Hannegan was really alarmed. "Meester Hannegan, Johnny Mac says you tells him I make sausenges out'en dead hogs!" yelled the butcher. "I makes nice, clean sausenges, and I wants to know about it." "Why, my good friend," said Mr. Hannegan, "who told you that?" "Vy, John Mac." "Did he; did the rascal say that? Let's go and see him." Excusing himself to his friends, Mr. Hannegan and the sausage man started out to hunt the jolly Irishman. Arriving at his house, he was called out, and when he appeared a broad smile upon his face soon developed into a loud laugh. "Now, Mr. Mac," began Hannegan, "did you intimate that I cast any reflections on this man or his business? Why, sir," growing more excited, "he was about to assassinate me." The Teuton began talking, also, and between the two, the noise was lively. After awhile there was a lull, and the joker said to the butcher, 'You don't make sausages out of live hogs, do you?" Light broke in upon the German, and uttering the words — —, he walked away. By this time Hannegan was somewhat mollified, and addressing the Irishman said: "Johnny Mac, jokes are jokes, but when they reach the point that a friend is in danger of assassination, it is carrying them a little too far." The story soon spread over town, and Hannegan enjoyed it as much as any one; but the sausage-grinder's occupation was gone. He could not stand the raillery to which he was subjected, so he left Covington and sought fields for peddling his sausage where jokes did not so much abound.

Mr. Hannegan was on the steamer Princeton, February 28, 1844, when a large gun exploded, killing Abel P. Upshur, Secretary of State, Thomas W. Gilmer, Secretary of the Navy, and several other distinguished men. President Tyler was on board, but was not injured by the explosion. In a letter to Dr. Stewart, of Delphi, dated March 1, 1844, Mr. Hannegan says:

"The horrible occurrence on the Princeton you will see in the papers. I was standing with General Jessup at the mainmast, some twenty-five or thirty feet from the explosion, and was the first person who pressed forward to the place. Colonel Benton had been prostrated by the awful concussion, having been standing immediately behind the breech of the gun. When I reached his side he was lifting a poor sailor in his arms whose

left arm was shot off; thoughtless of himself, he thought only
of the poor, suffering man. He was cool and collected. I asked
him if he was wounded. "No, Hannegan," was his reply;
"but look at this poor fellow. Bring a surgeon to him, quick."
Judge Phelps, of Vermont, was standing near Benton at the
time of the explosion, and acted likewise with great coolness and
courage. He declared publicly that injustice shall no longer be
done to Benton's generous and noble heart; that he will seek
an occasion in the Senate to pay him a tribute. He is, as you
know, a warm Whig. Benton and Phelps were standing immediately by the bulwarks which were swept away, and their
hats were also carried overboard, with the bonnet of a lady who
stood between them. Benton is out of danger, but not able to
sit up. The force of the concussion struck his breast; had it
struck his head, he must have been instantly killed."

When Mr. Hannegan was in the Senate, Bishop Simpson
was President of Asbury University at Greencastle. Mr. Hannegan had a high appreciation of Bishop Simpson's power as a
preacher, and invited him to go to Washington and speak to
the "Godless Congressmen." The bishop went, and notwithstanding Mr. Hannegan's effort to get him an audience, he
preached his first sermon largely to empty benches. But those
who did hear him were charmed with his discourse, and his
subsequent appointments drew crowded houses. He remained
at Washington over a month, preaching every Sunday, and always with much acceptability. Mr. Hannegan is entitled to the
credit of first introducing Bishop Simpson to the leading men
of the country, and of securing for him a hearing which was the
commencement of his reputation as one of the best pulpit orators
in the country.

In some respects Mr. Hannegan was a great man, but in others he fell far below several of his cotemporaries. He was
like the comet that flashes athwart the heavens, dazzling the
eye a moment with its brilliancy, and then disappearing. He
and Jesse D. Bright were in the Senate together, and although
he was Mr. Bright's senior in years and in public service, he
did not exercise anything like the influence of that gentleman,
either in the Senate or in the country. He was a more brilliant
man than Bright, but he lacked the latter's strength of charac-

ter and his knowledge of men. In speaking of the Indiana Senators of that day, it was always Bright and Hannegan, not Hannegan and Bright. Governor Willard used to say, "Start Hannegan down stream at high tide, and he can gather more driftwood than any man I know, but he isn't worth a curse to row up stream."

The following incident is related as illustrative of Hannegan's impulsive nature. A paper called the *Fountain Ledger* was started in Covington by J. P. Luse for the purpose of supporting the Whig cause in the then strong Democratic county of Fountain, and defeating Hannegan. It became very bitter and personal in its war with the *People's Friend*, then published by Solon Turman. It was especially severe on Hannegan, and hence the editor incurred the enmity of him and his friends. After the election, which resulted in the defeat of Hannegan, Mr. Luse bought the *Lafayette Journal* and removed to Lafayette. Shortly after the unfortunate homicide of Captain Duncan by his brother-in-law, Hannegan, occurred. It was expected that Mr. Luse would embrace that opportunity to denounce Hannegan and inflame the public mind against him. On the contrary, he published a very mild, kind and considerate editorial, referring most generously to Hannegan, and asking the calm judgment of the country on his awful deed. Some two years after, Mr. Hannegan accidentally met Mr. Luse at Danville, Illinois, rushed up to him, embraced him, and in his impulsive and characteristic way evinced his deep appreciation of his kindness. Ever after, till Hannegan's death, they were friends.

In person Mr. Hannegan was below the medium height; he was firmly and compactly built, and in his latter days was inclined to corpulency. He had a ruddy complexion, blue eyes, and light brown hair. He was a charming companion, a fascinating talker, and a public speaker of true eloquence. He was not a profound man nor a great scholar, but what he lacked in profundity he made up in brilliancy, and his deficiencies in scholarship were largely compensated for by his quick wit, his fertile imagination, and his power to express himself in the choicest of language. He was of Irish descent, and inherited many of the characteristics of that warm-hearted and impulsive race.

JESSE D. BRIGHT.

For twenty years prior to 1860, Jesse D. Bright was a leading man in Indiana. He was the autocrat of his party, and ruled it as absolutely as did Governor Morton the Republican party when in the zenith of his power. Indeed, in many respects these men were alike. Both loved power and knew the art of getting it; both loved a friend and hated an enemy, and both knew how to reward the one and punish the other.

Mr. Bright was born in Norwich, New York, December 18, 1812, and came to Indiana when a boy. His family located at Madison, and there young Bright grew up to man's estate. He had a good constitution, and was one of the healthiest and strongest men in the town. He was fond of athletic sports, and was always ready to test the strength and endurance of any who chose to challenge him. He would accommodate them with a friendly tussle or a regular knockdown—just as they pleased to have it. I do not mean by this that he was quarrelsome, for he was not; but I do mean that he had muscle and grit, and was not loth to let it be known. His physique was splendid. He weighed about two hundred pounds and had a well-proportioned body, save, probably, a little too much fullness in the abdomen. His face was cleanly shaven, and his clothes fitted him well and were of good quality. He had a good head and a good face, and he stood straight upon his feet and carried himself as one having authority. He was imperious in his manner, and brooked no opposition either from friend or foe. Indeed, he classed every man as foe who would not do his bidding, and made personal devotion to himself the test of Democracy. He had natural talents of a high order, but was deficient in education and cultivation. In his public speeches he was a frequent violator of grammar and of logic, but his manner was so earnest and his delivery so impressive, that what he said found a lodgment in the minds of his hearers. He was the Danton of Indiana Democracy, and was both loved and feared by his followers.

Mr. Bright was the best judge of men that I ever knew. Indeed he seemed to have an intuitive knowledge of men and their thoughts. He seldom or never gave his confidence to a man that abused it. He often withheld it from gentlemen of his own political household and bestowed it upon those of another faith. As an illustration of this fact the following incident is narrated: One evening in 1852 the editor of a Whig paper was in Mr. Bright's parlor on invitation, when the door-bell rang, and Mr. Bright said: "I must ask of you the favor to step into another room; that is John A. Hendricks at the door; I don't want him to meet you here; he wants my influence for Congress; I must humor him, but I can not trust him; he is uncertain anyhow, and if he is not nominated by the Democrats will leave us and go over to the opposition; if he sees you here he will suspect where you get some of your items about Joe Wright. Mr. Hendricks was not nominated by the Democrats, did go over to the opposition, and in 1856 was the candidate of the "People's" party for Congress in the Third District, and was defeated by the late Judge Hughes. He was killed at the battle of Pea Ridge during the rebellion, and his photograph may be seen in our State Library. He was a son of ex-Governor William Hendricks, and a cousin of Hon. Thomas A. Hendricks.

Mr. Bright was an earnest man, and whatever he undertook he did with all his might. There was nothing "'alf and 'alf" about him. He struck out from the shoulder, right and left, and his blows were those of a giant. He never conciliated; he demanded absolute obedience; he permitted no divided allegiance, and the Democrat that looked with favor upon his rival, Governor Wright, committed an offense for which there was no atonement. In those days Governor Wright was a strong man with the people of Indiana. His character was entirely different from that of Mr. Bright. He had not the boldness nor the courage of the Senator, and in the battle for the leadership had to go to the wall. Bright hated him with a healthy hatred, and was disposed to make war on him " to the knife, and the knife to the hilt." However, through the interposition of friends a truce was established ; but it lasted only a short time. The late James Blake and Judge S. E. Perkins once published a card in which they said that all matters of difference between these Democratic leaders having been submitted to them for settlement, were satisfactorily and honorably adjusted. How hollow the truce ! The fires smouldered and soon broke out again. Both wanted to go to the United States Senate, but the matter was finally settled by the return of Bright and the appointment of Wright as Minister to Berlin.

Mr. Bright chose the law for a profession, and was early admitted to the bar. At that time the Madison bar was the ablest in the State. Marshall, and Sullivan, and Stevens, and the elder Bright, and several other distinguished men were members of it, so when the young lawyer opened his office, business was slow in coming. He never mastered the philosophy of law, and did not equal his brother Michael as a lawyer, but he spoke well, and, being popular with the people, succeeded in getting a fair amount of business.

The county of Jefferson was Whig, and Mr. Bright was a Democrat of the strictest sect, but notwithstanding this he was elected Probate Judge of the county, and held the office for years. Subsequently he was appointed United States Marshal for Indiana, and it was while in this office that he laid the foundation of his political career. His business took him all over the State, and he made friends wherever he went. His knowledge of mankind was such that he never, or very rarely, mistook his man, and the friends he made were bound to him with hooks of steel. Afterwards, when he needed these friends to help on his political fortunes, he knew where to find them, and they failed him not.

Away back in the forties, the Whigs of Jefferson county nominated Williamson Dunn for the State Senate. He was a pioneer of the State, and commanded a company of rangers in the war of 1812. He was a man of great physical and moral courage and unquestioned integrity. But he was a Presbyterian elder and held to the faith and teachings of Calvin with the

15

greatest tenacity. He was ultra on the Sunday question, and was very active in trying to stop the Sunday mails. This caused dissatisfaction with his nomination, and the disaffected brought out Shadrach Wilber, also a Whig, as an independent candidate. The fight waxed warm between the supporters of Dunn and of Wilber, and much bad blood was aroused. When the blood was seething a new Richmond entered the field. He saw his chance and embraced it. He knew the passion between the friends of the other candidates was too intense to be allayed, so he entered the lists and won the fight. That Richmond was Jesse David Bright.

In the State Senate Mr. Bright took rank, at once, as the leader of his party. In fact, he was a born leader of men. He always stood at the fore-front of the line.

In 1843 Mr. Bright was nominated for Lieutenant-Governor on the ticket with James Whitcomb. He canvassed the State thoroughly, speaking in every county. He had not the grace nor the eloquence of his chief, but his speeches were equally or more effective. He had an earnestness of manner, and a certain rough and turgid eloquence that won the people's favor, and when the canvass closed he had established a reputation as a politician second to none in the State. He was elected, and came to Indianapolis the leader and beau ideal of the young Democracy.

No one in his party disputed his right to lead, and no one outside of it, except his great compeer, Joseph G. Marshall, dared cross swords with him in the city where he lived. His success in doing what he attempted was proverbial. He filled his office well, presiding with fairness and dignity, and so won the affections of the Senators and Representatives that they soon elected him to the Senate of the United States. At this time [when elected to the United States Senate], he was barely eligible to a seat on account of his age, he being the youngest man that had ever taken a seat in the Senate.

In 1850 he was a candidate for re-election to the Senate. Robert Dale Owen, who was also a candidate, openly charged him with having attempted to secure his return by bribery. Being advised of this charge a few days before the election he applied to Postmaster-General Campbell and obtained a special order to be taken to the Ohio river in the United States mail coach. [At that time no railroad crossed the mountains.] At Wheeling he took a steamer for Cincinnati, and from that city telegraphed to Madison to have an engine and car ready to convey him to Indianapolis. When he stepped ashore in the city of his home he at once boarded the car, which awaited him, and was borne to the State capital as fast as steam could propel him. Great was the wonderment among the politicians at Indianapolis when they saw him upon the streets of that city. They thought he was at Washington, and expected the election to come off in his absence. He sought Mr. Owen, and soon satisfied that gentleman that he had been misinformed about the alleged bribery. Mr. Owen thereupon withdrew from the race, and Mr. Bright was re-elected without further contest.

In 1856, his second term having expired, he again sought a re-election, but the Republican members of the Legislature refused to go into an election. They had met the Democratic members in joint convention to canvass the votes for Governor and Lieutenant-Governor, and when that was done took their leave and refused to go into joint convention again.

The Democratic members adjourned to a fixed day, and when it arrived again met, but did nothing but organize and adjourn until another day. The intention had been to elect the Senators [two were to be chosen] at the second meeting, but Mr. Bright refused to accept an election unless satisfied it would be legal, of which he had his doubts. At his suggestion, the question was referred to Samuel E. Perkins, James Hughes and Joseph W. Chapman, all eminent lawyers and jurists, who subsequently reported to a caucus that an election held under the circumstances existing would be legal. The Democratic and American members of the two houses soon after this met in joint convention and elected Messrs. Bright and Fitch to the Senate. The next Legislature, being Republican, declared this election illegal, and chose Henry S. Lane and William M. McCarty as Senators, and these gentlemen went to Washington and claimed their seats. They were, however, refused admission to the Senate by a party vote, with the exception of Senators Douglas, Mason and Broderick, Democrats, who voted to admit them. This vote of Douglas made Mr. Bright his enemy for life, and in 1860 he opposed Mr. Douglas's election to the Presidency with all the influence and power he possessed.

In the Senate of the United States Mr. Bright did not rank high as a debater, but he was good at committee work, and won and maintained a respectable standing. He was popular with the Senators, and enjoyed their personal friendship. Between him and Henry Clay there was a warm attachment, and more than once was he the guest of that gentleman at Ashland. When Mr. Clay introduced his omnibus bill, and the Committee of Thirteen was raised, Mr. Bright had a place upon it. He stood by the author of this bill during the bitter fight over it, and when it went to pieces clung to the fragments. Such was his standing that on the death of Vice President King, in 1853, he was elected President *pro tempore* of the Senate. He filled this office until the inauguration of John C. Breckinridge, in 1857, and thus for four years stood within one step of the Presidency.

While President of the Senate he did not assign Sumner, Chase and Hale to places upon the committees, and when asked his reason for failing to do so, replied: " Because they are not members of any healthy political organization." He did not see the seeds of the great Republican party which were then sprouting and about to burst through the ground.

In 1857, when forming his cabinet, President Buchanan offered Mr. Bright the secretaryship of State, which office he declined.

At the time of Mr. Bright's entrance into political life, and for many years afterward, public sentiment in Indiana was strongly Southern. Northern Indiana was but sparsely settled, and the immigrants to the southern and central parts of the State were mostly from the South. Mr. Bright lived on the southern border, and in sentiment and feeling was a Southern man. He owned a farm in Kentucky, well stocked with negroes, and was thus identified with the South by interest as well as feeling. Once he had the temerity to bring one of his slaves to Madison, but somehow or other she got away, probably by the help of Chapman Harris or Elijah Anderson. A Senator from a free State, he was the owner of slaves and a representative of Indiana, his largest material interests were in Kentucky. During most of the time for many years he lived at Washington and in Kentucky in the midst of slavery. So it is no wonder he became politically permeated with the virus of that abominable institution. When the war came and slavery was about to be destroyed, he had no heart for the contest. All the Southern Senators, save those from the border States, excepting Andrew Johnson only, left Washington and went home to help on the rebellion. Mr. Bright did not believe that war would restore the Union as it was, and therefore he opposed the war. He wanted the Union to stand dominated and controlled by Southern men, and rather than have any other Union he was willing to see the country go to pieces. It is but just to say that he was not a secessionist *per se*, and would gladly have had the Union remain as it was. He knew that war meant the destruction of slavery, and, being a slaveholder, he opposed the war. Just before the commencement of hostilities, but when it was apparent that the conflict must come, he wrote a letter to Jefferson Davis, the provisional President of the Confederate States, introducing an old friend and former fellow-townsman. The letter was as follows:

" WASHINGTON, D. C., March 1, 1861.

" MY DEAR SIR—Allow me to introduce to your acquaintance my friend, Thomas Lincoln, of Texas. He visits your capital mainly to dispose of what he regards a great improvement to fire-arms. I recommend him to your favorable consideration as a gentleman of the first respectability, and reliable in every respect. Very truly yours,   JESSE D. BRIGHT.
" To His Excellency Jefferson Davis, President of the Confederation of States."

Lincoln was arrested on his way to the Confederate capital with the letter of Mr. Bright upon his person. Proceedings were at once commenced against the writer, and after a short and angry contest, ended in his expulsion from a body in which he had sat for sixteen years and over which he had presided for a quarter of the time. He defended himself as best he could, and when the vote was taken, gathered up his books and papers, and left the Senate never to return. He came back to Indiana, and for some time quietly staid at his home. But when the Democracy, in 1862, elected a majority of the Legislature, he determined to be a candidate for his unexpired time in the Senate. When the Legislature met he came to Indianapolis and asked his party friends to vindicate him by sending him back to the body which had disowned him. But "the scepter had departed from Judah," and the boon was refused him. Judge Turpie was elected to the place, and Mr. Bright left Indianapolis, swearing vengeance against those who had brought about his discomfiture. He laid the principal blame of his defeat at the door of Governor Hendricks, and ever afterwards was a personal and political enemy of that gentleman.

In 1860 Mr. Bright organized and led the Breckenridge party in Indiana. He stumped the State for the young Kentuckian and gave the movement all the force and vitality that it had in this State. He made a speech at Franklin, in which he was very bitter on Douglas and his friends. After he had concluded his address and was going to his hotel, he observed an old personal and political friend on the opposite side of the street. He crossed over, and taking the friend by the hand, said: " Why were you not out to hear me speak?" He was answered : " Mr. Bright, I am sorry to see you engaged in such a work. I can give no countenance to your effort to break up the Democratic party." " I am endeavoring to place the Democratic party on a solid basis. A number of old Whigs and free-soilers are in the party, and they must not control it." He was reminded that the organization in Indiana had declared for Douglas, and that the mass of the Democratic voters were for him. " Yes," said he, " the State Convention did instruct for Douglas, but Hendricks and McDonald, Hammond and Dunham consented to these instructions without consulting me."

In June, 1868, he went to Indianapolis on a political mission, and stopped at the Bates House. One afternoon the author received a note from him, asking his presence at the hotel, and on going there met Mr. Bright, Hon. D. W. Voorhees, James B. Ryan and Robert S. Sproule. The conversation was upon political matters, and during it Mr. Bright asked Mr. Voorhees whom he favored for the Democratic nomination at New York. Mr. Voorhees answered, General Hancock, whereupon Mr. Bright asked Mr. Ryan the same question. Mr. Ryan replied that his choice was Mr. Hendricks, and the author, on being asked for his favorite, named the same gentleman. I then said: " Mr. Bright, we have named our choice, now name yours." Drawing his nether lip between his teeth, as if to give emphasis to what he said, he replied: " Not your man Hendricks. He is the Oily Gammon of the Democratic party. He paid his respects to me in 1863 ; I propose paying mine to him in 1868." Pausing for an instant, he continued: " Salmon P. Chase is the proper man for the Democracy to nominate at New York. He is a Democrat, now that slavery has gone, and there is no reason why Democrats should not support him. If he be nominated, he will be elected ; any other man will be defeated." In order that the reader may see how Mr. Bright kept his word, I will recall the fact that his nephew, Richard J. Bright, sergeant-at-arms of the United States Senate, was a delegate to the New York convention, and that he steadily voted against the nomination of Mr. Hendricks. Had Indiana been solid for Governor Hendricks he would undoubtedly have been the nominee instead of Governor Seymour.

In the summer of 1865 Mr. Bright came to Indianapolis, direct from Washington. The President, Andrew Johnson, had broken with his party, and there was much controversy among Democrats as to the proper thing to do. A number of Mr. Bright's old friends gathered about him, and one of them asked him what course the Democracy ought to pursue. " Support Johnson," he answered ; " he is right in his fight with Congress and Democrats should hold up his hands. God knows how I hate him, but I will stand by him in this fight. In 1842 I canvassed a part of the State with Dr. John W. Davis. of Sullivan county. One day while he was speaking a man kept interrupting him by asking him questions. At last Mr. Davis became tired of the interruptions, and, turning to the man, said : ' My friend, to save time and trouble, I will say that I am in favor of everything the Democratic party ever did do, or ever will do.' Now, gentlemen," continued Mr. Bright, " I will not ask you to indorse Andy Johnson as broadly as Dr. Davis did the Democratic party, but I will ask you to indorse him when he is in the right." In the same conversation Mr. Bright advised his party friends to do what they could to secure the election of

Judge Hughes to the United States Senate, as the successor of Governor Lane. Judge Hughes was then a Republican Senator from the county of Monroe, and had been as ultra as the most ultra upon the question of the war. " You can't elect a Democrat," said Mr. Bright, " and Mr. Hughes is far preferable to an old-time Republican. 'Tis true, he has strayed from the fold, but we Baptists believe in election and foreordination. Hughes is one of the elect ; he may go astray, but he will not be lost." It will be remembered that shortly afterwards Judge Hughes returned to the Democratic party, and remained in it while he lived.

Mr. Bright left Indiana soon after the Legislature of 1863 refused to return him to the United States Senate, and took up his residence in Kentucky. Subsequently he served two terms in the Kentucky Legislature, and at one time was prominently named for United States Senator from that State. He once told the author that he could have gone to the Senate from Kentucky had he chosen to make the contest.

Mr. Bright was a good business man, as well as a good politician. He had large interests in the coal mines of West Virginia, out of which he made much money. In 1874 he removed to Baltimore, but he was broken down in health, and on the 20th day of May, 1875, he died in that city, of organic disease of the heart. He was buried there, and all that was mortal of Jesse D. Bright is mouldering to dust near the banks of the " Blue Patapsco."

Most of the men who were cotemporaries of Mr. Bright are dead. At Madison, where he commenced his political life and where he lived so long, he had as devoted followers as any man that ever lived. The Old Guard was not more devoted to Napoleon than was the Democracy of Jefferson county to Jesse D. Bright. Of his captains, there are but three remaining—John Kirk, John Marsh and Rolla Doolittle. These men love the memory of their dead chieftain, and will tell you for the asking that Jesse D. Bright was a warm friend and a good hater—as true to his friends as the needle to the pole and as inexorable to his enemies as death itself.

JOHN WESLEY DAVIS.

From 1829, when he entered public life, until 1859, when he died, Dr. John Wesley Davis, of Carlisle, Sullivan county, was one of the prominent men of Indiana. He was judge of a court, often a legislator, repeatedly a Congressman ; he was a foreign minister and Governor of a Territory, and all these places he filled with credit to himself and to his adopted State.

The author has in his possession a manuscript autobiography of Dr. Davis. It is without date, but, as it speaks of matters which occurred in 1858 it must have been written but a short time before his death. He gives the incidents of his early life with more minuteness than is necessary for a paper like this, but as I do not wish to abridge or alter it, I copy it entire. It was written with his own hand, and is a valuable contribution to the history of the day. It is as follows :

" I was born in the village of New Holland, Lancaster county, Pennsylvania, on the 16th of April, 1799. A portion of my childhood was spent with my maternal grandfather, Jones. When I was about ten years old my father purchased a farm one mile east of Shippensburg, in Cumberland county, Pennsylvania, and settled upon it. Until I was seventeen years of age most of my time was spent upon my father's farm ; however, during that period I was bound an apprentice to a clock-maker by the name of Hendel M. Carlisle, but my health failed from confinement, and I quit that business and was next sent to learn storekeeping. Being changeful in my disposition, I did not long remain at it, and my father then sent me to a Latin school in Shippensburg, where I continued about a year, and then commenced the study of medicine in Carlisle, under the

direction of Dr. George D. Foulke. The winter of 1819-20 I
spent in attending medical lectures at the University of Maryland, Baltimore. The intervening summer, between the win-
ters of 1820 and 1821, I spent in practicing medicine in the village of Concord, Franklin county, Pennsylvania. In October,
1820, I married Ann Hoover, of Shippensburg, and shortly
afterward returned to Baltimore to attend a second course of
lectures. I graduated at the university on the 2d day of April,
1821. After graduating I attempted to practice my profession
at Shippensburg, but becoming discouraged with my prospects,
I moved, in August, 1821, to Old Town, Allegheny county,
Maryland, and there practiced medicine until early in the spring
of 1823, when I moved to Carlisle, Indiana, where I arrived in
April of that year with just three cents in my pocket. My professional prospects were anything but flattering for the first few
weeks of my residence here, but eventually I obtained my share
of the practice.

"In 1826 I thought to better my condition in some respects, and
in the spring of that year removed to Terre Haute, where, in
August following, myself and two children were taken sick with
bilious fever, and, after lingering several weeks, and partially
recovering, I returned to Carlisle, and am indebted to the kindness of Mr. John Widener, in his care and nursing at his house,
for my recovery. I continued the practice of my profession
until the summer of 1828, when I was induced to be a candidate
for the State Senate against William C. Linton, and was defeated by a few votes. The district then, as now, was composed
of the counties of Vigo, Clay and Sullivan. I went to Indianapolis at the opening of the Legislature and became a candidate
for clerk of the House, and was again unsuccessful, there being
four candidates in the field (Mr. Hurst, Mr. Sheets, Mr. Huntington and myself); my share of the ballots was only eleven,
and Mr. Hurst was elected. My successful competitor for the
Senate solicited me to be a candidate for sergeant-at-arms to
that body. I consented, and was elected. In the summer of
1829 I ran against Associate Judge John H. Eaton for Judge of
the Probate Court, under the new law, and was elected. I
served two years, and then (in 1831) was a candidate for the
Legislature, and was elected. In 1832 I was re-elected to the

Legislature without opposition, and at the session which followed I was elected Speaker over Harbin H. Moore. After my election in 1832, and prior to the meeting of the Legislature, I was appointed by the President one of three commissioners to hold treaties with the Indians, the other commissioners being Governor Jennings and M. Crume, Esq. After discharging our duties as commissioners we all resigned, and I repaired to my legislative duties. In 1833 I became a candidate, with five others, for Congress, and was defeated by Mr. John Ewing, he receiving two more votes than I. In 1835 I was again a candidate for Congress, and was elected over Mr. Ewing by nearly 1,000 majority. In 1849 I opposed Mr. Ewing again for Congress, and was elected (to the best of my memory) by a majority of 1,297.

"At a special session, held the first Monday in May, 1841, preparatory to a called session of Congress, R. W. Thompson and myself were the candidates, and he was successful, but not by so large a majority as that received by General Harrison the preceding fall. After my defeat for Congress in 1841, I was induced to be a candidate for the Legislature, and was successful. When the Legislature met I was again elected Speaker of the House. In 1842 I was again returned to the House of Representatives, but declined being a candidate for the chair. In 1843 I was again a candidate for Congress, my competitor being the talented George G. Dunn, whom I defeated by a majority of some 800 to 1,000 votes. [Mr. Davis's majority over Mr. Dunn was 962.]

" In 1845 I was again returned to Congress over Rev. Eli P. Farmer by a majority of about 3,000. [His majority was 2,930.] On the assembling of Congress I was elected Speaker of the House, by a party vote, over the Hon. Samuel P. Vinton, of Ohio.

" In 1847 I was nominated by several Democratic conventions for Congress, but as the conventions were not attended by delegates from all the counties in the district, I declined to run.

" In December, 1847, President Polk appointed me Commissioner to China. I very soon embarked on my mission in the United States sloop of war Plymouth. I was over four months on my voyage out, and had a most irksome and disagreeable journey. Early in the year 1850 I asked leave of my government to return home, and in the summer of that year started home by what is usually called the overland route, touching at Singapore, Penary, the Island of Ceylon, the Red Sea, Suez, across the desert to Cairo, down the Nile to Atfeh, thence by the Mamonda canal to Alexandria, and thence by the Mediterranean to England. I then visited France, returned to England, and then came home.

"In 1851 I was again returned to the Legislature, and again was elected Speaker of the House. During the session the House took some action which I construed into an implied censure, whereupon I resigned the speakership.

"On the 8th of January, 1852, I was appointed one of the delegates from Indiana to the Democratic national convention that met in Baltimore in June of that year. On the assembling of that body I was chosen its president; I had several times before been a delegate to Democratic conventions.

"Up to about this time I attended to the duties of my profession at all times when my public engagements permitted.

"In 1853 President Pierce sent me a commission as Governor of Oregon, unsolicited by myself, or by any one else, so far as I know. I declined this appointment at first, but, after an interview with the President, I went to Oregon in the autumn of 1853, and remained there about a year, and then resigned and returned home.

"In 1856 I was again elected to the Legislature by the most flattering vote I ever received from the good people of Sullivan county, among whom I have resided for more than thirty-five years.

"In 1858 I was appointed by the Secretary of War a visitor to West Point Military Academy, and while there I was elected president of the board of visitors."

Here Dr. Davis's autobiography ends.

The reader will not forget that Dr. Davis speaks of his resignation of the speakership in 1852, on account of what he considered bad treatment. It will be remembered that the session of the Legislature of 1851-2 was the longest and most important one ever held in the State. During that session the whole system of the law was revised so as to make it conform to the new constitution which had just been adopted. Dr. Davis and Hon. William H. English, then just entering upon his legislative career, were candidates before the Democratic caucus for nomination for Speaker, Dr. Davis receiving thirty-one votes and Mr. English twenty-two. Dr. Davis, being the nominee, was elected Speaker by the House on its organization, but early in March he resigned the position, as stated in his autobiography, on account of a disagreement between him and the House.

On Friday, March 5, 1852, both houses adopted a resolution for a temporary adjournment from the 10th of March to the 20th of April, and for the appointment on the part of the Senate of two members, and on the part of the House of four, to remain as a committee of revision during the recess. In the Senate Messrs. Eddy and Hester were elected by a *viva voce* vote. In the House a difference of opinion existed as to the power to appoint, some contending that the Speaker, under the rule, "He shall have the right to name any members to bear messages to the Senate, and to appoint all committees, subject to additional members to be added on motion," had such power, and others that the election should be by the House. The Speaker was of the former opinion. To settle the matter, however, on motion of Mr. English, the House adopted a resolution directing the Speaker to make the appointment, and he thereupon appointed Messrs. Gibson and English, Democrats, and Messrs. Bryant and Lindsay, Whigs, as such committee.

On Saturday, March 6, Mr. Mudget moved to reconsider the vote by which the House gave the power to appoint the committee to the Speaker. A lengthy and exciting debate ensued, and the motion to reconsider prevailed—yeas 52, nays 21. The question then recurred on the resolution authorizing the Speaker to appoint the committee.

Mr. English moved to amend the resolution by striking out all after the enacting clause and inserting "That the House will, the Senate concurring, rescind the resolution for a temporary adjournment."

Mr. Mudget moved to lay the resolution on the table, which was carried.

Mr. Mudget then moved to amend the original resolution by

striking out all after the enacting clause, and inserting the following :

" *Resolved*, That this House now proceed, by *viva voce* vote, to elect the joint committee on the revision." Carried—yeas 59, nays 16.

The question then recurred on the adoption of the resolution as amended—yeas 50, nays 27.

The Speaker decided that it took two-thirds to pass the resolution, and hence it was lost.

Mr. McDonald appealed from the decision of the chair.

The question being taken whether the decision of the chair should be taken as the judgment of the House, it was decided in the negative—yeas 15, nays 31.

Dr. Davis at once wrote his resignation as Speaker, and calling Mr. English to the chair, handed it to him and then descended to the floor. Mr. English then laid before the House the following communication :

" HALL OF REPRESENTATIVES, March 6, 1852.

" SIR—You will please lay this, my resignation of the place of Speaker of the House, before the body over which you are temporarily presiding, and oblige yours, respectfully,

" JNO. W. DAVIS."

" To Wm. H. English, Esq."

Dr. Davis remarked, after the resignation had been read, that he should be wanting in every element of self-respect if he had continued for a moment longer to occupy the chair. The rescinding of the resolution authorizing him to appoint the committee was a vote of censure, either for ignorance in the discharge of that trust by appointing incompetent or unworthy men, or else for maliciously violating the will and wishes of the House. He had on former occasions presided in this House and in the National Congress, and never before had his character for impartiality been impeached. It was the severest stab ever aimed at him.

Messrs. McDonald and Owen, for themselves and the House, disclaimed all intentions of the kind, renewed their expressions of friendship for the Speaker, and solemnly declared that they were governed only by a regard for the best interests of the State, and a desire to protect the rights of the House.

During the day there was much excitement. In the afternoon a caucus of the Democratic members was held, in which Dr. Davis was urged to resume the chair, but which he peremptorily refused to do. The meeting then nominated Mr. English for Speaker, and Messrs. Owen, Stover and Gibson for the revising committee, and, on Monday, March 8, 1852, these gentlemen were severally elected.

In speaking of Dr. Davis, Oliver H. Smith, in his "Early Indiana Trials and Sketches," says: "Few men in this or any other State have held so many prominent positions, or discharged their duties with greater ability." All who knew him bear similar testimony.

A writer in the *New Albany Press*—supposed to be Colonel Horace Heffren—in sketching the members of the Legislature of 1856-7, thus speaks of Mr. Davis:

"John W. Davis was from Sullivan. Of him I need not write, as all are, or ought to be, familiar with his history. He was an old-time gentleman, and had been in the Legislature, Speaker in Congress, Minister to China, and Speaker of the Indiana House of Representatives. He was a man of talent, of a high sense of honor, and very sensitive."

Dr. Davis was a solid rather than a showy man. His imagination was small, but his perceptive faculties were large. He thoroughly understood parliamentary law, and was one of the best presiding officers in the country. While his mind was not so active as that of Willard, it moved fast enough for him to readily reach his conclusions. These were seldom wrong, nor were they often questioned.

Throughout Dr. Davis's long career no one ever doubted his honesty. He kept his hands clean. With opportunities for money-making possessed by few, he contented himself with his legitimate earnings, and died a poor man.

Dr. Davis had fine social qualities. While he was at the capital, in attendance upon his public duties, it was his custom often to spend his evenings in the families of his friends. He was fond of music, was a good vocalist, and delighted in the singing of popular songs.

Dr. Davis did not rank high as a public speaker. He had none of the arts of the public orator, but nevertheless he was an entertaining talker. He was a good canvasser, could express himself intelligently and well, and if not an eloquent man, he was a sensible one. He knew how to reach the average voter, and how to get his vote.

Physically, Dr. Davis was a fine specimen of manhood. He was six feet two inches high, with a well proportioned body. He had light hair, blue eyes, and a florid complexion. As a presiding officer he ranked with the best, and as a safe and prudent legislator he was the equal of any man in the State in his day. He died in Carlisle, August 22, 1859, and was buried in the cemetery there.

GEORGE G. DUNN.

George G. Dunn, lawyer and statesman, was born in Washington county, Kentucky, in December, 1812. He came to Indiana when a boy, and settled in Monroe county, a county that has given the State several of her most eminent sons. Having acquired sufficient education to enter college, he became a student of the State University at Bloomington, and continued one until after he entered the junior class. While a member of this class he had trouble with the President, Dr. Wylie, which ended in his leaving college. Dr. Wylie said something Mr. Dunn did not relish, and he made a cutting retort. The Doctor then said to him, "Young man, do you see this cane?" shaking one he held in his hand. "Yes, sir," replied the young student, "but I don't feel it." He at once gathered his books and left the college, never to return as a student. He was then a boy, but was a brave and self-reliant one. He determined to strike out for himself, and at once went to Switzerland county and commenced teaching school. When he had saved one hundred dollars out of his earnings he gave up his school and started back to his old home. On the way he lost his money, and when he reached home he was as poor as when he left, save in the knowledge he had gained of the world.

In 1833, when he was twenty-one years old, Mr. Dunn went to Bedford and taught school awhile, and occupied his spare hours in reading law. In due time he was admitted to the bar, and soon afterward formed a partnership with Colonel Richard W. Thompson, late Secretary of the Navy.

In 1843 he ran for Congress against Dr. John W. Davis, and was defeated. After this he was made prosecuting attorney of his circuit, and was a terror to the evil-doers of that section of the State. He prosecuted law-breakers as he did everything else, with the vim and energy of a great mind.

Traveling over the circuit, he became acquainted with its leading men, and in 1847 his party friends again determined to make him their candidate for Congress. His district two years before had given Dr. John W. Davis, Democrat, 2,930 majority, but this fact did not deter Mr. Dunn from making the race. He was then thirty-five years old, was in good health and capable of great physical and mental labor. He made a searching canvass of the district, speaking in all the townships, and defeated his competitor, Dr. John M. Dobson, twenty-two votes. This race and its result astonished everybody save the young Whig standard-bearer, who, from its beginning, believed he would win. He served his term in Congress with credit, and at its close intended to return to private life, but he was not permitted to do so, for his party friends nominated and elected him to the State Senate the year his term expired.

In the spring of 1852 he resigned his seat in the Senate while the Legislature was in session and went home to attend to his legal business. He continued in active practice until the summer of 1854, when he again entered the political field. During that year the Know-nothing party sprang into life. It was composed of former Whigs, sore-headed Democrats and Abolitionists. Captain John A. Hendricks, who, until then, had been a Democrat, was nominated for Congress by a convention of political mongrels, most of whom had been Democrats. He at once took the field and commenced his canvass. Soon, however, he learned that Mr. Dunn was also a candidate. The candidacy of the latter, so far as the world knew, was solely of his own volition. He had been nominated by no convention, but it was soon discovered that the mass of the new party was rallying to his support. Captain Hendricks was in a quandary what to do. He had long been an aspirant for congressional honors, and now when the cup of fruition was at his lips another snatched it from him. He saw his friends deserting him, and, knowing his race to be hopeless, he left the field.

Mr. Dunn entered the contest in 1854 somewhat as he had done that of 1847. Two years before the district had given

Cyrus L. Dunham 931 majority over Joseph G. Marshall. But this had no terror for Mr. Dunn. He believed in his star, and went into the fight feeling confident of success. He visited all the townships in the district, sometimes speaking three times a day. He was in bad health, but his great will and determination kept him up until the canvass closed. He was elected, beating Mr. Dunham 1,660 votes, but his success was a poor compensation for his broken health. The labor of this contest was so severe that it undermined his constitution and he was never afterward a strong man.

In Congress Mr. Dunn occupied a somewhat anomalous position. He was mainly elected by the Know-nothings, but the Whigs of the district who refused to assume the new party affiliations voted for him. It will be remembered that the Know-nothing party had but an ephemeral existence. Out of its ruins sprang the Republican party, a party with which Mr. Dunn did not identify himself. In Congress he occupied an independent position, but generally voted with the opposition to the Democracy. He had made his canvass mainly in insisting that the Missouri restriction, which had been repealed, should be restored, and he remained faithful to that position. The anti-Nebraska party in Congress nominated Mr. Banks for Speaker, but Mr. Dunn persistently opposed his election. Congress convened on the 3d day of December, 1855, and did not organize until the 2d day of February following. During this interval great excitement prevailed throughout the country. One hundred and twenty-nine ballots had been taken for Speaker, when Mr. Smith, of Tennessee, offered a resolution that the House proceed to vote three times, and if no one had a majority for Speaker, then " the roll shall again be called, and the member who shall then receive the largest number of votes, provided it shall be a majority of a quorum, shall be declared duly elected Speaker of the House of the Thirty-fourth Congress. The resolution passed, Mr. Dunn voting against it.

The final ballot was as follows:

For N. P. Banks, 103; William Aiken, 100; Henry M. Fuller, 6; Lewis D. Campbell, 4; Daniel Wills, 1.

On this ballot Mr. Dunn voted for Campbell. During the contest he voted for Mr. Etheridge, Mr. Campbell, Mr. Pennington and Mr. Eddie, but never for Mr. Banks. His course during the organization of the House, no doubt, cost him the chairmanship of a leading committee, a place he was well qualified to fill. His position in this Congress could not have been a pleasant one, for he was not in accord with those in control of the House, and it must have been with a feeling of relief that he left Washington for his home at the end of his term. His health was now so bad that he could do little else than remain at home with his family. He gradually grew worse until September of that year (1857), when he died.

As an advocate, Mr. Dunn was always ready. He took no notes of the testimony in his cases, relying entirely upon his memory for his facts. He made the cause of his client his own, and in conducting his cases he was aggressive and bold. If such a course involved him in trouble with opposing counsel he let the trouble come. He had a difficulty with the late Judge Hughes, which grew out of a trial in court, and came near ending in a duel. He called Judge Hughes a pettifogger, and, refusing to retract, was challenged by that gentleman. He accepted the hostile invitation, but before going upon the field friends interfered and the trouble was settled.

Mr. Dunn made more reputation in the State Senate than in Congress. In the Senate he stood head and shoulders above his fellow members, with the single exception of Joseph G. Marshall, and in some respects he excelled that distinguished man. He was a better scholar and a greater master of ridicule and invective than the Senator from Jefferson, but he fell below him in breadth of comprehension and ability to move the passions of the people. The one was scholarly, argumentative and witty, the other impassioned, profound and convincing.

In an admirable portraiture of this subject by Miss Laura Ream, in 1875, that graphic writer, speaking of his oratory, says: "His voice was clear and resonant as a silver bell. His style of speaking was very impressive, enforced, as it was, by a personal magnetism which can scarcely be imagined in this age of tame leadership. His will was invincible, and he inspired others with such confidence in his strength that any law case he undertook was considered decided in his favor beforehand."

While in the Senate Mr. Dunn had a memorable debate with Colonel James H. Lane, then Lieutenant-Governor of Indiana, and afterwards a United States Senator from Kansas. David P. Holloway, a Senator from the county of Wayne, offered a resolution to present certain trophies of the Mexican war, then in the State Library, to a Catholic church in Indianapolis. In speaking on his resolution he animadverted on the Mexican war, and when he had concluded Colonel Lane took the floor and made a speech, in which he coarsely abused the Senator from Wayne. When he had taken his seat Mr. Dunn replied in a speech that will never be forgotten by those who heard it. He flayed the Lieutenant-Governor, taking off his hide, strip by strip; that is, if words can be made to do such a thing. Before taking his seat he said he wore no shad-bellied coat like the Senator from Wayne (Mr. Holloway was a Quaker), and that he was personally responsible for what he had said. It was supposed at the time that Colonel Lane, who recognized the "code," would call Mr. Dunn to account for this speech, but he did not—letting it pass without notice.

The greatest speech Mr. Dunn ever delivered was at the Whig State Convention of 1852. A few days before the convention was held he resigned his seat in the Senate, and in this speech he gave his reasons for the act. The main one was the fact that his party being in a minority in the Senate, he was without influence and unable to shape legislation. He was not the man to have influence with his political opponents; he was too bitter and choleric for that. He denounced the course of the Democratic Senators, and said, with a single exception he parted from them with the greatest pleasure. That exception he declared to be the Senator from Clark, Dr. Athon, for whom he said he had the warmest feeling. Dr. Athon, who was present, arose and said he highly appreciated the kind expressions of the speaker. He severely criticised the action of Governor Wright in appointing Messrs. March, Barbour and Carr commissioners to revise and simplify the Code. "When these men were appointed," said Mr. Dunn, "I was at a loss to know what place 'Squire Carr would fill in the commission. A little reflection, however, convinced me he had his place. March is to furnish the law, Barbour to read the version, and if Carr can understand, it will be within the comprehension of all." He took up the Democratic nominees for State offices one by one and thoroughly dissected them. He was particularly severe upon Governor Wright. Seeing the Governor in the hall, Mr. Dunn said: "I am glad you are here, Governor. Don't leave until I am done. I propose going through you with a lighted candle that all may see what a mass of putrefaction and political rottenness you are." When he came to speak of Judge Davidson, he said: "My objection to Davidson is that his eyes are too close together. When you farmers buy a horse you don't choose one whose eyes are in the middle of his head. You know that such a horse would run against the first fence-corner he comes to. You should exercise as much care in voting for a Supreme Judge as you would in buying a horse," But space forbids me further following Mr. Dunn in his criticisms of the Democratic candidates. When he was done with them he proceeded to speak of the Whig nominees. Mr. McCarty, who had just been nominated for Governor, was sitting but a few feet from the speaker. Mr. Dunn drew a dark picture of the condition of the Whig party until Mr. McCarty consented to be a candidate, and then, rising on tip-toe, and bending his body forward and pointing his finger at the nominee, he exclaimed with the power of a Booth :

> "Now is the winter of our discontent
> Made glorious summer by the sun of York ;
> And all the clouds that lowered upon our house,
> In the deep bosom of the ocean buried."

It is a great pity that this speech was not taken down at the time and preserved. It embodied the wit and drollery of Corwin, the invective and sarcasm of Randolph, and the eloquence of Clay, in one symmetrical whole. It lives only in the recollection of those who heard it, and, happily for the author, he was one. These men will be gone after awhile, and then this great forensic effort will be forgotten, or remembered only as it is handed down from father to son.

During the first State fair held in Indiana, just after the October election, 1852, the Democracy had a jollification meeting at the State capital. The Whigs, believing the time and occasion inopportune, and smarting under their recent defeat, cre-

ated so much "noise and confusion" that the speakers could
not be heard. The speaking took place on Washington street,
opposite the Wright House, where a large number of leading
Whigs were staying. Joseph E. McDonald and Ashbel P.
Willard, who had just been elected Lieutenant-Governor, attempted to speak, but their voices were drowned by the noise
of the tumultuous crowd. During Willard's attempt to speak,
Mr. Dunn, who was on the balcony of the Wright House, overlooking the crowd, appealed to those about him to stop their
noise and let Mr. Willard speak. Some of those who saw him
standing and gesticulating thought he was urging on the mob.
The Democrats, after awhile, countermarched down Washington street, and stopped at the State-house square, where the
speaking was resumed without further interruption. Both Colonel Gorman and Governor Willard charged Mr. Dunn with
having incited the disturbance, and criticised him severely for
it. The *Sentinel*, next morning, had an account of the meeting
and reported what the speakers had said. Mr. Dunn sought
Messrs. Gorman and Willard and told them they were mistaken
in attributing to him sympathy with the mob, that he had done
all he could to quell it. Governor Willard expressed himself
as entirely satisfied with Mr. Dunn's statements, and published
a manly letter withdrawing his offensive language. Colonel
Gorman also promised to retract the charge, and the next day
he published a card in the *Sentinel*, which, after giving an account of what he had said, closed as follows: "In a personal
conversation this morning with Mr. Dunn, he assures me that
my information was incorrect, and that he tried to suppress the
confusion and noise. I publish this to allow him the full benefit
of his denial, and to place myself in the right." This card did
not satisfy Mr. Dunn, but, on the contrary, incensed him the
more. He addressed Colonel Gorman a letter, in which he
asked to be informed if he was the author of the card signed
with his name. Colonel Gorman replied in a somewhat lengthy
letter acknowledging the genuineness of his card, and, after
answering other questions propounded, he closed as follows:
"If this is not satisfactory, it is out of my power to make it so
on paper." That it was not satisfactory is evidenced by the
following letter:

" BEDFORD, Ind., November 8, 1852.

" HON. W. A. GORMAN : Sir—Yours of the 5th inst. is just received, and is, I regret to say, objectionable in several respects. It is my purpose now to take the advice of some experienced friend in regard to the whole matter, and adopt such steps as may be due to my obligations to society.

" Being called to Louisville, Ky., the last of this week, I shall be happy to find you at the Galt House, in that city, at 10 o'clock A. M., on Saturday next. Respectfully yours,

" GEORGE G. DUNN."

To which letter Colonel Gorman made the following reply :

" BLOOMINGTON, Ind., November 9, 1852.

" HON. GEORGE G. DUNN : Sir—Yours of this date is before me. I will be at the Galt House, in Louisville, agreeably to your written request, on Saturday next, at 10 o'clock A. M., where my friend will receive any communication you may be pleased to make. Respectfully, your obedient servant,

" W. A. GORMAN."

Messrs. Dunn and Gorman met at Louisville, as agreed upon, and referred their difficulty to Professor John H. Harney and Mr. George A. Caldwell, who, after examining the correspondence, published a card announcing a settlement on the following terms :

" We are of opinion that the note of Colonel Gorman to Mr. Dunn amply exonerates that gentleman from all participation in the disturbance of the meeting referred to, and sufficiently explains the purpose of the card published in the *Sentinel*, and that nothing remains to disturb the peaceful relations of the parties except the language in which the notes are couched and their general tone.

" Mr. Dunn objects to the concluding sentence of Colonel Gorman's note of the 3d instant, and to the language in other passages, as offensive.

" Colonel Gorman objects to the general tone of Mr. Dunn's previous note of the 30th ult., and especially to the call upon him to retract.

"Mr. Dunn cheerfully withdraws the word 'retract,' and substitutes the word 'correct,' or any other word not deemed offensive, and disavows any purpose of giving offense by his note of the 30th, his only object being to obtain a respectful vindication of himself from whatever was injurious in the matters referred to in the note. Whereupon, Colonel Gorman promptly withdraws anything offensive in his note of the 3d.

"Therefore, the whole difficulty, we are happy to announce, is amicably and honorably settled.

"JOHN H. HARNEY,

"GEORGE A. CALDWELL."

And thus the matter ended.

Mr. Dunn was fond of fine stock and did much to improve the strain of horses and sheep in his section of the State. He was one of a company which imported the first Norman Percheron horse brought to Indiana. He purchased in Ohio a flock of Cotswold and Southdown sheep at $27 a head, an enormous price for that day. He took good care of his stock, giving it his personal attention and spending much of his time in looking after its comfort.

One of Mr. Dunn's chief characteristics was his contempt for shams and a love of independent thought. On the leaf of an old Latin dictionary used by him while at college, he wrote, "I despise your opinion." One day his oldest son, then a boy, put on his father's watch. Looking at the lad the father said: "If you go on the streets with that watch people will ask, as Cæsar did of a small lieutenant, 'Who tied you to a sword?'—or watch."

Again quoting Miss Ream, I give her description of his home, and also his death scene, as follows:

"Towards the latter part of his life he built a house in the country, in the center of a magnificent tract of land. The large domain abounded in rich and diversified scenery, especially on the line defined by a range of cliffs nearly two hundred feet in height and really picturesque, if not grand, in appearance. But Mr. Dunn built his house in the heart of a grove of royal growth, a bit of pasture land to the north, an orchard and the door yard

the only clearing. The house that he built was a story and a
half in height, but there its modest pretensions ended. There
was a great hall as wide as an ordinary house, and the rooms
opening out of it were fit for the audience chamber of a king.
The ceilings were lofty and elegantly frescoed, the furniture of
these rooms was in keeping, and the out-door complement,
which the great windows added to their state, were views of the
forest, meadow and sky. It was a home for a prince, for a poet ;
it proved the last earthly abiding place of a kingly soul. When
it was noised abroad that George G. Dunn was dying the people from all the country round came to see him. The lane leading to the house was lined with the horses and wagons belonging
to the friends who had come to bid him good bye. Among the
number was one Robert Rout, a man yet living, but weather
tanned and wrinkled ; why, you could not lay a pin-point anywhere on his face that would not touch a wrinkle. Well, when
Robert Rout heard that Mr. Dunn could not live long, he came
and took up his abode near. He said little or nothing, and his
presence was only noticed when his ready hand or step answered to the sick man's need. The very last day of Mr.
Dunn's life he observed Rout hovering about the room, and
said : ' Rout, take that glass pitcher and go to the well and
bring me a drink. Draw it from the north side of the well, Rout ;
I want it cold and fresh.' The fond and faithful friend did
his bidding, and when he came back into the room, the glass
pitcher filled to the brim and running over with the drops of
water sparkling like diamonds in the sunlight, the dying man
looked at him for a moment with grateful, tender eyes, and said :
'Rout, 'tis well, 'tis very well. Rout, you shall be cup-bearer when
I am king.' The voice which uttered these words had lost none
of its melody, but the strength to swallow was gone, and the
water was put down from his parched, feeble lips untasted. The
act which followed was not less in character—as brave as it was
human. He turned his face to the wall—himself shutting out
and bidding farewell to the world, the day, sunlight and friendship.''

Mr. Dunn's literary library was large. It was composed of
standard classical historical works and English political pamph-

lets and essays, and books treating on American history and politics.

Mr. Dunn left no manuscript copies of any of his speeches, nor, indeed, any manuscript whatever. He filed his letters carefully, leaving some five or six books of correspondence. He was a great lover of Shakespeare, and often quoted him in his speeches. He was also familiar with the Bible, and, in addressing juries, was in the habit of drawing largely from its pages.

In person, Mr. Dunn was tall and commanding. He had fair complexion, blue eyes and light hair. His talents were great and varied, and he is entitled to stand in the front rank of Indiana lawyers and statesmen.

WILLIAM W. WICK.

But few men of early Indiana were better known than William Watson Wick. He came to the State in 1820, being the first lawyer to locate in Connersville, and from that time until 1857 he was almost continuously in public life. He was a man of marked peculiarities. He had a sunny disposition, was of a genial nature, thoroughly understanding human nature, and knowing just what to do to maintain his hold upon the people. I can not give a better summary of his life, up to 1848, than the following letter written to a Texas gentleman named Payne. Payne had read one of Judge Wick's congressional speeches, and was so impressed with its quaint humor and ready wit that he wrote to Hon. D. S. Kauffman, then in Congress, asking about Judge Wick, and saying he would like "to know all about him." Mr. Kauffman gave Judge Wick the letter, and under date of June 12, 1848, the Judge sent Payne the following autobiography:

"William W. Wick is a full-blooded Yankee, though born in Cannonsburg, Washington county, Pennsylvania, February 23, 1796. In 1800 W.'s father, a Presbyterian preacher, settled in the woods in the poorest township in the Western Reserve of Ohio, adjoining the Pennsylvania State line. Here W. lived, going to school, toiling at ordinary labor, and indulging in day-dreams till the time of his father's death in 1814. He then renounced all interest in his father's estate (which was only some $3,000), and took himself off. Till spring, 1816, he essayed to 'teach the young idea how to shoot' in Washington county, Pennsylvania, when he descended the Monongahela and Ohio in a 'broad-horn' to Cincinnati. He taught school and studied, first medicine and then law, till December, 1849; read chemistry principally by the light of log-heaps in a clearing, and law of nights and Sundays (wrong so far as Sunday is concerned). December, 1819, settled in Connersville, Indiana, as a lawyer, and made and sent his mother a deed for his interest in his father's real and personal estate. December, 1820, was chosen clerk of the House of Representatives of Indiana, and served till January, 1822, when he was chosen judge of a new circuit, just formed, and removed to Indianapolis, where he has ever since resided. In three years he resigned the judgeship, because it was starving him, and was chosen Secretary of State, served four years, then chosen circuit prosecuting attorney, then judge again. He has also figured as quartermaster-general, and is a now a brigadier. He has committed much folly in holding offices, and only escapes the condemnation of his own judgment in consideration of the fact that he was never green enough to accept a seat in the State Legislature. In 1835 W. changed his politics; his party did not leave him—he left it. [In this he differs from most great men.] In 1839 he was chosen an M. C. as a Democrat, and as successor to Col. Kinnard, who died from the blowing up of a steamboat when on his way to Washington. [Colonel K. had been in Congress for some years.] In 1843 and 1847 W. was nominated and elected to Congress. He was a candidate for Congress in 1831, and got beat. Right. He was once a Clay candidate for elector, and got beat. Right. In 1844 was a Democratic candidate for elector—successful. Right.

" In the intervals of the above engagements he practiced law; never made much at that; did not know how to scare and skin a client. In 1821 he married a wife, who died in 1832. He has a son and daughter married, and five grandchildren living. His youngest boy (a third child and all), went last year 'to see the elephant' as a private in the Illinois volunteer regiment— then he was near seventeen years of age. He went without leave, but (good boy) he wrote for and got leave after he was gone. He has acquired Spanish enough to write a good Spanish letter, and unassisted by W.'s name, has worked his way. He is now clerk to the depot quartermaster at the city of Mexico. Says the climate in Mexico is better than in Indiana, and that the boys killed themselves drinking spirits, eating Mexican fruits, and 'cavorting.'

" Wick has committed much folly in his time—the principal of which has been holding offices, writing rhymes, playing cards for money, and paying other people's debts—all which he abandoned about the time he became a Democrat.

"At this present writing W. is fifty-two years of age ; fair, a little fat, having increased since 1833 from 146 to 214 pounds— six feet and one inch high, good complexion, portly—has been called the best looking man about town—but that was ten years ago—not to be sneezed at now—a little gray—has had chills and fever, bilious attacks, and dyspepsia enough to kill a dozen common men, and has passed through misfortunes sufficient to humble a score of ordinary specimens of human nature. His system being sluggish, he takes a sarsaparilla bitter, or some No. 6, in the morning, and takes a glass or two of wine (if good) at dinner when he can get it. He has acquired a good deal of miscellaneous knowledge, loves fun, looks serious, rises early, works much, and has a decided penchant for light diet, humor, reading, business, the drama, music, a fine horse, his gun, and the woods. W. owes nothing, and were he to die to-day his estate would inventory eight or nine hundred dollars. He saves nothing of his per diem and mileage, and yet has no vices to run away with money. He ' takes no thought for to-morrow,' but relies upon the same good Providence to which he is debtor for all.

" W. would advise young men to fear and trust God, to cheat rogues, and deceive intriguers by being perfectly honest (this mode misleads such cattle effectually), to touch the glass lightly, to eschew security and debt, tobacco, betting, hypocrisy and federalism, to rather believe, or fall in with new philosophical and moral humbugs, and to love woman too well to injure her. They will thus be happy now, and will secure serenity at fifty-two years of age, and thence onward."

This paper exhibits Judge Wick as he was—warm-hearted, humorous and improvident. He truly said he took no thought for the morrow.

In 1853 President Pierce appointed Judge Wick postmaster

at Indianapolis. He served a full term of four years, and in 1857 was superseded by John M. Talbott. He was an applicant for reappointment, and he took his defeat sorely to heart. In a letter to a friend, under date of May 8, 1858, he thus speaks of his retirement from office :

" I suppose my selfish interests in politics are closed, and closed forever. My health, activity and physical energies are much impaired by the wear and tear of the last few months. It is the first time in my life that I have been constrained to feel a consciousness of exceeding wrong, neglect and injustice, accompanied by fraud and dishonor. It came upon me unexpectedly, and it hurt badly. But no measure of age, ill-health or disgust could make me careless of the fate of the Democratic party."

After leaving the postoffice Judge Wick resumed the practice of the law. Like most men who forsake the law for public office, he found it hard to get back his legal business. Others had taken his clients, and now when he sought to regain them they would not come. But if the law was measurably closed to him, the political field was open, and as he had always loved politics he did not particularly grieve at the want of clients, but entered actively into political work.

The Thirty-fifth Congress was the most exciting one that had ever convened up to that time. The Kansas and Nebraska bill had passed, and the bill to admit Kansas under the Lecompton constitution which was before the House, aroused the fiercest passions of the people. The Democratic party, then in control of the government, was divided upon the bill, and the two wings fought each other with intense fury. There were in that Congress six Democrats from Indiana, and the six were equally divided in sentiment upon the bill. Messrs. Niblack, Hughes and Gregg favored the measure, and Messrs. English, Foley and Davis opposed it. Judge Wick was bitterly hostile to the bill, and by speech and by letter did what he could to defeat it. In a letter to Hon. W. H. English, then in Congress, dated February 8, 1858, he says: " I am opposed to Kansas's admission on the Lecompton constitution solely on the point of honor." He proceeds at some

length to show that the honor of the Democratic party demands
the submission of the constitution to the people, and closes by
saying : "The most foolish thing a politician can do is to grow
desperate and risk his all on a single question." He begs of
Mr. English not to "risk his all" by voting for a bill whose
passage would bring dishonor upon his party. Writing to Mr.
English under date of February 21, 1858, he says :

"'The wise man forseeth the evil and hideth himself; the
fool passes on and is punished.' I would not expect you to be
a fool, but on the contrary would expect your wariness, clear-
sightedness and high sense of honor to save you from minister-
ing to the ambitious plans of others, by surrendering yourself
to be led blindfold into the pit, and I see it is likely that I shall
not be deceived. I congratulate you."

Further on he thus refers to the bill introduced by Mr. English for the settlement of the Kansas question :

"Had I been at your elbow, I would have whispered these
things to you, and said : 'Now mind your compromise. It will
do no public good, and may be to the Jews (anti-Lecompton
men) a stumbling-block, and to the Greeks (Lecompton men)
foolishness, and so bring you little honor or profit.'"

When the campaign of 1860 opened, Judge Wick took the
stump as an advocate of the election of Douglas. He made
speeches in several places in Central Indiana, and with much
effect, for he was a very popular stumper. He was not particularly logical as a speaker, but his humor, his wit and pleasant-
ries supplied the place of argument with many and made him
a great favorite upon the hustings. Had Judge Douglas been
elected Judge Wick would undoubtedly have been rewarded
for his devotion to the fortunes of that remarkable man, but as
he was defeated all hopes of Judge Wick for political preferment disappeared. In a short time after the campaign closed
he left Indianapolis, which for so long had been his home, and
took up his abode at Franklin, with his daughter, Mrs. William
H. Overstreet. He died at her house, May 19, 1868, and was
buried in the Franklin cemetery.

William and Henry Wick, Judge Wick's father and uncle, settled at Youngstown, Ohio, in 1801. As previously stated, William was a Presbyterian preacher. He came to the then far West as a missionary, and labored zealously in his calling. In speaking of the location of his father and uncle at Youngs town, Judge Wick once said: "One chose piety and poverty, the other merchandizing and money-getting, and they both succeeded." One laid up treasures in heaven, the other on earth, and verily they both had their reward.

Judge Wick's father intended him for a Presbyterian minister, but the boy grew up doubting the truth of Calvinism and refused to become an organ for its propagation. He studied medicine, as stated in his autobiography, but soon abandoned it, giving as a reason that he did not like to be always contemplating the miseries of mankind. Law and politics were more congenial to his nature, hence he embraced them and became a good lawyer and a very astute politician.

Judge Wick, like Yorick, was "a fellow of infinite jest, of most excellent fancy." His exuberant humor often "set the table in a roar," making him one of the best and most jolly of companions. Fun and hilarity abounded wherever he was, not even leaving him when on the bench. The lawyers joked with him and played cards with him, often for money. He was once indicted by the grand jury of Bartholomew county for gambling, was tried before his associate judges, found guilty and fined. A few days after this one Job Gardner, who had been indicted for gambling with the Judge, was brought to trial, and, on being asked if he was guilty, replied: "Guilty, as Your Honor well knows." "You are fined $5 and costs," responded Judge Wick, whereupon Gardner cried out, "Have mercy, Judge, have mercy." "You will have to appeal to a higher court for mercy," said the Judge, with a twinkle in his eye, as he proceeded to call the next case upon the docket.

Judge Wick, like most of the public men of early Indiana, loved a social glass. Oliver H. Smith, in his "Early Indiana Trials and Sketches," tells this story:

"We started in fine spirits from Greensburg after breakfast. The day was cloudy, dark and drizzling. There was no road

17

cut out between Greensburg and Shelbyville; there were neighborhood paths only in the direction between them. Judge Wick rode a spirited animal, and at once took the lead. Away we went at a rapid traveling gait. All at once the Judge stopped at a little log cabin at the forks of the paths, upon the gate-post of which hung a rough board with the word 'whisky' marked upon it with chalk. The Judge hallooed at the top of his voice, the door opened, and out came the woman of the cabin. The Judge: 'Have you got any whisky?' 'Yes, plenty; but we have no license to sell, and we will be prosecuted if we sell by the small. You can have a gallon.' 'A gallon! I don't want a gallon. A tin-cupful, with some sugar, will do.' 'You can't have it.' 'Fetch it out. I am the president judge of the Circuit Court, and this is Mr. Smith. He can quash any indictment these woods prosecuting attorneys can find against you. Fetch it out; there is no danger of prosecution.' Thus assured, the old woman returned, brought out the whisky and sugar, the Judge took the lion's part, and away he went on his journey."

Judge Wick was kind and affectionate to his family. His youngest daughter was accidentally burned when a child, and when the wound healed it left a bad scar upon her face. While she was from home, at the house of a friend of the family, a thoughtless companion twitted her with the cicatrix. In her mortification and grief she wrote her father, asking to be brought home. In reply, he sent her the following touching and beautiful letter:

"INDIANAPOLIS, November 1, 1862.

"DEAR ALLY—I am delighted to hear from you. I was not uneasy about you, but I did want to see my little one—my beloved child. But, now I know you are well, all is well. I am truly glad that you are learning not to be afraid of the darkness, which is one of the foolishest things in the world.

"Nobody has slighted you because of your scars, I know, who was worth minding. I hope my little girl will remember that as she will never be very pretty there is so much more reason for her to be good. A pretty face may recommend one to light-hearted and foolish people, but it is goodness and talent and education which recommend one to the better sort of peo-

ple, whose good opinion is valuable. Be ever good and innocent and sincere, as you are now, and you will find enough people to love you, in spite of the burns. Perhaps they may, like
your old father, love you all the more for the scars. I long to
see my baby, but do not wish to say a word about your coming
home, but leave that to fix itself. Be good and obedient and
obliging, and your pa will not be ashamed of you. Dear Ally,
good bye. W. W. WICK."

This child, now an intelligent and thoughtful woman, in a
note to the author of this sketch, thus speaks of her father:

"After my father's first stroke of paralysis, when it was with
great difficulty that he walked, we had in our household a ca-
nine called 'Dainty,' for which I had a great fancy, but the rest
of the family a very decided dislike. I fear 'Dainty' must
have been a serious trouble to my father, owing to his unfortunate faculty for always being in the way. But my dear father
bore very patiently with the dog and his many pranks, for his
'baby's' sake, and one day crowned all by an act which was
much to me then, but more to me now, that I can better appreciate the loving thoughtfulness that prompted it. I was away
from home, and 'Dainty,' taking advantage of my absence,
took to the street for a frolic. But, alas! with his usual readiness, he got in the way of a heavy wagon, and thus ended his
somewhat active career. My father, hearing of the accident,
and knowing what a sad catastrophe it would be to me, went
out into the street, and bringing in the poor little body, laid it
down in a shady part of our yard, and then waiting my return,
told me that poor little 'Dainty' was no more, but that there
was a happy hunting-ground where all good dogs were supposed to go.

"And so it was always; his children's troubles were always his
troubles, too. They were never so small but he could and did understand them, and relieve them, too, when relief was possible.
Many a time has he stroked my head, saying: 'Never mind,
baby, it will all come right.' And so it did, or was forgotten,
which was about the same thing to my mind in those days."

A son of Judge Wick, now living at Springfield, Ohio, gives this incident in his father's career :

"I remember when a lad, during one of his canvasses for Congress, going to the old Court-house where he was making a speech. My boy eyes were wide open taking in the scene. The room was literally packed, and I noticed that by his eloquence his audience were affected to tears, and then by his wit and humor were convulsed with laughter. At the close of the speech two stalwart Clay Whigs gathered him upon their shoulders, and went out of the Court-house yard and down Washington street, hurrahing for Billy Wick."

Judge Wick's first wife was Laura Finch, a sister of Hon. Fabius M. Finch, of Indianapolis. As stated in the Judge's autobiography, Mrs. Wick died in 1832, and in 1839 he married Isabella Barbee. The issue of this marriage was two daughters, the youngest of whom is living, and is connected with the Indianapolis Public Library. The second Mrs. Wick survived her husband.

Judge Wick wrote well and correctly. His manuscript was a pattern of neatness and grammatical accuracy. It could be printed as written, something that can not be done with the compositions of most of our public men.

Judge Wick's grave is without even a headstone to mark it. It is several inches lower than the cemetery's level, otherwise there would be nothing to show that the ground where his ashes lie was ever disturbed. A foot or so from the head of the grave stands a monument erected to one who, though one of the best of men,* was unknown outside his neighborhood, and at its foot runs a roadway. On either side are monuments commemorating the virtues of those who exercised but little influence upon their kind, and whom the State's history will never mention. Amid such surroundings is the final resting-place of the genial pioneer, with nothing to mark it save an indentation in the ground. Some members of the Franklin bar have talked of putting a stone at the head of the grave, but nothing further has

---

*The author's father.

been done, and unless some one moves in the matter before long the last resting place of the first judge of the " New Purchase " will be unknown. Standing by it a thoughtful man must realize the instability of worldly honor and human greatness. Alas, how transient and fleeting they are!

TILGHMAN A. HOWARD.

THE term "Christian statesman" is so often applied to men who prostitute public office for private gain as almost to become a synonym of hypocrite ; but that it may be applied to Tilghman A. Howard in its literal sense, those who read this sketch will see.

Tilghman Ashurst Howard was born on the Saluda river, near Pickensville, South Carolina, November 14, 1797. His father was a Revolutionary soldier, and afterward a Baptist preacher ; so the son inherited patriotism and religion as a birthright. When a child Tilghman's mother died, and he went into the family of John McElroy, his half-brother. Soon afterward this family removed to North Carolina, and settled in the county of Buncombe. Here the subject of this sketch remained until he was nineteen years old, and then he started out in the world for himself. He traveled to East Tennessee, and liking the country, made it his home. He had gone to school in North Carolina altogether about a year, and soon after he settled in Tennessee he commenced to utilize his learning by teaching school. After awhile he quit teaching and became a merchant's clerk, and continued in that vocation until he entered, as a student, the office of Hugh Lawson White, one of the most eminent lawyers and statesmen of that day. When twenty-one years old he passed his examination, and was admitted to the bar. He practiced his profession with success, but having an aptitude and a love for public life, he entered it six years afteward as a Senator from his district. This was when he was twenty-seven years old ; but, young as he was, he took high rank as a debater, and became one of the most influential members of the body in which he sat.   He participated in all the leading debates, and his advocacy of, or opposition to, a measure did much to determine its fate.   While he was in the Senate of Tennessee he became intimate with General Sam Houston, then Governor of the State.   The intimacy was renewed years afterward, when he went as a representative of his country to the republic of Texas, whose executive head was his friend, the old-time Governor of Tennessee.   Governor Houston appointed him to a place on his military staff, and in other ways testified his high appreciation of his talents and patriotism.

In 1828 General Howard was put upon the electoral ticket for his district as the friend of Andrew Jackson.   He canvassed the State, and, being elected, cast his vote in the electoral college for his friend, both personal and political, the hero of New Orleans.   Two years afterward he left Tennessee and came to Indiana.   He settled at Bloomington, and at once opened an office for the practice of his profession.   In a short time he formed a partnership with James Whitcomb, afterward Governor of Indiana, and it is questionable if there ever was a stronger legal firm in the State than this.   He remained at Bloomington some three years, and removed to Rockville, Parke county, which was his home until he died.   He continued his business relation with Mr. Whitcomb until 1836, when he dissolved it and entered into partnership with Judge William P. Bryant. This connection continued three years, when Judge Bryant withdrew from it.   His place was taken by Joseph A. Wright, afterward Governor of the State, who continued to be General Howard's partner until the latter's death.

In 1835 it became necessary for the administration of General Jackson to appoint a commissioner to adjust and settle a number of claims against the government growing out of treaties with the Indians.   The place was an important one, requiring capacity and integrity of a very high order, and there being much difference of opinion among General Jackson's cabinet as to the proper man, the matter was referred to the President.

" Gentlemen," said General Jackson, " I will tell you whom to appoint.   Appoint General Howard, of Indiana ; he is an

honest man. I have known him long." He was selected, and
filled the place, as he did all his trusts, honestly and well.

In 1832 General Howard was appointed District Attorney for
Indiana, and held the office for seven years. In August, 1839,
he was elected a member of the Twenty-sixth Congress, his
district comprising nineteen counties in the western and northern parts of the State. The next year, 1840, he was nominated
by the Democracy for Governor. He reluctantly accepted, and
made the race. Like the waters of a mighty river, the great
popularity of General Harrison, who was a candidate that year
for President, carried everything before it. General Howard
went down with the tide, being beaten by Samuel Bigger 8,637
votes. How he bore himself under his defeat the following letter, written to a friend, will tell:

"ROCKVILLE, IND., 8th August, 1840.

"DEAR SIR—I have seen enough to convince me that Indiana has gone the entire Whig ticket—Governor, Lieutenant-
Governor, Congressmen, and a majority in both houses of the
Assembly. The close of the canvass found me worn down by
fatigue and disease, and only sustained by the tremendous excitement of the occasion. I am still very feeble, and part of my
time confined. Repose, however, and proper attention, I trust,
will restore me, and leave me to return to my profession, to
mend up my private affairs, and to forget as soon as I can what
I was and be content with what I am. My kind regards to our
friends.   Very truly yours,   T. A. HOWARD."

General Howard had made an able canvass, but Hercules
could not have withstood the Harrison tornado of that year. It
is pleasant to see with what philosophy the General took his defeat, and how easily he adjusted himself to the situation. As
bearing upon his nomination for Governor and his canvass for
the office, the following letters will be read with interest:

"WASHINGTON CITY, 30th Dec., 1839.

"MY DEAR SIR—Who will be Governor? We shall know
after the election. Will not Palmer run? You must have
harmony, union, prudence and patriotism—everything for the

principles of liberty, equality and sound State policy; no private bickering, no heartburnings. My whole soul is with you, and success and wisdom attend all your deliberations. Our committees have been announced, and the new Speaker has given the Democrats the Committees of Ways and Means, Foreign Relations (of which I have the honor to be a member), etc. We had a little Abolition breeze to-day, but it died away, and this evening all is tranquil, cool and peaceable.

"Your friend, T. A. Howard."

———

"Washington City, May 14, 1840.

"Dear Sir—I received your letter from New York. Am happy to hear that you will soon be in the Hoosier State. You should encourage in every way you can the formation of Democratic associations. Let it be done everywhere. You can, for example, write to Fisher, Law, Stuart, etc., etc.; never writing to any but men of discretion. Palmer ought to do the same. It is better to take this course, because it will bring our people together, and they will, unmolested, talk over their principles and compare their reflections. It is calculated to do good by diffusing political knowledge. Action and concert are necessary, but with these we can carry the State. I will be there the greater part of July. Truly yours, T. A. Howard."

———

"Washington City, May 30, 1840.

"Dear Sir—When I saw you something was said about the general assemblage of the Democracy at Indianapolis, with a view to a public dinner, etc. I have considered the matter. It is not Democratic, and would be to a certain extent, imitating the folly of our antagonists. Freemen ought to meet together to reason on public interests, when they assemble for political effect, and allow me to say to you that the mass of our people will not be any the more zealous by any public demonstration. They will turn out to hear debate. I shall have as many as I deserve to have to hear me, and my wish is to have no demonstration, no procession, no flags, no drums, nor any other exhibition unworthy of a free, thinking, orderly community. I shall leave here at the very earliest day, and hurry home, and you may rely on it, I will be at several points yet in Indiana before the election. Allow my suggestion to prevail. Let us be what Democracy should be, too independent to be deceived by shows or led away by them ; possessing too much respect for our fellow-men to attempt to mislead them on those great subjects that concern the general happiness. Your friend,

"T. A. HOWARD."

The Legislature chosen in 1842 having a United States Senator to elect, the canvass of that year was made mainly upon that issue. The Whigs supported Oliver H. Smith, and the Democrats General Howard. No other man was spoken of in connection with the office until after the Legislature met. The two candidates met just before the Legislature convened and had a talk about the senatorship. General Howard said to Mr. Smith that he knew one of them would be elected if the will of the people was carried out ; "but," said he, "the vote will be so close that a man or two may be found, who, like Judas, would sell his party for a few pieces of silver. There is nothing certain." That General Howard was correct events proved. On the first ballot he received 74 votes, Mr. Smith 72 votes, Edward A. Hannegan 3 votes, and Joseph G. Marshall 1 vote. It will be seen that Howard lacked two votes of election. It was said at the time these votes were offered him if he would promise office to the givers, but he scorned the proffer. On the sixth ballot Mr. Hannegan was elected, General Howard having withdrawn from the contest. The following letters from General Howard in reference to the election are not without interest :

"ROCKVILLE, IND., 5th Jan., 1843.

"MY FRIEND—I have received your two letters and agree with you and others, and have remained at home.

"I am very anxious respecting the nomination on one point, and that is the question of harmony. Never was a party in better condition for a contest, and if we 'pull all together,' success is certain. Then I hope there will be union and a hearty co-operation.

"Let me hear from you as soon as the nominations and business of the convention are over, and believe me to be most truly your obliged friend,   T. A. HOWARD."

"ROCKVILLE, IND., Jan. 16, 1843.

"MY DEAR SIR—I have received your letter, and two or three others, urging me to come to Indianapolis by the last of the present week, under the hope that the United States Senator would about that time be elected.

"Since my return from Indianapolis I have enjoyed poor health, and now it would be very painful to me, owing to the rheumatism with which I am afflicted, to travel there. Other things pressing upon me, connected with my private affairs and professional business, render it next to impossible that I should now leave home.

"I should be happy to be there, but I am satisfied that, so far as results are concerned, they will be the same whether I am present or absent. I have, therefore, concluded to trust my interests entirely to my friends. If any man may do this, I surely may, after the evidences which were afforded me during my four or five weeks' stay at Indianapolis this winter.

"I understand that counter-instructions have been gotten up in Monroe county in favor of a man who will vote for a bank and a high protective tariff. I am not acquainted with the particulars, and have no right to censure or complain. If the people of these counties (Monroe and Brown) are for a United States bank and a high protective tariff, they surely have the right to say so, but I am not the man to aid in carrying out their measures. I would rather remain in the ranks with the real anti-bank party, and aid in still further laboring to prove to the mind of our whole people the impracticability, as well as the inconsistency of such an institution with the fundamental principles of our government, until there shall be no party remaining in its favor, than to aid under any sanction or any circumstances to entail such a corporation upon the country.

"I will thank you to show this letter to Henly, Harris, Majors, Bright, and others of the Legislature who may feel any interest in knowing why I am not there. I shall be happy to hear from you.   Your friend,

"T. A. HOWARD."

The two following letters exhibit General Howard as a father and a Christian:

"WASHINGTON CITY, February 22, 1844.

"MY DEAR SIR—Before I left home, during the sickness of my favorite, who is now in her grave (a dear little daughter eighteen months old) I received your last letter. I started to this city the day after her death, and am now here, where I shall probably remain some time. I am engaged in promoting, as far as I may be able, the interest of our canal. I have written some of the citizens of your place on the subject. I expect to be at home in due time, and, unless my health should fail, visit the several parts of the State. I have not been here long enough to know what is going on; but I shall be an attentive observer of men and things while I stay, and will likely trouble you with an occasional line.

"I remain, as ever, faithfully yours,
"T. A. HOWARD."

———

"WASHINGTON CITY, March 12, 1844.

"DEAR SIR—I received your letter yesterday. I thank you for your kind and sympathetic expressions respecting my dear little girl whom I buried before I left home. I got a letter from my wife, a few days since, in which she seems perfectly resigned. It is a good thing to have the Christian's hope—it withdraws a veil when sorrow swells the bosom, and shows a vision so bright, so calm, so real, that the soul feels all its sorrows to be nothing compared with this overwhelming consolation.

"One word to you—I may be allowed to surmise and conjecture. Stand erect, conscious of your rights in society and among your friends, and do not let any future event, or thing that man can do, disturb you. Your friend,   HOWARD."

In 1844 the question of the annexation of Texas to the United States greatly agitated the public mind. Mr. Van Buren and Mr. Clay, both candidates for the presidency, wrote letters in which they argued against the policy of annexation. The following letter of General Howard gives his views upon this subject:

"WASHINGTON, April 29, 1844.

"DEAR SIR—You will see Van Buren's and Clay's letters on Texas. I do not agree with either of them, as I regard the ac-

quisition of Texas of great moment to the United States. Mr.
V. B.'s letter has given great dissatisfaction to the Southern
members here, and there is much confusion and misgiving in
the party. A third man is talked of, and Cass often mentioned.
I think Democrats should not be too prompt in taking ground
against Texas, as it will react, and the country will go for it, or
I am mistaken. I will write you again in a few days.

" Yours truly,   T. A. HOWARD."

General Howard was correct. The country did go for Texas,
the joint resolution for its annexation being approved by the
President on the 2d of March, 1845. All the letters contained
in this sketch, except the one which follows, were written to a
personal and political friend in Indianapolis, and are now published for the first time. Their chirography is beautiful, their
punctuation faultless and their style admirable, as the reader
will see. They are an important contribution to the history of
that time, and the author congratulates himself on being able to
give them to the public.

In the summer of 1844 General Howard was appointed by
President Tyler Charge D'affaires to the Republic of Texas.
He left home on the 4th of July, and reached Washington, the
capital of Texas, August 1, 1844. In a few days he was taken
sick with fever, and, in fifteen days from the time of his arrival,
he died. He breathed his last at the house of John Farquher,
a few miles from Washington. He was buried in Texas, and
for three years his remains rested in that far-off country.

In the spring of 1844 there was a great revival of religion at
Rockville, General Howard's home. A gentleman of the town
wrote Hon. Joseph A. Wright, then a member of Congress,
asking his opinion of the revival. Mr. Wright showed General
Howard the letter, and he at once wrote the inquirer as follows :

" MY DEAR FRIEND—I saw in your letter to friend Wright
this line, ' Is this enthusiasm or is it reality?' This prompts
me to drop you a line. I have asked myself in years past the
same question ; and I believe that God has answered it to my
moral nature. It is reality. My dear sir, I know of no man
who more needs the soothing consolation of religion than you.
It would bind up your wounded spirit, and shall I say how it is

to be obtained? I answer, be assured of one thing: God exists. Go to him in the silent hour, when he alone sees and knows your purpose; falter not, but ask him, as the fountain of eternal truth, to solve the question, to open your heart and moral vision that you may see and feel whether these things be so. Read the words of Christ to Nicodemus, his Sermon on the Mount, his prayer for his disciples while in the garden of Gethsemane, and his whole mission, and continue to read and pray, and you will find pardon, consolation and joy in believing."

General Howard was a member of the Presbyterian church, but he was not a sectarian. He believed there were many branches of the same vine, many paths leading to the strait gate. He was too great to be a bigot, too good to have no charity.

General Howard was always dignified in public. He seldom indulged in levity; but notwithstanding this, he had the faculty of drawing all classes of men to him. The sober and the gay, the lettered and the unlettered, alike followed his fortunes.

Although General Howard never attended an academy or a college, he was a very learned man. He was acquainted with the civil law, with theology, history, politics, geology, mineralogy, botany, philosophy, and the occult sciences. His mind was a vast storehouse of knowledge, it being questionable if there was another man in the State of such information as he.

During the canvass of 1840 a newspaper published at Greencastle sought to make political capital against General Howard by commenting upon his well-known opinions on temperance. When he spoke in that town he read the article and told the editor to get out another edition of his paper and throw it broadcast over the State. "I want every voter to know my opinions on this question," said Howard. "I am willing to stand by them, and, if need be, fall by them."

On another occasion, when speaking, he read aloud a newspaper article charging him with a disreputable act. When done reading he threw the paper from him and proceeded with his speech. He could afford to thus treat the charge with silent contempt; he stood too high to be affected by it.

In a debate with a gentleman who evaded the issues and went

out after side ones, General Howard told the following story, and applied it to his opponent: "Once," said he, "a representative from Buncombe county made a speech in the North Carolina Legislature, in which he talked of many things entirely foreign to the matter before the House, and on being called to order by the Speaker, and told to confine himself to the question at issue, replied: 'My speech is not for the Legislature; it is all for Buncombe.' 'All for Buncombe' became a common saying, and has remained such to the present day."

As has already been stated, General Howard died and was buried in Texas. But the people of Indiana were not willing that his dust should commingle with foreign soil. The Legislature of 1847 passed an act directing the Governor and General Joseph Lane "to have the remains of Tilghman A. Howard removed from their place of burial in Texas, and reinterred at such place in Indiana as his family might desire." The act was approved by his friend and former partner, James Whitcomb, then Governor of the State. The will of the Legislature was carried out, and the remains of Howard disinterred and brought to Indiana. They remained awhile at Indianapolis, receiving high honors. From thence they were taken to Greencastle, where like honors awaited them. They were then removed to Rockville, his old home, and interred in his orchard. Previous to placing the coffin in the ground, Professor William C. Larrabee, afterward Indiana's first Superintendent of Public Instruction, delivered a eulogy upon the dead statesman, replete with beautiful thoughts. It closed as follows:

"Take him and bury him among you. Bury him where the primrose and the violet bloom in vernal beauty, where the rose of summer sheds its fragrance, and where the leaves of autumn fall, to protect the spot from the cheerless blast of the wintry winds. Bury him in that rural bower on the hillside, within sight of his quiet cottage home. Bury him by the side of the pretty child he loved so well—the beauteous little girl, who, years ago, died suddenly, when the father was away from home. Bury him now by her, that child and father may sleep side by side. Ye need erect no costly monument, with labored inscription, over his grave. On a plain stone inscribe the name of Howard, of Indiana's Howard, and it shall be enough."

General Howard stood among the people of Indiana as did Saul, the son of Kish, among the people of Palestine. Although so very tall, his form was symmetrical. His hair and eyes were coal black, and his complexion corresponded with them. His nose and mouth were large and expressive; his forehead broad and high, and the whole contour of his face denoted energy and intellect of the highest order. In private life his deportment was simple, his conversation delightful, and he enjoyed the pastimes of the social circle with the zest of youth to such an extent that he sometimes half reproached himself with the remark that he "was afraid he should never be anything but a boy." Howard was a great man and a good one, and made a deep impression on the State of his adoption.

JAMES H. CRAVENS.

JAMES HARRISON CRAVENS, one of the ablest of the men who changed public sentiment in Indiana on the slavery question, was born at Harrisonburg, Rockingham county, Virginia, August 12, 1802. When a boy he was self-willed and self-reliant; was independent, plucky and thought for himself. His father designed him for the law, but in order to tame and take the wire edge off him, put him with a gunsmith, intending it only as a temporary expedient, but when the father wanted him to quit work and go to school, he obstinately remained throughout his whole apprenticeship and learned the trade. Afterward he went into the law office of Judge Kinney and studied law. He was admitted to the bar in 1823, and soon after removed to Franklin, Pa., and commenced the practice of his profession. He met with reasonable success, but the reports which reached him from the West made him dissatisfied with his location and prospects. He had confidence in his ability to successfully compete with the young men who were leaving the older States for Western homes, and his subsequent career proved that he did not overestimate his parts. He left Pennsylvania in 1829, and came to Indiana, locating in Jefferson county.

An incident of the journey, which illustrates some very interesting phases of character, is furnished by a member of the family now living at Franklin, Indiana. Before removing he had bought the black woman, "Aunt Mary," at the sale of effects of his wife's mother. Soon thereafter, having decided to come to Indiana, he determined to take the slave woman along. Mary had a husband, or a "man," who belonged to another master. Not wishing to part them Mr. Cravens bought

18

the man, Tom, for $600. He provided a "carry-all" and horse and started the two blacks for Madison, Indiana. As robbers frequently halted the stages in those days crossing the mountains, and as Mr. Cravens had about a thousand dollars more than enough to defray the expenses of himself and wife and the blacks to Indiana, he had such confidence in the honesty of the old woman "Mary," that he gave her the $1,000 in gold to secrete upon her person, telling her not to let "Tom" know she had any money about her, other than a few dollars to defray expenses. Well, they all left Virginia the same day. Cravens and wife, by stage, arrived about two weeks before the negroes. The former's friends at Madison learning what he had done with his money laughed at his "foolishness," and said he would never see his money nor negroes again. In due time, however, the blacks arrived at Madison, and the old woman "Mary" handed over the package of money saying, "*Here, Mars Jim, is yo money.*" The money proved to be all there as when given in charge of the old black woman. The two negroes would have sold for more money than all Cravens was worth besides. But his anti-slavery notions were such that he would never sell into slavery any human being.

At that time Madison, the capital of Jefferson county, was the leading town of the State, and contained a number of men who were, even then, noted for their ability. Marshall and Sullivan, the two Brights, Robinson and others resided there, and it would seem that the new comer's chances for success at the bar were meager indeed. He had settled on a farm some twelve miles from Madison, and had a law office in town, and between the two his whole time was employed. He was an ardent Whig, and took a deep interest in public affairs. Two years after he located in Jefferson county, in 1831, he was elected to the Legislature, defeating David Hillis, afterward Lieutenant-Governor of the State. The next year he was a candidate for re-election, defeating James H. Wallace, an able and popular man. He was now on the high road to political fortune. He was farming and practicing law, but his hand had not forgotten its cunning, and he could make a gun, and for that matter, could shoot it, too, as well, or better than any other man in the county. These accomplishments added to his popularity.

and particularly endeared him to the men who lived in the valleys of Indian Kentuck.

Mr. Cravens had an ambition to reach a leading place in his profession, and realizing the fact that the Madison bar was the ablest in the State, he determined to leave Jefferson county, and go where competition was not so strong. Therefore, in 1833, he removed to Ripley county, and remained a citizen of it while he lived. He opened an office at Versailles, and soon had a large and lucrative practice. Like most lawyers of that day, he took an active interest in politics, and although not an office seeker, he was always ready to speak for his party. In 1839 the Whigs of Ripley elected him to the State Senate, and the county never had an abler or more faithful representative. His reputation as a speaker was such that he was placed on the Harrison electoral ticket in 1840, a position of honor, and one to which the leading Whigs of the State aspired. Indiana never had so able an electoral ticket as the one upon which he was placed. Jonathan McCarty and Joseph G. Marshall were the electors for the State at large, and among the district electors were Joseph L. White, Richard W. Thompson, Caleb B. Smith and James H. Cravens. These men made the hills and valleys of Indiana resound with praises of "Tippecanoe and Tyler, too," and when the election was held and the votes counted it was found that Indiana had voted by a large majority to make her first territorial Governor the chief executive of the national government. It was in this campaign that Mr. Cravens became known throughout the State as one of the ablest debaters in it. During the canvass he and Robert Dale Owen had a joint discussion at Bloomington, which is still remembered, and will be while those who heard it live. As is known, Mr. Owen was the most learned and cultured of all the public men of Indiana of his time, but, as a debater, Mr. Cravens proved his equal. When the debate between them ended, Dr. Wylie, then president of the State University, publicly complimented Mr. Cravens on the ability he had displayed, and at the same time spoke in high terms of Mr. Owen's talents and learning.

The spring after General Harrison's election Mr. Cravens was nominated for Congress, and elected over his competitor, Colonel Thomas Smith, by over one thousand majority. He

took his seat at the called session which convened soon after
President Harrison died and Mr. Tyler, the Vice-President,
had become the acting President. Mr. Tyler soon broke with
his party, and failing to establish a party of his own, he naturally drifted to the Democracy. Mr. Cravens had often sounded
his praises upon the stump, and had voted for him in the electoral college, but when he separated from the party that elected
him, Mr. Cravens denounced him from his seat in Congress as
well as from the stump at home. In his family Bible he made
this record :

" For the Tyler vote I have sorely repented, and hope my
country will forgive me.   J. H. CRAVENS."

In Congress Mr. Cravens stood by and supported John Quincy
Adams in his fight for the right of petition, and in many other
ways testified to his belief in the rights and equality of all men
before the law. He hated oppression in all its forms, and he
hated that which was known as human slavery with an intensity
akin to madness. In it he saw nothing good ; for it he had no
charity whatever. But his party was thoroughly permeated
with its virus, and when he went before a convention and asked
a nomination for re-election he was put aside, and one with different views upon the question of slavery selected. He knew
he had been badly treated, but he accepted the situation without complaint. In 1846 a Whig convention nominated him for
the State Legislature, but a large portion of his party rebelled
against the nomination. The objection to him was on account
of his pronounced anti-slavery principles, and so hostile were
many Whigs to him for that reason that they demanded his
withdrawal from the ticket. That there might be no mistake
as to his views upon the slavery question, he published an address, from which I make the following extract :

" I understand that a portion of the Whigs of our country
charge me with being what they call an 'Abolitionist.' If I
knew in what sense they used the term abolitionist, as applied
to me, I would give a simple answer, ' Yes,' or ' No ; ' but,
inasmuch as I do not know what meaning they attach to it, in
reference to me, I deem it proper, in justice to them as well as

to myself, to give my views of slavery as it exists in the United States:

"1. I consider slavery a great moral and polit'cal evil.

"2. I am opposed to the extension of slave territory.

"3. I am opposed to the admission of any more slave States into the Union.

"4. I believe the admission of slave States into the Union out of territory acquired since the adoption of the Federal constitution to be a violation of the spirit of that instrument.

"5. I believe that whilst we are expending $1,000,000 annually for the suppression of the 'African slave trade,' we ought not to spend millions for the promotion and extension of the 'domestic' or American slave trade.

"6. I believe that Congress has the power to regulate the inter-state slave trade, and ought to exercise it.

"7. I believe that Congress has the power of abolishing slavery in the District of Columbia (the seat of the national government), and ought to exercise it whenever a majority of the citizens of the District desire it to be done, and that the 'slave mart' there ought to be abolished immediately.

"8. I believe that whenever a proposition is made to the nation to extend the peculiar institution, either directly or indirectly, that it then becomes, so far, *ipso facto*, a national question; and that the non-slaveholding States, and their citizens individually, ought, in self-defense, both in a moral and political point of view, to make use of every constitutional means within their power to prevent so great an injustice.

"9. I am utterly opposed to the abolition of the liberty of speech, and of the press, and of the rights of petition.

"10. I believe the slave States and slave owners have constitutional rights in reference to their slave property, with which the free States can not and ought not to interfere, nor ought their citizens, individually, to meddle with them, such as persuading a slave to escape from his owner, concealing them after they have escaped, and running them from the place clandestinely or otherwise, with a view of aiding them in finally making their escape.

"11. I would not arrest and return to his owner, nor harbor, nor conceal a fugitive slave.

"12. I should be more than gratified to see the slave States adopt some system of gradual emancipation by which we, as a people, should be entirely rid of slavery in some twenty-five or thirty years.

"13. I do not believe the Whigs have, nor am I prepared to believe they will, incorporate a pro-slavery article in their political creed. Should they do so they will drive many good and true men from their ranks in grief and sorrow."

At that time there was quite a number of abolitionists in Ripley county, the leader of whom was Stephen S. Harding. They met and resolved to support Mr. Cravens for the Legislature, whereupon several leading pro-slavery Whigs determined he should be driven from the ticket. Their antagonism caused him to ask for the reassembling of the convention which had nominated him, and when it met he placed his declination before it. It, however, unanimously indorsed him, and he continued a candidate. He was elected, and in the Legislature made a strong fight against the Butler bill; but it passed, notwithstanding his opposition. As will be remembered, it was a bill to compromise the debt of the State upon the basis of the surrender of the Wabash and Erie canal to the bondholders for one-half the debt, and the issuance of new bonds for the remainder.

Mr. Cravens opposed the Mexican war because he believed it was waged in the interests of slavery. In 1848 the Whig convention of his congressional district passed a resolution justifying the war, and offered him the nomination for Congress upon the condition that he would indorse the platform. He replied at once, " No, gentlemen, I will not do it. If it was in your power to give me a seat in Congress for life I would not do it." Where is the man now in politics who would not indorse his party's creed, when by so doing he could go to Congress?

Mr. Cravens saw that his party was wedded to slavery, and when it nominated General Taylor, a slaveholder, for the presidency, he determined to leave it. No one who has not passed the ordeal knows how hard it is for one to cut loose from his party. Personal friends desert him and the associations of years are broken up and destroyed. But Mr. Cravens saw his duty in a line different from that pursued by his party, and he determined to follow it. He went to the Buffalo Freesoil convention as a delegate, and actively participated in its proceedings. He supported its nominees—Van Buren and Adams—stumping the State in their behalf. They were defeated, and for awhile afterward Mr. Cravens affiliated with the Democracy. He was one of its nominees in 1850 for delegate to the constitutional convention, but was defeated at the polls. The Democratic party, like the Whig, had too many pro-slavery men in its ranks for a man of such pronounced anti-slavery principles as Mr. Cravens to be popular with it. As stated above, he was beaten, and the people of Indiana were debarred from having his valuable services in the formation of the constitution under which we live.

In 1852 both the Whig and Democratic parties declared in their national platforms that the question of slavery was settled. They also resolved that the further agitation of the question was unwise and unpatriotic. There really was no vital issue between the parties, their contest being merely to determine which should have the patronage and the spoils. In the canvass of that year Mr. Cravens supported Hale and Julian, the Freesoil candidates for President and Vice President, and was himself the candidate of that party for Governor of the State. Of course he was beaten, for although pro-slavery politics was then becoming weakened, it was strong enough to bind with its hateful cords the masses of the people.

When the Republican party was formed Mr. Cravens entered its ranks. Indeed, he was one of the men who made the party. Its opposition to the extension of slavery endeared him to it, and made him active in its behalf. At the Republican State convention of 1856 he was nominated for Attorney-General of the State, and he entered the canvass with all his old-time zeal and eloquence. He was defeated, but this canvass added largely to his already well-established reputation as a strong debater.

On the breaking out of the civil war, in 1861, Mr. Cravens took an active part in securing recruits, and in other ways furthering the cause of the government. He was, for a time, lieutenant-colonel of a regiment of infantry, but he was too old and feeble for active service, and soon resigned his commission.

When John Morgan made his raid through Indiana, Colonel Cravens rallied his neighbors, and tried to stop the invader's progress, but he and his soldiers were taken captive and paroled by the guerrilla chieftain. After this Colonel Cravens did not aspire to public employment, but remained at his home in Osgood until the 4th of December, 1876, when death called him hence. His remains were taken to Versailles and deposited in the cemetery there.

Colonel Cravens was one of those men, rarely met in life, who prefer principles to success. Elected to Congress before he had reached middle life, he could have continued in the public service had he not been truer to his convictions than to his ambition. But he preferred private station with self-respect to public office with self-abasement.

In early life Colonel Cravens was small of physique, but as he grew older he fleshened. His height was five feet six and one-half inches, and his weight about one hundred and sixty pounds. His complexion was light, his eyes blue and his hair inclined to be sandy. He was a brave, conscientious and able man, and well deserving a place in the history of the State.

ANDREW KENNEDY.

ONE of the best examples of the possibilities of the American boy may be seen in the life and career of Andrew Kennedy. Born poor, and growing to manhood illiterate, he became a lawyer of large practice, a statesman of enviable reputation, and died before he was thirty-eight years old, one of the best known and most honored men in the State.

Andrew Kennedy was born near Dayton, Ohio, July 24, 1810. When a child his father removed to Indiana and settled in the wilderness near where the city of Lafayette now stands. Here young Kennedy lived and worked until farm life became irksome and distasteful, and he determined to leave it. This was when he was about midway between boyhood and manhood. He left his home and went to Connersville, where he had an aunt living, and soon after arriving there he apprenticed himself to a blacksmith, to learn the trade of a smithy. In due time he became a master workman, and would, most probably, have continued at the anvil and bellows for life had not an accident happened to him, which, instead of being a misfortune, proved a blessing.

The late Samuel W. Parker then lived at Connersville, and was not only a brilliant lawyer, but was also a dear lover of the horse. He owned an animal which was so spirited and vicious that it was difficult to get him shod, but Kennedy undertook the task, and was badly injured by a kick from the horse. Being unable to work, he commenced to study, and, although he could scarcely read and could not write his name, with the help of Mr. Parker, who took great interest in him, he soon became able to read and understand what he read. Books were a revelation to him. They opened to him a new life. He soon came to the conclusion that the hammer and the anvil were not the proper instruments for him to fight with; that he was capable of wielding intellectual weapons as well as those only used by the hand. He therefore determined to abandon his trade and study law. In this he was encouraged by Mr. Parker, who placed at his command his library, and the young blacksmith laid aside his apron, washed the soot from his face and hands, and entered Mr. Parker's office as a student. He studied hard, and in a short time was licensed to practice. At that time admission to the bar was much more difficult than now. Good moral character was not the only thing necessary to enable one to be a lawyer. Before being admitted to the bar the applicant had to pass a rigid and critical examination, and he was only licensed when he passed this ordeal to the satisfaction of two judges of a court of record, so it is apparent that young Kennedy made good use of his time and opportunities, for otherwise he would not have been able to gain the admission he sought.

Soon after obtaining his license he removed to Muncie, and opened an office for the practice of his profession. At that time (1830) Muncie contained but few inhabitants, and these few lived in log cabins. The Court-house was a cabin, and in it the young lawyer's voice rang out in behalf of those who employed him. While not so good a lawyer as some who practiced at the Muncie bar, he excelled them all in the defense of those charged with crime. His fine presence, his magnetism and his fervid eloquence made him exceedingly effective before a jury, and fortunate indeed was the offender who secured him as an advocate. His fiery eloquence captivated the people, and he soon became noted as one of the most popular speakers as well as one of the most successful lawyers in the eastern part of the State. He had engaging manners, and, in 1836, when hardly eligible on account of his age, he was elected to the State Senate to fill a vacancy. The next year he was chosen a Senator for a full term, and while in the Senate he was noted for his attention to business and for his fidelity to the interests of those whom he represented. In 1840 he was placed on the Democratic electoral ticket, and made a thorough canvass of his district. The people flocked to hear him wherever he went, and at the close of the canvass, the "young blacksmith" was one of the best-known men in the State. In 1841 he was nominated for Congress and elected. He was re-elected in 1843 and in 1845, and in 1847 was again offered a nomination, but declined it. During his six years in Congress he attended strictly to his public duties and established a reputation for eloquence and effective services equaled by few.

Before the close of his congressional term Mr. Kennedy determined to be a candidate for the United States Senate. He aspired to a seat in the highest legislative body in the country, and had he lived would, most probably, have succeeded in obtaining it. He came to Indianapolis in December, 1847, to commence his canvass for the Senate, but he had been here only a few days when he was taken sick with a disease which proved to be small-pox. The Legislature was in session, and many of the members had called on him at his room in the Palmer House, and when it became known that the disease with which he was afflicted was small-pox the utmost consternation prevailed. Resolutions adjourning the Legislature until the second Monday in January, 1848, were introduced and passed on the 13th of the preceding month, and the members at once left for their homes. There was no case of small-pox in the city except the one, and why this one should so badly scare the assembled wisdom of the State seems to us of the present time exceedingly strange. Mr. Kennedy continued sick and confined to his room until the evening of the last day of 1847, when he died. His body was taken at the dead of night, wrapped in the clothes of the bed on which he died, to the cemetery, attended only by the hack-driver and sexton, and consigned to mother earth. The hackman and the sexton who performed the sad task of laying him away in his tomb contracted the fell disease which took him off, and in less than two weeks thereafter were laid by his side. A sad ending was this of a career which promised so much.

The death of Mr. Kennedy caused gloom throughout the State. In commenting upon his demise, the *Indianapolis Sentinel* said:

"In the death of Mr. Kennedy the State loses, in the prime

of his life and usefulness, one of her most honored and distinguished sons."

On the 1st day of January, 1848, the same paper thus spoke of Mr. Kennedy:

" The decease of this distinguished man will excite feelings of the profoundest regret, not only among the people of this State, but among all who had the pleasure of his acquaintance. He was emphatically one of 'nature's noblemen,' and, though born of poor parents, and in his early youth deprived of even common advantages for the cultivation of his mind, he was so richly endowed in mental qualities that he was able to overcome all obstacles, and ultimately to attain an elevated position among the most distinguished men of the State. He was socially, as well as politically, a Democrat. Possessing the most exalted mental attributes, he felt that no man could rightfully claim mastery over him ; and, having himself drunk of the bitter cup of poverty, he knew how to sympathize with and encourage the poor in the assertion of their rights."

When the Legislature convened in January following Mr. Kennedy's death, appropriate resolutions were introduced and several eloquent speeches were made. In speaking on the resolutions, Hon. A. J. Harlan, of Grant county, said:

" I hope and believe that I shall not be deemed by any one who hears me at all exaggerating when I assert that the lamented Kennedy, whilst connected with his public services, either in the Legislature of his adopted State, or in the Congress of the nation, gave constant and continued proof of his sound, practical and statesmanlike intellect, unyielding honesty of purpose, and a generosity of soul and will that ever qualified him for the performance of all generous, hospitable and noble deeds, and which at all times saved him from the charge of any act that was ignoble, sordid or illiberal.

" In his private life he was remarkably bland, courteous and interesting ; and his death has thrown a sorrow and disappointment to many a kind and innocent bosom which his living moments never failed to fill with the liveliest hopes of future goodness and prosperity."

Mr. Orr, a representative from Delaware county, the county in which Mr. Kennedy had lived, said:

"MR. SPEAKER—I arise to announce to you and the House the pleasing intelligence that that dreadful and loathsome disease, the smallpox, is measurably arrested. We had some thirty-odd cases at our county-seat, and but three deaths out of the number. Out of ten or fifteen cases in the county there was but one death, and for a week or ten days previous to my leaving home there was but one new case. Now, sir, although this was calculated to produce joy in our midst, yet we are cast into gloom and sadness at the news of the death of our highly honored and much esteemed fellow citizen, the Hon. Andrew Kennedy. Death, it is true, is not a respecter of persons, and in this case its victim was a shining and conspicuous mark; his social virtues were most appreciated by those who knew him best. As an instance of this, sir, I will tell you that in his own county, which always casts upwards of two hundred Whig majority, he reduced this majority to twenty-five. He was an ardent admirer and lover of our institutions, and well he might be, for it was owing to their benign influence that he rose to that conspicuous and enviable position he occupied in society. When talking on these subjects he seemed to soar, as it were, above himself, and to forget every other thing around him. As an instance of this, I will tell you a circumstance that transpired as he and I came down at the opening of the Legislature. Talking of our glorious institutions, which to me was always pleasing, he became quite eloquent; his eyes beamed with luster peculiar to the man; he sprang to his feet (unconsciously dropping the check-lines, though approaching a critical place in the road), and burst forth into one of his most grand and eloquent strains, just as though he had an audience of five hundred persons. He poured forth to my delighted ears, in the most glowing language, the glory of our country as it now is, and as I hope it will be a thousand years hence; during which time we had passed over considerable road. After sitting down he asked me how or when I took the check-lines from him. I told him the circumstances; he replied that he hoped the tree of liberty would ultimately become so large that all nations and kindreds might repose underneath its shade, and that its branches might extend to the nethermost parts of the earth, and that he believed republican principles would become so prevalent that they could peremptorily give the command, 'Tyrants, about face!' But he needs no eulogy from me; the history of this commonwealth is his history. Of this, the future impartial historians in writing it out will devote a page to the history of the Hon. Andrew Kennedy. Permit me, sir, in conclusion, to present the following resolutions:

"*Resolved, unanimously,* That we have heard with profound regret of the death of our distinguished fellow-citizen, the Hon. Andrew Kennedy, who departed this life on the 31st day of December, 1847.

"*Resolved, unanimously,* That in the death of Andrew Kennedy society has lost one of its brightest ornaments, and the State one of its faithful servants.

"*Resolved, unanimously,* That we deeply condole with his afflicted family in the loss they have sustained, and that we hereby tender to his bereaved widow our mutual sympathy.

"*Resolved, unanimously,* That His Excellency, the Governor, be requested to forward to the widow of the deceased a copy of the foregoing resolutions.

"*Resolved, unanimously,* That as an evidence of the high esteem entertained for the deceased this House do now adjourn."

Mr. Kennedy's widow still lives at the old homestead in Muncie, and a short time ago the author of this sketch heard from her lips the sorrowful account of her husband's death. She said she begged to be taken to Indianapolis that she might be with her husband in his illness, but the boon was denied her. The life of her husband went out when she was far away. His fevered brow and parched lips were cooled by stranger hands while the wife of his youth was praying that she might be permitted to perform those loving offices herself. But she prayed in vain.

The small-pox scare of 1847 caused a good deal of amusement among the people of that day. That the great Sanhedrim of the State should dissolve and its members go home on ac-

count of a solitary case of small-pox seems incredible, but it
was so. Many were the jokes that went the rounds of the newspapers of that time. Among them were the following:

"Why is the present Indiana Legislature like General Wilkinson?

"Answer—Because they ran away from Kennedy (Canada).
"Why is the Indiana Legislature like a young lawyer?
"Answer—Because it is highly excited over a solitary case.
"Why is the Indiana Legislature unlike Santa Anna?
"Answer—Because they ran when there was no danger; he
ran when there was danger."

A local poet thus poured out his soul in blank verse in an ode
to "Small-pox and the Legislature:"

> "Thou hast
> Alarmed the heels e'en from their boots, and
> Given their tattered coat-tails to the wind;
> And, with the vast velocity of fear, they
> Have outstripped the speed of railroad cars,
> And frost and mud have been like cobweb
> Barriers to their brave retreat. Avaunt!
> Fell devil, from our peaceful town, and
> Let the Legislature all come back."

This body of lawmakers was known at the time as the Leg-is-
lature.

Mr. Kennedy, while in Congress, made a speech on the Oregon bill, in favor of "fifty-four forty or fight." At the conclusion of his speech he fainted from exhaustion. However, he
revived in a moment and received many congratulations from
his friends. Among those who took him by the hand on that
occasion was John Quincy Adams, a bitter opponent of the bill,
but a great lover of oratory. He said: "Kennedy, let me
take by the hand the greatest natural orator in America."

In a speech, delivered in the Senate of the United States, by
Judge Douglas, of Illinois, the following reference is made to
Mr. Kennedy. (See *Congressional Globe*, part 3, Thirty-fifth
Congress.)

"I am reminded of the case of Hon. Andrew Kennedy, a
Democratic member of Congress from Indiana, who, some years

ago, was elected from a district which had about four thousand Whig majority.   One day he got up to make a speech in the House, when one of his colleagues asked him how he got there. He replied :   ' I come from the strongest Whig district in the State of Indiana, a district that gave General Harrison a bigger majority than any other in the United States of America.   I beat three of the ablest Whigs there were in the district, and I could have beaten three more if they had dared to run against me."

ROBERT DALE OWEN.

JUDGE BANTA, in his veracious history of "The Voyage of the Oscar Wilde," makes the observation: "Writing history is like making a bouquet in a garden of rare and beautiful flowers—there is such an array of material, so much to choose from, so little that can be chosen, and so much to be left untouched." In preparing this sketch I was forced to reject more material than I used; to cast aside more flowers than my bouquet contains. If I have had the judgment to select those which give forth the sweetest fragrance, those whose colors best blend in unison, I have been fortunate, indeed.

Robert Dale Owen, litterateur, reformer and statesman, was born at Glasgow, Scotland, November 7, 1801. His father was Robert Owen, the noted philanthropist, and his mother a daughter of David Dale, a rich cotton-spinner, renowned for his benevolence. When Robert was a child his father removed to New Lanark, a village near Glasgow, where he operated an extensive cotton mill. He had a delightful home, known as Braxfield House, where he lived in elegance, and at which he entertained many of the most distinguished men of his day, among them the Grand Duke Nicholas, afterwards Emperor of Russia. Here young Robert remained until he was sixteen years old, receiving all the advantages which wealth and cultured surroundings could bestow. At that age he left home, and with his brother William went to Switzerland, and for three years attended the school at Hofwyl, near Berne, conducted by M. Fellenberg, a noted Swiss scholar and statesman. On leaving Hofwyl he returned to New Lanark, and for several years assisted his father in conducting his business, a portion of the time it being under his entire control.

In 1824 Robert Owen bought of George Rapp a large tract of land on the Wabash river, where the town of New Harmony now stands. The next year Robert Dale left Scotland for America, that he might assist his father in the management of the New Harmony estate. On arriving at New York he at once went to the Prothonotary's office and declared his intention of becoming a citizen of the United States. In due time he arrived at New Harmony and zealously entered into his father's plans to build up a community where competitive labor should be unknown, where the work of each should be for the benefit of all. The experiment proved a failure, and was soon abandoned.

In 1828 Mr. Owen went to New York, and for three years conducted in that city, in connection with Frances Wright, a radical journal known as the *Free Enquirer*, a paper devoted to socialistic reform. In 1832 he married Mary Jane Robinson, a woman of great strength of mind, who entered heartily into her husband's efforts to change the social system. After a bridal trip to Europe, Mr. Owen and his wife returned to America, and in a short time located at New Harmony, where the greater portion of their lives was spent.

Mr. Owen was active in furthering the moral and material interests of the community where he lived. There was no town in the West, if in the whole country, where the standard of morality and intelligence was higher than at New Harmony. Philosophers, scientists—men of world-wide reputation—sought the little town on the Wabash for society and for homes. Among these men Mr. Owen was a central figure. His education, his intelligence, and his popularity among his neighbors combined to make him the most influential man in his section of the State.

It would have been almost impossible for a man of Mr. Owen's position at that time to keep out of politics, and in 1836 he became a candidate for the Legislature. He was elected, and during this, his first year of public life, we find him an influential member of the body in which he served. During the session he was mainly instrumental in setting aside, for the purpose

ROBERT DALE OWEN. 291

of education, two-thirds of the surplus revenue given Indiana
by the general government. He introduced a bill securing to
married women the right to own and control property, a measure with which his name is inseparably connected. But the
people were not prepared for such a radical change in the laws
of property, and the proposition was defeated.

Mr. Owen was returned to the Legislature the two following
years, and at the session of 1838-9, he prepared and offered a
bill known as the " Modification Bill," which passed, and arrested the gigantic operations which were loading Indiana with
debt.

In 1839 Mr. Owen was a candidate for Congress, his opponent being the gifted George H. Proffit. During the canvass
Mr. Owen was grossly attacked, being charged with infidelity,
licentiousness and other crimes against religion and morality.
Two days before the election, three clergymen of Posey county—
Mr. Owen's home—published a contradiction of the calumnies,
and bore testimony to the purity of his life, but the defense came
too late. He was beaten by Mr. Proffit 839 votes.

In an article published in *Scribner's Monthly* in 1877, Mr.
Owen gave this incident of his campaign with Proffit:

" I may mention here, as illustrative of the style of thought and
of idiomatic expression among the simple people with whom I had
made my home, an incident of a later date, when I was in the
field of Congress against George Proffit. It was in a rustic portion of the district, and after I had spoken I had been invited,
as usual, to spend the night at a neighboring farmer's. Happening to sit, during the evening, on my host's front porch, I
overheard, from just 'round the corner of the cabin, the conversation of two men who did not suppose I was within ear-shot.
Their talk was, as usual, of the candidates:

" ' Did you hear Owen speak?' asked one.

" ' Yes,' said the other, ' I hearn him.'

" ' Now, ain't he a hoss?' was the next question.

" ' Well, yes; they're both blooded nags; they make a very
pretty race.' "

Seldom, indeed, were better blooded animals than Proffit and
Owen entered for congressional sweepstakes.

In 1840 Mr. Owen was placed on the Democratic ticket as an elector for his district. He made a general canvass of the State, and established a first-class reputation as a public speaker. His standing as a writer was already established.

In 1841 Mr. Owen was again a candidate for Congress, and this time was elected, defeating John W. Payne 602 votes. During the canvass he published an address to the electors of the district, in which he said:

"Many conscientious and excellent men were misled by the outcry raised against me in 1839. I appeal from their votes then to their second sober thought now. I claim for myself, as the good and noble Roger Williams did of yore, that right of private judgment and free speech, which is our country's proudest boast, that every American citizen, be he citizen by birth or citizen by selection and preference, may demand at the hands of his fellow-citizens. To the greatest it has not been refused; to the humblest it may not justly be denied. Jefferson claimed it when he asked your fathers' votes for the office of Chief Magistrate of the republic. I am equally entitled to its sacred shield, though I stand before you but one among the undistinguished hundreds who now aspire to a seat in the councils of the nation."

In Congress Mr. Owen became prominent at once. His speeches on the Oregon question, on the annexation of Texas, and upon the tariff, were among the ablest delivered upon these subjects. That upon the tariff was adopted by the Democratic congressional committee as their tract upon this subject. It was this speech that first attracted the author's attention to Mr. Owen. I was then a boy, and lived on the peninsula between Chesapeake and Delaware bays, where political tracts did not often come. But I got hold of this speech of Owen, and well I remember the impression it made upon me. John Weathered, who then represented the Third Maryland district in Congress, was a manufacturer of cotton and woolen goods. In a speech upon the tariff he attacked Mr. Owen and twitted him for having been born in a foreign land. He declared that if Mr. Owen should go back to his native land he would be commanded to appear before the British Queen to receive an order of Knighthood for his services in her behalf in the American Congress.

I have not Mr. Owen's speech in my possession, nor have I seen it for nearly forty years, but I well remember much that he said. He commenced by saying that on looking around the hall he saw but two pictures, those of Washington and Lafayette. Continuing, he said: "While the gentleman from Maryland was speaking, the picture of Lafayette seemed imbued with life, and I expected to see its quivering lips cry out: 'Take me hence! This is no place for one born in a foreign land.'" He closed his speech in almost these very words: "Mr. Speaker, the gentleman from Maryland is an American by chance; I am one by choice. I had no control over the place of my birth; could I have chosen the spot, it would have been in the Pocket of Indiana." Twice I asked Mr. Owen for a copy of this speech, and twice he promised me I should have it. As I never received it, I presume he had no copy at his command.

In 1845 Mr. Owen was re-elected to Congress, his majority over Wilson, his competitor, being 1,015. In this Congress he introduced a bill creating the Smithsonian Institute, and for many years afterwards he was one of its regents.

Mr. Owen's congressional career terminated in March, 1847, and from that time until 1850, he remained at home, devoting most of his time to study and literary work. In August, 1850, he was elected a delegate from Posey county to a convention called to make a new constitution for Indiana. At the organization of the convention in October following he appeared and took his seat as a member. He was made chairman of the committee " on the rights and privileges of the inhabitants of the State ;" also, on the " committee on revision, arrangement and phraseology "—a most wise selection, for he was, by odds, the best writer of English in the convention.

Early in the session Mr. Owen proposed a section " prohibiting negroes and mulattoes from coming into the State ; and prohibiting any negro or mulatto from purchasing or otherwise acquiring real estate hereafter." He was naturally the friend of the downtrodden and helpless, but he lived in Southern Indiana, which was then as thoroughly pro-slavery in sentiment as the State of Kentucky. In a speech made in favor of this section he said :

"They can never obtain political rights here. They can never obtain social rights here. And for these reasons I think we ought not to have them amongst us. We ought not to have in our midst a race, daily increasing, who must, of necessity, remain disfranchised; a class of people to be taxed without being represented, on whom burdens are imposed, and who have no voice in deciding what these burdens shall be."

Mr. Owen lived to see the negro have political rights in Indiana, and he did much to secure them to him. When making this speech he did not see with the eye of a seer.

A few days after the convention was organized, Mr. Owen offered the following resolution :

"*Resolved*, That the committee on rights and privileges of the inhabitants of the State inquire into the expediency of incorporating in the bill of rights the following section : Women hereafter married in this State shall have the right to acquire and possess property to their sole use and disposal ; and laws shall be passed securing to them, under equitable conditions, all property, real and personal, whether owned by them before marriage or acquired afterward by purchase, gift, devise or descent ; and also providing for the registration of the wife's separate property."

The proposition was fiercely antagonized by nearly every lawyer in the convention. They declared that such a law would overturn organized society and break up the family relation. Mr. Owen combatted these assertions with power and earnestness. In one of his speeches he said :

"It will be thirteen years next winter since I (then a member of the Legislature and of its committee to revise the laws) reported, from a seat just over the way, a change in the then existing law of descent. At that time the widow of an intestate dying without children was entitled, under ordinary circumstances, to dower in her husband's real estate and one-third of his personal property. The change proposed was to give her one-third of the real estate of her husband absolutely, and two-thirds of his personal property, far too little, indeed ; but yet as great an innovation as Mr. Marshall, of Jefferson, and myself (we were the sub-committee to whom the law had been referred) thought it probable we could carry."

It will thus be seen that Mr. Owen's public life commenced with an effort to confer upon married women the right to own and control their separate property, and it may be said that his legislative life ended with it. In the last Legislature in which he sat this was the subject that engrossed his mind, and this the object for which he worked. Throughout the published proceedings of the convention of 1850 are scattered many gems of oratory by Mr. Owen in advocacy of his favorite measure. On one occasion he eloquently said:

"I appeal to the successful settler, who has raised his cabin first in the wild woods, has gradually opened a flourishing farm, and at last has seen flow in upon him comfort and plenty, whether he, alone and unaided, built up his fortune and made comfortable his home? I ask him whether there was not one who saved while he accumulated; whether, when his arm was busy without, her hand was idle within? I ask him whether his heart does not revolt at the idea that when he is carried to his long home his widow shall see snatched from her, by an inhuman law, the very property her watchful care had mainly contributed to increase and keep together?"

In the convention Mr. Owen advocated the section in the constitution prohibiting the State from contracting debt, except for the purposes therein specified. He also favored a provision securing a homestead for all heads of families. His efforts were generally directed to protect the weak against the strong. During the debate on the question of securing to married women the right to own and control property, Mr. Owen's views upon moral and religious questions were savagely attacked by Mr. Badger, a delegate from the county of Putnam. In his reply, Mr. Owen quoted Leigh Hunt's poem of "Abou Ben Adhem and the Angel." Abou Ben says:

"I pray thee, then,
Write me as one who loves his fellow-men."

"When there is a question in regard to my religious opinions," said Mr. Owen, "be my reply this: that I adopt and indorse the sentiment of Leigh Hunt's beautiful parable."

The convention refused, by a close vote, to engraft into the constitution Mr. Owen's section to secure property rights to women. Defeated but not vanquished, he afterward sought an election to the Legislature that he might secure by legislative enactment what he failed to do by constitutional provision. He was successful, and the women of Indiana are more indebted to him than to any other man—living or dead—for some of the most valuable of their legal rights. There were a few women in those days who appreciated Mr. Owen's labors in behalf of their sex, and among them was Sarah T. Bolton, a lady of great worth and talents, who still lives to grace her sex and honor the State. Knowing she was active in sustaining Mr. Owen in his contest for the rights of women, I addressed her a note asking for her recollection of the events connected with the presentation of a silver pitcher to him by the women of Indiana. A few days afterward I received the following reply:

"LAUREL, September 16, 1882.

" *William Wesley Woollen, Esq.:*

"DEAR FRIEND—Your favor of the 11th inst. is before me. Mr. Owen's efforts in the constitutional convention to which you allude were to get recognition in the organic law of women's rights of personal property; their rights of real estate were already secured. This measure excited a great deal of unprofitable discussion. It hung on for weeks—months, I think—was laid on the table, taken up and discussed *pro* and *con*, and laid on the table again. Men did not scruple to stand up and say: 'If women had the rights proposed by this measure under consideration, they would go out into the market to buy and sell, instead of darning the stockings, sewing on the buttons, cooking dinner and washing the children's faces. In short, the proposed law would throw a firebrand into a thousand happy homes.'

"In the meantime I was writing articles setting forth the grievances resulting from women's status, as under the common law, and the necessity of reform, and scattering these articles through the newspapers over the State to make public opinion.

"At length the measure passed, but was reconsidered and voted down. Then we rallied the few women who were in favor of it, and went to the convention in a body to electioneer with the members. The measure was brought up and passed again, reconsidered the next day and again voted down. This, to the best of my recollection, was repeated five or six times before it was finally lost.

"Then I wrote a circular setting forth Mr. Owen's efforts, and asking the women of the State to contribute one dollar each for the purpose of presenting to Mr. Owen a testimonial to show our appreciation of his endeavor on our behalf. Canvassing the city of Indianapolis to get lady signers to this circular, we got, I think, but four names—Mrs. Drake's and mine making six, and we obtained five more in different parts of the State. The women of Indiana, in answer to this circular, sent over one hundred dollars for the testimonial. With this money we procured one of the most elegant antique silver pitchers I have ever seen in any land, and had it engraved with a suitable inscription.

" Having obtained leave to use the hall of the House of Representatives on the occasion of the presentation, we decorated it with green garlands and fragrant flowers till it seemed a bower of beauty, and on the evening of the 28th of May, 1851, it was crowded and crammed with the *elite* of the city to see what had never occurred in Indianapolis before. Professor Larrabee, who had accepted our invitation to make the presentation, acquitted himself admirably in a beautiful and graceful address. Mr. Owen's reply on receiving the pitcher was a grand, logical, exhaustive argument in favor of woman's rights.

" I am not a ' woman's rights woman,' in the common acceptation of the phrase. I have taken no part in the present crusade, but am proud of my action in that long-ago battle for the property rights of my sisters.

" Mr. Owen, as you doubtless know, returned to the Legislature for the sole purpose of securing by statute the law he had tried to have incorporated in the new constitution, where it would not be subject to the action of every demagogue who chanced to have a little, brief legislative authority.

" Although the people of our State paid but little attention to the matter at that time it was taken up by the English newspapers. Mr. Owen's action in the convention, the spirit and bearing of the law equalizing the property rights of men and women, the testimonial in recognition of Mr. Owen's efforts, were all set forth and discussed in the *London Times* and the *Evening Star*, with the gracious comment: 'From this, we should judge that Indiana has attained the highest civilization of any State in the Union.'

" I have written this hastily, having no data with me, here among the hills.   Very respectfully,

"SARAH T. BOLTON."

An Indianapolis paper of the 30th of May, 1851, gives the following account of the presentation of the pitcher to Mr. Owen:

"THE OWEN TESTIMONIAL.

" This interesting ceremony came off in the Representatives' Hall on Wednesday evening. The hall was thronged with ladies, they occupying the bar exclusively long before 8 o'clock, the hour at which the presentation was to take place. The gentlemen were then admitted, filling up, almost to suffocation, the lobbies and galleries. Never before was there so large a crowd in that hall, and upwards of five hundred left, unable to get in.

" Hon. T. L. Smith was called upon to preside, and on taking the chair delivered a short and appropriate address. After music by Downie's Sax-horn Band, the silver pitcher was handed to Professor W. C. Larrabee, on behalf of the ladies, by Mrs. C. J. Allison. It is the finest specimen of silver plate we have ever seen, weighing forty-four ounces, and carved in the most beautiful manner.

" On presenting the testimonial, Professor Larrabee thus addressed Mr. Owen:

" 'The women of Indiana, sir, deeply impressed with the evident injustice of the laws now in force regarding the property of married women and of widows, and ardently desiring that those laws may be so changed as to afford protection to the unfortunate of their sex, have delegated me to tender you their heartfelt gratitude for your efforts in their behalf in the late constitutional convention, and as a slight token of their high appreciation of the nobleness of soul, the integrity of character and the singleness of purpose that impelled you to advocate, unselfishly and perseveringly, those invaluable and necessary rights, which custom, prejudice and inconsiderate legislation have hitherto withheld from them in regard to their power to possess property, and to be protected by the law of their country from the vicissitudes of life and the casualties of misfortune, they have commissioned me to present to you this piece of plate, on which I find the following inscription :

" ' Presented to the Hon. Robert Dale Owen by the women of Indiana, in acknowledgment of his true and noble advocacy of their independent rights to property, in the constitutional convention of the State of Indiana, convened at Indianapolis, 1850.' "

Mr. Owen's speech on this occasion was unusually eloquent, even for him. He closed it as follows :

" In after days it may need some such memorial as the rich and graceful gift that now stands before me to remind a more enlightened generation that time was when the law took from wives their property, and from parents the right to convey what they would to a child. That exertions of mine may have contributed, in manner how humble soever, to remedy injustice thus flagrant, will be to me a pleasant thought in that hour, the last of earth's pilgrimage, when all things, good or evil, put on their true garb, and when the deeds of a past life standing forth, as before God's throne, they might, unmasked, unveiled, receive judgment from a heart soon to be stirred no more forever by the fears or the promptings of censure or of praise."

Robert Dale Owen did much for Indiana, but nothing of more importance than in equalizing the property rights of men and women. For this the women of the State owe him a monument, and they should cause his remains to be brought to the Capital, and erect over them a shaft to commemorate his labors in their behalf. Will no one commence the work?

In an article like this it is impossible to narrate all that is

worth remembering of a man so prominent as was Mr. Owen.
At best, I can but skim the subject; albeit, I will try to get the
cream.

On the 24th of May, 1853, President Pierce appointed Mr.
Owen Chargé d'Affaires to Naples, and on the 29th of the next
June he was commissioned Minister Resident to the same country.
He remained at Naples in the diplomatic service until September 20, 1858, when he took leave and returned home. He remained in private life, engaged most of the time in literary
work, until the breaking out of our civil war, when he was appointed by Governor Morton an agent to purchase arms for the
State. He performed this service with great intelligence and
honesty. Subsequently, a committee of the Indiana legislature
investigated his dealings in this matter, and found them all correct. For this work he received no compensation and asked for
none, being content with the satisfaction he enjoyed for doing
that which he believed to be his duty.

Mr. Owen's facile pen was busy during the war writing tracts
and newspaper articles in defense of the war and of President
Lincoln and his administration. His writings did much to unify
the people and to cause them to stand by the government in its
war with the Confederacy.

Early in the war Mr. Owen advocated the emancipation of
the slaves by presidential proclamation. On the 17th of September, 1862, he addressed a letter to the President upon this
subject, and, in acknowledging its receipt, Mr. Lincoln thus
spoke of its effect upon him: "Its perusal stirred me like a
trumpet call." Mr. Chase, then Secretary of the Treasury,
wrote thus to Mr. Owen: "It will be a satisfaction to you to
know that your letter to the President had more influence on
him than any other document which reached him on the subject; I think I might say than all others put together. I speak
of that which I know from personal conference with him." Mr.
Owen considered this letter to President Lincoln the most useful service he ever rendered his country.

Mr. Lincoln had great confidence in Mr. Owen, and highly
prized his services. He appointed him to revise the contracts
for military supplies which were outstanding when Simon Cameron left the War Office.

Mr. Owen served as chairman of the commission known as the " Freedman's Inquiry Commission," an organization created after the slaves were freed.

When the war was over and reconstruction had taken place, Mr. Owen went back to his study and his books. He wrote much in favor of spiritualism, which doctrine he had embraced many years before, when he was minister to the court of Naples. He also wrote his autobiography, a most charming book, which he called " Threading My Way." At this time he seems to have been greatly engrossed in the study of spiritualism, and his writings upon it are very voluminous. He gave a pretended spiritualistic medium—one Katie King—his fullest indorsement, going so far as to write a magazine article in her praise, but investigation proved her a fraud, and her manifestations shams. This cut Mr. Owen to the quick, for he was an honest man, hating frauds and shams with a healthy hatred. About this time his mind gave way, and it was believed that this sad afflic-tion came upon him on account of grief caused by his connec-tion with the Katie King swindle. But this was a mistake. His mental troubles were caused by disease and overwork. His son, Ernest Dale Owen, in a letter to Dr. Taylor, of New York, dated July 13, 1875, says:

" You may remember that my father, for some time, has been residing at Dansville, New York. While there he was very ill with a nervous fever, the most severe sickness he has suffered for years. When he was recovering from his attack, and while he was still so weak that he was unable even to sit up, he in-sisted, against the advice of physicians and friends, on com-mencing a book, which he had for some time had in contempla-tion, by dictating for others to write. As soon as he was at all able to sit up, he employed much of his time at this labor. The book—a treatise on theology—dealing as it did in some of the most abstruse propositions, required the intensest mental appli-cation. This, under the circumstances, proved more than the brain could bear, and so its powers broke down. This is the real cause of his malady."

His daughter, Rosamond Dale Owen, in a letter to the *New York Post*, thus speaks of the cause of her father's illness:

" The cause of the calamity which has befallen us is simply an overworked brain. My father believed his strong Scotch constitution could, even in his old age, endure all things ; but richly endowed though he was with physical and mental vigor, he could not break God's laws of health with impunity, and we, his children, can not, with our love and care, shield him from the effects of his error."

Mr. Owen was received into the Indiana Hospital for the Insane July 10, 1875, and left it restored to health October 14, of the same year. A few days before he left the institution he addressed Dr. Everts, then its superintendent, a letter, from which I make the following extract :

" If a man wishes to be well spoken of by those who had hitherto slighted or reproved him, he had better either die or suffer a temporary civic death by confinement in a lunatic asylum. *De mortuis nil nisi bonum*—we speak with tender favor of the dead. This has been amply illustrated by the many newspaper notices of myself which have fallen under my observation since an inmate of this institution. I trust that on entering the world again I shall give no cause for retraction of these good opinions of the press, so kindly volunteered while temporarily secluded."

Soon after leaving the Insane Hospital Mr. Owen took up his residence at a cottage on the banks of Lake George, and resumed his literary work. He was engaged to write a series of articles for *Scribner's Monthly* on his recollections of matters in the West, but soon after finishing the first one, he sickened and died. The end came on the morning of the 24th of June, 1877, at his cottage home. His funeral services were conducted by a Mr. Huntington, a Presbyterian minister, in the presence of the family and neighbors of the dead philanthropist. After the services were over a procession was formed, which marched around the lake shore to the cemetery near the village of Caldwell. Here the remains of Mr. Owen were deposited in the earth. One who was present at the burial thus describes the scene :

" It was a scene for an artist. As the casket was being lowered into the grave we looked up to take in a glimpse of the
surroundings. In the company were persons representing various conditions of life. Here was a believer, there an infidel,
yonder several Christian neighbors, and beyond these a group
of Indians, watching with wonder every movement. The beautiful lake stretched out before us in full view ; upon its bosom
was the new steamer, coming rapidly toward us ; the sun gilded
the tops of the distant mountains, and its light reflected from a
thousand wavelets. From the grave you can see his former
home ; from his home you can behold some of the most pleasing
aspects of nature ; from nature as she is here revealed you
may, if pure in heart, see God ! "

Mr. Owen was twice married. His first wife's maiden name
was Mary Jane Robinson. He married her in New York, April
12, 1832. The marriage was performed by a notary public, in
the presence of the bride's family and a few of her neighbors.
Previous to the marriage, Mr. Owen drew up and signed a paper, from which I make this extract :

" Of the unjust rights which, in virtue of this ceremony, an
iniquitous law tacitly gives me over the person and property of
another, I can not legally, but I can morally, divest myself.
And I hereby distinctly and emphatically declare that I consider myself, and earnestly desire to be considered by others,
as utterly divested, now and during the rest of my life, of any
such rights, the barbarous relics of a feudal and despotic system, now destined in the onward course of improvement to be
wholly swept away, and the existence of which is a tacit insult
to the good sense and good feeling of the present comparatively
civilized age."

Mr. Owen lived to see the "iniquitous law swept away " in
Indiana, and had the pleasure of knowing that it was mainly
by his efforts that it was done.

Mrs. Owen lived to a ripe old age, and until her husband had
become one of the noted men of his day. When she died, Mrs.
Harriet Beecher Stowe wrote a hymn, which was sung at her
burial, and her husband delivered a eulogy upon her life and

character, as he stood by her open grave. In this eulogy he thus declared his faith in a hereafter :

"I do not believe—and here I speak also of her whose departure from us we mourn to-day—I do not believe more firmly in these trees that spread their shade over us, in this hill on which we stand, in these sepulchral monuments which we see around us here, than I do that human life, once granted, never perishes more. She believed, as I believe, that the one life succeeds the other without interval, save a brief transition slumber, it may be for a few hours only.   *   *   *   Again, I believe, as she did, in the meeting and recognition of friends in heaven. While we mourn here below, there are joyful reunions above."

Mr. Owen's second wife's maiden name was Lottie Walton Kellogg. He married her about a year before he died. His autobiography, which was mainly written at her house, was dedicated to her.

Mr. Owen was a devoted Odd Fellow, and was appointed by the Grand Lodge of Indiana to purchase ground, and upon it erect a Grand Lodge hall. The building in Indianapolis known as Odd Fellows' Hall was the result of this appointment.

Mr. Owen, having been one of the early settlers of Indiana, knew what it was to travel over bad and muddy roads. In 1851 and '52, he warmly advocated, by pen and tongue, the construction of plank roads, and did much to create the plank road fever of that time. These roads, like the block pavements of to-day, were smooth and delightful to travel upon when new, and like them, also, were exceedingly rough and difficult to get over when old and worn. They lasted but a few years, and gave place to the gravel and macadamized roads now so generally used.

In 1843 or 1844 Mr. Owen was invited by the Union Literary Society of Hanover College to deliver an address before it. So soon as it was known that the invitation had been given and accepted the faculty of the college and some of its trustees determined he should not speak. Rev. E. D. McMasters was the president of the college, and to him, more than any one else, was due the insult that was heaped upon Mr. Owen in this matter.

Knowing that Hon. James Y. Allison, of Madison, was then a resident of Hanover, I addressed him a note, asking for his recollection of the event. In Judge Allison's reply he said:

" I remember the circumstances well, as I was one of the committee of the Union Literary Society to confer with Dr. McMasters on the subject. Mr. Owen had been invited as the anniversary speaker for the society, and Dr. McMasters said, ' He, being an infidel, can not speak,' and we had to cancel the engagement."

The illiberality and dogmatism that prompted such a decision would have put upon Mr. Owen the iron boot and driven in the wedge, had the laws of the land allowed it. Thank God for the law that prevents bigots from putting men to the torture for a difference of opinion!

Mr. Owen's mother was a Presbyterian, and his father a deist. He adhered to the doctrines of his father until middle life, but the teachings of his mother had not been entirely lost upon him. In many of his speeches, and often in his writings, he spoke of Jesus, and always with reverence. In his latter days he became, as we have seen, a spiritualist, and he enriched the literature of his time with publications in favor of that doctrine. It has been charged that he recanted spiritualism before his death, but this is a mistake. He died in the faith he had so ably advocated and defended.

Mr. Owen was a radical of the most pronounced type. He tried to make the world better by uprooting and destroying that which he believed to be bad. He never advocated a measure because it was old; in fact, age was a reason for attacking it. He believed in progression. He thought the world should grow better as it grew older, and he labored hard to make it so. That in some respects he succeeded must be the verdict of mankind.

Mr. Owen was unusually prompt in meeting his engagements. If he made an appointment he kept it to the minute. He was

20

always on hand when the train started, never being left nor having to run to reach it.

Mr. Owen was five feet eight and a half inches high, and weighed about 150 pounds. He had a large head (he wore a 7½-inch hat) and a long face. His nose and mouth were large, his forehead broad and high. His eyes were a blue-gray, over which the lids drooped when he was absorbed in thought. The expression of his face was frank and mild. He had great earnestness in all his undertakings, from the most trivial to the most important. He would throw all his energies into an attempt to stop a street car rather than wait for the next one. To succeed in what he undertook, and to give pleasure to others, gave him the greatest happiness.

He was very fond of making presents. Indeed, this was almost a mania with him. In order to make an offering that would be a surprise, so as to give the greater satisfaction, he would take trouble out of all proportion to the result. He was impatient when forced to attend to business, particularly that relating to money matters. He had a contempt for money for its own sake, and spent it freely. He occupied but a small part of his time in money-getting, yet he made a good deal of it. His freedom, however, in spending money and giving it away prevented him from accumulating anything like a fortune. No traits of his character were more prominent than his buoyancy and hopefulness. In the severest reverses he saw something good. He lived in the faith that mortal affairs were presided over by a beneficent being and influenced by his spirit. In a trustfulness childlike in its simplicity, he believed that, in some way or other, everything that transpires, no matter what its immediate appearance may be, works out for good.

In politics, Mr. Owen was a Democrat. On the breaking out of the civil war he separated from his party, and during the great struggle affiliated with the friends of Mr. Lincoln's administration, but on those questions which usually divide parties he was essentially a Democrat.

I can not better conclude this sketch than by adopting the language of another, one who knew Mr. Owen, intimately and well, Mr. B. R. Sulgrove:

" His manner was courteous, unaffected and conciliating. He
never let his feelings displace his reason and force him to harsh
language or ungenerous allusions.   Even in the heat of a presidential campaign he never dealt in personal aspersions or im-
putations of bad motives.   Severity, irritation, invective, were
no parts of his rhetoric.   He abused neither individuals nor
parties, and was as little of a " rabble rouser " as a quiet man
could be, though one of the most powerful and altogether the
most winning of all speakers the Democracy ever had in this
State.   He relied on facts, and rational applications of them,
and he never made a stump speech that did not contain more
substance in a sentence than most stumpers could get into a
wind gust continued, like a Chinese play or a *Ledger* story, for
six months.   He was what a party orator never was then and
rarely is now—a scholar.   He knew something besides ' ante-
cedents,' and ' records,' and ' platforms,' and the stale drippings
of ten thousand watery effusions.   If he had any animating
principle to which all others were subordinated it was his humanity.   In all his lectures and legislation and fugitive publications his theme was social or individual improvement, effa-
cing mean prejudices, diffusing wholesome correction, elevating
human nature.   He inherited it from his father, and made it at
least as effective by good sense and practical statesmanship as
his father did by wealth and energetic preaching.

" In scholarship, general attainments, varied achievements,
as author, statesman, politician and leader of a new religious
faith, he was unquestionably the most prominent man Indiana
ever owned.   Others may fill now, or may have heretofore filled,
a larger space in public curiosity or interest for a time, but no
other Hoosier was ever so widely known, or so likely to do the
State credit by being known, and no other has ever before held
so prominent a place so long with a history so unspotted with
selfishness, duplicity or injustice.   He was a pure man, and in
two generations of politicians with whom he lived and labored
there can not enough more of the same kind be named to have
filled the bond of Sodom's safety.   It is noteworthy that, though
he began his public life an infidel, he ended it a believer in the
most irrational of superstitions, if it be not the most inaccessi-
ble of sciences ; his father did, too.   Mr. Owen, though, as

might have been expected from his tolerant and genial nature, was never bigoted or disposed to maintain that he must be right and everybody else damned for doubting, in the fashion of Wendell Phillips. He did a great deal for the State in his life, and always set a good example in industry, system and punctuality, and preached by acts many virtues that usually are most loudly inculcated in the pulpit."

THOMAS SMITH.

THOMAS SMITH, known in the days of his political activity as
·· Tom, the Tanner," was born in Fayette county, Pennsylvania,
in 1799. He was of Scotch-Irish descent, and inherited many
of the characteristics of that hardy and contentious race. Pluck,
endurance, tenacity of purpose and uncompromising devotion
to principles were his by birthright. When a boy of eighteen
he left his native State and sought a home in the West. He
located at Rising Sun in 1818, and commenced to learn the
trade of a tanner. He labored assiduously, and in due time became a master workman.

In 1821 he married Frances, daughter of Hon. John Watts,
and soon afterward removed to Versailles. He at once established a tanyard and went to work at his trade. His business
brought him in contact with nearly all the people who traded at
Versailles, for in those days it was the custom for a man who
killed a sheep or a bullock to take its hide to the tanner's and
have it made into leather. The affability of the young tanner,
his accommodating manner and his intelligence all combined to
give him influence and make him a power in the county in
which he lived. At that time much attention was paid to military affairs, the annual muster and drill being looked forward
to with as much anxiety as is now the county fair. The village
tanner became the militia colonel, and seldom was colonel more
popular with his soldiers than he. He thus laid the foundation
for a popularity that never deserted him.

Colonel Smith subsequently represented Ripley county in
both branches of the Legislature. While in the Legislature he
opposed the wild schemes of internal improvement which bank-
rupted the State and brought financial dishonor upon her name.

His course upon this subject added to his popularity at home, and was the immediate cause of his subsequent political advancement.

In 1839 Colonel Smith was nominated for Congress, and made a successful race against the Hon. George H. Dunn, the Whig candidate, his majority being 999. Mr. Dunn was an able man, and when Colonel Smith was nominated his friends were fearful that he would not be able to meet Mr. Dunn on the stump, but after the first encounter of the candidates these fears were dispelled. He developed unexpected powers as a debater, and proved himself a full match upon the stump for his competitor.

In 1841 Colonel Smith was a candidate for re-election, but was defeated by James H. Cravens 1,030 votes. This was the year after the ever-to-be-remembered Harrison campaign. Two years after this he was again a candidate, his opponent being John A. Matson, whom he defeated by a majority of 255. In 1845 he was a successful candidate for re-election, defeating Joseph Eggleston, Esq., an able and popular man, by a majority of 540 votes. He did not seek a re-election, but at the expiration of his term, in 1847, retired to private life. His congressional career was honorable both to himself and his State. He proved himself a ready and fluent speaker, and took rank among the best debaters in the House.

In 1850 the Democracy of Ripley county nominated Colonel Smith and Hon. James H. Cravens for delegates to the constitutional convention. They were unquestionably the ablest men in the county, and were peculiarly fitted for the place. Mr. Cravens had two years before broken with the Whig party and supported Van Buren for the presidency, and after the election was over had affiliated with the Democracy, but there he was not at home. He was an anti-slavery man of decided convictions, and was never loth to express them. His position upon the slavery question cost him many votes and caused his defeat. Colonel Smith was elected, although he, too, was an anti-slavery man, but he was not so radical in his views as Mr. Cravens, nor so open in expressing them.

In the convention Colonel Smith was made chairman of the committee " on county and township organization, powers and offices," and was also a member of the committee " on revision, arrangement and phraseology." He participated actively in the proceedings of the convention, and during its sittings made several speeches of great merit.

Colonel Richard M. Johnson, once Vice President of the United States, died while the convention was in session, and resolutions were introduced expressive of the sense of its members. During Colonel Smith's congressional service he had for three months been a member of Colonel Johnson's household, and for a part of the time was very ill with fever. His host had cared for and nursed him, and in other ways had endeared himself to his guest. Therefore, it is no wonder that Colonel Smith paid this beautiful tribute to his memory, in his speech seconding the resolutions:

" Sir, in war Colonel Johnson was as brave as Jackson; of death or danger he was fearless as Worth, or Scott, or Taylor. But as a man, in his affections he was tender as a child. The tale of sorrow never entered his ear and failed to draw a tear from his eye.

" If goodness of heart, kindness of soul and acts of charity form claims on heaven, then may we not say his spirit is blessed ? Mr. President, I second the motion for the adoption of the resolutions."

Colonel Smith offered a resolution in the convention in favor of a provision to make all banks organized in Indiana responsible for the issues of each other; also, that the banks so organized should issue no notes of a less denomination than ten dollars. The convention, however, voted it down. He made a speech against the re-eligibility of State and county officers, and the constitutional provisions upon these subjects are the work of his hands. Upon the question of erecting by the State a monument to those who fell at Tippecanoe, he said:

" Sir—It requires no monument of marble to perpetuate the memory of those who fought at Tippecanoe. Their monument exists in the hearts of their countrymen. To the soldiers who fell upon the battle fields of Mexico you need rear no huge column of granite or marble. Such things perish; but the memory of brave deeds never perishes. Go to the city of Washington and look at the monument that has been there erected to the memory of those who fell at Tripoli. See the mouldering condition in which it now is, whilst the memory of their deeds is fresh in the minds of Americans. Who is there that would fail to be convinced that they need no monument erected by human hands? Their deeds have erected for them a monument more durable than brass. *Erexerunt monumentum ære perennius.*"

Upon the question of prohibiting negroes from coming into the State Colonel Smith made a lengthy speech, from which I make the following extract :

" Whenever you make a law that we shall not feed these unfortunate people, under the penalty of presentment or indictment, or fine ; and whenever a man shall be brought into court under a presentment or indictment of this kind, and shall stand up and plead his cause and say : ' This man came to my house ; he was starving! he begged of me bread ; I gave it to him, and he did eat '—how, under such circumstances, could you enforce a penalty of this kind upon any man? You can not do it. I tell you, sir, I would feed the starving man, if black as Pluto. The dog does not live that I would not feed, if I knew he were starving. Your penalties would never quench these irresistible sympathies of the people of Indiana. I have too much confidence in their humanity to believe they would suffer even a black man to die at their door for want of food."

Seldom do we find better examples of true eloquence than these extracts afford. The tanner boy had become an orator of power and skill, and, springing as he did from the people, he delighted in pleading the cause of the poor and oppressed. He was " to all the world akin."

When the convention had completed its work, Colonel Smith went back to his home at Versailles, and never afterward held public office. He did not, however, cease to take an interest in public affairs. When Congress passed the Kansas-Nebraska act he left the Democratic party and went into the Fusion or People's party. On the formation of the Republican party he became a member of it, and remained in its ranks while he lived. He was a Democrat by education and from conviction, but he did not hesitate to sever his connection with his party when he believed the public interests required it. He was an opponent of banks, of a protective tariff, and of monopolies of all kinds, but he held these questions in abeyance while the war lasted and the Union was in danger of dissolution. He did not allow party to stand between him and what he believed to be public duty. He left the party with which he had trained so long, and which had honored him so highly, because he believed that, upon the issues then before the country, his party was wrong. In so doing he alienated many warm and devoted friends, but this he counted as naught. He never hesitated to go where he believed public duty called him.

As a politician Colonel Smith was decided in his views and frank in expressing them. He had no compromises to make with what he believed to be wrong. He opposed rings, cliques, and corruptionists in every form. In short, he was a man of the people; he sprang from their ranks, and was true to their interests.

Colonel Smith died at Versailles, April 12, 1876, and was buried there. His widow still lives, and shares, in a large degree, the affection the people bore her husband. It must be a comfort for her to know that her husband is not forgotten by the people of the State whose constitution he helped to make, and whom he served so long and so well, both in the councils of the State and of the Union.

Oliver H. Smith, in his "Early Indiana Trials and Sketches," thus speaks of Colonel Smith:

"In the winter of 1818 one evening I went to a little schoolhouse in Rising Sun to a debating society. I met there a number of young men of the place, among them the subject of this sketch; a young tanner in his apprenticeship; his face smooth, eyes and hair dark, forehead high, face narrow, countenance smiling and pleasant, below the common height, spare person. I heard him that night, and then said: 'That young man will yet be known in the State.' Time rolled on, Thomas Smith married a daughter of Judge John Watts, settled in Versailles, Ripley county, was soon after a member of the Senate of the

State, among the most able of that body. Soon after he was elected to Congress, and again re-elected, and served his constituents with decided ability in that body of distinguished men. His manner as a debater was plain, straightforward, emphatic, impressive. He was heard with attention whenever he spoke. He was a strong Democrat and a prominent leader of that party until the Missouri compromise line was effaced by the Nebraska and Kansas bill, when he took sides with the Republicans, and presided at their convention at Indianapolis. He maintained the integrity of the compromise acts, and placed himself firmly upon the principles of non-extension of slavery over territory that was ever free."

JOHN L. ROBINSON.

KENTUCKY has furnished Indiana many men of mark, and among them John L. Robinson. In his day he was a power in Indiana, and when he died one of the brightest intellects in the State went out. What manner of man he was, and what he did worthy of remembrance, I will try to tell.

John L. Robinson was a native of Mason county, Kentucky, and was born May 3, 1814. When eighteen years old he came to Indiana and settled in the county of Rush. He went into a country store, and for some time weighed coffee and sugar and measured calico for a living. After awhile he commenced business for himself, but, like Patrick Henry, he was not a success as a merchant, his experience as a storekeeper being more utilized in the study of character and in learning the different sides of human nature than in piling up a balance on the right side of the ledger. He paid more attention to the variations of the political compass than to the fluctuation of the markets, and was a better judge of men than of dry goods. He soon earned a reputation at home for political tact and sagacity, and in 1840, when but 26 years old, was placed upon the Democratic electoral ticket for his district. Until then he was but little known outside of his county, but when the canvass closed he was acknowledged to be one of the strongest debaters in Eastern Indiana. The campaign of 1840 was a memorable one, and terminated in the defeat and utter rout of the party to which Mr. Robinson belonged, but it served to bring out his great powers as a political debater.

During the canvass of that year the Whig leaders at Rushville, at the head of whom was the late General Pleasant A. Hackleman, proposed a debate between Mr. Robinson and

Caleb B. Smith. As is known, Mr. Smith was among the ablest
men of his party, and at that time had a reputation as a political
orator beyond the boundaries of the State, but this did not deter
the young Democratic chieftain from accepting the challenge.
He believed in the principles of his party, and had confidence
in his ability to advocate them in a convincing manner ; so he
entered the lists without hesitation, and valiantly strove for the
mastery.   When the lists were opened and the contestants entered, great was the wonderment of the people that one so
young and inexperienced should have the temerity to encounter
the Whig Goliah. But when the bugles sounded the charge and
the battle commenced, the wonderment ceased. Like the disin-
herited knight's assault upon Brian de Bois-Gilbert, that of the
young David was for victory or utter discomfiture. And although it can not be said he won the right to crown the Queen
of Love and Beauty, he showed his ability to handle his weapon
deftly and to measure spears with the best.   The debate lasted
three days, and Mr. Robinson came out of it with a reputation
as one of the very strongest political disputants in the State.

In August, 1842, Mr. Robinson was elected Clerk of the Circuit Court of his county, and in 1847, before his official term
had expired, he was nominated and elected to Congress. He
was re-elected the two succeeding terms, and on the accession
to office of President Pierce in March, 1853, he was appointed
United States Marshal of Indiana. President Buchanan continued him in this office, so he held it from the time of his appointment until his death.

In 1856 Mr. Robinson became a candidate for the Democratic
nomination for Governor. His opponent was Ashbel P. Willard, one of the most eloquent and dashing young men of that
day.   Each of the candidates had warm and devoted friends,
and the contest between them was so even that it took the closest
calculation to determine which was the stronger. Senator Bright
was understood to favor the nomination of Mr. Robinson, and
on being written to by Mr. Willard upon the subject, replied
that he would take no part in the contest, but that he loved Mr.
Robinson " as a very brother."   The candidates came to Indianapolis several days in advance of the meeting of the convention, and log-rolling and combinations were the order of the

day. John C. Walker and Robert Lowry were candidates for the nomination for Lieutenant-Governor. The friends of Walker combining with those of Willard, and the friends of Lowry with those of Robinson, made it almost certain that one or the other of the combinations would be the ticket. Mr. Robinson counted his friends, and finding he would be beaten unless he could draw upon Walker for support, went to him and proposed that if the delegations from Laporte, Porter and Stark would favor his nomination he would insure the withdrawal of Judge Lowry and the nomination of Colonel Walker for Lieutenant-Governor by acclamation. The offer was a tempting one, for to be nominated for the second office in the State government without opposition was no common honor; but as Colonel Walker was an avowed friend of Willard, he declined the proposition and took the chances. Mr. Robinson had so thoroughly canvassed the matter and so well understood the situation that he knew he would be defeated without the votes of these counties, and failing to secure them, he withdrew from the contest and left an open field for Willard. Willard and Walker were nominated, but the rebuff Mr. Robinson had received from the latter rankled in his bosom, and he determined to get even with the man who gave it. Suspecting that Colonel Walker was not old enough to legally hold the office of Governor, he went to Shelbyville, where the Colonel was born, and sought for information among the records there. He found his suspicions well founded, and that the nominee for Lieutenant-Governor was under the constitutional age. He thereupon went before the Democratic State Central Committee and demanded that Colonel Walker be taken off the ticket. The situation was an embarrassing one, but Colonel Walker, who had not before thought of his disqualification, relieved the committee by withdrawing from the ticket. The committee published an address at the time notifying the public of Colonel Walker's withdrawal and of the substitution of Judge Hammond, and saying that the action of the former had been such as to endear him more than ever to the Democratic party. It will be remembered that Governor Willard died before his term expired, and was succeeded by Judge Hammond, the Lieutenant-Governor. Had Colonel Walker remained upon the ticket, and received, as he would have done, a majority of the votes, it is almost certain that the Republican candidate for Lieutenant-Governor would have been declared elected, for the votes cast for an unconstitutional candidate would not have been counted. Thus it will be seen that Mr. Robinson's action in this matter—whatever may have been his motive—secured the succession of a Democrat to the governorship.

Mr. Robinson was the administration leader in the Democratic State convention of 1860. At that time the Democratic party was divided on the Lecompton question, and its different wings fought each other with great violence. Indeed, the administration men and the adherents of Douglas were more bitter and hostile to each other than to the Republican party. When the State convention met the two wings came together, but they did not fuse and become one body. The fight on the organization was bitter, but on the first ballot it was apparent that the friends of Douglas were in the majority. Mr. Robinson and Governor Willard fought gallantly, and contested the ground inch by inch, but the numbers were against them and they had to succumb. They retired with honor, having secured the nomination of several administration men on the State ticket, and they swallowed the instructions for Douglas with apparent gusto. But the pill was a bitter one, and the seeming complacency with which they took it served to prove them the consummate politicians they were.

The Legislature of 1855 passed a very stringent liquor law, known as the Maine law. It made impossible the buying of spirituous liquors, except from regular authorized agents, and then only on the certificates of practicing physicians. Mr. Robinson was accustomed to having liquors about his house, and not being able to procure them in the State, he sent to Louisville for a keg of the best Bourbon and ordered it shipped to him as lard oil. The keg reached Rushville in safety, but before it was taken to Mr. Robinson's house the true character of its contents was discovered. This incident was widely published at the time, and afterwards, while Mr. Robinson lived, he was often called "Lard Oil John L."

During one of the sessions of the Legislature, while Mr. Robinson was marshal, Silas Colgrove, a member from Randolph county, and afterwards a general in the Federal army, attacked Mr. Robinson in a speech delivered in the House. He charged him with having prostituted his office to political purposes. The speech was offensive to Mr. Robinson, and on the evening after it was delivered he met Mr. Colgrove in the office of the Palmer House, and called him to account for it. Angry words passed between them, and these were followed by a blow from Mr. Robinson. He was a small man, physically, and having his overcoat on at the time, the blow had little effect, save to excite Mr. Colgrove to anger. The latter was large and strong, and he struck his assailant a powerful blow, which felled him to the floor. Mr. Robinson was taken up limp and helpless by his friends and conducted to his room. After he had washed and dressed himself, one of his friends asked him what he proposed to do about the difficulty. He answered, "Nothing." "Why, you don't intend to let the matter rest where it is, do you?" inquired his friend. "Why not?" said Mr. Robinson : "I am satisfied, and I am sure Colgrove ought to be. A man can't always whip, but he can always fight. When he fights he satisfies his honor, and mine is satisfied." One of the gentlemen present went down stairs and told Mr. Colgrove what Mr. Robinson had said. In a moment that gentleman was knocking at Mr. Robinson's door. On its being opened, the two late antagonists met face to face. "I have come to your room," said Mr. Colgrove, "at the risk of being kicked down stairs, to offer you my hand. I have heard what you said about our difficulty, and it touched my heart. If you will take my hand, you may count on me as a friend while you live." Mr. Robinson took his hand and invited him to a seat. He ordered a bowl of punch, and the two drowned their difficulties in the exhilarating fluid. The seal of the punch-bowl was never broken.

One who knew Mr. Robinson intimately in all the relations of life thus sums up his character :

"Of all the public men I ever knew he was farthest removed from the time-server and the demagogue. He despised political intrigue, chicanery, dissimulation, tergiversation, untruth and injustice, and held with Jefferson that ' an honest heart is the first blessing, a knowing head is the second.'

"What his ambition compassed highly it compassed holily. In the assured confidence of an honest purpose for the achievement of the public weal he was bold, fearless and audacious, and yet always unerring in the precision of his aim.

"His was no spirit that palls in irresolution and doubts its own quivocation, nor did he consort with those juggling political fiends 'that palter with us in a double sense ; that keep the word of promise to the ear, and break it to the hope.'

"But what he was in pledge he ever fortified in performance. He knew nothing of that oily art, to speak and purpose not. No one was ever at a loss to know his convictions in regard to either measures or men. He was unreserved and candid in the avowal of his opinion as to both.

"His marked decision of character, his clear judgment, his unselfish devotion to the popular cause, his unfaltering faith in the masses of his own party, his pre-eminent abilities as the advocate and defender of popular rights, combined to make him, as acknowledgedly he was, the heart and head leader of the Democracy of Indiana."

Mr. Robinson died at his home in Rushville, March 21, 1860. Over twenty-one years have passed since he departed from among us, but he is still remembered by many who admired him living and mourn him dead.

Mr. Robinson was five feet nine or ten inches high, was sparely built, and weighed from 135 to 140 pounds. His mouth and nose were large and prominent, his forehead broad and high, his eyes coal-black and wonderfully expressive, and his hair was as the raven's wing. Such was John L. Robinson, one of the great men of Indiana twenty-five years ago.

CYRUS L. DUNHAM.

CYRUS LIVINGSTON DUNHAM was born at Dryden, Tompkins county, New York, January 16, 1817. His family was poor, and he worked in the spring, summer and fall for money to pay his schooling in the winter. In this way he grew to manhood, save that he once took service in a fishing-smack and made a trip to Newfoundland. By his labor he obtained sufficient means to pay his way in a seminary for awhile, and when he had obtained the requisite education he commenced teaching school and studying law. Soon after his admission to the bar he emigrated to Indiana and located at Salem, in Washington county. This was in 1841. He at once commenced the practice of law, and, considering the competition he had, succeeded remarkably well. But it was not until 1844 that he obtained much reputation as a speaker, and that was gained, not at the bar, but upon the hustings. In that year Dr. Elijah Newland was the candidate for elector upon the Democratic ticket in his district. He associated Mr. Dunham with him in the canvass, and the latter became noted throughout the district for his eloquence and ability as a speaker. The next year he was elected prosecuting attorney for his circuit, and soon became eminent as a criminal lawyer. In 1846 he was elected to the State Legislature from Washington county, and the next year was re-elected. He was active in the support of a bill authorizing the calling of a convention to make a new constitution for the State. In 1848 he was on the electoral ticket for his district, and cast his vote in the electoral college for Cass and Butler. The next year—1849—he was nominated by his party for Congress, and defeated William McKee Dunn for the place, his majority over

Mr. Dunn being 485. In 1851 he was re-elected, his competitor being Roger Martin, whom he beat 963 votes. The next year he defeated Joseph G. Marshall, one of the grandest men Indiana ever had, his majority over Mr. Marshall being 931. Two years after this, in 1854—the year of the Know-nothing avalanche—he was beaten by George G. Dunn 1,660 votes, which ended his congressional career. On the resignation of Daniel McClure, in 1859, Governor Willard appointed Mr. Dunham Secretary of State. He held this office until the election and qualification of his successor, Mr. Peelle, in the fall of 1860.

Soon after the breaking out of the civil war Mr. Dunham raised the Fiftieth regiment Indiana Volunteers and took it to the field. After serving about a year ill health compelled him to resign his commission and retire from the service. He settled at New Albany and opened a law office there. The next year, in 1864, he was elected to the Legislature and took a leading part in the proceedings of that body. In 1871 he was elected judge of the Floyd and Clark Criminal Circuit Court. While holding this office he removed to Jeffersonville, and remained a resident of that city while he lived.

James K. Marsh, Esq., had read law with Colonel Dunham in New Albany, and in 1867 or '68 the two lawyers formed a partnership, Mr. Marsh opening an office in Charlestown and Colonel Dunham remaining in New Albany. This relation continued until the election of Dunham as criminal judge. After his term expired he resumed his practice, and continued in it until November 21, 1877, when he died.

Colonel Dunham's death was deeply lamented by the people of Southern Indiana, to whom he was as well known as any man in the State. A meeting of the Jeffersonville bar was held to take action on his death, at which Hon. J. C. Howard acted as chairman. At this meeting invitations were extended to the lawyers of New Albany and Charlestown to participate in the funeral ceremonies, and necessary arrangements were made for the burial of his remains. The following resolution was adopted :

"*Resolved*, That in the death of Colonel Dunham our profession has lost a member possessed of eminent personal worth and rare legal attainments. Guided always by a strong sense of justice and right, his firmness, his fearlessness and independence in maintaining his convictions, won the confidence and respect of all who met him, either in professional, public or private life."

The day after the meeting of the bar, the remains of Colonel Dunham were followed to Walnut Ridge cemetery, near Jeffersonville, by a large concourse of people, and there interred. When the earth covered them, all that was mortal of a great man was hid from view.

Colonel Dunham was a very brave man. He proved his courage in many combats, both private and general. No one ever saw him quail at the sight of danger. His nerve and endurance were wonderful. Once his abdomen was so cut that his bowels protruded; he put them back with his own hand and walked some distance, unaided, to the office of a surgeon. In his contest for Congress, in 1851, with Roger Martin, he and that plucky Irishman had a set-to and knock-down.

One of the most striking illustrations of his genuine courage is an incident given while he was on the bench in Clark county. A family named Park, living near Henryville, had been murdered in their beds, and three negroes had been arrested on suspicion and lodged in jail. A mob of about fifty men entered Charlestown about midnight and overpowered the sheriff and broke the jail and took the men out and hung them. Court was in session at the time, and Colonel Dunham was loud the next morning in the denunciation of the mob. Business was entirely suspended in the town, and intense excitement had taken possession of every one. The streets were full of threats, that should any of the officers attempt to find out who were in the mob they would share the same fate of the negroes. When court assembled the room was crowded, and it was generally supposed that a majority of the mob were in the crowd. Judge Dunham had the grand jury brought in and delivered to them a special charge upon the mob, taking occasion to denounce it in the most vehement and bitter terms. It was a regular stump speech against mobs in general and that one in particular. In this Judge Dunham displayed more bravery than in any of his personal encounters.

While in the Legislature of 1865 he had, in open session of the House, a difficulty with Alfred Kilgore, a representative from Delaware county, and hit that gentleman with an inkstand. A few days afterward he got into a quarrel with the Speaker, John U. Pettit, and was ordered to take his seat. He refused to obey the order, whereupon the Speaker directed W. W. Browning, the doorkeeper, to enforce the command. Mr. Browning approached Colonel Dunham, and, laying his hand upon his shoulder, ordered him to be seated. Colonel Dunham at once drew back and struck the doorkeeper in the face. For this offense Judge Horatio C. Newcomb, then a representative from Marion county, offered a resolution to expel Mr. Dunham from the House, but the resolution never reached a vote. When these difficulties occurred, both Mr. Kilgore and Mr. Browning were Republicans. Soon afterward they became Democrats, whereupon a wag remarked that Dunham struck proselyting licks, that whomsoever he hit he converted.

Colonel Dunham's military career, though brief, was honorable. He fought Forrest at Parker's Cross Road, Tennessee, and behaved with great gallantry. He was in several skirmishes, and he always acted bravely and well. Colonel B. C. Shaw, in a letter to the author, thus speaks of Colonel Dunham's bearing at Mumfordsville:

" Your favor of the 14th instant, asking me to relate incidents in the military career of Colonel C. L. Dunham, is received. My only direct connection in service with that in many respects remarkable man, was at Mumfordsville, Kentucky, when the so-called fort at the crossing of Green river by the Louisville and Nashville railroad and turnpike was besieged by the Confederate forces of General Bragg, in their advance north on Louisville, in the fall of 1862. The position was held by about three thousand Indiana troops, all new regiments, or recruits, that there stopped off on their road south to join the commands for which they had been recruited. Among others thus detained with their detachments was Colonel Dunham, Colonel John T. Wilder, and others. Colonel Dunham, being the senior officer present, was placed in command of the post on the approach of Bragg's army. After the attack on the fort was made by Bragg's advance, General Dumont sent Colonel R. Owen, Sixtieth Indiana, and Colonel E. A. King, Sixty-eighth Indiana, as reinforcements. The writer was the lieutenant-colonel of the Sixty-eighth Indiana. When about to depart from Lebanon Junction on this mission, the General approached me with a warm grasp of the hand, remarking : 'Good-bye, Colonel. I never expect to see you again, unless after you have been a prisoner in the rebel army ;' saying, 'I know it will not change your action nor dampen your ardor when I tell you that the forces at Mumfordsville will either all be killed or taken prisoners inside of forty-eight hours.' This was the first intimation to the writer of the truly perilous expedition upon which the two regiments were embarking. Arriving at Mumfordsville, we found the devoted band, under command of Col. Dunham, had repulsed several direct attempts to carry the works by assault, but the whole force of Bragg was now fast surrounding the fort. During the last day the odds seemed so great against the Federals that the boys, being nearly all fresh troops, began to show some signs of discouragement. Several new guns had opened on us. The sharp twang of the Parrot shells and the whistling bullets of the muskets required men and officers to stick close to the ditches, as 'heads up' longer than necessary to take aim and fire was nearly certain death.

'' During the heavy firing Colonel Dunham mounted his horse and leisurely rode along the lines of the fort, starting along the left flank, encouraging the men, not only by his daring, but with words of cheer, and at the same time attracting the fire of the enemy on all sides. Arriving about the middle of the left face of the fort, where Colonel E. A. King was in command, that officer immediately jumped out of the ditch and approached Colonel Dunham. I was in command of the right face of the fort, and seeing the extraordinary scene, I supposed some new phase of the fight was to take place at once. My curiosity tempted me also out of the ditch, to run over at great risk to receive the orders at once, that Colonel Dunham might not expose himself unnecessarily. Running up to them I eagerly inquired, 'Have you anything new for us, Colonel?' The group thus fully exposed was receiving the compliments of the enemy in terrible, close and frequent calls. Colonel King at once

said: ' I was just saying to Colonel Dunham that he had no
more right to unnecessarily expose himself than I had, and if
he was going to make a d—d fool of himself I would, also : '
adding, in a jocular way, that the Colonel was an old bachelor,
and if he did get killed there would be no one to mourn his
loss. ' But,' said Colonel King, ' if by imitating his example
I should get killed, what would become of my poor wife?' Instantly straightening himself up more erect, if possible, than
usual, Colonel Dunham retorted: ' By G—d, sir, I'll marry
her.' Both laughed heartily at the rejoinder. The writer remarked: ' If that's all, I'll scoot to my ditch.' Colonel Dunham rode a few steps further, and, turning his horse, rode
leisurely back to headquarters, in the rear. He had revived
the spirits of all—officers and men—by his daring. An hour
afterward he was relieved of command by a telegraphic order
from General Boyle, at Louisville, and Colonel John T. Wilder
was placed in command."

In regard to his war record a correspondent of the *Indianapolis Journal*, who speaks from personal knowledge, relates
the following incidents to show how earnestly Colonel Dunham
was devoted to the Union, and how zealously he defended it
during the war :

" His command was on duty at Nashville, Tennessee, during
most of the summer of 1862. More than once I heard him complain because he could not get out to the front where the big
fighting was being done, notwithstanding his position, while he
was fighting small detachments of Rebel cavalry and keeping
them from approaching Nashville along the Nashville and
Louisville railroad, was attended with much danger, and he
did not know at what moment he would have to contend with
greatly superior forces, for that country was at that time full of
bushwhackers and wandering squads of rebel cavalry and infantry, ever ready to attack any unfortified position. He had,
therefore, to keep men on guard and scout duty all the time.

" John Morgan slipped in one day in broad daylight and rode
with fifty men behind an embankment thrown up for a railroad
track, and actually reached the bridge across the Cumberland

river, and would in ten minutes more, had he not been discovered, had the bridge on fire. He had just commenced applying turpentine when the alarm was given. No troops were for one hour safe from the risk of an attack by some of these dashing, daring men. Morgan had sent word by some prisoners who reached our lines from him, or, rather, he had said in their presence that he would come down to Nashville on the Fourth of July and learn the Yankees how he celebrated that day. When the word reached Colonel Dunham he said, ' I will send him an invitation to come, and I will teach him some new lessons of devotion to the old flag.' Colonel Dunham was too familiar with the reckless bravery of Morgan not to indulge some apprehensions that he might undertake to carry out his threat.

"A few days before the Fourth the Colonel announced that he was going to have the glorious old day of independence celebrated in camp, and everything was made to conform to his purpose. A large stand was erected, and a reader of the Declaration was appointed. Colonel Dunham was to be the principal orator of the day. Everything was put in readiness, not only for the celebration, but to defend the camp against the threatened attack of John Morgan.

"The day was a beautiful one. The men were dressed up in their best, and all that could be spared from duty were called around the stand. The Rev. Mr. Jackson, the chaplain, opened the exercises with prayer; the Declaration was read, and Colonel Dunham made one of the best speeches he ever made in his life, much of which was addressed to the citizens, who had gathered in to witness the ceremony. Quite a number were present, among them some of the best citizens of Nashville.

" I shall only give one or two of the impressive utterances of the Colonel on that occasion. In referring to General Jackson, whose tomb was almost in sight, he quoted his memorable utterance with reference to the preservation of the Union, that, ' By the Eternal, it must and shall be preserved.' He referred to the attempt made by the Confederates to stop the navigation of the Mississippi river, and said :

" ' We are standing upon the banks of the Cumberland river, and this stream bears off the products of your farms. It is the channel along which pass the trade and much of the travel that support and maintain the prosperity of your capital. Were we of the North to attempt to blockade this outlet, which the God of heaven has prepared for your use and for the expansion of your enterprise, you would be cowards if you did not fight till that wrong was redressed. I live up in Indiana. The farm that raises my bread gathers a part of the waters that flow down the channel of the Mississippi. It is the outlet that nature has provided for the products of the land. You men of the South now attempt to blockade that river, and tell me and my neighbors in Indiana that we must seek other channels of trade. I tell you, men of Old Tennessee, here to-day, on this anniversary of our national independence, under that flag, that you underestimate our manhood, and misapprehend the temper of the citizens of Indiana, if you for one moment suppose we will not fight till this blockade is raised. We will float our traffic down this stream if we have to do it on our hearts' blood. The spirit of the Revolutionary fathers will marshal the hosts of heaven to defend us in a cause so just as that in which we are struggling.'

" These remarks were made in a highly impassioned manner, and in that magnificent dash of oratory for which the Colonel was noted when he was warmed up by the magnitude of his utterances. The boys in blue cheered lustily, and the effect of this speech was wonderful. For fully one minute you could have heard a pin fall, so absorbed was every mind in contemplating the ideas so logically and eloquently presented.

" Other speeches were made, but I will not even name them at this time. The day, however, passed off pleasantly. The boys had a good dinner, and all seemed to enter into the spirit of the occasion. This was the only time I saw the Fourth celebrated in sight of and under the threats of the rebels. Dunham was the man, however, who had the pluck to do so. Though but little has been said of his war record I have seen him tried, and know that no braver man ever commanded a regiment or a brigade than Colonel Cyrus L. Dunham."

Colonel Horace Heffren, who was the lieutenant-colonel of Dunham's regiment, in a late note to the author, speaks of his chief with great affection. He also says: "Dunham was the idol of his men. No man ever took better care of his soldiers than he." When he left the army his soldiers parted from him with warm tokens of affection. They loved him as a friend.

In early life Colonel Dunham dressed very poorly; so much so that many believed he did it purposely to catch the rabble vote. I became acquainted with him in 1849, when he was making his race for Congress against William McKee Dunn, and I well remember his appearance and dress at that time. He was then in the strength of early manhood. In person he was tall and wiry, with not a surplus pound of flesh upon his body. He seemed an athlete trained for the ring. His clothes were scanty and of the commonest kind; a pair of nankeen breeches and a long, swinging linen coat, a hat made of wheat straw, with a rim a yard in circumference, and a pair of coarse shoes, constituted the sum total of his visible apparel. But if he didn't dress well, he spoke well. Indeed, he was eloquent. He captivated his audience, being one of the best speakers on the hustings in the State. The meeting was at Dupont, in Jefferson county; and after it was over I rode with him in his ramshackle buggy to Madison. It had no top. One of its shafts was broken and mended by a pole lashed to it with hickory withes. His horse would have made Sancho Panza's eyes glisten with delight. He would have much preferred him to his mule. Such was Dunham's mode of conveyance over his district. He was elected, but it could not have been his "turnout" that did the work, for the people of the district were ordinarily intelligent, being too smart to be influenced by claptrap and demagoguery. The majority were of his political way of thinking, and those who heard him speak knew he was a man of a very high order of intellect.

In 1859, when Daniel McClure resigned the office of Secretary of State, Governor Willard telegraphed Mr. Dunham to come to Indianapolis. At that time he lived in Jackson county, and was engaged in farming. The dispatch was taken to him in the field. He had barely time to reach the railroad station before the train for Indianapolis would arrive, so he left without changing his clothes. On his arrival in the city he went at once to the Governor's office and asked what was wanted.

Cockle burs and Spanish needles were clinging to his pantaloons and socks, and his dress otherwise was unfitted for any-
one pretending gentility. Willard told him to go to a clothing
store and dress himself as became an ex-member of Congress,
and he would tell him. Dunham left, and soon returned properly dressed, when Governor Willard handed him a commission
as Secretary of State.

In 1860 Mr. Dunham was a candidate for the Democratic
nomination for Governor. The intelligent reader will remember that at that time the Democratic party was divided upon the
Kansas and Nebraska question, one wing of it being known as
the administration wing and the other as the Douglas wing.
Mr. Dunham identified himself with the former, and was supported by it for the gubernatorial nomination. When the State
convention met it was found that the administration men were
in a minority, and that Mr. Dunham had but a small chance
for the nomination. After the convention was organized and
the time had come for the nomination to be made, Mr. Dunham arose, and in a most eloquent speech withdrew from the
contest, and moved that the Hon. Thomas A. Hendricks be
nominated by acclamation, which was done. During his speech
Mr. Dunham was several times interrupted by Colonel Allen
May, in a manner which was very offensive to the speaker.
Soon after the convention adjourned for dinner these gentlemen met in the street opposite the Bates House, when a personal altercation took place between them. Mr. Dunham got
the best of the difficulty, putting his antagonist *hors du combat.*
The convention put him and the late Dr. John C. Walker at
the head of the electoral ticket, by way of a compromise,
Dunham being an administration man and Walker an adherent
of Douglas. Dunham made a thorough canvass of the State,
and added much to his laurels as an eloquent political speaker.
His old-time friend Senator Bright, who stumped the State for
Breckenridge, tried hard to get him to withdraw from the regular Democratic ticket and take a position on that of the bolters,
but his efforts were in vain. Dunham was too good a party
man to falter when he carried the colors, and too good a soldier
to turn his back to the enemy, or engage in a diversion in his

favor, even when so commanded by a general whom hitherto he had delighted to follow.

Mr. Dunham was not a great lawyer. His professsonal reputation mainly rested upon his ability as an advocate. Before a jury he was always effective, often eloquent. His speech in defense of Dr. Benjamin Newland, tried for the killing of J. Madison Evans, was one of the finest forensic efforts ever made at the bar of Southern Indiana. Public sentiment justified Dr. Newland in taking Evans's life, and the speech of Mr. Dunham in his behalf struck a chord in the popular heart that vibrated throughout the State. Dr. Newland was acquitted, and the ladies of New Albany—where the trial was held—vied with each other in testifying their delight at the verdict. They showered bouquets upon Dr. Newland, upon Mr. Dunham and upon the jurors, making one of the most affecting and dramatic scenes ever witnessed in a court of justice.

In his later years Colonel Dunham abandoned the slovenly mode of dress he affected when younger, and clothed himself as became one of his character and standing. He was always courteous and polite, particularly to ladies, and whatever might be his garb, his manners were unexceptionable.

Colonel Dunham was over six feet high, was raw-boned, had black hair and eyes, and a pleasant countenance. He had his weaknesses and his faults, but they were not venal ones, but of the kind that often afflict the most eminent men of the world. " He that is without sin among you, let him first cast a stone."

JOHN LAW.

ONE of the prominent men of Indiana in early days was John
Law, the historian of Vincennes. He was born in New London,
Conn., in 1796, and, when 18 years old, graduated at Yale College, New Haven. He studied law, and, in 1817, was admitted
to the bar of the Supreme Court of Connecticut. The same year
he left his native State and came to Indiana, settling at Vincennes. He opened an office there and commenced the practice
of his profession. In a short time he was elected prosecuting
attorney of his circuit, a circuit which embraced nearly one-half
the settled portion of the State. In 1823 he was elected to the
Legislature from Knox county, and was an active member of
that body. His tastes, however, running in the line of his profession, he did not seek a re-election. In 1830 the Legislature
elected him Judge of the Seventh Judicial Circuit. In 1838
President Van Buren appointed him receiver of public moneys
for the Vincennes district, which office he held for four years.
In 1851 Judge Law removed to Evansville, and, with James B.
McGall, Lucius H. Scott and his brother, William H. Law, purchased 700 acres of land adjoining Evansville, and laid it out in
lots, giving it the name of Lamasco. In 1855 President Pierce
appointed him Judge of the Court of Land Claims for Indiana
and Illinois, the court to be held at Vincennes. This was a position of great importance, and he filled it with signal ability.
His mind was cast in a judicial mould, and he had both the patience and the industry to critically examine the cases brought
before him. His conclusions were reached after much research
and thought, and were seldom called in question.

In 1860 Judge Law was elected to Congress from the First
District, and served on the Library Committee and on the Com-

mittee on Revolutionary Pensions. It was as chairman of the latter committee that he drew and reported to the House a bill to pay the twelve remaining soldiers of the Revolutionary war each a pension of $100 a year. This bill was unanimously passed by the House, and the old soldiers made glad as they tottered to the grave. Where is the John Law who will get through a similar bill for the benefit of the soldiers of the Mexican war, a war that added a golden empire to the country? Judge Law was re-elected to Congress in 1862, and thus served in the national councils during the most perilous period of our country's history. His congressional career, though not brilliant, was eminently useful, and he left Congress with the respect of his fellow members and the regret of his constituents. He died at Evansville, October 7, 1873, and, according to his desires, his remains were taken to Vincennes and buried. A plain monument, one simply bearing his name, the date of his birth and the time of his death was erected at his grave. It was made plain and simple, in accordance with his oft-repeated requests.

During Judge Law's legal practice he had charge of the celebrated case of Vigo against the United States. This claim grew out of the fact that Colonel Vigo furnished General George Rogers Clark provisions and war material in 1779, when General Clark captured Vincennes from the British. Some forty years after the goods were furnished, Congress agreed to pay the principal of the draft drawn by General Clark, amounting to nearly eight thousand dollars, but he refused to accept it unless the interest was also paid. In 1877 the claim was paid, both principal and interest, but too late to be of any benefit to either Colonel Vigo or Judge Law, as previous thereto both of them had been gathered to their fathers.

Although of different politics, a warm friendship existed between Judge Law and the late Thaddeus Stevens. They frequently corresponded, and they kept up their friendly intercourse until Mr. Stevens's death. Judge Law was also a personal friend and correspondent of the late President Lincoln. He gave Mr. Lincoln his first case in the Illinois Supreme Court, and was a great admirer of the personal qualities of that remarkable man. When struck down by an assassin no one grieved for him more sincerely than Judge Law.

I have no recollection of any family in the country, except the Adamses, the Bayards and the Harrisons, that equals the Laws in length and distinction of public service. Judge Law's great-grandfather, Jonathan Law, was Chief Justice of Connecticut for many years, and Governor of the colony from May, 1741, until his death, in 1750. His grandfather, Richard Law, and his father, Lyman Law, both served in the national Congress, and as he was for four years a member of that body, it will be seen that for three generations the Laws sat in Congress as representatives of the people. His maternal grandfather, Amasa Learned, was a member of the first Congress under the constitution, and was cotemporary with, and an intimate friend of, those great men who formed our government and put its machinery in motion. Surely the children of Judge Law have reason to be proud of their ancestry.

Judge Law was not only a good lawyer, but also as a historian and an antiquarian he ranks among the first in the West. For some time he was President of the Indiana Historical Society, and took great interest in its transactions. On the 22d day of February, 1839, he delivered an address before the Vincennes Historical and Antiquarian Society which is standard authority on the matters of which it treats. Two thousand copies of the address were published at the time, but they were soon taken by an appreciative public. In 1858 he published a new edition, with additional notes and illustrations, and this, too, was soon exhausted, and it is now extremely difficult to get a copy of it. It exhausts the subject of the "Colonial History of Vincennes," and no one need look elsewhere to learn its history from its first settlement to the formation of the Territorial government of Indiana.

In person Judge Law was large and commanding. He weighed about two hundred and twenty-five pounds, and his general appearance was that of an intellectual, dignified man. His literary work will live, and he will be remembered when most of those who were cotemporary with him shall have been forgotten.

Michael C. Kerr.

Origin. Engraving & Printing.

MICHAEL CRAWFORD KERR.

MICHAEL CRAWFORD KERR, Speaker of the Forty-fourth Congress, was born near Titusville, Pennsylvania, March 15, 1827. His father was a man of moderate means, and the son was mainly self-educated. At the age of eighteen he graduated at the Erie Academy, and soon after married her who was his wife while he lived. He then emigrated to Kentucky, and for awhile taught school at Bloomfield, in that State. While teaching at Bloomfield " he laid the foundation of his subsequent career of usefulness and honor. There, in the intervals of his arduous duties as a teacher, which others would have devoted to idleness and pleasure, he mastered the fundamental principles of jurisprudence and political philosophy, with which, in after life, both as a lawyer and a statesman, he showed himself so remarkably familiar." After this he attended the Louisville University, where he received the degree of Bachelor of Laws. In 1852 he removed to New Albany, Indiana, and commenced the practice of the law. Soon afterward he was elected City Attorney of New Albany, and the next year was chosen Prosecuting Attorney of Floyd county. In 1856 he was sent to the State Legislature, where he served with distinction, and in 1862 was chosen Reporter of the Supreme Court of the State. In 1864 he was nominated for Congress by the Democracy of his district, his opponent being Rev. W. W. Curry, whom he defeated by a majority of 1,793. In 1866 he was re-elected, beating his opponent, General Walter Q. Gresham, 1,743 votes. In 1868 he again ran against General Gresham, and defeated him by 6,436 majority. In 1870 he was again elected to Congress from his district, beating his opponent, Carr, 5,834 votes. In 1872 Indiana having, by the last census, gained two members of Congress, and the State not having been redistricted, Mr. Kerr was nominated by the Democracy for Congressman for the State at large, and beaten by Godlove S. Orth, 162 votes. In 1874 he ran against General James A. Cravens for Congress, in his district, and beat him 1,209 votes.

The labor of the campaign of 1874 was so severe that Mr. Kerr's health gave way under it. He spent most of the next year in the far West, hoping to recruit his shattered constitution. He was benefited by the change of climate, and returned to Indiana in the fall of 1875, with his health measurably restored.

While Mr. Kerr was in Colorado inhaling the pure air of the mountains, the press of the country was discussing his qualifications for Speaker of Congress. His long congressional experience and knowledge of parliamentary law peculiarly fitted him for the place, and this the people readily saw. His views upon the currency question were in consonance with those entertained by his party friends in the East, and, besides, he was known to be honest and brave, qualities valuable in all public men, and particularly valuable in those charged to preside over the Congress of the United States.

The Forty-fourth Congress met on the 6th of December, 1875, and, after the roll-call, Mr. Lamar, of Mississippi, placed Mr. Kerr in nomination for Speaker, and Mr. Wheeler, of New York, Mr. Blaine. On the call of the roll, Mr. Kerr received 173 votes and Mr. Blaine 106. The clerk announced that Mr. Kerr, having received a majority of all the votes given, was duly elected Speaker, whereupon he took the Speaker's chair and thus addressed the House:

"I am heartily grateful for the honor you have conferred upon me in calling me to this exalted station. I profoundly appreciate the importance and delicacy of its duties. I shall, doubtless, many times need your patient indulgence. I pray that you will grant it; and, with nothing but kindly feelings toward every member of the House, I promise that in all my official acts I will divest myself, to the utmost of my ability, of all personal bias, and observe complete fairness and impartiality toward all the great and diversified interests of our country represented in this House."

Mr. Kerr was never well a day after he was elected Speaker. He presided during the sessions of the House while suffering intense pain. Disease was at his vitals, and it was apparent to all who saw him that he must soon succumb to its demands. At a time when he was barely able to be about, and was discharging the duties of his high office only on account of his indomitable will, a cruel charge was made against him which well nigh killed him outright. One Lawrence Harney, a Washington lobbyist, charged that, several years before, he had paid Mr. Kerr $450 for securing one Augustus P. Greene a position in the regular army. A committee was appointed to investigate the charge, and, on the 12th of June, 1876, the committee reported to the House that there was no evidence to sustain the charge. The report closes as follows:

"Your committee have found no difficulty in reaching the conclusion that the charge, as made by Harney, as to the payment of the amount of money stated, or any other sum, to Mr. Kerr for the object and purpose named, is unqualifiedly false; that Mr. Kerr stands fully exonerated from all implication in anywise affecting his personal honor or official integrity. Your committee find nothing throughout the whole progress of this investigation to impair or detract from the well-established reputation that he enjoys for unquestioned personal integrity and unsullied purity of official record."

Messrs. Clymer and Danford made speeches in favor of adopting the report, after which the following proceedings were had by the House:

"Mr. Clymer—I ask the previous question on the adoption of this report.

"The previous question was seconded and the main question ordered.

"Mr. Garfield—I ask that the question on the adoption of the report be taken by a rising vote.

"Mr. Clymer—I hope that will be done.

"Mr. Blackburn—I trust the suggestion of the gentleman from Ohio (Mr. Garfield) will be adopted.

22

" The affirmative vote being called for, all the members present rose.

" Mr. Banks—Let there be a count; it makes a record.

" Mr. Garfield—I ask unanimous consent that it be entered on the record that the report was unanimously adopted.

" Mr. Milliken—By a rising vote.

" The Speaker (pro tempore)—Unless there be objection the record suggested by the gentleman from Ohio will be entered.

" Mr. Banks—There should be a count of the votes; it makes a record.

" The negative vote being called for and no member rising, the result was announced—yeas, 210; nays, none.

" The Speaker (pro tempore)—The report is adopted by a unanimous vote.

" Mr. Garfield—I renew my request that it be recorded that the report was adopted unanimously by a rising vote.

" The Speaker (pro tempore)—It will be so recorded.

" Mr. Leavenworth—It seems to me, Mr. Speaker, that it would be highly proper that this House should furnish to Mr. Kerr, in the most formal manner, a certified copy of our proceedings on this occasion. I move that such copy be furnished to him by the Clerk of this House.

" The Speaker (pro tempore)—The chair hears no objection and the order is made."

Never was a man more completely vindicated than was Mr. Kerr. Few men so long in public life have escaped charges affecting their public reputation, and fewer still have been so grandly upheld. The charge, instead of being a blot upon his memory, but adds to his glory. In the language of Mr. Hurlburt, of Illinois, when speaking of the report of the committee : " The long record of an honorable life outweighs all charges of those loose defamers whom these base times encourage to detraction and scandal." He also declared that Mr. Kerr's blameless life was a shield to " protect him from the envenomed shafts of malice."

Mr. Kerr was now too sick to preside in the House, and, hoping that rest and mountain air would benefit him, he left Washington shortly after the warm weather set in, and went to

Rockbridge Alum Springs, in West Virginia. At first the water and the air helped him, but, in a short time, they lost their power for good. The base charge of Harney had done its work. The magnificent vindication of Congress came too late for him to rally. He continued to grow worse, and was conscious that his end was near. On the afternoon of the 15th of August, 1876, he telegraphed his friend, S. S. Cox, of New York, " My condition is very critical ; no change since morning." The dispatch was read in the House, and created great feeling. Mr. Banks, of Massachusetts, took the floor, and, after delivering a feeling speech, offered the following resolution :

"*Resolved*, That the House of Representatives, at the moment of closing the present session, tenders to Hon. Michael C. Kerr, its beloved and honored presiding officer, the unanimous expression of the heartfelt sympathy of its members in his affliction, and they hope that the recovery of his health may soon restore to his associates in the public service the wisdom of his counsel and the beneficent influence of his example."

The resolution was unanimously adopted, and the Speaker was requested to communicate the same to Mr. Kerr by telegraph.

The message came none too quickly, if it was to reach the Speaker alive, for four days afterward, on the 19th of August, 1876, he breathed his last.

A few days after the death of Mr. Kerr his remains were started on their way to the West, escorted by Senator Ferry, President pro tempore of the Senate, Mr. Adams, clerk of the House, Mr. Morrison, chairman of the Committee of Ways and Means, all under charge of John G. Thompson, door-keeper of the House. The widow and only son of the dead statesman were with the cortege. A special train, containing a large number of prominent citizens, left Indianapolis on the 23d of August, and met the remains at Knightstown, where they boarded the train containing the corpse. The party reached New Albany at 12 o'clock that night, and were met at the depot by an immense concourse of people, and the remains were taken to the Court-house. The casket was placed in the rotunda, where it lay in state until 8 o'clock the next evening, and was then taken to the home of the late Speaker.

New Albany put on the habiliments of woe. All her public buildings and many private ones were draped in mourning. The next day Dr. Conn preached an eloquent funeral discourse over the honored dead, after which the body was taken to the cemetery at New Albany and buried.

When Congress met, in December, action was taken on the death of the late Speaker, several eloquent eulogies being pronounced. In his address, Senator McDonald said:

" He filled every station to which he was called, public and private, with honor. He honored the city in which he lived, and his name is there cherished as a household word. He honored the district which had conferred upon him its highest favor, and his memory will be long held in reverence by his people. He honored the State of his adoption, and it will preserve his name upon the roll of its most illustrious citizens. He honored the high place to which he was called by the representatives of the whole people, and for that we this day place his name ' in memoriam ' upon the records of the Congress of the nation, there to remain for all time."

Senator Morton, in a very eulogistic speech, said of the dead Speaker:

" His name will be remembered with pride and with affection in Indiana. He was one of her most highly favored and gifted sons, and it gives me satisfaction to bear testimony to his patriotism. I believe he was a devout lover of his country, and went for that which he believed was for the best. I have always given him credit for his integrity, for his patriotism, and for love of his country, and the strongest testimony which I can bear to the character of Mr. Kerr is to say that he was regarded by men of all parties in Indiana as an honest man, an able man, a patriotic man, and that his death was mourned by all his neighbors, and by all who knew him, without distinction of party."

Those who know how chary Senator Morton was of compliments to political opponents will properly appreciate this eulogy

upon the life of Mr. Kerr.   It is a just tribute of one great man
to the memory of another.

Mr. Kerr was a patriot.   In 1864 he was a candidate for the
Democratic nomination for Congress, the late Colonel Cyrus L.
Dunham being his principal competitor.   The nominating con-
vention met at Jeffersonville, in the old Methodist church, on
Wall street.   Politics was at fever heat, and the contest between
Mr. Kerr and Colonel Dunham was very close.   An hour or so
before the convention was to meet Mr. Kerr called a caucus of
his friends in a room over the store of General Sparks.   There
were present at the caucus several of Mr. Kerr's friends from
New Albany; General Sparks and Mr. J. P. Applegate, from
Clark county; Hon. William H. English, then a resident of
Scott county; General James A. Cravens, of Washington county, and a few other gentlemen from different parts of the district.
The gentlemen thus called together supposed the purpose of the
meeting was to make arrangements for the management of the
convention.   When all were seated, Mr. Kerr arose, drew himself up to his full height of six feet or more, and, with sup-
pressed excitement but with perfect self-control, said he must
withdraw from the race for Congress ; that he was in possession
of the knowledge that a conspiracy existed against the government of the State ; that the conspirators were Democrats; that
he felt it his duty to go to Indianapolis and lay the facts before
Governor Morton; that such a course would embitter certain
Democrats and jeopardize his election should he be a candidate.
Mr. English and others made remarks after Mr. Kerr had taken
his seat, the purport of which was that he was right in his purpose to make known and denounce the conspiracy, but wrong
in determining to withdraw from the contest ; that only a few
hot-heads had gone wrong ; that the great body of the party was
loyal to the government.   Mr. Kerr persisted in his purpose to
decline, and it was formally announced that he was no longer a
candidate.   Afterward, however, several gentlemen were sent
to him by the various county delegations, who urged him to
stand.   He finally consented to do so, and was nominated.   He
came at once to Indianapolis to expose the conspiracy, and what
he did can be best told by giving the testimony of one of the

witnesses in the trials of Bowles, Milligan and others. Says
this witness :

"As I walked down Washington street I saw a gentleman
coming up rapidly, and I stopped him : "Hello! Kerr, what
has brought you here?' said I. He seemed very much excited.
'Do you know anything?' he said ; and I said, 'Do you know
anything?' 'Yes,' he replied. 'What is it?' said I. He then
said, 'The devil's to pay in our section of the State ; the people
of Washington, Harrison and Floyd counties, and that neighborhood, have got the idea that a revolution was impending ;
the farmers were frightened and were selling their hay in the
fields and their wheat in the stacks, and all the property that
could be was being converted into greenbacks.'"

Mr. Kerr was so deeply impressed with the danger of the
situation that he and the witness from whom I have quoted
went to the residence of Hon. Joseph E. McDonald in the
night, awakened that gentleman, and told him what they knew
about the conspiracy. It was agreed that a meeting of prominent
Democrats should be called next morning at Mr. McDonald's
office, to consider the situation. The meeting was held, and
during its sitting Mr. Kerr made a speech. I again quote from
this witness :

"He spoke about this excitement, this revolutionary scheme,
and said that he came up on purpose to put a stop to the thing.
I think he said it was our duty to stop it, and if it could not be
stopped¡ in any other way it was our duty to inform the authorities."

Mr. Kerr was sustained in his position by Mr. McDonald and
other prominent Democrats, but there is no gainsaying the fact
that he was the leading man of his party in the effort to destroy
the conspiracy, which, had it been inaugurated, would have
deluged Indiana with blood.

The action of Mr. Kerr in proposing to decline the race for
Congress in his district was in keeping with his character.
Young, and ambitious for political preferment, he was yet wil-

ling to stand aside for others when he believed duty called him to make the sacrifice.

Mr. Kerr was very resolute and persistent in any course he adopted. He fought three-fourths of the Democrats of his county on the question of a tariff, and he fought nearly all the prominent men of his party in the State on the currency question. On these questions he didn't consider policy. He bravely advocated what he believed to be right, regardless of policy.

Without being a professor of religion, Mr. Kerr was strictly moral. He had no vices, either great or small, being as pure a man as ever lived.

Mr. Kerr lived and died a poor man. With opportunities to make money possessed by few he chose to do that which was right, preferring a good name to great riches. When on his dying bed he said to his son and only child: " I have nothing to leave you, my son, except my good name. Guard it and your mother's honor, and live as I have lived. Pay all my debts, if my estate will warrant it without leaving your mother penniless. Otherwise pay what you can, and then go to my creditors and tell them the truth, and pledge your honor to wipe out the indebtedness." Such a father could trust his son to do his commands.

In 1862, when Mr. Kerr went into politics he had a fine law practice, which his entrance into public life measurably destroyed. At a bar which contained an Otto, a Crawford, a Smith, a Browne, a Howk, a Stotsenburg, and other leading men, he ranked with the best.

Mr. Kerr was not a pleasant speaker. He was too honest and conscientious to stand before an audience and troll off something he thought every intelligent man knew as well as himself. Although possessed of ambition, he was exceedingly modest, and a modest man rarely becomes an attractive extemporaneous speaker.

Such is a brief outline of the life and some of the leading characteristics of Michael C. Kerr, a man who reached the third office in the government of the country, and one whom Indiana delighted to honor.

ISAAC BLACKFORD.

Isaac Blackford, for thirty-five years a Judge of the Supreme Court of Indiana, was born at Bound Brook, Somerset county, New Jersey, November 6, 1786. When sixteen years old he entered Princeton College, from which, four years afterward, he graduated with honor. He then commenced the study of the law in the office of Colonel George McDonald, where he remained a year, and then entered that of Gabriel Ford, where he continued his legal studies. In 1810 he received his license, and two years afterward left New Jersey and came to Dayton, Ohio. He remained there but a short time, and then came to Indiana. He stopped at Brookville awhile, and then went to Salem and located. On the organization of Washington county, in 1813, he was chosen its first Clerk and Recorder. In after years he used to say that his principal duty while filling these offices was the recording of marks. At that time there were few inclosures for stock, and, as it ran at large, it was important that it be so marked that it might be identified by the owner; hence the marks. The next year Mr. Blackford was elected Clerk of the Territorial Legislature, which office he resigned on being appointed Judge of the first judicial circuit. He then removed to Vincennes, and in the fall of 1815 resigned the judgeship and opened a law office. The next year, 1816, he was elected a representative from the county of Knox to the first Legislature under the State government. There were many men in that body who afterward became distinguished in the history of Indiana, among them James Noble, Amos Lane, John Dumont, Williamson Dunn, Davis Floyd, Samuel Milroy and Ratliff Boon; but even at that early day Judge Blackford's reputation for judicial fairness was so well established that he was chosen Speaker without a contest. The next year Governor Jennings appointed him a Judge of the Supreme Court, a position he graced and honored for the next thirty-five years.

In 1853, his term as Supreme Judge having expired, he opened an office at Indianapolis for the practice of the law. He had been so long on the bench that he was ill at ease when he went into court with a case. His effort to get into practice was not successful, and in a short time he measurably abandoned it. General Terrell narrates this amusing incident in Judge Blackford's career at that time:

"One of his first cases was tried before a jury in the Marion Court of Common Pleas, Judge David Wallace presiding. The testimony on both sides had been submitted, and as the day was far spent court adjourned until next morning, when the attorneys were to make their arguments. Judge Blackford was on hand bright and early, apparently eager to proceed with the case. It was the first time in thirty-five years that he had appeared as an advocate before a jury. When the time came for him to make his argument he arose with some trepidation, and thrusting his hand into his coat pocket for the manuscript of his speech, discovered, to his astonishment, that he had left it in his office. Without the document he was entirely helpless, and he was compelled to beg the indulgence of the court and jury until he could go out and get it, which he did as quickly as possible; but he was evidently much embarrassed and humiliated by the unfortunate circumstance. He read his remarks in a stumbling, monotonous way, that probably made little impression on the minds of the 'twelve good and lawful' jurors, inasmuch as they brought in a verdict against him. It is not unlikely that this mishap and adverse verdict had some influence in his retirement from practice in the courts."

Judge Blackford was not at home at the bar, and he longed to be again upon the bench.. The opportunity soon came. In 1855, on the organization of the Court of Claims at Washington, President Pierce appointed him one of its judges. He held this office until his death, December 31, 1859. He discharged its duties in a way that added luster to a name already illustrious, and died the best known and most eminent jurist Indiana has ever produced.

When Judge Blackford's death became known at Washington a meeting of the Indiana congressional delegation was held to take action upon it. Albert G. Porter, then the representative from the Indianapolis district, in a speech delivered on that occasion, said:

"It is hardly possible, sir, for persons who reside in an old community to appreciate the extent to which, in a new country, the character of a public man may be impressed upon the public mind. There is not a community in Indiana, not a single one, in which the name of Judge Blackford is not a household word. He has been identified with our State from the beginning. He may almost be said to be a part of our institutions. Judicial ability, judicial purity, approaching nearly to the idea of the divine, private worth, singularly blending the simplicity of childhood with the sober gravity of age—these were represented, not simply in the mind of the profession, but in the universal popular mind of Indiana, in the person of Isaac Blackford."

At the same meeting General William McKee Dunn, then the representative from the Madison district, said: "For more than a quarter of a century Judge Blackford occupied a seat on the Supreme Bench of our State. He has done more than any other man to build up our jurisprudence on the broad foundation of the common law. His reports are not only an honor to him, but to the State of Indiana also. It has been well said here that he was an 'upright judge,' and not only was he so in fact, but so careful was he of his judicial character, and so regardful of all the proprieties of his position, that he was universally recognized and esteemed as 'an upright judge.'

"Indiana is proud of her great jurist, but to-day she mourns the loss of one of her most eminent citizens, and now by her united delegation in Congress claims that all that is mortal of Isaac Blackford may be entrusted to her care and have sepulture in her bosom. Let his body be borne back to the State with whose judicial history his name is inseparably connected, and there at its capital let him be buried, where those from all parts of the State who have so long known, revered and loved him may visit his tomb and pay affectionate tribute to his memory."

On Thursday, January 13, 1860, while the Democratic State convention was in session, Governor Willard announced to the convention that the remains of Judge Blackford had reached Indianapolis and were then lying in state at the Senate chamber. He also said the Judge's funeral would take place that afternoon, and invited the delegates to view the remains and attend the funeral. On the same day the Indianapolis bar held a meeting in reference to his death, at which Judge Morrison presided and John H. Rea acted as secretary. John L. Ketcham, chairman of the Committee on Resolutions, reported a series, including the following, which were unanimously adopted:

"*Resolved*, That while we receive, in the profoundest sorrow, the announcement of the decease of the late Hon. Isaac Blackford, we cherish for his memory the highest regard, acknowledging that he has contributed more than any other man in Indiana to the high character of her judicial reputation; that such judges are a blessing to any State, and deserve to be held in great respect by all the people.

"*Resolved*, That as we recognize in this removal the hand of God, we also acknowledge His goodness to the State in sparing so long one who presided over her highest judicial tribunal with such marked ability and spotless integrity."

Judge Blackford's remains have been interred in Crown Hill Cemetery, and at his grave stands a monument upon which is engraven the leading events of his life, the inscription closing as follows:

" The honors thus conferred were the just rewards of an industry that never wearied, of an integrity that was never questioned."

A year or so ago Mr. D. S. Alexander, now Fifth Auditor of the Treasury at Washington, contributed a valuable paper on the life and character of Judge Blackford to the *Southern Law*

Review. Mr. Alexander, however, does not do justice either
to the natural talents or legal attainments of the distinguished
jurist. He says that " at no time in his long career was he
(Judge Blackford) esteemed a great lawyer or a profound jurist." Again : " He was in no sense a great man, and candor
compels the admission that in some respects he was a very ordinary man." I must take issue with Mr. Alexander on this
subject. His verdict is not the verdict of the world. A man's
ability can be determined by what he accomplishes in life. By
this standard Judge Blackford was a great man, for he accomplished much. When he entered upon his public life there was
no scarcity of able men about him. The pioneers of Indiana
who reached distinction were all able, and most of them highly
educated. It would have been impossible for one " not a great
lawyer " to have reached Judge Blackford's eminence in judicature, and it would have been equally impossible for " a very
ordinary man " so early in life to have attained his distinction
in the politics of the State. While his talents were not of the
highest order, they were good, and his great industry enabled
him to accomplish more than many possessing greater natural
parts.

In 1825 Judge Blackford was a candidate for Governor of
Indiana, but was defeated by James Brown Ray by a majority
of 2,622 votes. Subsequently he was a candidate for United
States Senator, and was beaten by William Hendricks by a
single vote.

Judge Blackford was very careful in his expenditure of money.
He seldom parted with it without an equivalent.

In March, 1851, when Jenny Lind sang in the Madison pork-
house, he went to Madison to hear her. There was much excitement the evening she sang over the sale of tickets, but he
stood at the box office and patiently bided his time. When the
bidding became slack, and the price of tickets dropped to five
dollars he made his purchase. He was not a benevolent man,
but he seldom refused a contribution, when called on, for a
charitable purpose.

Judge Blackford had an only son, George, whose mother
died in giving him birth. The father was wrapped up in his
boy. He was not only an only child, but he was the only hope

of perpetuating the Blackford name. This boy, this child and companion of the cloisteral jurist, sickened and died while at Lexington, Kentucky, under medical treatment of Dr. Dudley. The father went to Lexington, and after seeing his boy laid away in his tomb, returned to his home. It was in the summer time, and he reached Indianapolis in the middle of the night. Instead of going to his room in the Circle, he went to the residence of Henry P. Coburn, and, without knocking, opened the door and entered the house, a house in which he was ever welcome. Soon afterward one of Mr. Coburn's sons was awakened by the stifled sobs of the mourner. He arose from his bed, and lighting a candle, beheld Judge Blackford, walking the floor and sobbing as though his heart would break. Not a word was said. The young man knew the cause of the great grief of his father's friend, and having no wish to intrude upon its sanctity, left the room. Judge Blackford remained at Mr. Coburn's for several days, and during the time held no conversation with any one. He took his meals in silence, and when they were over returned to his room. When narrating this incident, General John Coburn said to the author: "I have seen grief in all its forms; have seen the mother mourning for her son; have seen the wife at the grave of her husband, and heard her sobs, but I never saw such appalling agony as Judge Blackford exhibited that night at my father's house."

Judge Blackford had a room in the old building which used to stand in the Governor's Circle, in which he lived for many years. It was plainly furnished, but it contained everything necessary for his comfort. There were three tables in it, and these were always loaded with books. William Franklin, a colored man still living, used to sweep the Judge's room, make the fires and do other necessary things about the house. He was with Judge Blackford twelve years, and says that, during that time, he never saw him in a passion, nor heard him utter an angry word. He nursed the Judge when he was sick, and attended to his little wants when he was well, and had the best of opportunities of knowing him as he really was.

Judge Blackford was prudish in the manner of writing his opinions. The orthography must be perfect and the punctuation faultless before the matter left his hands. One who knew

him well says he paid as much attention to a comma as to a
thought. He has been known to stop the press to correct the
most trivial error, one that few would notice. The late Samuel
Judah, desiring to have a decision delayed, once asked him the
correct spelling of a word he knew would be in the opinion.
The Judge answered, giving the usual orthography. Mr. Judah
took issue with him and argued that the spelling was not correct. The Judge at once commenced an examination of the
word, dug out its roots and carefully weighed all the authorities
he could find. He spent two days at this work, and before he
got through the court had adjourned and the case went over to
the next term.

In politics Judge Blackford was originally a Whig, but in
1836 he supported Van Buren for the presidency, and afterward
acted with the Democracy. He hated slavery, and during his
whole life his influence was against it. Although the ordinance
ceding the Northwestern Territory to the United States provided that slavery should never exist in the Territory or the
States formed from it, it was covertly introduced into the Territory. Laws were passed authorizing the bringing of negroes
into the Territory, and providing for apprenticing males until
they were thirty-five years old, and females until they were
thirty-two. Children of colored persons born in the Territory
might be apprenticed until the males were thirty and the females
twenty-eight years old. It was also provided that slaves found
ten miles from home without permission of their masters might
be taken up and whipped with twenty-five lashes. Congress
was petitioned to suspend the sixth article of the ordinance of
1787 prohibiting slavery in the Territory, but happily without
effect. General Harrison was Governor of the Territory, and
approved of all these measures. He had about him, and enjoying his confidence, Waller Taylor, Thomas Randolph, and
other immigrants from Virginia, who were pro-slavery men of
the most decided cast. Judge Blackford hated slavery in all
its forms, and early allied himself with the free State party led
by Jonathan Jennings. He held General Harrison responsible
for the effort to make Indiana a slave Territory, and when the
General became a candidate for President, in 1836, Judge
Blackford refused to support him. His action in this matter put

him outside the Whig party and into the Democratic—a position he maintained while he lived.

Judge Blackford regarded Vincennes as his home for many years after he came to Indianapolis to live, and every year he spent a part of his time in that place. On one of his trips to Vincennes on horseback he came very near losing his life. Mounted on a stout horse, with overcoat, leggings, and saddle-bag full of law books, he undertook to ford White river, near Martinsville, while the river was much swollen by a freshet. He and his horse were swept down the stream a great distance, but eventually they landed on an island. The Judge was wet and cold, and it was several hours before he reached the mainland, being rescued by a farmer who had heard his outcries. He spent a couple of days in drying his law books and clothing, and in waiting for the waters to fall low enough for him to cross the river with safety, and then proceeded on his journey.

Judge Blackford was about five feet nine inches high, very erect, with a neat, trim, lithe figure; he was quick and active in motion and graceful in bearing. His face was long, though well proportioned and marked with intelligence, sensibility and refinement. His head was small but shapely. He was upright and scrupulously honest in his dealings; was a model of integrity and purity of character. He had great reverence for the Sabbath, and nothing could swerve him from his purpose to do no work on Sunday.

He lived the greater part of his life alone, having the habits of a student and the tastes of a scholar.

His legal opinions were prepared with the greatest care and precision. They were written and rewritten until they were brought to his critical standard. So, too, with his reports of the decisions of the Supreme Court, eight volumes of which he published. Each syllabus was wrought out as a sculptor chisels his marble. He did not report all the decisions of the court, many were omitted. Those only were published which he regarded as sound and just on the general principles of the law. The result of this was his reports are authority wherever the courts recognize the common law as their rule of action. Since they were published a law has been passed compelling a report of all the opinions of the court. There have been so many contradictory opinions given since then that the authority of our highest court is not, relatively, as high as it was when its decisions were only known through Blackford's Reports. Judge Blackford's reports were short and sententious, his style being clear and faultless. He did not write essays or treatises in his opinions, but treated of the essence of the case, and of nothing more.

Judge Blackford was not a member of any church, and he attended religious meetings wherever his taste or inclination led him. He was a believer in the Christian religion. He was, in short, a conscientious, modest, firm and incorruptible man. He was economical in habit, plain in dress, and unostentatious in manner. He was shy in deportment, avoided discussions, and made no enemies by his manner or treatment of men. He was a constant reader, and had an extensive miscellaneous as well as an excellent law library. He took the leading American and foreign magazines and carefully read them. He was great as a judge. He was not great as an advocate, or statesman, or scholar, or orator, or writer, but as a judge he stands in advance of any man our State has produced.

He was not a rapid thinker or powerful reasoner, but his sense of justice and fair dealing, his ability to weigh legal arguments, his untiring perseverance in the investigation of cases, put him in the front rank of Indiana judges, and there he will stand.

Without favor, fear or affection he held up the scales of justice before the world. His spotless rectitude and unswerving justice made his name a household word in Indiana, a State whose judicature he found in swaddling clothes and left clad in beautiful raiment.

STEPHEN C. STEVENS.

ONE of the leading lawyers of early Indiana was Stephen C. Stevens. He ran a political career at an early stage of his history in the State, which may be briefly summed up as follows:

In 1817 he was elected to the Legislature from Franklin county (he then lived at Brookville). He was made chairman of the Commission on Revision of the Laws. Soon after this he removed to Vevay, in Switzerland county, and in 1824 was sent to the Legislature from Switzerland county, and was elected Speaker of the House. The next year he was re-elected to the Legislature from Switzerland, and was appointed chairman of the Judiciary Committee.

In 1826 he was elected to the State Senate from Switzerland and Ripley counties, and in 1828 was re-elected to the Senate from said counties. He was always a prominent figure in the Legislatures in which he served.

He was an officer in the Vevay branch of the Bank of Vincennes, an institution chartered by the Territorial Legislature in 1814. Subsequently he removed to Madison, and remained a resident of that city while he lived. On the 28th of January, 1831, Governor Ray appointed him a Judge of the Supreme Court, a position he held until May, 1836, when he resigned and returned to the practice of the law.

Judge Stevens was not a great lawyer. However, he was a painstaking one, and his industry and care made him a successful practitioner. For years he had the largest collection business of any member of the Madison bar. He was a fair jury lawyer, and excelled most of his compeers in the preparation of legal papers and in the collection of claims. In these respects he was fully abreast of any member of the ablest bar in the State.

Judge Stevens was diffuse and prolix in his writings. He always told the whole story. I remember writing up the complete record of the case of Warfield *vs.* Warfield, a chancery case disposed of in the Jefferson Circuit Court in 1847. Judge Stevens was the plaintiff's attorney, and had prepared most of the papers. There were several depositions taken and published, the questions and answers of which were written by the Judge. Each deposition commenced as follows:

" The deposition of John Smith, a man of sound mind and discretion, taken before Hiram Harris, Esq., a justice of the peace in and for the township of Shelby, in the county of Jefferson and State of Indiana, duly elected, commissioned and qualified, at his office in the town of Canaan, in the township, county and State aforesaid," etc.

While I was making up the record Judge Stevens came into the Clerk's office, and I asked him why he prefaced the depositions so minutely and particularly. He answered, that when a school-boy the master once called him up and interrogated him about a difficulty he had had with one of the scholars, and ended with administering to him a pretty severe flagellation; that subsequently, on learning all the circumstances connected with the difficulty, the teacher said that if he had told the whole story he would have escaped punishment. "This was a lesson," said the Judge, "I have never forgotten. Since then I have made it a rule to tell the whole story."

Judge Stevens was an old-time Abolitionist. He was an anti-slavery man at a time when it required great courage to be one. It is impossible for those whose memory does not go back twenty years to realize the prejudice, and even bitterness, that then existed against the Abolitionists. They were not only considered " outside of any healthy political organization," but they were socially tabooed and ostracised. And particularly was this the case in Southern Indiana, where Judge Stevens lived. But opposition to slavery was with him a principle.

In 1845 the Liberty party nominated Judge Stevens for Governor of the State. From a speech he made during the canvass I make the following extracts, illustrative of his extreme views on the question of slavery and his bold style of presentation:

" Sir, let us know but two classes of men in church and state— the friends of slavery and its enemies.

" We are asked how slavery is to be abolished? Sir, I will tell you. We must reach the abolition of slavery over the dead bodies of both the old political parties : not slain by violence, but destroyed by the overthrow of their principles, the only thing which holds them together and gives them party existence. As long as those parties exist so long will slavery find a shelter under their folds. In the second place, we must reach the abolition of slavery through the doors of twenty thousand churches. I do not mean that we must destroy them, so that they will cease to be churches, but that we must bring them on the side of Jesus Christ instead of that of slavery. All this we must do by teaching the truth and correcting the errors of the people.

" But we are told that our plan is seditious and factious ; that we are agitators, yes, agitators. Well, Christ was an agitator. What makes agitation wrong is that it is error and not truth which agitates. The only question whether our agitation, like that of Christ and his apostles, is justifiable and necessary, is whether what we teach is the truth ; and it is the truth, God knows !

" 'But we shall divide the church !' Sir, division implies separation ; and what shall we separate? Why, the sin of slaveholding from Christianity. God send that division soon. We are told, too, that we shall divide the Union ; that we are disunionists. Now, sir, I am for the Union ; but I say if the only Union we can have with the South, in church and state, is to be and must be cemented by the blood of three millions of my brethren, I say, in God's name, let it go down. I am for no union the bond of which is open crime. No church can or will be recognized for Christ in the great day which is cemented together by blood. The doom of Sodom and Gomorrah will be more tolerable in that day than theirs.

"But we are told to remedy all our evils at home before touching slavery. Doctor, cure yourself.

"Sir, if we must wait till no injustice exists among men before we touch slavery we shall never touch it. Is that what they want?

"But our black laws in the free States, which they ask us to repeal before touching slavery, are a mere sequent—a tail—a following thing to slavery itself. When slavery is destroyed these laws, which are a mere consequence of slavery, will fall with it. Destroy the tree and you kill the branches."

He believed slavery wrong, and he lifted up his voice against it at all times, in season and out of season. In 1851 or 1852 a negro committed a rape on a white woman some thirty miles from Madison, and was lynched by an infuriated mob. The author, who was born and reared in a slave State, and taught to believe in the divinity of slavery, was talking with Judge Stevens about this case, when the latter remarked that, although rape was a great crime, and its perpetrators should be severely punished, yet there were mitigating circumstances in this case which should have shielded the negro from extreme punishment. Shocked at his words, I asked him what he meant. He answered that the commission of a criminal assault by a negro upon a white woman was not so great an offense as the commission of a similar assault by a white man. This was so contrary to my own feelings that I told him I was surprised at such an avowal; that I had not supposed there was a man in the State who entertained such sentiments. He replied that the white man had the school-room, the church and the Bible to enlighten and christianize him, while the negro was denied them all. Said he: "A man must answer according to his opportunities; when the educated white man makes a beast of himself he is more culpable in the sight of God, and should be in the sight of man, than the ignorant negro who does a similar thing." However contrary to my education and feelings this position of Judge Stevens was, I could not but admit its force.

Judge Stevens was a Presbyterian, and for some time was a member of the New School Presbyterian Church at Madison. As is known, the New School branch was formed on account of the conservatism of the Presbyterian church on the subject of slavery. The New School Presbyterians were anti-slavery, but they were not sufficiently so to suit the views of Judge Stevens. He refused to affiliate with any one in the church who upheld slavery, and therefore severed his connection with the church at Madison, and joined one located in the Abolition settlement some twelve or fourteen miles away. He remained a member of this church while he lived.

In his younger days Judge Stevens was an active member of the Masonic fraternity. He was one of the eleven men who met at Corydon, December 3, 1817, and laid the foundation for the Grand Lodge of Indiana. In his latter days he did not affiliate with the order, having left it at the time of the Morgan excitement, but he never ceased to have a high respect and regard for it while he lived.

Judge Stevens accumulated a competence by his profession, and lived in good but not extravagant style. In 1851 or 1852 he invested all his means in a contemplated railroad. Although he had seen much of the world, and was a close observer of men and things, he ignored the fact that those who build railroads seldom operate them. He put all the money he had, and even his home, into the road and lost it all. He soon found himself without a dollar of money or a home. The shock was too great for him to bear, and it impaired his mind. He imagined himself immensely rich, and traveled over the State in search of investments for his surplus money. Wherever he went he bargained for farms, for houses and lots, and for anything that struck his fancy. The author saw him at Franklin in 1861 or 1862, and remembers that he contracted for the finest residence property in that city. Having known him in the days of his intellectual strength and worldly prosperity, I was deeply pained to see what a wreck he had become. He was but a shadow—and a faint one, too—of his former self. Time did not improve his mental condition, and on the 29th of June, 1869, he was admitted into the Indiana Hospital for the Insane as a patient. He remained in that institution, with but little apparent benefit, until November 7, 1870, when death came to his relief. His remains were taken to Madison and buried in the cemetery there, and all that was mortal of Stephen C. Stevens rests near the homestead where he lived so long.

Judge Stevens was a large, raw-boned man. He was slightly stoop-shouldered, and in person was somewhat ungainly. He had an active mind and strong body, but the first gave way to misfortune and the latter to age. He was an old man when he died, but had not adversity overtaken him he would most probably be living now. Bodily disease is not the only thing that kills ; reverse of fortune often causes disease of mind, and when the mind dies it is a blessing for the body to follow.

Oliver H. Smith, in his Early Indiana Trials and Sketches, thus speaks of Judge Stevens :

" He stood high at the bar, and was one of the strongest advocates in the State, but the diffuseness of his opinions supplied to many *obiter dicta* for other cases, in the opinion of many sound members of the bar. He was one of the most laborious judges upon the bench, and furnished Blackford's Reports with many valuable opinions."

For the following additional incidents of interest the author is indebteded to the venerable Judge Test, yet living, who knew the subject personally and well :

"Judge Stevens came to Brookville with his mother about 1812. It was during the war, and the Indians were troubling us a great deal. Stevens reported one day that he had shot at an Indian that was coming up to his house, and that he had wounded him. Some were rather doubtful about the matter, and followed the trail of blood down to the river, but finding nothing, they accused him of having killed a chicken and passed it off as an Indian. This got him down a good deal. He was a merchant then on his own account. Before the close of the war he went to New Orleans and joined Jackson's army. He was one of the few men wounded in the battle of New Orleans, being wounded on the top of his head. This restored his reputation at home, and the people thought his Indian story might not be altogether untrue. He had studied law while operating as a merchant, and when he returned to Brookville he commenced the practice of law, building a little office in the south part of town. After this he moved to Vevay, living there with his mother. He was very devoted to his mother, taking good care of her and living for her. He was president of the Vevay bank, and after the bank broke he practiced law with some success. I became better acquainted with him at this time and came into collision with him in one case. He was a very diffuse man and covered a good deal of paper to express a small idea. The last time I saw him he was in the Insane Asylum. The superintendent asked me if I had known Judge Stevens. I told him I had known him very well, having lived in the same town. The superintendent informed me he was there and I found him lying on the bed in his drawers, while an old fellow named Musselman, from Logansport, was mending his breeches. He looked at me intently, as if trying to gather up his thoughts, and then said: 'I don't know you,' then added, 'Yes, of course I know you; but ever since the top of my head was cut off my memory is not as good as it used to be.' After leaving the asylum I went to the Governor's office and told him the circumstances, and how poor the old man was. Governor Baker pulled out a ten dollar bill, and going around to others, raised some fifty or sixty dollars within an hour, which was sent up to the superintendent with instructions to buy Stevens a suit of clothes. His measure was taken and when the suit was made, it was presented with the compliments of the bar. Stevens made quite a speech to the effect that he was glad to be remembered by the bar. In a few days after this he died and was buried in his new suit."

CHARLES DEWEY.

No name is more venerated by the bar of Indiana than that of Charles Dewey. Although not so learned in the books as his great compeer, Isaac Blackford, nor so elegant in his diction as his other companion on the bench, Jeremiah Sullivan, yet, in strength of intellect and ability to grasp legal questions, Judge Dewey was superior to either of them. Such is the judgment of those best qualified to know.

Charles Dewey was born in Sheffield, Massachusetts, March 6, 1784. He was well educated, having graduated at Williams College with the honors of his class. After completing his course at college he studied law, and in 1816 came to Indiana and located at Paoli, in Orange county. He opened an office and commenced the practice of the law, and soon had a large business, not only in the county where he lived, but in other counties on his circuit. In these days a lawyer did not confine his practice to a single county, but traveled over a large extent of territory, and took cases wherever they were offered him.

Mr. Dewey, like most lawyers of his time, and indeed of this also, took an interest in politics, and in 1821 was elected to the Legislature from his county. He served with such distinction as to attract the attention of the people throughout his section of the State, and the next year they demanded that he should run for Congress. His district comprised one-third of the State, and it was very thoroughly canvassed both by him and his competitor, General William Prince. General Prince had been with Aaron Burr in his Southwestern expedition, and it was charged that Mr. Dewey had favored the Hartford convention; therefore, the honors were even so far as charges went. But the pioneers of Indiana were more antagonistic to the Hartford con-

vention than to Burr's filibustering expedition, and, although
Mr. Dewey had not been a member of the Hartford convention,
the charge was " a good enough Morgan " to defeat him.

In 1824, two years after Mr. Dewey made his unsuccessful
race for Congress, he removed to Charlestown, in Clark county,
and lived there until his death. He devoted himself assiduously
to the practice of the law, and reached a high place in the profession. While taking an interest in politics he was not a candidate for office until 1832, when he ran for Congress against
General John Carr, and was beaten. This was the last race he
made for office before the people.

In 1836 Governor Noble appointed Mr. Dewey Judge of the
Supreme Court, to fill the place of Stephen C. Stevens, who had
resigned. Oliver H. Smith, in his " Early Indiana Trials and
Sketches," speaks thus of this appointment: "The Judge
brought with him a matured mind, and a large experience as a
practitioner. Many doubted, at the time, whether he could sustain on the bench his high reputation at the bar. But as his
judicial powers were developed he rose as a judge, and fully
sustained himself in the opinion of the bar, who are good judges
and safe depositories of the judicial reputations of the judges."

Judge Dewey sat on the Supreme bench eleven years, and
honored it as few have done. He came fully up to the mark,
the public having, by common consent, placed him in the very
front rank of Indiana judges.

Under the first constitution of Indiana, Supreme Judges were
appointed by the Governor, by and with the consent of the Senate. In politics Judge Dewey was a Whig. In 1843 James
Whitcomb, a Democrat, was elected Governor, and re-elected
in 1846. When the Governor came into office one of the Supreme Judges—Isaac Blackford—was a Democrat, and the
other two — Dewey and Sullivan — were Whigs. When the
terms of the judges expired, the Governor sent to the Senate
the name of Judge Blackford to succeed himself, and those of
Samuel E. Perkins and Thomas L. Smith to succeed Judges
Dewey and Sullivan. The Senate confirmed Judge Blackford,
but refused its consent to the appointment of Messrs. Perkins
and Smith. A long and acrimonious contest took place between
the Governor and the Senate over these appointments.

The Governor sent the names of several other gentlemen to the Senate, but they were promptly rejected. After the Legislature adjourned Governor Whitcomb gave Judges Dewey and Sullivan temporary appointments to last until the meeting of the next Legislature. When that body convened, the Senate, like that of the previous session, refused to confirm the Governor's nominees. A few days after it had adjourned the Governor sent Judge Dewey another temporary appointment. Before accepting it he had an interview with the Governor, and told him he should decline the appointment unless he had assurances that he would be regularly nominated to the next Senate. Governor Whitcomb told him that he should, as a compromise measure, nominate him and Judge Perkins to the next Senate, "unless he should be diverted from his purpose in respect to him—Judge Dewey—by the course the Whigs might take in the coming canvass for Governor." It was, undoubtedly, Governor Whitcomb's intention, at the time to re-appoint Judge Dewey, but he was diverted from the purpose, mainly through the influence of Ashbel P. Willard, afterward Governor of the State. Willard was then just rising to influence and power in the politics of Indiana, and Judge Dewey, being a Whig, was fiercely antagonized by the rising young politician. He succeeded in preventing the nomination of Judge Dewey, and in securing that of his friend and townsman, Thomas L. Smith, but, as many thought at the time, at the expense of the Governor's good faith.

In February, 1847, Judge Dewey published a letter in the *Indianapolis Journal*, in which he recounted at length his complaints against Governor Whitcomb. After reciting the several interviews he had had with the Governor, and naming the pledges which he asserted had been given him, he closed as follows: "I have only to add that the Governor's word has not been kept; his pledge is unredeemed."

On leaving the Supreme bench Judge Dewey resumed the practice of the law. He took into partnership George V. Howk, now of our Supreme Court, and for many years they practiced together. The firm had a large practice in Southern Indiana, as well as in the Supreme Court of the State, the reputation of the senior partner bringing it business, far and near.

In April, 1849, Judge Dewey, while riding in his carriage, was thrown out, and suffered the fracture of a leg. He never recovered from the hurt, being compelled during the remainder of his life to walk with crutches, but he continued the practice of his profession while he lived. He died at his home in Charlestown, April 25, 1862, and was buried in the cemetery there. Judge Dewey was cotemporaneous with the men who made Indiana a State. He was the friend and neighbor of Jonathan Jennings, and was his legal adviser in the trouble between him and Christopher Harrison about the governorship. He practiced at a bar which contained many able members, but none of them outranked him. He and Benjamin Parke, the first United States District Judge of Indiana, were friends, and usually came to Indianapolis together, when business called them there, although they lived many miles apart. Judge Dewey was a great reader of novels, and tried to have Judge Parke read them also, but the latter could not get interested in the fictitious creations of genius, and continued to prefer Coke and Blackstone to Fielding and Smollet. After Judge Parke's death Judge Dewey, at the request of the bar of the State, delivered a eulogy upon his departed friend worthy of the distinguished subject. The address was printed, and a few copies of it only are in existence. I have been unable to find any literary effort of Judge Dewey save this address and his published opinions, but these prove him to have been a writer of remarkable ability. The clean-cut sentences of his eulogy upon Judge Parke remind one of the writings of Burke. There is no superfluity of words. His meaning is never obscure. Judge Dewey was not blessed with the graces of oratory. He could, however, talk with ease and fluency, and was very effective when presenting his views to a court.

Judge Dewey was fond of anecdotes. Having been personally acquainted with most of the leading men of early Indiana, he was full of reminiscences and stories, which he was in the habit of recounting to attentive listeners. When on the bench he was dignified and somewhat austere, but when off it he was always ready to tell a story.

Throughout Judge Dewey's long life he was a supporter of the Christian church. A short time before he died he made a profession of the Christian religion, and joined the Presbyterian church, in whose communion he died.

I am indebted to Professor Campbell, of Crawfordsville, for the following characteristic anecdotes of Judge Dewey:

" On a certain occasion there were assembled a pleasant party in the parlor of the Washington House, Indianapolis, who were enjoying especially the joke of Dewey's menagerie, as they facetiously termed the traveling concern which happened at the time to be exhibiting at Indianapolis, and was located on some vacant lots on Washington street belonging to Judge Dewey, when a young man of somewhat diminutive stature and pompous manner approached the Judge with a ' Well, Judge, I think I shall patronize your menagerie to-night.' ' Glad to hear it,' replied Dewey; ' glad to hear it. Our pony has just arrived, and our monkey is sick; we shall need you.' Gifted as he was in this quickness of repartee, he enjoyed equally well a sally of wit, even though he himself were the subject. On another occsion, at the same hotel, in a company of lawyers, John L——, of Madison, with a little unwarranted liberty, remarked, in reference to the long nose and chin of Judge Dewey, that they would probably meet soon. The Judge replied, somewhat bitterly, that they never had met yet; whereupon Henry S. Lane, with ready wit, added: ' Yet a good many hard words have passed between them!' The merry twinkle with which this was received established a cordiality and friendship between them that lasted while they lived.

" On one occasion, in the argument on a demurrer, the law was plainly against him, and he was prepared to yield gracefully to the decision of the court against him in accordance with the presentation of the other side by Col. Wilson. Unfortunately, however, Judge John Thompson, instead of confining himself to the points made by the opposing attorney, was proceeding to make the ruling for other reasons, whereupon Mr. Dewey boldly spoke out, ' The law may be against me, Judge, but you are giving a —— poor reason for it.'

" ' Sit down, Mr. Dewey, sit down!' thundered the Judge in excited tones. With stern dignity and folded arms, Dewey replied, ' I am too much of a freeman, sir, to be directed by you, or any one, as to the attitude I must assume.' 'Be quiet, sir,' again spoke Judge T. 'That Your Honor has the right in this court to command,' responded Mr. D., and this passage at arms ended."

In person Judge Dewey was large and commanding. He was six feet high, and weighed about 200 pounds. His hair was black, his complexion dark, his forehead broad and high, and his mouth very expressive. His features were not regular, his nose and chin being too long to be symmetrical, but this defect was more than overbalanced by the look of intelligence and dignity that always pervaded his face.

Judge Dewey's widow is living in Indianapolis at the advanced age of eighty years. Her health is good, her mind unimpaired and her body exceedingly vigorous for one of her years. She gave the author many of the incidents mentioned in this sketch, and, when speaking of her distinguished husband, her eye plainly told of the love she bore him.

JEREMIAH SULLIVAN.

Among the men who impressed themselves upon the morals of the people and the institutions of the State in early days was Jeremiah Sullivan. He had much to do in laying the foundations of the State government and in giving character to its judiciary, and he well deserves a place in the list of distinguished men.

Mr. Sullivan was of Irish descent. He was born in a small Virginia town eighty-seven years ago, and was designed by his father, who was a Roman Catholic, for the priesthood. He was educated at William and Mary's College, graduating from that institution with honor. He chose the law for a profession, but before being admitted to the bar he enlisted in the army and soon earned a captain's commission. This was during the last war with Great Britain, and when hostilities ceased the young soldier laid aside his military trappings and resumed his books. He was admitted to the Virginia bar, but his chances for rising in his profession there being but meager, he determined to seek a more inviting field. So he bade his friends farewell and started West on horseback in search of a location. His destination was Louisville, Kentucky, but on arriving at Cincinnati he heard there was a good opening for a lawyer at Madison, Indiana, so he changed his mind and went to that town. It was in the fall of 1817 when he reached there, and he settled and lived there until he died.

At Madison Captain Sullivan practiced his profession with success, and it was very seldom that he left it for any other business. In 1820, three years after he came to the State, he was elected a member of the Legislature from his county. He proved to be an industrious and painstaking one, and was as influential in shaping legislation as any member of the House. It was he who gave Indianapolis its name, as will be seen by the following letter to ex-Governor Baker, when that gentleman was Governor of the State:

" I have a very distinct recollection of the great diversity of opinion that prevailed as to the name the new town should receive. The bill was reported by Judge Polk, and was, in the main, very acceptable. A blank, of course, was left for the name of the town that was to become the seat of government, and during the two or three days we spent in endeavoring to fill that blank there were some sharpness and much amusement. General Marston G. Clark, of Washington county, proposed ' Tecumseh' as the name, and very earnestly insisted on its adoption. When that failed he suggested other Indian names which I have forgotten. They also were rejected. Somebody suggested ' Suwarro,' which met with no favor. Judge Polk desired the blank to be filled with ' Concord;' " that also failed. Other names were proposed, but they were all voted down, and the House, without coming to any agreement, adjourned until the next day. There were many amusing things said during the day, but my remembrance of them is not sufficiently distinct to state them with accuracy. I had gone to Corydon with the intention of proposing ' Indianapolis' as the name of the town ; and on the evening of the adjournment above mentioned, I suggested to Mr. Samuel Merrill, the representative from Switzerland county, the name I preferred. He at once adopted it, and agreed to support it. We together called on Governor Jennings, who had been a witness to the amusing scenes of the day previous, and told him to what conclusion we had come. He gave us to understand that he favored the name we had agreed upon, and that he would not hesitate to so express himself. When the House met and went into committee on the bill I moved to fill the blank with ' Indianapolis.' The name created a shout of laughter. Mr. Merrill, however, seconded the motion. We discussed the proposition freely and fully, the members conversed with each other informally, and the name gradually commended itself to the committee, and was accepted. The principal reason given for its adoption, to wit: that its

Greek termination would indicate the importance of the town, was, I am sure, the reason that overcame opposition to the name. The town was finally named Indianapolis.

"JER. SULLIVAN."

In early life Judge Sullivan had a taste for politics, but it left him as he grew older. He once made an unsuccessful race for Congress against William Hendricks, and this defeat seemed to have cured him of politics and caused him to adhere more closely than ever to his profession. I believe he never was a candidate for office before the people after this until the year he died. He was appointed by the Governor of the State a commissioner to adjust the land question between the States of Ohio and Indiana, growing out of the construction of the Wabash and Erie canal. After this he was appointed a Judge of the Supreme Court of Indiana, and he sat upon the bench of that court from 1837 to 1846. It was while a judge of this court that he earned his fame, and it is as a Supreme judge that he will be best remembered. During the nine years he sat upon the Supreme bench he graced and honored the place. His associates were Judges Blackford and Dewey, and it is only saying what is well known that at no time since the organization of the court has it stood so high as when Blackford, Dewey and Sullivan were its judges. These men were different in their mental make-up, but they were all able. Sullivan was the ablest writer of the three, as may be seen by reading the reports of the court of that era. His opinions, as recorded by Blackford, are models of legal composition. There are a grace and perspicuity in his style but seldom found, and had he chosen to be a writer of legal books, he would, unquestionably, have won a reputation even exceeding that which he earned upon the bench.

In 1869 a criminal court for Jefferson county was created, and Judge Sullivan was appointed its judge. At the first election afterwards he was chosen judge for a full term, but on the very day he would have taken his oath of office he died. He had been in bad health for some time, but notwithstanding this, his death was unexpected, and it greatly shocked the community where he lived. He had resided so long at Madison, and had been so closely connected with public affairs, that when the end came his old friends and neighbors keenly felt the loss.

In his early life Judge Sullivan was an active Freemason. In January, 1818, representatives for the different Masonic lodges in the State met at Madison and formed the Grand Lodge of Indiana. Judge Sullivan was a member of this body, and was elected grand orator of the lodge. He continued his connection with Masonry for many years, but about the time of the Morgan excitement he withdrew his membership from the order, and never afterwards renewed it.

Judge Sullivan was a member of the Presbyterian church, and in his daily walk and example was a Christian man. On the division of that church he allied himself to the New School branch. He was an active member of the church and a regular attendant upon the services. He was a ruling elder, and ever demeaned himself as should one who occupies that high position.

There were two places which Judge Sullivan always entered with reverence, the church and the temple of justice. I remember an incident which occurred many years ago that will serve to illustrate his respect and reverence for the latter. A store-house and stock of goods, belonging to William Brazleton, were burned by incendiaries. Suspicion fell upon a couple of men in the neighborhood, and, on following it up, sufficient evidence was obtained to secure their indictment. They were in due time put upon their trial, and Mr. Brazleton appeared as a witness against them. While the trial was going on, and the Court-house was filled with people, a pistol in Brazleton's coat-pocket exploded. It was loaded with buckshot, but fortunately no one was hurt. Brazleton's coat-tail was badly shattered and the chair in which he was sitting was filled with shot, but no other damage was done. The unfortunate witness, who was frightened almost to death, drew the pistol from his pocket, but no sooner had he done this than Judge Sullivan snatched it from him, and, seizing him by the arm, demanded of the court that he be sent to prison. "He comes into court," said the Judge, " a walking arsenal, and must be punished. I ask Your Honor to maintain the dignity of your office and pro-

24

tect the lives of those whose duty it is to be here." Judge Downey, or Judge Chapman, I have forgotten which, was upon the bench, and no doubt would have complied with Judge Sullivan's demand had not one of the lawyers present asked to be heard in Mr. Brazleton's behalf. He read a letter to Brazleton, without signature, threatening him with death if he appeared as a witness in the case. The judge considered this a sufficient reason for the witness's arming himself, and therefore excused him. Judge Sullivan acquiesced in this decision, but said the witness should have left his pistol outside the court-room. He declared the court-room to be a place where controversies were decided by the law, and not by violence, and that its precincts should never be profaned by the presence of a deadly weapon.

Judge Sullivan seldom took an active part in politics. He was a Whig while that party existed, and afterwards a Republican, but he usually contented himself with voting his party ticket. The only exception to this which I remember was in 1850, when the Whig candidates for the constitutional convention were nominated. He was very anxious that delegates should be sent to the convention from Jefferson county who would not be under the control of corporations. He declared that the people were in danger from corporations, and if they were not controlled by constitutional provisions the time would come when they would dictate the legislation of the country. He opposed the nomination of William McKee Dunn, a personal friend, because he was a son-in-law of Mr. Lanier, a gentleman who had large interests in banks and in railroads. His opposition to Mr. Dunn was unavailing, that gentleman being nominated and elected.

Judge Sullivan was a humorist of the first water. His humor seldom showed itself, but when it did it sparkled like a gem. Just before the breaking out of the Mexican war Thomas J. Henley, then a representative in Congress, and Senator Bright made speeches at Madison, in which they ridiculed the idea of war, and said if it came they would undertake to clean out Mexico with a regiment of women armed with broomsticks. When the war came, and blood commenced to flow, Judge Sullivan wrote a series of articles for the *Madison Banner*, over the signature of " Colonel Pluck," that were the perfection of humor and ridicule. In them he called on Messrs. Bright and Henley to make good their promises at once, or he would take the field with his "Invincibles" and mop up Mexico before the women with their broomsticks could get into the field. He and Senator Bright were personal friends, and fearing, if the authorship of the letters was known, the Senator would be offended, he had the papers copied before they went to the printer.

Soon after the adoption of the constitution of 1850 he wrote some papers ridiculing the provision prohibiting the immigration of negroes and their employment in the State. In one of these papers he gave his reflections as he sat in a barber's chair getting shaved. These papers were inimitable, and no one who read them will question that they were written by a master hand. I do not think Judge Sullivan ever had a superior in this State as a humorous and satirical writer, and I question if he ever had an equal. He wrote so little, and so few knew what he did write, that I doubt not this statement will be questioned by many who knew him well, but nevertheless it is true.

While Judge Sullivan was upon the Supreme bench he was particularly intimate with Judge Dewey, one of his associates. Judge Dewey used to come to Madison and stay with Judge Sullivan for days. It was understood that they met for conference and consultation, but I suspect that friendship and congeniality of tastes had more to do with bringing them together than the law.

In 1852, when General Scott was making his Western tour, he was invited to Madison and given a grand reception. Judge Sullivan made the welcoming address, and it was a model one of the kind.

In 1861, on the breaking out of the rebellion, Judge Sullivan entered actively into furthering the interests of the government. His oldest son had been an officer in the war with Mexico, and his youngest son, Jere, raised a company and entered the service in the war for the Union. He was afterwards promoted to a colonelcy, and subsequently to a brigadiership, and he served in all these positions with bravery and distinction. Another son, Algernon S., an eminent lawyer of New York, was arrested early in the war and imprisoned at Fort Lafayette. It will be remembered that the administration of Mr. Lincoln at first determined to treat Confederate privateers as pirates. It denied them counsel and notified lawyers not to undertake their defense. But notwithstanding this order, Mr. A. S. Sullivan accepted employment as counsel for the captured privateers, and commenced to prepare for their defense. He sent to Richmond for copies of the commissions under which they acted, but his messenger was arrested before he crossed the lines. For doing this Mr. Sullivan was arrested and sent to Fort Lafayette, and for some time confined as a prisoner of state. Judge Sullivan was an ardent patriot, and, like Abraham of old, would have offered his son as a sacrifice had it been necessary, but he was also a lawyer, and had decided notions as to the duties of lawyers to their clients. He believed his son's employment legitimate and his arrest an outrage. These things he did not hesitate to say, and in a short time, through his influence and that of his friends, his son was released from imprisonment and restored to his family.

In person Judge Sullivan was tall and commanding. His height was over six feet, and his body was well proportioned. He had a good head and a good face. His eyes were dark brown, his hair light and thin, and usually long, and his complexion was ruddy. His carriage was good and his manners dignified. He was always polite—was always a gentleman. He was not an aggressive man, and did not have the influence of Marshall or of Bright, but he was a good citizen and an upright judge, and had the respect of all who knew him.

A HISTORICAL TRIO.

Politics ran as high in Indiana seventy-five years ago as it does to-day. William Henry Harrison was appointed Governor of Indiana Territory July 4, 1800, and early in 1801 he entered upon the duties of his office. On the 6th of February, 1801, he appointed William McIntosh Territorial Treasurer, and about the same time he commissioned John Rice Jones Attorney-General of the Territory. These men occupied very close relations with the Governor, and for some time had his confidence. They, however, became jealous of Benjamin Parke, a warm friend of the Governor, and one of the purest men Indiana has ever had. Seeing that Mr. Parke was supplanting them in the Governor's favor, they determined to break him down, and at the same time destroy the Governor. Their quarrel with the latter was ostensibly on account of his position on the question of the Territory's entering the second grade of government, but in reality it was because others enjoyed a greater share of his favor than themselves.

The contest was a bitter one. Mr. Parke ably defended Governor Harrison with his pen, and challenged McIntosh to mortal combat for traducing him. McIntosh refused, but, with Jones and Elijah Bachus, a newspaper writer, continued to abuse the Governor. That the reader may know something of the virulence of the fight between Governor Harrison and his enemies, I copy the following from the *Western World*, a paper published at Frankfort, Ky. It was written at Vincennes, and appeared in the *World* in its issue of March 3, 1808.

JOHN RICE JONES.

" The pieces which appeared in your paper of the 31st ult. and 7th inst. over the signature of Philo-Tristram, and Tristram are the productions of William McIntosh, John Rice Jones and Elijah Bachus, of this Territory, a triumvirate worthy of each other and the vile cause of slander and detraction in which they are engaged. I feel, most sensibly feel, the humiliation of entering into a controversy with men who have no character to lose, and who have long since (if they ever possessed them) bid adieu to those sentiments of honor which characterize the gentleman. Convinced that from a victory over such opponents I could derive neither triumph nor consolation, I shall confine myself to the relation of some circumstances and the exhibition of a few documents to show the credit which ought to be attached to this respectable fraternity. The existence of a combination to write Governor Harrison out of office was communicated to me by a gentleman of veracity, who had it from Jones himself. To the industry and ingenuity of Jones was assigned the task of hunting up the charges; these were to be reduced to form by the classical pen of Bachus, and the Scotchman (McIntosh) undertook to usher them to the world. From a conversation which Jones had with a gentleman of this place, it appears that his exertions in finding a proper subject to commence the attack were for a long time unsuccessful. After indulging himself in some violent and indecent abuse of the President of the United States, he declared in general terms his dissatisfaction with the conduct of Mr. Harrison as Governor, and his determination to commence a decided opposition to all his measures. The gentleman expressed a favorable opinion of Mr. Harrison's character and conduct, and requested him to mention an instance of maladministration on his part. After frequent evasions, he asserted that his treatment of a Mr. Jennings was most cruel and tyrannical. Mr. Jennings was referred to, who expressed the utmost astonishment, and declared, from his first acquaintance with Governor Harrison he had only received from that gentleman friendship and politeness. From this anecdote we may with certainty conclude that the worthy associates will never be in want of materials for their slanders.

" The following queries, published upward of two years ago in the *Farmer's Library*, contain a few anecdotes of Jones's life. The name of the author (one of our most respectable citizens) was left with the printer, but no attention has been paid to it by

Jones. It is hinted that a new edition, with additions, is shortly to be given to the world by the same author:

" *To John Rice Jones, one of the Legislative Council of Indiana Territory:*

" By answering the following queries you will not only satisfy an inquiring public, but relieve yourself from the load of infamy which your conduct through life has heaped upon you:

" Did you come with General Clark's expedition to Vincennes in the fall of the year 1786? Was Bazadonne not robbed of merchandise to the amount of $6,626?

" Did you not receive the merchandise so taken from Bazadonne, and did you ever account to Bazadonne, to General Clark, or to any other person else for them?

" When Bazadonne was about to commence suit for the recovery of damages for the merchandise thus fraudulently taken from him, did you not, in order to secure to yourself that safety which you knew your guilt would not entitle you to, tell Bazadonne General Clark was the only person against whom he could maintain an action; that your testimony was all he wanted to reinstate him in everything he had lost, and until he gave you a release General Clark might, and would, contend that you were an improper witness, being the person who seized the goods (though by his order), therefore, interested, and deprive him of your testimony?

"And did you not, through your intrigue, swindle Bazadonne out of a release?

" Did General Clark ever receive one cent of the merchandise taken from Bazadonne, but yourself the only person benefited by them?

" Was not your general character so infamous in the government of Spain as to induce an officer of that government to forbid you putting foot on his Catholic Majesty's dominions?

" Did you not, during the period in which you acted as Attorney-General for the Indiana Territory, receive testimony of acknowledgments from I. B. Laplante and I. Barron, against whom there were public prosecutions, to enter a *nolle prosequi* to these indictments, and thereby filch the country out of its revenue?

"Did you not, to answer your own sinister views, prevail upon Mr. Clark to have the Judge's library appraised and sold at private sale for their appraisement? Did not your intrigues procure you the appointment of appraiser, and did you not value such of his library as you wanted 300 per cent. less than they could be purchased in the city of Philadelphia? Did any person know the manner your vile imagination had suggested for the disposal of the Judge's books until you were seen loading them off? Were you not met by a gentleman who offered you $18 for 'Coke on Littleton,' which you had valued and taken at $6, and you refused to take it? For shame! Will you, clothed with the garb of friendship, deprive the widow and fatherless of their property?

"Were you not frequently at the loo-table, in a circle of your neighbors, discovered hiding cards, and, in consequence of that vile disposition, were you afterward admitted to the loo-table?

"Did you not cheat James Sullivan and Lee Decker out of £50?

"Have you ever settled your account with the administrator of Judge Clark? Don't you dispute payment because you know it can not be proved?   PETER, PAUL AND POMPEY."

John Rice Jones was a Welchman, and was born in 1750. He emigrated to America soon after the Revolutionary war, and came to the Northwestern Territory in 1786. He was the first lawyer in Illinois, and one of the ablest she ever had. He was a classical scholar and an accomplished linguist. His practice extended from Kaskaskia to Vincennes, and even to Clarksville. He was not, like most pioneers, a hunter, but devoted his whole time to the practice of his profession and to politics. He was a brilliant speaker, a perfect master of satire and invective. He removed to Vincennes previous to the Territorial organization, and in 1805 was appointed by President Jefferson a member of the Legislative Council of Indiana Territory, having, in the meantime, served as Attorney-General of the Territory. In 1809 he and John Johnson revised the laws of the Territory, most of the work being done by him.

Soon after the organization of Indiana Territory there was born to John Rice Jones a son who became eminent in the politics of the country, and who still lives in the city of Dubuque, Iowa. He was called George Wallace, after a son-in-law of General Gibson, then Secretary of the Territory. He was bred to the law, but never practiced it. He was Clerk of the United States District Court of Missouri in 1826, and was aid-de-camp to General Dodge (who was also born at Vincennes) in the Black Hawk war; was subsequently a colonel, and then a major general of militia, and then a judge of a county court. In 1835 General Jones was elected a delegate to Congress from the Territory of Michigan, and subsequently was elected to Congress from the Territory of Wisconsin. Afterwards, he served as Surveyor-General of the Northwest, and in 1848 he was elected to the United States Senate from Iowa, and in 1852 was re-elected. Mr. Buchanan appointed him Minister Resident at Bogota, which office he held until 1861, when he was recalled by President Lincoln. Soon after his return home he was arrested, and for sixty-four days he was a prisoner of state at Fort Lafayette. No reason was ever given General Jones for his arrest, but it is supposed that it was made on account of one of his sons going South and entering the Confederate service.

On the 1st day of June, 1883, there was a meeting of the pioneers of Iowa, at Burlington, which was largely attended. General A. C. Dodge presided, and on introducing General Jones to the people said:

"In early days the pioneers always estimated a workman by his chips. Here, ladies and gentleman, is the hand (grasping the hand of General Jones) that chipped Wisconsin out of Michigan; that chipped Iowa out of Wisconsin; that chipped for us 640 acres of land covering this original town at a mere nominal price, and to him, more than to any other man or representative, we are indebted for our railroad grants."

The evening after the celebration the pioneers had a dance, and in a description of it the *Burlington Gazette* says:

"The venerable statesman, General Jones, took part in the dances, and was quite as frisky as the youngest participant."

Another son of John Rice Jones, his eldest, I think, was killed at Kaskaskia, Illinois, in a street rencounter, before Illinois became a State. He was a very brilliant man, and his death caused great sorrow at the time. Thus it will be seen that the talents of the first Attorney-General of Indiana Territory descended to his children.

In 1786 news came to the West that Congress had, by a secret treaty with Spain, agreed to relinquish the free navigation of the Mississippi river. This greatly incensed the people, and they determined to resist it. At Vincennes General George Rogers Clark enlisted a body of men known as the Wabash regiment, and by his orders all the Spanish traders at Vincennes and in Illinois were despoiled of their property, in retaliation for similar offenses alleged to have been committed by the Spaniards at Natchez, Miss. In these despoliations John Rice Jones took a leading part. He was the commissary-general of the marauders, and sold such goods as the regiment could not use. This raid of General Clark came near embroiling the country in a war with Spain, but being disowned by the government, it escaped it. Some time after this Mr. Jones removed to Missouri, where he became a leading man. He was a member of the convention that made the first constitution of Missouri, was afterward a candidate for United States Senator against Colonel Benton and defeated. He was one of the first Judges of the Supreme Court of Missouri, and held the office until his death, which occurred in 1824. Like Ratliff Boon, he was a pioneer of both Indiana and Missouri, and prominent in both.

WILLIAM McINTOSH.

In the same issue of the *Western World* is an article on William McIntosh, one of the three leaders of the organization to destroy Governor Harrison's influence. The reader will note its extreme bitterness. Seldom, indeed, do we find in the press of the present day an article so personal and so denunciatory. It is from the pen of the same writer that so mercilessly criticised John Rice Jones in the extract previously copied. The writer says :

" William McIntosh is by birth a Scotchman. In the Revolutionary war he held a subaltern's commission in one of the temporary regiments that were raised for the protection of the King against his external and internal foes. He made his first appearance at Vincennes as a trader, but, not succeeding in this business, he took the sure road to the acquirement of a fortune, by undertaking to act as agent for many of the French citizens whose claims to land were to be decided by the Governor. By magnifying the difficulty of obtaining confirmations, and other vile deceptions upon those illiterate and credulous people, he succeeded frequently in obtaining two hundred out of four hundred acres for barely presenting the claim. In the year 1804 his portrait was given to the world by Mr. Parke, and crimes of the blackest hue charged upon him. The Scotchman retorted upon him some abusive language, which produced from Mr. Parke a challenge; the acceptance of this was, however, declined by McIntosh until he could clear his character of the charges that had been made against it, and which he declared would take but a short time. To this day, however, upwards of three years have elapsed and no attempt of the kind has been made (I can safely aver), nor ever will, for two powerful reasons: The first is that his character is of too deep a dye to require even a century to cleanse it of its stains; the other, his unutterable aversion to the smell of gunpowder. He surely is the veriest coward that ever bit the dust. It is not my intention to give a history of that man's iniquities, but shall content myself with the exhibition of the following documents, taken from the office of the land companies of this district." [Here follow several affidavits showing that McIntosh had obtained land from the makers by duplicity and fraud.]

McIntosh was not only involved in a personal difficulty with Benjamin Parke on account of his opposition to Governor Harrison, but he had an altercation with Thomas Randolph, a warm personal and political friend of the Governor, growing out of the same matter, in which the latter came near losing his life. McIntosh cut Randolph with a knife, and he lay for weeks in a most dangerous condition.

The personal friends of the Governor were enemies of McIntosh, and did what they could to drive him out of the Territory, but without success. His intelligence and wealth gave him an influence that could not be entirely destroyed.   When Governor Harrison left Vincennes to take command of the Northwestern army he turned over the executive affairs of the Territory to John Gibson, its Secretary.   During General Gibson's term as Acting Governor McIntosh was a large contractor for supplying the army with rations.   General W. H. H. Terrell, of Indianapolis, has in his possession a manuscript letter of McIntosh, which I have been permitted to copy.   It is as follows :

"SIR—At Vincennes the contractor has not any quantity of flour in store, and for several days I have been entirely supplied from the country. Measures have been taken by him to import from the State of Kentucky a quantity sufficient to meet the several requisitions which have been made, but I am as yet without information of the time in which any part of it may arrive here. Of meat, whisky and the other component parts there is a sufficiency at my disposal to comply with the requisitions.
"I have the honor to be, sir, your most obedient servant,
"WILL McINTOSH, *for the Contractor.*
"*Vincennes, September 25, 1812.*
"GENERAL GIBSON."

The letter has never before been published, and is valuable in showing the condition of the commissariat, and the kind of articles then believed to be necessary to support an army in the field.

On the 4th of July, 1883, I had a very interesting interview with Mrs. Adeline D. Wolverton, of Vincennes, and obtained from her much valuable information. Mrs. Wolverton is a daughter of Dr. Elias McNamee, and is the widow of Dr. Wolverton, both of whom were prominent in early Indiana history. She remembers William McIntosh well, and says he was a rich Scotch merchant, of elegant manners and good social position, notwithstanding the fact that he had a negro mistress, by whom he had a family of children.   McIntosh was an infidel, and he and Beaubien, Currie, Flowers and Burbeck—all European Free-Thinkers—purchased a large body of land on the Illinois side of the Wabash river, upon which they located a city and called it " Mount Carmel." McIntosh removed to Mount Carmel and lived there until he died. Rev. Aaron Wood, in a recent publication, thus speaks of McIntosh and his death :

" It is well known that the infidel, W. McIntosh, of the Grand Rapids of the Wabash, was the father of illegitimate mulatto children by old Lydia, his black housekeeper. I saw him carried to his grave, and Lydia, her two daughters and one son were left poor, and others got his land. His son became a distinguished preacher in the African Methodist Episcopal Church, for it is due to Colonel McIntosh to say that he gave him a good education in the English and Latin languages and mathematics, so that he was, in his time, among the few educated men of his church."

The education given the mulatto boy did much to atone for the lax morals of the infidel, as it enabled the former to assist in elevating the race to which his mother's blood allied him.

William McIntosh was nearly related to Sir James McIntosh, a distinguished English philosopher and statesman, and had he not become involved in a quarrel with Governor Harrison must have risen to the front rank in power and influence in the new Territory. His antagonism to the Governor put him under the ban of those who controlled the affairs of the Territory, and prevented him from reaching the position his education and talents entitled him to. He and Jones, and Bachus, charged the Governor with having cheated the Indians out of their lands, and the Governor determined to sue McIntosh in a court of law for slander, believing that would be the best way to vindicate himself and show the correctness of his conduct. Dawson, in his life of General Harrison, goes into this matter with particularity, and asserts that in instituting the suit the General was governed solely by a desire to protect his reputation from slanderous assaults. Dawson says that McIntosh had been for many years hostile to the Governor, and was not believed to be very partial to the government of the United States.

It appears by a deposition made in 1811 by Colonel John Small, that prior to the year 1805, McIntosh had been upon the best terms with Governor Harrison, but that, in that year, the Governor gave him great offense by his advocating and promoting the measure of the Territory going into the second grade of government; from which circumstance Mr. Small believed, and asserted on his oath, that McIntosh bore the greatest enmity towards Governor Harrison.

It thus appears that the Governor's exertions to improve the condition of the Territory by giving it a representative government had drawn down upon him the enmity of McIntosh, who strictly adhered to the declaration he had made to do the Governor all the injury in his power.

Suit was brought against McIntosh in the Supreme Court of the Territory, and was, from its character, well calculated to draw the attention and excite a strong interest in the minds of the people of the Territory. Of the three judges, one was a personal friend of the Governor, and another of McIntosh. Both these gentlemen, when the suit was called, left the bench, and the Hon. Waller Taylor, then recently arrived in the Territory, was left to preside alone in the suit. To insure an impartial jury the court named two elisors, who chose forty-eight citizens as a panel from which the jury was to be taken. From this forty-eight the plaintiff and defendant each struck twelve, and from the remaining twenty-four the jury was drawn by lot.

" Before a crowded audience the trial was continued from 10 A. M. till 1 o'clock at night. Every person concerned in the Indian Department, or who could know anything of the circumstances of the late treaty at Fort Wayne, was examined, and every latitude that was asked for or attempted by the defendant in the examination permitted. Finding that the testimony of all the witnesses went to prove the justice and integrity of the Governor's conduct, the defendant began to ask questions relating to some points of the Governor's civil administration. To this the jury, as well as the court, objected, the latter observing that it was necessary that the examination should be confined to the matter at issue. But, at the earnest request of the Governor, the defendant was permitted to pursue his own course, and examine the witnesses upon every point which he might think proper. The defendant's counsel, abandoning all idea of justification, pleaded only for mitigation of damages. After a retirement of one hour the jury returned a verdict of $4,000 damages. To pay this sum a large amount of McIntosh's lands were exposed to sale, and, in the Governor's absence in command of the army, was bought in by his agent. Two-thirds of this property he afterward returned to McIntosh, and the remaining part he gave to some of the orphan children of several distinguished citizens who fell in the war of 1812."

The writer in the *Western World*, from whom I have already quoted, closes his article with this scathing notice of

Elijah Bachus.

" From the specimen which Mr. Bachus has exhibited of his principles in the short time he has resided in the Territory, there is every reason to believe that, if the history of his previous life was as well known, that it would be found to contain as many acts of perfidy as that of his worthy coadjutors. To say nothing of his official conduct, which has been severely arraigned, he has been convicted, by a gentleman of respectability, of the most egregious falsehoods and as vile a swindling trick as ever was committed by a man who professed to be a gentleman.

" The sole intention of this publication, Mr. Editor, is to show the world the real characters of those who, to gratify their malignant dispositions, have attempted, under the mask of patriotism, to undermine the character of Governor Harrison by the foulest aspersions."

The fight against Governor Harrison, as the reader must know, resulted disastrously to his assailants. It served to draw his friends the closer to him, as it always will when one is unjustly attacked. He was afterward elected President of the United States, the highest office in the world, and the history of his country makes honorable mention of him as soldier and statesman. But few there are who know anything about John Rice Jones, William McIntosh, or Elijah Bachus. In assailing the Governor they made it impossible for them to reach a high position among a people who loved and revered him, and the only one of the three who ever held office afterward was Jones, and to attain it he had to leave Indiana and go west of the Mississippi river.

BENJAMIN PARKE.

In *Drake's Dictionary of American Biography* is this notice of Benjamin Parke: " Parke, Benjamin, jurist; born in New Jersey in 1777; died at Salem, Ind., July 12, 1835. A Western pioneer. He settled in Indiana about 1800; was a delegate to Congress in 1805–8; was soon after appointed by Mr. Jefferson a Judge of the District Court, and held the office until his death. President Indiana Historical Society."

Reader, isn't this the first time you ever heard of Benjamin Parke? And yet he was a leading man in Indiana under both the Territorial and State governments, and a county on the Wabash bears his name. If Benjamin Parke is so soon forgotten, what hope for earthly immortality have you or I? I have not been able to learn anything about Benjamin Parke's boyhood, further than that he obtained a good common school education. When twenty years old he emigrated to Kentucky and settled at Lexington. He soon afterward entered the law office of James Brown, once Minister to France, and in due time was admitted to the bar. Between him and his preceptor a friendship was formed which lasted while they lived.

In 1801 Judge Parke and his young wife came to Indiana, and took up their abode in the town of Vincennes, then the capital of the Territory. He opened a law office, and was soon appointed Attorney-General of the Territory—the second one appointed. He was a member of the first Territorial Legislature, which met in Vincennes July 20, 1805. The Legislative Council and House of Representatives elected him a delegate to Congress, and he served in that capacity from that time until 1808, when he was appointed by President Jefferson a Territorial Judge. He remained in this office until Indiana became

a State. He was a member of the convention that met at Corydon on the 10th day of June, 1816, to form a State constitution,
and took a leading part in its deliberations. On the admission
of Indiana into the Union President Madison appointed him
United States District Judge, with circuit court powers, a position he held until his death.

But it was not only as a legislator and magistrate that Judge
Parke endeared himself to the people of Indiana. When the
savage warrior, with tomahawk and scalping-knife, marched
against the defenseless settlers of the frontier, Judge Parke
raised a company of dragoons and went to their relief. He was
in the bloody battle of Tippecanoe, and greatly distinguished
himself for bravery. When the gallant Major Daviess fell Captain Parke was promoted to the majority and became commander of the cavalry. General Harrison thus speaks of him
as a military officer: " He was in every respect equal to any
cavalry officer of his rank that I have ever seen. As in everything else which he undertook, he made himself acquainted
with the tactics of that arm, and succeeded in bringing his
troops, both as regards field maneuvering and the use of the
saber, to as great perfection as I have ever known."

During the Territorial government, for several years Judge
Parke acted as Indian agent, and acquired great influence over
the savage men of the forest. He was peculiarly fitted for the
duties of this position, by reason of his knowledge of the Indian
character, and his patience, fortitude and bravery.

The late Hon. John I. Morrison many years ago conducted,
at Salem, a seminary of a very high grade. Judge Parke took
great interest in this school, as he did in everything that was
calculated to make men wiser and better. Mr. Morrison furnished the author the following beautiful and touching tribute to
the memory of his early friend and benefactor:

" KNIGHTSTOWN, IND., Jan. 23, 1882.
" *William Wesley Woollen, Esq.:*

" DEAR SIR—In the spring of 1827 I became acquainted with
Hon. Benjamin Parke. Sarah B. and Wm. Barton, his only
children, both of whom he survived, were pupils of my first

25

school in Salem, Washington county, Indiana. In person the Judge was tall, nearly six feet, but spare in habit, and of a rather delicate frame. His dignified appearance impressed me with awe and reverence. He looked so much like a philosopher —like my ideals, Socrates and Plato—I fancied I might admire him as I was wont to admire them, but concluded I could never love him. What a mistake! I soon felt that I had found a second father, one whom I could not help but love and venerate. In all matters pertaining to my school he manifested the liveliest interest. If I had been his own son he could have done nothing more. He never failed to invite his distinguished guests from abroad, who frequently shared his hospitality, to visit the school. Among the number I remember well Governor William Hendricks, Governor Jonathan Jennings and General William Henry Harrison. On such occasions the Judge showed a singular partiality for the class in Colburn's mental arithmetic, and seemed unwilling to withdraw before his friends had an opportunity to witness the drill of his favorite class. I wondered many a time what there could be in operations so simple and practical to interest the mind of a jurist so learned and profound.

"At home and abroad he spared no pains to present the claims of the seminary to the public, and to his active efforts and potent influence justly belongs a large share of the success achieved in former days by that institution.

" He was ever on the lookout for opportunities to do good, especially to the young, the poor, and the wayward. What made other people happy seemed to increase his own happiness, and if ever there was a man who performed works of disinterested benevolence he surely was the man.

"The training and education of his own children claimed much time and attention. The result was, they were regarded by all as model pupils in deportment and scholarship.

" He never permitted his son to leave school without first obtaining leave of absence, even when failing health required his presence and watchful care while court was in session at Indianapolis.

" Judge Parke could not endure anything like arrogance and pride. He was very careful to guard his son on this point. He encouraged him to ring the seminary bell, and associate, at stated times, with the children of a very poor neighbor, who came from the country to enjoy the advantages of the seminary. Thus did he strive to crush out any false notions of superiority which might be entertained on account of his father being a Judge of the United States Court.

"Judge Parke was a hard student. He had a large library of very select books, not wholly confined to the law, but well supplied with standard works of history, philosophy, and classical literature. The Judge was scrupulously exact in all his dealings and engagements.

" He never failed to attend the regular sessions of this court, so long as he was able to make the journey to Indianapolis on horseback.

" He was not long confined to his bed. His last hours were calm and peaceful, and as I stood by his bedside and watched his last pulse, and closed his eyes when he ceased to breathe, my heart bled for the loss of my dearest friend and constant benefactor. Yours truly, JOHN I. MORRISON."

Honorable Barnabas C. Hobbs was for many years an inmate of Judge Parke's family. He has great reverence for the dead jurist's memory, and in a note to the author gives this graphic description of the Judge and his family :

" His wife's maiden name was Eliza Barton. They were married at Lexington. Parke was an intimate of Henry Clay. He took his wife to Vincennes when he entered upon service, that being then the chief town in the State and the residence of Governor Harrison. While there a great intimacy existed between his family and the Governor's. He was on the Governor's staff in his treaty with Tecumseh and in the battle of Tippecanoe, and could relate some very interesting events in connection with this service. He traveled on horseback during all his judicial service. His last saddle-horse was a magnificent fellow, presented to him by his son-in-law, Abram Hite, a merchant of Louisville, Kentucky. He reached Wayne County Court by a circuitous journey along the Ohio river to Lawrenceburg, and then up the Whitewater valley. His first case in Wayne county was a criminal case. He sat on a log, the court being held in the forest. The case was a theft. A young man had stolen a twenty-five cent pocket-knife from John Smith's store. Judge Parke rode all the way from Vincennes to try this case, the only one on the docket.

"Judge Parke was honest and generous to the core. He scorned all subterfuge, dishonesty and hypocrisy. While at Vincennes he was induced to unite his fortunes with two other men in the organization and management of a bank. He, of course, was busy with professional duties, and left the management of the bank and his own fortune to the other partners. They found a desirable time and way to let the bank break and to hide its resources, leaving Judge Parke to attend to its liabilities. These reverses made him bankrupt for life, or nearly so. All who knew him knew his honesty and integrity, and admired his patience and resignation to his fate. After Governor Harrison left Vincennes Judge Parke moved to Salem, in Washington county, a place at that time more central. He took an inexpensive house, and year by year used all his savings to cancel his bank indebtedness. He closed it all out a short time before he died. He was for years afflicted with tubercular consumption, and must have struggled with much infirmity while steadily and faithfully performing his judicial duties. He suffered also from paralysis of his right side, so that he could not use his right hand in writing. He overcame this disadvantage by learning to write with his left hand, which he used with elegance and dispatch.

"He had two children, a daughter and a son. He took his daughter with him to New Albany—being a delicate and beautiful maiden of fifteen—to join in his country's welcome of Lafayette, in his visit to America, in 1825, when Abram Hite, an accomplished young merchant of Louisville, became fascinated and afterward married her. She died young, leaving a little son, whom the grandmother claimed and took to her Salem home.

"Barton was the son's name. He was a delicate but talented boy, and accompanied his father very often in his rides into the country. He was a student in the county seminary, and was making good progress in a preparation for college when, in

1833, the town of Salem lost one-twentieth of its citizens by cholera. Barton and his sister's little boy were both taken, and Benjamin and Eliza Parke were left childless.

" Not long after this, in his loneliness he invited me to board with him while I was attending school at the seminary, and to have a care of the family garden and stable, while he was away at court in Indianapolis.

" On one occasion we were agreeably surprised to have a call from General Harrison, who was making a visit by saddle from North Bend to Vincennes, and dined with us. I was much interested in witnessing the old-time friendship of these pioneer officials. After dinner I brought out the General's horse and helped him to his stirrup, and they parted to meet on earth no more. During the summer of 1835 the destroyer finished his work. I was by him in his last hours, saw him expire, and, assisted by David Campbell, Professor Campbell's father, of Crawfordsville, prepared him for his narrow resting-place on the hill west of Salem.

" Benjamin Parke was a Christian in the true acceptation of the term, though he identified himself with no religious denomination. He attached much value to the spiritual acceptation and experience of Christian life. To him it must be a true life in the soul. He could not be satisfied with appearances without a practical exhibition of its genuineness. He very often rode out three miles into the country to sit in silence with the Friends at their midweek meetings, as well as on the Sabbath, and was as appreciative of their spiritual communion as themselves. He read and enjoyed their books, and kept them in his library, which was perhaps the best, at that time, in the State. When death was near he was very conscious and calm, and smiled at all my little attentions ; and when the last suffocating cough was over he seemed quite ready, with Kirke White, who sank under like circumstances,

> " Henceforth, O world, no more of thy desires,
> No more of hope, of anxious, vagrant hope.
> I abjure all. Now other cares engross me,
> And my tired soul, with emulative haste,
> Looks to its God and plumes its wings for Heaven."

While a resident of Vincennes Judge Parke was mainly in-

strumental in the formation of a public library. Under his care
it grew until it contained over 1,500 choice books, embracing
standard works in many branches of science and departments
of literature. He was a member of the first Board of Trustees
of Vincennes University, and helped to organize and start that
institution of learning. He was the father of the movement
that established at Indianapolis a law library which has grown
to be one of the best of the kind in the country. It was largely
by his influence and activity that the Indiana Historical Society
was formed, once an institution of much promise, but now
scarcely known. Would that we had another Benjamin Parke
to put life into this corpse, in order that the rich treasures of
Indiana history now going to waste might be preserved. If
the spirits of the departed are permitted to know what transpires on earth, that of Benjamin Parke must view with horror
the wreck of the edifice he helped to build.

A warm friendship existed between Judge Parke and the late
Judge Dewey. In going to court at Indianapolis it was the
custom of Judge Dewey, who lived at Charlestown, to come by
way of Salem, that he might have Judge Parke's company to
the capital. Mrs. Parke used to say that her husband's eyes
shone at the sight of Dewey as they did at the sight of no other
man. When Judge Parke died the bar of Indiana selected
Judge Dewey to deliver an address commemorative of his
virtues. This address was a magnificent tribute of one great
lawyer to the memory of another. It closes as follows: "His
venerable form is in the tomb, but his example is with us in
that his spirit lives and still kindly admonishes us to consecrate
the remainder of our lives to life's great purposes, to duty and
to usefulness."

THOMAS RANDOLPH.

THOMAS RANDOLPH, third Attorney-General of Indiana Territory, was born in Richmond, Virginia, in 1771. He belonged to the celebrated family of that name, and was a second cousin of John Randolph of Roanoke. He graduated with high honor at William and Mary's College, and subsequently studied law. He served one term in the Virginia Legislature, a position at that time of much honor and influence. He married, when a young man, a daughter of Sir John Skipwith, who bore him one child, a daughter, and shortly afterwards died. He was an applicant for a position in the regular army, and in May, 1808, was appointed to a lieutenancy, but having previously emigrated to Indiana Territory, where he had many influential friends, he declined the commission. Soon after coming to Indiana Governor Harrison appointed him Attorney-General of the Territory, a position of honor, but one which brought him but little money.

In June, 1810, he married Catherine Lawrence, a step-daughter of General James Dill, and a grand-daughter of General Arthur Saint Clair. By her he had one daughter—Mrs. William Sheets, of Indianapolis—a lady of culture and high breeding, and to whom the author is indebted for much of the material used in the preparation of this sketch.

Mr. Randolph was one of a coterie of young Virginians who came to Indiana in early times, and whose influence upon the manners, customs and politics of the Territory was widespread and deep. Their chief was William Henry Harrison, then Governor of the Territory, to whose fortunes they clung with great steadfastness and fidelity.

Chaperoned as Mr. Randolph was by Governor Harrison, he

at once took rank among the leading men of the Territory. At that time there was an effort being made to nullify the provisions of the ordinance of 1781, forbidding slavery in the Northwestern Territory. At the head of this movement was Governor Harrison, and he had as aids the Virginians about him, among them Mr. Randolph. The leader of the Free State party, or the party opposed to any change in the compact between Virginia and the United States in relation to the territory northwest of the Ohio river, was Jonathan Jennings, afterwards Governor of the State. In 1809 Jennings became a candidate for delegate to Congress. The Virginia, or pro-slavery party, chose Randolph to make the race against him, and the contest which ensued was active, bitter and exciting. When the votes were counted it was found that Jennings's majority was thirty-nine, but Mr. Randolph and his friends contended that this majority was made up by votes illegally counted. A contest was determined upon, and money raised to prosecute it. Mr. Randolph went to Washington, having previously given Mr. Jennings notice of contest, and appeared before the Committee on Elections. He commenced a speech before the committee, but was interrupted by Mr. Jennings, who moved that he be required to reduce his objections to writing. The committee ordered this to be done, and Mr. Randolph complied with the order. A sharp and acrimonious debate took place before the committee between the contestant and the contestee, during which Mr. Randolph said :

" MR. CHAIRMAN—I have but a few observations to make in reply, for I certainly am not disposed to controvert arguments and positions perfectly in accord with my ideas on this subject, and which I have contended for before this and the committee to whom was referred the memorial from the Territory. I most sincerely wish that the arguments of the gentleman may convince you of the legality of the election, as I myself believe it to have been. Much rather had I that this should be your decision than the seat of the delegate should be vacated, unless on the other points before you, because this has been seized on by a pettifogging faction (who, like drowning men, catch at straws), to prove the arbitrary conduct of the Governor. Such

are their contemptible artifices to render unpopular a virtuous
and great man, by representing that he had trampled upon the
rights and privileges of the people. I am not a little astonished,
sir, to see the change in sentiment which has taken place in that
gentleman. I did not expect a change of situation would have
so metamorphosed him. He has chimed in with this faction in
the clamor against this man in the vain hope of rendering him
unpopular. Such a change should not be produced in me by
personal considerations." [Here Mr. Randolph was called to
order. He apologized by declaring that his surprise had produced these observations, but added, he stated nothing but the
truth.]

The committee came to the conclusion that the election for
delegate was without authority of law, and, therefore, that Mr.
Jennings was not entitled to his seat. They closed their report
by submitting the following resolution :

"*Resolved*, That the election held for a delegate to Congress
for the Indiana Territory, on the 22d of May, 1809, being without authority of law, is void, and, consequently, the seat of
Jonathan Jennings as a delegate for that Territory is hereby declared to be vacant."

The report of the election committee was considered in committee of the whole and adopted, but on coming before the
House for final action that body refused to concur in it, but
confirmed Mr. Jennings in his seat.

This contest between Mr. Jennings and Mr. Randolph begat
much bad blood. They both resorted to the hand-bill—a
weapon much used by the politicians of that day. Randolph
hand-billed Jennings, and Jennings hand-billed Randolph. Each
was severe on the other, but Randolph's invective and sarcasm
were the more cutting and biting of the two. He closes one of
his letters to the public as follows :

"If at any time I have been led into indiscretion in my defense it has proceeded from the injustice and violence of my
opponents. Truth may sometimes, with propriety, be sup-
pressed—it will always have most force when mildly expressed—

but though uttered in the warmest language, with the keenest satire, it may often be excused. The feelings of the man too frequently gain the mastery of sober judgment. I confess my natural sanguine disposition, impatient at injustice, often forces me to express myself in terms which might be softened. In whatever garb, however, it may be decked, truth will at length prevail."

The feud between Randolph and Jennings extended to their friends, and many bitter things were said by the latter of each other. Waller Taylor, then a Territorial judge, and afterwards a Senator in Congress, thus writes to Mr. Randolph:

"JEFFERSONVILLE, June 3, 1809.

" DEAR SIR—There has no circumstance transpired to throw further light on the result of the Dearborn election since I saw you. Jennings's conduct is a little mysterious, but he still says he is elected. He states that he got 143 votes, that you got 67, and Jones an inconsiderable number; one township he had not heard from when he left there, but he apprehends no injury from that, as it was in a part of the county the least populous. I expected the fellow would have been so much elated with his success that he would have been insolent and overbearing, but he says very little on the subject, and is silently preparing to go on to the city. Our meeting was not cordial on my part; I refused to speak to him until he threw himself in my way and made the first overtures, and then I would not shake hands with him. He has heard, I am told, of everything I said against him, which, by the by, was rather on the abusive order, but he revenges himself on me by saying that he never did anything to injure me, and professes esteem. He is a pitiful coward, and certainly not of consequence enough to excite resentment nor any other sentiment than contempt. He may rest in peace for me. I will no longer continue to bother myself about him. I expect, before you receive this, you will have passed through the list of your enemies in asking them over the Wabash to partake of your company and the amusement you wish to afford them. I make no doubt they will decline your invitation, although it may be couched in the most polite and ceremonious style; if they do, you will have acquitted yourself agreeable to the rules of modern etiquette, and can be then at liberty to act afterward to them in whatever way may best suit your humor. I hope the junta will be put down like Lucifer, ' never to rise again.' I have no news to communicate. I shall expect you on shortly. In the meantime, believe me to be respectfully yours,

"WALLER TAYLOR."

William McIntosh, who had been Territorial Treasurer, became inimical to Governor Harrison, and headed a movement intended to destroy his character and influence. He made slanderous statements about the Governor, which, coming to the latter's knowledge, highly incensed him. He brought a suit against McIntosh for slander, and employed Randolph to prosecute it. The latter called to his aid General W. Johnston and Ellis Glover, two eminent lawyers of that day, and the three successfully prosecuted the suit, obtaining judgment in favor of the Governor against McIntosh for $4,000. McIntosh was a Scotchman of large fortune, who, for many years, had been hostile to Governor Harrison, and who was not believed to be very partial to the government of the United States. Governor Harrison had a sufficient amount of McIntosh's property executed and sold to pay the judgment, but to show that his suit was not instituted for money, but to maintain his good name, he afterwards returned to McIntosh two-thirds of this property, and gave the remaining third to some of the orphan children of persons who fell in the last war with Great Britain.

A bitter feud between McIntosh and Randolph grew out of this suit, which culminated in a personal altercation between them. McIntosh stabbed Randolph in the back with a dirk, and Randolph cut McIntosh in the face with a small pocketknife, the only weapon he had about him. McIntosh was but slightly hurt, but Randolph was so badly injured that for weeks it was supposed he would die. In a letter of General James Dill to Mr. Randolph, dated October 19, 1809, that gentleman says :

" I am glad to hear you are out of danger, and am really astonished you came off so well, considering the precipitate and inconsiderate manner you engaged. I hope, however, it will have the effect of stopping the slanderous and libelous publications of that wretch, McIntosh, and if it does this you will not have risked your life for nothing."

Under date of October 15, 1809, Jonathan Taylor thus writes him :

" I had been much distressed for your recovery until I received your letter by Mr. Tanahill, having before heard of the affray between you and McIntosh. I have with great pleasure, I assure you, heard, to-day, by Mr. Jones, that you were entirely over the wounds."

Under date of October 13, 1809, Waller Taylor, in a letter to Mr. Randolph, says :

" I am happy to hear that you are so nearly recovered from the wound given you by Sawney. I wish you could batter his Scotch carcass well for it."

During the summer of 1809 several articles appeared in the *Vincennes Sun* severely denunciatory of Mr. Randolph. They had fictitious signatures, but Mr. Randolph suspected they were either written by Mr. Jennings or were instigated by him. On the 3d of June, 1809, he addressed a letter to Mr. Stout, the editor of the *Sun*, demanding the name of the author or authors of these objectionable communications. Mr. Stout replied, giving the name of Dr. Elias McNamee. The next day Mr. Randolph sent Dr. McNamee a letter by the hands of Major Jonathan Taylor, demanding redress for the injury done him. Dr. McNamee replied, saying, " I must leave you to seek that redress you may think most proper." The same day Mr. Randolph wrote him, saying : " I hope a polite invitation to meet me on the other side of the river Wabash, in the Illinois Territory, will be accepted." Instead of accepting the " polite invitation," Dr. McNamee went before Judge Vanderburg and swore " that Thomas Randolph, of the county of Knox, Esquire, hath challenged him to fight a duel, and that he hath good reason to believe, and doth verily believe, that the said Thomas

Randolph will take his life or do him some bodily harm." Mr. Randolph was arrested and put under bonds to keep the peace.

Dr. McNamee was born and bred a Quaker, and consequently was opposed, on conscientious grounds, to accepting Randolph's challenge. If Randolph knew this when he challenged him his action was not in accordance with the code.

In the next number of the *Sun* he published a long communication, reciting the correspondence between him and Dr. McNamee, and closing as follows:

"In taking leave of you, Dr. McNamee, as a scoundrel no longer worthy of my notice, I pronounce you a base slanderer, an infamous liar and a contemptible coward."

Such was the "modern etiquette" to which Waller Taylor, in the letter copied above, referred.

Mr. Randolph was of such a fiery nature that he often got into trouble. In a letter written by him to Captain Samuel C. Vance, of Lawrenceburg, he thus speaks of his relations with John Johnson, afterwards a judge of the Supreme Court:

"J. Johnson's address to me as the author of 'Alpheus,' I suppose, has reached you before this. It excited my risibility without creating in the slightest degree sentiments either of irritation or mortification; and believing it unworthy of notice I have passed it over in silence. On his appearance in this place he prepared and walked with a large hickory stick for some days. Informed by my friends that they had good reason to believe it was intended for me, and earnestly urged by them to place myself in a situation for defense, I thoughtlessly followed their advice, and carried also a stick for one evening and then threw it away, censuring myself for the folly of suspecting his intentions. A day or two afterwards, however, the truth was discovered that his was a weapon of defense and not offense, for he apprehended an assault on him by me, for which I had no cause save his hostile appearance. Warlike appearances have vanished, and we treat each other politely in court, and touch hats as we pass on the streets."

In a letter to Captain Vance, dated January 10, 1811, Mr. Randolph says:

"I have nothing to expect from Mr. Jennings more than all the injury he can do me. His unremitted exertion to identify me in all things with the Governor proceeds from his inimical disposition toward me. If he means, in this side way, to produce on the minds of his hearers that I am the echo of the Governor, he is a fool and a liar."

My purpose in drawing so copiously on the letters at my disposal is to show the reader the temper of the men who were prominent in the politics of Indiana in Territorial days. In no other way could I convey to him so forcibly their principles and manner of action.

When General Harrison inaugurated the Wabash campaign of 1811 it was his intention to give Mr. Randolph a command, but circumstances made this impossible. Mr. Randolph, however, accompanied him as a volunteer aid, and fell at the battle of Tippecanoe, pierced by an Indian bullet. The gallant Jo Daviess also fell, and Waller Taylor, a major in the army, and a bosom friend of Randolph, caused them to be buried side by side on the sanguinary field. Before committing their bodies to the grave he took a pin from Randolph's bosom, cut off a lock of his hair, and on his return home gave them to Randolph's widow. He also cut the initials of the names of the dead soldiers on the tree under which they were buried, and years afterward Mrs. Sheets, Randolph's daughter, visited Tippecanoe and found the spot where her distinguished father was laid at rest.

General James Dill, the husband of Mrs. Randolph's mother, thus broke the sad news of Randolph's death to his family. His letter was written at Vincennes and dated November 12, 1811:

"MY DEAR BESS—It appears as if misfortune were to attend us in all situations and circumstances. News has at length arrived from the army. They have had a severe conflict, but a signal victory. The worst of it is that many brave men have been killed, more especially amongst those who were immediately around the Governor. I wrote to you that Randolph had joined the army. I wish it had not been so, but it is now too late to wish. You will no doubt endeavor to support the trials heaven has thought proper to inflict. I wish I were with you. but that is impossible. The man who filled the place to which I was appointed (a Colonel Owens), was shot through the heart by the side of the Governor. Many have been killed and more wounded, but there is one consolation for the friends of those slain—they died gloriously and in the arms of victory. I hope you are all well. May God protect you. Yours, as ever,

"JAMES DILL."

Mrs. Sheets has an oil portrait of her distinguished father, which was painted in Richmond in 1806. It is that of a man in the prime of life, with high, broad forehead, over which the hair falls in ringlets, a long and delicate nose, dark hazel eyes and a large mouth. The lower part of the face is too small for the face to be symmetrical. A long queue hangs down the back, and the whole appearance is that of a high-bred, intellectual man. Had the original of this picture lived to the alloted age of mankind he must have risen to great eminence in the history of the State, for he had unquestionable talents, a classical education, a fine person and a host of friends.

WILLIAMSON DUNN.

WOULD that I had the pen of Dickens that I might draw Williamson Dunn as he was. I design no panegyric of the old pioneer, and if what I say appears extravagant, I beg to assure the reader that Judge Dunn was one of the grandest men I ever knew. I knew him well; he was my friend when I needed friends; he was my counselor when I needed counsel, and if I can do aught to honor his memory, I shall only be paying a debt I owe.

Williamson Dunn was born December 25, 1781, near Crow's station, within a few miles of Danville, Kentucky. He was the third son of Samuel Dunn, a native of Ireland, who at the age of thirteen emigrated from the north of Ireland to America, and settled in Rockingham county, Virginia. The family were Scotch-Irish Presbyterians, and transmitted to their descendants the characteristics of that tenacious and combative race. Samuel Dunn was in the bloody battle fought with the Indians at the mouth of the Big Kanawha, October 10, 1774, and afterwards served with distinction as a soldier in the Revolutionary war. He afterward removed to Kentucky, where Williamson, the subject of this sketch, was born and reared to manhood. The son inherited his father's bravery and patriotism, and these qualities descended to his children. As evidence of this fact there has never been a call to defend the country's flag since Williamson Dunn had issue, without his children and his grandchildren answering, "We are here."

In September, 1806, Williamson Dunn was married to Miriam Wilson, in Garrard county, Kentucky, and three years afterward, with his wife and two children, he emigrated to Indiana Territory and settled in the woods where Hanover now is. This continued his home until his death, except while he was register of the land office at Crawfordsville.

When Mr. Dunn came to Indiana he brought with him three negro slaves. They were a part of his inheritance from his father's estate, and constituted a large part of it. But he hated slavery, and brought his slaves to Indiana that they might be free.

In 1811 General Harrison, then Governor of Indiana Territory, gave Mr. Dunn two commissions—one as a Justice of the Peace, the other as Judge of the Court of Common Pleas of Jefferson county. He held these offices for some time, and honestly discharged their duties.

In 1812 President Madison commissioned Judge Dunn a captain of rangers. He soon raised a company, among the members being two of his brothers and two of his brothers-in-law. On the 13th of April, 1813, the company was mustered into the service of the United States, at Madison, and at once entered upon active service. For some time it was employed in erecting block-houses in the counties of Switzerland, Jefferson and Scott, for the protection of the settlers.

In June, 1813, Captain Dunn and his company made a raid upon the Delaware towns on the west fork of White river, and next month, with three other companies, all under the command of Colonel Russell, marched against the Indian towns on the Wabash river, at the mouth of the Mississiniwa. During this expedition Captain Dunn's company encamped one night on the spot which is now known as Circle Park, Indianapolis. In September, 1813, Captain Dunn's rangers marched to Fort Harrison, near Terre Haute, to relieve Captain Zachary Taylor's company of United States regulars. Dr. David H. Maxwell, a brother-in-law of Captain Dunn, and a member of his company, in a petition to Congress asking compensation for medicine and medical services rendered the members of his company, gives this graphic description of the situation at Fort Harrison when Captain Dunn arrived:

"After this campaign (the Mississiniwa), and without a respite, Captain Dunn's company of rangers was ordered to Fort

26

Harrison to relieve a company of United States infantry which had charge of that garrison.

"No language which your petitioner can command can adequately describe the situation of this infantry company when the Rangers took charge of the fort. Of the whole company four only were able to perform duty. The physician who was stationed at the fort had been sick and confined to his bed for weeks. At his request your petitioner attended upon the sick of his company until those who recovered (for some died) were able to leave the fort. Within the short space of three months after Captain Dunn's company of rangers was stationed at Fort Harrison there were eighty-five men out of one hundred and six who were sick and confined. Such was the rapid increase of disease that your petitioner was wholly unable to attend personally upon the sick, and he was obliged to apply to the officers to obtain the aid of three or four intelligent individuals to assist him in preparing and administering medicines, and to attend on the sick during their operation. Nearly all the sick were affected with remitting and intermitting fever, some few from dysentery or bloody flux. The rangers were continued at Fort Harrison for four months, and during that time, and, in fact, until the company was discharged, in March, 1814, the sick were often requiring additional medicines. Of the whole number of rangers at the fort, only one died during the service; but more than twenty never perfectly recovered, and died within eighteen months afterward."

Such were some of the hardships the pioneers of Indiana endured that this fair land might be opened to settlement and its inhabitants made secure in their persons and property.

On Captain Dunn's return to his home he put aside the sword and put his hand to the plow. Soon afterward he joined the Presbyterian church at Charlestown, twenty-five miles from his home, and continued a member of it until the establishment of a Presbyterian church at Madison, to which he removed his membership. In February, 1820, a church was organized at Hanover, of which Judge Dunn became a ruling elder, and he continued to occupy this high office until he died.

In 1814 Governor Posey commissioned Judge Dunn an Associate Judge of the Circuit Court of Jefferson county. He held this office until 1816, when he was elected to the first Legislature under the State constitution. He was re-elected to the second, third and fourth Legislatures, and during the sessions of the third and fourth was Speaker of the House. While a member of the Legislature he was virtually offered a seat in the United States Senate, but he declined the honor because it would have taken him away from his family.

In May, 1820, Judge Dunn was commissioned, by President Monroe, Register of the Land Office for the Terre Haute district. Three years afterward the land office was removed to Crawfordsville. Judge Dunn and Major Whitlock, the Receiver of the Land Office, entered the land where Crawfordsville stands, and laid out the town. Judge Dunn was re-appointed Register in 1827 and held the office until 1829, when he was superseded by General Milroy. A short time after leaving the Land Office he returned to Hanover and remained a citizen of that town while he lived.

Judge Dunn donated fifty acres of land to establish Hanover College, and also donated the ground upon which Wabash College, at Crawfordsville, was erected. Thus it will be seen that these colleges are mainly indebted to him for their establishment.

In 1832 Judge Dunn was a candidate for the State Senate, but on account of his views upon temperance and the Sunday mail, was defeated by David Hillis. At the end of his term Mr. Hillis was re-elected, and in 1837, having been elected Lieutenant-Governor of the State, resigned his seat in the Senate, and Judge Dunn was chosen to fill the vacancy.

In 1843 Judge Dunn was nominated for the Senate by the Whigs of Jefferson county. Shadrach Wilber, also a Whig, became an independent candidate, and the Hon. Jesse D. Bright, a Democrat, received a plurality of the votes cast and was elected. This was the real beginning of his long political career.

In 1846 Judge Dunn was elected Probate Judge of Jefferson county over George S. Sheets, a very brilliant young lawyer of Madison. He was re-elected at the end of his term and held the office when the court was abolished.

In September, 1854, while overlooking some improvements of a plank road of which he was president, Judge Dunn was sunstruck, and taken to his home in a helpless condition. He remained an invalid until November 11, 1854, when he died. When his life went out one of the best men of Indiana was no more.

The children and grandchildren of Judge Dunn inherited his bravery and love of arms. His sons, David and Thomas, served in the Mexican war, the first as a lieutenant and the latter as a private soldier. In the war of the rebellion they again enlisted in the service of their country. David became lieutenant-colonel of the Ninth Indiana regiment of volunteers, and Thomas the captain of a company. He was afterward appointed to a captaincy in the regular army, and is now a major in that service. Judge Dunn's son James was also lieutenant-colonel in the volunteer service, and his son Williamson served as a surgeon throughout the war. Another son, William McKee, who was a member of Congress when the war broke out, was offered a colonelcy by Governor Morton, and a brigadiership by President Lincoln, but declined them both, that he might fill out the term for which he was elected. When it expired he was appointed Judge Advocate of the department of Missouri, and served for some time in that capacity. Subsequently he was appointed Assistant Judge Advocate-General, and on the retirement of Judge Advocate-General Holt he was selected to fill the vacancy.

All of Judge Dunn's grandsons, except two, who were boys, served in the war of the rebellion. One of them, William McKee Dunn, Jr., who is now a major in the regular army, was a member of General Grant's staff, and was distinguished for his coolness and bravery. General Grant once said of him: " He is as brave as Julius Cæsar. Had I ordered him to a place where it was certain death to go I do not believe he would have hesitated a moment to obey the order." He is a true descendant of Williamson Dunn. His grandfather never hesitated to go where duty called him. If there ever was in this State a family that equaled the Dunns in bravery and soldierly qualities I hope some one will point it out. I have no knowledge of such an one.

Judge Dunn took great interest in public affairs. He started the movement which culminated in the election of Zachary Taylor President of the United States. A meeting was held at Madison in 1848, which formally put forward General Taylor for the presidency. Judge Dunn was the moving spirit of that meeting. He introduced the resolutions favoring General Taylor's nomination, and supported them in an earnest speech. In February, 1849, when on his way to Washington to assume the presidency, General Taylor stopped off at Madison and was given a public dinner. Judge Dunn presided at this dinner, and, on arising to propose the health of the guest, read an order he had received from him at Fort Harrison in 1813. He then paid a high tribute to the soldierly qualities and strong common sense of General Taylor, and ended by proposing his health. The toast was drunk with water, a cold-water banquet being the only kind at which Judge Dunn ever presided.

Judge Dunn had moral bravery as well as physical bravery. He did what he believed to be right, and would have suffered burning at the stake rather that do an act he knew to be wrong. He was of the stuff of which martyrs are made.

In 1848 or '49 a temperance wave swept over Southern Indiana, and at Madison petitions were numerously signed praying the repeal of the license law and the enactment of a law to make the selling of liquor a felony, punishable with fine and imprisonment. A year or so afterward, when the temperance movement had waned, the liquor men procured copies of these petitions and had them published in the Madison papers. This played havoc with the aspirations of several men who were ambitious to serve the public in an official capacity. A candidate for the mayoralty of Madison on being confronted with one of these petitions with his name to it sought to evade responsibility by claiming that he did not know its contents when he signed it. A day or two after his card to this purport had appeared in the *Madison Courier* I was at Hanover, and seeing Judge Dunn in his porch, approached him and took a seat by his side. We conversed awhile upon politics, and the canvass for the mayoralty of Madison being mentioned, Judge Dunn said:

" I see by the *Courier* that —— —— is trying to crawfish out of having signed the temperance petition. I have a contempt for a man who, having done a proper thing, turns his back upon it to please the public. I, too, signed that petition. I did it with my eyes open, and I stand by the act. It was right, and I will do it again if the opportunity offers."

It was his unyielding devotion to conviction that twice cost him a seat in the Senate of the State.

In appearance General William McKee Dunn is the counterpart of his father. At the late meeting of the Army of the Tennessee in Indianapolis, while sitting on the platform at the Park Theater, I saw General Dunn in the parquette, and, had I not known his father was dead, I would have thought he was before me. I never knew a son more like his father.

Judge Dunn was five feet ten and one-half inches high, and was very strong and muscular. He had a fair complexion and bright blue eyes. In his latter years his head was entirely bald, save a fringe of hair behind his ears. His sons were all good and patriotic men, but none of them was so good and patriotic as he. He was a model citizen, and a Christian without reproach.

Rev. Jonathan Edwards, once president of Hanover College, in an address at the dedication of the Presbyterian Theological Seminary of the Northwest, at Chicago, thus speaks of Judge Dunn:

"Early and intimately associated with Dr. Crowe in the founding and fostering of this institution (Hanover College) was his neighbor, Williamson Dunn, once Register of the Land Office at Crawfordsville, but for the last thirty years of his life a resident of Hanover. He had been a judge, but was best known as a farmer and an elder of the church. Comparatively hidden as was his light, Judge Dunn was yet widely known and highly appreciated. His general intelligence, his practical sense, his prudence, his great firmness, his rare integrity of character, are still embalmed in the traditions of his State, and he lives in the recollection of those who knew him as one of the best specimens of the American citizen."

ABEL C. PEPPER.

ABEL C. PEPPER was born in Kentucky, and emigrated to Indiana Territory in 1815. He was a soldier in the war of 1812, having been a private in Captain William Garrard's troop of volunteer light dragoons. He was mustered out of the service by Lieutenant-Colonel James V. Bell, at Lower Seneca, August 10, 1813, and received from his captain the following certificate:

"FRANKLINTON, August 18, 1813.

"By virtue of the within order, Abel C. Pepper, a private in my troop of volunteer light dragoons, who has served under my command twelve months, is hereby honorably discharged from the service, and is entitled to the privileges and emoluments provided by the acts of Congress upon such discharge.

"WILL GARRARD, JR.,
"*Captain of Volunteer Light Dragoons.*"

When he came to Indiana he settled in Dearborn county, and soon afterward became one of her leading citizens. He had a taste for military affairs, and had been in the Territory but a short time until he became a militia captain. He was advanced to the office of colonel, and subsequently to that of brigadier-general, although he was generally called by the title of Colonel. He served as County Commissioner of Dearborn county, as her Sheriff, and for several terms represented her people in the Legislature of the State. In 1828 he was a candidate for Lieutenant-Governor, but was defeated by Milton Stapp a few hundred votes. In 1830 General Stapp was a candidate for Governor, and during the canvass made a speech at Rising Sun, in which he said the people of Dearborn county ought to support him, for they did but little for him when he ran for Lieutenant-Governor. Continuing, he said:

" When the returns came in from every portion of the State, except old Dearborn, I felt rejoiced at the result. But when the votes of Dearborn were counted, it was 'Pepper,' 'Pepper,' 'Pepper,' and I assure you it came near peppering me."

In 1829 Colonel Pepper was appointed sub-Indian agent at Fort Wayne by General Jackson. He was afterward promoted to the office of Indian agent, and then superintendent for the removal of the Indians in Indiana, Michigan, Illinois and Wisconsin. In 1839 he resigned this office. Subsequently he was elected a Sinking Fund Commissioner, and in 1845 was appointed by President Polk United States Marshal for Indiana. He held this office until 1849, when he was superseded by John L. Robinson. In 1850 he represented Ohio and Switzerland counties in the constitutional convention, and took a very active part in its proceedings. He served on the committees of elective franchises, apportionment and representation, banks and banking, arrangement and phraseology, and of the militia, being chairman of the last.

In the convention Colonel Pepper took a decided stand against a State bank. Early in the session he offered a resolution. " That from and after the expiration of the charter of the State Bank of Indiana all connection between the State and banks shall cease." He made a speech in favor of the resolution, in which he declared himself in favor of free banks and opposed to a State bank.

During the session of the convention Colonel Pepper offered a resolution of inquiry in relation to the unsold lots and land included in the donation by the national government to the State. In speaking on this resolution, he said:

" My object in offering the resolution is to secure the preservation of these lots for the use and pleasure of the people of the State as well as the citizens of Indianapolis, as public grounds. In all the large cities of our country it became an object of great interest to secure squares and open plats of ground in their midst, to be ornamented with trees and shrubbery, and to serve the double purpose of public use and private gratification. While it is yet possible to secure such lots here I wish to see it done."

Colonel Pepper died at his home in Rising Sun, March 20, 1860, and was buried in the cemetery there. His death caused much grief among his neighbors, and he was also mourned throughout the State, for he was well known to the people as a good and patriotic man.

Colonel Pepper was a devoted member of the Masonic fraternity. He was made a Mason in 1816, and afterward received the highest honors of the craft, serving both as Grand Master and Grand High Priest of the order in the State. He was one of the brightest and most zealous Masons ever within the jurisdiction of the Grand Lodge of Indiana.

When Colonel Pepper was a young man he determined to study and practice medicine. Accordingly he entered the office of a physician as a student, and soon afterward a man came to get medicine for a sick person while the doctor was away. The student thought he would act the doctor for the nonce, and put up what he thought was a dose of salts, gave it to the messenger, and sent him away. The doctor soon returned, and, on being told by Mr. Pepper what he had done, ordered him to mount a horse at once and overtake the messenger, as what he had given him was the rankest poison. The student did as directed, and succeeded in reaching the house of the sick man just in time to prevent him from taking the poison. This narrow escape from causing the death of a human being induced Colonel Pepper to quit the study of medicine, and hence he did not become a physician.

After this Colonel Pepper concluded to study law. He purchased some law books, and for a time diligently studied them. Soon after commencing these studies a farmer came to him and narrated a difficulty he had had with a neighbor, and urged the Colonel to take the case. He had no license, but knowing the suit could be brought before a justice of the peace, he accepted the employment. The case was tried, decided against his client, and then appealed to the Circuit Court, which confirmed the judgment of the justice. The costs were so heavy that the farmer had great difficulty in saving his farm from being sold to pay them. This ended the Colonel's aspirations to become a lawyer.

After this Colonel Pepper engaged in merchandising, and continued at it most of the time he was not in public life.

Mr. Shadrach Hathaway, eighty-eight years old, and now living at Rising Sun, in 1883, says that he and Colonel Pepper once walked from Rising Sun to Cincinnati, some thirty miles or more. Their route was through Kentucky. When they were near Covington they encountered a hill, and the Colonel, being much fatigued, said he would give "a quarter" if he were at its top. Mr. Hathaway took him upon his back and safely carried him to the top of the hill. The "quarter" was paid.

A gentleman of this city, who was a lad of thirteen when he looked upon the face of the Colonel at his funeral in March, 1860, has very pleasant recollections of the last years of the Colonel's life. During a series of lectures at Rising Sun by home talent—doctors, lawyers, clergymen and "statesmen"—the Colonel lectured upon his experience among the Indians, occupying the old fashioned high pulpit in the Universalist church. As he proceeded with his description he gave forcible illustrations by means of his Indian relics. With the aid of the county sheriff dressed up with a buffalo's head, tinkling bells, and other instruments of terror to eye and ear, he presented to the audience the "medicine man" as he appeared in his native forests. The boys were impressed and the adults amused by the spectacle and the vivid description, punctuated by tosses of the head and jangling of the bells. The fright of the young folks was tempered by a suspicion that they knew the man in costume.

In the winter of 1860 a committee of boys from a literary society called upon Colonel Pepper one evening and solicited his patronage to the society, and asked him to address it. They found him tired with a hard day's work in killing hogs, but were received with kindness, and with a dignity that reminded them of the Father of his Country.

Colonel Pepper presided at the ceremonies of laying the corner-stone of the Court-house of Ohio county, at Rising Sun. The stone-mason, who supplemented speculative masonry with limestone and mortar, had trouble in convincing the Colonel which corner should be honored, as the building did not front due east and west, the street upon which it stands running 36° north of west by 36° south of east.

For a time after the election at which Colonel Pepper was a candidate for Lieutenant-Governor it was supposed that he had been elected, and preparations were being made to do him honor, when unexpected returns from distant parts crushed the hopes of his friends, and left him a defeated candidate for the second office in the State.

Colonel Pepper was slightly above medium height, spare and sinewy, of easy and pleasing address. He was urbane and dignified in his intercourse with his fellow men, and was particularly polite to ladies. He was a useful and patriotic citizen, and his memory should be perpetuated in the history of the State.

JOSEPH LANE.

THE Lanes have been prominent actors in the politics and history of Indiana. Amos Lane was a leading lawyer in early times, and served in Congress from 1832 to 1836. His son, James H., was a colonel in the Mexican war, was Lieutenant-Governor of Indiana from 1849 to 1852, and a member of Congress from 1853 to 1855. Subsequently he removed to Kansas, and from March, 1861, until 1866, when he died by his own hand, he was a Senator of the United States from Kansas. Henry S. Lane was a gallant soldier, an eloquent speaker, and a conscientious man, and, after receiving the highest honors his State could confer upon him, died in 1882. But the Lane who was best known to the country, and who served Indiana longer than any of his name, was Joseph Lane, a pioneer of the State and a distinguished soldier of the Mexican war.

Joseph Lane was born in Buncombe county, North Carolina, December 14, 1801. In 1814 his father's family emigrated to Kentucky, and two years afterward the future general, then a boy of fifteen, crossed the river and came to Darlington, then the county seat of Warrick county, Indiana. He worked alternately in the office of the County Clerk and in a dry goods store until 1821, when he married and settled on a farm in Vanderburgh county, just across the Warrick line. The next year, before he was twenty-one years old, he was elected to the State Legislature from the counties of Vanderburgh and Warrick, and had to wait until he reached the legal age before he could take his seat. From that time until 1846 he was almost continuously a member of one branch or the other of the State Legislature.

The breaking out of the Mexican war found him a member

of the Senate, but he laid aside his official robes and joined Captain Walker's company of infantry as a private soldier. When the volunteers were organized at New Albany he was elected colonel of the Second regiment, and on the 1st day of July, 1846, he was appointed a brigadier-general and given command of the Indiana troops. He started at once for Mexico, and when he reached the seat of war his brigade was assigned to the First division, under command of Major-General Butler.

A thrilling episode in the shape of a personal difficulty just prior to the battle of Buena Vista is described by the *New Albany Ledger* of February, 1876. It was between General Jo Lane and Colonel James H. Lane :

"While General Taylor's army was encamped at Agua Nueva, fourteen miles south of Buena Vista, the quarrel was brought about by a trivial occurrence. It commenced in General Lane's tent, and in the presence of Colonel B. C. Kent, of this city, Lieutenant A. L. Robinson, aid to the General, and several other officers. They were engaged in the discussion of the relative merits of two companies of the brigade (incidental to a discussion with reference to the organization of another regiment at the close of the service of the regiments then in the service), General Lane championing Captain Sanderson's company, of the second regiment, of this city, while Colonel Lane was equally enthusiastic in regard to the qualities of the company of Captain Ford, of the third regiment, of Madison, this State. Both of these companies were excellent, and it was the utmost difficulty to decide which was really the better of the two. During the discussion the Lanes became very much excited, and something aroused the General to such a pitch that he deemed it necessary to fight it out then and there, and, reaching to his camp chest, produced a pair of very excellent dueling pistols, and handing them toward Colonel Lane, asked him to take his choice. The latter endeavored to secure one of the pistols, but the parties were separated by Lieutenant Robinson and others, when Colonel Lane withdrew from the tent.

"Both of these officers were highly exasperated, and were with difficulty prevented from laying violent hands on each other. This occurred in the afternoon, near the time for the usual dress parade of the several regiments. When the third regiment was assembled on the parade ground, ready for the exercise, Colonel Lane being present, General Lane came down the line of tents with an old-fashioned rifle on his shoulder, and called upon the Colonel to arm himself, for he had come to demand satisfaction for the insult offered him in the tent. Colonel Lane promptly directed one of the color guards to load his gun with ball cartridge, which was done at once. In the meantime intelligence had been conveyed to Major J. A. Cravens, of the second Indiana regiment, who was officer of the day, and he at once repaired to the parade ground and arrested the two officers just as they were about to take their places for an exchange of shots. Their swords were surrendered and sent by Major Cravens to General Wool's headquarters.

"It was very fortunate that Major Cravens was so prompt in action, for there is no doubt but that one or both of these officers would have been killed, both being men of courage and at the time exasperated to the highest degree. Nor would the feud have ended there, for the members of the second regiment were devoted to General Lane, and looked upon him with the reverence usually bestowed upon a father and confidence as a commander. During the excitement in the camp previous to the arrest many of the members of the second regiment seized their arms, loaded them, and were prepared to take a hand in defense of the General, and, no doubt, if he had fallen, would have sought revenge in an attempt to take the life of Colonel Lane. The devotion of the second regiment to the General was no greater than the love and admiration of the third for their chivalrous Colonel, and they would have sought the life of General Lane had their commander been killed. These were the feelings that pervaded the camp in these two regiments at the time.

"These events occurred in the early part of February, and the two officers made no effort to reconcile their differences, nor would they permit their friends to interfere. They both remained under arrest until the evening of the 21st of February, when General Wool sent their swords to them by the then Captain McDowell, since promoted to major-general, with the information that he presumed they would have an opportunity within a few days of drawing them on a common enemy, it then being known to General Wool that Santa Anna was advancing on his position from the San Louis road, and that a conflict would occur within forty-eight hours, which was realized in the famous battle of Buena Vista, where less than five thousand American volunteers put to flight a trained army of twenty-two thousand Mexicans. Shortly after the battle, and while the army was encamped at the ranche of Buena Vista, the former friendly relations of these two officers were re-established, and continued until the second and third regiments returned to their homes. They were frequent visitors to their several quarters, and those then best acquainted with them would never have dreamed that the former bitter feud existed."

At the battle of Buena Vista General Lane commanded the left wing of the division, and during the day was badly wounded in the arm. He behaved with distinguished bravery, and was warmly commended by General Taylor for his action in that sanguinary conflict. The next June he brought his brigade to New Orleans, where it was disbanded. But, although the men he had led at Buena Vista returned to their homes when their term of enlistment expired, he went back to Mexico, was given command of 3,000 men at Vera Cruz, and at once started for the Mexican capital. He defeated Santa Anna at Huamantla, attacked and routed a large body of guerrillas at Atlixco, scattered other bands of these partisan soldiers at Flascala, then took Matamoras and captured a large quantity of military stores, and soon after reached the headquarters of General Scott, the commander-in-chief of the army. Early in 1848 he was sent out by the commanding general to break up and destroy the many bands of guerrillas roaming over the country. He came so near Santa Anna at Tehuacan that he captured his carriage containing his private papers and wooden leg. He moved with such rapidity, and was so successful in beating the enemy, that he was called "The Marion of the Mexican War," a name that clung to him while he lived. He did the last fighting in Mexico, and his services brought him a brevet major-general's commission, an honor he fairly won.

A writer in *Cist's Advertiser* gives the following item of history :

" It may not be amiss to state how he obtained his military appointment, taken, as he was, from the farm, to lead armies to victory.

"When it became the duty of the President to make the appointment of brigadier-general it was felt by every Western member of Congress to be a prize for his constituents. Probably some fifty names had been handed in to the President, accordingly. Robert Dale Owen, in whose district Lane resided, entertaining no such local pride, would probably not have furnished any name, but for a suggestion to that effect from one of the Indiana Senators, 'Whom do you intend recommending?' 'Why,' said Mr. Owen, 'I had no thought of offering a name. There are no applications to me from my own district, but if you think it due to it to offer a name I shall hand in that of Jo Lane.'

"The Senator approved of the choice, and it was accordingly suggested. The President, as usual, said he would give it his favorable consideration. A few days afterwards Mr. Owen was transacting some private business at the White House. After it was through—'By the by, Mr. Owen,' observed the President, 'I shall have to appoint your friend Lane to the brigadier-generalship. I hope you have well considered your recommendation, for the office is a very responsible one.' 'I know nothing,' replied Mr. Owen, 'of Lane's military talents, but there are about him those elements of character which in all times of difficulty prompt every one to rally instinctively, around him as a leader. This has been the case in early days when lawless men infested the river border. Whether on shore or among boatmen on the river, Lane was the man relied on to keep such men in order, and he was always found equal to every emergency. I would select him for the office before any other man I know, if I had the appointment to make.'

"Lane was appointed. The sequel is history, and justified the penetrative judgment of Mr. Owen. Lane developed qualities which place him in the front rank of military service.

"When the news of the battle of Buena Vista reached Washington Mr. Owen called on President Polk.

"Well, sir," exclaimed he, "what do you think of our Hoosier general?"

"Ah!" said the President, with a quiet smile, "Mr. Owen, you are safe out of that scrape!"

When the war had ended General Lane came back to Indiana, but his residence here was of short duration. In August, 1848, he was appointed by President Polk Governor of the Territory of Oregon, and in March he reached its capital. He organized the Territorial government and remained at its head until August, 1850, when he was removed by President Taylor, a Whig, he being a Democrat. The next year he was elected a delegate to Congress, and continued as such until Oregon became a State, when he was chosen to represent her in the United States Senate. In 1860, while he was in the Senate, he was nominated for Vice-President on the ticket with John C. Breckenridge, and received seventy-two electoral votes. General Lane left the Senate on the 4th of March, 1861, and returned to Oregon. He remained in private life until April 20, 1881, when he died at Rosenberg, which for many years had been his home.

General Lane's long service in the public councils, and his brilliant career as a soldier, made him very popular in Indiana. A large convention of the Democracy declared in his favor for the presidency, and several of its shrewdest leaders at once went to work to pave the way for his nomination. Robert Dale Owen, a leading Democrat and a master of the English language, wrote a pamphlet in which General Lane's claims and qualifications for the presidency were elaborately set forth. John L. Robinson, than whom there was no more effective political worker in the State, took charge of the movement and threw into it all the energy and ability he possessed. In order that the reader may have an inside glimpse of the political workings of that day, and know something of the extent of the effort to nominate General Lane for the presidency, the following letters from Mr. Robinson and from General Lane to a gentleman of Indianapolis, are now published for the first time:

"WASHINGTON, January 23, 1852.

"DEAR SIR—Some of my letters from Indianapolis indicate some discouragement on the part of General Lane's friends. I

27

see no sufficient reason for this; on the contrary, there is much to encourage them. It is the opinion of all the General's friends here with whom I have conversed, and I have given it my unceasing attention, that things are working as well for him as could be reasonably expected. It is true, not much is said about him in the papers; in fact, at present he is not in the fight that is so actively going on between the other aspirants and their friends, and this very fact is most favorable to him. While Cass's, Buchanan's, Douglas's and Butler's friends are active and noisy, exciting prejudices against each other, Lane and his friends, here, at least, are quietly awaiting the issue and striking occasionally when we find something is to be made. We desire to keep him in the position he now occupies; that is, friendly with all, hostile to none, so that he may eventually get votes from all, for we do not believe that any of the others can possibly reach a two-thirds vote, so as to be nominated. Lane has kept very still since he has been here, but has nevertheless made some strong friends and a most favorable impression with every one with whom he has come in contact. I have never known a man so uniformly and certainly successful in making all whom he meets friends, and keeping them so, as General Lane. I hear that there is a possibility that our convention on the 24th of February will name a second choice. No friend of General Lane ought to listen for a moment to such a proposition; it would be fatal to him. If you appoint his reliable friends as delegates there is no need of absolute instructions at all, but pass strong resolutions in his favor like Kentucky did for Butler. But if you instruct, begin and end with Lane, and nobody else.

"The Douglas bubble has exploded. Conventions have been held in New York, Ohio and Kentucky, and delegates appointed. He expected much from each and all of them, and has signally failed. Lane is, in my opinion, stronger than Douglas in all these States. At present Douglas can't rely upon any State but Illinois. The contest at first in the national convention will be between Cass and Buchanan. Douglas will be put in as a rival of both, and hence not likely to get their friends after they abandon them.

"Ultimately the race will be between Lane, Marcy and Butler. I think there can be no doubt of this. I write thus freely to you just what I think. I intend to devote every energy to the service of Lane, and I really have sanguine hopes of success. Much, however, very much, depends upon the action of your convention on the 24th, and the sort of men you name as delegates. Very truly yours,

"JOHN L. ROBINSON."

———

"WASHINGTON, March 28, 1852.

"DEAR SIR—I have been prevented by indisposition from writing you for some time, but being now well, I propose to give you a few of my thoughts and views about things connected with the interests of our friend Lane. I will begin by saying that his prospects for the nomination are, in my opinion, getting better daily. This is owing to the fact that he keeps very quiet, pursuing the even tenor of his way, and by his unobtrusive but frank and generous bearing winning the affections of all who make his acquaintance. His conduct and that of his friends is in such wide and favorable contrast with that of other candidates and their friends, particularly Douglas and his, that it is having a happy effect. You have noticed that some sharp shooting has occurred in the House between Douglas's friends and Butler's; it has resulted much to the injury of Douglas, as it ought. I never knew such an organization as exists around Douglas, and it reaches into most of the States, too, but it embraces but few but trading politicians who expect to live off of speculation and spoils. Their game is brag. They will impudently assert that every man and every State is for Douglas, wherever it will serve a purpose. In our delegation Gorman, Davis and Mace, I think, play a little at the game. Speaker Boyd told me that he was in Gorman's company last night, and that Gorman said Indiana would go for Douglas, the second ballot certain, and the first if necessary; that this was an ascertained fact. Still these gentlemen say they are for Lane, but that 'he has no chance.' In short, their conversations are calculated to aid Douglas only; I mean Gorman and Davis particularly. Fitch, Lockhart and myself, and Bright, when he is here, are doing what we can for Lane.

Cass is proving much stronger than was expected, and may be nominated, but I think not; to let Douglas beat him, however, would be a shame. Buchanan may now be considered out of the ring; his failure, so considered, in Virginia kills him. Douglas's friends will now claim Virginia, but I am assured he can not get it. Many Southern Democrats have recently indicated a strong leaning towards Lane; it is generally of that class who do not like to go for Cass. It will require but little management to get many of the Southern States to go in convention for Lane in the event, which, I think, is almost certain to occur, to wit: a repeated and protracted balloting. But if we have delegates who come up to Baltimore ostensibly for Lane, but really for Douglas, determined to vote for Douglas as soon as possible, a candidate from whose friends Lane has nothing to expect—I mean who has no intrinsic strength to transfer if he fails—why, I would rather have no delegates from Indiana at all. It is therefore all important that Lane's friends come up. You may rest assured Douglas's will, for they will be paid for coming, if necessary.

"In haste, truly yours,   JOHN L. ROBINSON."

———

"WASHINGTON CITY, January 31, 1852.

"DEAR SIR—While I was on the Pacific side of the Rocky Mountains the people of Indiana, at a great mass-meeting held in Indianapolis, in which every portion of the State was represented, unanimously presented my name for the presidency, subject to the decision of the national convention. It was their voluntary act, without my knowledge or wish (as you well know I had no agency in the matter). It was, however, gratifying to me, and fairly placed my name before the country as the choice of that State for the highest office in the world. Knowing the people as I do, having in them the utmost confidence, and feeling under great obligations for the high honor conferred, I returned to the State of my adoption, in which so large a portion of my life has been spent, with a heart full of gratitude. I love my country, her honor and integrity. The perpetuation and progress of our glorious institutions have been the aim and desire of the Democratic party from the beginning of our government; with that party I have acted from manhood to the present time, and shall continue so to do till the day of my death. I have never deceived a friend or acted hypocritically toward any one. I have always considered the Democratic party as a band of brothers, bound by the strongest ties, with one great object in view, namely, the promotion and perpetuation of the institutions of our common country.

" Indiana occupies a high political position. She has within her borders many natural advantages and artificial advantages over any State in the Union of her age, with a generous, intelligent, industrious and patriotic population. I love her honor and reputation as I love life, and I feel confident that she never will do a dishonorable thing ; therefore I have no fears about her course toward me, notwithstanding it is rumored here that an effort is now being made to give me the go by, by instructing the delegation to vote for a second choice as soon as your humble servant can be disposed of.

" It is not my wish to embarrass the Democracy of Indiana. So far from it, I stand ready to support the election of any man who may receive the nomination of the State or national Democratic convention. With this view of the case, I hope that Indiana will send to the national convention delegates, each and every one of them good personal friends, who would rather see me nominated than any other man, without instructions, to act as circumstances may require.

" Now, my friend, let me beg you to say to my friends that I hope good delegates may be appointed without instructions as to first or second choice.

" With great respect, I am, sir, your obedient servant,
" JOSEPH LANE."

The Democratic State convention of 1852 convened at Indianapolis February 24, and was presided over by Judge Thomas L. Smith. The committee on resolutions, of which Robert Dale Owen was chairman, was a very strong one, being composed of the leading Democrats of the State, among them Oliver P. Morton, afterward the great War Governor of Indiana. Two of the resolutions reported by the committee, and unanimously adopted by the convention, were as follows :

"*Resolved*, That Joseph Lane, the State legislator, the gallant general, the Territorial Governor, tried in the executive chair and never found wanting, is, of the people of Indiana, their first choice for the presidency. While we repose entire confidence alike in his administrative capacity, in his firmness, in his honesty of purpose and in his unswerving devotion to Democratic principles, at the same time, desiring, above all things, union and harmony in the support of the nominee of the national convention, we will support him, let the choice of the majority fall as it will; and, fully trusting the judgment and devotion to principles of our delegates to that convention, we leave them free to exercise their judgment.

"*Resolved*, That, if General Lane should be the Democratic nominee for President, we pledge him the vote of Indiana, of that State the honor of whose sons he has so nobly vindicated, by a majority, as we confidently hope and truly believe, of twenty-five thousand votes."

It will be observed that the views of General Lane, as expressed in his letter, were adopted and carried out by the convention.

The Democratic national convention met at Baltimore the next June, and for thirty ballots the solid vote of Indiana was cast for General Lane. On that ballot Judge Douglas developed unexpected strength, and the delegates from Indiana being particularly hostile to his nomination, on the next ballot cast their thirteen votes for General Cass, his strongest competitor. As is known to the intelligent reader the convention eventually nominated Franklin Pierce, of New Hampshire, who was elected President over General Scott, the Whig candidate.

General Lane had great influence with the Indians of Oregon. He learned to speak their language, and often hunted with them. One day while in the woods with a party of Indians he was assaulted by one of them, a powerful man, who struck at the General, but the latter dodged the blow. Seizing a club, he struck his assailant and knocked him down. For a a time he lay limp and almost lifeless, and when he recovered sufficiently to arise upon his feet he expressed himself satisfied, and he desired no further contest with the General. It took a brave man to maintain himself, single and alone, with a drunken Indian, flanked by a number of his red-skin friends.

During Mr. Pierce's administration General Lane, being in Washington attending to his official duties, was requested by the President to return to Oregon and take command of the troops then employed in suppressing an insurrection of the Indians. He did so, and entered the field at the head of the army, determined to bring the war to a speedy close. He found the Indians, several hundred strong, intrenched and well protected by fallen trees and brushwood, awaiting his coming. Stopping his command near their lines, he advanced alone, waving a handkerchief, and when near enough to be heard he asked for a parley. He was fired upon as he approached, and shot through the shoulder, but this did not cause him to turn back or abandon his effort to have a conference with the Indian chieftains. When they saw who it was several of the leaders came out from their cover and approached him. He asked that the men in their camp who had murdered the settlers and burned their houses be delivered up that they might be punished. He told them they had better surrender these men, for if they did not he would take them, and if they did, and would agree to prevent such murders in the future, he would retire with the army and not further molest them. The Indians delivered up the criminals, who were hung, and peace between the red men and the settlers was restored.

While General Lane lived in Oregon he was a great hunter, and once, on his return from a trip in the woods, a pistol in his coat pocket went off as he was alighting from his horse. The ball entered his back and came out in front, near the hip joint, without striking a vital part. In speaking of this wound he was wont to say that he would never die by powder and ball, and that he felt entirely confident that he would die a natural death. His faith was well founded, for, although he was wounded by a Mexican bullet at Buena Vista, by an Indian bullet in the wilds of Oregon, and by the accidental discharge of his own pistol, he survived all these wounds and died in a natural way. When he died the life of a brave man went out. A pioneer of Indiana, a gallant soldier of the Union, and he who fashioned Oregon into a State, was no more. But his memory lives. No history of Indiana, none of the Union, and none of Oregon, can be truthfully written without honorable mention of his name. His memory will live while there is a man to read of the deeds of those gallant soldiers who added to the country its richest jewels.

In an eloquent sketch from the *San Francisco Chronicle*, by Joaquin Miller, that nervous writer says:

" On the day he was sixty-five he and his son, since a member of Congress, went out shooting, and I saw the old Senator bring in a seven-pronged buck on his shoulders.

" Ten years later, on my return from Europe, I sought him out. ' He lives three miles east and four miles perpendicular now,' said one of his sons, pointing up the mountains. Poverty had driven him from his ranch in the valley.

" I found this old man, now approaching eighty years, felling a tree in front of his little log cabin. He came forward, ax in hand, to meet me, his aged wife shading her eyes with a lifted hand as she looked from the cabin door, wondering what stranger could possibly have climbed this mountain to their humble hermitage.

"And what a talk we had ; how he wanted to know all about Europe, a world he had never seen, but which he knew so well. How interested he was in my work, patting me on the head and calling me his own boy, believing in me entirely, bidding me to go with God's blessing ; to be good, to be great if I could, but be good always.

"And here, on the mountain top, with the companion of his bosom for more than fifty years, the sun of this old Roman senator's life went down. Nothing was said of him at his death, for no one knew him in his life. I lay this handful of leaves on my dear dead. It is all I have to give ; I, a robin, bring leaves for one who was lost in the woods, one who lay down alone and unknown and died in the wilderness of this life. He lived frugally and died poor, while others lived extravagantly and grew rich. Not a dollar of this nation's money ever found its way into this simple and sincere man's pocket. He died not in want, for his children were well-to-do, but poor ; very poor and very pure, as he had lived.

" I may almost say literally this man taught me to read. He certainly taught me to read a dozen well-thumbed old masters, which he knew so well that if I misread a single word as we lay under the oaks—I reading, he lying on his back looking up at the birds—he would correct me. I know there is a vague impression that General Lane was an ignorant man. Well, I am not learned enough to be good authority, but I have mixed with many educated men since, and I am bound to say, so far as I can judge, he was the best read man I have ever yet met with. His letters are the most perfect in all respects I have ever received. He wrote in the old-fashioned, full, round style, every letter like print, not even a comma missing in letters of the greatest length. Using the simplest Saxon, he always said much in little—a duty of every writer of everything."

General Lane was about five feet nine inches high ; his complexion was ruddy, his eyes hazel, and his hair dark and inclined to curl. In person he was strong and muscular ; in disposition brave and chivalrous. He was a pioneer of Indiana, the founder of Oregon, and the people of these States will remember him with affection and gratitude.

JAMES GREGORY.

JAMES GREGORY, an Indiana pioneer, was born in Buncombe county, North Carolina, in the year 1783. When twenty-two years old he married Elizabeth Lee, and five years afterward left his native State and removed to Kentucky. He remained there three years, and in 1813 came to Indiana Territory. He located in Washington county, where he built a cabin in the woods, and in it placed his earthly goods, which were few, even for a Western pioneer. A large number of those who settled in Washington county were North Carolinians, so the young pioneer had countrymen for neighbors. I say countrymen, for at that time, and indeed at the present day, people from the Southern States consider those who were born in the same State as themselves friends and countrymen. The young settler was strong and courageous, and in his neighborhood was a man of influence and a leader whom the people delighted to follow. The frontier was then menaced by Indians, and the pioneers were wont to carry their rifles in their hands, as they visited from cabin to cabin. Such were the surroundings of the subject of this sketch for many years after he made his home in the Territory north of the Ohio river.

Three years after Mr. Gregory settled in Washington county he was an unsuccessful candidate for delegate to the convention that made our first State constitution. Two years after this, in 1818, he removed to Lawrence county, then just organized.

He was elected State Senator from the counties of Washington, Orange, Jackson, Lawrence and Monroe, and took his seat November 27, 1820.

In 1818 Lewis Cass, Jonathan Jennings and Benjamin Parke, as commissioners on behalf of the United States, pur chased of the Indians all the central part of the State, and, with the exception of some small reservations, all the Indian lands south of the Wabash river. This large territory was known as the New Purchase, and among the first to locate upon it was James Gregory, the subject of this sketch. He bought a tract of land in Shelby county, about four miles west of where Shelbyville now stands, and again built a cabin and opened up a farm in the wilderness. He at once became a leading man of his county, was made a colonel of militia, and in 1822 was elected to the State Senate from his district. The district then comprised eight counties, including Marion, a county which now sends two men to the Senate upon a basis much larger than that upon which Mr. Gregory was elected from the eight. The other seven counties of the district were Hamilton, Madison, Johnson, Decatur, Shelby, Rush and Henry.

The constitution of 1816 required that "Corydon, in Harrison county, shall be the seat of government until 1825, and until removed by law." The Legislature met on the first Monday of December in each year, and, therefore, that of 1824-25 must have met at Corydon, unless the time for its meeting was changed. Soon after Colonel Gregory took his seat in the Senate he went to work to get a law passed changing the time of the meeting of the Legislature to the first Monday in January in each year. He was assisted in his work by John Paxton, the representative from Marion county, by James Rariden, of Wayne, Milton Stapp, of Jefferson, and others. At the head of those opposed to it was Dennis Pennington, Senator from Harrison, a man of much influence, and Ratliff Boon, then Lieutenant-Governor of the State. These gentlemen succeeded in uniting the members from the southwestern part of the State against the measure, but there were not enough of them to defeat it. It went through both houses and was approved by the Governor. The constitutional restriction being thus removed, Colonel Gregory succeeded in getting a law passed changing the capital to Indianapolis. The act was passed on the 28th of January, 1824, and provided that the offices and archives should be removed to the new capital by the 10th of the January following, one year earlier than it could have been done had it not been for Colonel Gregory's bill.

The hostility of the people of Corydon toward Colonel Gregory for his course in relation to the removal of the capital, was intense. Caricatures of him were posted on the walls of the State-house and in other places about the town. Indignities were offered him in public and threats were made to lynch him. The reasons which caused the people of Corydon to insult and abuse Colonel Gregory, endeared him the more to his constituents of Marion county. James Blake, Calvin Fletcher, Samuel Henderson, Colonel Paxton and James M. Ray inaugurated a movement to give him a public dinner in recognition of his services. The dinner came off at Washington Hall, and was attended by most of the leading citizens of the town. Calvin Fletcher, Harvey Gregg, Colonel Paxton, John Hawkins, Nicholas McCarty and others made speeches. The late James M. Ray, in a letter to Judge Gregory, of Lafayette, thus speaks of the dinner:

"The speeches, and your father's happy and graceful reply, were cheered in the highest pitch. Sismond Basye (afterwards of Lafayette) was present; also, B. J. Blythe, Hervey Bates, Alfred Harrison, O. Foote, Douglas Maguire, Nat Bolton, George Smith, Dr. Coe, D. Mitchell and others. It was a jolly good time, and a hearty proof of the high estimate of your father's prominence and popularity in our part of the 'New Purchase.' In decisive force of character, for executive ability and magnetic influence over his associates, Colonel Gregory had much of the force and stamp of Governor Morton."

Colonel Gregory continued in the Senate until 1831, when he left Shelby county and removed to Warren. Before he left his home his neighbors and friends met at Shelbyville in mass convention to bid him good-bye. Judge Gregory, of Lafayette, was at this meeting, and, in a letter to the author, says: "I thought the speech of my father to his old friends and neighbors very touching and eloquent." He left them to again found a home in the wilderness.

Very soon after Colonel Gregory removed to Warren county he was sent to the Legislature. Wherever he went the people had use for him in a public capacity. In 1833 he ran for Congress against the eloquent Edward A. Hannegan, and was defeated. In 1837 he was a candidate for Lieutenant-Governor of the State, and was defeated by David Hillis. Colonel Gregory, while in the Legislature, opposed the vast schemes of internal improvement, then so popular in Indiana, and it was upon that issue he made his race for Lieutenant-Governor.

In the winter of 1842 Colonel Gregory went to New Orleans on a trading expedition. The next May he chartered a vessel in that city, loaded it with pork and flour, and sailed for Yucatan, in Central America. Soon after his arrival there he took the black vomit and died. A young man named Johnson was with him, and at his death took charge of his affairs, but nothing is definitely known about his sickness or the circumstances of his death. It is known, however, that he breathed his last at a small town on the coast, and was buried there. But no stone marks his resting place, and none of his family know the place where he sleeps. The ashes of the old pioneer mingle with foreign soil, but his memory will be preserved by the people of the State he helped to found.

When Colonel Gregory settled in Warren county the supplies of the settlers were brought from Chicago. The farmers would take their grain to Chicago in wagons, and return with them loaded with salt, leather and such other things as they needed. Colonel Gregory was a large trader in cattle, sheep and hogs. He once took a drove of cattle to Chicago and sold them to an ancestor of the Chicago sharper of to-day. Soon after getting possession of the cattle the purchaser sold them, put the money in his pocket and ran away without paying Colonel Gregory a dollar. As soon as the latter found out that he had been swindled, he got a rifle and a fast horse and put out after the swindler. He caught him, made him disgorge, and then, with a healthy malediction, let him go.

During Colonel Gregory's service in the Legislature his son Benjamin opened an office at Newport and commenced the practice of the law. His father wrote him a letter from Indianapolis, which is still preserved in the family, and contains sentiments worthy of a philosopher. He was not an educated man, and reached his enviable standing by reason of his strong common sense and correct dealings; but if he had not studied the philosophers, he was not a stranger to their teachings. The letter is as follows:

"Dear Son—I received your letter from Newport. You have now settled down as a lawyer; you are young in experience and amongst strangers. On your course now as a young man of your profession much of your future standing in society depends. You must be steady. Meddle not with anything that you are not called on to take part in, saying nothing in your speeches in any tryal you may be engaged that is qualifyed to injure the feeling of any person; be faithful to your client and honest in all your dealings; take exercise for your health; walk where you can; avoid drinking strong drink, you can do well without. I have not and I think I shall not taste one drop of anything that tends in the least to stimulate, and I have just as good health as any member here that uses it. One other injunction, and in this and from this you must in nowise deviate: Never, never, in no case, do you gamble—not the most innocent games. Never put your hands on a card—they have a bewitching quality about them. Go to meeting and other moral societys, so that you can always be numbered with those that respect the morals of the country. Dabble as little in politics as possible. You must have always before your eye that your brothers are moral men—so I want all my children to be when they leave me. I will send your books to you so soon as they come to hand. Your Father and Friend,

"James Gregory.
"Mr. Benjamin F. Gregory, Newport, Indiana."

The orthography of the letter may be faulty, but no one will find fault with its sentiments.

Colonel Gregory was not only a pioneer of Indiana, but was one of four counties. He didn't like to be crowded, and when population came about him he sold out and moved away. He was never better satisfied than when building cabins and clearing up land. He was essentially a pioneer.

Colonel Gregory was a strong man, both in mind and in body. He weighed 244 pounds, had fair complexion, black hair and eyes. He was of commanding presence, would have been a man of mark in any company. He was one of those who opened up Indiana to civilization, and the people owe him much. He left a family which has honored his name. Three of his sons and a grandson have sat in the Legislature of the State, and one of them, Hon. Robert C. Gregory, of Lafayette, served a term as Supreme Judge. Right worthily they bear their father's name.

JOSEPH GLASS MARSHALL.

" He was a man, take him for all in all,
I shall not look upon his like again."

SCOTCH-IRISH and cavalier blood mingled in the veins of
Joseph G. Marshall. Like the North of Ireland man, he got
all the contention out of a thing there was in it; and like the
cavalier, he was warm-hearted, impulsive, and brave. When
contending for a principle he believed to be right you would
imagine him a born son of Carrickfergus; when at the fireside, or around the social board, he would impress you as one
born on the banks of the York or the James. His father was a
Scotch-Irishman and his mother a Virginian, so his leading
characteristics were his by inheritance.

Joseph Glass Marshall was born in Fayette county, Kentucky, January 18, 1800. His father was a Presbyterian minister, and he thoroughly indoctrinated the son in the principles
of the Scottish Church. He was fitted for college at home, entering Transylvania University as a junior, and graduating from
that institution in 1823. In 1828 he came to Indiana and settled at Madison, where he resided until he died. He had studied
law in Kentucky, and although a young man in a town noted
for the strength of its bar, he soon obtained a lucrative practice.
Two years after coming to Indiana he was elected Probate
Judge of his county, and discharged the duties of the office with
signal ability. When he left the judgeship he returned to the
bar. In 1836, 1840, and 1844, he was on the Whig electoral
ticket, and each time made an active canvass of the State. In
1846 he was nominated for Governor and was beaten by James
Whitcomb 3,958 votes. In 1849 President Taylor appointed

Joseph G. Marshall.

him Governor of Oregon, but he refused the place. Before declining, however, he went to Washington and personally thanked the President for the tender of the office. In 1850 he was elected Senator from his county, and served the legal term. In 1852, much against his wishes, he was nominated for Congress in his district, and was beaten by Cyrus L. Dunham 931 votes. This was the last race he made before the people. In addition to the offices named, he represented his county several times in the lower branch of the State Legislature.

Mr. Marshall had an ambition to go to the United States Senate, but his ambition was never gratified. In the Legislature of 1844 the Whigs had ten majority on joint ballot. They nominated him for the Senate, but the Democrats refused to go into an election. Each party had twenty-five members in the Senate, and Jesse D. Bright, then Lieutenant-Governor, gave the casting vote against going into the election. In 1845 the Democrats carried the Legislature, and elected Mr. Bright to the Senate, his vote being eighty, and Mr. Marshall's sixty-six. His defeat the year before incensed him against Mr. Bright, and ever afterward he hated him.

In the Legislature of 1854 the People's, or anti-Nebraska party, had a majority of fourteen on joint ballot, but the Democrats, having two majority in the Senate, prevented the election of a Senator. Mr. Marshall was the nominee of the dominant party, and had an election been held he would have been chosen. Thus it will be seen that he was twice kept from going to the Senate by the refusal of the Democrats to perform a legal duty.

Mr. Marshall was at Indianapolis most of the time during the session of the Legislature of 1854-5, and while there contracted a deep cold. The cold settled on his lungs, and soon became alarming. Early in the spring of 1855 he started on a Southern trip, in hopes of regaining his health. When he reached Louisville, being too sick to proceed further, he took to his bed, and, on the 8th of April, 1855, died. His remains were brought to Madison and there interred. When the sad news reached Indianapolis a meeting of the bar was held to take action upon his death. Governor Wright presided at the meeting, and James

28

Rariden was the secretary. A committee consisting of Oliver H. Smith, Samuel C. Wilson and Simon Yandes was appointed to prepare suitable resolutions, and reported the following :

"The members of the bar have recently heard with deep regret that their professional brother, Joseph G. Marshall, is no more.

"The profession has been deprived of one of its brightest ornaments, and our State and country of a distinguished citizen. We who have witnessed the pure example of the deceased can not permit an event so solemn and affecting to pass unnoticed. Few men of his age in any country have left behind stronger proofs of eminent professional abilities, or higher claims to private and public confidence. While we feel a just pride in the professional attainments and distinguished character of the deceased we will long cherish a recollection of his social qualities and amiable deportment in private life which endeared him to his friends and acquaintances.

"Therefore, in order to testify our regard for the memory of the deceased,

"*Resolved*, That we hold in the highest estimation the pure and exalted private and professional character of Joseph G. Marshall, and deeply lament the loss which the profession and the country have sustained by the death of one so eminently qualified for the high position which he occupied. *   *   *"

The meeting appointed Oliver H. Smith to present the preamble and resolutions to the United States Circuit Court, then in session. The next day Mr. Smith performed the duty, and Judge McLean ordered them recorded. Before making the order he said :

"The court sympathizes with the bar in the loss of one of its distinguished members. Our social and professional relations teach us how uncertain is the tenure of our earthly existence. Among all the members of the bar there was no one who, from his apparent strength of constitution and healthful vigor, appeared to have a stronger hold on life than the friend whose death we now deplore.

"Mr. Marshall was a man of vigorous intellect and of strong

reasoning powers. His mind had a basis of common sense, without which learning and experience are of little value. In the strength of his views he more than compensated for any want of polish in his manner. He was always sensible, often convincing. At any bar in the Union his ability would have been marked, and he would have been considered as an antagonist worthy of the highest efforts. His professional bearing was elevated and honorable. The loss of such a man can not but be deeply felt and deplored by the public, and especially by the bench and the bar, to whom he was best known.

"The court directs the proceedings presented to be placed upon the records."

Indiana never had the equal of Mr. Marshall in breadth and strength of intellect. Neither did she ever have his equal in ability to stir the passions and sway the feelings of the people. She has had men of greater culture and of more general information, but in those qualities which enable the orator to melt the hearts and fire the passions of his auditors he was without a peer. He was called the "Sleeping Lion," and, when fully aroused, he was a lion indeed.

On such occasions his oratory was like the hurricane that sweeps everything before it. Ordinarily, he did not show his power, but when engaged in a case that enlisted his feelings and his conscience his words were like hot shot from the cannon's mouth. I will name but two examples of his power to sway the people. One was his speech in defense of John Freeman, charged with being a fugitive slave. Of this effort Miss Laura Ream gives the following account:

"The trial of the case excited unusual interest from the fact that Freeman had long resided in that place, and, with his family, was held in personal esteem. He alleged, under oath, and his counsel brought testimony to prove, that he was a free man, but the presiding judge did not care to brave the popular sentiment in favor of the fugitive slave law, and at the close of the argument asked if there was no other reason why the prisoner should not be returned to his master? On the instant, a man on the outskirts of the bar, in the old Court-house, was seen to rise to his feet. He did it slowly, grasping the table before him with both hands as if to steady his quivering nerves ; and towering to his full height, with breast heaving and eyes aflame, in trumpet tones began : 'Your Honor, though not of counsel for this unfortunate man, I think I can answer the question why he should not be remanded to slavery. I will answer that question. The law presumes every man to be free. It is a fundamental question going back to the first principles of free government. It is essential to State sovereignty. For it we went to war with Great Britain in 1812 ; shall we surrender it now? The writ of *habeas corpus* was not suspended by the fugitive slave law. It is the inalienable right of every citizen, whether black or white, whether bond or free. The State is not required to deliver up a person held to service in another State before she knows whether that person is a slave or not. In this case the fact of slavery is denied, and there is no power in the world that has the right to determine the point but the sovereign State of Indiana, to whom this man belongs.' The above is but the imperfect summary of a speech which electrified the audience, which did not need to be told that the speaker was 'Jo Marshall,' as he was familiarly called. In a moment the court-room, every window, was crowded with people, eager, breathless, in tears, and ready to protect the prisoner with their lives. The incident has been related to me by different men who were present, but none could define the secret of Mr. Marshall's eloquence. ' He was like one inspired,' said one gentleman. ' He was the incarnate majesty of right. I could no more define the quality of his eloquence than I could explain the wonders of the deep.' "

The other case was his defense of Delia A. Webster, charged with running off slaves from Kentucky. Miss Webster lived on the Kentucky side of the Ohio river, opposite the city of Madison. Previous to her residence there she had served a term in the Kentucky State prison for assisting slaves to escape. While residing opposite Madison she was an object of suspicion on the part of her Kentucky neighbors. Several slaves in the neighborhood escaped, and investigation showed that she prompted their leaving. For this she was indicted in the Trimble Circuit Court, but before being caught she crossed the river to Madison. She was arrested on a requisition from the Governor, but before the officers could get her away Mr. Marshall had her brought before a judge on a writ of *habeas corpus*. In his speech at the trial he so maddened the people that they drove the Kentucky officers from the Court-house and from the State. Indeed, they had to run for their lives, so frenzied were the people.

In some respects Mr. Marshall's oratory was faulty, but it was none the less effective. He seemed to speak from his throat, and not from his chest. When excited he enunciated so rapidly and sent his words after each other so swiftly that they ran together. His voice was not musical, like that of Hannegan, but his matter was so strong that one hardly noticed his defects. In his day the Madison bar was a strong one, but he was its king. Michael G. Bright, Judge Sullivan, Judge Stevens, William McKee Dunn and Abram W. Hendricks, all lawyers of eminence, practiced at it, but none of them approached Mr. Marshall in ability to convince courts and sway juries. The litigant who had him for an advocate was fortunate, indeed. In fact, it was almost impossible to get a verdict against him when he was thoroughly aroused and " shook his mane."

A man with Mr. Marshall's power to arouse passion in others must have passion himself. He had plenty of it, and, although like his eloquence, it was usually dormant, yet when it was stirred it was hot and burning. The late John Dumont once demurred to a complaint drawn by Marshall, and made his points so well, and argued them so strongly, that it seemed almost certain he would be sustained. At that time a demurrer was a more serious matter than it now is, for, if maintained, it drove the plaintiff out of court; therefore, Marshall fought Mr. Dumont with all his might. When it became evident that the court would decide against him he asked for a suspension of judgment until he could bring a certain authority into court. The favor being granted he thrust his hat upon his head and started for his office almost on the run. At that time Judge Woollen, now of Franklin, had a sleeping-room adjoining Mr. Marshall's office, and was in it when Mr. Marshall reached his door. He tried to open it, and, finding it locked, cried out fiercely : " Woollen, have you the key to this door?" "No, sir," replied Mr. Woollen; "I do not carry your key, Mr. Marshall." The hall leading to his office was some six feet wide, and Marshall, backing up against the wall, and drawing his lips between his teeth, shouted, " d—n the door," and with a bound and a kick he went through it like a flash. Mr. Woollen went down the stairs, but, being desirous of seeing the result of the storm, stopped in the doorway. In a few minutes Mr. Marshall came down the stairway, and observing Mr. Woollen, he said, with a smile, " Woollen, I had the key in my pocket. My passion has cost me a door."

Mr. Marshall and Judge Otto were once opposing counsel in a case at Charlestown, and during the trial had a personal difficulty. Mr. Marshall, becoming incensed at something Judge Otto said, retorted very severely. During the wrangle Judge Otto called him a liar, whereupon Mr. Marshall knocked him down. Jndge Otto arose, and, coming at Mr. Marshall in a belligerent manner, was knocked down again. He then got up and went out of the house to arm himself preparatory to renewing the fight. While he was gone some one told Mr. Marshall that he was to blame for the commencement of the difficulty, whereupon he sat down and wrote Judge Otto a letter in which he apologized for his conduct and asked his pardon. He was too great and brave to refuse justice when justice was due.

Mr. Marshall and the late George G. Dunn loved each other like brothers. They roomed together during the session of the Legislature of 1851, both being members of the Senate. In the latter part of the session they had a difficulty, and a gentleman who witnessed their reconciliation thus describes it:

" Marshall and Dunn roomed together in 1851-2, when they were in the Senate. They had a difficulty in debate, and though they continued to occupy the same room to receive their friends, were known not to speak to each other for weeks. The Senate adjourned. Marshall was in one corner packing an old carpet-bag and crowding into it his soiled clothing. Dunn was in another corner crowding things into an old trunk. Neither of them spoke. Finally Marshall walked up to Dunn, held out his hand and said: ' Well, good-bye, George.' Dunn took it, and they both cried like children."

This was Marshall to the life. He belonged to that fiery class of men who are all ablaze in their affections and their hates.

In 1851 the contest for the Legislature in Jefferson county was made upon the question of the State selling her interest in the Madison and Indianapolis Railroad. Joseph W. Chapman, a law partner of Senator Bright, was in the Legislature the year before, and opposed a bill authorizing the sale. Mr. Marshall canvassed the county in 1851 in support of candidates favoring the sale, and Senator Bright in support of those opposing it. In a speech at Ritchey's Mills, Mr. Marshall said he was surprised at Senator Bright's course in the canvass, as he had told him before it commenced that if he had said to him, Mr. Bright, that he, Mr. Marshall, desired Mr. Chapman's support the winter before, he would have seen that he got it. Mr. Bright, who was present, cried out in a loud voice: "Judge Marshall, I deny that statement." Marshall stopped a moment, and looking Bright straight in the eye, said, with an emphasis I shall never forget: "And I, sir, reiterate it." "We will see about it hereafter," said Mr. Bright. "As you please," replied Mr. Marshall, who then proceeded with his speech. This trouble resulted in a challenge and almost a duel, as will be seen further along.

In 1852 the author conducted a newspaper at Madison which supported Mr. Marshall for Congress. During the canvass he received a letter from some half dozen Quakers of Jackson county asking him to give the particulars of the difficulty between Mr. Marshall and Senator Bright. They said that while anxious to vote for Mr. Marshall they could not conscientiously do so if he had ever sought the blood of a fellow man. The day I received this letter I sent Mr. Marshall a note asking him to call at my office. When he came I handed him the letter. He read it carefully, and, handing it back to me, said: "I fear we must get along without the support of our Quaker friends. You were present when the trouble between Bright and myself culminated, but it had been brewing a long time. Bright has ever been in my pathway. I never go out of a door without seeing his shadow. He prevented me from going to the Senate in 1844, and the next year beat me for the place. The day after the trouble at Ritchey's Mills, while at my home, Jonathan

Fitch was announced. He came into my library and handed me a note from Bright. It was not a challenge, but was intended to provoke one. Its contents were so insulting that I became enraged, and resolved to kick Fitch out of my house. But in a moment I changed my mind. He was in my house, and, being a respectable man, I could not treat him thus. I told him Mr. Bright would either see or hear from me soon, and then he left. I studied over the matter that afternoon and evening, and concluded that the world was not big enough for me and Bright—that one of us must die. Next morning I came to the city, went to the hardware store of H. K. Wells & Co., and bought a bowie-knife. I put it in my pocket, and, knowing that it was Bright's custom to go for his mail at 10 o'clock, I walked up and down Second street, between the post-office and West street, from 10 to 10:30, waiting for him, but he did not appear. Had he come I should have attacked him and killed him, if I could. I knew he was always armed, so I would not be taking him at a disadvantage. I then went to my office, and wrote him a note, asking him to meet me at Louisville, on a day I named, to settle our difficulty. The day before we were to meet I told McKee Dunn what I had done, and asked him to accompany me to Louisville. He agreed to go down that evening on the mail-boat. I left him, and at noon took the Louisville packet, got off at Charlestown landing, and walked out to Charlestown. I called on Dr. Athon, told him I had challenged Bright, and asked him to go on the field as my surgeon. He consented, and he and I then hunted up Captain Gibson, who agreed to serve as my second. That evening Athon, Gibson and myself went to Louisville, and next morning found Dunn at the hotel. Bright was also in the city, and negotiations for a meeting began. Before they were completed friends interfered and the matter was settled." "How was it settled, Mr. Marshall?" I asked. "The particulars are not for the public. All it will ever know is contained in the card published by our friends. It was satisfactory to us, and the difficulty is ended." This is the substance of what he said, and very nearly the words he used.

Knowing that General William McKee Dunn, of Washington, was very near Mr. Marshall in his difficulty with Senator

Bright, I wrote him a short time ago asking him to give me his recollection of it. I suggested that, as the principals and every one connected with the trouble but himself were dead, there could be no impropriety in giving the facts to the public. The following is a copy of General Dunn's reply:

"WASHINGTON, January 5, 1882.

" *W. W. Woollen, Esq., Indianapolis, Ind.:*

"DEAR SIR—I have been so occupied and distracted by vari, ous causes that I have too long delayed to answer your letter asking for information about the difficulty between Senator Bright and Joe Marshall, which caused them a trip to Louisville, with a prospect of a duel. I do not think I can add much, if anything of consequence, to the information you already have. I can not give you dates.

"You remember when the two law offices of Marshall & Walker and Dunn & Hendricks were adjoining in the Sering House. One hot day in August, I think, Mr. Marshall called me out of my office to the street. He was equipped, as he usually was when he would start out on the circuit, *i. e.*, with an old carpet-sack, with very little in it, stuck under his arm, and his hat full of papers down over his eyes. He told me he was on his way to Louisville to meet Senator Bright, with a view of challenging him to fight a duel, unless he (Bright) qualified or retracted some statement he had made. He said he wished me to meet him the next morning at the Louisville Hotel. I told him I knew nothing about the code, did not believe in dueling, and could be of no service to him. He explained that he was going down by the Louisville and Madison packet, that he would stop at the Charlestown landing, walk out to Charlestown, and get Captain Gibson to act as his second, and all that he wanted of me was to act as an outside friend. I told him, with that understanding I would go, as requested, hoping to be of some use in bringing about an adjustment. He immediately started on his way, and I shall never forget the appearance of that great big-headed, big-hearted man, as he walked down the street on his way, with the evident purpose of having matters brought to a satisfactory conclusion. The friends and neighbors whom he passed on the street little suspected the errand on which he was going. He had requested me, of course, to say nothing of the matter. I went down to Louisville that night on the mail-boat, without having informed any one of the object of my trip. On the boat I met Senator Bright, his brother Michael, Jonathan Fitch, I think, and Charley Shrewsbury, who were of Senator Bright's party. The next morning, at the Louisville Hotel, I met Mr. Marshall and Captain Thomas W. Gibson. Senator Bright's party were at the Galt House.

"I do not remember the particulars of the correspondence that ensued between the parties belligerent. I remember that Hon. James Guthrie, afterward United States Senator and Secretary of the United States Treasury, seemed to be Mr. Bright's principal adviser. Judge Huntington, of the United States District Court for Indiana, happening to be in Louisville at the time, became one of Mr. Marshall's advisers. No conclusion was reached the first day, and by night rumors of a hostile meeting expected between the parties were in the air. In consequence of these rumors I went to the Galt House and took Captain Shrewsbury's room, Shrewsbury took Marshall's and Marshall took mine at the Louisville Hotel. My recollection is that a police officer visited Marshall's room that night, where he found Captain Shrewsbury, who threw him entirely off his trail. The next day we were amazed by the arrival of Rev. Samuel V. Marshall, a brother of Joe, and I had great difficulty in preventing him from procuring the arrest of the parties by the police. You remember how Joe deceived a police officer who did not know him by pointing out his brother Sam as the Joe Marshall to be arrested.

" The correspondence was brought to what was accepted as a satisfactory conclusion that afternoon. It was part of the arrangement that the parties should return to Madison on the little packet. They shook hands when they met on the packet, but I do not think they ever spoke to each other afterward. On the arrival at Madison we landed at the depot wharf. Several of Mr. Bright's friends met him, apparently with great rejoicing. No one met Mr. Marshall. He walked up with me as far as my house, and then, with his old carpet-sack under his arm, he broke for his home on the hill. How grand and yet how simple he was in his tastes and ways.   Yours truly,

"W. M. DUNN."

The morning after Messrs. Marshall and Bright had settled their difficulty the following card appeared in the Louisville papers:

"The difficulty between Joseph G. Marshall, Esq., and Hon. Jesse D. Bright having been referred to us by mutual (not official) friends, we are happy to say has been honorably adjusted, and to the mutual satisfaction of the parties.

"HENRY PIRTLE.
"JAMES GUTHRIE.
"ALFRED THURSTON.
"W. O. BUTLER.

"*Galt House, August 29, 1851.*"

Mr. Marshall always traveled on foot or horseback. For several years the author saw him almost every day, and never knew him to ride in a carriage. He kept one for family use, but did not use it himself. He lived on the hill just north of Madison, and in going to and from his home to his office he invariably walked. When he started out on the circuit he threw a pair of saddle-bags, containing a few articles of clothing, over his saddle and mounted his horse. He made his canvass for Governor in 1846 on horseback. The author is informed by Judge Julian that during Mr. Marshall's canvass for Governor in 1846 he came to the Judge's house and remained with him over night. He was to speak next day at a town some ten miles distant, and Judge Julian proposed taking him to the place in his carriage. He said he preferred riding his horse, and it took a good deal of persuasion to get him to take a seat in the Judge's carriage.

Mr. Marshall loved the horse and was a most excellent judge of that animal. He always rode a good one and treated it most affectionately.

Although a leading politician Mr. Marshall seldom did more on election day than deposit his ballot. I remember only two occasions when he was a worker at the polls. One of them was when General Stapp ran for the Legislature, and the other when Captain Meek was a candidate for County Treasurer. When a candidate himself he kept away from the voting place. He was too big and too proud a man to work for himself. He left to others the responsibility of his election or defeat.

Mr. Marshall was particularly fond of pictures. He has been known to buy a book for its pictures, and, when he had examined them, to give the book away. He loved the beautiful and the true.

Mr. Marshall was a consummate actor. He knew how to "suit the action to the word, and the word to the action." In his arguments to a jury his force was not in the comparisons he made, but in the deductions he drew from his premises. In other words, he argued not by comparison, but from cause to effect. His ability to present his facts in the strongest possible manner was excelled by no man. He wasted no time in dallying with the graces of oratory, but at once hurled the javelins of his logic at the weakest points in his adversary's armor. He had the element of pathos. At times he would have a jury he was addressing in tears, and in a minute thereafter convulsed with laughter. He knew when to do this, and never made the mistake of provoking mirth when sadness would better serve the interests of his client.

Mr. Marshall was kind to young lawyers, but held those that aspired to be his peers to the strictest accountability. After demurring a young attorney out of court he would graciously permit him to amend his pleadings and go on with his case. But if he got a fair advantage of Judge Sullivan, Mr. M. G. Bright, or attorneys of their standing, he would not relax his hold upon them one iota. He held them rigidly to the "bond," even though it took the "pound of flesh."

Mr. Marshall had the reputation of being an indolent man, and the reputation was a correct one. He had a habit of putting off labor to "a more convenient season," but in justice to him it must be said that he could do more work with less labor than any of his competitors at the bar. Indeed, he could do better work with little preparation than they could do with much study. His mind was so great that it could grasp a difficult problem in law at once, while his less able compeers could accomplish this only by much study and labor.

Mr. Marshall was a wit as well as an orator. He often said things that were worthy of Dean Swift. They came from him, not as studied efforts, but as naturally as the water runs from the spring. One day, as the attorneys were gathering in the Madison Court-house previous to the opening of court, a bright boy—son of the deputy sheriff—came within the bar, when a Democratic lawyer addressed him thus: "Jeff., what's your politics?" "I'm a Democrat, sir," answered the hopeful three-year-old. "There, gentlemen," said the lawyer, "you see that little children that know no sin are Democrats by nature." "Yes," said Mr. Marshall, "the Good Book tells us that we are all brought forth in sin, but through grace we are saved. We may be Democrats by nature, but through grace we become Whigs."

Again, the venerable John H. Thompson, who died in Indianapolis a few years ago, was at one time Judge of the judicial circuit that embraced the county of Scott. Mr. Marshall had a case in this court, and introduced a witness that "surprised" him, and, desiring to destroy the force of his testimony, sought to impeach him. This was objected to by the opposing counsel, and Judge Thompson sustained the objection. The same day a law student applied to the Judge for license to practice, and was referred to Mr. Marshall for examination. Marshall took the young man outside the bar and spoke a few words to him, when the student left the court-room and Mr. Marshall resumed the seat he had just vacated. The Judge asked him if he had examined the applicant and was prepared to report. "Yes, your honor," replied the lawyer. "Your examination was a very brief one," remarked the Judge. "I only asked him a single question, your honor." "What was the question, sir?" "I asked him if a party could, under any circumstances, impeach his own witness. He said no; and I told him to return to his books, as a man that knew no more of law than that was not fit to practice before a justice of the peace."

Sometimes Mr. Marshall was very domineering in his manner. He even carried this into court, and neither judge nor counsel was spared when the humor was on him. A young man was indicted in the Jefferson Circuit Court for larceny, and Mr. Marshall volunteered to defend him. The prisoner was charged with stealing a watch that was found in a room occupied by him in a Madison hotel. It came out in the evidence that the person indicted was decoyed out of the city by the Sheriff and City Marshal, and threatened with flagellation if he did not produce the watch. He confessed the stealing, and told them where the watch could be found. To this testimony Mr. Marshall objected because the confession was made under duress. Judge Courtland Cushing was on the bench, and ruled that although the confession of the prisoner could not go to the jury, yet, if they found that the watch was discovered in the prisoner's room, in the place named by him, they might infer that it was placed there by him, and would be justified in bringing in a verdict of guilty. To this ruling Mr. Marshall excepted with much warmth. After the evidence was closed he addressed the jury in one of the ablest efforts he ever made. The adverse decision of the judge had angered him, and the "Sleeping Lion," as he was called, was aroused. He commenced his speech by saying that the liberty of the humblest citizen in the land was as dear to him as though he was "clothed in purple and fine linen" and sat among the rulers of the land. Continuing in an excited manner, he said: "The prisoner at the bar stands charged with crime without a particle of evidence to sustain it. The court, in its infinite wisdom, has permitted testimony to go to you which should have been excluded." At this point Judge Cushing interrupted him, and said that he must be more respectful to the court. With forced calmness, for he was seething with excitement, he said: "I must confess my inability, your honor, to be more respectful than I am." "The court will teach you, then," replied the Judge in a testy manner. Folding his arms and bowing his head, he said: "Will the court commence its lessons now?" The Judge gave way to the lawyer, who remained for some time as immovable as a statue, and only relaxed his features and resumed his argument when he saw that he had cowed the court. Had it been any other member of the Madison bar he would have been fined, if not imprisoned, for contempt of court. But Judge Cushing could not assert the authority necessary to maintain the dignity of his office when the transgressor was Joseph G. Marshall.

In social circles he was facetious and witty, but in public he seldom indulged in pleasantry. When he did so it was to illustrate a point or ridicule the position of his adversary.

No man ever questioned Mr. Marshall's integrity. He was as honest in politics as in private dealings. He was conscientiously opposed to the use of money in elections. In 1852, when a candidate for Congress, the chairman of the Whig State Central Committee wrote him that the National Committee had sent him money to be used in Mr. Marshall's district, and asking what should be done with it. Mr. Marshall replied: "Return it to Washington. The use of money in elections is both corrupt and corrupting. I shall have nothing to do with it."

In his sketches of Indiana men, Oliver H. Smith says of Mr. Marshall: "As a lawyer Mr. Marshall stood among the very first in the State. His great forte as an advocate was in the power with which he handled the facts before the jury. He seemed to forget himself in his subject, and at times I have thought him unsurpassed by any man I ever heard in impassioned eloquence." It should be remembered that Mr. Smith had sat in the Senate of the United States, and had heard speeches from Clay, Webster and Calhoun. Colonel Abram W. Hendricks, in a recent address, thus speaks of Mr. Marshall: "He was one of the most transcendently powerful advocates that have figured at the Indiana bar. His intellect was colossal. He seemed to know the law by intuition. His logic was surrounded by a glowing atmosphere of passion. He could sweep through his subject like a tempest or crush through it like an avalanche." Colonel Hendricks had practiced at the bar with him for years, and knew whereof he spoke.

John D. Defrees, in a letter published in the *Madison Courier*, says that Mr. Marshall was "the Webster of Indiana."

John Lyle King, of Chicago, in a recent letter, said that Mr. Marshall "was, by odds, the greatest man Indiana ever produced."

Making all due allowance for the partiality of his friends the reader must conclude that Joseph G. Marshall was a great man —the peer of any man living in Indiana in his day.

Mr. Marshall was very careless of his dress. He didn't care whether his coat fitted him or not, or whether the bow on his neck-stock was under his ear or his chin. He usually wore low shoes, and there was often quite a distance between his shoe-tops and the bottom of his pantaloons. He carried his papers in his hat instead of his pockets, and wore his hat pulled low down up-on his head. He had a great big head, thickly covered with sandy hair. His forehead, mouth and nose were large and prom-inent. His eyes were a light blue, and were the least expressive of his features. He stood over six feet high. His body was not symmetrical, being from his shoulders to his hips almost the same in size. It was his head and face that told you the manner of man he was. These were magnificent, and his uncouth form and careless dress served to show them to the best advantage. Had he gone to the Senate, as he should have done, he would have made a reputation equal to any one in the land. He had the ability to shine anywhere and would not have suffered by comparison with the ablest men in that body.

MICHAEL GRAHAM BRIGHT.

MICHAEL GRAHAM BRIGHT, lawyer and financier, was born at Plattsburg, N. Y., January 16, 1803. He was a son of David J. Bright, who came with his family to Indiana in 1820, and settled at Madison, where he conducted a hat manufactory for many years. Mr. David J. Bright was a man of commanding presence and great force of character. He lived to see his sons Michael and Jesse leading and influential men, and died suddenly, at Madison, many years ago. His son Michael studied law with the late Judge Sullivan, and became one of the first lawyers of the State. He was the last of the legal coterie which, thirty-five years ago, made the Madison bar so famous. Marshall and Sullivan and Stevens passed away years ago. William McKee Dunn and Abram W. Hendricks were then young men, and can hardly be considered as cotemporaneous with the legal giants we have named, but they followed close after, and did much to maintain the high character of the Madison bar. As a lawyer Mr. Bright was astute and full of expedients. He had not the logical mind of Marshall, nor was he as elegant and polished as Sullivan, nor as painstaking as Stevens, but in resources he was as fertile as any of them. His watchful eye took in the situation at a glance, and his ingenuity enabled him to make the most of it.

The county of Jefferson was, in the days of Mr. Bright's activity, Whig, as it is now Republican. Notwithstanding this fact, Mr. Bright, a Democrat, was chosen to represent it in the State Legislature. He was in no sense an office seeker. The offices he held came to him unsought. They were the free-will offerings of his neighbors and friends.

For a time he edited a newspaper at Madison, but then, as for many years afterward, his main business was the law. In 1832 he was elected to the State Legislature, and served with distinction, but he was satisfied with one term, and did not seek a re-election. In 1844 he was elected Agent of State, and discharged the duties of the office with very great ability. When he entered upon his official duties he found the office in great confusion, but he soon restored it to order. At that time the State had a large suspended debt, but Mr. Bright collected a large part of it, and paid the money to the State's creditors. Indeed, his administration of the office was such as to receive the commendation of the public, and was in striking contrast with that of his predecessor. When his term expired he went back to the bar, but he was indifferent about obtaining business, and did not give his profession that care and attention he had previously done.

In 1850 Mr. Bright was elected a member of the constitutional convention from the county of Jefferson, defeating Moody Park, a Whig, for the office. He was chosen chairman of the Committee on the Legislative Department, was second on the Committee of Revision, Arrangement and Phraseology, and was also a member of the Committee on Salaries, Compensation and Tenure of Office. He was not a speaking member, but he sometimes addressed the convention, and when he did he was listened to with the greatest interest. He took much concern in the provision authorizing the taking of private property for public use, and addressed the convention several times upon it. He opposed that part of section 21 of the bill of rights which forbids the taking of private property for public use without first tendering the money for the damages assessed. In discussing the question, he said : "Every member of the community holds his property, whether real or personal, subject to the rights and requirements of the State. It is a duty which the State owes to itself and to all the members who compose it to maintain its sovereignty and its authority inviolate. It is a right inherent in sovereignty to take private property for public use without compensation being first made. The State is amenable to no one, save to a sense of right."

During the debate on this question, Mr. Walpole, a delegate

from the county of Hancock, charged Mr. Bright with being the representative of the Madison and Indianapolis Railroad upon the floor of the convention. Mr. Bright replied to the accusation in the following dignified words:

"MR. PRESIDENT—I have no interests to represent upon this floor which will conflict with the rights and interests of the State at large. I do not consider myself as holding a seat in this convention for the purpose of exclusively representing Jefferson county. I am here to represent and support the interests of the whole people of Indiana—not the interests of a section as opposed to the general welfare. I am not the representative of a local or personal interest; I came up here to aid in the formation of a constitution which shall be, as I trust, the beneficent organic law for this generation of the people of the State, and for the generation to come, as well as for myself and my children. I am a constituent part of the people—an unit in the great aggregate—and I can not, if I would, separate my interests or the interests of my immediate constituents from the interests of the people of the State. We are all interested together and alike in the formation of a good constitution; we shall all be benefited by its wise provisions or injured by its bad ones."

Mr. Bright was the author of several sections in our State constitution, and had much to do in moulding into shape many others. The day the convention adjourned it thanked the Committee on Revision, of which he was a leading member, for the able manner in which it had discharged its duties.

Mr. Bright never held public office after the constitutional convention adjourned. He had large farming interests, and devoted much time to railroad matters. He projected several railroads, some of which were built and others not. He did not do much at the law, nor did he care to, his office being in his yard, away from the business quarter. He had accumulated a handsome estate, and did not wish to be bothered with cases in court. He seldom accepted employment as an attorney, and never did unless it was to oblige a friend.

Among his last cases in court was that of Stephen Lanciscus, indicted for the killing of Ebenezer Hollis. Lanciscus being the son of an old personal and political friend, Mr. Bright entered upon his defense with great earnestness and conducted it with all his old-time ability and energy. Lanciscus, however, was convicted and sentenced to the State prison for life, but through the influence of Mr. Bright and others he was afterward pardoned.

Mr. Bright owned a railroad running from Columbus to Knightstown, and it being unprofitable he put it on the market for sale. It was purchased by the Jeffersonville Company, and thereby Mr. Bright became a large stockholder in that corporation. Previous to this sale John Brough, then president of the Madison and Indianapolis Railroad Company, and afterward Governor of Ohio, asked the Legislature to pass a certain law in the interest of his road, but Mr. Bright antagonized the measure and it was defeated. Mr. Brough publicly charged that Mr. Bright offered to champion the measure if the Madison Company would buy his road, and that his opposition to the legislation sought was caused by the company's refusal to do so. Mr. Bright denied the charge and asked Mr. Brough to retract it, and upon his refusal to do so challenged him to fight a duel. Mr. Brough published the cartel and his answer in a newspaper, and, Mr. Bright declining to fight on such a field, the matter ended. Early in February, 1865, Mr. Bright was stricken with paralysis at the Fifth Avenue Hotel, New York, and never afterward was able to walk. He left Madison in 1868 and removed to Indianapolis, where he remained until he died.

On the 24th of April, 1878, Mr. Bright celebrated his golden wedding, and it was as beautiful as it was touching to see him on that eventful day. As he sat in his chair with a bouquet pinned to the lapel of his coat, the wife of fifty years by his side, and all his children and grandchildren around him, he seemed like the patriarch of old, ready to say: "Lord, now lettest Thou Thy servant depart in peace, according to Thy word, for mine eyes have seen Thy salvation."

On the 19th of January, 1881, when seventy-eight years and three days old, Mr. Bright departed this life. His remains were taken to Crown Hill Cemetery and there interred.

Mr. Bright was a member of the Episcopal Church, and in his younger days was an active Freemason. His affliction in his latter years debarred him from the privilege of the lodge room, but he often attended church after he became an invalid.

Mr. Bright was an able and ingenious lawyer. He was well read in the books, and in practice was as good as the best. He was ever on the alert, and if an opponent had a weak place in his lines he pierced it. In speaking he sometimes hesitated or stammered, and frequently repeated his words; but if he was not an eloquent man he was a sensible and a plausible one. He ranked high at the bar as a business lawyer, standing at the very head of his profession in the State. He made a study of finance, and once prepared a lecture upon it, which, however, he never delivered. He loved social games, and was an adept in playing them. He was public-spirited, and liberal with his means in assisting such enterprises as were for the public good.

Mr. Bright was an ardent Democrat, and the best party manipulator in his section of the State. He was not ambitious for office, and was never a candidate from choice. He lived in a Whig county, but, when a candidate, he was always elected. His party opponents knew his ability, and his power to serve them, and, therefore, many of them voted for him.

Mr. Bright was a born diplomatist. No one knows how much his brother Jesse was indebted to him for his successful political career. He was his brother's mentor and counselor. All his movements on the political chess-board were to check the king of his brother's antagonist. The following letters, written by him to a friend, and hitherto not published, will show his interest in his brother's fortune:

"BROOKELAND, Nov. 21, 1852.

"DEAR SIR—I received your late favor and mark its contents. I hope things will all come out right. I do not fear, if prudence and discretion mark our management. Jesse will not go into the Cabinet—at least I think so. In the first place, a position there will not be offered him; in the second place, I think that it would be inexpedient, under all circumstances, to accept it if it were offered. He can be of as much service to his friends and more to himself by remaining where he is. Judge Borden wants to be Recorder of the Land Office in place of Tenney, who was appointed from our State not long ago.

How would he do? My notion is, it would be a very proper appointment.

"As to United States Senator we in the South must follow the lead of our Northern friends. If they want Pettit, then Pettit is the man; if they prefer Dr. Fitch, then Fitch must be our candidate. We shall leave it to them to say whom they will have. If they can not agree among themselves (which will be most likely), and it devolves upon us in the South to make the selection, I say to you in confidence, I should not hesitate one moment about the choice. Pettit, with all his goodness, is too much identified with the Douglas faction to receive my cordial support. On the other hand, Fitch is a real gentleman—known to be right, and as true as steel. I hope to be out next week or the week after, and shall be pleased to see you.

" Ever your friend,   M. G. Bright."

———

"Madison, Jan. 31, 1853.

"Dear Sir—I acted on your suggestion and visited Washington. I returned last Friday, and one day this week I shall pay you a visit, for I have much that I wish to say to you.

" Who are to compose the Cabinet of General Pierce no one can tell. On this subject you know as much as I, and I knew as much before I left home as I learned by my trip. All is in the dark. Pierce, if indeed he has made up his own mind upon the subject, which it is believed he has not, keeps it entirely to himself. Cass and Hunter, and all those men, are as profoundly ignorant on the subject as we are ; at least they say so, and I do not doubt it. Fears are entertained by many of our friends that extreme men will be taken into the Cabinet whose appointment will create distrust, and produce dissatisfaction to the National Democracy. I fear such a thing, though I hope for the best.

" On the whole, I am gratified that I went. I found things much better than I feared they would be, and I am entirely easy in reference to the effect which any effort of Jo. W. and Bill B. can have upon my brother. He can laugh them to scorn. I shall try to be out this week ; if not early next.

" Truly your friend,   M. G. Bright."

It will be seen by these letters that the interests of his brother Jesse were ever uppermost in his thoughts. He says nothing about his own affairs ; it is of those of his brother that he speaks. These two distinguished men were the most affectionate of brothers. When you struck one you hit the other. In many respects they were unlike. Michael was insinuating, diplomatic, and conciliatory ; Jesse, magnetic, frank, and outspoken. They were both proud of their family, and both loved their father's children.

John Pettit and Graham N. Fitch were candidates for United States Senator before the Legislature of 1853. As will be seen from Mr. Bright's letter printed above, he favored the election of Dr. Fitch. He came to Indianapolis at the beginning of the session, and worked hard for his favorite. Mr. Pettit, however, was elected, and this result greatly chagrined Mr. Bright, for he felt it was a blow at his brother Jesse. The evening after the election he and Mr. Pettit met at the Palmer House, and warm words passed between them. Pettit told him that, having been elected to the Senate, he would have influence with the appointing power, and that he intended that he (Mr. Bright) should be sent as Minister Plenipotentiary to the Guano Islands. After this, Mr. Bright and Judge Pettit became friends and remained such while they lived. It will be remembered that Judge Pettit was nominated for Supreme Judge in 1870 by the Democratic State Convention. The evening after the convention adjourned he called upon Mr. Bright at his home. They had a long conversation on old times, and when Judge Pettit arose to leave, Mr. Bright ordered his carriage for the purpose of having the Judge taken to his hotel. Judge Pettit declined the offer, saying he was too heavy and clumsy to get in and out of the carriage. He then walked up to Mr. Bright, and taking his hand, said : "Michael, God bless you. I am glad to see you looking so well, and I hope you will be dancing with the girls before spring. Good-by."

On the 24th of April, 1828, Mr. Bright married Betsy Brooke Steele, who survives him. Twelve children were born to them, six of whom are living. Among the dead is the lamented Michael Steele Bright, who lost his life by trying to save the lives of others in the memorable conflagration of the steamers United States and America, which burned on the Ohio river in December, 1868. The children living are, Richard J. Bright, Sergeant-at-Arms of the United States Senate ; Mrs. Rachel Haldeman, Mrs. Martha Griffin, Mrs. Hannah Nichol, Mrs. Mary Korbly and William L. Bright.

Mr. Bright's eldest daughter married Dr. J. R. Haldeman, who, during the war, was a Confederate surgeon. Mrs. Haldeman was taken sick while her husband was in the army, and was kindly nursed and cared for by the Sisters of Charity in Vicksburg. When she convalesced she passed the lines and came to her father's home. After the war had ended Mr. Bright made a trip to New Orleans, and finding the steamer upon which he traveled would stop awhile at Vicksburg resolved to personally thank the Sisters for their attention to his daughter. When the boat landed at the Vicksburg wharf he was taken ashore in his chair and conducted to the Sisters' hospital. Reaching the hospital he called for the Superior, and on her appearance said : "My name is Bright. I am the father of Mrs. Haldeman, whom you so kindly treated during her sickness, and I could not pass your city without calling in person and thanking you for your goodness to my child." He was then taken to the steamer and proceeded on his way.

In person Mr. Bright was large and portly. He was quick in speech and in action. When animated his face and eyes were peculiarly expressive. His hair was a dark brown, his eyes hazel, his features good, and his whole appearance that of a well-bred gentleman. He was a good lawyer, an adept in finance, and a diplomatist of very decided ability.

NICHOLAS McCARTY.

Indiana has had many men of more learning and greater natural talents than Nicholas McCarty, but she has had few who exercised a more healthful influence, and whose life-work redounded more to the public good. He was a pioneer of the State, and impressed himself deeply upon its morals and politics.

Nicholas McCarty was a native Virginian, being born in that part of the Old Dominion now included in the boundaries of West Virginia. When but a child his father died, and he was thrown upon his own resources for a living. Not only this, but he had a mother to care and provide for, and he discharged this sacred duty with the same fidelity with which he ever executed his trusts. When a boy in his teens he left Pittsburgh, where he had gone soon after his father's death, and emigrated to Newark, Ohio. He soon obtained employment in a dry goods store, and such was his faithfulness and aptitude for business that in a short time his employer placed him at the head of a branch house in a neighboring town. This increased responsibility was met by increased industry and more strict attention to his duties, and the fidelity with which he served his employer laid the foundation for a friendship which lasted while they lived. Soon after this he went into business for himself, and met with reasonable success, but becoming infected with the emigration fever then pervading the country he sold his store and started towards the setting sun. When in the vicinity of Indianapolis he became impressed with the fertility of the soil, and on reaching that town he stopped and pitched his tent. From that time (1823) until he died he was an inhabitant of Indiana's capital.

The pathways of some men are easily traced. By the furrows they cut others follow them as readily as huntsmen follow the trail. Nicholas McCarty was such a man. From the time he settled in Indianapolis until he died he was a leader in everything that went to build up the city and conduce to the public weal. He was the first man to establish a large mercantile house in the town, and his manner of dealing was such as to draw to it a large and lucrative trade. After awhile he instituted branch houses in several towns throughout the State, and unquestionably he did more to create a correct code of mercantile ethics than any other man in Indiana. Although he had his vicissitudes, his ups and downs in trade, no one ever questioned his integrity or doubted his fair dealing. If he did not always do just as he agreed, he ever had a reason for the failure, and the one he gave was accepted without question.

Mr. McCarty was of a sanguine temperament, and engaged in several enterprises which were not successful, but the faith he had in the future of the city where he lived never forsook him. He bought large tracts of land in its immediate vicinity which have become exceedingly valuable, and his descendants are now reaping the benefit of his judgment and foresight.

As commissioner of the canal fund Mr. McCarty effected the first loan ever made to Indiana. His action in this matter was such as to commend him to those in authority, as well as to the people at large, and no man ever acquitted himself in a fiducial capacity with more conscientiousness and fidelity than he.

Mr. McCarty had a taste for politics, and it is a wonder he did not cultivate it more than he did. He was emphatically a man of the people, and had the faculty of endearing himself to all classes, but he preferred a private business to public employment, and was seldom a candidate for office. He was a Whig and a leader of the party, and could have had almost any office in its gift for the asking. In 1847 he was the Whig candidate for Congress in his district, and was beaten 298 votes by the late Judge Wick. Judge Wick's majority over his competitor two years before was 1,676, and William J. Brown's majority over his opponent in the same district two years afterwards was 1,497. Thus it will be seen that Mr. McCarty was over 1,200 votes stronger in the district than his party.

In 1850 Mr. McCarty was nominated and elected to the State Senate. He was made chairman of the Senate's Committee on Corporations, and jealously guarded the interests of the people. The author remembers an incident which illustrates this fact. During Mr. McCarty's service in the Senate some gentlemen at Madison sent William McKee Dunn and Captain David White to Indianapolis to secure from the Legislature a charter for an insurance company. They wanted the charter to run ninety-nine years, and to be secure against legislative interference. But Mr. McCarty, while favoring a charter, insisted that the Legislature should reserve the right to alter or repeal it at will. Messrs. Dunn and White reported this fact to their clients, and were directed to get the charter through the Senate when Mr. McCarty was absent. This was done, and the charter secured without any provision for its alteration or repeal.

In 1852 the Whig State convention nominated Mr. McCarty for Governor. He did not desire the nomination, and strenuously opposed its being made. Marshall and Dunn and Thompson were spoken of, but none of them wanted the race. And, besides, it was believed that Mr. McCarty, on account of his business connections and large agricultural interests, was stronger than any other man. When the convention met it was apparent that he would be nominated if he would accept, but it was so generally understood that he would not stand that the convention hesitated to make the nomination. Therefore, after appointing a committee to see him and solicit his consent, it adjourned until the following day. That evening the committee met Mr. McCarty for conference, and found him firmly fixed in his determination not to make the race. It labored with him long and earnestly, but he continued obdurate. At last George G. Dunn, one of the most gifted Indianians of that or any other day, arose and, in the name of the Whigs of Indiana, demanded that Mr. McCarty cast behind him his personal wishes and accept the standard his party wished to place in his hands. This touched him deeply, and asking until the next morning for consideration, he left the room. It was felt at once that Mr. Dunn's shot had hit the mark. 'Tis said, if a woman hesitates she is lost, and it may with equal truth be said that the man who hesitated when George G. Dunn urged him in another direction was also lost. So next morning the committee notified the convention that Mr. McCarty would make the race, and he was nominated by acclamation.

After this the convention was addressed by several distinguished speakers, among them James T. Suitt and George G. Dunn, who were particularly severe upon Governor Wright. At last the nominee for Governor appeared and took the stand. He looked troubled and careworn, and seemed as one offering himself as a sacrifice. He thanked the convention for the honor it had conferred upon him; said that, being a candidate, he wished to be elected, and would do all he honorably could to succeed: that his competitor was able and honorable and had made a good Governor, and he hoped his friends would not belittle his opponent nor traduce his character. The convention had been wrought to a high state of excitement by the previous speakers, and these words, for the moment, fell on stony ground. But the appearance and manner of the speaker, his frankness, his earnestness and his simplicity, soon touched the hearts of his auditors, and they cheered him to the echo. They saw they had nominated a good and an honest man, and one whom it would be an honor to follow. That the sentiments he avowed were from his heart, his subsequent actions abundantly proved. He and Governor Wright made the canvass with the utmost good feeling. They went from place to place together, often riding in the same carriage, and nearly always stopping at the same hotel. They had no petty bickerings nor angry words, their intercourse being more like that of members of the same family than of leaders of hostile parties. On the stump there was great difference between them. Governor Wright was educated; Mr. McCarty was not. Governor Wright was a good talker and a good reasoner; Mr. McCarty was also a good talker, but not a good reasoner. He dealt in repartee and in anecdotes, and was peculiarly happy in his application of the latter. At their meeting at Madison, Governor Wright led off in a long speech, in which he claimed credit for developing the agricultural resources of Indiana and for the State's improved financial condition. When he had concluded Mr. McCarty took the stand, and addressing himself to the audience, said: "If my friend Governor Wright's foresights were as good as his hindsights, what a wonderful man he'd be." The crowd laughed and cheered him, and although he was no match for the Governor as a debater, he excelled him in wit and anecdote, and made a deeper impression on his hearers.

Eighteen hundred and fifty-two was a bad year for Whig candidates, and Mr. McCarty went down with the tide, being beaten 20,031 votes. Having resigned his seat in the Senate when he accepted the gubernatorial nomination, he was now a private citizen, and he remained one while he lived.

Mr. McCarty was a good story-teller, and was fond of jokes. His was a sunny disposition, and when he visited friends of evenings the young folks always remained at home. There are men with gray beards now living who are wont to tell of the many funny things said and done by the old pioneer in the long, long ago. The sunshine he brought to the homes of his friends still lingers on the door-steps, and lights the way of those who traverse the halls of their fathers.

Mr. McCarty loved practical jokes, and often indulged in them. He was a believer in the integrity of men and a disbeliever in the doctrine that every man had his price. In the early history of the State he sometimes went South to purchase tobacco and other Southern products. On one of these occasions he took with him a large amount of the bills of the bank of the State of Indiana. The bills were brand new, never having been used. On his passage up the Cumberland river on a steamer he made the acquaintance of a Kentucky farmer who was also on his way to Tennessee. Mr. McCarty found out that the Kentuckian was a Baptist, and being a half-way one himself, the two soon became intimate and treated each other as old friends. He had often heard the assertion that every one had his price, and he thought he had a good opportunity of testing the truth of the saying. So one day he whispered to his friend in a mysterious way that he wished to see him privately, and led the way to his state-room. Entering it with his companion, he drew the curtain over the window, bolted the door, and opened his carpet-bag. Taking from it a large roll of bank bills, and looking under the berths to see that no one was present, he spread the money on his bed and said: " There, Mr. Smith, is as good money as though it had been issued by a bank. It will pass anywhere, and I can let you have it on such terms as will enable you to make a handsome thing out of it." Seeing that Mr. Smith was surprised and astonished, he proceeded: "Don't be afraid of the money, Mr. Smith; it is as good as the bank and will go anywhere. I can let you have it at twenty-five cents on the dollar, and you can pay it out for tobacco dollar for dollar." By this time the Kentuckian had recovered from his surprise and replied: "I had rather not, Mr. McCarty; I believe I had rather not." Mr. McCarty used to tell this story with great zest, and declare that he had found one man in his life who had not " his price."

But he was also an accommodating man, and took delight in serving others. He would go out of his way to do one a favor, and was always glad to make others happy. He had a keen sense of the ridiculous, and enjoyed a joke as well as the best of them. Years ago, when postage was high, a letter written on two pieces of paper was subjected to double postage, which could be prepaid or not, at the option of the writer. An acquaintance from a distance wrote him upon a subject in which he had no manner of concern, and failed to prepay the postage. Mr. McCarty attended to the business, and in his reply to his correspondent said: "Your postmaster is dishonest. He did not mark your letter prepaid. Of course you intended to prepay it, as no one writes to another on his own business without doing so. That you may have the evidence of his dishonesty I return your letter herewith." This act mulcted his correspondent in double postage.

Mr. McCarty wrote rapidly. His chirography was poor, but his writing was generally correct, although he knew but little or nothing of grammar. Realizing his deficiency as a scholar he did what he could, in private life and public station, to secure to others what had been denied himself. When a candidate for the State Senate he visited a neighborhood where opposition to public schools was active and strong, but he boldly said that, if elected, he would vote money to make tuition free. His courage and frankness won him friends, and many who went to hear him speak, opposed to free schools, went home their advocates. When Mr. McCarty was nominated for Governor so well was his reputation for frankness established that the *In-*

dianapolis Sentinel had this to say of him : " Like Henry Clay, everybody who knows Nicholas McCarty knows his politics. The same yesterday, to-day and forever."

Mr. McCarty was five feet eight inches high, and weighed about 160 pounds. His complexion was fair, his hair light, and his eyes of a hazel color. His head and face indicated shrewdness rather than profundity. In movement he was quick and active. He was not a great man, but he was an intelligent and influential one, and his influence was always for the good. Although not a church member he had a great reverence for Deity, and his daily walk and example were without reproach.

At Crown Hill, that beautiful city of the dead, there stands a granite shaft with this inscription :

NICHOLAS M'CARTY,
Born September 26, 1795 ;
Died May 17, 1854.

And there, beneath the now green sod, and beside that shaft pointing heavenward, lie the earthly remains of Nicholas McCarty.

CALVIN FLETCHER.

TTHERE stands at Crown Hill a massive granite shaft—the largest in the cemetery—bearing the name of Fletcher. On its north face are engraven these words:

CALVIN FLETCHER,
Born in Ludlow, Vt., February 4, 1798 ;
Emigrated to Indianapolis October 1, 1821 ;
Died May 26, 1866.

The monument is fitly chosen. It is plain, as was the man whose name it bears ; it is solid and enduring, as is his fame.

The following extract from a letter dated March 25, 1861, written by Mr. Fletcher to the Secretary of the New England Historical Society, gives the main incidents in his active and remarkable career:

" At that period (1815), I had only had the advantage of two months each year at the school in the district where my father lived. For two years I labored for others at wages, a portion of the time, and the residue I spent at the academies of Randolph and Royalton in my native State. In 1817 I determined on a seaman's life, and in April of the same year went to Boston, a total stranger, and tried my best to obtain a berth on board an East Indiaman, but failed. I then turned my face toward the country west of the Alleghenies. In two months I worked my way, mostly on foot, to the western part of Ohio, and stopped at Urbana, then the frontier settlement of the northwestern part of that State. I knew not an individual in the State—had no letter of introduction. I obtained labor as a hired hand for a short time, and then a school. In the fall of 1817 I obtained a situation in the law office of the Hon. James Cooley, a gentleman of talent and fine education—one of a large class which graduated at Yale under. Dr. Dwight. He was sent to Peru under John Quincy Adams's administration and died there. In the fall of 1821 I was admitted to the bar and became the law partner of my worthy friend and patron, Mr. Cooley. In the summer of 1821 the Delaware Indians left the central part of Indiana, then a total wilderness, and the new State selected and laid off Indianapolis as its future capital, but did not make it such for four or five years thereafter. I had married, and, on my request, my worthy partner permitted me to leave him to take up my residence at the place designated as the seat of government of Indiana. In September of that year (1821) I left Urbana with a wagon, entered the wilderness, and after traveling fourteen days, and camping out the same number of nights, reached Indianapolis, where there were a few newly erected cabins. No counties had been laid off in the newly acquired territory; but in a few years civil divisions were made. I commenced the practice of law, and for about twenty-two years traveled over, twice annually, nearly one-third of the northwestern part of the State, at first without roads, bridges or ferries. In 1825 I was appointed State Attorney for the Fifth Judicial Circuit, embracing some twelve or fifteen counties. This office I held about one year, when I was elected to the State Senate; served seven years, resigned, and gave up official positions, as I then supposed, for life. But in 1834 I was appointed by the Legislature one of four to organize a State bank, and to act as Sinking Fund Commissioner. I held that place also seven years. From 1843 to 1859 I acted as president of the branch of the State Bank at Indianapolis, until the charter expired. During the forty years I have resided in Indiana I have devoted much of my time to agriculture and societies for its promotion, and served seven years as trustee of our city schools. I have been favored with a large family—nine sons and two daughters. Three of the former have taken a regular course, and graduated at Brown University, Providence, R. I., and two a partial course at the same institution. I have written no books, but have assisted in

30

compiling a law book. I have kept a journal of daily events, confined mainly to my own routine of business."

Mr. Fletcher's death, which occurred May 26, 1866, caused much public sorrow. His acquaintance was large, and extended to all classes. He had long been a banker, and had made for himself an honorable record as such. The day after he died . the bankers of Indianapolis met to take action in relation to his death, and among other resolutions passed the following:

" That we do not believe mere success in worldly aims was the controlling inspiration of his career. His devotion to every patriotic impulse; his vigilant and generous attention to every call of benevolence; his patient care of all wholesome means of public improvements; his interest in the imperial claims of religion, morals and education, and his admirable success in securing the happiness and promoting the culture of a large family, show conclusively that whatever importance he attached to the acquisition of wealth he never lost sight of his responsibility to that Great Being who smiled so graciously on his life, and whose approbation made his closing hours serene and hopeful."

The funeral of Mr. Fletcher was largely attended. Among those present were a large number of colored people. He had long been a friend to this down-trodden race. He had aided the negro with advice and money, and in return received his love and veneration.

He was an anti-slavery man from principle; was one when it cost something to be one. No person who was not living thirty or forty years ago can realize the bitter prejudice that then existed against the old-time abolitionist; he was considered an enemy of his country, and was subjected to both social and political ostracism. But this did not deter Mr. Fletcher, nor cause him to alter his course. He once said to one of his sons: " When I am in the Court-house, engaged in an important case, if the Governor of the State should send in word that he wished to speak to me I would reply that I could not go; but if a Quaker should touch me on the shoulder and say, 'A colored man is out here in distress and fear,' I would leave the Court-

house in a minute to see the man, for I feel that I would have
to account at that last day when He shall ask me if I have visited the sick in prison or bondage and fed the poor. The great
of this world can take care of themselves, but God has made us
stewards for the down-trodden, and we must account to Him."

Mr. Fletcher's funeral discourse was preached by Rev. A. S.
Kinnan, after which his remains, followed by a large concourse
of people, were taken to Crown Hill and there interred.

Mr. Fletcher had large farming and banking interests, as well
as a large law practice, and he was successful in them all. Few
men were capable of doing so much work, and fewer still of
doing it so well. As a lawyer he was remarkably fortunate in
obtaining satisfactory results for his clients. He discharged his
professional duties as he did all his work—faithfully and well.
The author is indebted to one of Mr. Fletcher's law students for
many of the incidents that follow. They will give the reader
an insight into the life of this remarkable man, and must be of
interest to all who read this sketch. They testify of his fidelity
to duty, of his devotion to the interests of those who intrusted
their business to him. In practicing his profession, he investigated the cases of his clients to the bottom, and for this purpose
was in the habit of cross-examining them and making note of
the facts both pro and con. He was, on one of these occasions,
much amused by a remark made by a brother of the client, who
had been brought along to help state the case and assist in understanding and remembering the instructions. The client stated in detail all he could prove, and by whom. He could prove
much, but at the end of the conference the brother spoke out
and said: " Yes, lawyer, and they can prove a power on the
other side."

Mr. Fletcher viewed his cases dramatically. He realized
them in actual life, then the points and authorities were examined and the questions arising were settled after cautious and
labored deliberation. On the trial he was not oratorical, but he
had a fine, clear voice, and was a shrewd and effective speaker.
His most prominent talent was an insight into the motives of
parties and witnesses, and he was especially strong in cross-
examining witnesses. In one case, a witness who was compelled by him, on cross-examination, to disclose facts which con-

tradicted his evidence in chief, fainted, and his evidence was disregarded by the jury.

Mr. Fletcher's earliest practice was very miscellaneous, ranging from justice of the peace to the Supreme Court, including both law and chancery cases, civil and criminal, with, however, an undue proportion of criminal and tort cases, among the last slander suits being quite common. In early times there was less appeal to authority and more to the feelings of the jury than now. In new counties the court-rooms were always crowded, and often by citizens who had no business at court, but only came to see and hear. The lawyers were much tempted to make speeches for the lobby, and it was quite an object to entertain and amuse the audience, and even those who were indisposed to encourage this abuse occasionally gave it countenance.

Mr. Smith, in his "Reminiscences," gives several instances of Mr. Fletcher's fondness for quizzing and practical jokes. A few specimens may be added. In early times lawyer Forsee, who was not distinguished for his law or logic, but was fond of display, made the quotation "*Otium cum dignitate*," for the purpose of making a grand impression on the 'squire. In reply Mr. Fletcher pretended he said, "Oh, come and dig my taters," which, he argued, was not applicable to the case, for the reason that there was not a word of evidence about digging taters. However trivial the fun, it plagued Forsee, who wanted to explain that it was Latin, etc., all of which amused the crowd the more.

There was formerly a lawyer of distinction at the Indianapolis bar who was a fine speaker and a wit, but a little too fond of metaphysical distinctions. Hugh O'Neal, when Prosecuting Attorney, to break the force of this kind of argument, sometimes in closing the case, would tell the jury this story: That this lawyer, so successful in his fine-spun distinctions, had been employed to defend old man Van Blaricum for shooting a neighbor's dog; that the proof was clear that the defendant said he would shoot the dog; that he brought out the gun in open day and loaded it; that he took deliberate aim at the dog, and that at the crack of the rifle the dog fell dead with a bullet hole through him; that thereupon this ingenious lawyer was stimulated by the difficulties in his case to unusual ingenuity, and contended that this was a case of circumstantial evidence merely, and that in such cases it was well settled that if a single link in the chain of evidence was wanting the whole evidence was worthless; and although there was proof of the threat, the loading of the gun, the firing, and that the dog was killed, "Yet," said he "what witness has testified that he saw the bullet hit the dog?" O'Neal told the story so well that he was sure to bring down the house, and that brought his opponent to his feet to explain that that was one of the stories invented by Fletcher.

Mr. Fletcher and William Quarles were employed by an old Quaker farmer unused to courts, but as full as other people of human nature. The case was before Judge Wick, in chancery, and the question was whether he would grant an injunction in favor of the Quaker. Mr. Fletcher's argument exhausted the points and authorities, so that, when Quarles closed the argument, his remarks were principally directed to reviving some pungent scandals against the Quaker's adversary, to all which the Quaker gave earnest attention. Judge Wick sustained the injunction, but criticised, with some severity, the personalities which had crept into the case. The Quaker sat just outside the bar, and Mr. Fletcher, thinking he might not have understood the purport of the decision, said to him: "The court has decided in our favor." "Yes," was the answer, "but did thee hear Quarles?"

Occasionally, however, the fun was on the other side. On one occasion, when the mails only went once a week to Martinsville, Mr. Fletcher desired to forward a letter to that town in advance of the mail, and so informed Mr. Gregg, a waggish pioneer lawyer. Mr. Gregg found a Methodist preacher who was on his way to Martinsville, and who was much in the habit of holding up before sinners the terrors of future punishment. Mr. Gregg hurried into the court-room and found Mr. Fletcher busy. He told him, however, with a sober face, that he had found a "brimstone peddler," who was on his way to Martinsville, and would be in soon for the letter. Mr. Fletcher was writing the letter as fast as possible when the minister came in, and Mr. Gregg introduced him as the gentleman he had spoken of. The letter being hurriedly completed, and the minister about to leave, Mr. Fletcher, without reflecting, inquired how he succeeded in peddling brimstone. The minister was, of course, surprised, and Mr. Gregg, with a smile, explained that the peddler was a different man. Such are the specimens of the humors of the bar, which, though interesting at the moment, effervesce and disappear. But, perhaps, the less the incident the greater the comic talent required to make the fun effective. It will not be supposed that these casual diversions indicated any want of earnest purpose.

One of Mr. Fletcher's peculiarities was his ingenious mode of criticising and stimulating his students. He would think of something praiseworthy in the student, which he would eulogize, and thus please and gratify him; then he would, with touches of humor, state the faults to be corrected. By this course he avoided all offense.

During the process of making up his decision upon a question of law or policy he preserved entire impartiality. He was ready at any moment to abandon an untenable position. He was not satisfied until all sides had been examined, and he had the art of appropriating from those about him all that could be known. In consequence of this his decisions were not rapid, but they were sound and well considered.

One of his most serviceable powers was his remarkable memory, which seemed to hold all that was committed to it. In his law office it was he who kept in mind all the business and who watched all the points of danger.

He held himself bound to give satisfaction to his client, and if there was dissatisfaction he was willing to consider it his fault. He explained, especially to non-residents, the services performed and difficulties encountered, and thus demonstrated the reasonableness of the charges made. This he considered both his duty and his interest.

He had, when young, felt the pressure of poverty, and had learned life from actual contact with its difficulties; and while this gave additional force and edge to his good sense, and acquainted him with the details of humble life, it also aroused his disposition to take the part of the poor, the helpless and the oppressed. To them his services were often rendered gratuitously, or for meager compensation. His sympathies were always active, and he had the faculty of conferring great benefits, not so much by direct aid as by teaching others how to help themselves. His power of stimulating others to exertions was one of his leading traits, and was more valuable than mere gifts of money.

Notwithstanding his fees were moderate, his business was so extensive, and his industry and effectiveness achieved so much, that his income was large. His judicious investments, and his plain and unostentatious mode of living, led to the rapid accumulation of wealth.

This success did not enervate him; he was essentially the same, whether poor or rich. He was opposed to litigation when it could be avoided, and had great success in adjusting cases by agreement.

In forming his judgment of men he paid more attention to character than to talent, and he had the faculty of inferring character from circumstances generally overlooked.

When introduced to a stranger he would, for some minutes, give him his exclusive attention. He would notice every remark and movement, every expression of feature, and even the minutiæ of dress, yet he did all this without giving offense. He seemed to be ever under some controlling influence which led him to study character. In early times the bar, judge and people were thrown much together, and social and conversational talents were of great advantage to the lawyer. Here Mr. Fletcher was remarkably well endowed. Attachment to his friends was one of his prominent qualities, and he often had them at his house enjoying his hospitality. Toward those in his office he was most attractive and amiable. He gave them his confidence and directed them to open and read the letters which came in his absence.

Among his other good qualities he was an example of temperance. He avoided the use of liquor and even of tobacco in all their forms. He never played cards, although card-playing was a common pastime among the lawyers in his day.

It is noticeable that he contrived to find his amusements along the beaten path of every-day duties. Mr. Fletcher held the office of Prosecuting Attorney at an early day, and afterwards served some time as a State Senator.   His services for the public were always his best.

No one guarded the interest of the public more scrupulously than he.   As Senator he gave great offense to some of his constituents by opposing the first charter proposed for the organization of a State bank.   He resigned the Senatorship, and the next year another charter was prepared which obviated his objections.   This charter passed the Legislature, and on the organization of the bank he became a director on the part of the State, and thenceforth gave banking and finance a large portion of his time and attention.

At one time Mr. Fletcher was, for a few days, a candidate against William Herod for the Whig nomination for Congress. He had every prospect of success, but he withdrew from the race because he thought it bad policy to leave his family and his business.   At another time Governor Noble tendered him the nomination for Supreme Judge, but he refused to accept it.

For a short time Mr. Fletcher was president of the Bellefontaine railroad, and for ten years he was superintendent of Roberts Chapel Sunday-school.   It was his custom to have family worship every morning, and all his household, including his servants, were required to be present.

Mr. Fletcher kept a diary in which he recorded everything of importance that took place under his notice.   This diary is a compendium of the history of Indianapolis during Mr. Fletcher's residence here, and it is understood that one of his sons is now preparing a biography of his father, and that this diary will be largely drawn upon in the preparation of the work.

John B. Dillon, the historian of Indiana, in a paper not hitherto published, thus sums up Mr. Fletcher's leading traits of character :

"I do not doubt that those peculiar traits of character which made Mr. Fletcher a remarkable man as a private citizen were influential forces in regulating and controlling his conduct as a member of the legal profession.   As a private citizen he was a man of great industry, of unquestionable integrity, with a healthy, robust body, a mind naturally strong, fairly educated, cautious, and inquisitive about men and things.   He was a good judge of men, and active supporter of the interests of practical Christianity, popular education, temperance and charitable institutions. In the expenditure of money his habits were prudent and economical, but not parsimonious. He was firm, courageous and persevering in what he regarded as the line of duty. He was fond of children, and sometimes he would stop in his rapid walk on the street, to arouse into activity and ambition the dull sluggishness of

> " 'The whining schoolboy, with his satchel
> And shining morning face, creeping like a snail
> Unwillingly to school.'

" Mr. Fletcher was often very much amused with laughable stories, especially when such stories illustrated cases in which dandies, fops or other vainglorious pérsons were made the subject of comical practical jokes.

" Holding his place in the first rank among the lawyers of Indiana while he was an active member of the bar, the duties of Mr. Fletcher in prosecuting and defending suits in the courts were numerous, important and often burdensome. As a speaker his language was forcible. His reasonings were generally brief and pointed, and were always understood by those to whom they were addressed. He belonged to the class of ' business speakers,' and he seemed to care very little for the arts of rhetoric and logic. He could, on proper occasions, use the power of sarcasm with great skill.

"As a prosecuting attorney in the pioneer time of the Fifth Judicial Circuit in Indiana, he was diligent and faithful in the discharge of his professional duties, but, if well authenticated tradition be true, he sometimes, in very extraordinary cases, availed himself of the use of novel and irregular powers in order to prevent the defeat of the ends of justice by the ignorance and stubborness of foolish men."

A gentleman who knew Mr. Fletcher well and intimately, gives this estimate of his character:

" He was, as he appeared to me, a man of remarkable physical constitution ; of abounding animal spirits, yet without vicious indulgence ; with great industry, energy and endurance ; of active, sympathetic, moral and Christian character and public spirit; of shrewd, clear and vigorous intellect, well stored with a vast fund of knowledge, all resulting in a very high order of practical wisdom, and as a natural consequence he achieved marked success in his professional and other pursuits in life."

Oliver H. Smith, in his "Early Indiana Trials and Sketches," speaks thus of Mr. Fletcher:

"He was a remarkable man. He combined all the elements of an effective pioneer in a new country—an iron constitution, clear and vigorous common sense mind, an energy that never slumbered, integrity never questioned, a high conception of morality and religion, social qualities of the first order, a devoted friend to the cause of education, a good lawyer and a forcible speaker."

While the Whig party existed Mr. Fletcher was a member of it, and when it dissolved he became a Republican. Had he sought office it would have been given him, but he preferred a private business to public employment, hence his official life was short.

Mr. Fletcher was one of the men who made Indianapolis what it is. No one impressed himself more deeply upon the people than he, and no one dying left behind him more friends and a better name. His influence was always for the good. Education and religion had in him a friend and an exemplar.

Mr. Fletcher was about five feet eight inches high, and was strongly and compactly built. He had dark brown hair and gray eyes, the latter being unusually penetrating and expressive. His features were symmetrical, and his complexion unusually white, although of a healthy hue. He was a good and honest man, and his memory is revered by all who knew him.

WILLIAM H. MORRISON.

THE winter of 1880–'81 will long be remembered by the people of Indianapolis, not only on account of its extreme cold, but for the further reason that during it several of the city's most prominent citizens were called away. First, Governor Williams died, and although he was not properly a citizen of the capital, his almost four years of official residence seemed to make him so. Then Michael G. Bright, in his prime one of the foremost men of the State, departed this life; and soon after him General John Love, a respected and well-known citizen, went to " the undiscovered country, from whose bourne no traveler returns." Following quick after him—almost in his shadow—James M. Ray, one of the oldest and best beloved of our pioneers, departed from among us. Then Mr. Morrison was called away.

Mr. Morrison was born in New York, in July, 1806, and when fourteen years old came to Indiana and settled in the county of Clark. Nine years afterward he came to Indianapolis and entered the office of his brother, the late Judge James Morrison, as deputy Secretary of State. At the expiration of his brother's official term he engaged in mercantile pursuits, and continued in active business until he died. On the first day of March, 1870, he became a member of the Indiana Banking Company, and was president of that institution until 1878, when he left it to take the presidency of the First National Bank of Indianapolis. He remained at the head of the First National until March 18, 1881, when he died.

To properly estimate the character of a man other things besides his business career ought to be considered. Mr. Morrison was a good business man, but he was something more.

His influence was for good. He was active in most things that favored correct morals and the building up of Christianity. He was free from all the smaller vices, as well as the larger ones. His daily walk was above reproach, and his activity in the building of churches and in supporting the ministry was proverbial. He was instrumental in the building of Christ Church, Indianapolis, and to him more than to any other man must be ascribed the erection of St. Paul's Cathedral, in the same city. It was in this church that he worshiped during his latter days, and for years before his death no stranger entered there without noting an elegant and dignified man in a pew near the chancel. That man was Mr. Morrison.

Mr. Morrison, like all mortals, had his failings. They were not in the line of laxity of morals, or a want of religious activity, for in these respects he was above reproach; but his nature was so positive and his will so strong that at times he seemed obstinate and illiberal. This trait in his character was so marked that some thought him hard-hearted and unkind, but, in fact, he was neither. In his intercourse with friends and in the transaction of his business he was ever courteous and obliging. It was only when he felt himself wronged that his combativeness arose, and at such times he was unyielding.

Mr. Morrison was both by nature and practice a gentleman. He never so forgot himself as to give way to passion or to act in an angry manner, but when he differed from a man it was in a courteous way. He never acted the bully nor played the role of a blackguard.

Mr. Morrison belonged to a distinguished family. His brother, the late Judge Morrison, was an eminent lawyer, and filled many places of honor and profit with great ability. He was Secretary of State when a young man, and he was Indiana's first Attorney-General. For many years he was president of the old State Bank of Indiana, and performed the duties of that responsible place honestly and well. Another brother—Alexander H.—was prominent in politics in his day, and he left his impress upon the city in which he lived in more ways than one. The youngest brother, the subject of this sketch, never asked for public office, but contented himself with commercial affairs. Had he sought public employment it would have been given him, and the record of his business life is an earnest of what he would have done had he chosen to be a public man.

Mr. Morrison was an active business man until the sickness overtook him from which he died. Although he had passed the age allotted to man, three-score years and ten, he stood upright and walked with grace and ease so long as he was able to get about. His was not the tottering gait of old age, but the steady one of vigorous manhood. He was often seen upon the streets of Indianapolis taking his regular walks, with a son of his old age beside him; and the elegant old gentleman and the bright boy side by side, engaged in thoughtful converse, brought to mind those great creations of Dickens—Dombey and Son. Had the great novelist known Mr. Morrison and his boy many would have thought that they were the originals of his picture.

The funeral of Mr. Morrison took place in St. Paul's Cathedral, on Saturday, March 19, after which his remains were taken to Crown Hill and buried. The Indianapolis Clearing House Association and the directors of the First National Bank of Indianapolis met and passed resolutions extolling his virtues. But in no other place, outside his family, was Mr. Morrison so missed as in his church. In church influence he was first among the laity, and his advice was sought and his counsel heeded by the clergy. He was Senior Warden of St. Paul's Cathedral when he died.

JAMES S. ATHON.

Dr. James S. Athon was born in Louden county, Virginia, April 1, 1811. Soon after his birth his parents removed to Murfreesboro, Tennessee, and after remaining there awhile emigrated to Kentucky. They lived there but a year or two and then came to Indiana Territory and located upon Clark's grant, on the southern border of the State.

The father of Dr. Athon was an unpretentious farmer of firm integrity, and stood high in the community where he lived. For many years he was a member of the Methodist church, and living near the town of Charlestown his family had the benefit of church privileges. The church in town and the log schoolhouse in the country afforded all the facilities young Athon had in his boyhood to obtain an education. He worked on his father's farm until he reached manhood, and then he commenced the study of medicine. He afterwards graduated at the Medical College at Louisville, Ky., after which he removed to Lexington, in Scott county, and opened an office for the practice of his profession. He remained at Lexington but a short time and then went to Charlestown, where he afterwards became eminent in his profession, ranking among the first practitioners of the State.

On the breaking out of the Mexican war Dr. Athon was appointed surgeon of the Third Indiana regiment and remained with it until it was mustered out of service. Subsequently the Fifth Indiana regiment was formed and Dr. Athon went to Mexico as its surgeon, and continued with it until the end of the war. Being then vigorous and in his prime he was active in the discharge of his army duties, and many a brave man owed his life to the skillful and attentive surgeon.

On the return of Dr. Athon from Mexico he was elected to the State Senate from his county, and served as Senator one term. While in the Senate, although a Democrat, he had many personal friends on the Whig side of the chamber, among them being Joseph G. Marshall, of Jefferson, and George G. Dunn, of Lawrence county. He accompanied Mr. Marshall to Louisville as his surgeon when that gentleman challenged Senator Bright to mortal combat, and he and Mr. Dunn were very warm personal friends while the latter lived.

In 1852 the Democratic State convention of Indiana placed Dr. Athon on the ticket as a presidential elector for his district. He was elected, and cast his vote in the electoral college for Pierce and King. The next year the Legislature elected him Superintendent of the Indiana Hospital for the Insane. He filled the place with distinguished ability, earning for himself a fame that will go down to later generations.

In 1862 Dr. Athon was elected Secretary of State, and held the office for a full term of two years. When his term expired he resumed his medical practice, and was actively engaged in it until attacked by the disease from which he died.

On the 28th of September, 1875, Dr. Athon was stricken by paralysis. He lingered until the 25th of the next month when death came to his relief.

Dr. Athon was a man of great physical and moral courage. What he believed to be his duty he did at once. Always prompt and energetic, he nearly always succeeded in his undertakings. He did not wait for others to act before determining his course, he determined it himself.

Dr. Athon left a widow and three children when he died, one of the latter being the gifted Hettie Athon Morrison, well-known throughout the West as a song and sketch writer of very great ability. Another daughter is the widow of the late General Jefferson C. Davis, the most distinguished soldier Indiana has ever produced. Dr. Athon's fame rests mainly upon his professional actions. Although he served the State well in the offices he held, he did her a greater service in healing the diseased bodies and minds of her citizens.

MICHAEL C. GARBER.

MICHAEL CHRISTIAN GARBER was born in Augusta county, Virginia, April 7, 1813. His father served, for several terms, as sheriff of Augusta county, and for awhile was mayor of the city of Staunton. For many years he was engaged in conducting a line of stage coaches, in which business he was assisted by his son Michael. In this way the latter became familiar with the transportation business, and he availed himself of this knowledge later in life to the great benefit of the government.

Before Mr. Michael Garber reached his majority he left Staunton and went to Hollidaysburg, Pa., and engaged as a clerk for an uncle. After this he and his uncle became contractors on the Chesapeake and Ohio canal, then under construction. From 1832 until 1840 he was engaged in the forwarding busi ness, and for a short time afterwards was a partner of George McFarland in the conduct of a foundry.

In 1843 Mr. Garber left Hollidaysburg and located at Rising Sun, Indiana, as a merchant. In 1849 he bought the *Madison Courier* of Samuel F. and John I. Covington, and at once removed to Madison and assumed control of the paper. It was as the conductor of this paper that he became known to the people of Indiana, and his fame is inseparably connected with it.

When Mr. Garber took charge of the *Madison Courier* he was without newspaper experience. He associated with him in the editorial conduct of the paper Charles P. Baymiller, a brilliant though erratic man, who died in Indianapolis several years ago. At that time the *Courier* was a Democratic paper of the strictest sect, and being published at the home of Jesse D. Bright, was looked upon as his personal organ. But the new editor was not fitted to be a personal grinder of tunes for any man, and he soon became restive under the restraints which such a position imposed. The contest between Senator Bright and Governor Wright for the leadership of the Indiana Democracy was then pending, and the *Courier* gave evidence of weakening in the Bright cause by publishing complimentary notices of Governor Wright, copied from other papers. By doing this its editor incurred the mortal displeasure of the Senator, for he was a man who allowed no divided allegiance. From his place in the Senate chamber at Washington he wrote a letter to the late Judge William M. Taylor, of Madison, in which he hurled his anathemas at the editor, and declared he would drive him out of the Democratic party. The letter did not reach the man for whom it was intended, but went to another Taylor, who gave it to Mr. Garber. The latter was, therefore, put in possession of irrefragable proofs of Senator Bright's hostility, and being a man not given to turning the other cheek when smitten on one, he placed the *Courier* squarely on the side of Governor Wright.

When Mr. Bright came home he called a meeting of Democrats in the old Madison Court-house to consider the situation. All the leading Democrats of the county were there, and to them Mr. Bright delivered a two-hours speech, in which he denounced Mr. Garber as no Democrat, and demanded that he be publicly read out of the party. He ended by offering a series of resolutions to that effect, but before the question was put upon their adoption Mr. Garber arose and asked to be heard. He protested against being politically ostracised, and declared himself a Democrat in whom there was no guile. He read a letter from Governor Wright certifying to his Democracy, but Governor Wright was not Democratic authority in Jefferson county, and his certificate of the editor's political orthodoxy went for naught. Mr. Bright's resolutions were adopted with but three dissenting voices, and Mr. Garber was declared outside the Democratic pale. But the condemned man refused to abide the decree, and continued to advocate Democratic principles and policy. He supported Pierce for President and Wright for Governor, and rendered his party very efficient service the year they were elected. But he had no affiliation with the Demo-

31

cratic leaders of his county. They had started the *Madisonian* to crush the *Courier* and drive its editor from Madison. But their efforts were in vain. The *Courier* lived and prospered, while the paper which was intended to supplant it struggled a few months and died. The bad feelings engendered by the efforts of Mr. Bright and his friends to break down the *Courier* terminated in a personal difficulty, which came near costing Mr. Garber his life.

The citizens of Madison held a public meeting and appointed a committee to receive Kossuth when he visited Madison in the winter of 1852. Hamilton Hibbs, a devoted friend and follower of Senator Bright, was on this committee, and so was Mr. Garber. The former published a card in the *Madisonian*—the Bright organ—declining to serve, for the reason that Mr. Garber was a member of the committee, and saying he would rather serve on a committee with a " buck nigger " than with M. C. Garber.

Now, Mr. Garber was a Democrat, and in those days to be likened to a " nigger " was more than Democratic nature could bear, so, on meeting Hibbs the afternoon his card appeared, he spat in his face and struck him with a cane. Hibbs, who was a house-carpenter, was returning home from his work with his tools in his hands, and on being thus assaulted he drew a chisel and stabbed Garber three times in his left side, each time cutting the lung. The wounded man was taken home faint and bleeding, and for many days lay halting between life and death. He recovered, however, from the injury in a few weeks and resumed control of his paper. Nothing was done with Hibbs for the stabbing.

When the People's party was organized in 1854 Mr. Garber cut loose from the Democracy and entered the new party. In 1856, when the Republican party made its first campaign in Indiana, he attached himself to it, and continued in its ranks until he died. He assisted in making the State platform of the party that year, and in 1858 he was chosen chairman of the State Central Committee. He filled the place with signal ability, and at the expiration of his term turned over the party machinery to his successor in good working condition. His paper—the *Madison Courier*—has been an active and able supporter of the Republican party since its birth. It is now, and for several years has been, mainly under the editorial control of Colonel Garber's eldest son, Michael C. Garber, Jr.; but its policy was determined, while he lived, by the one who, for more than a quarter of a century, was its head.

Colonel Garber made an unsuccessful race for Treasurer of Jefferson county in 1860, the only time he was ever a candidate for office before the people.

In 1861 the late David C. Branham, then in the secret service of the government, suggested to the Secretary of War the appointment of Mr. Garber as an army quartermaster. General Cameron, the Secretary, had known Mr. Garber in Pennsylvania, and was well acquainted with the fact that the latter had great knowledge of the subject of transportation. He at once caused Mr. Garber to be commissioned as brigade quartermaster with the rank of captain. Mr. Garber at once entered upon the duties of his office, and so well and satisfactorily did he perform his official duties that he was twice promoted, once to the rank of major and then to that of colonel. He was chief quartermaster of the Army of the Tennessee, and was with it during the Atlanta campaign.

When Sherman started on his march to the sea Colonel Garber was ordered to Louisville, Kentucky. Subsequently he joined Sherman at Savannah, and was appointed chief quartermaster of Sherman's army. He remained with that general until the war ended, and was present at the grand review at Washington, when General Sherman refused to take the hand of Secretary Stanton, and publicly turned his back upon him. He remained in the army about one month after the war had ended, and then resigned his commission and went back to his work on the *Courier*.

On the 25th of July, 1865, General Sherman wrote Colonel Garber a very complimentary letter, closing it as follows: "I hope you will enjoy health and prosperity and live long to enjoy the peace and security you aided to establish for our common country."

As editor of the *Courier*, Colonel Garber sharply criticised Governor Morton's Richmond speech, and antagonized his views in other particulars. The *Courier* was known throughout the State as an anti-Morton paper, and was really a sharp thorn in the side of the War Governor.

In 1872 Colonel Garber was appointed postmaster at Madison, after which time the *Courier* was mainly conducted by his oldest son. The new director changed its course towards Governor Morton, and from thence onward until the latter died gave him a very cordial support.

On the morning of April 3, 1881, Colonel Garber was attacked with hemorrhage of the brain. For five days he lay in an unconscious state, and then breathed his last. Two days after his death he was buried at Madison, with Masonic honors, in the presence of a large assemblage of sympathizing friends.

In his younger days Colonel Garber was able to do two men's work, and he did it. He was a man of indomitable pluck and perseverance, and he never tired in his undertakings. Although he had nearly reached the allotted life of man—three score and ten years—he was a worker until he died. He was at his office the morning on which he was struck with the malady that caused his death ; so it may be said that he died at work, with his harness on.

Colonel Garber was a man of splendid physique. His form was full, even to rotundity, and his carriage was manly and graceful. He had white hair and beard, and his appearance denoted an old man in vigorous life, one who had retained his strength as he grew old. He was greatly missed by the people of Madison, where he had lived so long, and the press of the State deplored the loss of its oldest representative and one of its most honored and influential leaders.

JOHN D. DEFREES.

JOHN D. DEFREES was born at Sparta, Tennessee, November 10, 1810. He attended a country school when a boy, and obtained a fair education, and when thirteen years old went into a printing office to learn "the art preservative of all arts." Subsequently he emigrated to Ohio, and entered the law office of the late Governor Corwin, at Lebanon, as a student. After being admitted to the bar he removed to South Bend, Indiana, and opened an office for the practice of his profession. He took an interest in public affairs, and was elected to the State Senate from his district, becoming one of the leading members of that body. On the resignation of Jesse D. Bright, then Lieutenant-Governor of the State, to take his seat in the Senate of the United States, there was a severe struggle over the election of a President of the Senate. The two parties—Whig and Democratic—were equally divided in the Senate, and many fruitless ballots were had for a presiding officer of that body. The Democrats claimed the office on the ground that the State was Democratic on a popular vote, and were answered by the Whigs that if they wished a Democratic presiding officer they should not have elected Mr. Bright to the United States Senate. After wrangling several days over the matter, each party met in caucus to determine what to do. The Democrats made a list of ten Senators and sent it to the Whigs, with the word that the selection of any one of the ten would be satisfactory to them, when Mr. Defrees, on the part of the Whigs, made a counter proposition, naming the twenty-five Whig Senators, and saying the selection of any one of the twenty-five would be acquiesced in by his political friends. The matter was finally settled by a compromise. Godlove S. Orth, Whig, was elected President, with the agreement that he should resign on the last day of the session, which he did, and James G. Read, Democrat, was elected in his place. This contest and settlement were mainly managed by Mr. Defrees for the Whigs.

In February, 1846, while a member of the State Senate, Mr. Defrees bought the *Indianapolis Journal* and became its editor. He controlled its columns until the fall of 1854, when he sold the paper and retired from newspaper work. In July, 1855, Mr. Defrees, in connection with other gentlemen, established the Central Bank, and for some time he was its president. In 1858 he was a candidate for nomination for Congress in the Indianapolis district. His competitors were William Sheets, Albert G. Porter, and, for a time, Jonathan W. Gordon, who, however, withdrew from the contest before the convention was held. Mr. Porter was nominated and elected, beating Martin M. Ray, Esq.

In July, 1859, Mr. Defrees started the *Atlas*, a daily paper, and continued in its control until March, 1861, when it was absorbed by the *Journal*. The *Atlas* favored the nomination of Edward Bates, of Missouri, for the presidency, and its editor was Mr. Bates's principal manager in Indiana. The plan was to nominate Mr. Bates on his record, without a platform, a scheme which proved successful in 1848 in the election of General Taylor. Early in 1861 President Lincoln appointed Mr. Defrees Government Printer, in the place of Cornelius Wendell, who had long held the office. Mr. Defrees did not dispense the patronage of his office to the satisfaction of the Republican members of Congress, and in 1869 Congress passed a law making the office of Government Printer elective by the Senate. The Senate elected A. M. Clapp, then of the *Buffalo Express*, to the place, and Mr. Defrees became a private citizen. There had been ill feeling between Senator Morton and Mr. Defrees for a long time, which was deepened on account of this election, and the estrangement lasted while the Senator lived. For many years Mr. Defrees and Hon. Schuyler Colfax had been particular friends. Mr. Defrees aided Mr. Colfax in his canvass for the Republican nomination for the vice-presidency in 1868, and was as influential in securing it as any other man. When the law was pending in Congress to make the office of Public Printer elective Mr. Defrees appealed to Mr. Colfax to use his influence against it, and was refused. This caused an estrangement between these gentlemen which lasted until about the time of the scandal of the Credit Mobilier. As is known, Mr. Colfax was sought to be implicated in that matter, but Mr. Defrees believed him innocent, and publicly defended him. This coming to the knowledge of Mr. Colfax he sought Mr. Defrees and offered him his hand, which was taken, and ever afterward they were friends.

In 1872 Mr. Defrees supported Horace Greeley for the presidency. He was originally a Whig and afterward a Republican, and had nothing in common with the Democracy. It is no wonder, then, that when the Liberal Republican party disbanded, Mr. Defrees should have resumed his former party affiliations. In 1876 Mr. Defrees supported General Hayes for President, and soon after that gentleman was inducted into office was appointed to his old post as Government Printer, Congress having in the meantime repealed the law making the office elective. He continued to discharge the duties of Government Printer until the 1st of April, 1882, when he resigned the office, and again became a private citizen.

For many years Mr. Defrees was one of the most influential politicians in Indiana. In 1852 he was chairman of the Whig State Central Committee, and in 1856 he filled the same position for the Republicans. His conduct of the canvass of 1856 was pretty freely criticised at the time, and in the light of future events it was faulty, but at the time it had the approbation of the leading Republicans of the State. Southern Indiana was not actively canvassed for Fremont, and many of the border counties gave him but a meager vote. Had Republican speakers gone into these Democratic strongholds and discussed the questions at issue, it is quite certain that the anti-Democratic vote would have been cast for Fremont and not been thrown away on Fillmore, as a large portion of it was. But it is much easier to know a thing after it has transpired than when it is pending. Mr. Defrees's mistake in managing the canvass of 1856 was one the most astute politician might have made.

Since March, 1861, Mr. Defrees did not reside in Indiana. His home was at Washington and Berkeley Springs, Virginia.

When in practice Mr. Defrees was a good lawyer. He was not a strong speaker, but he could talk sensibly and well. He was a writer of very considerable power, and he will be best remembered by the work he did with his pen. In his day he was one of the prominent men of the State, and as the conductor of a leading public journal he exercised great influence in shaping public sentiment.

Mr. Defrees died at his home in Berkeley Springs, Virginia, October 19, 1882. The next day S. P. Rounds, Mr. Defrees's successor in the office of Public Printer, issued an order, that on account of Mr. Defrees's death, "The flag will be placed at half-mast, and the office and all its branches will be closed on the day of the funeral."

On the 21st of October the remains of Mr. Defrees reached Indianapolis, and on the afternoon of that day were taken to Crown Hill and buried. The funeral services were conducted by Rev. S. T. Gillette, and Messrs. John Lee Mothershead, John, Milton and David Morris and Morris Ross, all nephews of the deceased, acted as pall bearers. The grave was lined with twigs of cedar, and the fresh earth from the grave was covered with the same material. In such a receptacle was placed all that was mortal of one who made a deep impress upon the politics and legislation of Indiana.

FREEMASONRY IN INDIANA.

HISTORICAL SKETCH FROM THE ORGANIZATION OF THE GRAND
LODGE TO THE BUILDING OF THE SECOND GRAND TEMPLE.

MASONRY is one of the oldest if not the very oldest organized
body of men existing in the world. Its history is found in the
earliest records. It dates away back to the cradle of the race
and the morning of recorded time. Its legends extend beyond
the historic age. It has raked up in its ashes the essence of all
sciences and of all human history. It is common to all nations
and to all religions. Its altars now extend around the world.
Its light shines in all lands. Its brotherhood is the most complete of any in the world. It unites in one body men of all
countries, sects and opinions. It contains in its archives the
condensed wisdom of all time. The intelligent Mason stands
upon the highest eminence of human observation. He finds in
his cosmos the histories of all nations, ages and religions. He
finds the teachings of the order in the Vedas of Hindostan, in
the sacred books of Confucius and Boodah, in the Avesta of
Zoroaster, in the ancient scrolls and hieroglyphics of Egypt, in
the writings of the prophets and sages of Judea, in the beautiful and enduring philosophies of Socrates, Plato and Aristotle, in
the teachings of Jesus and Mohammed, in the laws and religion
of Rome, and in the myths and legends of the Scandinavian
and Teutonic races. He traces the footsteps of our ancient
brethren from the cradle of the seven great races in Bactriana,
in Central Asia, among the Judean hills about Jerusalem, among
the fallen columns and broken arches of ruined cities and deso-
lated empires, around the pyramids and the Sphinx, throughout

the marble wilderness of Greece, and among the mouldering temples of Roman power. Wherever man has wandered, suffered and died there he finds the footprints of Masonry and the grave of a brother. From all these sources he culls lessons of wisdom. While Masonry embraces in its tenets the fundamental teachings of the Christian religion, as well as of all other great religions, it does not profess to be a religious institution. It regards the whole human species as one family, the children of one Great Parent, and strives to do good to all men without distinction. It visits the sick and the afflicted. It buries the dead with the honors of the order. It protects and provides for the widows and the orphans, and spreads the broad mantle of its charity over the weaknesses, frailties and errors of mankind. Its mission is love and good works. It seeks to do good to all and harm to none. Many of the greatest and best of men whose names brighten the pages of history, and whose good deeds have rendered them immortal, were members of the order. It numbers more than half a million men in the United States, and over 27,000 in the State of Indiana. Many of the best men in every town or city in this State are proud to say that they are members of this ancient and honorable order.

The early settlers of Indiana organized Masonic lodges and held their meetings in the log cabins of the wilderness. The first lodges were organized at Vincennes, Lawrenceburg, Vevay, Rising Sun, Madison, Charlestown, Brookville, Salem and Corydon. These lodges received their dispensations or charters from Ohio or Kentucky. On the 3d day of December, A. D. 1817, delegates from these various lodges met at the old town of Corydon to make arrangements for organizing a Grand Lodge for the Territory of Indiana. Brother William Hacker, who compiled the proceedings of this meeting and many others that followed it, wisely says:

"The opinions and acts of the far-seeing and true-hearted men of the past, who had but the good of Masonry at heart, constitute landmarks for the present generation; and the volume which contains their transactions should be the study of those who are guiding the destinies of the order now."

But eleven Masons were present at this meeting. They laid

the foundation of the Grand Lodge and what has indeed become a *grand* body in Indiana. They have all passed to the Grand Lodge above, but their names will ever be commemorated as the founders of Masonry in Indiana. Some of them have children and grandchildren now prominent members of the fraternity. The eleven were General W. Johnston, S. C. Stevens, Abel C. Pepper, Christopher Harrison, Henry P. Thornton, Joseph Bartholomew, John Miller, Davis Floyd, Hezekiah B. Hull, James Dill and A. Buckner. These delegates addressed a communication to the Grand Lodges of Ohio and Kentucky, expressing their desire to sever their connection with their mother lodges as soon as a Grand Lodge could be organized in Indiana. This body adjourned to meet at Madison on the 12th day of January, 1818. Delegates from the various lodges of the State met pursuant to this adjournment, and were in session four days. The Grand Lodge of Indiana was duly organized, and the following officers were elected: M. W. Alexander Buckner, Grand Master; R. W. Alexander A. Meek, Deputy Grand Warden; W. John Tipton, Senior Grand Warden; W. Marston G. Clark, Junior Grand Warden; W. Samuel C. Tate, Grand Treasurer; W. Henry P. Thornton, Grand Secretary; W. Jeremiah Sullivan, Grand Orator; W. Isaac Howk, Grand Senior Deacon; W. Jonathan Woodbury, Grand Junior Deacon; W. Nicholas D. Grover, Grand Pursuivant; W. Alexander McCrosky, Grand Steward and Tyler. A constitution was then adopted for the government of the Grand Lodge, most of which still remains in force. The account of expenses of this Grand Lodge shows the spirit of economy that prevailed in those early days. The aggregate expenses were $52.62½. It appears by the bill of expenses that the one-half cent was for "refreshments, etc." The following resolution was adopted:

"*Resolved*, That a committee be appointed, whose duty it shall be to prepare and forward an address to the several Grand Lodges within the United States, from this Grand Lodge, explanatory of their reasons for forming a Grand Lodge in the State of Indiana, and requesting of them a reciprocation of correspondence and communications."

The Grand Lodge was now fairly organized. Sixty-six years

have elapsed since that time. This long period must be briefly sketched. September 14, 1818, the Grand Lodge met at Charlestown. The ordinary business was transacted, and Alexander A. Meek was elected Grand Master. In 1819 the Grand Lodge met at Madison; the same Grand Master was re-elected. The expenses of the communication amounted to $16.00, and the Grand Lodge had in the possession of its various officers $316.50.

During the next five years the Grand Lodge met at Jeffersonville, Corydon, Madison and Salem. John Tipton, John Sheets, Jonathan Jennings and Marston G. Clark served during this period as Grand Masters. The largest number of lodges represented at the annual communications during this period was twenty-eight. At the communication held at Corydon in 1822 a communication was presented of peculiar interest. It was from the Hon. Henry Clay, of Kentucky, John Marshall, of Virginia, and other prominent Masons and statesmen. The following appears in the records of the Grand Lodge proceedings of that year:

"The Grand Secretary presented the following communications on the subject of organizing a General Grand Lodge of the United States: 'Masonic Notice—Those members of Congress who belong to the Masonic fraternity, and those visitors of the city who are or have been members of any State Grand Lodge, are respectfully invited to attend a meeting to be held in the Senate chamber this evening, at 7 o'clock, to take into consideration matters of general interest to the Masonic institution.' "*March 9, 1822.*"

Pursuant to the above notice published in the *National Intelligencer* (printed in the city of Washington), a number of members of the Society of Free Masons from various parts of the United States, composed of members of Congress and strangers, assembled at the capitol in the city of Washington, March 9, 1822. Brother Thomas R. Ross, a member of Congress from the State of Ohio, was appointed chairman; and Brother William Darlington, member of Congress from Pennsylvania, Secretary. Much conversation took place on the expediency of the general objects of this meeting; various propositions were submitted; and several brethren offered their views at large. Finally, the following resolutions, offered by Brother Henry Clay, of Kentucky, were adopted unanimously:

"*Resolved*, That in the opinion of this meeting it is expedient for the general interests of Free Masonry to constitute a General Grand Lodge of the United States.

"*Resolved*, That it be proposed to the several Grand Lodges in the United States to take the subject into their serious consideration at their next annual communications; and that if they approve of the formation of a General Grand Lodge, it be recommended to them to appoint one or more delegates, to assemble in the city of Washington on the second Monday of February next, to agree on the organization of such a Grand Lodge."

Other resolutions follow and a long address written by Henry Clay, the eloquent orator and classical scholar, who so often thrilled the hearts of his countrymen in later years. It is a powerful argument in favor of a General Grand Lodge of the United States. The following paragraph quoted from it shows its spirit:

" These reflections, drawn from the external circumstances of Masonry, are strengthened by the consideration of its intrinsic nature. Its foundation is fixed in the social feelings of the best principles of the human mind. Its maxims are the lessons of virtue reduced to their practical application. It stands opposed to sordidness, to jealousy or revengeful temper; to all the selfish and malevolent passions; it coincides with the highest motives of patriotism, the most expanded philanthropy; and concentrates all its precepts in reverence to a Divine Creator and good will to man."

In another part of this address Mr. Clay says: " The United States are supposed to contain 80,000 Free Masons. They are generally in the vigor of manhood, and capable of much active usefulness." It is needless to say the suggestions of Clay and his associates were not adopted by the various Grand Lodges, and no General Grand Lodge of Masons for the United States has yet been formed. More than fifty years ago the " Mill-boy of the Slashes " had left his old home at Hanover, Virginia, and had become " Harry of the West." His clarion voice rang out through the Western forests, rousing his countrymen as no one before had done. In the halls of Congress he spoke for the rights of man with a power that thrilled the nation. If his wise suggestions regarding Masonry had been adopted it is reasonable to suppose the fraternity would have been strengthened and benefited. His remains have long rested in his tomb at Lexington, but his eloquent words have not yet faded from the memory of his friends and his brethren. In 1826 the Grand Lodge met at Salem, a little town nestled among the hills of Washington county. Thirty-two lodges were represented, covering a territory extending from the Ohio river to the Wabash. Then there was not a railroad in the State, and no public conveyance between the towns where lodges were located. Some of the delegates rode more than a hundred miles on horseback. We can see in imagination the sturdy yeomen assembled in a log cabin, the grand old primeval forest about them, and the wolves for sentinels. Less than four hundred Masons were then represented by all the lodges of the State. The records show that the Grand Lodge met at Corydon in 1817, 1821 and 1822; at Madison in 1818, 1819, 1823 and 1824; at Salem in 1825, 1826, 1827 and 1832; at Vincennes in 1831, and there was an adjourned meeting at Charlestown in 1818. During the first ten years of the existence of the Grand Lodge of Indiana, Indianapolis was too insignificant a town to be recognized by the Grand Lodge. The first meeting of the Grand Lodge in that city was on the 28th day of November, 1828. The record does not show the number of lodges represented. From the best information accessible it appears that there were about thirty lodges and about four hundred Masons in the State. Indianapolis was in the midst of a dense wilderness, with less than a thousand inhabitants. Fifty-four years have passed; a great change has taken place. It has become a city of nearly one hundred thousand inhabitants, with a system of railroads binding it to all parts of the country, bringing to and carrying from it the products of all lands. In place of the rude hovel, where the delegates of a few feeble lodges assembled, is the Grand Masonic

Temple. Where four or five hundred Masons were represented then, more than twenty-eight thousand are represented now. The city alone contains more than twice as many Masons as were in the State when the first Grand Lodge met at Indianapolis. For the next twenty years the Grand Lodge met at Indianapolis. It had a steady and prosperous growth. During this period we find nothing of especial interest except what is shown in the biographical notices in this article, with the exception of the preliminary steps which were taken for the erection of the Grand Lodge Hall, now known as

" THE OLD MASONIC HALL."

At the annual communication of the Grand Lodge of the most ancient and honorable fraternity of Free and Accepted Masons for the State of Indiana, begun and held at Indianapolis, on Monday, the 24th day of May, Anno Lucis, five thousand eight hundred and forty-seven, Anno Domini, one thousand eight hundred and forty-seven, the following proceedings were had in relation to the purchase of a site and the erection of a Grand Lodge Hall, to-wit: On motion of Brother William Sheets, of Indianapolis, *Resolved*, That a committee of five on the part of this Grand Lodge, and five to be appointed on the part of the Grand Chapter of Indiana, now in session, report at their earliest convenience, as to the expediency of procuring a site in this city for a Grand Masonic Hall. *Resolved*, That the Grand Secretary furnish a copy of the foregoing resolution to the Grand Chapter. The M. W. Grand Master laid before the Grand Lodge the following communication:

" HALL OF GRAND CHAPTER OF
" STATE OF INDIANA, May 27, A. L. 5847.

" *To the M. W. Grand Lodge of Indiana:*

" I am instructed to inform you that the Grand Chapter concur in the resolution providing for the appointment of a committee to confer with a similar committee appointed by your body on the expediency of procuring a site in this city for a Grand Masonic Hall, and have appointed Companions Taylor, Colestock, Deming, Sopris and King the committee on the part of this Grand Chapter. Respectfully,

" WILLIAM SULLIVAN, G. S."

Brother Sheets, from the committee on that subject, made the following report:

"The committee to which was referred the resolution directing them, in conjunction with a committee from the Grand Chapter, to inquire into the expediency of procuring a site for a Grand Masonic Hall in this city, and if, in their opinion, such a site should be secured, to recommend such location as in their judgment promises the most revenue to the institution in the way of rent, respectfully report that they have met the committee of the Grand Chapter, and, after a full investigation of the first branch of the resolution, are unanimously of the opinion that the Grand Lodge ought no longer to delay the procuring of a site for the erection of a hall. The committee, after coming to this conclusion, then took into consideration the second branch of the resolution, the selection of a site. The committee weighed the subject in all its bearings, as connected with the present and prospective business of this city, are alike unanimously of the opinion that such site should be located on Washington street, as the only one that promises a fair interest upon the investment in the way of rent. They are also clearly of the opinion, from the past history of the city, as well as facts intimately and inseparably connected with its future growth, that the increase and spread of business will greatly preponderate in the direction west from the present center of business. This opinion is based partially upon the fact that a large majority of the produce business of the country will flow into the city from that direction, and from the fact that all the manufacturing power is on the western border of the city, no small element, as they conceive, in the future growth of the place. For these reasons the committee directed their attention in the selection of a site to that part of the city, and recommended, without a dissenting voice, the purchase at once of lots Nos. 7 and 8, in square 67, fronting 63 feet on Washington street, running south on Tennessee street 350 feet to Kentucky avenue, thence on said avenue 121 feet. This property can be had now on very advantageous terms, the whole for $4,200, one thousand in hand and the balance in four equal annual instalments with 6 per centum interest. The committee believe this is as good an investment of the surplus funds of the lodge as could be made.

" The committee have learned that there will be, at the close of the present meeting, a surplus of funds on hand amounting to over a thousand dollars, nearly or quite enough to make the first payment, as it is likely the payment of one-fourth in hand will be received. The committee recommend that funds be raised by stock subscription for the payment of the remainder of the purchase money and for the erection of a hall, the cost of which shall not exceed $10,000, with the right reserved to the Grand Lodge of sinking or purchasing at pleasure the individual stock at par, and they recommend that the Grand Lodge subscribe for stock equal to the advanced payment on the lot, and for the probable annual net revenue of the lodge, and the subordinate lodges such amount as their means might warrant; the Grand Chapter and subordinate chapters such amount, in like manner, as they may think fit, and individual brethren in the same way; and that so soon as a sufficient amount has been thus realized to erect and enclose the building, to have it done, so as to bring the store-rooms on the first floor into use. They recommend that the second story be prepared for a hall suitable for celebrations, concerts, town meetings, etc., and the third story for two halls, one for the Grand Lodge and the other for the Grand Chapter. If this plan should be adopted, a house can be erected without involving the Grand Lodge or any subordinate lodge in a dollar of debt. We therefore recommend the adoption of the following resolutions, viz:

" *Resolved*, That three commissioners be appointed to make the purchase for the Grand Lodge of the lots named in said report; that they procure subscriptions of stock upon the plan proposed; that they invite the presentation of plans for an edifice not to cost exceeding $10,000; that they procure materials, to the extent that the stock subscription will warrant, so as to commence the building early in the spring of 1848, and that said commissioners adopt such plans as, in their judgment, combine in the greatest degree neatness of exterior, cheapness of construction and internal convenience.

"*Resolved*, That the Grand Secretary be directed to subscribe stock to the amount of the funds on hand at the close of the

32

present meeting, and for such additional sum as the annual receipts will meet.

"*Resolved*, That the Grand Treasurer pay to the said commissioners, when called upon, any funds in his hands in the way of bank stock, ready money or otherwise.

"All of which is respectfully submitted.

" GEO. W. WHITMAN,

" WM. SHEETS,

" JOHN TAYLOR,

" JOSEPH ROSEMAN,

" J. S. FREEMAN,

" *Committee on part of Grand Lodge.*

" R. SOPRIS,

" ISAAC BARTLETT,

" FRANCIS KING,

" HENRY COLESTOCK,

" E. DEMING,

" *Committee on part of Grand Chapter.*"

The hall was commenced during the year of Masonry 5848, and was constructed in conformity to plans furnished by Brother Joseph Willis, architect, Indianapolis. The corner-stone was laid on the 25th day of October, Anno Lucis, 5848, A. D. 1848, in the presence of the Grand Lodge and before the assembled craft of the State, a large body of the Independent Order of Odd Fellows of Indianapolis, the Grand Division of the Sons of Temperance of Indiana, all in their appropriate jewels and regalia, and a numerous concourse of citizens, by the Most Worshipful Elizur Deming, Grand Master of Masons in Indiana.

There were present: Officers of the Grand Lodge of Indiana—Most Worshipful Elizur Deming, Grand Master; Right Worshipful G. W. Whitman, Deputy Grand Master; Right Worshipful John W. Spencer, Senior Grand Warden; Right Worshipful S. P. Anthony, Junior Grand Warden; Right Worshipful Rev. John W. Sullivan, Grand Chaplain; Right Worshipful Austin W. Morris, Grand Secretary; Right Worshipful Charles Fisher, Grand Treasurer; Brother William Fogg, Senior Grand Deacon; Brother William N. Doughty, Junior

Grand Deacon ; Brother Charles I. Hand, Grand Steward and Tyler. Building committee, William Sheets, James Whitcomb, Austin W. Morris. Architect, Joseph Willis.

The Grand Secretary then read the following schedule of deposits :

"BRETHREN—There will be deposited in the cavity of the corner-stone, now about to be laid, as follows, viz : The Holy Bible, square and compass, the Master's mallet, the twenty-four-inch rule, three lights, the globes, the letter G, the plumb and level, a lamb-skin apron, a sprig of evergreen, the trowel, sword, spade and coffin, the constitution and by-laws of the Most Worshipful Grand Lodge of Indiana, the printed minutes of the proceedings of the Grand Lodge and Grand Chapter of this State, of their respective sessions, held in May, 1848. An abstract from the minutes of the several Grand Lodges of the respective States for 1848, showing the names of officers, time and place of meeting, and names and number of subordinate lodges. A printed copy of the proceedings of the last General Royal Arch Chapter and General Grand Encampment of Knights Templar of the United States, held at Columbus, Ohio, in 1847. A copy of the *Free Masons' Magazine*, edited by Brother C. W. Moore, of Boston. A copy of the last *Masonic Review*, edited by Brother Cornelius Moore, of Cincinnati. A copy of the last newspapers issued at Indianapolis. Several pieces of coin of the United States of America, dated in 1848. A scroll containing the names, organization and present condition of the several churches in Indianapolis. A scroll containing the names, organization and present condition of the several divisions of the Sons of Temperance in Indianapolis. A scroll containing the date of organization, names of officers, and present condition of Sigourney Union of the Daughters of Temperance in Indianapolis. A scroll containing the date of organization, names of officers, number of members of Center Lodge of I. O. O. Fellows of Indianapolis."

AN ORIGINAL ODE FROM MRS. BOLTON.

The following original ode, prepared for the occasion by Mrs. Sarah T. Bolton, of Indianapolis, was sung by the breth-

ren and citizens, to the tune of " Hail to the Chief," led by
Mr. Willard and others of the choir of the Second Presbyterian
Church :

" ODE.

" Sons of a glorious order anointed,
   To cherish for ages the ark of the Lord,
Wearing the mystical badges appointed,
   Come to the temple with sweetest accord.
     Come lay the corner-stone,
     Asking the Lord to own
Labors that tend to His glory and praise ;
     Long may this mercy seat,
     Where angels' pinions meet,
Rest in the beautiful temple ye raise.

" Brothers united, to you it is given,
   To lighten the woes of a sin-blighted world,
Far o'er the earth, on the free winds of heaven,
   Now let your banners of love be unfurled.
     Write there the blessed three,
     Faith, hope and charity,
Names that shall live through the cycle of time ;
     Write them on every heart,
     Make them your guide and chart
Over life's sea to the haven sublime.

" Go forth, befriending the wayweary stranger,
   Bright'ning the pathway that sorrow hath crossed,
Strength'ning the weak in the dark hour of danger,
   Clothing the naked and seeking the lost.
     Opening the prison door,
     Feeding the starving poor,
Chiding the evil, approving the just,
     Drying the widow's tears,
     Soothing the orphan's fears,
Great is your mission, ' in God is your trust.'

" Go, in the spirit of Him who is holy,
   Gladden the wastes and the by-ways of earth,
Visit the homes of the wretched and lowly,
   Bringing relief to the desolate hearth.
     Bind up the broken heart,
     Joy to the sad impart,
Stay the oppressor and strengthen the just ;
     Freely do ye receive,
     Freely to others give,
Great is your mission, ' in God is your trust.'

"Go forth with ardor and hope undiminished,
   Ever be zealous and faithful and true,
  Still, till the labor appointed is finished,
   Do with your might what your hands find to do.
     Narrow the way and strait,
     Is heaven's guarded gate,
   Leading the soul to the regions of love ;
     Then with the spotless throng,
     Swelling the triumph song,
  May you be found in the Grand Lodge above."

On the evening of the 24th day of May, 1850, the members of the Grand Chapter and a large number of citizens and strangers met in one of the city churches for the purpose of presenting to Mrs. Bolton the silver cup voted her by the Grand Chapter for the beautiful ode copied above. The presentation speech was made by Judge Morrison, and was in the following words:

" MRS. BOLTON—The Grand Chapter of Indiana are gratified to be permitted thus publicly to assure you of their warm personal esteem and high appreciation of your poetic merits, but especially do they congratulate themselves that the opportunity thus afforded enables them, in the name of Ancient Free Masonry, to thank you for your noble and disinterested vindication of the principles of the Order. In the ancient and appropriate symbolic ceremony of laying the corner-stone of the Grand Masonic Hall of Indiana, you, madam, were so kind and intrepid as to voluntarily come forward, in the face of wide-spread and deep-rooted prejudice, to animate us in the work then just begun. And when the edifice shall be completed, as we trust it soon will be, we can never look upon its imposing and symmetrical proportions, looming out on the blue arch of heaven—a monument of the taste and liberality of the Masonic fraternity of Indiana—without associating a recollection of the beautiful and soul-inspiring ode chanted at the laying of the corner-stone. To speak of the poetic excellencies of the ode is not, of course, the object of this manifestation; that has been done by those more competent to the work than the individual addressing you. Nor, madam, do your claims to high poetic merit rest alone, or even mainly, on this or any other single production. Far from it. Many, very many gems, rich and rare, are enwreathed in your coronet of song ; and, ever and anon, another and another brilliant is made to flash upon the eye of an admiring public.

If, therefore, you have been emulous of fame, you must feel that you have already attained a most enviable niche in her temple. As Masons, madam, we attach peculiar value to the signal service done our order by this free-will offering of your muse, for we so consider it. I repeat the sentiment—we do consider it a most noble, glowing and truthful defense of the cardinal principles of ancient Free Masonry ; principles, alas, most grievously maligned and misrepresented because they are not generally understood. Penetrated, therefore, with a due sense of the obligations under which you had brought the whole Masonic fraternity, the Grand Chapter, at its last annual meeting, unanimously adopted the following resolutions :

" '*Resolved unanimously*, That the thanks of this Grand Chapter are due to Mrs. Sarah T. Bolton, of Indianapolis, for the beautiful Masonic ode composed by her, which was sung on the occasion of laying the corner-stone of the Grand Masonic Hall, in said city, on the 25th day of October last.

" '*Resolved unanimously*, That, as a token of the high regard which the members of the Grand Chapter entertain for the character of Mrs. Bolton, and to manifest their appreciation of her merits as a poetess, the Grand Chapter will present for her acceptance a silver cup with an appropriate device and inscription.

" '*Resolved*, That a committee be appointed to carry these resolutions into effect, and that a copy of the resolutions, under the seal of the Grand Chapter, be furnished Mrs. Bolton with the presentation.

"And now, madam, as the honored organ of the Grand Chapter, in their name and presence, I present for your acceptance this cup, the main device of which, you will notice, is the Royal Arch, and under which, and between its sustaining columns, is this inscription :

"'THE GRAND CHAPTER OF THE STATE OF INDIANA,

TO

MRS. SARAH T. BOLTON,

As a token of acknowledgment for her excellent Masonic ode

ON THE

Laying of the corner-stone of the Grand Masonic Hall,

At Indianapolis,

October 25, A. D. 1848; A. L. 5848.'

" The minor device represents a craftsman in the act of adjusting a corner-stone to its proper place. The inscription is one quite familiar to you, being three lines from your own inspiring ode :

" 'Come, lay the corner-stone,
Asking the Lord to own
Labors that tend to his glory and praise.'

" This token, Mrs. Bolton, you will please receive as an acknowledgment, by Masons, of a debt that neither time nor circumstances will cancel or efface."

Mrs. Bolton replied :

" I have no language to express my sense of the honor conferred on me by the Grand Chapter of Indiana in the presentation of this beautiful cup ; but let me assure that honorable body, through you, sir, that I will treasure it up with the proudest care, and that it will be to me, in future years, the nucleus of a thousand bright and cherished recollections. The ode, in consideration of which it is presented, was but the simple and spontaneous outpouring of a heart alive to the dictates of humanity, a heart well taught in the school of adversity to appreciate human aid and human sympathy. When a little child on my mother's knee, I listened to many a story of the stranger cared for, the widow relieved, and the orphan cherished by Masonic charity, I learned to love and honor your noble and venerable institution. The seed then sown has ripened with my years, and I now believe that Free Masonry is the sister of Christianity. Both have gone out into the wastes and by-ways of earth, ' giving beauty for ashes, the oil of joy for mourning, and the garment of praise for the spirit of heaviness.' Both have been subjected to the ordeal of persecution, and both, like the Hebrew children, came forth unscathed by the furnace and the flame. When, bowed and broken-hearted, our first parents were driven from the Garden of Eden, to reap the bitter fruits of disobedience, the spirit of Free Masonry was commissioned, in heaven, to bless and cheer them in their loneliness. She has fed the hungry, reclaimed the wandering, ministered consolation by the bedside of the dying, and brightened the pathway of the bereaved and desolate.   Mortals have witnessed her labors of love, and angels have recorded her annals in the archives of eternity.   When the lion shall lie down with the lamb, when the new heavens and the new earth are created, then, and not till then, may she fold her white wings on her spotless bosom, and proclaim that her mission is accomplished.''

In the spring of 1851 the Grand Lodge Hall was dedicated to the purposes for which it was erected.   The editor of the *Masonic Review*, who was present, thus writes of the dedication :

"The recent session of the Grand Lodge was, in some respects, the most interesting one ever held in the State.   The Grand Hall, to complete which the members had been toiling for years, was finished, and at the annual meeting was to be dedicated in solemn form.   A great crowd had assembled to witness the imposing ceremonies, and the craft especially were represented by delegates from every part of the State.   We need not describe the procession and the ceremonies, for these things are familiar to our readers ; it is enough to say that the Grand Master, Dr. Deming, officiated on the occasion, and with his usual skill and ability.   The great hall of the building was filled to overflowing.   Age and childhood were commingled in that throng, man in his rugged strength, and woman in her loveliness and purity.   The Governors of Indiana and Ohio were both in the throng ; judges and officers of State, with representatives from professional, mechanical and agricultural lives, were all present to give eclat to the occasion and honor the completion of the noble work.   The Rev. Brother Lynch delivered an address that was well received, and gave general satisfaction to the crowded assembly.   The song written expressly for the occasion by Mrs. Bolton, the poetess of Indiana, was sung with fine effect. Mrs. Bolton was in the audience, and her daughter, a beautiful girl of ' sweet sixteen,' was one of the leading singers in the choir.   It is right that the mother should be a poetess and the daughter a musician.   Indiana may be proud of her gifted and accomplished daughters.   The following is the poem referred to :

"DEDICATION ODE.

" Brothers, rejoice ! for our task is completed,
  After the pattern appointed of yore;
Let the reward to the craftsmen be meted,
  While, with thanksgiving, we bow and adore,
    Low at the feet of Him,
    Throned where the seraphim
And the archangels sing anthems of praise,
    Born of the lowly dust,
    Wanting in faith and trust,
How shall we worship Thee, Ancient of Days.

Darkly we grope through the light of being,
  Weary we wait for the day dawning bright;
Father omnific, supreme and all-seeing,
  Come to Thy temple and fill it with light.
    Write here Thy great name,
    Kindle the altar flame.
Sacred to Thee in the most holy place;
    And where the cherubs fling
    Light from each golden wing,
Leave us the Ark with its symbols of grace.

" Show us the Truth and the pathway of duty;
  Help us to lift up our standard sublime,
Till earth is restored to the Order and Beauty
  Lost in the shadowless morning of time.
    Teach us to sow the seed
    Of many a noble deed;
Make us determined, unflinching and strong—
    Armed with the sword of right,
    Dauntless amid the fight,
Help us to Level the bulwarks of wrong.

" Prompt us to labor, as Thou hast directed,
  On the foundation laid sure in the past,
And may 'the stone which the builders rejected'
  Crown our endeavors with glory at last.
    Then, at the eventide,
    Laying the Square aside,
May we look calmly on life's setting sun;
    And, at the mercy seat,
    Where ransomed spirits meet,
Hear from the Master the plaudit, 'well done.'"

The building was 63 feet front on Washington street by 110 feet deep on Tennessee street, and three stories high. It was built in the Grecian Doric order of architecture, with a portico in front 11 feet deep, extending across the entire front. The entablature was supported by six Doric columns, 4¼ feet in diameter, and 33 feet high; said columns commencing on a platform on a level with the second story floor. The sides and rear end were finished with pilaster or antæ the same height of the columns, 4 feet face and projecting 9 inches, and the whole building crowned with a heavy Doric entablature. The roof was covered with composition, and the whole external surface of the walls with stucco, in imitation of cut stone, giving the building the appearance of a cut stone edifice. The first or basement story was 11 feet high in the clear, and was divided into three store-rooms, each 17 feet wide by 107 feet deep, and a passage and stairway 6 feet wide. The second story was in one large room for a public hall, 54 feet by 96 feet, and 20 feet high, finished with a paneled ceiling and cornice around the room in a good, neat style; the entrance to said room was from the front, on Washington street, with a private entrance from the rear end. The windows on the front end extended to the floor and opened out on the portico, and those on the west side, on Tennessee street, also extended to the floor and opened out to a handsome balcony, inclosed with a neat iron railing. The third story was appropriated exclusively to Masonic purposes, and consisted of a lodge room 37 by 60 feet, and a chapter room 26 by 60 feet, the ceilings 19 feet high. There were also several other rooms of different sizes, which were used for various purposes in the labor of the craft, and also an encampment room 32 by 50 feet, and 11 feet high.

The building was designed by J. Willis, architect, of Indianapolis. The lot on which it was erected is 63 feet front by 350 feet deep. Entire cost of lot and building was about $20,000.

GRAND MASTERS OF THE STATE.

The following is a list of the Grand Masters of Indiana in the order in which they served: In 1818, Alexander Buckner; in 1819, Alexander A. Meek; in 1820, John Tipton; in 1821–2, John Sheets; in 1823–4, Jonathan Jennings; in 1825, Marston G. Clark; in 1826, Isaac Howk; in 1827, Elihu Stout; in 1828, John Tipton; in 1829, Abel C. Pepper; in 1830, Philip Mason; in 1831, William Sheets; in 1832, Woodbridge Parker; in 1833,

Philip Mason; in 1834, Daniel Kelso; in 1835, John B. Martin; in 1836, James L. Hogan; in 1837, Caleb B. Smith; in 1838 to 1844, Philip Mason; in 1845, Isaac Bartlett; in 1846, Johnson Watts; in 1847 to 1850, Elizur Deming; in 1851–2–5–6–9 and 1860, A. C. Downey; in 1857-8, Solomon D. Bayliss; in 1861, Dr. Thomas R. Austin; in 1862, John B. Fravel; in 1863–4, William Hacker; in 1865–6–7, Harvey G. Hazelrigg; in 1868–9,1870–1, Martin H. Rice; in 1872–3, Christian Fetta; in 1874, Lucian A. Foote; in 1875, David McDonald.

John Tipton was a United States Senator; John Sheets, a paper manufacturer of Madison; Jonathan Jennings, a Governor of Indiana; Abel C. Pepper, United States Marshal of Indiana; William Sheets, a well-known merchant and manufacturer of Indianapolis; Daniel Kelso, a lawyer and politician of some prominence in Southern Indiana; Caleb B. Smith, a well-known statesman and jurist, whose remains are deposited in a vault at Crown Hill; A. C. Downey, a distinguished jurist; William Hacker, an historian of the order, and probably the best versed man in Indiana in the literature and jurisprudence of the craft; Martin H. Rice, who is a native of Vermont, and in early life followed the profession of a civil engineer. He was made a Mason at Plymouth, where he lived until a few years ago, when he became a resident of Indianapolis. He is the present editor and proprietor of the *Masonic Advocate*, a Masonic journal of great influence and popularity. He is in the prime of life, and bids fair to live many years to instruct his brethren in the principles of an order which four times honored him with its highest office. It will be observed that Judge Downey's term of service was longer than any of the other Grand Masters, it being for six years, and that next to him in length of service is Past Grand Master Rice, who was Grand Master for four years.

One of the best known Masons of Indiana, was Past Deputy Grand Master Caleb Schmidlapp, of Madison. Mr. Schmidlapp was born in Germany in 1798. He came to this country in 1818, and settled in Cincinnati, where, in 1825, he became a brother of the "Mystic Tie." During his residence in Cincinnati he had the pleasure of sitting in a lodge with the Marquis de Lafayette, who visited the Masonic lodge in the Queen City, when last among the people for whom he had done so much and who loved him so well. He emigrated to Indiana in 1830, and settled in Madison. He was first a member of the Grand Lodge in 1838, and was present at every meeting of that body since, until the convocation of 1875, which he did not attend on account of physical infirmities.

Past Deputy Grand Master M. D. Manson, of Crawfordsville, deserves honorable mention in the sketch of Indiana Masonry. He was a valiant soldier in the Mexican war and in the war of the rebellion, and is no less distinguished in peace than he was in war. He was once the candidate of his party for the office of Secretary of State, and was afterwards elected to Congress from his district. In 1872 he was elected Auditor of State and served his term. He is still living, and is in vigorous health.

Grand Secretary Morris—One of the best known and most influential Secretaries the Grand Lodge of Indiana ever had was Austin W. Morris, who died on the 21st day of June, 1851, while filling that office. He was a son of Morris Morris, and a brother of General Thomas A. Morris, of Indianapolis. He was born in Kentucky on the 9th day of August, 1804, and was in the prime of life when he died. He was much in public life, and every position he filled was honored and dignified by his actions. He left his impress upon the city of his adoption, and to-day his name is honored and revered by all who knew him. Particularly is his memory dear to his Masonic brethren who knew him as Grand Secretary of the highest body of their order and an active worker in all things appertaining to the good of Masonry. The following article, written by the editor of the *Masonic Review*, and published shortly after the death of this distinguished Mason, is so beautifully conceived and is such a truthful estimate of his character that we reproduce it just as it was written :

"We have known many excellent men in our day, men of rare piety and uniform, consistent goodness, but we have known few, if any, who combined so many traits of excellence, so good, so kind, so true, as the subject of this notice. We knew him well ; we had known him long, and we loved him. As Secretary of the Grand Lodge of Indiana, and as a prominent and leading Mason of that State, we have been familiar with his deportment as a Mason for a number of years. He was, in our eye, the beau ideal of a Free Mason. Frank, generous, firm, consistent, unwavering in his attachment to the principles of the order, determined and consistent in his efforts to preserve Masonry in its purity, and exhibiting in his own character a living illustration of what a Mason ought to be. He taught by example. Few, very few, have passed from this earth who left behind a more stainless reputation than Austin W. Morris."

The Grand Lodge of Indiana, in order to testify its appreciation of his services, and to commemorate his name, erected to his memory an imposing monument, and the visitor to-day will see at Crown Hill, the beautiful cemetery where rest so many of our friends and loved ones, a column upon which is engraved an epitome of the virtues of one whom the Masons of Indiana loved while living and whose memory they now revere.

James F. D. Lanier, the founder of the eminent banking house of Winslow, Lanier & Co., was Grand Secretary of the Grand Lodge of Indiana in 1830. At that time he lived at Madison and was a practicing lawyer. Subsequently he was president of the Madison Branch Bank, and went to New York in 1848 to start the banking house which now bears his name.

Judge Sullivan—Among the officers of the first Grand Lodge of Indiana were Jeremiah Sullivan and Nicholas D. Grover. The first was a native of Virginia, and came to Indiana when a young man. He settled at Madison, and remained a resident of that city until his death, which occurred a few years ago. He was dignified in his manners and of the strictest integrity. He was a lawyer by profession and attained great distinction. He was a Judge of the Supreme Court of Indiana for many years, and, with his associates, Judges Blackford and Dewey, constituted a legal triumvirate whose decisions were authority wherever they were known. He was the father of General Sullivan, who attained distinction in the war of the rebellion, and the grandfather of Thomas L. Sullivan, a promising young attorney of Indianapolis.

General Grover, who died at Logansport in 1875, was the last member of the first Grand Lodge of the State. He was originally from Madison, where he lived for many years, and was well known in both the southern and northern portions of Indiana.   He survived but a short time his friend and associate in the first Grand Lodge, John B. Rose, of Wabash, who died a few years ago.

Stephen C. Stevens, who represented his lodge at the first meeting of Masons at Corydon, was originally from Brookville, but many years ago removed to Madison.   He was a lawyer by profession, and at one time was a Judge of the Supreme Court of Indiana.   He was active in politics and a pioneer in the abolitionist movement.   In his old age misfortunes overtook him and his mind became clouded.   He was an inmate of the insane asylum at Indianapolis, where he died eleven years ago.

Francis King, who held the office of Grand Secretary from 1851 to 1868, a period of fourteen years, will be remembered by many of the readers of this sketch.   He was the private secretary of Governor Wright during the time he held that office, and as such came into contact with men from all parts of the State. After Governor Wright went out of office Mr. King was elected Treasurer of the city of Indianapolis and served for some time. Subsequently he was elected Grand Secretary of the Grand Lodge, and continued in office until he died.   He was an honest and conscientious man, and his death was much lamented by the citizens of Indianapolis, both Masons and non-Masons, as well as by the fraternity throughout the State.

The present Grand Treasurer of the Grand Lodge of Indiana is Charles Fisher.   No history of Masonry in this State would be complete without a biography of this worthy man.   It is believed that there is no other member of the fraternity in the United States who has seen so many years of continuous service as an officer of the order as Mr. Fisher.   In all his official life there has never been a breath of suspicion against his integrity.   He is a model citizen as well as a model Mason, and his example is worthy of emulation by all men who aspire to be good citizens and good Masons.   He was born in Dauphin county, Pennsylvania, on the 26th day of February, 1806, and came to Indianapolis in October, 1834, and has resided there continuously ever since.   He was made a Mason by Center Lodge on New Year's day, 1836.   In 1840 he was elected Secretary of his lodge, and held the office, without interruption, for thirty-five years. He was Recorder of Indianapolis Chapter of R. A. Masons from 1855 to December, 1882, Recorder of Raper Commandery from 1855 to December, 1877, Treasurer of the Grand Commandery since 1860, Treasurer of the Grand Council since 1861. In 1838 he was elected Grand Secretary of the Grand Lodge of Indiana and held the office one year. In 1848 he was elected Grand Treasurer of the Grand Lodge, and holds the office to-day, having been custodian of the funds of the Grand Lodge for thirty-six years. In addition to these offices, on the formation of the Masonic Mutual Benefit Society of Indiana, in 1870, Mr. Fisher was elected Treasurer and held the office fourteen years. As Treasurer of this society more than one million of dollars passed through his hands. His accounts have always been correctly kept, and there has never been a dollar of discrepancy between his books and those of the Secretary. Surely this is a record of which any man may be proud, and his many friends in Indiana—Masons and non-Masons—will be gratified to know that he bids fair to live many years to honor the position he fills so well.

John M. Bramwell, ex-Grand Secretary of the Grand Lodge of Indiana, is a native of Jefferson county, Indiana. He was a merchant's clerk for several years in Madison, and afterwards went into business on his own account. He was the first Auditor of Jefferson county, being elected in 1841, and serving until 1848, when he resigned and came to Indianapolis to engage in mercantile pursuits. He was made a Mason in Marion Lodge in 1850, and ever since has been an active and zealous worker. He was elected Grand Secretary of the Grand Lodge in 1868, and is the oldest active member of the Grand Lodge. At the meeting of the Grand Lodge, May, 1882, the Grand Secretary, W. H. Smythe, prepared a full list of all the officers of the Grand Lodge since its organization in 1818. From the recapitulation the following items of general interest are hereto appended:

"Since the organization of the Grand Lodge the following brethren have been elected and installed Grand Masters: Alexander Buckner, Alexander A. Meek, John Tipton, John Sheets, Jonathan Jennings, Marston H. Clark, Isaac Howk, Elihu Stout,

Abel C. Pepper, Philip Mason, William Sheets, Woodbridge
Parker, Daniel Kelso, John B. Martin, James L. Hagin, Caleb
B. Smith, Isaac Bartlett, Johnston Watts, Elizur Deming, Alexander C. Downey, Henry C. Lawrence, Sol. D. Bayless, Thomas
R. Austin, John B. Fravel, William Hacker, H. G. Hazelrigg,
Martin H. Rice, Christian Fetta, Lucien A. Foote, Daniel McDonald, Frank S. Devol, Andrew J. Hay, Robert Van Valzah, Ballamy S. Sutton.   By this it will be seen that but thirty-five brethren have had the honor of presiding over the Grand Lodge, and
of this number there are now living the following :   Thomas R.
Austin, A. C. Downey, William Hacker, Martin H. Rice, Christian Fetta, L. A. Foote, Daniel McDonald, Frank S. Devol, A.
J. Hay, Robert Van Valzah, Ballamy S. Sutton.

" Those who have served as Grand Secretaries are as follows :
Henry P. Thornton, William C. Keen, J. F. D. Lanier, A. W.
Morris, Daniel Kelso, A. W. Harrison, Charles Fisher, William
H. Martin, Francis King, William Hacker, John M. Bramwell,
William H. Smythe.   Of this number the following are now
living :   Charles Fisher, William Hacker, John M. Bramwell,
William H. Smythe."

The intelligent reader will observe that this list contains the
names of men as renowned in the State as they were in Masonry.   The lessons they had learned in the lodge room qualified them the better for the discharge of their duties as citizens.
A good Mason is always a good man.

MADISON FROM 1844 TO 1852.*

THE PUBLIC BUILDINGS.

I FIRST knew Madison in 1844. In October of that year I landed, one evening, at the city wharf, and put up for the night at a hostelry known as the Light House. It stood on the east side of Mulberry street extended, between Ohio street and low-water mark. It was a two-story brick and frame house of the ordinary style, and was the only building then in the city between Ohio street and the river, and it was the only one that ever stood within these bounds since I have known the city. It long since passed away, but its location and its appearance are indelibly written upon my memory.

At this time Madison was a well built city of 4000 or 5000 souls. Its streets were graded and its sidewalks paved much as they are to-day. The exception I now remember is High street, which then, east of Main street, was neither graded nor graveled. The principal hotels in the city at that time were the Madison Hotel and the Washington House. The former stood on the site of the Academy of Our Lady of the Angels, and was kept by George D. Fitzhugh, now of Indianapolis, and the latter, which was under the direction of Enoch D. Withers, still stands as a monument of hotel architecture of the olden time. The Court-house was a two-story brick building of modest pretensions, standing on the site of the present one. Southeast of the Court-house was the jail, an old, dingy building two stories high, fronting on an alley, with cells in either story, and rooms for the

---

* An address delivered at the High School building in Madison, on Thursday evening, March 13, 1879.

jailer on the south.   On the northeast corner of the Court-house lot was the Clerk's office, a squatty one-story brick house of two rooms, fronting on Main Cross street.   At the northwest corner of the lot, on the corner of Main Cross and Main streets, stood a two-story building, having two rooms in the first story, and three in the second, with a platform on a level with the latter running the entire length from east to west.   The platform was reached from both Main Cross and Main streets by wooden stairways, over which people passed to reach the offices above. The main room below was occupied by Bramwell & Phillips as a dry goods store, and the other was the office of Dr. Joseph H. D. Rogers whose presence is not yet denied you.   The west room above was the Recorder's office, the center one the Auditor's office, and the east one the office of the County Treasurer. Around the Court-house lot was a brick wall four feet high, capped with stone.   Such were the public buildings of Madison thirty-five years ago.

THE CHURCHES.

Saint Michael's Catholic church then stood, and the priest who ministered to the spiritual wants of the parish was Maurice de St. Palais, afterwards the distinguished Bishop of Vincennes. This prelate was succeeded by Father Dupontavice, who was known to you all.   The Rev. Harvey Curtis was pastor of the Second Presbyterian church, the Rev. Mr. Leavenworth of the First Presbyterian church, and the Rev. E. D. Owen of the Baptist church on Vine street.   The policy of the Methodist church is such that its clergy remain but a short time in charge of a particular congregation, but I remember the Rev. W. C. Smith and the Rev. Prescott as pastors of Wesley Chapel, and the Rev. John Keiger and the Rev. Dr. Daily as pastors of Third street church.   Saint John's church was not then in existence.   This church was an offshoot from Wesley Chapel. Among its leading members were the Taylors—Gamaliel, John H. and William M.—Caleb Schmidlapp and Charles W. Basnett.   The church building was erected in 1849 or 1850, near the site of the first Methodist church built in Madison.   The Rev. John S. Bayliss was the first pastor of Saint John's.

Christ Episcopal church and the United Presbyterian church

were erected during this time. The former was built mainly by the exertions of Joseph M. Moore, then cashier of the Madison Branch Bank, and of its worthy rector, the Rev. Dr. Claxton. Dr. Claxton was a gentleman of acknowledged ability and was esteemed outside his parish as well as within it. He was, probably, the most popular minister in the city of his day.

The Reverend James Browne, pastor of the United Presbyterian church, was a man of earnest convictions and of deep piety. He was an active worker in the anti-slavery cause, and did much to create public sentiment among us in opposition to human slavery. He used to declaim against this abomination from the pulpit, and was ever ready to espouse the cause of the oppressed. It is to the labors of such men as Mr. Browne that the world is indebted for that public sentiment which eventually strangled this monster in his lair.

THE NEWSPAPERS.

At this time there were two weekly newspapers published in Madison, the *Banner* and the *Courier*. The first was edited by Daniel D. Jones, known as Davy Jones, and the latter by Rolla Doolittle. Mr. Jones was a dapper little gentleman, a Welshman by birth, and in his day the foremost newspaper writer in the State. His sentences were short and terse, and their meaning always apparent. He seldom wrote his editorials; he set them at the case and composed them as he handled the types. He was a genial, social man, delighting in fun and practical jokes. I was once at a social party at his house when a most ludicrous incident occurred. He kissed a young lady, who turned upon him as if to box his ears. His wife, a large, portly woman, was present, and to her Mr. Jones ran for protection. She was seated, and he cuddled by her side, sitting on the floor with his head under her arm, and looking into her face, his eyes sparkling with merriment, he said: "Mother, protect your boy." I need say nothing of Mr. Doolittle, the editor of the *Courier*, as he is of and with you at the present time.

William W. Crail, now, as then, of Louisville, Kentucky, bought a half interest in the *Banner*, and soon afterwards it was converted into a daily. On Mr. Jones's death, in 1851, his late interest in the paper was purchased by the Hon. John R.

Cravens, who, in March, 1851, sold it to William Wesley Woollen. Subsequent to this time Mr. Woollen bought Mr. Crail's interest, and in 1853 sold the *Banner* to General Milton Stapp, who soon afterwards disposed of it to Captain W. H. Keyt, in whose hands it died.

Samuel F. and John I. Covington bought the *Courier* in 1848, or thereabout, and changed it to a daily. In 1849 they sold it to Mr. M. C. Garber, now its senior proprietor. Mr. Garber is the ranking newspaper publisher in the State, having been continuously engaged in the business for twenty-nine years and over.

In 1851 Milton Gregg and John G. Sering established the *Madison Daily Tribune*. After publishing the *Tribune* for a short time Mr. Sering withdrew from the firm, and Mr. Gregg removed the paper to New Albany, where it was published for several years under his direction.

In 1852 the *Daily Madisonian* was established by a company of Democratic politicians. Rolla Doolittle was its publisher, and Robert S. Sproule its editor. It lived during the Scott and Pierce campaign, and soon thereafter it yielded up the ghost.

A daily paper was published a week or so during this time by B. F. Foster and Ben. F. Reed, but its life was too short for it to be properly classed among the journals of Madison.

A Free-soil paper was established in 1848 to advocate the election of Van Buren and Adams. Its editor was Riley E. Stratton, who afterwards went to Oregon and became a leading jurist of that State.

With the exceptions of two religious weeklies—one a Baptist and the other a Universalist—these are all the newspapers published in Madison during the time covered by this address.

THE BAR.

At this time the bar of Madison was very able. Marshall, the giant intellect of Indiana, was of it; so was the suave and polished Sullivan; the painstaking and prolix Stevens; Glass, vigorous in mind and body; the polite and affable Dunn; the brilliant and erratic Sheets; the scholarly King; the methodical Markley; the sarcastic Chapman; the studious and careful Troxell; the brusque Daily; the two Brights, the elder a lawyer of much ability, and the younger, who gathered in the Senate chamber the laurels which would have been his had he continued at the bar. The two William Hendrickses, senior and junior, were of it—the elder an ex-Governor and an ex-Senator ; the younger genial in disposition and with a heart ever responsive to distress :

> " Green be the turf above thee,
> Friend of my better days;
> None knew thee but to love thee,
> None named thee but to praise."

There were two Abram Hendrickses—John Abram and Abram W. There were the two Hillises—William C. and John S. ; Oliver S. Pitcher, once a partner of the elder Bright ; Hull, and Thom, and Crittenden, and Walker, and Shaw, and perhaps others whom I have forgotten. One whom I have not named I first knew as a wagon-maker in the neighboring town of Hanover. One-half the day he worked at his bench ; the other half and well into the night he studied law. Weekly, under the summer's sun and through the winter's snow, he walked to Madison to recite his lessons, for he was too poor to pay for riding. In due time he stood his examination and was admitted to the bar. He came here and opened an office, but clients came not. Weekly board bills were to pay, clothing had to be bought, and other necessary expenses to be met, and how to do these things was the problem this courageous young man was to solve. More than once he consulted with me in regard to abandoning his profession and returning to his trade. I advised against it, and the advice was followed. After awhile " the tide which, taken at its flood, leads on to fortune," turned. He was elected City Attorney, then County Attorney, then a Senator, and now he is the honored Judge of your Circuit Court.*

> " Honor and shame from no condition rise ;
> Act well your part, there all the honor lies."

Many of those I have named have pleaded their last case and gone to judgment. Marshall sleeps near your city, mourned by a State, and he would be mourned by a nation had his theater of action been larger ; Sullivan left you but yesterday, like a ripe sheaf garnered in the field ; Stevens, overtaken

---

* Hon. J. Y. Allison.

in old age by poverty, his mind gave way, and he died at the Indiana Hospital for the Insane ; Dunn fills an honorable place in the military service of the country ; Glass was cut down in the prime of a vigorous manhood ; Sheets died young, a victim of an unfortunate appetite ; King is practicing his profession in Chicago ; Markley is a prosperous merchant in the same city ; Troxell lives in North-western Indiana, still engaged in the practice of the law ; Daily, after representing Nebraska in the National Congress, died while yet a young man ; the elder Bright is an invalid, and lives at the capital of the State, an honored citizen ; and the younger Bright, after serving seventeen years as a Senator of the United States, died a few years ago in the Monumental City, and his remains now lie mouldering on the banks of the blue Patapsco. The two William Hendrickses died in your midst many years ago ; John Abram Hendricks fell at Pea Ridge while leading his regiment against the enemy ; Abram W. Hendricks is an eminent lawyer at Indianapolis ; William C. Hillis lives in Northern Missouri, where he has filled several offices of honor and profit ; Shaw is a retired merchant of Dayton, Ohio ; John S. Hillis died in his youth, and was laid in the shade of the old homestead where he first saw the light of day ; Walker lives among you ; Pitcher is a thrifty business man in a sister State ; Crittenden is practicing his profession at Washington City ; Hull and Thom are dead and they were buried in your midst.

THE CIRCUIT JUDGES.

In this connection it is proper that I should say something of the Judges before whom these men practiced their profession. When I first knew Madison the Circuit Judge was Miles C. Eggleston. He was then in feeble health and well stricken in years. He was small in stature, a good lawyer, and although at times cross and petulant, he never forgot the dignity of his station.

Courtland Cushing succeeded Judge Eggleston upon the bench. He had respectable talents, was very dressy and quite a beau among the ladies. While serving as judge he was appointed Chargé d'Affaires to Ecuador. After serving out his term he entered the service of the Nicaragua Transit Company, and soon thereafter died on the Isthmus of Panama.

Alexander C. Downey, now, as then, a resident of Rising Sun, followed Judge Cushing as presiding judge of the Madison Circuit. Judge Downey is, or was at this time, an inveterate wag. I will relate two incidents which will show the truth of this:

In these days full beards were unknown, and a moustache was as rare as a disinterested friend. The Rev. Frederick T. Brown once apologized from his pulpit for wearing a full beard, and no other public man of the day had the temerity to offend in a similar manner. A young man noted as a wit, and who, since that time, has attracted much attention by reason of a rencounter which resulted in death, removed to Madison at this time. He had a red moustache which he cultured with the greatest care. He was often in the Court-house, and one day while he was there Judge Downey wrote the following order and handed it to the clerk:

"Ordered by the court, that the young man with the red moustache be taken into the custody of the sheriff and by him conducted to the nearest barber shop and there shaved within an inch of his life; and may the Lord have mercy on his soul."

On another occasion, when the term of the court was nearly ended and order was lax, Abram W. Hendricks and John S. Hillis lay down at full length within the bar of the court-room. Observing their posture, Judge Downey wrote the following order and passed it to the clerk:

"Ordered by the court, that Abram W. Hendricks and John S. Hillis, two members of this bar, be, and each of them hereby is, fined five dollars for contempt of court for lying at full length within the bar during the sitting of the court." And on a line below the order, and in brackets, he added: "Which may be satisfied by bringing into court, at once, twelve good, ripe watermelons." The dozen watermelons were soon in the Temple of Justice and the wrath of the Judge appeased.

JUDGES OF THE PROBATE COURT.

At this time William Hendricks, junior, was the Judge of the Jefferson Probate Court. This court was one of limited jurisdiction, its business being to settle the estates of deceased persons, and to care for their minor children. Judge Hendricks was one of the kindest men I ever knew. Of a genial nature, he had the esteem and love of all who knew him. I never heard him say an unkind word of any one, nor any one say an unkind word of him. He was one of those rare men whose province is to make happy every one they meet. I can recall the memory of no one with more pleasure than that of this good and modest man. In the language applied to another by one of the most gifted daughters of Indiana, " He was good enough to be a woman."

Williamson Dunn, of Hanover, succeeded Judge Hendricks. He was a man of marked character. He was a soldier of the war of 1812, and had served the State in many important positions. He was of unquestioned courage, and although an elder of the Presbyterian church, he never pleaded his religion in bar for not resenting an insult. In the year 1848 a meeting was held in the Court-house to put forward General Taylor for the presidency. It was the first meeting for that purpose held in the country, and as it was mainly inspired by Judge Dunn, it will be seen that he was the author of the movement that culminated in the election of old " Rough and Ready " to the presidency. The Judge offered a resolution nominating General Taylor and supported it in an earnest speech. Charles Woodward submitted an amendment, putting forward Tom Corwin, of Ohio, for Vice-President. This Judge Dunn opposed. He said that its adoption would militate against the interests of General Taylor. It will be remembered that Governor Corwin opposed the Mexican war. In a speech delivered in the Senate of the United States, he said :

" If I were a Mexican I would tell you, ' Have you not room in your own country to bury your dead men? If you come into mine we will greet you with bloody hands, and welcome you to hospitable graves.' "

Referring to this speech Judge Dunn said that while he could cordially support its author for Vice-President, many friends of General Taylor would be driven from him if his name were coupled with that of the man who had uttered such a sentiment. Mr. Woodward replied to him with some warmth, and during his speech said: "The gentleman admits that the nomination of Governor Corwin would be a good one, but says he is afraid to have it made." Slapping his breast with his hand as was his custom when speaking earnestly, he exclaimed, "Cowardice, sir, cowardice." Judge Dunn sprang to his feet, and approaching Mr. Woodward, said in a loud voice: "I am an old man, and never before was cowardice imputed to me. I ask the gentleman to take back his words. Will he do it?" Whether it was the sight of the judge's fist, or whether it was a sense of justice that caused Mr. Woodward to withdraw the offensive words, I know not, but I remember they were withdrawn.

THE ASSOCIATE JUDGES.

Previous to the adoption of the present constitution each county had two associate judges. These officials, usually denominated side judges, sat on either side of the presiding judge, and acted as guy-ropes to hold him level. As a rule they were neither Blackstones nor Mansfields, but were possessed of good common sense, an important requisite of the righteous judge. William M. Taylor and Robert Kinnear were the associate judges in Jefferson, and they were the last of their line. They went out of office with the old constitution, but their deeds live after them. Judge Taylor was a low, chunky man with a kindly face, was a saddler by trade and a gentleman by nature. He dressed neatly, wore a fob-chain with a large seal dangling at his side, and walked with a cane. Judge Kinnear was a farmer, and lived near Bryantsburgh. He was a large man with stooped shoulders and an ungainly walk. These judges sometimes, though rarely, held court in the absence of the presiding judge. When they did so the lawyers would call up their cases which had no merit and have them decided. I remember one case which was tried in the absence of Judge Cushing that caused much merriment at the time. It grew out of a horse trade, and Mr. Michael G. Bright was the defendant, and acted as his own attorney. It was of that class of suits which, under the old practice, was brought when the plaintiff was not the party in interest. Mr. Bright called the case, and, as attorney for the plaintiff, ordered it dismissed. "Not so fast, Mr. Bright," said Mr. Marshall, rising to his feet. "I have something to say about that." He proceeded to state the case, and succeeded in satisfying the court that it should not be dismissed. The trial proceeded, and Mr. Bright made an ingenious speech in which he quoted much law, and when he sat down it seemed certain that his case was won. Mr. Marshall arose, and with unusual deliberation addressed the court. He said that as the case was a small one—the amount involved being but sixty dollars—he had given it but little thought; that Mr. Bright knew the law, and as he was attorney for the plaintiff, attorney for the defendant, and defendant, himself, he had no doubt thoroughly familiarized himself with the case; that, if what he had laid down to the court as law was the law, he was entitled to a finding in his favor; therefore, he moved the court that Mr. Bright be put upon his oath, and required to answer as to whether or not the law he had given the court was the law of the land. Turning to Mr. Bright, and pointing at him with his finger, he exclaimed: "Will you swear, Mr. Bright, will you swear, sir?" The effect was electrical. Mr. Bright would not swear, and Mr. Marshall won the case.

THE COUNTY COMMISSIONERS.

The County Commissioners in these days were Nathan Robinson, John E. Gale, John Kirk, John Smock and James W. Hinds. It was during the administration of the first three of these gentlemen that the present jail and jailer's residence were built. Before undertaking a work requiring so large an outlay of money they concluded to go on a tour of observation and examine the best models of such buildings they could find. Accordingly, accompanied by their architect, Monroe W. Lee, they went to Ohio to inspect the prisons of that State. They journeyed in a stage-coach—for in those days railroads were not so common as they are to-day—and one afternoon during the trip they had for a fellow-passenger a loquacious gentleman who made himself exceedingly agreeable to "the innocents abroad." When night drew her curtains over the earth and the bright eyes of the stranger could no longer light the stage-coach, the honorable gentlemen from Jefferson went to sleep. They could not retire to the arms of Morpheus, for there was no couch to repose upon, so they contented themselves with sitting still and doing homage to the sleepy god by reverentially bowing their heads. "Some wee short hour ayant the twal" the coach stopped at a country town to permit the stranger to alight. Having touched *terra firma*, he sought his baggage in the dark, and as Captain Kirk sat sleeping, with his head nearly touching his knees, the stranger seized him by the nose. The clutch of the stranger awoke the Captain and brought him to his senses. He angrily demanded the cause of the assault. "Pardon me, sir," replied the stranger, "I thought I had hold of my carpet-sack."

THE COUNTY CLERK.

John H. Taylor was Clerk of the courts during the time of which I speak. He was a small man, of light complexion, affable in manner and a fluent talker. Dr. Tefft, at that time editor of the *Ladies' Repository*, declared, in an article published in his magazine, that Mr. Taylor's house was the home of the prophets—referring to the fact that it was the uniform stopping-place of the Methodist clergy.

Mr. Taylor was a great lover of tobacco. He chewed it constantly when not asleep, and was never seen, in-doors or out-doors, at home or abroad, without his cheek being distended by an enormous quid of the narcotic plant. About this time Daguerrean artists first appeared in the West, and one of them came to Madison. There was a rush to his rooms for pictures, and among others was Mr. Taylor. He succeeded in securing a good likeness of himself, and took it home to show it to his family. Handing it to his wife he asked her how she liked it. "Better than the original," replied the good dame; "the tobacco is there but not the spittle."

THE SHERIFFS.

The sheriffs of Jefferson county during this time were William H. Phillips, Robert Right Rea, Henry Deputy, and Robert M. Smith. Mr. Phillips still lives among you, so it is unnecessary to speak of him, but I can not pass Messrs. Rea and Deputy without notice. They were both men of marked peculiarities of character and took active parts in the public affairs of their

day.   Mr. Rea was a well built man of ordinary size, with a
bald head and kindly face.   He was unlettered but was unusually shrewd and cunning.   He was a natural detective and a
terror to absconding thieves and runaway cows.   He was also
feared by runaway slaves, for many a panting fugitive was
arrested by him and returned to bondage.   I never could satisfactorily account for this trait in his character, for he had a
kind heart and was no slave to Mammon.   It probably was the
effect of his early education.   Mr. Rea was easily teased and
had no relish for a practical joke when he was the subject.
Cool White, a negro minstrel, once offered a gold pen as a prize
for the best conundrum.   The offer brought a large audience to
the entertainment, and among others present was Mr. Rea.
When the exercises were ended White announced that the prize
had been awarded to Captain Horace Hull for the following
conundrum :

> " Why is our sheriff like old Uncle Ned ?
> Because he has no hair on the top of his head."

Captain Hull walked to the platform amid shouts of laughter
and cries of " bravo," to receive the prize.   He returned with
it down the aisle to where Mr. Rea was seated, and bowing, offered it to him.   " Which, which," said the sheriff; " damn it,
which? "   Captain Hull kept the prize.

Henry Deputy was a large man, of dark complexion and with
black hair and beard.   He was affected in his voice and manners and very particular in his dress.   He wore shirts with ruf-
fled fronts and was seldom on the street with hands ungloved.
He was long in the service of Sheriff Rea, first as clerk and
barkeeper in the old hotel that stood on the south side of the
public square, and afterwards as deputy sheriff.   The late Dr.
Cross used to tell a good story on Mr. Deputy.   He said he was
in the hotel one day when a Kentuckian entered, and addressing Mr. Deputy, said : " How is it that every time I come here
Right Rea has a new barkeeper.   What is your name, sir? "
" My name, sar, is Deputy, sar."   " Then, Mr. Deputy, sar,
will you please, sar, hand me a cigar? "   " With pleasure, sar,"
and he handed the Kentuckian a cigar, accompanied with a
lighted match.   " I tell the tale as it was told to me," and with

out vouching for its truth, but it is entirely consistent with Mr. Deputy's character and manners. If there was a Beau Brummell in Madison, it was he, and if he was not a Chesterfield it was for the want of ability rather than desire. While he was deputy sheriff he was the keeper of the jail and lived in the front rooms of the jail building. One night the prisoners made an effort to escape, and had almost succeeded before they were discovered. When Mr. Deputy reached the cell door and found them engaged in picking the wall, he called out in his blandest tones : " Gentlemen, gentlemen, desist from your operations, or I shall be under the disagreeable necessity of putting handcuffs upon you." The " gentlemen" desisted, but whether it was the polite and persuasive manner of the officer or the fear of handcuffs that stayed their hands, is not written in the chronicles of these days. Poor, Deputy! He afterwards became penniless, but his pride did not forsake him. I remember that on a cold day, several years after the time of which I am speaking, he came to me in the Court-house and asked for money to buy a load of wood. His clothes were seedy and threadbare, and as he sat in a chair before the fire, he drew the tail of his well worn overcoat over his knees to hide the rents in his clothing. It was the ruling passion, strong in death.

A PATRIOT.

At this time Joseph B. Stewart was a student in the law office of Marshall & Glass. He was six feet tall or over, and of gigantic frame ; vain and pompous. He was loud of speech, and ever ready to talk in public. On the breaking out of the Mexican war a meeting was held in the Court-house to stimulate enlistments. It was addressed by General Milton Stapp and John Lyle King, and perhaps by others. Stewart was present, but was not called upon for a speech. After the meeting adjourned and the crowd were leaving the Court-house there were loud calls for Stewart. He mounted the wall which surrounded the public square and commenced to harangue the people. He eloquently descanted upon the glory to be won at the cannon's mouth and upon the beauty of the halls of Montezuma. He closed his speech about as follows : " Business prevents me, my fellow citizens, from drawing my sword in this glorious cause. I would gladly unsheath it in my country's defense, but duty to others forbids. But there are some things I can and will do. Those of you who go to war and die in the service will not be forgotten by me. I will assist in settling your estates on the most reasonable terms. I will advise your widows of their legal rights, and see that your orphans are not defrauded of their patrimonies. These things I will do at a considerable reduction on regular rates for such services." Stewart is now, and for many years has been, one of the most noted and successful of Washington lobbyists. He has engineered several of the largest jobs ever put through the National Congress, and if the political morals of the country do not improve it is probable that he will engineer many more.

GENERAL MILTON STAPP.

One of the prominent men of these days was General Milton Stapp. He was a public spirited man, and was as brave as Julius Cæsar. He had filled many responsible offices, and had filled them well. He was vain of his talents and his honors; so much so that his vanity at times was very marked. He was a soldier in the war of 1812, and he commanded the Madison brigade in the Irish war. On that occasion he, like

> "The King of France, with forty thousand men,
> Went up a hill, and so came down agen."

General Stapp was Mayor of Madison, and never did the city have a better one. He often arrested offenders on the street and, unaided, marched them to jail. On one occasion he had a difference with a prominent citizen which led to angry words. He pronounced the man a liar and a scoundrel to his face. The prominent citizen retorted: "You dare not repeat those words." General Stapp went to the door of the office he was in and called to several gentlemen who were near. In their presence he said: "I have called you gentlemen to witness that I here pronounce Mr. —— a liar and a scoundrel." The insult was not resented. General Stapp was president of the convention held at Charlestown, in 1849, that nominated William McKee Dunn for Congress. I well remember the speech he made on taking the chair. He complained of his neglect by the Whig party, and declared himself entitled to more consideration than he had received. He said he had recently returned from Washington where he went to get an office from General Taylor, but his application was refused. He declared that he experienced great difficulty in getting an interview with Mr. Clayton, the Secretary of State, while others who had done nothing for the party were admitted without trouble. Continuing in this strain for awhile, he said: "When I first met Mr. Clayton, he inquired who I was. I told him I was General Stapp, of Indiana. He said he had never heard of me before. 'What, sir,' said I, 'never heard of Milton Stapp, and you the Secretary of State of the United States?'" The General had supposed his fame was national, not provincial.

M'KINLEY, NEWBERRY AND MURRAY.

Three noted men in these days were McKinley, Newberry and Murray. They were demented but harmless. McKinley believed he owned the major part of the city. His possessions also included lands in foreign countries, and sometimes he thought himself the governing power of at least one European monarchy. At times he would saw a load of wood, or perform other manual labor, but usually he was upon the street discoursing upon his riches. Sometimes he would disappear and be gone for awhile, but he would soon return and repeat "his thrice told tale." He was about as well known at Indianapolis as at Madison, and I have seen him more than once in that city and at Franklin with a crowd about him listening to his wondrous stories. He once became very angry with me because I told him that he and Murray (who also claimed to own the city) should settle the question of title before he disposed of some property he was trying to sell. He said Murray was "nothing but a damned old Yankee, and had no sense no how."

Newberry was a very different man. He approached you as stealthily as a cat, and would be bending over you and whispering in your ear before you were aware of his presence. He talked in a low voice, and his words were generally incoherent and sometimes meaningless. He always had a short gun strapped to his back, and his appearance was anything but inviting. He harmed no one, but the wonder is that he did not. His whispered words, his wild look and the gun upon his back always inspired me with terror, and made me watch him like a hawk. In his young days he was a prosperous man of business, and he became insane by trying to solve an impossible problem.

Murray was the worst man of the three, if not the greatest lunatic. He was given to liquor, and was terribly abusive when in his cups. At such times he would walk the streets, and " swear like the army in Flanders." He was particularly abusive of Moody Park, the Mayor of the city, who had often sent him to jail for drunkenness. He believed he was owner of all the property in the city by virtue of a judgment he had recovered for one million of dollars for false imprisonment. This hallucination ever possessed him. Whether drunk or sober he thought himself the lord proprietor of Madison, and her citizens his tenants. He threatened suits of ejectment against those in possession, and was often exceedingly abusive in his notices to quit. The only way to manage him was by force, and it was frequently employed. He was often committed to jail, and there compelled to remain for months. At that time the Mayor's office was in the row of buildings on Main Cross street known as the buzzard roost, and the jail was immediately south of and back of it. Every morning Murray would be at the window of his cell when the Mayor opened his office. So soon as he saw that official he would commence to curse and abuse him. On these occasions it was his custom to sing a doggerel song, running thus :

> " When first King Moody began to reign, began to reign,
>   He bought a peck of buckwheat bran, of buckwheat bran,"

and so on for quantity.

CAPTAIN DAVID WHITE.

No man in his day more deeply impressed himself upon Madison than David White. He came here in 1846 from Pennsylvania, where he had been engaged in the wool trade. He was about six feet tall, with rather less than the average flesh for one of his height, had stooped shoulders, and walked with his head well forward and his eyes upon the ground. His life was one of vicissitudes. He was rich to-day and poor to-morrow.

He failed in business in Pennsylvania, in Madison, in Iowa and, I believe, in St. Louis. But failure with him was but a stimulus to new exertions. Most men sink under adversity; not so he. If he touched the bottom it was to reach a foundation for a rebound. He went down under one wave and sprang in triumph upon the top of the next. His energy never gave way and his industry never tired. He was a leader in every public enterprise of his day. Madison is mainly indebted to him for her gas works, for her marine railway, and for the establishment of one of her insurance companies. He labored hard to connect her with the world by a net-work of railroads, but in this effort he failed. He saw the trade which had been hers directed to other cities, and the sight made him sad. He left us and went elsewhere, but so long as the great enterprises he inaugurated remain he will not be forgotten. It was eminently proper that his mortal remains should be brought here and consigned to rest among a people for whom he had done so much.

WILLIAM G. WHARTON.

William G. Wharton was a prominent man at the time of which I speak. In stature he was tall and straight. His physique was splendid. In earlier days he had been both a major of militia and a justice of the peace. Apropos to this: Some years previous to this time he was in New York, and meeting General Stapp at the Astor House he was prevailed upon to call upon General Scott. Major Wharton was not given to running after great men, nor to crowding himself anywhere uninvited; therefore, it was with reluctance that he consented to call upon the hero of Lundy's Lane. But the persistency of General Stapp prevailed, and the two went to the rooms of General Scott. General Stapp approached the great captain and said: "General Scott, allow me to present my friend, Major Wharton." "I am happy to know you, Major," said the General; "to what part of the service do you belong?" "I am an officer by brevet," said the Major; "I am from the great West where every man is a major or (bowing to Stapp) a general." Major Wharton used to tell this story with great gusto.

At this time, deeds signed by married women, to be valid had

34

to be acknowledged by the wives, separate and apart from and without the hearing of their husbands. Major Wharton was a notary public, as also was William McKee Dunn. The latter took the acknowledgment of a deed from Wharton and his wife and inadvertently signed the Major's name to the certificate instead of his own. Judge Billy Hendricks saw this deed in the Recorder's office and determined to have some fun out of the mistake. Observing Wharton on the street he called him to the office. "How is it, Major," said the Judge, "that you certify under your oath of office that you have examined your wife separate and apart from and without the hearing of her husband?" "What do you mean?" asked the Major. "I mean," answered the Judge, "that you have done this thing, and here is the evidence of it." With that he proceeded to read as follows:

"STATE OF INDIANA,   } ss:
   COUNTY OF JEFFERSON, }

"Before me, the undersigned, a notary public within and for said county, this day personally came William G. Wharton and Eliza Wharton, his wife, the grantors in the foregoing deed, and acknowledged the signing and sealing of the same to be their voluntary act and deed for the uses and purposes therein named. And the said Eliza Wharton, wife of the said William G. Wharton, being by me examined separate and apart from and without the hearing of her said husband, declared that she signed and sealed the same of her own free will and accord, and without any fear of or compulsion from her said husband.
   (Signed)   "W. G. WHARTON, Notary Public."

"Go and get Newberry's gun and strap it on my back," said the astonished Major.

Major Wharton was a devoted Mason. He was a Methodist, but he placed his lodge above his church. One day he came into the office of the Firemen and Mechanics Insurance Company and applied to the late Caleb T. Lodge, then president of the company, for a permit to smoke meat in his warehouse, on which that company had written a policy. There was a controversy about the rate to be charged, when Wharton petulantly said : " I'll have nothing to do with your company ; all insurance companies are swindling concerns." "I am surprised, 'Squire," said Mr. Lodge, "that a good Methodist, like yourself, should belong to a swindling concern." (Mr. Wharton was a stockholder in the company.) "Don't quote Methodism to me," responded the 'Squire ; "the other day I wanted some shingles and went to the yard of Mr. ———, a brother Methodist, to buy them. I selected the shingles I wanted and ordered them sent to my house. Those received were not those I bought, but were greatly inferior. Had I bought the shingles of old man Todd—a hell-bound sinner—I should have received what I bargained for. He is a good Mason, and show me a good Mason and I'll show you a good man."

REV. GAMALIEL TAYLOR.

Gamaliel Taylor, familiarly called " Uncle Gam," was known to every one in the city. His form was lithe and erect, although his locks were white and deep furrows were in his face. He was both a minister of the gospel and a minister of justice. On Sunday he dispensed gospel truths with a pure hand, and during the week he dispensed justice with an even one. He united in wedlock young men and maidens, and when death came he preached the funerals of the fathers and mothers. Gold and silver he had none, but he was passing rich in the love of all who knew him. His memory, like sweet incense, perfumes this hall as I speak, and if the spirits of the blest are permitted to leave their heavenly abode that of the old patriarch, so dear to us all, is hovering o'er us now.

MADISON'S CONTRIBUTIONS TO THE MEXICAN WAR.

In May, 1846, war was declared between the United States and Mexico. The war feeling at Madison ran high. Two companies of soldiers were formed and organized at once. The first was the Washington Guards, commanded by William Ford, who had for several years been the captain of an independent military company. His lieutenants were Samuel G. Cowden, J. P. A. M. Channey and John M. Lord. The second company, the Madison Rifles, was commanded by Thomas L. Sullivan, who had for lieutenants Horace Hull, John Har-

rington and Americus O. Hough.   War not having been antic-
ipated by the Federal Government, no provision had been made
for clothing and feeding the soldiers.   To meet the emergency
the Madison Branch Bank, then under the presidency of Mr.
J. F. D. Lanier, tendered Governor Whitcomb a sum of money
sufficient to clothe and feed the Madison soldiers until they
were mustered into service.   The Governor having made other
arrangements declined the offer, but his action in the premises
was such as to occasion much criticism at the time.   The Madison companies went into camp at New Albany, and on the 24th
of June were mustered into the service of the United States.
They formed part of the Third Indiana regiment commanded
by Colonel James H. Lane, and their members fought valiantly
at Buena Vista.   None of the Madison boys were killed in that
sanguinary battle, but the anxiety of their friends at home as to
their fate was intense.   Several members of these companies
died in Mexico from accident and disease, but none were killed
in battle.   The next summer, having served out the term of
their enlistment, the survivors returned home and were discharged.

In the summer and fall of 1847 the Fifth Indiana regiment
was formed.   It rendezvoused at Madison, its camp being in
the western part of the city, near the bend in the railroad.
Madison and Vernon contributed a company to this regiment.
It was commanded by Captain Horace Hull, who had for his
lieutenants DeWitt C. Ritch, John M. Lord and John M. Lat-
timore.   This regiment never was in battle, but one day it came
so close to Santa Anna that, in his hurry to get away, he left
behind his wooden leg.   It became a trophy of the war and was
highly prized by the Hoosier soldiers.

It was by the action of these three companies of Madison men
and others of like patriotism that the United States conquered a
peace with Mexico and added to her territory a golden empire.
By the treaty of Guadalupe Hidalgo, she became possessed of
the richest mineral lands in the world, and surely she owes a
debt of gratitude to the brave men who made it possible for her
to obtain them.   The denial to these men of a reasonable pen-

sion gives color to the charge sometimes made that republics are ungrateful.

THE CROOKED CREEK FLOOD.

Early in September, 1846, Crooked creek overflowed its banks, whereby eleven persons were drowned and over $100,000 worth of property destroyed. The flood was in daylight, otherwise the loss of life would have been much greater. Skiffs were taken from the river to the creek, and the lives of many persons thereby saved. At that time Crooked creek flowed through a culvert under the railroad track. This culvert was completely blocked with houses that had been swept from their foundations. The pent up water overflowed the banks of the creek and submerged the adjacent bottom lands. The woolen mill of Whitney & Hendricks, the oil mill of Jacob Shuh, a large part of the pork-house of Mitchel & McNaughten, and several dwelling houses were borne away by the raging water. The bodies of the drowned were recovered and inquests held upon them; and to illustrate the public economy of those times, it may be proper to say that the Board of County Commissioners considered the holding of these inquests unnecessary, and objected to paying their cost out of the county treasury.

A MURDER.

The current of events ran smoothly in these days, for Madison was a peaceable city. Burglaries and other high crimes were uncommon, and homicides were almost unknown. There was, however, one murder committed in Madison, and it created intense excitement at the time. It was the killing of Joseph Howard by Henry Holtzclaw. The Holtzclaws—William, the father, and Henry, Eli and Thomas, the sons, came from Kentucky and opened a wholesale grocery store on West street. Thomas created a disturbance one Sunday evening at Wesley Chapel, and the next day a warrant for his arrest was issued, and placed in the hands of Howard, who was a constable. Howard went to the Holtzclaw store to make the arrest, where he got into a personal difficulty with the father and the sons. He was a strong man as well as a courageous one, and seizing Thomas by the collar of his coat, he dragged him out of the

house.   He was followed by the father and brothers, and when
in the middle of the street was shot by Henry and mortally
wounded.   The Holtzclaws were arrested and admitted to bail,
and then fled the country.   Sometime afterwards Eli was re-
arrested in the South and brought here by a brother of his victim.
By this time two of the most important witnesses were gone.
Langtree had been drowned and Weide had removed to Minnesota ; so their testimony could not be had.   Holtzclaw took a
change of venue to an adjoining county, and in the absence of
these witnesses was tried and acquitted.

PUBLIC SENTIMENT.

Situated on the line between the free and the slave States,
Madison was a *quasi* Southern city.   The opinions and sentiments of her inhabitants were moulded, to a great extent, by
the opinions and sentiments of their Kentucky neighbors.
Runaway slaves were hunted over the hills and through the
valleys of Jefferson.   The abolition settlement in Lancaster
township was considered a plague-spot on the body politic.   The
Hoyts, the Nelsons and the Tibbettses of that neighborhood,
although honorable and peaceable men, were tabooed because
they believed in the equality of all men before the law.   The
Euletherian school at College Hill received the maledictions of
the people, because in it the fountain of knowledge was as free
to the negro as to the white man.   Dwelling houses which had
been erected near this college for the use of colored students
were burned and destroyed.   It is no wonder that in a community where Southern sentiments were so common the duel
should be considered a proper method for settling disputes.
Although we never had a duel here, we had several narrow
escapes from meetings under the code.   John Abram Hendricks challenged John Lyle King, Joseph G. Marshall challenged Jesse D. Bright, Michael G. Bright challenged John
Brough, and Robert S. Sproule challenged John A. Hendricks.
The difficulty between Messrs. Hendricks and King occasioned
much feeling in the city.   They were both young men of promise and were sons of leading citizens.   Mr. Hendricks had
been an officer in the regular army, but had resigned and come
home.   Mr. King, in a communication to the *Indianapolis*

Journal, over the signature of " Ion," mentioned this fact in the following words :

" Captain John A. Hendricks, formerly of the United States Infantry, but now of the peace establishment, has resigned his commission and returned home.

> "' Farewell the plumed troop and the big wars
> That make ambition virtue! O, farewell!
> Farewell the neighing steed, and the shrill trump,
> The spirit-stirring drum, th' ear-piercing fife,
> The royal banner, and all quality,
> Pride, pomp and circumstance of glorious war.
> And, O, you mortal engines, whose rude throats
> The immortal Jove's dread clamors counterfeit,
> Farewell! Othello's occupation's gone!'

" Ill health and an inability to weather the Mexican climate are the causes, I hear, assigned for his return."

Captain Hendricks was offended at this reference to him and to his return, and published in the Madison *Banner*, over his own name, a letter, in which he pronounced " Ion " a liar and a coward. Mr. King, still maintaining his *incognito*, replied in a bitter letter, in which he quoted the couplet from Hudibras,

> " For those that fly may fight again,
> Which he can never do that's slain,"

and said his name was with the *Banner* editor and was at the service of the Captain. Captain Hendricks went to Bedford, Kentucky, and from there wrote Mr. King a challenge and sent it by a Mr. Rowan. Mr. King refused acceptance of the challenge, giving as a reason for the refusal that he was not on equal terms with his enemy ; that his acceptance would subject him to the penalty of the law of Indiana, while Mr. Hendricks would escape such penalty by reason of having written the challenge in another State. Upon receiving this reply Mr. Hendricks came to Milton, opposite this city, and wrote another challenge, without naming the place where it was written. This paper was delivered to Mr. King by Abram W. Hendricks, Esq., and the invitation declined because it lacked a venue. By this time the difficulty was widely known, and coming to the knowledge of

Governor Hendricks and Victor King, the fathers of the belligerents, they interfered and prevented a hostile meeting.

The difficulty between Messrs. Marshall and Bright origi-
nated at a political meeting which took place at Ritchey's Mills
in this county. Inasmuch as I wrote an account of this matter
some years ago for the *Indianapolis Journal*, which embodied
all I know about it, I shall say nothing further of it here.

The trouble between Mr. Bright and Mr. Brough grew out
of a controversy in relation to selling the State's interest in the
Madison and Indianapolis Railroad. Mr. Bright challenged
Mr. Brough, but, instead of accepting the challenge, the latter
published it in the *Madison Banner* with the reasons for his refusal. In speaking of this difficulty the late George D. Prentice
said in his paper that most persons would think Mr. Bright
would have the advantage of Mr. Brough in a duel, on account
of the great size of the latter, but, in fact, the advantage would
be on the other side, as it was doubtful if the pistol was then
made which could send a bullet to Mr. Brough's vitals. He
was a behemoth in size.

The difficulty between Messrs. Sproule and Hendricks grew
out of political differences, and was not generally known.
Sproule was the challenger, and he sent the hostile message by
Michael Steele Bright. Nothing came of it, and the matter was
soon adjusted.

THE GOLDEN ERA.

This was Madison's golden era. She was the *entrepot* of the
merchandise sold and consumed in Indiana. She was the gate
at which the traveler entered the State. She had three wholesale dry goods houses, and as many wholesale groceries and
boot and shoe establishments. She was one of the largest pork-
packing points in the country. No less than four establishments
were engaged in the killing and packing of hogs, one of them
being the largest then in the world. She had a starch manufactory on Crooked creek and a glue factory just outside the
city limits. She had several of the largest flouring mills west
of the Allegheny mountains. She had three large iron foun-
dries, a brass foundry, a boiler manufactory, and many other
establishments of great value. She had a chamber of com-
merce, a reading-room and a public library. In addition to the

magnificent Pike and the Ben Franklin, which landed daily at her wharfs, she had daily lines of steam packets to Cincinnati and to Louisville, and a regular one to Frankfort. Her wharfs were covered with hogsheads of sugar and molasses from New Orleans, and with boxes and bales of merchandise from the Atlantic slope. Her streets were crowded with men who came to buy her merchandise and her manufactured goods. Her citizens were jostled on the sidewalks by strangers who came hither to view her greatness, or to enter Indiana through her portals. Such was Madison from 1844 to 1852, when the zenith of her prosperity was reached.

HER PRESENT POSITION.

Although Madison is not now what she then was, she is a city of which her people may well be proud. Her material interests are great and her memories are glorious. Her starch has a market in the old world ; her saddle-trees are sold in every State of the Union, and her furniture and her steam engines are floated down the beautiful river that flows at her feet to distant markets. The men she has educated and sent out from her midst have played no mean part in the drama of life. The Madison colony at the State capital is noted for the intelligence and business worth of its men and the beauty and goodness of its women. Many of the leading men of Chicago were reared in your city, and the same is true of Saint Louis. Go where you will in the West you will find Madison men. In the East, too, she is represented, for the head of one of the most eminent banking houses in America* was a resident of Madison when I first saw it. The late Chief Justice of Oregon was a Madison boy, and Justice Beck, of the Supreme Court of Iowa, is an old time Madisonian. " I am a Roman citizen " was the proudest boast of the dweller on the banks of the Tiber, and " I am a citizen of Madison " should be the proudest boast of every one whose home is in the healthy and beautiful city under the hills.

*J. F. D. Lanier.

THE INDIANA PRESS OF THE OLDEN TIME.*

I PROPOSE giving you some sketches of the press of Indiana as it was from twenty-five to thirty years ago. I hope they will interest you; the subject they seek to illustrate interests me. The sketches will of necessity be short, for the subjects are too numerous to be profusely illustrated within the time allotted to an address like this.

I speak of a time within the memory of men now living. I speak of a time within the memory of some who hear me. These will bear witness to the truth of what I say.

In 1850 the population of Indiana was 988,416. To-day it is 2,000,000. At the State election in 1852, 187,121 votes were cast; at the election last October, 470,738 ballots went into the box. In 1852 there were but 350 miles of railroad in the State; now there are over 6,000. I give these figures to remind you of the great strides in population and wealth Indiana has taken since the time of which I speak. Has the press of Indiana kept pace with population? I shall not answer the question, but content myself with showing what the press then was; you know what it now is, and when you have heard what I have to say you can answer the question yourselves.

Thirty years ago the Indiana newspaper was not what it now is. It was printed on inferior paper, with larger type, and its make-up was not so symmetrical or attractive. The editor's name was always at the head of the editorial column. There was no shirking of responsibility nor hiding behind the backs of others. The editor was answerable for the conduct of the paper, and there was no mistaking who he was.

---

*An address delivered before the Democratic State Editorial Convention at Michigan City, June 30, 1881.

The editorial " we " was more frequently used then than now. Indeed, it was sadly abused, for the editor took it wherever he went. " We took a ride yesterday," or "we have been sick," or " we shall be absent from our office for a day or so," might often be found in the papers of those days. It is now a rare thing to see in a respectable journal such abuse of this useful word, the public having concluded that it should never, in a newspaper, represent the personality of the writer.

At that time the telegraph was sparingly used by the press. The news by it came over the O'Reilly line, and seldom filled over half a column. It came from New York and from Washington and from the other large Eastern cities, and was mainly confined to the markets and to political affairs. The special correspondent and the special telegram were unknown. Nor was the interviewer abroad in the land. This species of newspaper workers has come upon the stage of action since the time of which I speak. But few journals had a distinctive department for local news. In most of them general and local news were mixed and published in the same columns. George Bennett, of the *Cincinnati Enquirer*, was the first distinctive local editor in the West. Some of the Indiana papers followed the *Enquirer's* example and established local departments, but most of them mixed news and opinions indiscriminately.

The first side of a newspaper in those days contained a love story complete in itself, or a serial story which ran through many numbers. I remember that the *Ripley County Index* published the whole of " Pilgrim's Progress." The *Madison Banner* facetiously advised its editor to commence on the " Bible " when the Pilgrim reached the land of Beulah. It was common to see at the foot of the last column on the first page the words, " To be continued." At a party in Madison a gentleman was asked who was his favorite author. He replied that he believed he liked " To be continued " better than any other writer he knew. He was then a prosperous dry goods merchant, and afterwards went to New York and became a millionaire. After this, who will say that culture is a factor in money-getting?

There were three daily papers then published at Madison, and for a time there were four. The *Banner* had grown into influence under the direction of Daniel D. Jones, a little chubby Welshman of decided talents. He set his editorials as he composed them, and they were among the best that appeared in the press of that day. When he died his interest in the *Banner* was bought by John Robert Cravens, who in a few months sold it to the speaker. Milton Gregg started the *Tribune* at Madison in 1851 ; but there was no room for it, and the next year he took it to New Albany, and published it there until he died. Mr. Gregg was an easy, flowing writer, but was not a particularly strong one.

Michael C. Garber, whose death occurred but a few months ago, edited the *Madison Courier*. He was an independent, plucky man, and a vigorous, though not a polished writer. He was ill suited to conduct an organ, such as the *Courier* had been, and his foot was on the pedal but a short time until he kicked the machine to pieces. His assistant—the brilliant and erratic Baymiller—was as independent as his chief, and the two practiced independence to such a degree that they soon vaulted outside the Democratic party. To strangle the *Courier* and have a personal organ Senator Bright and some of his friends started the *Madisonian*, and put it in charge of Robert S. Sproule. It had a sickly existence of a year or so and died, as all personal organs are apt to do. Many of you will remember poor Bob Sproule. He was an impulsive, big-hearted Irishman, improvident and reckless. "Alas, poor Yorick ! Where be your gibes now? your gambols? your songs? your flashes of merriment that were wont to set the table in a roar?" There comes no answer.

The *Ledger*, at New Albany, was established by John B. Norman and Phineas M. Kent. Mr. Kent soon sold his interest in the paper to Lucien G. Matthews, who was associated with Mr. Norman in the conduct of the *Ledger* so long as the latter lived. Mr. Norman edited the paper, and those who remember his writings will class him among the best writers in the State. He died in October, 1869, of apoplexy. "Of gentle nature, modest and unassuming, he was ill suited to breast the turbulent waves of life. He was honest and true in his friendships, affectionate and devoted in his family and social relations. He was no orator, but with his pen expressions he was facile, graceful, forcible and oft eloquent. In political contests he wielded a trenchant blade, and with logic he could combine sarcasm as keen as polished steel." When Jenny Lind was at Madison in

1851, there being no large hall in the city, she sang in a pork-house. Norman's description of the concert was one of the nicest pieces of newspaper work ever done in Indiana. It went the rounds of the press, and Jenny Lind in the Madison pork-house was as noted as Whittington in London town. Messrs. Kent and Matthews still live, but neither of them is engaged in newspaper work.

The *Indianapolis Sentinel* was then edited by William J. Brown. Mr. Brown is better remembered as a politician than as an editor, but he wrote well and conducted the *Sentinel* with ability. He held several offices in the State and was repeatedly elected to Congress. At one time he came near being made Speaker of the House, and would have been had not some of the Southern members refused to vote for him. He was deeply chagrined at his failure, and in a letter to a friend, after re-counting his services to the South and the treatment he had received from the Southern members, he said: " I am done." After this he was called by his political opponents, " Done Brown."

The *Indianapolis Journal* was then controlled by John D. De-frees. Mr. Defrees went to Indianapolis as the Senator from Saint Joseph county. He conducted the *Journal* for several years and then sold it. When Mr. Lincoln became President Mr. Defrees went to Washington, where he has since resided. Most of the time he has held office, and is now superintendent of the government printing office.

Dr. E. W. H. Ellis, a resident of Goshen, was elected Audi-tor of State in 1850, and soon afterwards, in connection with John S. Spann, established the *Indianapolis Statesman*. The *Statesman* was published weekly, and after existing a year or so was absorbed by the *Sentinel*. It advocated the nomination of General Jo Lane for the Presidency, and as the *Sentinel* also claimed to favor his nomination, Dr. Ellis asked Mr. Brown why he did not fly the General's flag. Mr. Brown replied that first-class hotels never put up signs ; that it was only cross-roads tav-erns that did so. Dr. Ellis was a strong and pungent writer and a poet of decided merit. He died at Goshen a few years ago, being postmaster of that city at the time.

About this time a series of sketches appeared in the *Indian-*

apolis Locomotive, a weekly paper published by Elder & Harkness, which attracted much attention. They were so much above the average of newspaper contributions that there was great speculation as to who the writer was. He proved to be Berry R. Sulgrove, then a young lawyer, but now one of the most noted writers in the State. His *nom de plume*, Timothy Tugmutton, will be remembered by those who were familiar with the newspapers of that day. Mr. Sulgrove afterwards edited the *Indianapolis Journal*, and since his withdrawal from that paper he has been a contributor to most of the journals published at the State capital. His information is vast and varied, and he writes with ease and grace upon almost all subjects. There is probably no man in the State of so extensive information, and none who excels him in ability to give it to the public in an attractive form.

James P. Luse then owned and conducted the *Lafayette Journal*. In 1853 he sold it to William G. Terrell, and six years afterwards purchased it again. He again sold it, and for the third time bought it. In 1866 he left Lafayette and went to New Albany to edit the *Commercial* of that city. He is now, and for some time has been, the leading editorial writer on the *Indianapolis Journal*. Mr. Luse is a scholarly man and a vigorous writer, and is well acquainted with public men and measures. There are few men in the State who equal him in information, and fewer still who have his ability to write. His pen is as prolific and his style as vigorous as they were a quarter of a century ago. In 1852 he and I were of a party of editors that went to Louisville to escort General Scott, then the Whig candidate for President, to Indiana. When we were introduced to the General, Mr. Luse remarked that we were Whig editors from Indiana, and were working hard to make him President. "Ah, gentlemen," replied the old hero, "the people of Indiana, then, have heard of Lundy's Lane."

The *Lafayette Courier* was then conducted by William R. Ellis. Mr. Ellis is still living,* but he abandoned journalism long ago. He sold the *Courier*, in 1854, to William S. Lingle, its present owner. Mr. Lingle was one of the Madison colony

---

* W. R. Ellis was a brother of Dr. Ellis, named above, and he died at Lafayette since this lecture was delivered.

that went to Lafayette with Mr. Terrell when he bought the *Journal*. He wields a caustic pen, as I have good reason to know. When I edited the *Madison Banner* I published a communication from Lingle that well nigh cost me a fight or a foot-race. Had not Providence favored me I should have had to fight or run. I have thought, ever since, that Lingle did not properly appreciate the vicarious offering I made for him twenty-nine years ago.

In these days A. H. Sanders edited the *Evansville Journal*. Evansville was not then even relatively what it now is, and the *Journal's* field was a circumscribed one. This paper has grown with the prosperous city in which it is published, and is now understood to be one of the most valuable pieces of newspaper property in the State. There was then no Democratic paper published in Evansville. Several attempts had been made to establish one, but without success, Charles P. Baymiller, a lieutenant of Garber and of Terrell, being one of those who made the effort. The *Evansville Courier*, now so ably conducted by the Shanklin brothers, was not then in existence.

In 1852 Enos B. Reed and Alf. Burnett started the *Democratic Union*, a weekly paper, at Vernon. It was profusely illustrated with wood cuts which had done previous service. Reed edited the paper and Burnett was its traveling correspondent. In a letter from New York he spoke of calling on N. P. Willis, the poet, *incog*. The press made so much sport of this piece of silly vanity that his letters stopped.

Mr. Reed, then as now, was a lover of the "foaming lager." One day he invited a prominent citizen of Vernon to take a social glass in a grocery store. The "prominent citizen" declined the beer, but remarked that, as the cost was the same, he would take a mackerel. As the people of Vernon liked mackerel better than beer they were not congenial to the poet-editor. So, in a short time,

> "He folded his tent like the Arab,
> And as silently stole away."

I well remember one incident connected with his career at Vernon. A ballad over my name was published, which attracted the poet's attention. He critically tore it into shreds, for which I thank him sincerely. From that day to this I have not attempted rhyme, being satisfied, with him, that if I have talents they do not lie in that direction.

Some ten years ago Mr. Reed started the *Indianapolis People*. It "took" from the start, and is now a valuable piece of property. It circulates chiefly among the working people, and is probably as influential with that class as any journal published at Indianpolis. Mr. Reed is a florid, rotund, jolly man, and is warm in his friendships. He is a devoted disciple of Izaak Walton, and deftly handles the hook and line. A hooked bass or red-eye throws him into ecstasies.

In 1855 Jacob B. Maynard bought the *Cannelton Reporter* and entered journalism. From that time until now he has been engaged in editorial work; in Cannelton, in Evansville, in Louisville, in St. Joseph, Missouri, and in Indianapolis. For more than four years he has been the leading writer on the *Indianapolis Sentinel*. As a statistician he has no equal in the Indiana press. He has the figures on his finger's end, and can tell all about the exports and the imports; how many bushels of wheat and corn are raised and how many consumed; how many gallons of whisky—Bourbon or Robinson county—are manufactured and how many drunk, and how much *per capita* it costs to run the government. He can dash off a political leader as easily as he can prepare a statistical table. He can also write a charming sketch, and, when necessary, successfully court the muse. A pen equally versatile I do not know. Those who judge him by his political leaders are apt to mistake the man. These are often denunciatory and vituperative, whereas he is naturally gentle and kind. He fashions a leader as a potter his clay—to suit the purpose for which it is designed. The late George Harding used to say that when the manager of the *Sentinel* wished a particularly savage article prepared he threw Colonel Maynard a piece of raw beef over the transom of his door. He works seven days in the week, year in and year out, and the quantity and quality of his work are marvelous. It is questionable if there be another man in the State who can do so varied work and do it so well. From the day of the presidential election in 1876, until the day Mr. Hayes was inaugurated, the *Sentinel's* rooster appeared as regularly as the paper, but when, for the first and only time in our country's history, a man not elected put on the presidential robes, Mr. Maynard took down his rooster. Six days before he took the chicken from his perch he thus addressed him:

"OUR ROOSTER.

"At twilight's shades and morning's dawn
    Our Rooster's watched the course of crime,
He's seen the perjured villains fawn,
    And heard the thieving kennel whine.

"On watch when Grant, the second Nero,
    Ordered troops to murder law,
He's stood his ground like Spartan hero,
    With indignation in his craw.

"Grandly he crowed the glory
    When triumph flashed, where Rads lay slain,
Till all the world caught up the story,
    And vict'ry was the grand refrain.

"He heard the crime-forg'd fetters rattle
    And queried, 'Are the victors slaves?
Or will there be another battle,
    Where freemen on its surging waves

"'Will fight for rights their fathers willed them,
    Till hope is lost to mortal vision,
Or fate a funeral pyre shall build them
    To save their names from curs'd derision?'

"Our Rooster has but lofty scorn
    For crime-stained Rads and perjured thieves,
And loud will crow on that glad morn
    When each in hell his pay receives.

"He'll crow when Morton pleads for ice
    To cool that lying tongue of his'n;
He'll crow when Bradley's in the vise
    The devil keeps in darkest prison.

"He'll crow when Wells goes plunging under
    Hell's hottest waves in search of Stearns;
He'll crow when both, with stolen plunder,
    Receive their pay in bonds and burns.

"Undismayed, our Rooster's crowing,
    And though the dawn is not serene,
He'll crow till man, defiant growing,
    Will by his courage change the scene.

35

" He'll crow till man, though fierce the fight—
   No matter where God gave him breath—
 At freedom's shrine will pledge his might
   For freedom or a freeman's death."

William G. Terrell bought the *Lafayette Journal* of James P.
Luse in the fall of 1853 and conducted it until 1859. When he
purchased the *Journal* he was a resident of Madison, and he
took with him from that city, to assist him in editing it, Charles
P. Baymiller and William S. Lingle. Mr. Terrell was a slow
but a careful and correct writer and an inveterate punster. He
was known as the newspaper joker of that day and some of his
sayings are not yet forgotten. In 1852 he attended a Whig
convention at Niagara Falls at which Horace Greeley was a
speaker. In his speech Mr. Greeley declared that while he
favored the election of the Whig candidate for President, General Scott, he "spat upon the platform." In a letter to the
Madison Banner, giving an account of this convention, Mr.
Terrell said that Mr. Greeley could not spit upon the platform
and expect-to-rate as a Whig. This *bon mot* went the rounds
of the press of that day.

On the breaking out of our civil war Mr. Terrell assisted in
raising a Union regiment in Kentucky, and afterwards was appointed paymaster in the army with the rank of Colonel. After
the war ended he was postmaster at Newport, Kentucky, and
held the office several years. Subsequent to this time he became involved in a personal difficulty with a lawyer of Covington named Meyers, which resulted in the lawyer's death. For
this he was tried and acquitted, the jury finding that the killing
was justifiable homicide. Colonel Terrell still lives, and at
present is engaged on the *Cincinnati Commercial*.

At this time Rev. William W. Hibben owned and controlled
the *Lawrenceburg Press*. He was a Methodist clergyman and
one of the pioneer preachers of that denomination in Indiana.
He was a smooth and a prolific writer, and was well known
throughout the State. His letters to the *Cincinnati Enquirer*
and to the *Indianapolis Sentinel*, and his contributions to the
Masonic Advocate, over the signature of Jefferson, proved him
a writer of merit. He died a few months ago at Indianapolis,
old and poor.

William W. Crail was a partner of Daniel D. Jones when the *Madison Banner* first became a daily. He continued his connection with the paper until 1854, when he sold his interest and left the State. He is not a brilliant man, but he is what is better, an honest and true one. While on the *Banner* he was the news editor, and he could boil down an article and get its marrow as well as any one I ever knew. He still lives, and is now working at the case on the *Louisville Courier-Journal.*

The *Brookville American*, edited by C. F. Clarkson, was then a leading journal of the State. Mr. Clarkson was identified with the temperance movement, and a large portion of his paper was devoted to that cause. He afterwards sold the *American* to Rev. Thomas A. Goodwin, and removed to Iowa, where he now lives. After conducting the *American* awhile at Brookville, Mr. Goodwin took it to Indianapolis, where it died on his hands.

Oliver B. Torbet edited the *Lawrenceburg Register*, then, as now, a leading journal of Southeastern Indiana. He was elected to the Legislature in 1851 and again in 1852, the latter year being chosen Speaker of the House. Subsequent to this time he removed to Indianapolis and became a partner of the late General Dumont in the practice of the law. He has been dead some sixteen years, and is better remembered as a politician than as a newspaper man.

One of the best weekly papers then in Indiana was the *Greensburg Press*, edited by Daviess D. Batterton. Mr. Batterton was an educated, scholarly man, and as a writer ranked with the very best in the State. He died at Greensburg many years ago.

The *Columbus Democrat*, a paper now published by Mrs. Laura C. Arnold and Mr. Addison Arnold, was founded in 1848 by John P. Finkle. In 1850 it went into the hands of Aquilla Jones and William F. Pidgeon, who published it for a year or so, and then sold it to W. C. Statelar. Mr. Statelar introduced a power press, but finding it too expensive for his small circulation, soon abandoned it. In 1855 Mr. Statelar died, and the *Democrat* was sold to I. C. Dillie. Dr. Nathan Tompkins, a brother-in-law of Hon. William J. Brown, was the editor. The Doctor was a ready, graceful writer, and the

paper, with improved typography, gained a respectable standing and a good paying patronage. The editor died, and in
1861 Dillie entered the Union army and was killed by guerrillas in Tennessee.

The *Soup Spiller*, a campaign paper, was issued by Mr.
Statelar, from the *Democrat* office, during the presidential campaign of 1852. The name was chosen in derision of General
Scott's "hasty plate of soup" letter. A committee of nine
Democrats did the editing, and several ingenious jack-knife
artists prepared the engravings with which the paper was profusely illustrated.

Shortly after the *Democrat* was started Samuel A. Moore and
William A. Holland began the publication of a Whig paper
called *The Spirit of the West*. Holland remained in the concern but a few weeks. Moore was a well-informed politician,
a practical printer, and wrote with force and pungency. He
was also an off-hand speaker of considerable ability. In May,
1849, Mr. Moore was appointed postmaster at Columbus, and
the next year was elected to the lower House of the State Legislature. In 1853 he removed to Iowa, where he served as a
county judge and as a State Senator. He is now postmaster
at Bloomfield, Iowa, and occasionally he appears on the rostrum
as a lecturer on literary subjects.

Mr. W. C. Statelar succeeded Mr. Moore, in 1849, as publisher of the *Spirit*, and soon afterward associated himself with
Columbus Stebbins as co-proprietor. Mr. Stebbins was a green
farmer-boy, twenty-three years old, strong and awkward, of no
experience in life, but of good, hard, native sense. He had
occasionally contributed short articles to the local press and
believed he was destined by the "bent of his genius" for a
brilliant career in journalism. In a short time he bought out
his partner's interest in the paper and became sole proprietor
and editor. His mind developed rapidly, and though not a
polished writer, his articles were bold, aggressive and argumentative, especially those on the questions of slavery and in-
temperance. Radical as the *Spirit* was under his management
it became doubly so in 1854, on the admission of Mr. J. Fred.
Myers as a partner. Mr. Myers was an excellent printer, a
German liberal, who hated slavery with all the intensity peculiar

to the original Abolitionists of the olden time. He was a writer of great force and clearness, indifferent to party expediency, and as pugnacious as a man well could be. In 1854 the proprietors changed the name of the paper to the *Columbus Independent*. Know-nothingism was then sweeping over the State like a mighty hurricane, gathering within its intolerant embrace the bulk of the defunct Whig party and thousands of discontented Democratic "sore-heads." Among all the papers of the State of Whig proclivities the *Independent* was the only one to boldly grapple with the wild fanaticism. Its proprietors were threatened with loss of patronage, but they courageously stood their ground and prospered, while Know-nothingism went down in disaster almost as suddenly as it had arisen.

In February, 1856, an anti-Democratic editorial convention was held at Indianapolis, a large proportion of the members being Know-nothings. Mr. Stebbins was a member of the committee on resolutions, the majority of which presented a report susceptible of a favorable construction of Know-nothingism, and which gingerly touched the question of slavery. Mr. Stebbins brought in a minority report, his resolutions embracing the main principles upon which the Republican party was founded. He advocated his report in an argumentative and fervid speech, and with the assistance of the late M. C. Garber, of the *Madison Courier*, and Theodore Hielcher, of the *Indianapolis Frie Press*, the minority report and resolutions were adopted. The first State convention of the Republican party was held at Indianapolis the next day, and Mr. Stebbins's resolutions were embodied in the platform.

In the fall of 1856 Mr. Myers withdrew from the *Independent*. He has since been connected with many journalistic enterprises, and is now publishing a paper at Denison, Iowa, of which town he is the postmaster. Mr. Stebbins continued the *Independent* until May, 1857, when he removed his printing establishment to Minnesota and started the *Hastings Independent*, at Hastings. He died there in December, 1878.

Rushville then had two journals, the *Jacksonian* and the *Republican;* the first under the control of John L. Robinson, and the latter under that of Pleasant A. Hackleman. Mr. Robinson was, for many years a member of Congress, and died United

States Marshal of Indiana. He was one of the ablest speakers in the State. Mr. Hackleman was a leading Whig, and on the dissolution of that party became a Republican. He was a delegate from Indiana to the Peace Conference held at Washington just before the breaking out of our civil war. When hostilities commenced he became a soldier, and was killed in battle at Corinth while holding the commission of a brigadier general.

In 1852 William M. French published the *Indiana Republican* at Rising Sun. Two years afterward he went to Jeffersonville to edit the *Republican* of that city. In 1861 he removed to Indianapolis, where he has since resided. He is the author of a life of the late Governor Morton, and is a frequent contributor to the daily press. He writes with ease and grace, and was a man of mark in the olden time.

The *Richmond Palladium* was then conducted by David P. Holloway. It was the leading Whig journal in Eastern Indiana and had quite a circulation in other parts of the State. Its editor was a member of the State Senate and afterward was elected to Congress from his district. In 1861 he was appointed Commissioner of Patents, and removed to the city of Washington, where he has since resided. Since his retirement from the patent office he has practiced law, making a specialty of that relating to patents. Mr. Holloway is the father of Colonel William R. Holloway, the well-known ex-postmaster of Indianapolis.*

The late Judge James Hughes then edited the *North Western Gazette*, a weekly paper published at Bloomington. As a writer Judge Hughes was aggressive and strong, but it was as a lawyer and politician that he became distinguished. His editorial career was but an episode, but had he made journalism a life work he would, no doubt, have become eminent in it. He was no common man, but was a master in any work he undertook. He was one of the strongest men Indiana has produced. He died some ten years ago.

James H. McNeely, at this time, was local editor of the *Indianapolis Journal*. He afterward went to Evansville, and for a long time was connected with the *Journal* of that city. About

* Mr. Holloway died September 9, 1883.

one year ago he removed to Terre Haute and became manager of the *Terre Haute Express*. He is a thorough newspaper man, is an intelligent and painstaking writer and ranks among the best as he is one of the oldest editors in the State.

A brilliant young man was John C. Turk, of the *Greencastle Argus*. A graduate of Farmer's College, Ohio, he came to Greencastle in 1849 and studied law with Judge Eckles, and in 1853 started the *Argus*. In 1856 he went to Keokuk, Iowa, and edited a paper there. From Keokuk he removed to Columbia, Missouri, and assumed control of a paper in that place. During the war he lived at Council Bluffs, Iowa, and was engaged in practicing law and writing for the press. He died at Council Bluffs in the fall of 1871. Mr. Turk was a good lawyer, a fascinating speaker and a strong writer. He was bold and fearless in his utterances and left his impress wherever he went. But few men in the State at that time excelled him in ability and culture.

Solon Turman then conducted the *People's Friend* at Covington. He was a member of the State Senate and the youngest man in that body. He afterwards removed to Greencastle, and subsequently became Judge of the Circuit Court. He died at Greencastle a few months ago.

The *Times*, a weekly paper then published at Laporte, was under the editorial direction of John C. Walker. It was a leading journal of Northern Indiana, and was as influential as any published in that section of the State. It may be mentioned as a matter of history that it was among the first, if not the very first paper, in Indiana, to antagonize the dogmas and methods of the Know-nothing party which sprang into existence in 1854. There was no more promising man of his age in the State than its editor. He was elected a member of the State Legislature of 1853, and took high rank in that body. In 1855–6 Colonel Walker owned and edited the *Indianapolis Sentinel*, and on the 8th of January of the latter year he was nominated for Lieutenant-Governor on the ticket with the eloquent Willard, but being under the constitutional age he did not make the race. In the latter part of 1857 he resumed charge of the *Laporte Times*, and in 1858 made a gallant race for Congress against the Hon. Schuyler Colfax. Two years after this he was placed at the head of the Democratic electoral ticket, and made a thorough canvass of the State in behalf of Judge Douglas for the presidency. On the breaking out of the civil war he was appointed Colonel of the Thirty-fifth (First Irish) Regiment of Indiana volunteers, and commanded the regiment about two years. The Legislature of 1863 elected Colonel Walker Agent of State, which required him to take up his official residence in New York. At the expiration of his term of office—in the spring of 1865—he went to England, and remained there eight years. During this period he studied and acquired a good knowledge of medicine, attending lectures at King's College, one of the oldest and best institutions of learning in London. In 1873 Dr. Walker returned to the United States, and in 1875 went to Shelbyville and opened an office for the practice of his profession. He remained at Shelbyville until the spring of 1879, when he was appointed assistant physician of the Indiana Hospital for the Insane. From that time till this he has filled that important position with credit to himself and to the satisfaction of the public.

Doctor Walker is a good speaker and a good writer, talents not often found in the same person. He is warm and true in his friendships, and courteous and urbane in his manners. He is as gentle and kind as a woman, but is utterly fearless of danger. Although he has not reached the high position his early life gave promise of he occupies a respectable place in his chosen profession, and has the good will of all who know him.*

In 1855 Dr. Orpheus Everts succeeded John C. Walker in the management of the *Laporte Times.* He edited that paper with marked ability for some two years, when it again went into the hands of Colonel Walker.

In 1857 Dr. Everts was appointed receiver of a Minnesota land office and removed to that State. On the breaking out of the civil war he was appointed Surgeon of the Twentieth regiment of Indiana volunteers, and remained in the service until the end of the war. In 1868 he was chosen Superintendent of the Indiana Hospital for the Insane, and continued as such until the spring of 1879. He is now Superintendent of the Sanitarium, near Cincinnati, an institution of first-class reputation for the treatment of the insane.

---

* Dr. Walker died April 14, 1883.

Dr. Everts is a big man, intellectually and physically. He has distinguished himself in every position he has filled. He is an artist of no mean ability, a prolific prose writer and a poet of genius. As a physician and surgeon, and as a specialist in the treatment of the insane, he ranks deservedly high. He designed the new hospital for the insane, and it was mainly built under his direction. It is a monument to his genius, his fidelity and his integrity, and one of which he may well be proud.

The *Practical Observer* was published at Valparaiso in 1850 by W. C. Talcott. Mr. Talcott now conducts the *Porter County Vidette*. Both the *Observer* and the *Vidette* have been ably edited by him and have exercised a large and legitimate influence within the sphere of their circulation.

Mr. Talcott is not a brilliant man, but he has energy and perseverance, qualities which nearly always win. He is one of the few men in Indiana who has successfully published a country newspaper for more than a quarter of a century.

The *Porter County Democrat* was established at Valparaiso in 1856 by L. H. Miller. Mr. Miller was succeeded in the conduct of the paper by J. L. Rock, an able writer and an influential politician. After several years of successful management of the *Democrat*, Mr. Rock went upon the staff of the *Chicago Times*, and as he is lost to public gaze he is most probably entombed in the bowels of that mammoth concern.

After publishing the *Indiana Tocsin* at Laporte for a time, Mr. Thomas Jernegan went to Michigan City, and in 1846 established the *News*. The office of the *News* was burned in 1853 and the paper discontinued. Shortly after this the *Michigan City Transcript* was established, and Richard W. Colfax made its editor. Mr. Colfax left the paper in 1854 and was succeeded by Wright & Heacock. Mr. Heacock withdrew from the paper in a short time and went to California. Mr. Wright changed the name of the paper to the *Enterprise* and continued to edit it until the fall of 1859, when he went to Waukesha, Wisconsin, and took charge of a paper there. As a writer Mr. Wright was vigorous and sometimes brilliant. When Mr. Wright left Michigan City, in 1859, the *Enterprise* went into the hands of Mr. Thomas Jarnegan, who controls it to-day. Mr. Jarnegan is one of the oldest editors and publishers in the

State. With but a few years intermission he has been engaged continuously in the business for nearly half a century. In a green old age he still pursues the chosen calling of his youth with honor both to himself and to the profession.

John and William Millikan were the proprietors of the *Laporte Whig* from 1845 to 1854. In the fall of the latter year they sold the paper to F. M. Horan and Richard Holmes, who changed its name to the *Union*. In a short time Mr. Horan retired, Mr. John Millikan taking his place. These gentlemen conducted the *Union* until 1866, when they sold it to the proprietors of the *Laporte Herald*. The Millikans are now over seventy years old, and have devoted more than half their lives to the conduct of country newspapers. They are practical printers, and are plain, temperate, honest and substantial men.

The *Laporte Herald* was started at Westville, in Laporte county, in 1856. Mr. Charles G. Powell took charge of the office in December of that year, and in 1859 removed the paper to Laporte. The success of the *Herald* is a valuable example of what industry, energy and perseverance will accomplish.

When the *Herald* was first issued in Laporte it came in direct competition with five papers which seemed to have possession of the field. It succeeded, however, in 1867, in swallowing the *Laporte Union*, one of the oldest journals in Northern Indiana. The *Laporte Chronicle*, started by the Hon. Joseph Packard in 1874, was also merged into the *Herald* at the beginning of last year. The *Herald* establishment is now one of the largest and best pieces of newspaper property in the northern part of the State, and the *Herald-Chronicle* is recognized as one of the leading Republican papers of Indiana. Mr. Powell was an obscure country boy when he entered journalism, but he has proved himself to be a fluent writer and a first-class business manager. He has never aspired to political position, but he is recognized as a leader in his party. He is one of the postoffice editors of Indiana, having been appointed postmaster of Laporte in 1877.

The *Pilot* was started at Plymouth, in 1851, with John Q. Howell as editor. Mr. Howell is now a resident of Kewanna, Indiana, and is engaged in practicing medicine and selling drugs.

Richard Corbaley conducted the *Plymouth Banner* in 1852 and 1853. He now lives at Healsburgh, Colorado, and is an Advent preacher.

William J. Burns edited the *Banner* from 1853 to 1856. He afterward started the *Stark County Ledger*, and died several years ago.

William G. Pomeroy succeeded Mr. Burns in the conduct of the *Banner*. He now resides at Rolla, Missouri, and is engaged in the practice of the law.

Thomas McDonald established the *Plymouth Democrat* in 1855. His sons, Daniel and Platt, were associated with him in the conduct of the paper, and two years afterward they became its sole owners. Mr. Thomas McDonald died at Plymouth in 1875. Daniel McDonald now owns and edits the *Democrat*. He has been a member of the State Legislature, has been Clerk of his county, and one year ago was the Democratic candidate for Congress in his district. He is a good writer, and makes one of the best weekly papers published in the State. Mr. Platt McDonald lives in Colorado, and is engaged in mining.

Ignatius Mattingly became editor of the *Marshall County Republican* in 1856, and continued as such until 1868. He is now postmaster at Bourbon, and editor of the *Bourbon Mirror*. He commenced the printing business in 1822, and has been in it almost continuously since. He is, therefore, without doubt, one of the oldest, if not the very oldest, editor in the State.

Schuyler Colfax then edited the *St. Joseph Valley Register*, a paper he established in 1845 and conducted until 1855. It is now the *South Bend Register*.

Mr. Alfred Wheeler was associated with Mr. Colfax in the conduct of the *Register* for many years. Since his withdrawal from the paper he has served as Auditor of St. Joseph county, and is now a resident of South Bend.

It would seem to be a work of supererogation to speak of the career of Mr. Colfax. Of all the men who were engaged on the press in Indiana in the olden time he became the most distinguished. He was an influential member of the convention which formed the constitution under which we live. He was elected to Congress in 1854, and continued a member of that body until 1868. During his last two terms he was Speaker of the House. In 1868 he was elected Vice President of the United States on the ticket with General Grant. Since the expiration of his term as Vice President he has not been in politics, but has devoted his time to literature. He is now one of the best known and most popular lecturers in the country.

The *South Bend Forum* was established in 1852, by A. E. Drapier, and was published by him and his son, William H. Drapier, until 1862. Both father and son were fluent and elegant writers, and while their paper did not reach great influence, it was, nevertheless, ably conducted, in a literary point, being one of the very best papers in the State. Mr. A. E. Drapier died at Mishawaka some three years ago. William H. Drapier now lives at Indianapolis. He is widely known as the publisher of the *Brevier Legislative Reports*.

Robert Lowry then edited the *Goshen Democrat*. He afterwards removed to Fort Wayne, and is now Judge of the Circuit Court of the Fort Wayne circuit.

Samuel A. Hall started the *Logansport Pharos*, in 1844, and published it until 1869. The *Pharos*, under his direction, was a sound, conservative Democratic paper. Mr. Hall was not a brilliant man or a fluent writer, but he had a retentive memory, and his head was full of local and general political history. He labored industriously in his chosen profession for twenty-five years, and, while he was a good editor and made a good paper, he died a poor man. He breathed his last in April, 1870, aged 47 years. Poor Hall! Those of you who knew him will, I am sure, drop a tear to his memory. Indomitable of will, energetic, honorable, honest, straightforward, unselfish and constant in his friendships, he was beloved by all who knew him and died without an enemy. *Requiescat in pace.*

The *Logansport Journal*, the organ of the Republican party of Cass county, was conducted by Thomas H. Bringhurst from 1854 to 1870. Mr. Bringhurst still lives and resides at Logansport.

John D. Howell established *The Flag*, a Democratic paper, at Rochester, in 1852, but it soon died.

The *Howard Tribune* was started at New London in 1849. It was designed to represent all political shades of opinion then in vogue, and in order to do so had three political departments—

Whig, Democratic and Abolitionist. The first was presided over by Charles D. Murray, afterwards a State Senator; the second by Moses R. Wickersham, and the last by Dr. J. F. Henderson. In 1852 the paper was removed to Kokomo, its name changed to the *Kokomo Tribune*, and Clinton Hensley was installed as editor. It was then, as now, a weekly journal, but at that time it was published somewhat irregularly on account of the scarcity of quinine. It may seem strange to you that this anti-periodical drug should be used as a motive power to run a newspaper, but nevertheless this was the case in the Indian Reserve thirty years ago. More than once were the weekly visits of the *Tribune* interrupted by the ague, but when the merchants replenished their stock of quinine it renewed its visitations.

In 1856 the *Tribune* was purchased by Theophilus C. Phillips, who was its editor on the 4th day of July, 1877, when he died. Since then it has been published by his sons.

Charles D. Murray and Moses R. Wickersham, two of the first editors of the *Tribune*, are dead, and the other editor, Dr. Henderson, still lives at Kokomo. His sons now own and conduct the *Kokomo Dispatch*, as do those of Mr. Phillips the *Kokomo Tribune*. The *Tribune* and the *Dispatch* are two of the very best papers published in the State.

The *Vincennes Sun*, the first paper established within the boundary of Indiana, deserves more than a passing notice. It was established by Elihu Stout on the 4th of July, 1804. The material for the paper was taken to Vincennes on pack-mules from Lexington, Kentucky. Mr. Stout conducted the *Sun* until 1845, when he sold it to John R. Jones, who had previously published the *People's Friend* at Covington. Mr. Jones conducted the paper with varying success until 1856, when it was purchased by a company of prominent Democrats of Knox county, who, in September of that year, disposed of it to George E. Greene, then of Louisville, Kentucky, who, in addition to publishing a weekly edition, started a semi-weekly one. Both Mr. Jones and Mr. Greene are dead. On the death of the latter, in 1870, the *Sun* went into the hands of Dr. A. J. Thomas and General R. E. Kise. These gentlemen conducted it until November, 1876, when it was purchased by Royal E. Purcell, its present owner, who for some two years has been publishing a daily edition.

In 1830 Robert Y. Caddington started the *Vincennes Gazette*. He continued its publication until 1854, when he sold it to Harney, Mason & Co., who published it, with the addition of a daily edition, until 1859. In that year they sold the paper to Dr. H. M. Smith, who published it until 1871, or thereabouts, when it died.

Mr. Caddington's editorial work showed care and precision, and he had the full confidence of his political friends. He was a bitter partisan, but his politics never interfered with his social relations. During a residence of more than forty years in Vincennes he was held in high esteem by those who knew him. He is probably the oldest man now living in Indiana who has been identified with the press, his age being fully eighty years. He resides in the city of Laporte.

William E. McLean became editor of the *Terre Haute Journal* in December, 1851. The *Journal* was then issued weekly, and was the only Democratic paper published in the Terre Haute congressional district. Mr. McLean conducted the *Journal* until the spring of 1856, when it was sold to Grafton F. Cookerly and Thomas J. Browne. Colonel McLean has served in both branches of the State Legislature, and during the war he raised and commanded the Forty-third Regiment of Indiana volunteers. He is now a citizen of Terre Haute.

David S. Donaldson then conducted the *Wabash Express*. Sometime in the spring of 1851 a daily edition of the *Express* was issued, it being the first daily paper published in Terre Haute, but in a short time it was abandoned. Mr. Donaldson is still living and resides at Terre Haute.

Thomas Tiger then conducted the *Fort Wayne Sentinel*. He and Mr. S. V. B. Noel, formerly of Indianapolis, established the *Sentinel* in 1833. Mr. Noel withdrew from it in about one year, and from that time until 1865, with but a brief intermission, Mr. Tiger was the *Sentinel's* sole owner and manager. He saw it grow from a small weekly into a daily of large circulation and influence. He died at Fort Wayne in February, 1875, in the 68th year of his age. One who knew him well thus speaks of him : " He did not usually write much, but he wrote

well, and for years his party had not an abler editor in the
State. He was peculiarly happy as a paragraphist, often con-
densing into a few sentences, pointed and expressive, the substance of a column in other hands. Had he been as ambitious
as he was able he might have risen to distinction as a party
leader."

John W. Dawson conducted the *Fort Wayne Times* from 1854
to 1860. He was a native Indianian, and was lame from his boyhood. He was a bright, precocious boy, and became a strong,
intellectual man. He was a vigorous writer, radical in his
views and uncompromising in his opinions, warm in his friendships and unrelenting in his animosities. He was appointed
Governor of Utah in 1861, but soon resigned and returned to
Fort Wayne, where he died some four years ago.

A number of editors—notably, Colonel Isaiah B. McDonald,
of Columbia City ; Judge E.V. Long, of Warsaw ; Rufus Magee,
of Logansport, and Joseph J. Bingham, of Indianapolis, followed
so closely in the footsteps of those I have named as to tempt me
to sketch them, but as I can not do so without transgressing the
limits I imposed upon myself before commencing this address,
I am forced to pass them by. There are, no doubt, other papers
and other editors worthy of mention, but I have forgotten them ;
and, besides, it would be impossible in the time allotted me, to
sketch all the papers and their editors of twenty-five to thirty
years ago. Those entitled to be named who are not should at-
tribute the omission to want of memory and want of time, and
not to a deliberate purpose to ignore them.

I have thus sketched the newspapers and newspaper men of
Indiana of the olden time. What I have said has been mostly
from memory, so I doubt not some mistakes have been made,
but I feel confident they are neither great nor many. If I shall
be instrumental in preserving the memory of a single one from
forgetfulness I shall be well paid for my labor. Many of those
I have named have gone to " the undiscovered country from
whose bourne no traveler returns," and those who remain must
feel they are nearing its borders. When we are all gone may
those who come after us be able to truthfully say that our work
redounded to the public good and that the world is better for our
having lived.

INDEX

NAMES OF PERSONS MENTIONED IN THIS BOOK.

INDEX. 563

Dunn George G., mention of.........
235, 438, 459, 479
Sketch of 241
Dunn George H., mention of...........
78, 178, 310
Dunn James, mention of................ 404
Dunn Thomas, mention of............ 404
Dunn Williamson, mention of......
162, 179, 344, 520
Sketch of 400
Dunn Williamson Dr., mention of 404
Dunn W. M., mention of.. ....
107, 320, 370, 404, 406, 437, 440,
441, 459, 516, 530
Remarks of 346
Dunn W. M., Jr., mention of......... 404
Dupontavice Father, mention of... 514
Durham Jesse B., mention of......... 189

Eaton John H., mention of......... 234
Edwards Jonathan, mention of 406
Eggleston Miles C., mention of.....
70, 197, 519
Ellis E W. H., delegate to Peace
Congress................ 117
Mention of........................... 541
Ellis W. R., mention of 542
Emerson Thomas, mention of...... 190
English W. H., remarks of............ 154
Mention of............237, 238, 255, 341
Evens J. M., mention of............... 331
Everts Orpheus, mention of......302, 552
Ewing John, mention of 235

Fetta C., mention of 507
Finch F. M., mention of............... 260
Finkle John P., mention of.. 547
Fisher Charles, mention of......498, 510
Fishback, W. P., mention of........... 154
Fitch Graham N., mention of........
...............................112, 419, 455
Fitch Jonathan, mention of 439
Fitzhugh George D., mention of..... 513
Fogg William, mention of............. 498
Foote L. A., mention of................ 507
Foley James B., mention of........... 255
Fordham E. P., mention of............ 165
Foster B. F., mention of................ 516
Fletcher Calvin, mention of..63, 82, 428
Sketch of............................. 464
Floyd Davis, mention of...179, 344, 491
Franklin William, mention of...... 349
Fravel John B., mention of........... 507
Freeman, J. S., mention of............ 498
Freeman John, mention of 435
French W. M., mention of............ 550

Garber M. C., Jr., mention of........ 483
Garber Michael C., sketch of 480
Mention of 540, 549
Gibson George, mention of 14

Gibson John, sketch of................. 11
Mention of............................ 380
Gibson, T. W., mention of........... 441
Gilliland John, mention of........... 189
Glass James D., mention of........... 516
Glover Ellis, mention of.............. 395
Gooding David S., mention of 150
Goodwin T. A., mention of 547
Gordon Jonathan W., mention of...
150, 200, 486
Remarks of........................ 155
Gorman Willis A., mention of..247, 419
Greene George E., mention of 557
Gregg Harvey, mention of 428, 469
Gregg James M., mention of 255
Gregg Milton, mention of.........516, 540
Gregory James, mention of........... 175
Sketch of.. 426
Gregory Robert C., mention of...... 431
Gresham, W. Q., remarks of 125
Mention of 153, 335
Griffin William, mention of 103
Grover N. D., mention of. 509
Guthrie James, mention of 443

Hacker Wm., mention of.............. 507
Hackelman P. A., delegate to Peace
Congress 117
Mention of 315, 549
Hall H. B., mention of................. 491
Hall S. A., mention of................. 556
Hammond A. A., sketch of 113
Mention of...................... 200, 317
Hand Charles I., mention of......... 499
Hanna Robert, mention of............ 191
Hannegan E. A., mention of........
120, 199, 204, 428
Sketch of 211
Harding George, mention of......... 544
Harding Stephen S., mention of... 278
Harney John H., mention of 249
Harlan A. J., remarks of 284
Harrington John, mention of......... 531
Harris Chapman, mention of......... 228
Harris Horatio J., mention of 88
Harrison Alfred, mention of 428
Harrison A. W., mention of 512
Harrison Benjamin, Governor of
Virginia.............. 3
Harrison Benjamin, Senator from
Indiana 3
Remarks of..................125, 155
Mention of 150, 157
Harrison, Christopher, acting Gov-
ernor 36
Sketch of 160
Mention of 363, 491
Harrison W. G., mention of 167
Harrison W. H., sketch of............ 1
Mention of...........................
189, 374, 378, 383, 385, 386

www.ingramcontent.com/pod-product-compliance
Lightning Source LLC
Chambersburg PA
CBHW060546280326
41932CB00011B/1414

* 9 7 8 0 7 8 8 4 5 6 4 3 5 *